JavaServer Faces

Hans Bergsten

O'REILLY®

Beijing · Cambridge · Farnham · Köln · Paris · Sebastopol · Taipei · Tokyo

JavaServer™ Faces

Other Java™ resources from O'Reilly

Related titles

Java™ in a Nutshell
Head First Java™
Head First EJB™
Programming Jakarta Struts
Tomcat: The Definitive Guide
Learning Java™
Java™ Extreme Programming Cookbook
Java™ Servlet and JSP™ Cookbook™
Hardcore Java™
JavaServer™ Pages

Java Books Resource Center

java.oreilly.com is a complete catalog of O'Reilly's books on Java and related technologies, including sample chapters and code examples.

OnJava.com is a one-stop resource for enterprise Java developers, featuring news, code recipes, interviews, weblogs, and more.

Conferences

O'Reilly & Associates brings diverse innovators together to nurture the ideas that spark revolutionary industries. We specialize in documenting the latest tools and systems, translating the innovator's knowledge into useful skills for those in the trenches. Visit *conferences.oreilly.com* for our upcoming events.

Safari Bookshelf (*safari.oreilly.com*) is the premier online reference library for programmers and IT professionals. Conduct searches across more than 1,000 books. Subscribers can zero in on answers to time-critical questions in a matter of seconds. Read the books on your Bookshelf from cover to cover or simply flip to the page you need. Try it today with a free trial.

JavaServer™ Faces
by Hans Bergsten

Printed in the United States of America.

Published by O'Reilly Media, Inc., 1005 Gravenstein Highway North, Sebastopol, CA 95472.

O'Reilly Media, Inc. books may be purchased for educational, business, or sales promotional use. Online editions are also available for most titles (*safari.oreilly.com*). For more information, contact our corporate/institutional sales department: (800) 998-9938 or *corporate@oreilly.com*.

Editor: Mike Loukides

Production Editor: Colleen Gorman

Cover Designer: Emma Colby

Interior Designer: David Futato

Printing History:

April 2004: First Edition.

This book uses RepKover™, a durable and flexible lay-flat binding.

ISBN13: 978-0-596-00539-9

[M] [4/08]

Table of Contents

Preface

JavaServer™ Faces (JSF) is the latest Java™ web application technology, building on the experience gained from Java Servlets, JavaServer™ Pages (JSP), and numerous commercial and open source web application frameworks. JSF defines an event-driven, component-based model for web application development, similar to the model that has been used successfully for standalone GUI application for years. This is an area that has received a lot of attention from vendors over the last few years. The highly anticipated publication of a Java Community Process (JCP) developed specification that addresses this need means that vendors can now focus on developing first-class development tools and user interface components based on the JSF specification rather than reinventing the wheel with proprietary APIs, and you will reap all the benefits of a larger market.

In This Book

This book covers Version 1.0 of the JSF specification, which was released in March 2004.

The first four chapters gives an introduction to what JSF has to offer and how it relates to other Java enterprise technologies. You'll also learn about the fundamentals technologies—HTTP, Java web containers, servlets, and JSP—and how to install and setup a Java web container.

Next, you will learn how to use all the standard JSF components and other features (such as input validation, data type conversion, page navigation, and internationalization), as well as how to develop customized versions of these items. Each chapter illustrates how to use a specific feature through stepwise refinement of a sample web application. In addition to showing you what to do, the book also describes what's happening behind the scenes, helping you gain a deeper understanding of how JSF works and how to use this technology in your own applications.

The sample application used in this book is an expense report system, where users create, edit, and submit expense reports for approval, and managers accept or reject reports. It's a realistic example that guides you through solutions to common JSF application design problems, such as authenticating users, connecting the business logic objects to the user interface while still keeping each aspect decoupled, distinguishing between user interface events and application events, customizing and localizing messages, and building a complete user interface in a modular fashion. The last three chapters describe advanced topics, such as how to develop custom components and custom presentation layers.

Audience

Developing a web application takes people with different skills, and the JSF specification associates these skill sets with role names. A *page author* is a person who knows the client-side technology (e.g., HTML, CSS, and JavaScript) but isn't a programmer. An *application developer* is a Java programmer who understands the application domain and how to develop solutions in terms of business objects. A *component writer* is a person who develops custom components and connects the user interface developed by the page author to the business objects developed by the Application Developer. The Component Writer must know both Java and the JSF API, and have a good idea about how JSF processes requests and produces responses. This book covers the tasks for all these roles.

What You Need to Know

I assume that the readers of this book have experience with HTML; consequently, I don't explain the standard HTML elements used in the examples. If you want to learn more about HTML, I recommend *HTML and XHTML: The Definitive Guide* by Chuck Musciano and Bill Kennedy (O'Reilly Media, Inc.). But even if you're an HTML wiz, this may be your first exposure to web applications. I have therefore included a thorough introduction to the HTTP protocol that drives all web applications.

I also assume that you're a programmer familiar with Java programming and object-oriented concepts. If that's not the case, you must learn Java before you continue reading this book. There are plenty of introductory Java books available, for instance *Head First Java* (O'Reilly) by Kathy Sierra and Bert Bates, and *Learning Java* (O'Reilly) by Patrick Niemeyer and Jonathan Knudsen.

The JSF specification builds on the Java Servlets specification and supports using JSP for page layout. I've included an introduction to both these technologies, enough for you to understand the examples. Before you develop any large, real-world application, though, I recommend that you learn more about these technologies. My own *JavaServer Pages* (O'Reilly) and *Java Servlet Programming* by Jason Hunter and William Crawford (O'Reilly) are two good books for these subjects.

Organization

The book consists of 15 chapters and 6 appendixes.

Chapter 1, *Introducing JavaServer Faces*
: Explains how JSF fits into the big picture of web applications and how it compares to alternative technologies.

Chapter 2, *JSF Development Process Overview*
: Provides an overview of what it means to develop an application with a JSF-based user interface.

Chapter 3, *Setting Up the JSF Environment*
: Describes how to install the Tomcat 5 web container and how to install the book examples, including the JSF reference implementation.

Chapter 4, *Servlet and JavaServer Pages Basics*
: Describes the fundamental HTTP, servlet, and JSP concepts you need to know in order to use JSF to its full potential.

Chapter 5, *Developing the Business Logic and Setting Up Authentication*
: Provides an introduction to the sample application used for most examples in this book and the business logic classes for this application.

Chapter 6, *Creating and Rendering Components*
: Gives a first look under the hood of JSF, focusing on how components are created and rendered at both the API and JSP level.

Chapter 7, *Validating Input*
: Describes how converters and validators are used to validate user input, and how to develop your own custom validators and customize error messages.

Chapter 8, *Handling Events*
: Explains how to deal with different types of events triggered by clicking on buttons and links or changing input components values, and how these events may affect the user interface or invoke the backend code.

Chapter 9, *Controlling Navigation*
: Takes a look at the JSF page navigation feature and how the outcome of event processing can control which page to display next.

Chapter 10, *Working with Tabular Data*
: Describes alternative ways to display and edit tabular data, including how to best handle large tables.

Chapter 11, *Internationalization*
: Explains internationalization and localization, the Java features available to implement an internationalized application, and describes how JSF takes advantage of these features for development of multilingual web sites.

Chapter 12, *Odds and Ends*
: Covers various areas not discussed in previous chapters, such as composing a page from multiple files, integration with the Struts application framework, debugging tips, and more.

Chapter 13, *Developing Custom Renderers and Other Pluggable Classes*
: Describes how to develop custom JSF renderers for standard components to provide alternative rendering and input capabilities, and discusses how to replace other pluggable classes with custom versions.

Chapter 14, *Developing Custom Components*
: Shows how to develop custom JSF components in different ways, from simple customization of existing components to development of brand new components.

Chapter 15, *Developing a Custom Presentation Layer*
: Describes how JSF supports other presentation layer technologies besides JSP and how to develop a custom layer inspired by the Tapestry open source product.

Appendix A, *Standard JSF Tag Libraries*
: Describes the JSP custom actions included in the two standard JSF tag libraries.

Appendix B, *JSF Expression Language Reference*
: Contains a description of the JSF EL syntax and rules.

Appendix C, *Standard JSF Components and Render Kits*
: Contains descriptions of all standard JSF component classes along with the standard render kit.

Appendix D, *Infrastructure API Reference*
: Contains descriptions of all JSF infrastructure classes, including converters, validators, and error messages.

Appendix E, *JSF Configuration File Reference*
: Contains descriptions of all JSF configuration file elements.

Appendix F, *Web Application Structure and Deployment Descriptor Reference*
: Contains a description of the standard web application structure and all elements in the web application deployment descriptor.

The chapters build on each other, so I recommend that you read them in sequence.

About the Examples

This book contains many examples that demonstrate useful techniques for dealing with requirements common to most JSF-based web applications. The code for all the examples is contained within the text and is also available for download from the O'Reilly web site at *http://www.oreilly.com/catalog/jsvrfaces/*. You can also download the example code, ask me questions, and more at *http://www.hansbergsten.com/*.

The examples use features of the Servlet 2.4 and JSP 2.0 specifications, even though the JSF specification depends on the previous versions of these specifications: Servlet 2.3

and JSP 1.2. I use the latest specifications, released in November 2003, because they make life so much easier in many areas, and I expect them to be supported by the major Java web containers by the time you read this book (or shortly thereafter). All examples have been tested with the official JSF 1.0 reference implementation on Windows ME and Linux (Red Hat Linux 7.2) using Sun's Java 2 SDK, Standard Edition (1. 4.2) and Tomcat 5.0.18.

Conventions Used in This Book

Italic
: Used for pathnames, filenames, program names, compilers, and options, new terms where they are defined, and Internet addresses such as domain names and URLs.

`Constant width`
: Used for anything that appears literally in a JSP page or a Java program, including keywords, data types, constants, method names, variables, class names, interface names, and commands, all JSP and Java code listings, and HTML documents, tags, and attributes.

`Constant width italic`
: Used for general placeholders that indicate that an item is replaced by some actual value in your own program.

`Constant width bold`
: Used for text that is typed in code examples by the user.

This icon designates a note, which is an important aside to the nearby text.

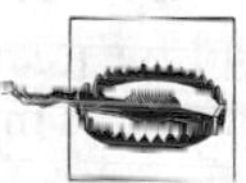

This icon designates a warning relating to the nearby text.

How to Contact Us

Please address comments and questions concerning this book to the publisher:

O'Reilly & Associates, Inc.
1005 Gravenstein Highway North
Sebastopol, CA 95472
(800) 998-9938 (in the United States or Canada)
(707) 829-0515 (international or local)
(707) 829-0104 (fax)

O'Reilly's web page for this book, where we list errata, examples, or any additional information. You can access this page at:

http://www.oreilly.com/catalog/jsvrfaces/

To comment or ask technical questions about this book, send email to:

bookquestions@oreilly.com

For more information about our books, conferences, Resource Centers, and the O'Reilly Network, see our web site at:

http://www.oreilly.com/

Acknowledgments

The JSF specification is developed through the Java Community Process (JCP) by representatives from companies large and small, as well as individuals like me. I'd like to thank all JSF Expert Group (EG) members that actively participated in this effort, especially Oracle's Adam Winer—I'm not sure what we would have done without you. Kudos also to the specification leads: Ed Burns for keeping track of all the issues we had to resolve and Craig McClanahan for his patience when I lost mine.

I'm also grateful to all those who helped me review the book and spot errors: Adam Winer, Craig McClanahan, Steve Bang, Pierre Delisle, and Janne Andersson; your comments definitely improved the material presented in this book. Thanks also to Dan Malks for connecting my design ideas to the J2EE patterns described in his *Core J2EE Patterns: Best Practices and Design Strategies* book (Prentice Hall). Unfortunately, it was too late to include the references in this edition of the book, but I hope to do so in a future edition.

It takes a lot of people to turn my words into a real book. I like to thank everyone at O'Reilly for their hard work and for giving me the opportunity to write, especially my editor Mike Loukides for his thoughtful suggestions, Colleen Gorman for great copyediting and for being so flexible, and Robert Romano for making art out of my simple drawings.

Many thanks also to my family and friends around the world for their support and encouragement, and for Friday nights at the Lighthouse with my friends in Vesica Pisces (*http://www.vp-unleashed.com/*—Kelly, Brian, Adam, and Nuss), Rob, Dave, Becky, James, Tamie, and the rest of the gang. Cheers!

—Hans Bergsten

CHAPTER 1

Introducing JavaServer Faces

Over the last few years, Java has established itself as the leading technology for web application development. Developers are using technologies like servlets and JSP to develop scalable and robust browser-based user interfaces for countless applications with great success. But as web applications become more complex, some developers are longing for the good ol' days of traditional graphical user interface (GUI) frameworks with rich, powerful user interface widgets and event-driven development models. Servlets and JSP have served us well, but HTTP's stateless nature and simple, coarse-grained request/response model forces application developers using these technologies to struggle with details that are handled behind the scenes by GUI frameworks like AWT/Swing, the standard GUI framework for Java.

To make it easier to develop sophisticated web application user interfaces, open source projects and commercial companies have developed frameworks that mimic traditional GUI frameworks as far as possible. Some notable examples are Enhydra's Barracuda, Apache's Tapestry, Oracle's UIX, and Sun's JATO. In the spring of 2001, a Java Community Process (JCP) group was formed with representatives from most of these efforts (including yours truly) to come up with a standard solution that all frameworks can use. The result is JavaServer Faces; the 1.0 version of the specification was released in March 2004.

What Is JavaServer Faces?

JavaServer Faces (JSF) simplifies development of sophisticated web application user interfaces, primarily by defining a user interface component model tied to a well-defined request processing lifecycle. This allows:

- Java programmers to develop the application backend without worrying about HTTP details and integrate it with the user interface through a familiar event-driven model with type-safe interfaces.
- Page Authors without programming knowledge to work with the user interface "look and feel" aspects by assembling components that encapsulate all user

interaction logic—thereby minimizing the need for program logic embedded directly in the user interface pages.

- Vendors to develop powerful tools for both frontend and backend development.

More specifically, JSF is a specification with implementations offered by multiple vendors. It defines a set of user interface (UI) components—basically, a one-to-one mapping to the HTML form element set plus a few extras—that can be used right out of the box, as well as an Application Programming Interface (API) for extending the standard components or developing brand new components. Validators attached to the components validate user input, which is then automatically propagated to application objects. Event handlers are triggered by user actions, such as clicking on a button or a link, and can change the state of other components or invoke backend application code. The outcome of the event processing controls which page is displayed next, with help from a pluggable navigation handler.

While HTML is the markup language of choice for most web applications today—and used for most examples in this book—JSF is not limited to HTML or any other markup language. Renderers that are separate from the UI components control the actual markup sent to the client, so the same UI component coupled with different renderers can produce very different output—for instance, either HTML and WML elements. If you're familiar with Swing, think "pluggable look and feel" (PLAF).

JSF gives you lots of flexibility in how you actually develop the user interface. All JSF implementations are required to support JavaServer Pages (JSP) as a presentation layer technology, with JSF components represented by JSP custom action elements (also commonly known as *custom tags*). The JSF API, however, is flexible enough to support other presentation technologies besides JSP. For instance, you can use pure Java code to create JSF components, which is similar to how a Swing UI is developed. Alternatively, you can bind JSF components to nodes in templates described by plain HTML files, the approach explored by projects such as Barracuda/XMLC and Tapestry. I use the JSP layer for most examples in this book because it's the only approach that's completely specified in JSF 1.0, but I also show examples of other approaches.

If you've developed Java web applications for some time, you've probably heard of (and have likely used) application frameworks like Apache Struts (*http://jakarta.apache.org/struts/*) or Maverick (*http://mav.sourceforge.net/*). Even though JSF overlaps a bit with the features offered by frameworks like these (for instance in the areas of validation and navigation support), it's also designed to play well with them. I discuss the options available for Struts applications to use a JSF user interface in Chapter 12, so you'll see exactly how JSF fits together with this popular application framework.

How Does JSF Compare to Traditional Technologies?

JSF brings a component-based model to web application development that is similar to the model that's been used in standalone GUI applications for years. Let's look at some of the advantages this gives you compared to more traditional web application technologies.

Less Code in the User Interface Templates

Java web applications user interfaces have typically been implemented as a set of JSP pages (or pages for similar template-engine technologies, such as Velocity or FreeMarker), where static content (e.g., text and HTML elements for layout) is mixed with elements that generate dynamic content when the page is processed. A problem with this approach is that the pages often end up with logic for maintaining the user interface state—for instance, code for marking checkboxes and list items as selected and for displaying current values in input fields.

When you use JSF with JSP as the presentation layer technology, special elements (JSP custom actions) represent the JSF components. Here's a snippet of a page with a form showing a user's food preferences as a set of HTML checkboxes:

```
...
<h:form>
  <table>
  ...
    <tr>
      <td>Favorite Foods:</td>
      <td>
        <h:selectManyCheckbox value="#{cust.foodSelections}">
         <f:selectItem itemValue="z" itemLabel="Pizza" />
         <f:selectItem itemValue="p" itemLabel="Pasta" />
         <f:selectItem itemValue="c" itemLabel="Chinese" />
       </h:selectManyCheckbox>
      </td>
    </tr>
    ...
  </table>
</h:form>
...
```

The details are not important at this stage, but note that there are no loops or conditional tests in the page. This logic is instead encapsulated in the JSF components represented by the `<h:selectManyCheckbox>` and `<f:selectItem>` elements. When the form is submitted, the JSF framework saves the list of current selections in an application object on the server (referenced by the `#{cust.foodSelection}` expression specified by the `value` attribute in this example). When the response is rendered, JSF uses the list to check off the corresponding boxes. Separating logic from the layout in this manner makes the page author's life easier.

With JSP as the presentation layer, the page author must still learn how to use the special JSF elements, and many standard page development tools don't know how to deal with them. As I mentioned earlier, JSF supports presentation layer technologies other than JSP. No alternative is fully described by the specification, but one can be implemented on top of the JSF API by third parties or in-house staff. Such a presentation layer may allow you to use just plain markup elements (e.g., HTML) in the templates instead. Anyone familiar with the markup language can then develop the user interface look and feel using standard tools, while Java programmers create JSF components that take care of the dynamic parts of the page:

```
...
<form action="validate_jstl.jsp" method="post">
  <table>
  ...
    <tr>
      <td>Favorite Foods:</td>
      <td>
        <input id="pizza" type="checkbox" name="food" value="z">Pizza<br>
        <input id="pasta" type="checkbox" name="food" value="p">Pasta<br>
        <input id="chinese" type="checkbox" name="food" value="c">Chinese<br>
      </td>
    </tr>
    ...
  </table>
</form>
...
```

The only thing that's a bit out of the ordinary here is the `id` attribute for the elements representing dynamic content. An identifier like this is typically needed by the custom presentation layer to tie JSF components to the elements in the template, so the components know which element to modify. We'll look at a custom presentation layer implementation that uses this approach at the end of this book.

Even for such a simple example (a page with a few checkboxes), both of these sample pages are a lot simpler to develop and maintain than a traditional JSP page with the same functionality. Here's a typical plain JSP page version of this example:

```
...
<form action="validate_jstl.jsp" method="post">
  <table>
  ...
   <c:forEach items="${paramValues.food}" var="current">
     <c:choose>
       <c:when test="${current == 'z'}">
         <c:set var="pizzaSelected" value="true" />
       </c:when>
       <c:when test="${current == 'p'}">
         <c:set var="pastaSelected" value="true" />
       </c:when>
       <c:when test="${current == 'c'}">
         <c:set var="chineseSelected" value="true" />
```

```
        </c:when>
      </c:choose>
    </c:forEach>
    <tr>
      <td>Favorite Foods:</td>
      <td>
        <input type="checkbox" name="food" value="z"
          ${pizzaSelected ? 'checked' : ''}>Pizza<br>
        <input type="checkbox" name="food" value="p"
          ${pastaSelected ? 'checked' : ''}>Pasta<br>
        <input type="checkbox" name="food" value="c"
          ${chineseSelected ? 'checked' : ''}>Chinese
      </td>
    </tr>
    ...
  </table>
</form>
...
```

If you're not familiar with JSP and the JSP Standard Tag Library (JSTL), don't worry about the details. The main thing to note is that this page contains a lot of code (in the form of XML-like JSP action elements and Expression Language expressions, but it's still code) in addition to the HTML elements. It first loops through all values received through a request parameter named food and sets flags when it finds values it recognizes. It then uses these flags to decide whether to add a checked attribute for the corresponding checkbox elements it generates. That's quite a mouthful (pun intended) for something as simple as handling food choices. Imagine the amount of code needed in a page that displays all kinds of dynamic state, such as the one in Figure 1-1.

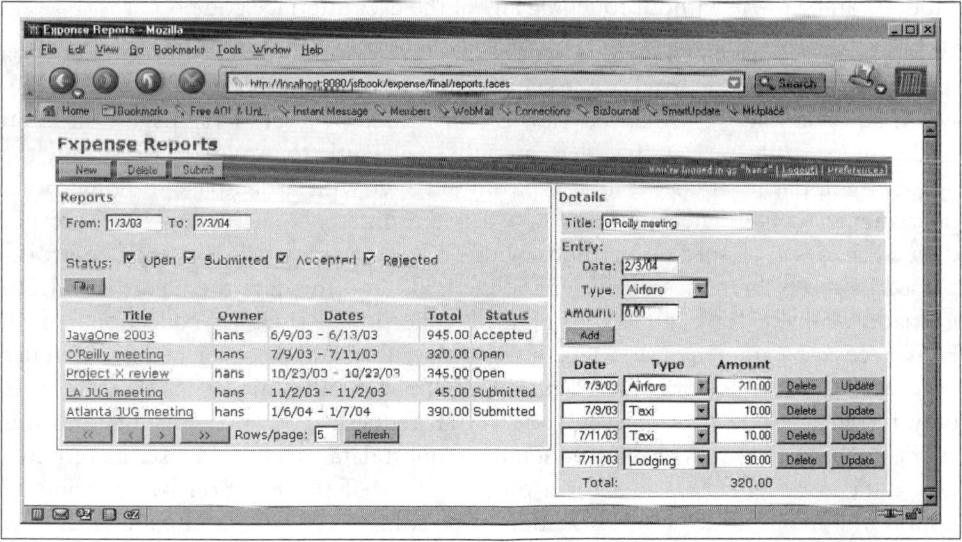

Figure 1-1. A complex web application user interface

This is the main screen for the sample application we'll develop in this book. It contains numerous buttons that are enabled or disabled depending on who's logged in and the business object status, plus scrollable and sortable tables and input fields that keep their previous values between requests. The application must also distinguish between different types of requests, triggered by clicking different buttons and links. For an application like that, JSF really shines.

More Modular User Interface Code

The web application architecture most experienced developers recommend is loosely based on the Model-View-Controller (MVC) design pattern. MVC was first described by Xerox in a number of papers published in the late 1980s, in conjunction with the Smalltalk language. This model has since been used for GUI applications developed in all popular programming languages. The basic idea is to separate the application data and business logic, the presentation of the data, and the interaction with the data into distinct entities labeled the Model, the View, and the Controller, respectively.

The *Model* represents pure business data and the rules for how to use this data; it knows nothing about how the data is displayed or the user interface controls used to modify the data. The *View*, on the other hand, knows all about the user interface details. It also knows about the public Model interface for reading its data, so that it can render it correctly, and it knows about the *Controller* interface, so it can ask the Controller to modify the Model. Using the MVC design pattern results in a flexible application in which multiple presentations (Views) can be provided and easily modified, and changes in the business rules or physical representation of the data (the Model) can be made without touching any of the user interface code.

While Java web application frameworks like Struts support the MVC model on a high level, it's not supported in the same strict, fine-granular way as in a GUI framework. For example, in Struts, the View is represented by a set of JSP pages, the Controller by a Struts servlet that delegates the real work to Action classes, and the Model by application classes that typically interact with a database or some other permanent storage. The interfaces between the different pieces, however, are not defined as a set of specific methods with declared parameters. Instead, control is passed between the pieces using generic methods, and the data the next piece needs is made available through coarse-grained collections—such as collections of all HTTP request parameters, headers, attributes, and so on. Another major difference between a GUI framework and a typical web application framework is that the latter only recognizes one type of event: the HTTP request. The code that handles this coarse-grained event has to dig through the request data to tell if the user has entered new data in any fields, asked for a different type of presentation by selecting an option in a menu, ordered a transaction to be completed, or something else. A GUI framework, on the other hand, is based on fine-granular events, such as "value changed," "menu item selected," and "button clicked," with separate event handlers dealing with each event.

The JSF MVC design is similar to Swing and other GUI frameworks, as shown in Figure 1-2.

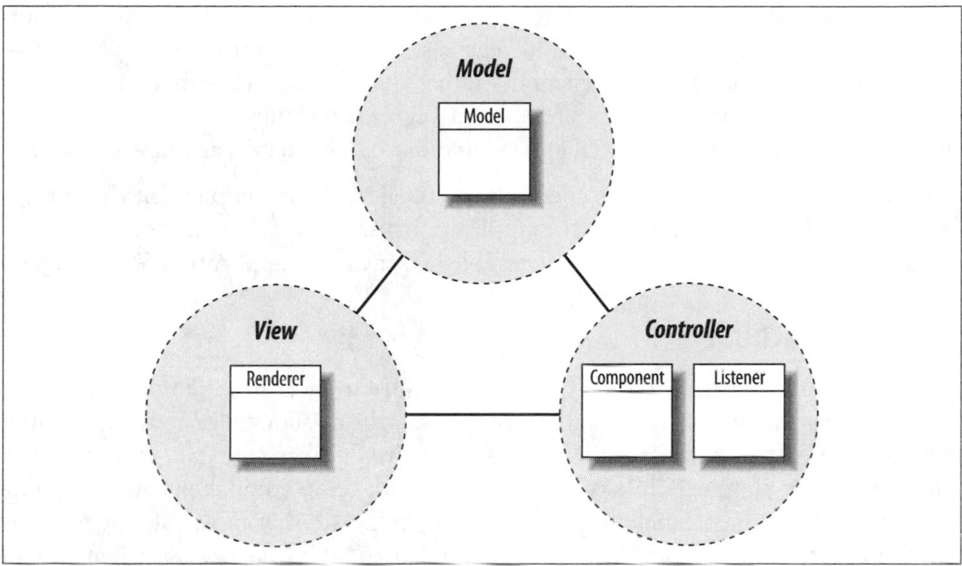

Figure 1-2. JThe JSF MVC design

The Model is represented by properties of application objects, e.g., a `username` property on an application object holding user information. JSF UI components declare what events they can fire, such as "value changed" and "button clicked" events, and external event listeners (representing the Controller) attached to the components handle these events. An event listener may set properties of the JSF components—for instance, adjust the set of rows shown in a table—or invoke backend code that processes the submitted data (say, verify that a credit card is valid or update a database). A separate renderer class (representing the View) renders each JSF UI component, making it possible to render instances of the same component type in different ways (e.g., either as a button or a link, or using different markup languages) just by attaching different renderers.

Besides the UI components, JSF also defines artifacts like validators and converters, each with a well-defined purpose. The end result is a very modular user interface code model that is easy to maintain, familiar to GUI application developers, and lends itself well to tools support.

Where Does JSF Fit in the Big Picture?

JSF may *not* be a good fit for all web applications. If you develop a web site where the dynamic aspects are limited to things like pulling content from a database, generating dynamic navigation menus, adding dynamic "cookie trails" to the pages, and other features that just make it easier to maintain the site content and simplify access to different parts of the site, JSF may be overkill. The best fit for JSF is a true *web application*—a web site with a lot of user interaction—rather than a web site with some dynamic content. A simple dynamic web site is probably easier to implement and maintain using only servlets and JSP, or even just JSP and the JSP Standard Tag Library (JSTL).

JSF does not necessarily replace current technologies. It's a complement that brings structure and maintainability to the application user interface. The following sections describe how JSF fits with some established Java web application technologies.

Using JSF with JSP

As you have already seen, JSF plays nicely with JSP. In fact, all JSF implementations must support JSP and provide tag libraries with custom actions for representing the standard JSF UI components in JSP pages. If you're familiar with JSP, adding JSF to the mix is fairly simple. While you can use JSP to develop complete, simple applications without writing a single line of Java code, be aware that most JSF applications require event handlers and backend logic implemented as Java classes; hence, you must have a Java programmer handy when you use JSF.

Using JSF with Struts and Other Application Frameworks

You may have noticed that I refer to Struts and similar frameworks as application frameworks, and to JSF as a user interface framework. I do this to emphasize that they have different objectives. An *application framework*'s objective is to support the development of complete applications; it's concerned with the Big Picture. This type of framework acts as a traffic cop, routing HTTP requests to request handling code and internal view requests to response rendering code based on mappings between symbolic names and the different types of application components. An application framework doesn't care about details, such as how the user interface is rendered, or make any distinction between user actions that only affect the user interface (e.g., asking for the next set of rows to be displayed in a table) and actions that need to be processed by backend code (e.g., processing an order on an e-commerce site). Struts, for instance, can use JSP, Velocity, XSLT, or any other presentation layer technology to render a response. The Struts servlet just routes requests to application classes that process them and then tell Struts which page to display next.

A *user interface framework*, on the other hand, focuses on the user interface details and isn't concerned with how the rest of the application is implemented. It defines a detailed API for user interface components, for how user actions result in user interface events and how these events are handled, how the components are tied to the business data they visualize, and so on.

With these differences in mind, it should come as no surprise that it's possible to use JSF with an application framework like Struts. Basically, all requests are processed by JSF until it's clear that backend code needs to be invoked. The control is then passed on to Struts, and eventually comes back to JSF for rendering of the response.

There's some overlap between Struts and JSF, though. Both define mechanisms for page navigation and validation, for instance, but they are so flexible that you can pick and choose which should be in charge of these tasks. The JSF custom tag libraries also make some of the Struts counterparts obsolete, but the Struts Action and model classes can be used without any modification in most cases.

Another class of application frameworks includes component-based presentation layers that are very similar to JSF. Examples include the Barracuda/XMLC and Tapestry open source products, as well as a number of commercial products. These frameworks can be modified to support JSF components in such a way that it would be almost transparent to the applications built on top of them. This will likely happen for most commercial products and possibly for the open source products if there's enough interest.

Using JSF with Enterprise JavaBeans

Enterprise JavaBeans and other J2EE technologies are often employed in complex web applications to support different types or clients (e.g., HTML browsers, WML browsers, and standalone GUI applications) with tight security and transaction handling requirements. These technologies are used to implement the backend code and are not directly tied to the user interface code. As a result, you can use JSF safely with these technologies.

What You Need to Get Started

Before we begin, let's quickly run through what you need in order to work with the examples in this book and develop your own applications:

- A PC or workstation, with a connection to the Internet so you can download the software you need
- A Java 2–compatible Java Software Development Kit (Java 2 SDK)
- A JSP 2.0–enabled* web server, such as Apache Tomcat 5 from the Jakarta Project
- A JSF 1.0 implementation, such as Sun's Reference Implementation

* The JSF 1.0 specification depends on the Servlet 2.3 and JSP 1.2 specification, but I take advantage of the many enhancements made in JSP 2.0 for the examples in this book.

All the examples in the book were tested on Tomcat 5 with the JSF Reference Implementation, but they should work with any JSP 2.0–compliant web container and JSF implementation. In Chapter 4, I'll show you how to download, install, and configure the Tomcat server to run the examples.

In addition, there are a variety of other tools and servers that support JSF, from open source projects and commercial companies. IBM, Oracle, and Sun are some of the companies that have announced plans for JSF development tools, and many others are expected to follow. Two sites to keep an eye on for what's available are *http://java.sun.com/j2ee/javaserverfaces/* (Sun's JSF site) and *http://www.jamesholmes.com/JavaServerFaces/* (an independent JSF resources site run by James Holmes). You may want to evaluate some of these tools when you're ready to start developing your application, but all you really need to work with the examples in this book is a regular text editor, such as Notepad, vi, or Emacs, and of course the Tomcat server.

Let's take a closer look at what JSF has to offer. The next chapter starts with an overview of what it takes to use JSF in an application.

CHAPTER 2

JSF Development Process Overview

Imagine building a flight reservation application with a web interface. The user first enters the departure and destination airports and dates, and preferences such as ticket type, airlines, and number of stops. This information is then validated and the user is presented with matching flight choices. When the user picks his preferred flights, the application ensures that the seats are available and marks them as reserved, calculates the cost, verifies credit card information, and finalizes the purchase.

People who are not computer gurus use applications like this, so the user interface must be intuitive and easy to use, error messages must be understandable, and the underlying problems must be simple to correct. For instance, the interface may let the user pick the destination airport by first asking for a country, state, or city name, and then present a selection of airports matching the criteria, provide calendars for choosing the dates, and display tables with flights to choose from. And the interface must be easy to enhance with accumulated user feedback and usage log analysis. The backend code requirements are also complex: accessing real-time flight schedules and reservation information, interfacing with credit card companies, and providing secure tracking of all transactions.

Clearly, this is not an application that can be slapped together without careful design. Applying the Model-View-Controller (MVC) principles briefly introduced in Chapter 1, we first break the application into classes that represent the business data and logic (the Model, including things like Customer, Airport, Flight, Seat, and so on), the user interface (the View, including things like Departure Input Field, Airport List, and so on), and the code that ties it all together (the Controller).

The View can be implemented in many different ways, using both client-side and server-side technologies. For instance, any of the traditional Java server-side technologies like JSP, Velocity, or plain servlets can render an HTML page with input fields, selection lists, and tables representing calendars. For complex user interfaces like this, however, the traditional technologies tend to result in pages with so much code that it becomes hard to make purely visual changes, such as changing the layout of a table.

With a JSF-based implementation, separate objects represent each user interface element, each keeping track of its UI state (e.g., brief or detailed display, number of rows to display, and the current start index) and its application data (e.g., the selected flight). The user interface objects also know how to render themselves in a way that can be customized based on developer or user settings, or even on the device type making the request. User actions, such as switching from brief to detailed display by clicking a button, are represented as events that can be handled either by the user interface object itself or an external event listener provided by the application developer. This type of event-driven component model has made it easier to develop very complex user interfaces for standalone applications over the years and, with a few twists, it simplifies web application development as well.

Developing an Application with a JSF-Based User Interface

To get an idea of how JSF simplifies development and maintenance of complex web-based user interfaces, let's implement a simple newsletter subscription application. The application contains a form where the user enters an email address and selects the newsletters of interest from a list, plus a button for submitting the form. Figure 2-1 shows this user interface.

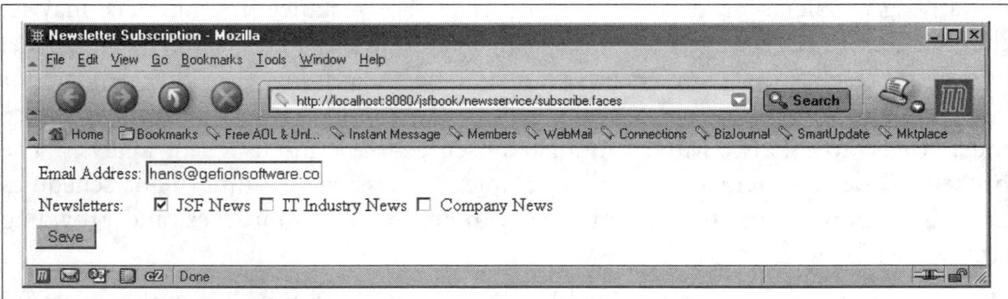

Figure 2-1. Newsletter subscription form

When the user submits the form, the email address and subscription list is saved in a database. Other parts of the application use this information to send the newsletters, but we'll focus on this single page here.

JSF-based application development involves a number of different activities. It helps to define the different roles that the developers play, and then discuss the application aspects each role is responsible for. One person can, of course, take on more than one role. First, you need an implementation of the JSF framework itself. This is the responsibility of the *JSF implementor*, a role that's usually performed by web container vendors. Another role, the *tool provider*, is responsible for developing tools to support JSF application development. Some web container vendors take on this role as well, but vendors specializing in development tools, such as Macromedia, are also likely candidates. Remember that JSF is a specification, not a product, so you have a choice of many competing implementations.

Most development projects use an existing JSF framework and tools, so let's focus on the remaining roles: the *application developer*, the *component writer*, and the *page author*. Implementing the newsletter subscription example shows you what parts each role is responsible for and gives you a glimpse of how JSF works.

Developing the Application Backend

The application developer is primarily responsible for developing the backend part of the application; in other words, the classes that handle business logic and data.

For the newsletter subscription form, the application developer may create a class called `Subscriber` to hold the subscriber information:

```
package com.mycompany.newsservice.models;

public class Subscriber {
    private String emailAddr;
    private String[] subscriptionIds;

    public String getEmailAddr( ) {
        return emailAddr;
    }

    public void setEmailAddr(String emailAddr) {
        this.emailAddr = emailAddr;
    }

    public String[] getSubscriptionIds( ) {
        return subscriptionIds;
    }

    public void setSubscriptionIds(String[] subscriptionIds) {
        this.subscriptionIds = subscriptionIds;
    }
}
```

The `Subscriber` class adheres to the JavaBeans method naming conventions—"properties" are defined by methods for getting their values, named `get` plus the name of the property, and methods for setting their values, named `set` plus the property name. As you'll see shortly, this makes it easy to use properties of this class as JSF UI component models.

When a subscription is registered or updated, the information must be saved somewhere, likely in a database. The application developer may decide to develop a separate class responsible for this task or put this logic in the `Subscriber` class. To keep the example simple, we'll add a method that represents this behavior to the

Subscriber class. Also, instead of saving the information in a database, we just write it to System.out:

```
public void save( ) {
    StringBuffer subscriptions = new StringBuffer( );
    if (subscriptionIds != null) {
        for (int i = 0; i < subscriptionIds.length; i++) {
            subscriptions.append(subscriptionIds[i]).append(" ");
        }
    }
    System.out.println("Subscriber Email Address: " + emailAddress +
       "\nSubscriptions: " + subscriptions);
}
```

This is all the backend code we need for this simple application. Note, however, that none of these application classes refer to JSF classes; the same classes could be used with any type of user interface.

Developing Components and Integration Code

The component writer develops all application-specific Java code needed for the user interface, ranging from simple classes that tie the user interface to the application backend code developed by the application developer to custom user interface components when the ones provided by JSF aren't sufficient.

Figure 2-2 shows the main classes and interfaces used by the newsletter application.

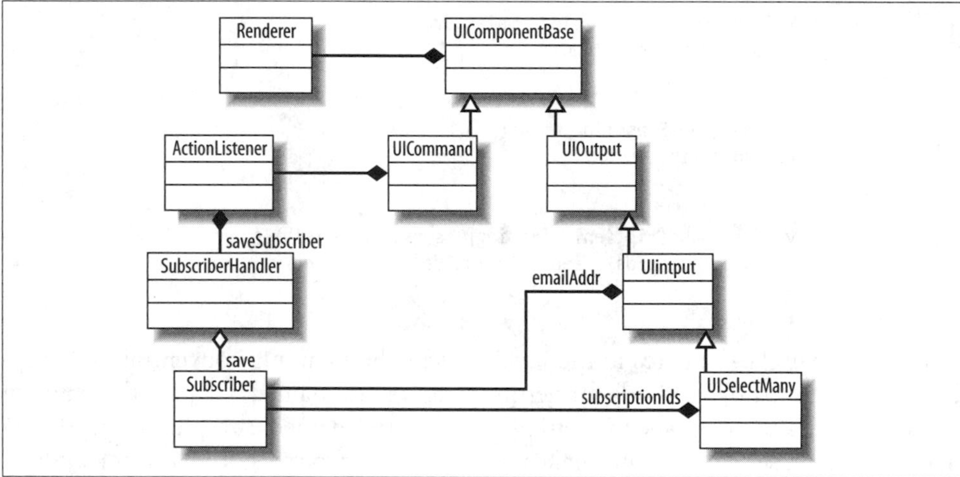

Figure 2-2. JSF component-related classes and the Subscriber application class

You probably recognize the Subscriber class from the previous section. The component writer develops the SubscriberHandler class, as shown in this section. All the other classes in Figure 2-2 are provided by the JSF implementation.

The UIComponentBase class is the base class for all JSF UI components. Subclasses represent specific interface elements, such as text fields, links and buttons, labels, menus and selection lists. JSF includes a set of component classes that can be used right out of the box, such as the ones shown in Figure 2-2, but a component writer can also implement custom components if needed. The UIInput class represents an input field and lets you bind the component to an application model through a *value binding*. When a component is rendered, it pulls its value from the application model object based on this value binding. Similarly, when an input component processes a request, it updates the model it's bound to with the value received with the request. In this example, value bindings for the UIInput and the UISelectMany (the checkbox group) components bind the components to the corresponding properties in the Subscriber application class.

The components fire events in response to user actions (such as clicking a button) and event listeners attached to the components handle the events (for example, by updating a database). Instead of implementing and registering listeners for each component, most JSF applications take advantage of shortcuts in the form of *method bindings*. A method binding is similar to a value binding, but it binds a component to an application method instead of an application property value. For instance, the UICommand component has a property that takes a method binding value. When the component fires an ActionEvent, a default ActionListener provided by JSF and automatically attached to the component invokes the method that the method binding points to. All the component writer needs to do is implement the method.

For the subscription example application, let's say that the component writer implements the action event processing method in a new class called SubscriberHandler:

```
package com.mycompany.newsservice.handlers;

import com.mycompany.newsservice.models.Subscriber;

public class SubscriberHandler {
    private Subscriber subscriber;

    public void setSubscriber(Subscriber subscriber) {
        this.subscriber = subscriber;
    }

    public String saveSubscriber( ) {
        subscriber.save( );
        return "success";
    }
}
```

The SubscriberHandler class has two methods: a setter method for associating it with an instance of the Subscriber class and a method for handling the Save button ActionEvent. The saveSubscriber( ) method simply calls the save( ) method on the Subscriber instance and returns success. In a real application, it would return one or more other values if things didn't go as planned, e.g., `systemFailure` if the database wasn't available.

It may seem like overkill to create a new class with the only purpose of calling a method in the application backend class, and in this simple example, it probably is. As you'll see when we start implementing a more complex application, there's a lot more that typically goes into this type of class. Its main purpose is to bridge the gap between the pure application objects and JSF components. For instance, it would be a bit odd for the `save()` method in `Subscriber` to return a `String`, but it serves a purpose for a JSF action event processing method to do so, because JSF can use the returned value to decide what to do next. But let's save that for later and move on to the next component writer task.

JSF creates and configures instances of application classes, such as the `Subscriber` and `SubscriberHandler` classes, based on information specified in a configuration file named *faces-config.xml*. It makes the instances available through variables that the page author uses in value and method binding expressions, as you'll see in the next section. Creating the configuration file is a task that also falls on the component writer's shoulders because it's part of tying the user interface and the backend together. Here's a snippet of the configuration file with the declarations for the example application classes:

```
<faces-config>
  ...
  <managed-bean>
    <managed-bean-name>subscr</managed-bean-name>
    <managed-bean-class>
      com.mycompany.newsservice.models.Subscriber
    </managed-bean-class>
    <managed-bean-scope>session</managed-bean-scope>
  </managed-bean>
  <managed-bean>
    <managed-bean-name>subscrHandler</managed-bean-name>
    <managed-bean-class>
      com.mycompany.newsservice.handlers.SubscriberHandler
    </managed-bean-class>
    <managed-bean-scope>request</managed-bean-scope>
    <managed-property>
      <property-name>subscriber</property-name>
      <value>#{subscr}</value>
    </managed-property>
  </managed-bean>
  ...
</faces-config>
```

As is customary these days, the configuration file is an XML document. The application objects are declared by `<managed-bean>` elements. The first `<managed-bean>` element declares that an instance of the `Subscriber` class should be made available as a session scope variable named `subscr`. I'll get back to the scope in Chapter 4, but declaring the scope as session (as in this example) means that a unique instance is created for each user and remains available as long as the user actively uses the application.

The second `<managed-bean>` element contains a similar declaration of a variable named `subscrHandler` as an instance of the `SubscriberHandler`, but it also contains a `<managed-property>` element, saying that its `subscriber` property must be initialized with the value of the `subscr` variable. This is how the `SubscriberHandler` instance is linked to the `Subscriber` instance.

Developing the User Interface Pages

With the Java classes defined and implemented in some form (maybe just prototypes initially), the page author can get to work.

The page author is the person who is responsible for developing the pages that make up the application's user interface, typically as templates that interleave static content (text, graphics, tables for layout, and so on) with dynamically generated content. A page is represented by a set of UI component instances bound to the application's data and methods. The static content and the dynamic content generated by the components is combined and sent to the browser. When the user clicks a link or a button in the page, the request is processed by the methods bound to the UI components. Depending on the outcome, the same page may be rendered again or the application may select a new page to send back to the user.

As I mentioned earlier, JSF can be combined with different presentation layer technologies, so the details of what the template looks like may vary depending on the options supported by the JSF implementation. For better or for worse, JSF 1.0 requires all implementations to support JSP as one of the possible presentation layer technologies. On one hand, JSP is familiar to many developers, so it lowers the barrier of entry to JSF. On the other hand, JSP has its own mechanism for adding dynamic content to a static template; when mixed with JSF UI components, there's a risk for confusion and clashes between the two technologies. I use JSP for the newsletter application and for most of the other examples in this book, but you should be aware that it's not the only option. Don't worry too much about the potential clashes between JSP and JSF. I'll explain the issues and show you how to steer clear of the potential problems as we encounter them.

When JSP is used as the presentation layer technology, the page author creates a JSP page with the static content plus special elements that represent JSF components. Example 2-1 shows a JSP page with JSF elements for the newsletter subscription form.

Example 2-1. JSP page with JSF elements for the subscription form (newsservice/subscribe.jsp)

```
<%@ taglib uri="http://java.sun.com/jsf/html" prefix="h" %>
<%@ taglib uri="http://java.sun.com/jsf/core" prefix="f" %>
<html>
  <head>
```

Example 2-1. JSP page with JSF elements for the subscription form (newsservice/subscribe.jsp)

```
    <title>Newsletter Subscription</title>
  </head>
  <body>
    <f:view>
      <h:form>
        <table>
          <tr>
            <td>Email Address:</td>
            <td>
              <h:inputText value="#{subscr.emailAddr}" />
            </td>
          </tr>
          <td>
            <td>News Letters:</td>
            <td>
              <h:selectManyCheckbox value="#{subscr.subscriptionIds}">
                <f:selectItem itemValue="1" itemLabel="JSF News" />
                <f:selectItem itemValue="2" itemLabel="IT Industry News" />
                <f:selectItem itemValue="3" itemLabel="Company News" />
              </h:selectManyCheckbox>
            </td>
          </tr>
        </table>
        <h:commandButton value="Save"
          action="#{subscrHandler.saveSubscriber}" />
      </h:form>
    </f:view>
  </body>
</html>
```

At the beginning of Example 2-1, you find two JSP custom tag library declarations. If you're not familiar with JSP, don't worry. I'll explain what you need to know in Chapter 4. For now, just accept that these declarations identify all elements with the specified prefixes as special JSF elements. Elements with the prefix `h` (short for HTML) represents the standard JSF UI components combined with HTML renderers; elements with the prefix `f` (short for Faces) represent validators, event listeners, etc. that can be attached to the UI components.

Following the custom tag library declarations, there are HTML elements for layout and JSF elements corresponding to the JSF UI components. Ignoring the `<f:view>` element for now, the first JSF element of interest is the `<h:form>` element, representing a JSF form component. The same as in HTML, JSF input components must always be nested within a form component.

The email address input component is represented by the `<h:inputText>` element. The `value` attribute contains a value binding expression that binds the component to the `emailAddr` property of an application bean named `subscr`. As you may recall, this is the name assigned to the `Subscriber` bean in the JSF configuration file. The list of newsletter choices is represented by an `<h:selectManyCheckbox>` element with a nested `<f:selectItem>` element for each choice. The `<h:selectManyCheckbox>` element `value` attribute is set to a value expression that binds the component to the `subscriptionIds` property of the `Subscriber` bean available through the `subscr` variable.

Finally, there's an `<h:commandButton>` element representing the Save button, with an `action` attribute containing a method binding expression that binds it to the `saveSubscriber()` method of the `SubscriberHandler` bean available through the `subscrHandler` variable.

Figure 2-3 illustrates what happens when a user requests the JSP page for the first time, and how the value and method binding expressions for the JSF elements in the JSP page combined with the bean declarations in the *faces-config.xml* file ties the whole thing together.

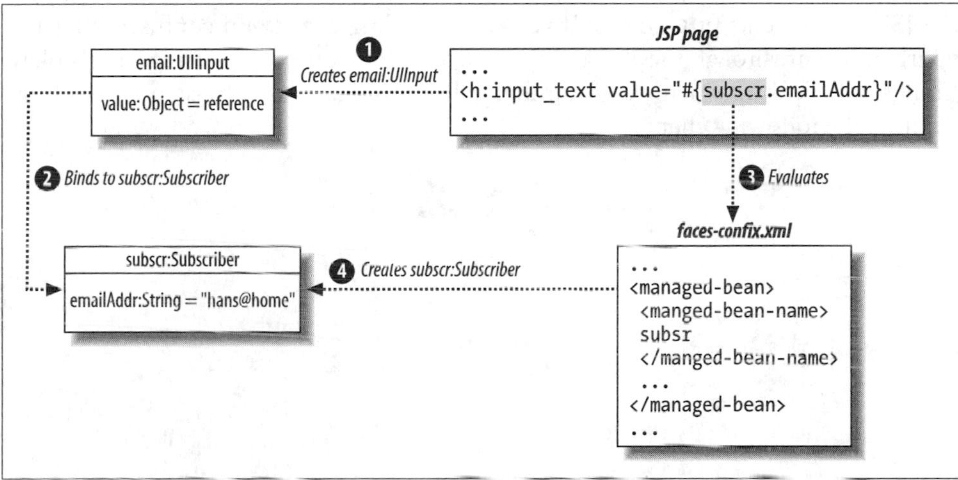

Figure 2-3. Object creation when processing the JSP page the first time

When the `<h:textInput>` element is processed, the corresponding `UIInput` component is created and bound to the bean property specified by the value binding expression. The component is then asked to render itself. It evaluates the value binding expression and, if the bean doesn't already exist, JSF creates it based on the information in the *faces-config.xml* file. The input component pulls its value from the property of the bean specified by the rest of the value binding expression and uses it as the value of the HTML `<input>` element it renders. The other JSF elements are processed in the same way, and the combination of static content and the content generated by the JSF components is sent to the browser.

When the user enters values in the form and clicks the Submit button, JSF processes the request by asking each component to get its value from the request. Each input component sets the bean property it's bound to, and the command component fires an event that causes the method it's bound to be invoked. The method typically saves the new values to a database or does some other backend processing, but in this simple example, as you may recall, it just writes the values to the console.

JSF then creates a response by processing the same or another JSP page (depending on the event processing method's return value and configuration-options we haven't talked about yet). If the same page is used, the component and application objects already exist, so no new objects are created. Other than that, the JSP page is processed exactly as for the first request.

This is a very simplified description of what really occurs at runtime. As you will learn, there's a lot more that may happen when a form is submitted, such as input value conversion and validation, error message queuing, forced redisplay of the same page without updating any bean properties, and more. But I've tried to keep it simple in this chapter to help you understand the basics of how the application code and the JSF components fit together. If you're still feeling dazed and confused after this whirlwind tour through the JSF architecture and the request processing, that's okay. Things will clear up when we go through all of this again, step-by-step and in more detail in the following chapters.

CHAPTER 3

Setting Up the JSF Environment

You need two things to run a JSF application: a Java web container and an implementation of the JSF specification.

There are plenty of Java web containers available, including commercial offerings, such as Caucho Technology's Resin, the BEA WebLogic Server, the IBM WebSphere Application Server, and the Oracle Application Server, and open source products, such as the Apache Tomcat server, Mortbay's Jetty server, and Gefion Software's LiteWebServer. JSF requires a web container that implements at least the Servlet 2.3 and JSP 1.2 specifications (part of J2EE 1.3), but the examples in this book use some features introduced in JSP 2.0, so to run them as is, you need a web container that implements the Servlet 2.4 and JSP 2.0 specifications (part of J2EE 1.4). All examples have been tested with the open source Tomcat 5 server (on which the reference implementation for these specifications is based) and I recommend that you use it as you read this book and develop your own JSF applications.

JSF is such a new technology that as of this writing, there aren't many implementations besides the reference implementation from Sun Microsystems available yet.* This will change during 2004, though, so when you read this, your favorite web container may bundle a JSF implementation. The web application containing all the book examples includes a version of the reference implementation, and I recommend that you use it. You can always download the latest version of the JSF reference implementation from Sun's site at *http://java.sun.com/j2ee/javaserverfaces*. For deployment of your applications, you may want to use the JSF implementation supported by your production server instead, if any.

In this chapter, you will learn how to install the Tomcat server and deploy the web application containing all the examples used in this book. You can, of course, use

* As of this writing, there are two open source implementations that I know of, but none of them complies with the final version of the standard. That may have changed by the time you read this, so if you want to check them out, they are available at *http://smile.sourceforge.net/* and *http://sourceforge.net/projects/myfaces/*.

any web server that supports JSP 2.0, but Tomcat is a good server for development and test purposes. You can learn more about the Jakarta project and Tomcat, as well as how you can participate in the development, at the Jakarta web site: *http://jakarta.apache.org/*.

Installing the Java Software Development Kit

Tomcat 5 is a pure Java web server with support for the Servlet 2.4 and JSP 2.0 specifications. In order to use it, you must first install a Java runtime environment. If you don't already have one, you can download a Java runtime for Windows, Linux, and Solaris at *http://java.sun.com/j2se/*. I recommend that you download and install the Java 2 SDK (a.k.a. JDK), as opposed to the slimmed-down Runtime Environment (JRE) distribution. The reason is that JSP, and therefore JSF applications that use JSP, requires a Java compiler, included in the SDK but not in the JRE.

Another alternative is to use the JRE plus the Jikes compiler from IBM (*http://www10.software.ibm.com/developerworks/opensource/jikes/*). Tomcat can be configured to use Jikes instead of the *javac* compiler available in the Java 2 SDK from Sun; read the Tomcat documentation if you would like to try this. To make things simple, though, I suggest installing the Java 2 SDK from Sun. The examples were developed and tested with Java 2 SDK, Standard Edition, v1.4.2. I suggest that you use the latest version of the SDK available for your platform.

If you need an SDK for a platform other than Windows, Linux, or Solaris, check your operating-system vendor's web site. Most operating-system vendors have their own SDK implementation available for free. Installation of the SDK varies per platform, but it is typically easy to do. Just follow the instructions on the web site where you download the SDK.

Before you install and run Tomcat, make sure that the `JAVA_HOME` environment variable is set to the installation directory of your Java environment, and that the Java *bin* directory is included in the `PATH` environment variable. On a Windows system, you can see if an environment variable is set by typing the following command in a command prompt window:

```
C:\> echo %JAVA_HOME%
C:\jdk1.4.2
```

If `JAVA_HOME` isn't set, you can set it and include the *bin* directory in the `PATH` on a Windows system like this (assuming Java is installed in *C:\jdk1.4.2*):

```
C:\> set JAVA_HOME=C:\jdk1.4.2
C:\> set PATH=%JAVA_HOME%\bin;%PATH%
```

On a Windows 95/98/ME system, you can add these commands to the *C:\AUTOEXEC.BAT* file to set them permanently. Just use a text editor, such as *Notepad*, and add lines with the set commands. The next time you boot the PC, the environment variables will be set automatically. For Windows NT, you can set them permanently from the Environment tab in the System Properties tool in the Control Panel, and for Windows 2000 and Windows XP, you can do the same with the Control Panel System tool by first selecting the Advanced tab and then Environment Variables.

If you use Linux, Mac OS X, or some other Unix-based platform, the exact commands depend on which shell you use. With *bash*, which is commonly the default for Linux, use the following commands (assuming Java is installed in */usr/local/jdk1.4.2*):

```
[hans@gefion /] export JAVA_HOME=/usr/local/jdk1.4.2
[hans@gefion /] export PATH=$JAVA_HOME/bin:$PATH
[hans@gefion /] echo $PATH
/usr/local/jdk1.4.2/bin:/usr/local/bin:/bin:/usr/bin
```

Installing the Tomcat Server

Tomcat supports many features and configuration options. In this section, I only describe the basics that you need to know to get Tomcat up and running. If you plan to use Tomcat extensively for development or as a production server, you'll find extensive information in Jason Brittain and Ian Darwin's *Tomcat: The Definite Guide* (O'Reilly).

You can download the Tomcat server in binary format or as source code that you compile yourself. If you're primarily interested in learning about JSF, I recommend that you use the binary download for running the examples in this book and to develop your own applications. If you're a Java programmer and are interested in seeing how Tomcat is implemented, feel free to download the source as well and take a look at the internals.

The binary distribution is available at *http://jakarta.apache.org/site/binindex.cgi*. On this page, you will find three types of builds: release builds, milestone builds, and nightly builds. *Release builds* are stable releases that have been tested extensively and verified to comply with the supported specifications. *Milestone builds* are created as intermediary steps towards a release build. They often contain new features that aren't yet fully tested but are generally known to work. A *nightly build*, however, may be very unstable. It's actually a snapshot of the latest source code and may have been tested only by the person who made the latest change. You should use a nightly build only if you're involved in the development of Tomcat.

I recommend that you download the latest release build. All examples in this book were developed and tested using Version 5.0.18, but any release later than 5.0.18 should work fine as well. The release builds are available as archive files of different formats. Which one to pick and how to install it varies a bit, depending on your platform.

Windows Platforms

For Windows, select *jakarta-tomcat-5.0.18.zip*[*] and save it to your hard drive—for instance, in a directory named *C:\Jakarta*. Unpack the package either with a ZIP utility program such as *WinZip* or use the jar command included in the Java distribution. Use the Command Prompt window where you set the JAVA_HOME and PATH environment variables, change to the directory in which you downloaded the ZIP file, and unpack it:

```
C:\> cd Jakarta
C:\Jakarta> jar xvf jakarta-tomcat-5.0.18.zip
```

This creates a directory structure that has a top directory named *jakarta-tomcat-5.0.18* and a number of subdirectories. Like most software packages, the top directory contains a file named *README.txt*; do that. Software distributions change and if, for instance, the instructions in this chapter no longer apply when you download the software, the *README.txt* file should contain information about how to get started. Additional details are found in the file named *RUNNING.txt*.

You should also set the CATALINA_HOME environment variable to point to the Tomcat installation directory:

```
C:\Jakarta> set CATALINA_HOME=C:\Jakarta\jakarta-tomcat-5.0.18
```

If you wonder about the variable name, *Catalina* is the name of the servlet container and *Jasper* is the name of the JSP container; together, they are known as the Tomcat server.

The Tomcat installation directory contains a number of subdirectories, described later. The *bin* directory contains Windows batch files for starting and stopping the server. The batch files are named *startup.bat*, *shutdown.bat*, and *catalina.bat*. The *catalina.bat* file is the main script for controlling the server; it's called by the two other scripts (*startup.bat* and *shutdown.bat*). To start the server in a separate window, change to the *bin* directory and run the *startup.bat* file:

```
C:\Jakarta> cd jakarta-tomcat-5.0.18\bin
C:\Jakarta\jakarta-tomcat-5.0.18\bin> startup
```

A new Command Prompt window pops up; you see startup messages similar to this:

```
Feb 29, 2004 12:53:59 PM org.apache.coyote.http11.Http11Protocol init
INFO: Initializing Coyote HTTP/1.1 on port 8080
Feb 29, 2004 12:53:59 PM org.apache.catalina.startup.Catalina load
INFO: Initialization processed in 2260 ms
...
INFO: Server startup in 7408 ms
```

Just leave this window open; this is where the server process is running.

[*] There's also a file with an *.exe* extension in the list of downloads. This is a GUI installer for Windows. While it simplifies the installation, it makes it almost impossible to debug installation problems and it doesn't work at all for older versions of Windows, e.g., Windows ME. I suggest that you use the command-line installation process described in this chapter, at least until you're familiar enough with Tomcat to handle the GUI installer issues.

If you're running this on a Windows 95/98/ME platform, you may see an error message "Out of environment space," when you try to start the server. That's because the default amount of space allocated for environment variables isn't enough. To be able to run Tomcat, run this command in the Command Prompt window before you run the *startup.bat* file again:

```
C:\Jakarta\jakarta-tomcat\bin> COMMAND.COM /E:4096 /P
```

This command sets the environment space to 4,096 bytes (4 KB). That should be enough for running this batch file. If you still get the same message, use a higher value.

For some installations, this command may not work. If it doesn't, try this instead:

1. Close the Command Prompt window, and open a new one.
2. Click on the MS-DOS icon at the top left of the window.
3. Select the Properties option.
4. Click on the Memory tab.
5. Change the Initial Environment value from Auto to 4096.
6. Click on OK and try to start the server again.

At this point, the server may not start due to other problems. If so, the extra Command Prompt window may pop up and then disappear before you have a chance to read the error messages. If this happens, you can let the server run in the Command Prompt window with this command instead:

```
C:\Jakarta\jakarta-tomcat-5.0.18\bin> catalina run
```

On Windows NT/2000 and Windows XP, you should first make sure that the Command Prompt window has a large enough screen buffer so that you can scroll back in case the error messages don't fit on one screen. Open the Properties window for the Command Prompt window (right mouse button in the upper-left corner), select Layout, and set the screen buffer size height to a large value (for instance, 999). Unfortunately, the Command Prompt screen buffer can't be enlarged for Windows 95/98/ME, so scrolling back isn't an option. If you run into problems on these platforms, double-check that you have installed the Java SDK correctly and that you have set the JAVA HOME and PATH environment variables as described earlier.

Unix Platforms (Including Linux and Mac OS X)

For Unix platforms, you can download the *jakarta-tomcat-5.0.18.tar.gz* file, for instance to */usr/local*, and use these commands to unpack it (assuming you have GNU *tar* installed):

```
[hans@gefion /] cd /usr/local
[hans@gefion local] tar xzvf jakarta-tomcat-5.0.18.tar.gz
```

If you don't have GNU *tar* installed on your system, use the following command:

```
[hans@gefion local] gunzip -c jakarta-tomcat-5.0.18.tar.gz | tar xvf -
```

This creates a directory structure that has a top directory named *jakarta-tomcat-5.0.18* and a number of subdirectories. As in most software packages, the top directory contains a file named *README.txt*; do that. Software distributions change and if, for instance, the instructions in this chapter no longer apply when you download the software, the *README.txt* file should contain information about how to get started. Additional details can be found in the file named *RUNNING.txt*.

You should also set the CATALINA_HOME environment variable to point to the Tomcat installation directory:

```
[hans@gefion local] export CATALINA_HOME=/usr/local/jakarta-tomcat-5.0.18
```

Catalina is the name of the servlet container, and *Jasper* is the name of the JSP container; together, they are known as the Tomcat server.

The Tomcat installation directory contains a number of subdirectories, described later. The *bin* directory contains Unix scripts for starting and stopping the server. The scripts are named *startup.sh*, *shutdown.sh*, and *catalina.sh*.

Start the server in the background with this command:

```
[hans@gefion jakarta-tomcat-5.0.18] ./startup.sh
```

If you want to have Tomcat start each time you boot the system, you can add the following commands to your */etc/rc.d/rc.local* (or equivalent) startup script:

```
export JAVA_HOME=/usr/local/jdk1.4.2
export CATALINA_HOME=/usr/local/jakarta-tomcat-5.0.18
$CATALINA_HOME/bin/startup.sh
```

Testing Tomcat

The Tomcat installation directory contains a number of subdirectories. All of them are described in the *README.txt* file, but the most important ones are:

bin
: Scripts for starting and stopping the Tomcat server.

conf
: Tomcat configuration files.

webapps
: Default location for web applications served by Tomcat.

Two more subdirectories under the Tomcat home directory are created the first time you start the server:

logs
: Server log files. If something doesn't work as expected, look in the files in this directory for clues as to what's wrong.

work
: A directory for temporary files created by the JSP container and other files. This directory is where the servlets generated from JSP pages are stored.

To test the server, run the startup script as described in the platform-specific sections, and (assuming you're running Tomcat on the same machine as the browser and that you're using the default 8080 port for Tomcat) open a browser and enter this URL in the Location/Address field: *http://localhost:8080/*.

The Tomcat main page is shown in the browser, as in Figure 3-1. You can now run all examples bundled with Tomcat to ensure everything works.

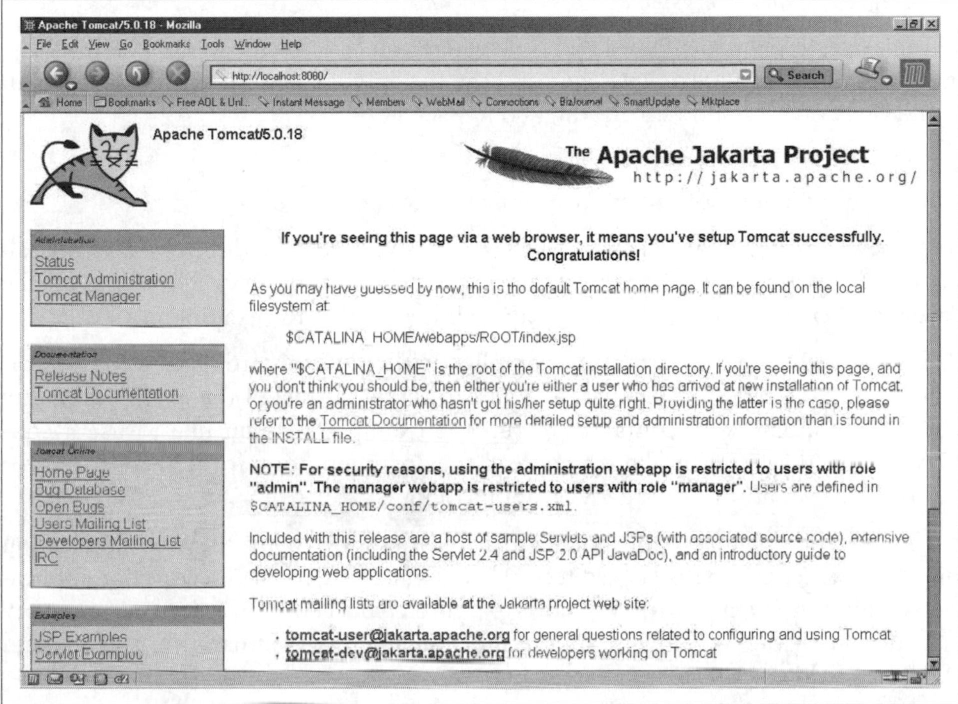

Figure 3-1. The Tomcat main page

If you're trying this on a machine that sits behind a proxy—for instance, on a corporate network—and instead of Tomcat's main page you see an error message about not being able to connect to `localhost`, you need to adjust your proxy settings. For Netscape and Mozilla, you find the proxy settings under Edit → Preferences → Advanced → Proxies, and for Internet Explorer, you find them under Tools → Internet Options → Connections → LAN Settings. Make sure that the proxy isn't used for local addresses, such as `localhost` and 127.0.0.1.

When you're done testing Tomcat, stop the server like this:

```
C:\Jakarta\jakarta-tomcat-5.0.18\bin> shutdown
```

Installing the Book Examples

All JSP pages, HTML pages, Java source code, and class files for the examples can be downloaded from the O'Reilly site at *http://www.oreilly.com/catalog/jsvrfaces/*.

They can also be downloaded from my personal web site, where you also find articles, tips, and other resources:

http://www.hansbergsten.com/

On this site, you'll find a Download page where you can download the examples distribution file, called *jsfexamples.zip*. Save the file on your hard drive (for instance, in *C:\JSFBook* on a Windows platform) and unpack it:

```
C:\JSFBook> jar xvf jsfexamples.zip
```

You can use the same command on a Unix platform.

Two new directories are created: *jsfbook* and *src*. The first directory contains all examples described in this book, and the second contains the Java source files for the JavaBeans, custom components, and other classes used in the examples.

The examples directory structure complies with the standard Java web application format described in Chapter 4. You can therefore install the examples in any JSP 2.0-compliant web container to run the examples. If you like to use a container other than Tomcat, be sure to read the documentation for that container for instructions on how to install a web application.

To install the example application for Tomcat, simply copy the web application directory structure (the *jsfbook* directory) to Tomcat's default directory for applications, called *webapps*. On a Windows platform, you can copy/paste the directory structure with the Windows Explorer tool, or use this command in a Command Prompt window:

```
C:\JSFBook> xcopy /s /i jsfbook %CATALINA_HOME%\webapps\jsfbook
```

On a Unix platform it looks like this:

```
[hans@gefion jsfbook] cp -R jsfbook $CATALINA_HOME/webapps
```

As you'll learn more about in Chapter 4, each web application in a server is associated with a unique URI prefix (the context path). When you install an application in Tomcat's *webapps* directory, the subdirectory name is assigned automatically as the URI prefix for the application (*/jsfbook*, in this case).

To run the examples, you must also define a couple of usernames. If you use the Tomcat server, edit the *CATALINA_HOME/conf/tomcat-users.xml* file and add these lines somewhere within the `<tomcat-users>` element (this process is described in more detail in Chapter 4):

```
<tomcat-users>
  <role rolename="manager" />
  <role rolename="employee" />
  ...
  <user username="mike" password="boss" roles="manager" />
  <user username="hans" password="secret" roles="employee" />
  ...
</tomcat-users>
```

At this point, you must shut down and restart the Tomcat server. After that, you can point your browser to the *jsfbook* application with the following URL:

http://localhost:8080/jsfbook/

You should see a start page, as in Figure 3-2, that contains links to all examples in this book.

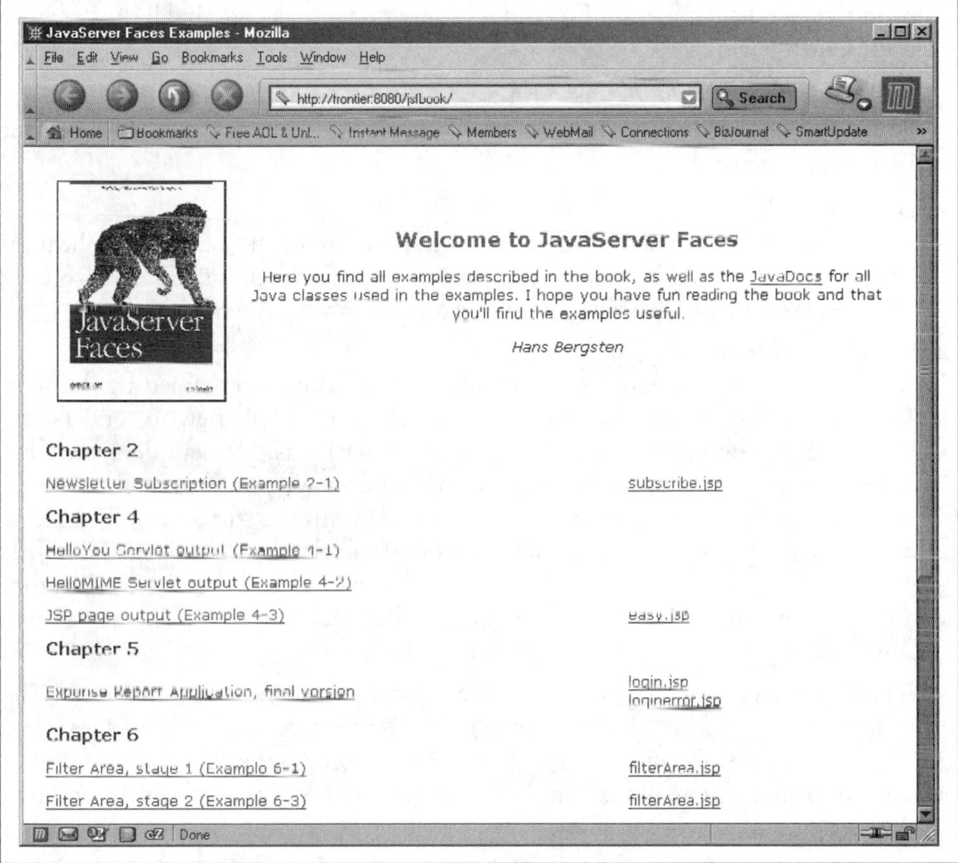

Figure 3-2. JSF book examples start page

Example Web Application Overview

The examples for this book are packaged as a standard Java web application. All servers compliant with the JSP 2.0 specification support this file structure, so you can use the example application as a guideline when you create your own web applications. How a web application is installed isn't defined by the specification, though, and it varies between servers. With Tomcat, you simply copy the file structure to the special *webapps* directory and restart the server. To modify the configuration information for an application, you must edit the application's *WEB-INF/web.xml* file using a text editor. Other servers may offer special deployment tools that copy the files where they belong, and let you configure the application using a special tool or through web-based forms.

If you look in the *jsfbook* web application directory, you'll see that it contains an *index.html* file and a number of directories. These directories contain all the example JSP and HTML pages.

There's also a *WEB-INF* directory with a *web.xml* file, a *lib* directory, and a *classes* directory. We will look at this in much more detail later, starting in Chapter 4, but here's a quick review:

web.xml file
: The *web.xml* file contains configuration information for the example application in the format defined by the servlet and JSP specifications. It's too early to look at the contents of this file now; we will return to parts of it when needed.

Lib and classes directories
: The *lib* and *classes* directories are standard directories, also defined by the servlet specification. A very common question asked by people new to servlets and JSP (prior to the standard web application format) was, "Where do I store my class files so that the server can find them?" The answer, unfortunately, differed depending on which implementation was used. With the standard web application format, it's easy to answer this question: if the classes are packaged in a JAR file, store the JAR file in the *lib* directory; otherwise, use the *classes* directory (with subdirectories mirroring the classes' package structure). The server will always look for Java class files in these two directories.

: The *lib* directory for the example application contains a number of JAR files. The *custom_jsf_lib_1_x.jar* and *sample_app_1_x.jar* files contain all the Java class files for the book examples. The other JAR files contain the JSF and JSTL Reference Implementation, plus all the classes that these implementations depend on.

: The *classes* directory contains the class for the `JSPSourceServlet` that displays the raw source code for the example JSP pages, so you can see what they look like before the server processes them. It also contains all *.properties* files with localized text for the example in Chapter 11 and a few test servlets described in Chapter 4.

If you want to try out some of your own JSP pages, beans, and other classes while reading this book, simply add the files to the example application structure: JSP pages in any directory except under *WEB-INF*, and Java class files in either the *classes* or the *lib* directory—depending on whether the classes are packaged in a JAR file or not. Alternatively, you can, of course, create your own web application structure and copy the JAR files you need from the example application.

CHAPTER 4

Servlet and JavaServer Pages Basics

A JSF-based application runs as a web application in a Java web container. While the Java Servlet API dependencies are limited to a few classes, and a simple JSF application never needs to be exposed to it, the main concepts defined by the Servlet specification must be understood to develop and deploy a JSF application. In addition, JavaServer Pages (JSP) technology—which is based on the Servlet API—is often used as the presentation layer in a JSF application.

This chapter is a brief introduction to the Hypertext Transport Protocol (HTTP), servlets, and JSP, focusing on the areas that are important for a JSF application. This chapter contains the bare minimum you need to know to understand the rest of this book. I recommend that you read books dedicated to the subjects of servlets and JSP before you embark on a real development project. Two books I can recommend are Jason Hunter's and William Crawford's *Java Servlet Programming* (O'Reilly) and my own *JavaServer Pages* (O'Reilly). If you're already familiar with these technologies, you can safely skip this chapter.

HTTP

The Hypertext Transport Protocol (HTTP) is the lingua franca of the web. In order to develop any type of web application, you must understand at least the basics of this protocol. Before we dig into servlets and JSP, let's see what HTTP is all about.

HTTP is based on a very simple communications model. Here's how it works: a client, typically a web browser, sends a *request* for a *resource* to a server, and the server sends back a *response* corresponding to the resource (or a response with an error message if it can't process the request for some reason). A resource can be a number of things, such as a simple HTML file returned verbatim to the browser or a program that generates the response dynamically. The request/response model is illustrated in Figure 4-1.

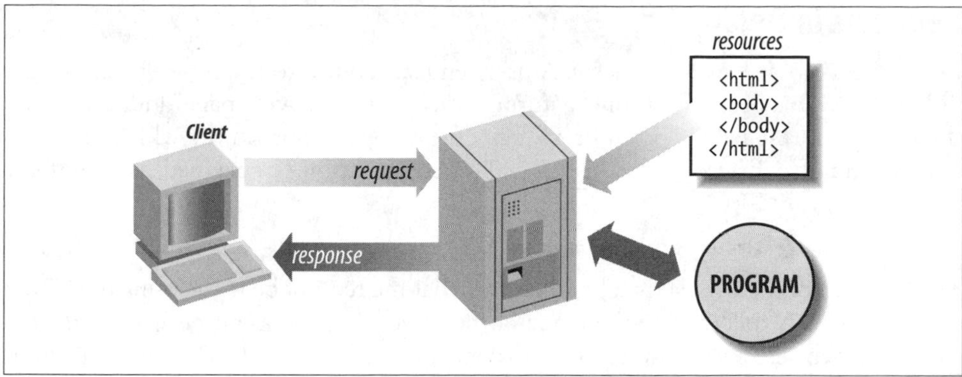

Figure 4-1. HTTP request/response with two resources

This simple model implies three important facts you must be aware of:

- HTTP is a stateless protocol; the server doesn't keep any information about the client after it sends its response, and therefore can't recognize that multiple requests from the same client may be related.
- Web applications can't easily provide the kind of immediate feedback typically found in standalone GUI applications, such as word processors or traditional client/server applications. Every interaction between the client and the server requires a request/response exchange. Performing a request/response exchange when a user selects an item in a list box or fills out a form element is usually too taxing on the bandwidth available to most Internet users.
- There's nothing in the protocol that tells the server how a request is made; consequently, the server can't distinguish between various methods of triggering the request on the client. For example, the server can't differentiate between an explicit request caused by clicking a link or submitting a form and an implicit request caused by resizing the browser window or using the browser's Back button. In addition, HTTP doesn't provide any means for the server to invoke client specific functions, such as going back in the browser history list or sending the response to a certain frame. Also, the server can't detect when the user closes the browser.

Over the years, people have developed various tricks to overcome HTTP's stateless nature—the first problem. JSF uses these tricks behind the scenes, so you rarely need to worry about it, but we'll look at how it's done later. The other two problems—no immediate feedback and no details about how the request is made—are harder to deal with, but some amount of interactivity can be achieved by generating a response that includes client-side code (code executed by the browser), such as JavaScript or a Java applet. JSF user interface components can generate this code for you.

Requests in Detail

Let's take a closer look at requests. A user sends a request to the server by clicking a link on a web page, submitting a form, or typing in a web page address in the browser's address field. To send a request, the browser must know which server to talk to and which resource to ask for. This information is specified as a *uniform resource locator* (URL):

```
http://www.gefionsoftware.com/index.html
```

The first part of the URL shown here specifies that the request be made using the HTTP protocol. This is followed by the name of the server, in this case *www.gefionsoftware.com*. The web server waits for requests to come in on a specific TCP/IP port. Port number 80 is the standard port for HTTP requests. If the web server uses another port, the URL must specify the port number in addition to the server name. For example:

```
http://www.gefionsoftware.com:8080/index.html
```

This request is sent to a server that uses port 8080 instead of 80. The last part of the URL, */index.html*, identifies the resource that the client is requesting.

A URL is actually a specialization of a *uniform resource identifier* (URI, defined in the RFC 2396* specification). A URL identifies a resource partly by its location, for instance, the server that contains the resource. Another type of URI is a *uniform resource name* (URN), a globally unique identifier that is valid no matter where the resource is located. HTTP deals only with the URL variety. The terms URI and URL are often used interchangeably, but unfortunately they have slightly different definitions in different specifications. I'm trying to use the terms as defined by the HTTP/1.1 specification (RFC 2616), which is pretty close to how they are mostly used in the servlet, JSP, and JSF specifications. Hence, I use the term URL only when the URI must start with `http` (or `https`, for HTTP over an encrypted connection) followed by a server name and possibly a port number, as in the previous examples. I use URI as a generic term for any string that identifies a resource, where the location can be deduced from the context and isn't necessarily part of the URI. For example, when the request has been delivered to the server, the location is a given, and only the resource identifier is important.

The browser uses the URL information to create the *request message* and send it to the specified server using the specified protocol. An HTTP request message consists of three things: a request line, some request headers, and possibly a request body.

The request line starts with the request method name, followed by a resource identifier and the protocol version used by the browser:

```
GET /index.html HTTP/1.1
```

* The RFC 2396 specification is available at *http://www.ietf.org/rfc/rfc2396.txt*.

The most commonly used request method is named GET. As the name implies, a GET request is used to retrieve a resource from the server. If you type a URL in the browser's address field, or click on a link, the request is sent as a GET request to the server.

The request headers provide additional information the server may use to process the request. The message body is included only in some types of requests, like the POST request, discussed later.

Here's an example of a valid HTTP request message:

```
GET /index.html HTTP/1.1
Host: www.gefionsoftware.com
User-Agent: Mozilla/5.0 (Windows; U; Win 9x 4.90; en-US; rv: 1.0.2)
Accept: image/gif, image/jpeg, image/pjpeg, image/png, */*
Accept-Language : en
Accept-Charset : iso-8859-1,*,utf-8
```

The request line specifies the GET method and asks for the resource named */index.html* to be returned using the HTTP/1.1 protocol version. The various headers provide additional information.

The Host header tells the server the hostname used in the URL. A server may have multiple names, so this information is used to distinguish between multiple virtual web servers sharing the same web server process.

The User-Agent header contains information about the type of browser making the request. The server can use this to send different types of responses to different types of browsers. For instance, if the server knows whether Internet Explorer or Netscape Navigator is used, it can send a response that takes advantage of each browser's unique features. It can also tell if a client other than an HTML browser is being used, such as a Wireless Markup Language (WML) browser on a cell phone or a PDA device, and generate an appropriate response.

The Accept headers provide information about the languages and file formats the browser accepts. These headers can be used to adjust the response to the capabilities of the browser and the user's preferences, such as using a supported image format and the user's preferred language. These are just a few of the headers that can be included in a request message. The HTTP specification, available at *http://www.w3c.org/*, describes all of them.

The URI doesn't necessarily correspond to a static file on the server. It can identify an executable program, a record in a database, or pretty much anything the web server knows about. That's why the generic term *resource* is used. In fact, there's no way to tell if the */index.html* URI corresponds to a file or something else; it's just a name that means something to the server. The web server is configured to map these unique names to the real resources.

Responses in Detail

When the web server receives the request, it looks at the URI and decides how to handle it based on configuration information. It may handle the request internally by simply reading an HTML file from the filesystem, or it may forward the request to some component that is responsible for the resource corresponding to the URI. This can be a program that uses database information, for instance, to dynamically generate an appropriate response. To the browser it makes no difference how the request is handled; all it cares about is getting a response.

The response message looks similar to the request message. It consists of three things: a status line, some response headers, and an optional response body. Here's an example:

```
HTTP/1.1 200 OK
Last-Modified: Mon, 20 Dec 2002 23:26:42 GMT
Date: Mon, 16 Jun 2003 20:52:40 GMT
Status: 200
Content-Type: text/html
Servlet-Engine: Tomcat Web Server/5.0
Content-Length: 59

<html>
  <body>
    <h1>Hello World!</h1>
  </body>
</html>
```

The status line starts with the name of the protocol, followed by a status code and a short description of the status code. Here the status code is 200, meaning the request was executed successfully. The response message has headers just like the request message. In this example, the `Last-Modified` header gives the date and time for when the resource was last modified. The browser can use this information as a timestamp in a local cache; the next time the user asks for this resource, the browser can ask the server to send it only if it's been updated since the last time it was requested. The `Content-Type` header tells the browser what type of response data the body contains, and the `Content-Length` header how large it is. The other headers are self-explanatory. A blank line separates the headers from the message body. Here the body is a simple HTML page:

```
<html>
  <body>
    <h1>Hello World!</h1>
  </body>
</html>
```

Of course, the body can contain a more complex HTML page or any other type of content. For example, the request may return an HTML page with `<img>` elements. When the browser reads the first response and finds the `<img>` elements, it sends a new request for the resource identified by each element, often in parallel. The server returns one response for each image request, with a `Content-Type` header telling what type of image it is (for instance, `image/gif`) and the body containing the bytes that make up the image. The browser then combines all responses to render the complete page. This interaction is illustrated in Figure 4-2.

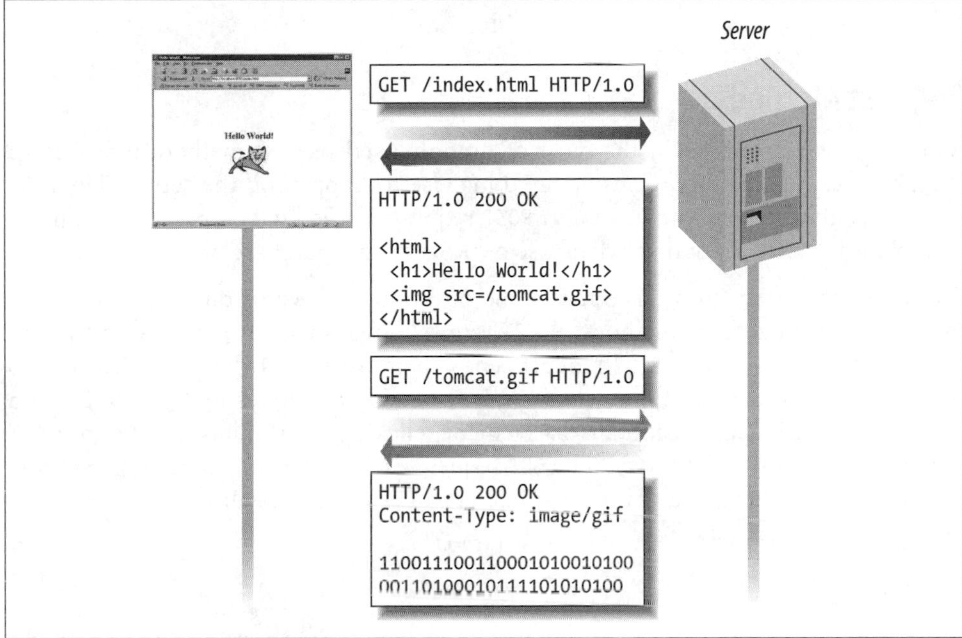

Figure 4-2. Interaction between a web client and a server

Request Parameters

Besides the URI and headers, a request message can contain additional information in the form of parameters. If the URI identifies a server-side program for displaying weather information, for example, request parameters can provide information about which city the user wants to see a forecast for. In an e-commerce application, the URI may identify a program that processes orders, using the customer number and the list of items to be purchased as parameters.

Parameters can be sent in one of two ways: tacked on to the URI in the form of a query string or sent as part of the request message body. This is an example of a URL with a query string:

```
http://www.weather.com/forecast?city=Hermosa+Beach&state=CA
```

The query string starts with a question mark (?) and consists of name/value pairs separated by ampersands (&). These names and values must be *URL-encoded*, meaning that special characters, such as whitespace, question marks, ampersands, and all other nonalphanumeric characters are encoded so that they don't get confused with characters used to separate name/value pairs and other parts of the URI. In this example, the space between Hermosa and Beach is encoded as a plus sign. Other special characters are encoded as their corresponding hexadecimal ASCII value; for instance, a question mark is encoded as %3F. When parameters are sent as part of the request body, they follow the same syntax: URL-encoded name/value pairs separated by ampersands.

Request Methods

As mentioned earlier, GET is the most commonly used request method, intended to retrieve a resource without causing anything else to happen on the server. The POST method is almost as common as GET. POST requests some kind of processing on the server; for instance, updating a database or processing a purchase order.

The way parameters are transferred is one of the most obvious differences between the GET and POST request methods. A GET request always uses a query string to send parameter values, while a POST request sends them as part of the body (it can also send some parameters as a query string, just to make life interesting). If you insert a link in an HTML page using an <a> element, clicking on the link results in a GET request being sent to the server. The GET request uses a query string to pass parameters, so you can include hardcoded parameter values in the link URI:

```
<a href="/forecast?city=Hermosa+Beach&state=CA">
  Hermosa Beach weather forecast
</a>
```

When you use a form to send user input to the server, you can specify whether to use the GET or POST method with the method attribute, as shown here:

```
<form action="/forecast" method="POST">
  City: <input name="city" type="text">
  State: <input name="state" type="text">
  <p>
  <input type="SUBMIT">
</form>
```

If the user enters "Hermosa Beach" and "CA" in the form fields and clicks on the Submit button, the browser sends a request message like this to the server:

```
POST /forecast HTTP/1.1
Host: www.gefionsoftware.com
User-Agent: Mozilla/5.0 (Windows; U; Win 9x 4.90; en-US; rv: 1.0.2)
Accept: image/gif, image/jpeg, image/pjpeg, image/png, */*
Accept-language: en-US
Accept-charset: iso-8859-1,*,utf-8

city=Hermosa+Beach&state=CA
```

Due to the differences in how parameters are sent by GET and POST requests, as well as the differences in their intended purpose, browsers handle the requests in different ways. A GET request, parameters and all, can easily be saved as a bookmark, hardcoded as a link, and the response cached by the browser. Also, the browser knows that no damage will be done if it needs to send a GET request again automatically; for instance, if the user clicks the Reload button.

A POST request, on the other hand, can't be bookmarked as easily; the browser would have to save both the URI and the request message body. A POST request is intended to perform some possibly irreversible action on the server, so the browser must also ask the user if it's okay to send the request again. You have probably seen this type of confirmation dialog, shown in Figure 4-3, numerous times.

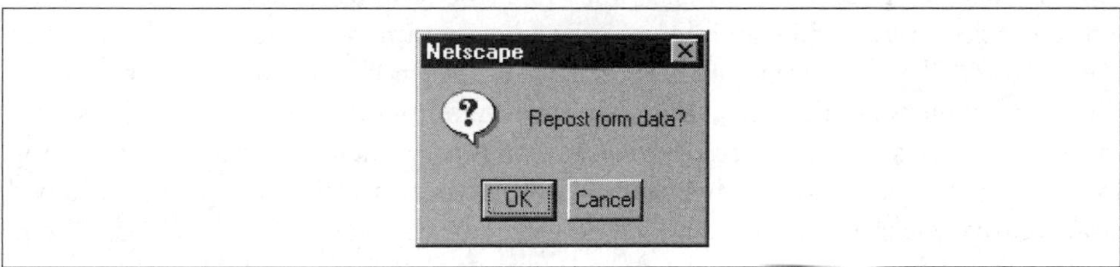

Figure 4-3. Repost confirmation dialog

Web Application Deployment and Runtime Environment

A JSF-based application consists of a lot of different pieces: user interface template files (e.g., JSP pages), static HTML files and image files, as well as class files for business logic, custom components, and so on. All pieces are packaged and deployed as a *web application archive* (WAR). The servlet specification describes the internal structure of the WAR and an application *deployment descriptor* containing configuration and metadata for the application.

The WAR structure contains directories for files accessed directly by browsers, such as HTML files and JSP pages, and directories for configuration files and classes seen only by the application. Here's part of the WAR structure for the example application we'll develop in this book:

```
/cover.gif
/index.html
/expense/reports.jsp
...
/WEB-INF/web.xml
/WEB-INF/classes/JSPSourceServlet.class
...
/WEB-INF/lib/commons-logging.jar
/WEB-INF/lib/jsf-api.jar
/WEB-INF/lib/jsf-ri.jar
/WEB-INF/lib/jsfbook.jar
...
```

The top level in this structure is the document root for all public web application files; in other words, all the files requested directly by the browser. For instance, the *index.html* file is a page with links to all book examples, and the *expense/reports.jsp* file is a JSP page used as a template in an example application.

The *WEB-INF* directory is the root for internal application files and it's inaccessible to a browser. This directory contains the application deployment descriptor (*web.xml*), as well as subdirectories for other types of resources, such as Java class files and configuration files. Two *WEB-INF* subdirectories have special meaning: *lib* and *classes*. All application class files must be stored in these two directories. The *lib* directory is for Java archive (JAR) files (compressed archives of Java class files). Class files that aren't packaged in JAR files must be stored in the *classes* directory, which can be convenient during development. The files must be stored in subdirectories of the *classes* directory that mirror their package structure, following the standard Java conventions. For instance, a class in a package named `com.mycompany.expense.model` must be stored in the *WEB-INF/classes/com/mycompany/expense/model* directory.

You can add other subdirectories under *WEB-INF* directory to organize the application files, but they have no special meaning except that they can't be accessed directly by a browser.

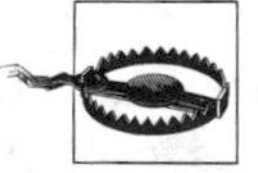

As with pretty much everything related to Java, directory and filenames in the web application structure are case-sensitive. If something doesn't work right, the first thing to check is that the *WEB-INF* directory is created with all caps, and that the case used for a page in the request URL matches exactly the case used in the filename. On a Windows platform, you may want to use a Command Prompt window and the `DIR` command to check this, because the names shown in the Windows Explorer tool adjusts the names and sometimes shows a directory name like *WEB-INF* as *Web-inf*.

A WAR file has a *.war* file extension and can be created with the Java `jar` command or a ZIP utility program, such as *WinZip* (the same file format is used for both JAR and ZIP files).

Web Containers and Servlet Contexts

The WAR file is deployed to what's called a *web container*. A web container provides the runtime environment for a Java web application. For instance, it translates request and response data between the raw protocol format and the Java object representations the web application works with and maintains shared resources (such as database connection pools and logfiles). All web containers provide tools for installing a WAR file, or a special directory where a WAR file is automatically picked up (such as the *webapps* directory in Tomcat). Most containers also support web applications deployed directly in a filesystem using the same file structure as is defined for the WAR file, which can be convenient during development.

There are many different types of web containers. Some containers are called *add-ons*, or *plug-ins*, and are used to add support for Java web applications to regular web servers (such as Apache and IIS). They can run in the same operating-system process as the web server or in a separate process. Other containers are standalone servers. A *standalone server* includes web server functionality to provide full support for HTTP in addition to the web application runtime environment. Containers can also be embedded in other servers, such as a climate-control system, to offer a web-based interface to the system. A container bundled as part of an application server typically distributes the execution over multiple hosts and can provide fail-over capabilities in case a host crashes.

Within the container, each web application is represented by a *servlet context*. Each context is self-contained and doesn't know anything about other applications running in the same container. References between the servlets and JSP pages in the application are commonly relative to the context path, and therefore are referred to as *context-relative* paths. By using context-relative paths within the application, a web application can be deployed using any context path.

The servlet context (i.e., the web application) is assigned a unique URI path prefix called the *context path* when the application is deployed. Figure 4-4 shows how the context path is used by the container to send the request to the right application.

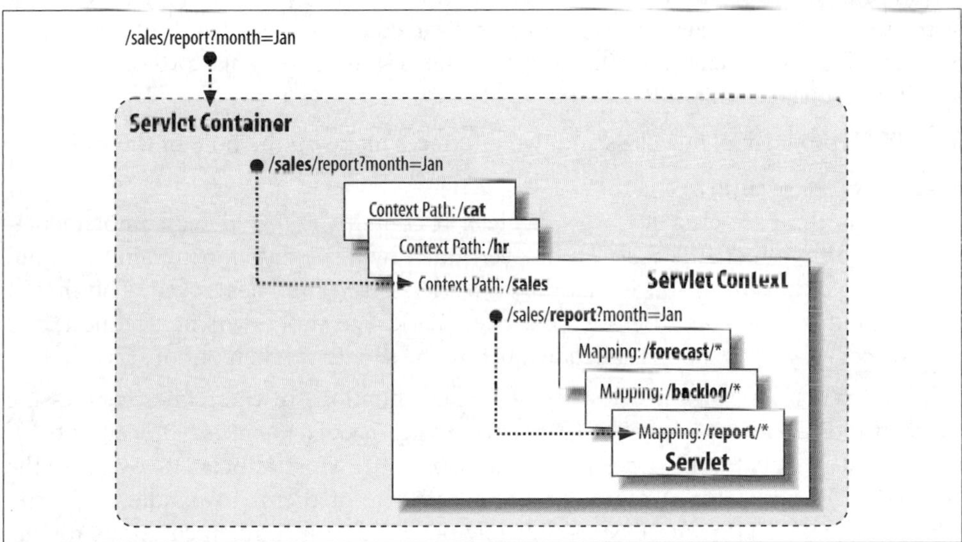

Figure 4-4. Request dispatching based on context paths

In Figure 4-4, a human resources application is associated with the context path */hr* and a sales tracking system with the context path */sales*. This allows the web container to distinguish between the different applications it serves and dispatch requests like */sales/report?month=Jan* to the sales-tracking application and */hr/emplist* to the human-resources application.

The remaining URI path is then used within the selected context to decide how to process the request by comparing it to path-mapping rules defined by the application's deployment descriptor. Rules can be defined to send all requests starting with */report* to one servlet and all requests starting with */forecast* to another. Another type of mapping rule can say that one servlet handles all requests with paths ending with a specific file extension, such as *.jsp*. This is how JSP page requests are handled. Figure 4-4 shows how the different parts of the URI path are used to direct the request processing to the right resource through the container and context.

Servlets, Filters, and Listeners

All new Java web-tier technologies, such as JSP, JSF, and portlets, are defined on top of the API that started it all: the Servlet API. A *servlet* is a Java class that processes a request from a client and produces a response. Most implementations of the JSF specification use a servlet as the entry-point for the page requests, and some JSF-based applications may also include a few servlets and other classes defined by the servlet specification, such as listeners and filters.

The Servlet API is general enough to allow servlets to deal with any request/response-based protocol, but it's almost exclusively used with HTTP. The API consists of two packages: the `javax.servlet` package contains classes and interfaces that are protocol-independent, while the `javax.servlet.http` package provides HTTP-specific extensions and utility classes.

For HTTP processing, one class and two interfaces make up the bulk of the API:

`javax.servlet.http.HttpServlet`
: This is the base class for most servlets. It contains empty default implementations of two methods that can be overridden by a subclass for initialization and release of internal resources used by a servlet: `init()` and `destroy()`. The `init()` method is called once before the servlet is asked to process its first request, and the `destroy()` method is called just before the servlet is taken out of service.

  The base class also provides default implementations of the request processing methods, one for each HTTP request type: `doGet()`, `doPost()`, `doDelete()`, `doHead()`, `doOptions()`, `doPut()`, and `doTrace()`. Most subclasses override the `doGet()` and `doPost()` methods (or at least one of them) to handle the corresponding HTTP request types, but rely on the default implementations for the other request types.

`javax.servlet.http.HttpServletRequest`
: This interface represents the HTTP request, with methods for reading request parameters, headers, and the request URL. Other methods let you add, read, and

remove application data—called *request attributes*—associated with the request. This mechanism comes in handy when the servlet delegates some of the processing (e.g., the rendering of the response) to another application class, as I describe later.

`javax.servlet.http.HttpServletResponse`
: This interface represents the HTTP response sent back to the client. It provides methods for setting response headers and obtaining a stream for the response body.

The web container loads the servlet class—either when the container is started or when the first request for the servlet is received—and calls its methods, converting raw HTTP request messages into `HttpServletRequest` objects and `HttpServletResponse` objects into raw HTTP response messages. It's important to realize that the container creates only *one* instance of each servlet. This means that the servlet must be thread safe—able to handle multiple requests at the same time, each executing as a separate thread through the servlet code.

Using Request Data

Example 4-1 shows a servlet that uses many of the `HttpServletRequest` methods.

Example 4-1. Using HttpServletRequest methods

```
import java.io.IOException;
import java.io.PrintWriter;
import java.util.Iterator;
import java.util.Map;
import javax.servlet.ServletException;
import javax.servlet.http.HttpServletRequest;
import javax.servlet.http.HttpServletResponse;

public class HelloYou extends HttpServlet {
    public void doGet(HttpServletRequest request,
        HttpServletResponse response)
        throws ServletException, IOException {

        String name = request.getParameter("name");
        if (name == null) {
            name = "you";
        }
        response.setContentType("text/html");
        PrintWriter out = response.getWriter( );
        out.println("<html><body>");
        out.println("<h1>Hello " + name + "</h1>");

        out.println("I see that:<ul>");
       String userAgent = request.getHeader("User-Agent");
        out.println("<li>your browser is: " + userAgent);
       String requestURI = request.getRequestURI( );
        out.println("<li>the URI for this page is: " +
            requestURI);
```

Example 4-1. Using HttpServletRequest methods (continued)

```
        String contextPath = request.getContextPath( );
        out.println("<li>the context path for this app is" +
            contextPath);
        String servletPath = request.getServletPath( );
        out.println("<li>this servlet is mapped to: " +
            servletPath);
        String pathInfo = request.getPathInfo( );
        out.println("<li>the remaining path is: " + pathInfo);
        Map parameters = request.getParameterMap( );
        out.println("<li>you sent the following params:<ul>");
        Iterator i = parameters.keySet().iterator( );
        while (i.hasNext( )) {
            String paramName = (String) i.next( );
            out.println("<li><b>" + paramName + "</b>:");
            String[] paramValues =
                (String[]) parameters.get(paramName);
            for (int j = 0; j < paramValues.length; j++) {
                if (j != 0) {
                    out.print(", ");
                }
                out.print(paramValues[j]);
            }
        }
        out.println("</ul></ul></body></html>");
    }
}
```

The HelloYou class in Example 4-1 extends the HttpServlet class, which makes it a valid servlet. It implements the doGet( ) method to process GET requests.

The doGet( ) method uses the getParameter( ) method to get a single value for a request parameter named name. For a request with multiple parameters of the same name, you can use a method called getParameterValues( ) instead. It returns a String array with all values. Further down in the example, note that you can also use the getParameterMap( ) to get a Map containing all parameters in the request. Each key is a String with the parameter name, and the values are String arrays with all values for the parameter. The getParameterMap( ) method was added in the Servlet 2.3 API. It comes in handy when you need to pass all parameters around or process all parameters without knowing their names. All these parameter access methods work the same for both GET and POST requests.

Example 4-1 also shows you how to use the getHeader( ) method for reading request header values, the getRequestURI( ) method for getting the complete request URI, and various getXXXPath( ) methods for getting different parts of the URI path.

To write all the information received from the request back to the browser, the doGet( ) gets a PrintWriter from the HttpServletResponse object by calling the getWriter( ) method. It then generates the response body simply by writing content to the writer.

Compiling, Installing, and Running a Servlet

To compile a servlet, you must first ensure that you have the JAR file containing all Servlet API classes in the CLASSPATH environment variable. The JAR file is distributed with all web containers. Tomcat 5 includes it in a file called *servlet-api.jar*, located in the *common/lib* directory. On a Windows platform, you include the JAR file in the CLASSPATH like this (assuming Tomcat is installed in *C:\Jakarta\jakarta-tomcat-5*):

```
C:/> set CLASSPATH=C:\Jakarta\jakarta-tomcat-5\common\lib\servlet-api.jar; %CLASSPATH%
```

You can then compile the HelloYou servlet from Example 4-1 with the *javac* command, like this:

```
C:/> javac HelloYou.java
```

To make the servlet available to the container, you can place the resulting class file in the *WEB-INF/classes* directory for the example application:

```
C:/> copy HelloYou.class C:\Jakarta\jakarta-tomcat-5\webapps\jsfbook\WEB-INF\classes
```

The container looks automatically for classes in the *WEB-INF/classes* directory structure, so you can use this directory for all application class files. The `HelloYou` servlet is part of the default package, so it goes in the *WEB-INF/classes* directory itself. If you use another package, say `com.mycompany`, you must put the class file in a directory under *WEB-INF/classes* that mirrors the package structure, as described earlier. Alternatively, you can package the class files in a JAR file (see the Java SDK documents for details) and place the JAR file in the *WEB-INF/lib* directory. The internal structure of the JAR file must also mirror the package structure for all your classes.

Next, you must tell the container that it should invoke your servlet when it recieves a request for a specific URL. You do this with `<servlet>` and `<servlet-mapping>` elements in the application deployment descriptor (*WEB-INF/web.xml*) file:

```
...
<servlet>
  <servlet-name>helloYou</servlet-name>
  <servlet-class>HelloYou</servlet-class>
</servlet>

<servlet-mapping>
  <servlet-name>helloYou</servlet-name>
  <url-pattern>/hello/*</url-pattern>
</servlet-mapping>
...
```

The `<servlet>` element gives the servlet class a unique name, and the `<servlet-mapping>` element links a URL pattern to the named servlet. Here I use a pattern that says that all requests with a path starting with */hello/* followed by any other characters (the "*" is a wildcard character) should be served by the servlet named `helloYou`. Appendix F contains a complete reference for the deployment descriptor format.

After compiling and installing the `HelloYou` servlet, and mapping it to the */helloYou/** URL pattern in the deployment descriptor, you can test it with this URL, assuming the context path for the application is */jsfbook*:

http://localhost:8080/jsfbook/helloYou/extra?name=Mike&a=1&a=2

The result should be similar to that shown in Figure 4-5.

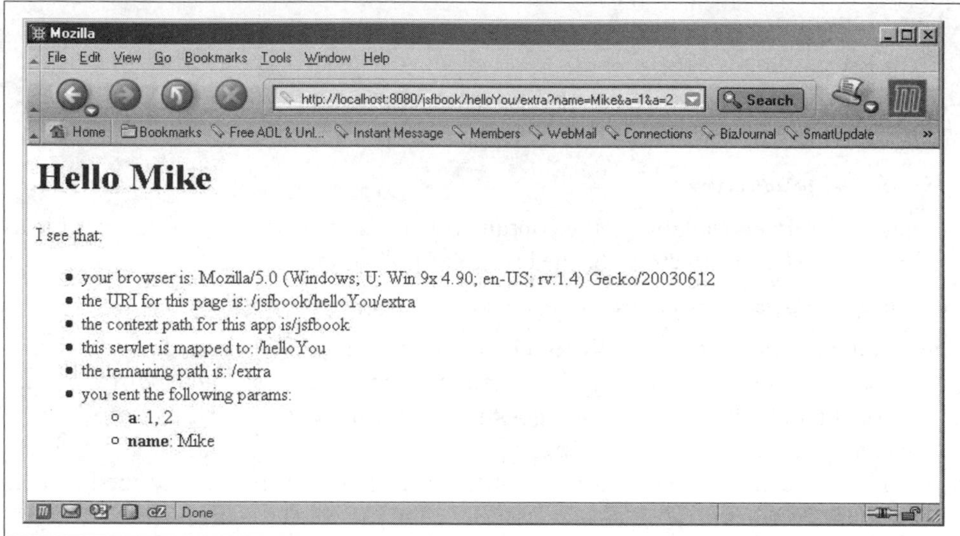

Figure 4-5. Response generated by the HelloYou servlet

Generating Responses of Different Types

Besides the request object, the container passes an object that implements the `HttpServletResponse` interface as an argument to the `doGet( )` and `doPost( )` methods. This interface defines methods for getting a writer or stream for the response body. It also defines methods for setting the response status code and headers. Example 4-2 contains the code for a servlet that uses some of these methods.

Example 4-2. Using HttpServletResponse methods

```
import java.io.IOException;
import java.io.InputStream;
import java.io.OutputStream;
import java.io.PrintWriter;
import javax.servlet.ServletContext;
import javax.servlet.ServletException;
import javax.servlet.http.HttpServletRequest;
import javax.servlet.http.HttpServletResponse;

public class HelloMIME extends HttpServlet {
    private static final int TEXT_TYPE = 0;
    private static final int IMAGE_TYPE = 1;
```

Example 4-2. Using HttpServletResponse methods (continued)

```
    public void doGet(HttpServletRequest request,
        HttpServletResponse response)
        throws ServletException, IOException {

        String greeting = "Hello World!";
        int majorType = TEXT_TYPE;
        String type = request.getParameter("type");
        if ("plain".equals(type)) {
           response.setContentType("text/plain");
        }
        else if ("html".equals(type)) {
            response.setContentType("text/html");
            greeting = "<html><body><h1>" + greeting +
                "</h1></body></html>";
        }
        else if ("image".equals(type)) {
            response.setContentType("image/gif");
            majorType = IMAGE_TYPE;
        }
        else {
            response.sendError(HttpServletResponse.SC_BAD_REQUEST,
              "Please specify a valid response type");
            return;
        }

        if (majorType == TEXT_TYPE) {
            PrintWriter out = response.getWriter( );
            out.println(greeting);
        }
        else {
            OutputStream os = response.getOutputStream( );
            ServletContext application = getServletContext( );
            InputStream is =
                application.getResourceAsStream("/ora.gif");
            copyStream(is, os);
        }
    }

    private void copyStream(InputStream in, OutputStream out)
            throws IOException {
        int bytes;
        byte[] b = new byte[4096];

        while ((bytes = in.read(b, 0, b.length)) != -1) {
            out.write(b, 0, bytes);
            out.flush( );
        }
    }
}
```

In Example 4-2, a request parameter named type is used to choose between a plain text, an HTML, or a GIF response. The response must include the Content-Type header to tell the browser what type of content the response body contains. The servlet used the setContentType( ) method to set this header. The method takes the MIME type for the content as its single argument. The HttpServletResponse interface contains a number of methods like this for setting specific response headers. For headers not covered by specific methods, you can use the setHeader( ) method.

If no type or an invalid type is specified, the servlet in Example 4-2 returns an error response using the sendError( ) method. This method takes two arguments: the HTTP response status code and a short message to be used as part of the response body. If you prefer to use the container's default message for the status code, you can use another version of the sendError( ) method that omits the message argument.

With the content type setting out of the way, it's time to generate the response body. For a body containing either plain text or a markup language such as HTML or XML, you acquire a PrintWriter for the response by calling the getWriter( ) method and just write the text to it. For a binary body, such as an image, you must use an OutputStream instead, which is exactly what the getOutputStream( ) method provides. When the type parameter has the value image, I use this method to grab the stream and write the content of a GIF file to it.

The way the GIF file is accessed in Example 4-2 is the recommended way to access any application file:

```
ServletContext application = getServletContext( );
InputStream is = application.getResourceAsStream("/ora.gif");
```

The getServletContext( ) method returns a reference to the ServletContext instance for this servlet. As you may recall, a ServletContext instance represents a web application and provides access to various shared application resources. The getResourceAsStream( ) method takes the context-relative path to a file resource as its argument and returns an InputStream. The Servlet API contains methods that let you open a file using the standard Java File class as well, but there's no guarantee that this will work in all containers. A container may serve the application files directly from a compressed WAR file, from a database, or any other way that it sees fit. Using a File object in such a container doesn't work, but using the getResourceAsStream( ) method does, because the container is responsible for providing the stream no matter how it stores the application data.

Filters and Listeners

The servlet specification defines two component types beside servlets: *filters* and *listeners*. These compont types are also often used in a JSF-based application.

Filters

A filter is a component that can intercept a request targeted for a servlet, JSP page, or static page, as well as the response before it's sent to the client. This makes it easy to centralize tasks that apply to all requests, such as access control, logging, and charging for the content or the services offered by the application. A filter has full access to the body and headers of the request and response, so it can also perform various transformations. One example is compressing the response body if the `Accept-Encoding` request header indicates that the client can handle a compressed response.

A filter can be applied to either a specific servlet or to all requests matching a URL pattern, such as URLs starting with the same path elements or having the same extension. Jason Hunter's *JavaWorld* article about filters, *http://www.javaworld.com/javaworld/jw-06-2001/jw-0622-filters.html*, is a good introduction to how to develop various types of filters, such as filters for measuring processing time, click and click-streams monitoring, response compression, and file uploading.

Listeners

Listeners allow your application to react to certain events. Starting with Version 2.3 of the servlet specification, there are listener types for servlet context, session and request lifecycle events ("created" and "destroyed" events), session attribute events ("added" and "removed" events), as well as for session activation and passivation events (used by a container that temporarily saves session state to disk or migrates a session to another server).

All these listener types follow the standard Java event model. In other words, a listener is a class that implements one or more listener interfaces. The interfaces define methods that correspond to events. The listener class is registered with the container when the application starts, and the container then calls the event methods at the appropriate times.

JavaServer Pages

You can use JSF in a couple of fundamentally different ways: use the JSF API in pure Java code to generate the complete web page, or use JSF together with some sort of template that holds static markup for the overall page layout and place holders for JSF components that generate dynamic content. JavaServer Pages (JSP) fits the bill for the latter scenario and is supported out-of-the-box by all JSF implementations.

The JSP specification was created to allow all `println()` calls for adding HTML elements to the response that you see in Example 4-1 and 4-2 to be moved from the servlet code to a separate file. This file can be managed by someone who knows HTML but is not a programmer, allowing programmers to focus on developing the application business logic instead of changing details in the user interface look every so often. Figure 4-6 illustrates this separation of concerns on different application component types.

The servlet is still in charge of request processing, but it uses JSP pages to render the response. The business logic can also be forked off to separate JavaBeans components, typically created and populated with data by the servlet, and read by the JSP pages.

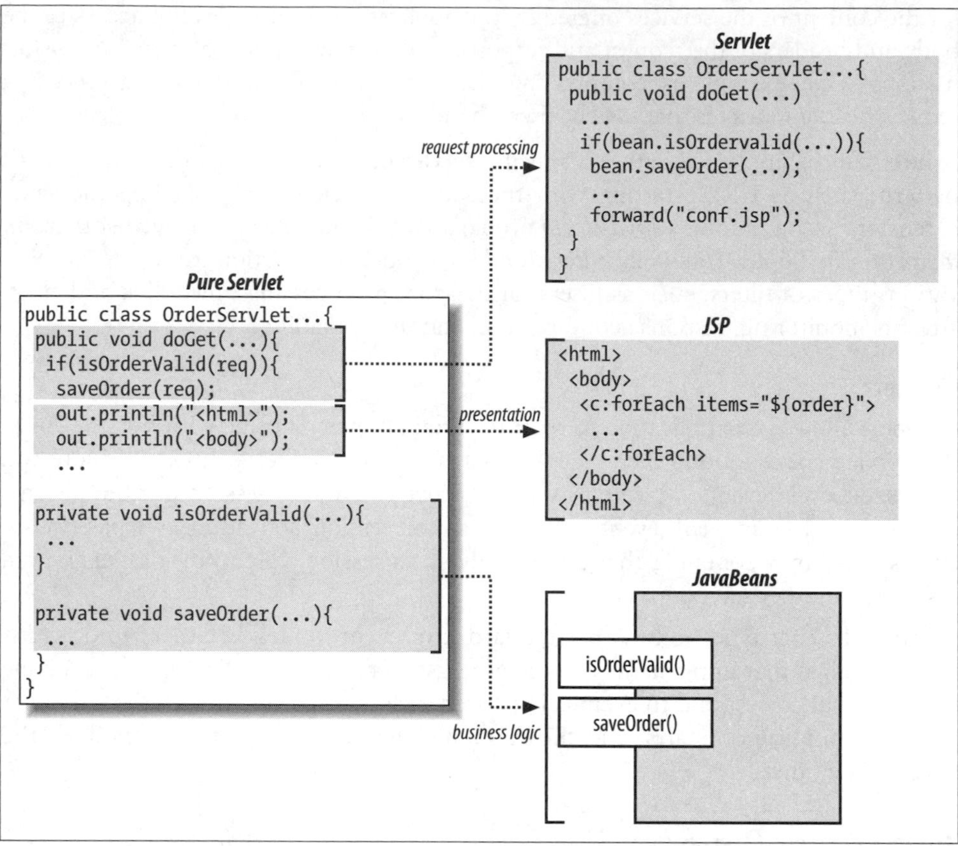

Figure 4-6. Separation of request processing, presentation, and business logic

The result of this separation is a much more efficient development process. It also makes it possible to change different aspects of the application independently, such as changing the business rules without touching the user interface.

JSP Processing

A JSP page is simply a regular web page combining static markup with JSP elements that generates the parts that differ between requests, as shown in Figure 4-7.

Everything in the page that isn't a JSP element is called *template text*. Template text can be any text: HTML, WML, XML, or even plain text. When a JSP page request is processed, the static template text and the dynamic content generated by the JSP elements are merged, and the result is sent as the response to the browser.

A web container that supports JSP intercepts all requests for JSP pages. To process all JSP elements in the page, the container first turns the JSP page into a servlet (known as the *JSP page implementation class*). The conversion is pretty

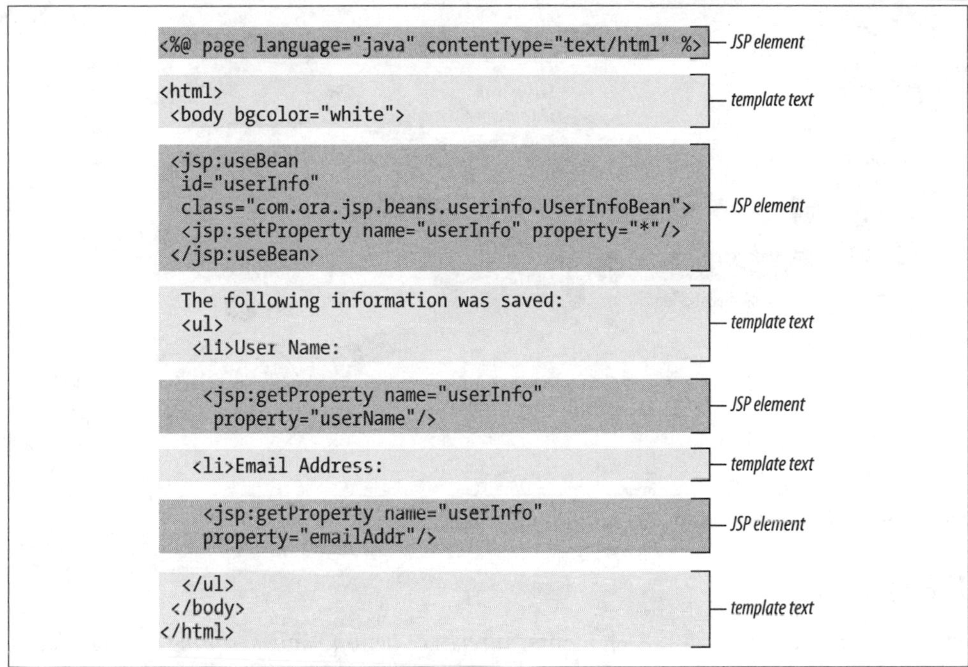

<%@ page language="java" contentType="text/html" %>
JSP element
<html>
<body bgcolor="white">
template text
<jsp:useBean
id="userInfo"
class="com.ora.jsp.beans.userinfo.UserInfoBean">
<jsp:setProperty name="userInfo" property="*"/>
</jsp:useBean>
JSP element
The following information was saved:
<ul>
<li>User Name:
template text
<jsp:getProperty name="userInfo"
property="userName"/>
JSP element
<li>Email Address:
template text
<jsp:getProperty name="userInfo"
property="emailAddr"/>
JSP element
</ul>
</body>
</html>
template text

Figure 4-7. Template text and JSP elements

straightforward; all template text is converted to `println( )` statements similar to the ones in the servlets shown in Example 4-1 and 4-2, and all JSP elements are converted to Java code that implements the corresponding dynamic behavior. The container then compiles the servlet class.

Converting the JSP page to a servlet and compiling the servlet form the *translation phase*. The JSP container initiates the translation phase for a page automatically when it receives the first request for the page. The translation phase takes a bit of time, so the first user to request a JSP page notices a slight delay. To avoid the delay, the translation phase can also be initiated explicitly before any requests are served; this is referred to as *precompilation* of a JSP page. Most web containers provide a tool for precompiling all JSP pages in an application (for Tomcat, it's done with the *jspc* utility, typically invoked by an *Ant* build file).

The web container is also responsible for invoking the JSP page implementation class (the generated servlet) to process each request and generate the response. This is called the *request processing phase*. The two phases are illustrated in Figure 4-8.

As long as the JSP page remains unchanged, subsequent requests go straight to the request processing phase (i.e., the container simply executes the class file). When the JSP page is modified, it goes through the translation phase again before entering the request processing phase.

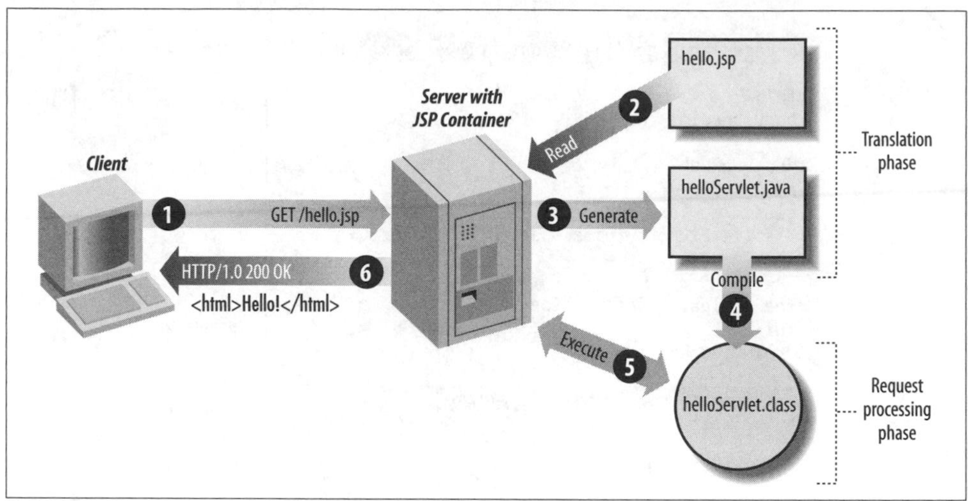

Figure 4-8. JSP page translation and processing phases

JSP Elements

There are three types of JSP elements: *directive*, *action*, and *scripting*. A new construct added in JSP 2.0 is the Expression Language (EL) expression; let's call it a fourth element type, even though it's a bit different than the other three. Example 4-3 shows a simple JSP page with most of these element types.

Example 4-3. JSP page showing a dynamically calculated sum

```
<%@ page contentType="text/html" %>
<%@ taglib prefix="c" uri="http://java.sun.com/jsp/jstl/core" %>
<html>
  <head>
    <title>JSP is Easy</title>
  </head>
  <body bgcolor="white">

    <h1>JSP is as easy as ...</h1>

    <%-- Calculate the sum of 1 + 2 + 3 dynamically --%>
    1 + 2 + 3 = <c:out value="${1 + 2 + 3}" />

    <jsp:include page="footer.jsp" />
  </body>
</html>
```

The page in Example 4-3 displays static HTML plus the sum of 1, 2, and 3, calculated at runtime and dynamically added to the response. It also includes the output produced by another page, *footer.jsp*, in the response. The result of processing the page is shown in Figure 4-9.

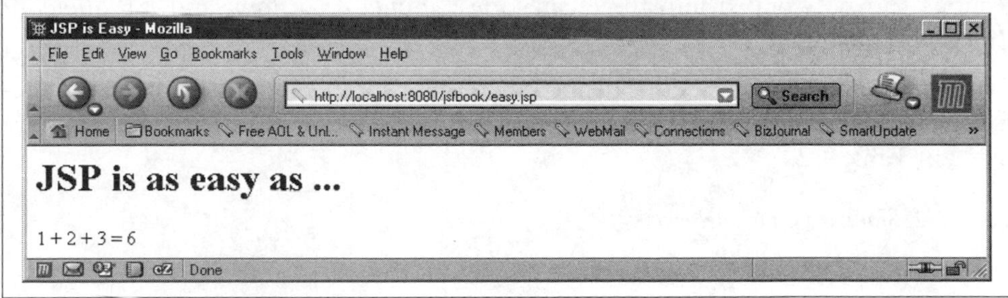

Figure 4-9. Sample JSP page output

Directive elements

The directive elements you can use in a JSP page, shown in Table 4-1, specify information about the page itself that remains the same between requests—for example, if session tracking is required, buffering requirements, and the name of a page that should be used to report errors, if any. Directives are also used to build a complete page from multiple segments and to declare custom tag libraries used in the page.

Table 4-1. Directive elements

Element	Description
`<%@ page ... %>`	Defines page-dependent attributes, such as session tracking, error page, and buffering requirements
`<%@ include ... %>`	Includes a file during the translation phase
`<%@ taglib ... %>`	Declares a tag library, containing custom actions, that is used in the page

Example 4-3 includes two directives: `page` and `taglib`. A JSP directive element is delimited by the character sequences `<%@` and `%>`, and consists of the directive name plus one or more attribute name/value pairs:

```
<%@ directive_name attr1="value1" attr2="value2" %>
```

Note that JSP element and attribute names are case-sensitive and in most cases, the same is true for attribute values. All attribute values must be enclosed in single or double quotes.

Action elements

Action elements are executed when a JSP page is requested (i.e., in the request processing phase), as opposed to JSP directives, which are used only during the translation phase (when the JSP page is turned into Java servlet code). An action can add text to the response or do other things such as write to a file on the server, send an email, or retrieve data from a database that is later added to the response by other actions.

Actions can be grouped into three categories: *standard*, *custom*, and *JSP Standard Tag Library* actions.

Standard actions are the actions defined by the JSP specification itself and are therefore available for use in any JSP application. Most of the JSP 2.0 standard actions are listed in Table 4-2.*

Table 4-2. Standard action elements

Action element	Description
`<jsp:useBean>`	Makes a JavaBeans component available in a page
`<jsp:getProperty>`	Gets a property value from a JavaBeans component and adds it to the response
`<jsp:setProperty>`	Sets a JavaBeans component property value
`<jsp:include>`	Includes the response from a servlet or JSP page during the request processing phase
`<jsp:forward>`	Forwards the processing of a request to servlet or JSP page
`<jsp:param>`	Adds a parameter value to a request handed off to another servlet or JSP page using `<jsp:include>` or `<jsp:forward>`
`<jsp:plugin>`	Generates HTML that contains the appropriate browser-dependent elements (`OBJECT` or `EMBED`) needed to execute an applet with the Java Plug-in software

Custom actions are developed using the JSP API or as special tag files (a new feature added in JSP 2.0) by in-house staff or third parties to make it easy for nonprogrammers to include custom behavior in a JSP page. They must be installed and declared before they can be used in a JSP page.

JSTL actions represent the third category; they are implemented as custom actions but their behavior is defined by an official specification. Until JSTL was defined, programmers had to develop proprietary custom actions even for very generic tasks, such as selecting different parts of a page based on a runtime condition or looping through a collection of data; none of the JSP standard actions support these common tasks. While the name of the standard contains the word "library" (singular), it's in fact a set of libraries that group related actions:

Core
: Conditional processing and looping, importing data from external sources, etc.

XML processing
: Processing of XML data, such as transforming and accessing individual elements

Internationalization (I18N) and formatting
: Formatting and parsing localized information, inserting localized information in a page

* There are a few more action elements used in combination with these standard actions or custom actions, or in very special cases.

Relational database access (SQL)
: Reading and writing relational database data

Functions (added in JSTL 1.1)
: Providing a set of generic Expression Language functions

The `<c:out>` action in Example 4-3 is part of the JSTL core library. It adds the result of the expression (written in the Expression Language, described later in this section) specified as the `value` attribute to the response.

Any action, whether it's a standard, custom, or JSTL action, is represented by an HTML-like element in a JSP page. An action element starts with an opening tag, possibly with attribute/value pairs, followed by a body, and a closing tag:

```
<prefix:action_name attr1="value1" attr2="value2">
  action_body
</prefix:action_name>
```

This is identical to the HTML element syntax, and as with HTML elements, the body of an action element can contain text or other action elements.

The standard action element in Example 4-3 doesn't have a body, so this shorthand syntax is used:

```
<jsp:include page="footer.jsp" />
```

Note that the single tag for an element without a body (an empty element) ends with `/>`, instead of just `>`. If you think this looks like XML syntax, you're absolutely right. The shorthand is equivalent to an opening tag, an empty body, and a closing tag:

```
<jsp:include page="footer.jsp"></jsp:include>
```

Action elements, or *tags* as they are often called, are grouped into libraries (known as *tag libraries*). The element name, used in the opening and closing tags, is composed of two parts: a prefix and the action's name, separated by a colon, with no space characters between any parts. Again, if you're familiar with XML syntax, you may recognize the prefix as an XML namespace. The `jsp` prefix is used for all standard actions.

With the exception of the standard action prefix (because it's defined by the JSP specification), you must declare the prefix you want to use for a tag library with the `taglib` directive:

```
<%@ taglib prefix="c" uri="http://java.sun.com/jsp/jstl/core" %>
  ...
  <c:out value="${1 + 2 + 3}" />
```

The prefix serves two purposes: it makes it possible for actions in different libraries to have the same name, and it makes it possible for the container to figure out which library a specific action belongs to. When the container finds an action element, it locates the `taglib` directive that declares the library with the corresponding action name prefix. The `taglib` directive's `uri` attribute is a unique identifier for the tag library, which the container uses to find the information it needs to process the action.

Scripting elements

Scripting elements, shown in Table 4-3, allow you to add small pieces of code (typically Java code) in a JSP page, such as an `if` statement to generate different HTML, depending on a certain condition. Like actions, they are executed when the page is requested. You should use scripting elements with extreme care: if you embed too much code in your JSP pages, you end up with the same kind of maintenance problems as with servlets embedding HTML.

Table 4-3. Scripting elements

Element	Description
`<% ... %>`	Scriptlet, used to embed scripting code.
`<%= ... %>`	Expression, used to embed scripting code expressions when the result shall be added to the response. Also used as request-time action attribute values.
`<%! ... %>`	Declaration, used to declare instance variables and methods in the JSP page implementation class.

I don't use any scripting elements in this book. If you believe you need to use them in your application, you can read about them in most JSP books, such as my *JavaServer Pages* book (O'Reilly).

Expression Language expressions

The Expression Language (EL) is a new feature in JSP 2.0; it was originally developed as part of the JSTL 1.0 specification. The JSP EL is a simple language for accessing request data and data made available through application objects. Its syntax is similar to JavaScript but much more forgiving when a variable doesn't contain a value, and data-type conversions are handled automatically for the common cases. These are important features for a web application, because the input is mostly in the form of request parameters, which are always text values but often need to be converted to application datatypes, such as numbers and Boolean values. The JSP EL is deliberately constrained in terms of functionality, because it's not intended to be a full-fledged programming language. It main purpose is rather to be used for tying together action elements and other application components.

To give you a feel for how the JSP EL is used, let's look at the expression used for the JSTL `<c:out>` action in Example 4-3:

```
<c:out value="${1 + 2 + 3}" />
```

A JSP EL expression always starts with the ${ delimiter (a dollar sign plus a left curly brace) and ends with } (a right curly brace). JSP EL expressions can be used to assign values to JSP action element attributes, as in Example 4-3, as well as directly in the page. This snippet can replace the JSTL `<c:out>` action in Example 4-3, for instance:

```
1 + 2 + 3 = ${1 + 2 + 3}
```

The <c:out> action is needed in a JSP 1.2 container, however, because prior to JSP 2.0, JSP EL expressions could be used only in JSTL action attribute values. The <c:out> action also converts special characters (e.g., < and &) to character entity codes (e.g., > and &) to avoid browser rendering problems, which doesn't happen when the JSP EL expression is used directly in the page.

Table 4-4 lists all JSP 2.0 EL operators.

Table 4-4. Expression Language operators

Operator	Operation performed
.	Access a bean property or Map entry
[]	Access an array or `List` element
()	Group a subexpression to change the evaluation order
? :	Conditional test: *condition ? ifTrue : ifFalse*
+	Addition
-	Subtraction or negation of a value
*	Multiplication
/ or div	Division
% or mod	Modulo (remainder)
== or eq	Test for equality
!= or ne	Test for inequality
< or lt	Test for less than
> or gt	Test for greater than
<= or le	Test for less than or equal
>= or ge	Test for greater than or equal
&& or and	Test for logical AND
|| or or	Test for logical OR
! or not	Unary Boolean complement
empty	Test for empty variable values (`null`, an empty `String`, or an array, Map, or `List` without entries)
func(args)	A function call, where *func* is the function name and *args* is a comma separared list of function argument

The JSP EL expression operators use literals, variables, or subexpressions as operands. Literals can be integer and floating-point numbers (e.g., 1 and 0.98), Booleans (`true` and `false`), strings ("enclosed by double quotes" or 'enclosed by single quotes'), and the keyword `null` to represent the absence of a value.

Variables are named references to data (objects) created by the application or made available implicitly by the JSP EL. Application-specific variables can be created in many ways. In a JSF application, the JSF framework can create them automatically based on configuration information, or they can be created explicitly by application code—for instance, by a JSF event listener.

A set of JSP EL implicit variables, listed in Table 4-5, provide access to all the information about a request as well as other generic information.

Table 4-5. Implicit EL variables

Variable name	Description
pageScope	A collection (a java.util.Map) of all page scope variables
requestScope	A collection (a java.util.Map) of all request scope variables
sessionScope	A collection (a java.util.Map) of all session scope variables
applicationScope	A collection (a java.util.Map) of all application scope variables
param	A collection (a java.util.Map) of all request parameter values as a single String value per parameter
paramValues	A collection (a java.util.Map) of all request parameter values as a String array per parameter
header	A collection (a java.util.Map) of all request header values as a single String value per header
headerValues	A collection (a java.util.Map) of all request header values as a String array per header
cookie	A collection (a java.util.Map) of all request cookie values as a single javax.servlet.http.Cookie value per cookie
initParam	A collection (a java.util.Map) of all application initialization parameter values as a single String value per value
pageContext	An instance of the javax.servlet.jsp.PageContext class, providing access to various request data

Most implicit variables are of type `java.util.Map`. You can use the property access operator (a dot) to access individual elements of a `Map` and properties of an object with JavaBeans-style acessor methods:

```
${param.userName}
${pageContext.request.requestURI}
```

The first expression accesses a request parameter named `userName`. The second accesses the `request` property of the `pageContext` implicit variable, and then the `requestURI` property of the bean held by the `request` property, corresponding to this Java code:

```
((HttpServletRequest) pageContext).getRequest().getRequestURI( );
```

Elements of an array or a `java.util.List` are accessed with the array element operator (square brackets):

```
${paramValues.subscriptions[0]}
```

This expression accesses the first element in the array of values for a parameter named `subscriptions` held by the implicit `paramValues` variable.

If a bean property name or a `Map` key contains characters that might be confused with operators (e.g., a dot or a dash), you must use the array element operator instead of the property operator. You can do the same if the property name is determined by evaluating a subexpression:

```
${param['user-name']}
${param[currentUser.name]}
```

A variable is always of a specific Java datatype, and the same is true for action attributes and bean properties. The EL operators also depend on type information. The EL takes care of type conversions in the "expected way," however, so you rarely have to worry about it. For instance, if you add a number and a string, the EL tries to convert the string to a number and perform the addition.

JSP comments

Example 4-3 also shows what a JSP comment looks like:

```
<%-- Calculate the sum of 1 + 2 + 3 dynamically --%>
```

Everything between `<%--` and `--%>` is ignored when the JSP page is processed. You can use this type of comment to describe what's going on in the page or to temporarily comment out pieces of the page to test different alternatives.

Creating, Installing, and Running a JSP Page

You can create a JSP page with a regular text editor. A JSP page should have the file extension *.jsp*, which tells the server that the page needs to be processed by the JSP container. Without this clue, the server is unable to distinguish a JSP page from any other type of file and sends it unprocessed to the browser.

JSP pages are requested directly from a browser (although the container intercepts the request and does its magic before the response is returned); you must place the page in the public part of the WAR structure. For instance, the page in Example 4-3 is contained in the *easy.jsp* file in the top directory of the WAR for the book examples:

```
/cover.gif
/easy.jsp
/footer.jsp
/index.html
/expense/reports.jsp
...
/WEB-INF/web.xml
/WEB-INF/classes/JSPSourceServlet.class
...
/WEB-INF/lib/commons-logging.jar
/WEB-INF/lib/jsf-api.jar
/WEB-INF/lib/jsf-impl.jar
/WEB-INF/lib/jsfbook.jar
/WEB-INF/lib/jstl.jar
/WEB-INF/lib/standard.jar
...
```

If the page uses actions from a custom tag library, you must also install the tag library. The page in Example 4-3 uses actions from the JSTL core library, so I use this library as an example here. Be aware, though, that because JSTL is defined by a public specification, a web container may bundle a shared implementation of the JSTL tag libraries so you don't have to install them for each application. A true custom library, e.g., one developed in-house, must always be installed, though.

Installing a custom tag library is very easy: just place the JAR file for the library in the *WEB-INF/lib* directory for the web application. If you look in the *WEB-INF/lib* directory for the book examples application, you see a JAR file named *standard.jar*; that's the JAR file for the reference implementation of the JSTL libraries, developed at the Apache Jakarta Taglibs project (*http://jakarta.apache.taglibs/*). It depends on a number of classes delivered in other JAR files, such as the *jstl.jar* file that contains all public JSTL API classes and interfaces; all dependent JAR file must also be installed in the *WEB-INF/lib* directory.

As I mentioned earlier, the container uses the `taglib` directive's `uri` attribute as a unique identifier for the tag library to locate the information it needs to process the action. More precisely, the information it needs is found in what's called a *tag library descriptor* (TLD). The TLD is an XML file with a *.tld* extension, containing information, such as mappings between the action names and the classes that implement their behavior. It also contains the unique identifier (the default URI) that should be used as the `taglib` directive's `uri` attribute value.

When the web application is started, the container scans through the *WEB-INF* directory structure for files with *.tld* extensions and all JAR files containing files with *.tld* extensions in their *META-INF* directory. In other words, the container locates all TLD files. For each TLD, the container gets the library's default URI and creates a map from the URI to the TLD that contains it. In your JSP page, just to use a `taglib` directive with a `uri` attribute value that matches the default URI. This is illustrated in Figure 4-10.

With the JSP page in the right place and the custom tag libraries installed, all you need to do in order to run the JSP page is type in an appropriate URL in a browser.

Assuming you're using Tomcat and have installed the book examples WAR as a subdirectory named *jsfbook* under Tomcat's *webapps* directory, as described in Chapter 3, the URL for the *easy.jsp* page is *http://localhost:8080/jsfbook/easy.jsp*. Note how the */jsfbook* part of the URL matches the Tomcat *webapps* subdirectory name for the application. This part of the URL is called the application's *context path*. As described earlier, every web application has a unique context path, assigned one way or another when you install the application. Tomcat uses the subdirectory name as the context path by default, but other containers may prompt you for a path in an installation tool or use other conventions. When you make a request for a web application resource (an HTML or JSP page, or a servlet), the first part of the URL (after the hostname and port number) must be the context path, so the container knows which application should handle the request.*

If you try this out, your browser will display a page like the one in Figure 4-9.

* There's one exception to this rule: a web container may let you install one application as the default, or root, application. For Tomcat, this application is installed in *webapps/ROOT* by default. Resources in the default application are accessed without a context path.

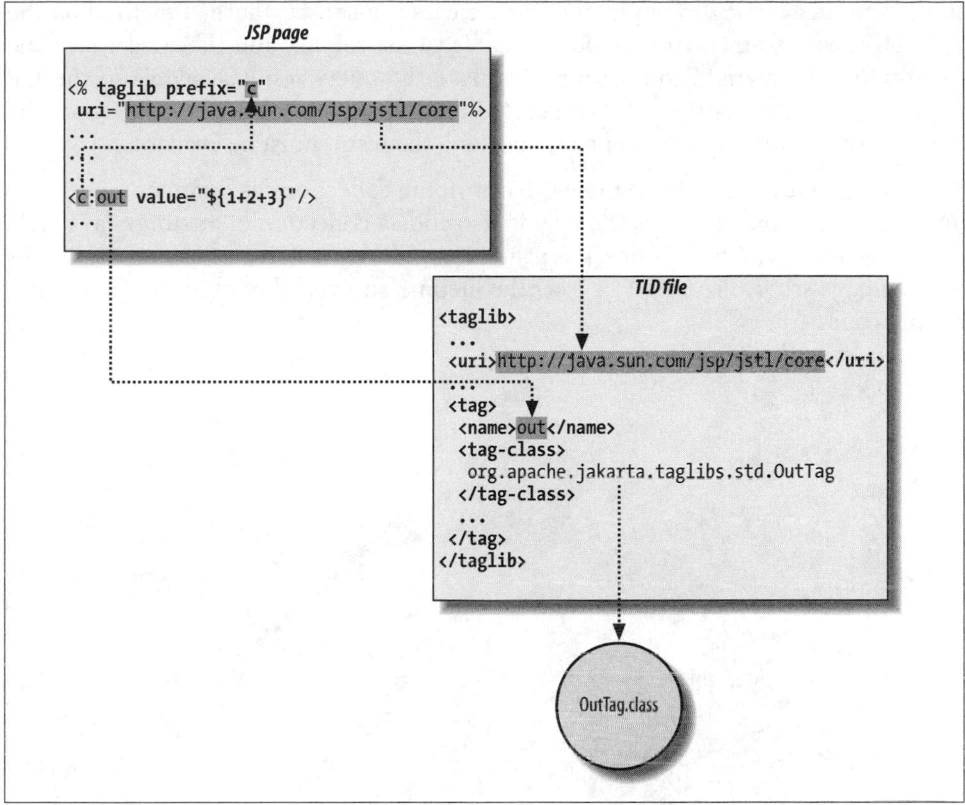

Figure 4-10. Relation between the taglib directive, the TLD, and the implementation (tag handler) for the custom actions

Accessing Application Data

The different parts of a Java web application need to be able access the same data objects. For instance, a product catalog object a listener creates at application start must be accessible by a servlet that processes a user query against the catalog, and the result of the query must be available to the JSP page that renders the response showing the result.

The Servlet API includes methods for managing this type of data as attributes of the objects representing the application, the user session, and the request, defined by these classes, respectively: `javax.servlet.ServletContext`, `javax.servlet.http.HttpSession`, and `javax.servlet.ServletRequest`.

All three classes contain these methods for managing the attributes:

```
public void setAttribute(String name, Object value);
public Object getAttribute(String name);
public void removeAttribute(String name);
```

In the product catalog example, the listener uses the `setAttribute()` method on the `ServletContext` to make the catalog available to the servlet, and the servlet uses the `getAttribute()` method to obtain it. To make the query result available to the JSP page, the servlet calls the `setAttribute()` method of either the `HttpSession` or the `ServletRequest` object (depending on how long the result must be available).

The JSP specification refers to these three attribute collections as different scopes: the *application*, *session*, and *request scope*. It also adds a collection of attributes available only to objects within the same JSP page during the processing of a request. It calls this the *page scope*. Figure 4-11 shows the lifetime and visibility of objects in the different scopes.

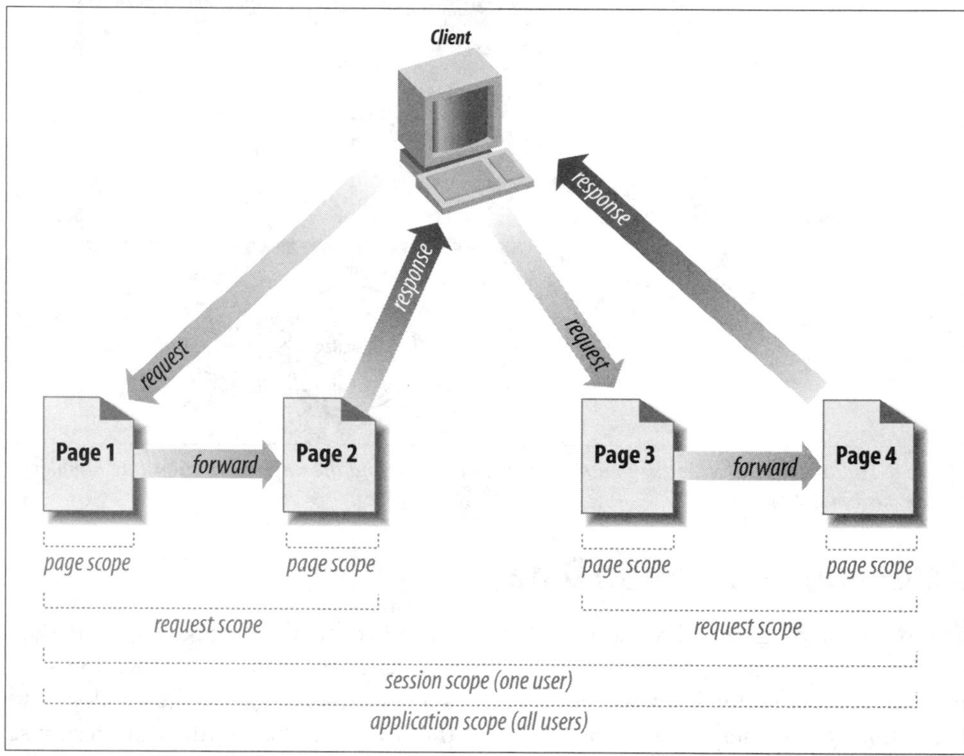

Figure 4-11. Lifetime and visibility of objects in different scopes

The JSP EL provides implicit variables that represent the scopes as `java.util.Map` instances, as shown in Table 4-5. Assuming the servlet in the product catalog example saves the query result as a bean with properties named `rowCount` and `rows` in a request attribute named `result`, the JSP page can access and use the data like this (using JSTL core actions):

```
<c:if test="${requestScope.result.rowCount == 0}">
  Sorry, not products match your criteria
</c:if>
<c:if test="${requestScope.result.rowCount != 0}">
```

```
    These products were found:
    <ul>
      <c:forEach items="${requestScope.result.rows}" var="row">
        <li>${pageScope.row.prodName}</li>
      </c:forEach>
    </ul>
  </c:if>
```

EL expressions actually look for attributes in all scopes if no scope is specified, in the order page, request, session, and application, so the example can be simplified like this:

```
  <c:if test="${result.rowCount == 0}">
    Sorry, not products match your criteria
  </c:if>
  <c:if test="${result.rowCount != 0}">
    These products were found:
    <ul>
      <c:forEach items="${result.rows}" var="row">
        <li>${row.prodName}</li>
      </c:forEach>
    </ul>
  </c:if>
```

This concludes our tour through HTTP, servlets, and JSP. While we've barely scratched the surface of these technologies, we have covered the most important aspects that you must be aware of in order to use JSF. If all of this is new, you may want to return to this chapter to refresh your memory when the other chapters rely on an understanding of what's covered here.

CHAPTER 5

Developing the Business Logic and Setting Up Authentication

The best way to learn a new technology is to use it. In this book, I guide you through the development of an application with a JSF-based user interface. Along the way, we look at all the fundamental JSF concepts and use most of the JSF components. As we progress through the chapters, we'll build the application in stages, starting with a simple but functional version and then adding pieces to make it easier to maintain and make it look nicer. In this chapter, we'll walk through the layout and functionality of the final version of the application.

All versions of the application use the same business logic classes. This is a nice illustration of the separation of concerns supported by JSF: the business logic stays the same even when the user interface goes through significant changes. We look at all the business logic classes in this chapter. In the following chapters, we'll develop additional classes that make it easy to tie JSF components to these business logic classes.

The sample application relies on information about who the user is and adapts the functionality based on this information. In the last part of this chapter, we therefore look at how to configure the web container to handle identification of the user.

Sample Application Overview

The sample application is a web-based expense report system. Employees enter their expense reports and submit them for approval; a manager looks at the reports and either accepts or rejects them. All users have to log in before they can access the application.

The main user interface consists of a single screen, shown in Figure 5-1. Employees and managers both use this screen, but different options are enabled depending on who's logged in.

The screen is divided into three main areas: a menu area at the top, a report list area to the left, and a report details area to the right. The menu area contains buttons for

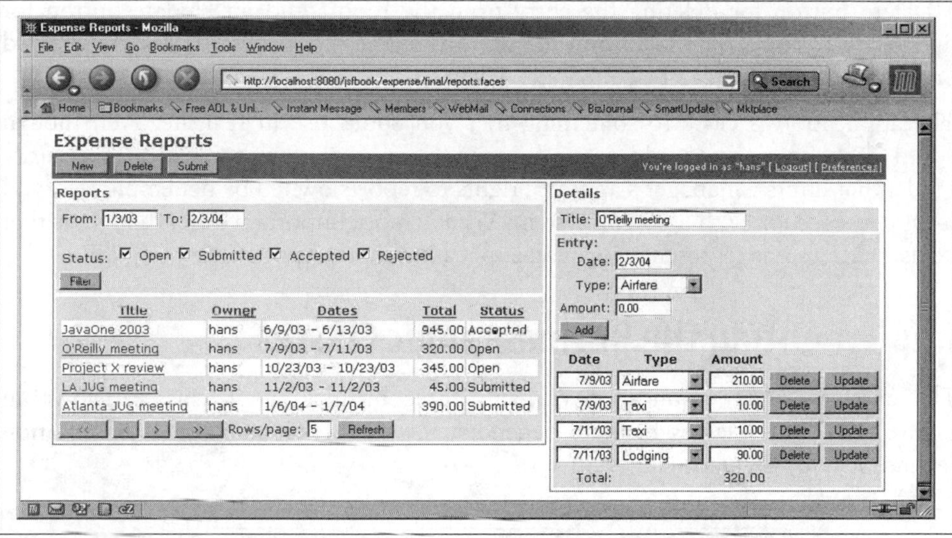

Figure 5-1. The expense reports screen

operations that affect the report displayed currently in the report details area. Its content differs depending on whether the user is an employee or a manager. An employee gets buttons for creating a new report, deleting the current report, and submitting the current report for approval. The buttons are enabled or disabled depending on the report's status. For instance, as long as the report has the status New (i.e., no entries have been added to it yet), all buttons are disabled; when at least one entry has been added (status Open), all buttons are enabled; when the report has been submitted (status Submitted), only the New button is enabled. If a manager is logged in, the menu area contains additional buttons for accepting or rejecting the report. These buttons are enabled only if the current report is submitted for approval.

The report list area provides access to existing expense reports. It contains two subareas. The filtering criteria area contains fields for a date range, report status choices, and a Filter button for applying the criteria. There's also an implicit filtering criteria: a regular employee sees only her own reports, but a manager sees reports owned by any employee.

The report list area contains a table with all reports matching the filtering criteria. The table rows can be sorted by clicking on the column labels. To make a report the current report, with the details shown in the report details area, the user clicks on the report title in the table.

The report details area is where the expense report information is edited or viewed (depending on its status). An expense report consists of a title and a number of entries, each with a date, an expense type, and an amount. This information is entered in the report entry subarea and added to the current report by clicking the Add button. The entry list area shows all entries in the report. For each entry, there's a Delete button for deleting the entry from the report and an Update button for updating the entry. The fields and the buttons in the report details area are enabled only when the report can be edited, i.e., when its status is New, Open, or Rejected.

The application is close to something that you could use in real life, even though you'd probably need to add a few features, such as a more sophisticated security model that limits a manager's approval rights to reports owned by her employees, and maybe integration with a payroll system. What's more important here, though, is that its user interface is representative of an application that benefits from using JSF.

Implementing the Business Logic Classes

The expense report application contains three business logic classes, shown in Figure 5-2. These classes have no dependencies on JSF (or any other presentation technology, for that matter).

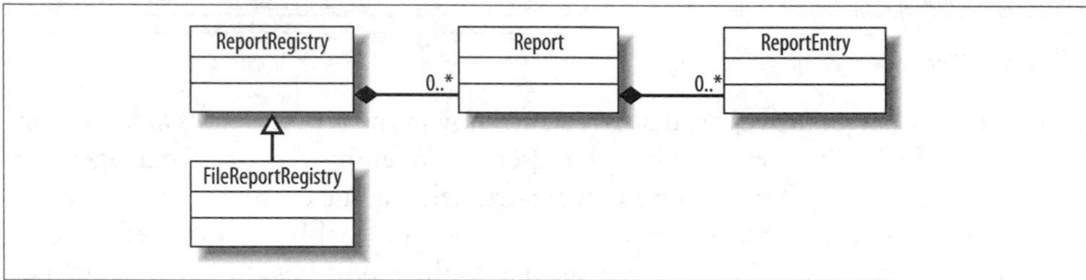

Figure 5-2. The business logic classes

A `Report` contains `ReportEntry` instances, and `Report` instances are saved in a `ReportRegistry`, which is an abstract class with concrete subclasses for different storage medias. The `FileReportRegistry` implements a simple filesystem-based storage facility.

The ReportEntry Class

The `com.mycompany.expense.ReportEntry` class, shown in Example 5-1, is a simple bean, with properties for all expense report entry items—the date, the expense type, and the amount—plus the entry's ID, unique within a `Report`.

Example 5-1. The ReportEntry class

```
package com.mycompany.expense;

import java.io.Serializable;
import java.util.Date;

public class ReportEntry implements Serializable {
    private int id = -1;
    private Date date;
```

Example 5-1. The ReportEntry class (continued)

```
    private int type;
    private double amount;

    public ReportEntry( ) {
    }

    public ReportEntry(ReportEntry src) {
        this.setId(src.getId( ));
        this.setDate(src.getDate( ));
        this.setType(src.getType( ));
        this.setAmount(src.getAmount( ));
    }

    public int getId( ) {
        return id;
    }

    public void setId(int id) {
        this.id = id;
    }

    public Date getDate( ) {
        if (date == null) {
            date = new Date( );
        }
        return date;
    }

    public void setDate(Date date) {
        this.date = date;
    }

    public int getType( ) {
        return type;
    }

    public void setType(int type) {
        this.type = type;
    }

    public double getAmount( ) {
        return amount;
    }

    public void setAmount(double amount) {
        this.amount = amount;
    }

    public String toString( ) {
        return "id: " + id + " date: " + date + " type: " + type +
            " amount: " + amount;
    }
}
```

Each property is represented by standard JavaBeans accessor methods: getId( ) and setId( ), getDate( ) and setDate( ), getType( ) and setType( ), and getAmount( ) and setAmount( ). The ReportEntry class also has a copy constructor, i.e., a constructor that initializes the new instance's properties to the values found in the instance provided as an argument. I'll return to how this constructor is used shortly when we look at the Report class.

In addition to the property accessor methods and the copy-constructor, the ReportEntry class implements the Serializable interface, so that the FileReportRegistry can save instances of this class to a file.

While implementing the java.io.Serializable interface is all it takes to make a class serializable, it's not something to be done without careful consideration. Serialization comes with potential maintenance and security issues that need to be dealt with, e.g., by implementing the readObject( ) and writeObject( ) methods and declaring a static serialVersionUID variable. The classes in this book are intended only as basic examples to illustrate how to use JSF, and are serializable only so that I can use a simple filesystem-based permanent storage. I therefore ignore dealing with versioning issues and other details. I recommend reading Joshua Bloch's *Effective Java* (Addison-Wesley) if you want to learn more about robust serialization strategies.

The toString( ) method in the ReportEntry class returns a String with all the property values, which is handy when writing log entries, e.g., for debugging.

The Report Class

Example 5-2 shows part of the com.mycompany.expense.Report class.

Example 5-2. The Report class variables and constructors

```
package com.mycompany.expense;

import java.io.Serializable;
import java.util.ArrayList;
import java.util.Collections;
import java.util.Comparator;
import java.util.Date;
import java.util.HashMap;
import java.util.Iterator;
import java.util.List;
import java.util.Map;

public class Report implements Serializable {
    public static final int STATUS_NEW = 0;
    public static final int STATUS_OPEN = 1;
    public static final int STATUS_SUBMITTED = 2;
    public static final int STATUS_ACCEPTED = 3;
    public static final int STATUS_REJECTED = 4;
```

Example 5-2. The Report class variables and constructors (continued)

```
    private int currentEntryId;
    private int id = -1;
    private String title;
    private String owner;
    private int status = STATUS_NEW;
    private Map entries;

    public Report( ) {
        entries = new HashMap( );
    }

    public Report(Report src) {
        setId(src.getId( ));
        setTitle(src.getTitle( ));
        setOwner(src.getOwner( ));
        setStatus(src.getStatus( ));
        setEntries(src.copyEntries( ));
        setCurrentEntryId(src.getCurrentEntryId( ));
    }

    public synchronized int getId( ) {
        return id;
    }

    public synchronized void setId(int id) {
        this.id = id;
    }

    public synchronized String getTitle( ) {
        return title;
    }

    public synchronized void setTitle(String title) {
        this.title = title;
    }

    public synchronized String getOwner( ) {
        return owner;
    }

    public synchronized void setOwner(String owner) {
        this.owner = owner;
    }

    public synchronized int getStatus( ) {
        return status;
    }

    public synchronized void setStatus(int status) {
        this.status = status;
    }
```

Just like ReportEntry, the Report class implements Serializable to make it easy to save reports to a file. Also like ReportEntry, it's a bean with a number of properties: id, title, owner, and status. The status is represented as an int value defined by static final variables: STATUS_NEW, STATUS_OPEN, STATUS_ACCEPTED, and STATUS_REJECTED. A java.util.Map holds the report entries, with the report entry IDs as keys and the ReportEntry instances as values. The Report class assigns an ID to each report entry when it's added to the report, and it uses an int variable to keep track of the next available ID.

The Report class has a copy constructor that initializes the new instance with the values from another Report instance by calling the property accessor methods plus four private methods: setEntries( ), copyEntries( ), setCurrentEntry( ), and getCurrentEntry( ). These private methods are shown in Example 5-3.

Example 5-3. Private initialization methods for the Report class

```
    private int getCurrentEntryId( ) {
        return currentEntryId;
    }

    private void setCurrentEntryId(int currentEntryId) {
        this.currentEntryId = currentEntryId;
    }

    private Map copyEntries( ) {
        Map copy = new HashMap( );
        Iterator i = entries.entrySet().iterator( );
        while (i.hasNext( )) {
            Map.Entry e = (Map.Entry) i.next( );
            copy.put(e.getKey(), new ReportEntry((ReportEntry) e.getValue( )));
        }
        return copy;
    }

    private void setEntries(Map entries) {
        this.entries = entries;
    }
}
```

The getCurrentEntryId( ) and setCurrentEntryId( ) methods get and set the variable holding the next available report entry ID.

The copyEntries( ) method loops through all report entries and returns a new Map with copies of all ReportEntry instances. This is where the ReportEntry copy constructor first comes into play. The setEntries( ) method simply saves a reference to the provided Map as the new entries list.

All four methods are private because no one should ever mess with these values directly; these methods are to be used only by the Report copy constructor. A set of other methods provides public access to the report entries instead. Example 5-4 shows the addEntry( ) method.

Example 5-4. Adding a report entry to the Report

```
public synchronized void addEntry(ReportEntry entry) {
    entry.setId(currentEntryId++);
    entries.put(new Integer(entry.getId( )), new ReportEntry(entry));
}
```

First, note that this method is synchronized. This is true for all methods accessing report content, in order to ensure that multiple threads can access the report at the same time without corrupting its state. Multithreading issues and thread-safety strategies are out of scope for this book, but it's a very important consideration when developing server-side applications. For a web application, all objects held in the application scope must be handled in a threadsafe manner; because all users and all requests have access to the objects in this scope, it's very likely that more than one thread will access the same object. Objects in the session scope must also be threadsafe, because they are shared by all requests from the same user. If the user makes parallel requests, e.g., by submitting the same form over and over without waiting for the response, making requests from multiple browsers tied to the same session, or requesting pages that contain references (e.g., frame references) to other pages that modify session scope objects, a session scope object's state can be corrupted. To learn more about thread-safety strategies, I recommend that you read *Java Threads* by Scott Oaks and Henry Wong (O'Reilly) or another book that deals exclusively with this subject. Joshua Bloch's *Effective Java* (Addison-Wesley) is another good source for tips about thread safety and a lot of other topics of importance to most large-scale Java projects.

The `addEntry( )` method first sets the ID of the `ReportEntry` instance argument to the next available ID and increments the ID counter in preparation for the next time the method is called. It then adds a copy of the `ReportEntry` instance to its entries `Map`. Saving a copy of the `ReportEntry` instance is important, because it's the only way to guarantee that what's in the report isn't accidentally modified if another part of the application makes changes to the argument instance later. Imagine what would happen if an employee, still holding on to the instance used as the argument, could change the amount of an entry in a report the manager has already approved.

The methods for removing an entry, getting a specific entry, and getting all entries are shown in Example 5-5.

Example 5-5. Removing and retrieving entries

```
public synchronized void removeEntry(int id) {
    entries.remove(new Integer(id));
}

public synchronized ReportEntry getEntry(int id) {
    return new ReportEntry((ReportEntry) entries.get(new Integer(id)));
}

public synchronized List getEntries( ) {
```

Example 5-5. Removing and retrieving entries (continued)

```
        return new ArrayList(copyEntries().values( ));
    }
```

The removeEntry( ) method simply removes the entry with a matching ID from the report's Map. The getEntry( ) and getEntries( ) methods return a copy of a single ReportEntry and a java.util.List with copies of all ReportEntry instances, respectively.

Example 5-6 shows the remaining methods in the Report class.

Example 5-6. Entries-based property accessor methods

```
    public synchronized Date getStartDate( ) {
        Date date = null;
        if (!entries.isEmpty( )) {
            List l = getEntriesSortedByDate( );
            date = ((ReportEntry) l.get(0)).getDate( );
        }
        return date;
    }

    public synchronized Date getEndDate( ) {
        Date date = null;
        if (!entries.isEmpty( )) {
            List l = getEntriesSortedByDate( );
            date = ((ReportEntry) l.get(entries.size() - 1)).getDate( );
        }
        return date;
    }

    public synchronized double getTotal( ) {
        double total = 0;
        Iterator i = entries.values().iterator( );
        while (i.hasNext( )) {
            ReportEntry e = (ReportEntry) i.next( );
            total += e.getAmount( );
        }
        return total;
    }

    public String toString( ) {
        return "id: " + id + " title: " + getTitle( ) +
            " owner: " + getOwner( ) +
            " startDate: " + getStartDate() + " endDate: " + getEndDate( ) +
            " status: " + getStatus( );
    }
    private List getEntriesSortedByDate( ) {
        List l = getEntries( );
        Collections.sort(l, new Comparator( ) {
                public int compare(Object o1, Object o2) {
                    Date d1 = ((ReportEntry) o1).getDate( );
                    Date d2 = ((ReportEntry) o2).getDate( );
                    return d1.compareTo(d2);
```

Example 5-6. Entries-based property accessor methods (continued)

```
            }
        });
        return l;
    }
```

The first three public methods are property accessors for read-only properties based on the list of report entries. `getStartDate()` gets a list of all entries sorted by the `date` property from the `getEntriesSortedByDate()` method and returns the `date` property value for the first one. The `getEndDate()` method is similar; it gets the sorted entries list and returns the `date` property value for the last entry in the list. `getTotal()` loops through all entries and returns the sum of their `amount` property values.

The private `getEntriesSortedByDate()` method uses a `java.util.Comparator` that compares `ReportEntry` instances by their `date` property values, combined with the `java.util.Collections` `sort()` method to sort the entries.

Finally, the `toString()` method is just a handy method for debugging, returning a `String` with the property values.

The ReportRegistry and FileReportRegistry Classes

`ReportRegistry` is an abstract class that defines a generic interface for maintaining a list of expense reports, shown in Example 5-7.

Example 5-7. The ReportRegistry class

```
package com.mycompany.expense;

import java.util.Date;
import java.util.List;

public abstract class ReportRegistry {
    public abstract void addReport(Report report) throws RegistryException;

    public abstract void updateReport(Report report) throws RegistryException;

    public abstract void removeReport(Report report) throws RegistryException;

    public abstract Report getReport(int id) throws RegistryException;

    public abstract List getReports(String owner, Date from, Date to,
                                    int[] status) throws RegistryException;
}
```

It defines methods for adding, updating, removing, and getting a single `Report`, and one method for getting a set of `Report` instances that matches a search criteria.

The concrete subclass of the `ReportRegistry` used in this book is called `FileReportRegistry`. It's a simple implementation that uses a file in the user's home directory for persistence. The constructor initializes the registry from the file, and all methods that modify the registry also save the updated registry to the file. This is okay as a proof-of-concept, but it would be too slow for a registry with many reports. In a real application, I would use a subclass that keeps the registry information in a database instead. Example 5-8 shows the instance variables and the constructor for the `FileReportRegistry` class.

Example 5-8. The FileReportRegistry variables and constructor

```
package com.mycompany.expense;

import java.io.File;
import java.io.FileNotFoundException;
import java.io.FileInputStream;
import java.io.FileOutputStream;
import java.io.IOException;
import java.io.ObjectInputStream;
import java.io.ObjectOutputStream;
import java.util.ArrayList;
import java.util.Collections;
import java.util.Date;
import java.util.HashMap;
import java.util.Iterator;
import java.util.List;
import java.util.Map;

public class FileReportRegistry extends ReportRegistry {
    private int currentReportId;
    private Map reports;

    public FileReportRegistry( ) throws RegistryException {
        reports = new HashMap( );
        try {
            load( );
        }
        catch (IOException e) {
            throw new RegistryException("Can't load ReportRegistry", e);
        }
    }
    ...
```

The `FileReportRegistry` is similar to the `Report` class, except that it maintains a set of reports instead of report entries. It keeps the `Report` instances in a `java.util.Map` variable, with the report IDs as keys and the `Report` instances as values. It assigns an ID to a report when it's added to the registry and uses an `int` variable to keep track of the next available ID.

The constructor calls the `load( )` method, shown in Example 5-9.

Example 5-9. Loading the FileReportRegistry information

```
    ...
    private void load( ) throws IOException {
        File store = getStore( );
        try {
            ObjectInputStream is =
                new ObjectInputStream(new FileInputStream(store));
            currentReportId = is.readInt( );
            reports = (Map) is.readObject( );
        }
        catch (FileNotFoundException fnfe) {
            // Ignore
        }
        catch (ClassNotFoundException cnfe) {
            // Shouldn't happen, but log it if it does
            System.err.println("Error loading ReportRegistry: " +
                               cnfe.getMessage( ));
        }
    }
```

The `load( )` method gets a `java.io.File` for the persistence file by calling the `getStore( )` method and opens a `java.io.ObjectInputStream` for the file. It then initializes the next available report ID and the `Map` containing all entries with data from the file. It catches the `java.io.FileNotFoundException` and ignores it, so that things work fine even if no file has been created yet, but it lets all other types of `java.io.IOException` subtypes through to signal problems, such as insufficient file permissions or corrupt data.

The `save( )` method, shown in Example 5-10, is called every time a report is added, updated, or removed from the registry.

Example 5-10. Saving the FileReportRegistry information

```
    private void save( ) throws IOException {
        File store = getStore( );
        ObjectOutputStream os =
            new ObjectOutputStream(new FileOutputStream(store));
        os.writeInt(currentReportId);
        os.writeObject(reports);
    }
```

The `save( )` method is the reverse of the `load( )` method: it gets the persistence file, opens an `ObjectOutputStream( )` for it, and writes the current report ID index and the entries `Map`. It also throws a potential `IOException` back at the caller.

Example 5-11 shows the `getStore( )` method.

Example 5-11. Creating a File instance for the persistence file

```
    private File getStore( ) {
        File store = null;
        File homeDir = new File(System.getProperty("user.home"));
```

Example 5-11. Creating a File instance for the persistence file (continued)

```
        File persistenceDir = new File(homeDir, ".expense");
        if (!persistenceDir.exists( )) {
            persistenceDir.mkdir( );
        }
        return new File(persistenceDir, "store.ser");
    }
```

The persistence file is named *store.ser*, located in a subdirectory named *.expense* in the home directory for the account running the application. The `getStore( )` method first creates a `File` instance for the subdirectory, and if the directory doesn't exist in the filesystem, the method creates the directory. `getStore( )` then creates a `File` instance for the persistence file and returns it.

Let's look at the methods that deal with the registry content next, starting with the `addReport( )` method shown in Example 5-12.

Example 5-12. Adding a report to the FileReportRegistry

```
    public synchronized void addReport(Report report)
        throws RegistryException{
        report.setId(currentReportId++);
        reports.put(new Integer(report.getId( )), new Report(report));
        try {
            save( );
        }
        catch (IOException e) {
            throw new RegistryException("Can't save ReportRegistry", e);
        }
    }
```

Just as with the `Report` class, the `addReport( )` method and all other methods that access registry content are synchronized to allow multiple threads to call them without corrupting the registry state.

The `addReport( )` method first sets the ID of the `Report` instance argument to the next available ID and increments the ID counter. It then adds a copy of the `Report` instance to its reports `Map`, to prevent later changes to the argument object from affecting the state of the registry. Finally, the `addReport( )` method saves the updated registry information by calling `save( )`.

The `updateReport( )` and `removeReport( )` methods shown in Example 5-13 follow a similar pattern.

Example 5-13. Updating and removing a report to the FileReportRegistry

```
    public synchronized void updateReport(Report report)
        throws RegistryException{
        checkExists(report);
        reports.put(new Integer(report.getId( )), new Report(report));
        try {
```

Example 5-13. Updating and removing a report to the FileReportRegistry (continued)

```
            save( );
        }
        catch (IOException e) {
            throw new RegistryException("Can't save ReportRegistry", e);
        }
    }

    public synchronized void removeReport(Report report)
        throws RegistryException{
        checkExists(report);
        reports.remove(new Integer(report.getId( )));
        try {
            save( );
        }
        catch (IOException e) {
            throw new RegistryException("Can't save ReportRegistry", e);
        }
    }
    ...
    private void checkExists(Report report) {
        Integer id = new Integer(report.getId( ));
        if (reports == null || reports.get(id) == null) {
            throw new IllegalStateException("Report " + report.getId( ) +
                                            " doesn't exist");
        }
    }
```

The `updateReport( )` and `removeReport( )` methods call `checkExists( )` to verify that the provided `Report` instance corresponds to an existing report in the registry. If it doesn't, `checkExists( )` throws an `IllegalStateException`. The `updateReport( )` method then replaces the `Report` instance that matches the argument with a copy of the argument instance, while `removeReport( )` simply removes the matching report.

Example 5-14 shows the `getReport( )` method.

Example 5-14. Getting a report from the FileReportRegistry

```
    public synchronized Report getReport(int id) {
        return (Report) reports.get(new Integer(id));
    }
```

No surprises here: `getReport( )` simply returns a copy of the `Report` with an ID matching the specified one, or `null` if it doesn't exist.

The `getReports( )` method shown in Example 5-15 is more exciting.

Example 5-15. Getting a set of reports from the FileReportRegistry

```
    public synchronized List getReports(String owner, Date fromDate,
                                        Date toDate, int[] status) {
        List matches = new ArrayList( );
        Iterator i = reports.values().iterator( );
```

Example 5-15. Getting a set of reports from the FileReportRegistry (continued)

```
        while (i.hasNext( )) {
            Report report = (Report) i.next( );
            if (matchesCriteria(report, owner, fromDate, toDate, status)) {
                matches.add(new Report(report));
            }
        }
        return matches;
    }

    private boolean matchesCriteria(Report report, String owner,
                                    Date from, Date to, int[] status) {
        boolean matches = false;
        if ((owner == null || owner.equals(report.getOwner( ))) &&
            (from == null || (report.getStartDate( ) != null &&
             report.getStartDate().getTime() >= from.getTime( ))) &&
            (to == null || (report.getStartDate( ) != null &&
             report.getStartDate().getTime() <= to.getTime( )))) {
            if (status == null) {
                matches = true;
            }
            else {
                for (int i = 0; i < status.length; i++) {
                    if (report.getStatus( ) == status[i]) {
                        matches = true;
                        break;
                    }
                }
            }
        }
        return matches;
    }
```

The `getReports( )` method loops through all reports and calls `matchesCriteria( )` for each one. If the report matches the criteria, the method adds a copy of the `Report` instance to the `List` it returns after checking all reports.

The `matchesCritieria( )` method compares all criteria arguments that have non-`null` values with the corresponding properties of the `Report` argument and returns `true` if they all match. The owner criterion matches reports only with the specified owner; the date range criterion matches reports with start dates that fall within the range; and the status criterion matches reports in one of the listed statuses.

Authentication and Authorization

In the sample application, each expense report has an owner; the actions a user can perform on a specific report depends on whether she owns it, and whether she's a manager or a regular employee. To implement these requirements, we need a way to identify application users and tell what type of user they are.

A process referred to as *authentication* identifies users. To access the application, the user has to provide personal information that only a real, registered user would know. The application authenticates the information, e.g., by comparing it to information in a registry of known users. If the information is authentic, the application recognizes the user as a specific person. Once the application knows who the user is, it can use this knowledge to decide what the person is allowed to do (also known as *authorization*).

Authenticating the User

A Java web container typically supports four methods of authentication, described in the servlet specification: *HTTP basic authentication*, *HTTP digest authentication*, *HTTPS client authentication*, and *form-based authentication*.

HTTP basic authentication is a simple and not very secure authentication scheme that I'm sure you've encountered. When a browser requests access to a protected resource, the server sends back a response asking for the user's credentials (username and password). The browser prompts the user for this information and sends the same request again, but this time with the credentials in one of the request headers so the server can authenticate the user. The username and password are not encrypted, only slightly obfuscated by the well-known base64 encoding; it can easily be reversed by anyone who grabs it as it's passed over the network. Security can be improved by using an encrypted connection between the client and the server, such as the Secure Sockets Layer (SSL) protocol.

HTTP digest authentication is a slightly more secure method introduced in HTTP/1.1. As with basic authentication, the server sends a response to the browser when it receives a request for a protected resource. But with the response, it also sends a string called a *nonce*. The nonce is a unique string generated by the server, typically composed of a timestamp, information about the requested resource, and a server identifier. The browser creates an MD5 checksum, also known as a *message digest*, of the username, the password, the given nonce value, the HTTP method, and the requested URL, and sends it back to the server in a new request. The use of an MD5 message digest means that the password cannot easily be extracted from information recorded from the network. Additionally, using information such as timestamps and resource information in the nonce minimizes the risk of "replay" attacks. The digest authentication is a great improvement over basic authentication. The only problem is that it requires HTTP/1.1 clients and servers, and there are still plenty of old HTTP/1.0 clients and servers out there.

HTTPS client authentication is the most secure authentication method supported today. This mechanism requires the user to possess a Public Key Certificate (PKC). The certificate is passed to the server when the connection between the browser and server is established, using a very secure challenge-response handshake process. The server uses the certificate to uniquely identify the user. As opposed to the mechanisms previously described, the server keeps the information about the user's identity as long as the connection remains open.

These three methods are defined by Internet standards. They are used for all sorts of web applications, Java-based or not. The servlet specification defines only how an application can gain access to information about a user authenticated with either one.

The final mechanism, form-based authentication, is unique to the servlet specification. Unlike basic and digest authentication, form-based authentication lets you control the appearance of the login screen. That's why I picked it for the sample application. Figure 5-3 shows the custom login screen for the sample application.

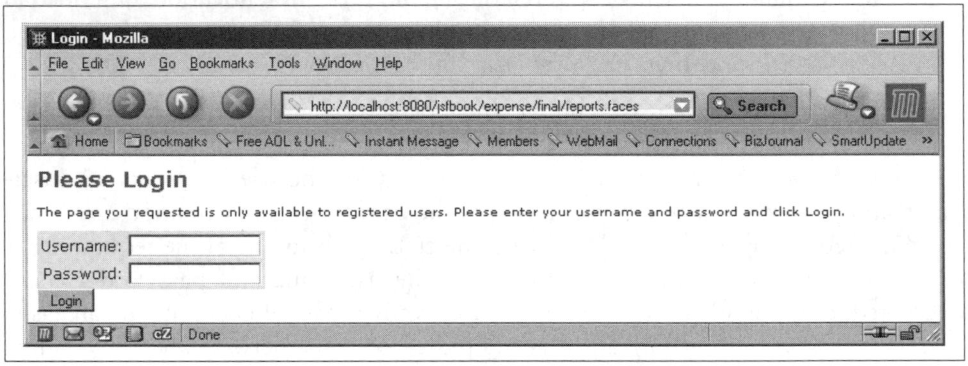

Figure 5-3. Expense report login screen

From the user's point of view, form-based authentication works just like HTTP basic and digest authentication. When the user requests a protected resource, the login form is shown, prompting the user to enter a username and password. When the user submits the form, the container authenticates the user; if the authentication is successful, it returns the requested resource; otherwise, it returns an error page. Form-based authentication is as insecure as HTTP basic authentication for the same reason: the user's credentials are sent as clear text over the network. To protect access to sensitive resources, it should be combined with encryption such as SSL.

You tell the container which type of authentication the application needs by adding a few elements to the web application deployment descriptor (i.e., the *WEB-INF/web.xml* file). Here's how you tell the container to use form-based authentication for the sample application:

```
<?xml version="1.0" encoding="ISO-8859-1"?>
<web-app xmlns="http://java.sun.com/xml/ns/j2ee"
  xmlns:xsi="http://www.w3c.org/2001/XMLSchema-instance"
  xsi:schemaLocation="http://java.sun.com/xml/ns/j2ee
    http://java.sun.com/xml/ns/j2ee/web-app_2_4.xsd"
  version="2.4">

  <login-config>
    <auth-method>FORM</auth-method>
```

```
        <form-login-page>/login.jsp</form-login-page>
        <form-error-page>/loginerror.jsp</form-error-page>
      </login-config>
      ...
    </web-app>
```

The <login-config> element contains an <auth-method> element that defines which authentication method to use. The FORM value tells it to use the form-based variety. For form-based authentication, you must also use the <form-login-page> and <form-error-page> elements to define the location of the login and error pages as context-relative paths. Other authentication methods require other nested elements, as described in Appendix F.

Example 5-16 shows the sample application login page.

Example 5-16. The login page (login.jsp)

```
<html>
  <head>
    <title>Login</title>
    <link rel="stylesheet" type="text/css"
      href="${pageContext.request.contextPath}/style.css">
  </head>
  <body bgcolor="white">
    <div class="title">Please Login</div>
    <p>
      The page you requested is only available to registered users.
      Please enter your username and password and click Login.
    </p>
    <form action="j_security_check" method="post">
      <table class="tablebg">
        <tr>
          <td align="right">Username:</td>
          <td><input name="j_username"></td>
        </tr>
        <tr>
          <td align="right">Password:</td>
          <td><input type="password" name="j_password"></td>
        </tr>
      </table>
      <input type="submit" value="Login">
    </form>
  </body>
</html>
```

The login page contains an HTML <form> element with the value j_security_check as the value of the action attribute, and two <input> elements with the names j_username and j_password. The action and input field names are defined by the servlet specification so you must use them exactly as in Example 5-16 for this to work.

The sample application's error page is shown in Example 5-17.

Example 5-17. The error page (loginerror.jsp)

```
<html>
  <head>
    <title>Login</title>
    <link rel="stylesheet" type="text/css"
      href="${pageContext.request.contextPath}/style.css">
  </head>
  <body bgcolor="white">
    <div class="title">Login Failed</div>
    <p>
      The username or password you entered is invalid.
      Please use the Back button to return to the Login screen
      and try again.
    </p>
  </body>
</html>
```

The only reason for using JSP pages rather than plain HTML pages for the form-based login and error pages is that I link to a stylesheet from both pages, highlighted in Example 5-17. I do this to illustrate an important point. The servlet specification demands that a web container return the login page when a user requests a protected resource, but it leaves it up to the web container vendors to decide *how* to return the page. The web container can send a redirect request with a URL matching the login page, telling the browser to get it with a new request, or it can return the login page directly (technically, this is called *forwarding* to the page). Which method it uses makes a big difference when it comes to references to other resources within the page, such as the stylesheet reference in Example 5-16 and 5-17, or references to image files and links to other pages.

If the container uses a redirect, the browser makes a new request and resolves relative references in the returned page, such as *style.css* and *images/logo.gif*, as relative to the URL for the login page. This is what most people expect, so when the redirect approach is used, there are typically no surprises. If, however, the container returns the page directly, the browser resolves relative references in the page as relative to the URL for the protected resource; it's the only URL it knows about. So if the protected URL is */jsfbook/expense/reports.faces* and the login page includes a relative URL like *style.css*, the browser tries to load the stylesheet from */jsfbook/expense/style.css*. Unless you're aware of this little quirk, you can spend endless hours trying to figure out why the referenced pages weren't found.

The solution to this problem is to always use absolute paths for resources referenced in the login and error pages; absolute paths work no matter how the container returns the pages. Because the first part of an absolute path is the application's context path, which may vary between deployments, the best approach is to use JSP pages and dynamically prepend the context path, e.g., with an EL expression (as I do in Example 5-16 and 5-17).

Controlling Access to Web Resources

Combining the result of authentication with rules for what different users are allowed to see and do is called authorization. The most basic authorization rule—what type of users are allowed to access certain web resources—can be expressed in the web application deployment descriptor for a Java web application. Other rules can be implemented by the application code with the help of methods in the servlet API.

Both types of authorization require information about users and types of users. How users, and groups of users, are defined depends on the web container you're using. Some containers use the operating system's user and group definitions. Others have their own user directory or use an external LDAP server, or let you define this information in a database. The security mechanism defined by the servlet specification describes how to specify the access-control rules for web application resources in terms of *roles*. Real user and group names for a particular container are mapped to the role names used in the application. How the mapping is done depends on the container, so you need to consult the container documentation if you don't use Tomcat.

Tomcat, by default, uses a simple XML file to define users and assign them roles at the same time. The file is named *tomcat-users.xml* and is located in the *conf* directory. To run the sample application, you must define at least two users like this:

```
<tomcat-users>
  <user name="hans" password="secret" roles="employee" />
  <user name="mike" password="boss" roles="manager" />
</tomcat-users>
```

Here, the user hans is assigned the employee role and mike is assigned the manager role. You can pick different usernames if you like, but you need at least one user defined for each role. Note that this is not a very secure way to maintain user information (the passwords are in clear text, for instance). The *tomcat-users.xml* file is intended only to make it easy to get started with container-based security. Tomcat can be configured to use a database or a JNDI-accessible directory instead, and for a production site, you should use one of these options. See the Tomcat documentation for details.

The type of authorization that should be enforced for web application resources, such as a JSP page or all files in a directory, is defined in the web application deployment descriptor (i.e., the *WEB-INF/web.xml* file).

Here's how you define the authorization rules for the pages used in the sample application:

```
<?xml version="1.0" encoding="ISO-8859-1"?>
<web-app xmlns="http://java.sun.com/xml/ns/j2ee"
  xmlns:xsi="http://www.w3c.org/2001/XMLSchema-instance"
  xsi:schemaLocation="http://java.sun.com/xml/ns/j2ee
    http://java.sun.com/xml/ns/j2ee/web-app_2_4.xsd"
  version="2.4">
```

```
    <security-constraint>
      <web-resource-collection>
        <web-resource-name>restricted</web-resource-name>
        <url-pattern>/expense/*</url-pattern>
      </web-resource-collection>

      <auth-constraint>
        <role-name>manager</role-name>
        <role-name>employee</role-name>
      </auth-constraint>
    </security-constraint>

    <security-role>
      <role-name>manager</role-name>
    </security-role>
    <security-role>
      <role-name>employee</role-name>
    </security-role>
    ...
  </web-app>
```

The rule is defined by a `<security-constraint>` element, with nested elements to define the resources to protect and the users that have access to the resources.

The `<web-resource-collection>` contains a `<web-resource-name>` element that associates the set of resources defined by the `<url-pattern>` element with a name. You can use any name, as long as it's unique within the application. The resources to protect are specified by a URL pattern. Here the pattern identifies all context-relative URLs starting with */expense/*. The asterisk at the end of the pattern is a wildcard character that means "any string." This pattern matches all requests for the sample application pages we'll develop in this book.

You can also use more than one `<url-pattern>` within a `<web-resource-collection>` and add `<http-method>` elements to restrict access for only some HTTP request types (e.g., only POST requests). Appendix F describes these options in detail.

The `<auth-constraint>` element contains nested `<role-name>` elements, declaring the roles a user must be associated with in order to access the resources. For the sample application, they say that a user must be associated with either the `employee` or the `manager` role to gain access.

All role names used by an application must also be defined in the deployment descriptor with `<security-role>` elements. A deployment tool may use these elements to ask for mappings to real users for each role when the application is installed.

With the security requirement declarations described in this chapter, the web container takes care of the authentication for the sample application and ensures that only registered users in the role of `employee` or `manager` can access the application pages. As you'll see in the following chapters, application code handles more fine-grained authorization, such as allowing only a manager to accept an expense report and restricting the set of reports a regular employee sees to the ones she owns.

CHAPTER 6

Creating and Rendering Components

JSF is a very powerful framework with lots of different features and options you can tweak to satisfy your needs. Trying to grasp everything at once would be overwhelming, so we'll take it one step at a time, looking at each feature in the context of the sample expense report application. This chapter focuses on how JSF components are created and rendered, using the sample application filtering criteria and menu areas as concrete examples.

The Basics

At the core, JSF is a Java API built on top of the Servlet API. In addition, it defines JSP custom tag libraries that hide the API layer to make it easy for Page Authors to include JSF components in a JSP page. Figure 6-1 shows both these layers and how JSF applications can be developed on top of either one or both.

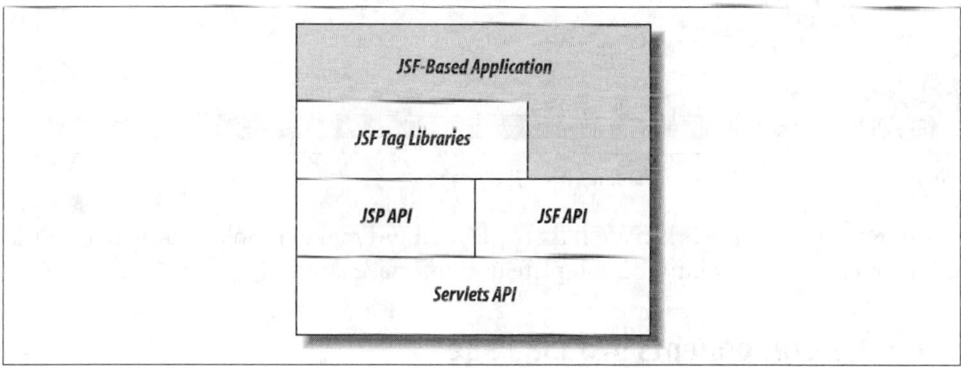

Figure 6-1. JSF layers

As you may recall from Chapter 4, a JSP custom tag library is a collection of custom actions, represented by XML elements in a JSP page and implemented as Java tag handler classes. If the term "custom action" sounds unfamiliar, you may be more familiar with the "custom tag" term. To make a long story short, an XML element includes an opening tag, an element body, and a closing tag, but the word "tag" is commonly used to refer to both tags and elements because it's easier to say and shorter to type. Hence, most people use the term *custom tag* for what formally should be called a *custom action* (the functional entity) as well as what formally is a *custom action element* (its representation in a page). Because I'm a stickler for correct terminology, I try to use the terms custom action and custom action element in this book, but if I slip, be aware that custom action, custom action element, and custom tag can all refer to the same thing.

When you use JSP as the presentation layer technology for JSF, you don't use the JSF API at all for creating and rendering components. Instead, you use the custom actions from the JSF custom tag libraries to say which components you need, and the tag handlers use the JSF API to create and render the corresponding component objects for you.

Even so, it helps to peek at the API to really understand what's going on. Let's start with something fairly simple, namely, the filtering criteria form from the sample expense report application, and look at both the JSP layer and what's going on behind the scenes at the API level. Figure 6-2 shows what the first incarnation of this part of the application looks like in a browser.

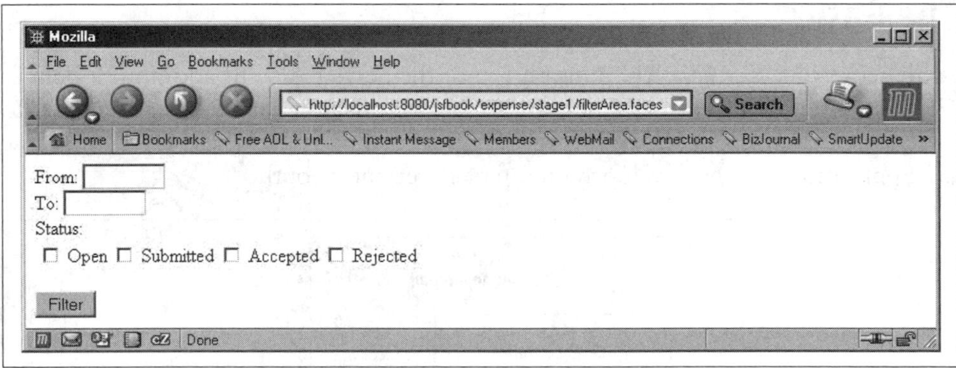

Figure 6-2. The first version of the filter area JSP page

It's not pretty, but it works. We'll fix the layout and make it look nicer when we put all the pieces together into the complete user interface later.

Using JSF Components in a JSP Page

The JSP page for the initial version of the filtering criteria form is shown in Example 6-1.

Example 6-1. Initial filtering criteria form JSP page (expense/stage1/filterArea.jsp)

```
<%@ page contentType="text/html" %>
<%@ taglib uri="http://java.sun.com/jsf/html" prefix="h" %>
<%@ taglib uri="http://java.sun.com/jsf/core" prefix="f" %>

<f:view>
  <h:form>
    From: <h:inputText size="8" />
    <br>
    To: <h:inputText size="8" />
    <br>
    Status:
    <h:selectManyCheckbox>
      <f:selectItem itemValue="1" itemLabel="Open" />
      <f:selectItem itemValue="2" itemLabel="Submitted" />
      <f:selectItem itemValue="3" itemLabel="Accepted" />
      <f:selectItem itemVvalue="4" itemLabel="Rejected" />
    </h:selectManyCheckbox>
    <p>
    <h:commandButton value="Filter" />
  </h:form>
</f:view>
```

The page starts with a JSP page directive, saying that the page generates HTML, and two `taglib` directives that declare the tag libraries used in the page. Each `taglib` directive contains two attributes: the `uri` attribute specifies the unique identifier for the library and the `prefix` attribute defines the namespace prefix used for elements from the library in this page. Note that even though the `uri` attribute value looks like a URL, it doesn't mean that the tag library is accessed over the Internet when you run the page. It's just a string that uniquely identifies a specific library, and a URL is typically used for public libraries because it's a pretty good guarantee that it won't clash with the identifier for other libraries.

The tag libraries used in Example 6-1 are the two tag libraries defined by JSF:

http://java.sun.com/jsf/core
: The core library contains action elements that represent JSF artifacts that are independent of the page markup language, such as converters and validators. The default prefix is `f` (short for "Faces"), but as with any JSP tag library, you can use any prefix you want as long as it's unique within the page.

http://java.sun.com/jsf/html
: The HTML library contains action elements that represent JSF components tied to renderers for rendering them as HTML elements. The default prefix is `h` (short for "HTML").

The fun starts after the tag library declarations, where you find a number of JSF action elements mixed with template text. Each JSF action represents an instance of a JSF component class defined at the API level.

The first action element in the page, `<f:view>`, is very important. The combination of the components that make up a specific user interface screen is called a *view* in JSF. A view contains an instance of the `javax.faces.component.UIViewRoot` class. This class is a nonvisual component type that acts as a container for all the other components in the view. Components representing UI widgets, such as input fields and buttons, are children of the `UIViewRoot` and can have children of their own. Together, the components form a tree, with the `UIViewRoot` at the top. The `<f:view>` action element represents the `UIViewRoot` component and you *must* make sure it encloses all other JSF action elements in the page; otherwise, they aren't included in the view.

Note that there's a one-to-one relationship between a JSF view and an HTTP response. Hence, you must use only one `<f:view>` element in the JSP page. A JSP page can, as you may know, include other JSP pages dynamically. Such included pages represent *subviews* in JSF, and are represented by an `<f:subview>` element. I'll discuss different ways to compose a view from subviews in Chapter 12.

The next JSF action element, `<h:form>`, represents a form component, acting as a container for input components that hold values that should be processed together. Within the `<h:form>` element in Example 6-1, you find action elements that represent the two input fields, the status choice checkboxes, and the Submit button (`<h:inputText>`, `<h:selectManyCheckbox>`, and `<h:commandButton>`).

The element names for all these actions are composed from a component type name and renderer type name. The core JSF components represent pure behavior and know nothing about how they are represented on a screen. This task instead falls on renderers associated with each component, making it possible to represent the same type of component in different ways. Take `<h:inputText>`, for example. It represents an input field component, i.e., a component type that holds a value that can be changed by the user. Such a component can be rendered in different ways. The `<h:inputText>` action associates the input component with a text renderer, which renders the component as an HTML `<input>` element with the `type` attribute set to `text`. Another action element named `<h:inputSecret>` associates an input component with a renderer of type "secret," which renders the component as an HTML `<input>` element with the `type` attribute set to `password`. Table 6-1 shows some other examples, and all combinations are described in Appendix A.

Table 6-1. Examples of actions representing component/renderer combinations

Action element	Component type	Renderer type
`<h:commandButton>`	Command	Button
`<h:commandLink>`	Command	Link
`<h:panelGroup>`	Panel	Group
`<h:panelGrid>`	Panel	Grid
`<h:selectOneMenu>`	SelectOne	Menu

The other elements that are in the form in Example 6-1 follow the same pattern. The `<h:selectManyCheckbox>` action element represents a "select many" component with a checkbox renderer, which renders the component as a group of HTML checkboxes. The `<h:commandButton>` represents a command component with a button renderer, rendering an HTML button. Most component types can be combined with more than one renderer type, and each valid combination is supported by an action element following the `<h:`*`componentTypeRendererType`*`>` naming convention.

So why doesn't the `<h:form>` element name follow the same convention? Because the only renderer type for the form component type is the form renderer. To avoid action element names like `<h:formForm>`, JSF uses an abbreviated element name when the component type and the renderer type have the same name.

The `<h:selectManyCheckbox>` element contains nested `<f:selectItem>` elements that define a label and a value for each choice. This makes it easy to define a number of fixed choices. Later, we'll look at other options that allow you to determine the choices at runtime instead.

The components are configured through action element attributes. Some attributes are defined by the JSF specification, but all actions in the JSF HTML tag library also support most of the same attributes as their HTML element counterparts. The `size` attribute used for the `<h:inputText>` elements in Example 6-1 is one example and Appendix A describes all attributes for all JSF action elements in detail. These are called *pass-through attributes*, and the renderer associated with the component adds these HTML-equivalent attributes as is to the HTML element it renderers.

Creating JSF Components

Example 6-1 shows a JSP page with JSF action elements representing a combination of component types and renderer types. When the page is processed, the tag handlers create and configure the component objects. That's all you really need to know to use JSF, but if you're a programmer, you're probably saying, "Okay, that's cool, but how are the components *really* created?" Let's take a look, but be aware that you don't need to worry about these details unless you're creating your own custom components, and in that case, you should read Chapters 13 and 14 to get the whole story. The intention here is only to give you an idea about how the JSF custom actions use the JSF API to make things happen. If you don't care about these details, you can safely skip the next two sections.

When the JSP container processes a page, it sends all template text to the browser as is, but when it encounters a custom action element it invokes the corresponding tag handler. All JSF tag handlers use the JSF API to create components and associate them with renderers the first time the user requests the page. For instance, the `<h:inputText>` tag handler contains code similar to this:

```
import javax.faces.application.Application;
import javax.faces.context.FacesContext;
import javax.faces.component.UIComponent;
```

```
import javax.faces.component.UIInput;
import javax.faces.webapp.UIComponentTag;
...
public class InputTextTag extends UIComponentTag {
    public int doStartTag( ) {
        FacesContext context = getFacesContext( );
        Application app = context.getApplication( );
        UIInput comp = (UIInput) app.createComponent("javax.faces.Input");
        comp.setRendererType("javax.faces.Text");
        ...
    }
    ...
}
```

It first gets a reference to the current instance of a class named javax.faces.context.FacesContext. An instance of this class is associated with each request and contains information about the request parameters, headers, session data, and a lot more. The javax.faces.webapp.UIComponentTag class that all JSF component tag handlers must extend implements the getFacesContext( ) method so it's available to all component tag handlers. In other types of classes, you can use the static FacesContext getCurrentInstance( ) method to obtain the current FacesContext instance when it's not available through other means, as long as the code that calls it runs in the context of a JSF request.

The FacesContext class provides an accessor method for an instance of the javax.faces.application.Application class. The Application class contains a number of methods for creating instances of configurable classes, such as the component type implementation classes. All JSF implementations provide default implementation classes for all component types defined in the specification, but you can replace them with specialized subclasses and register your own custom component types. The createComponent( ) method returns a new instance of the class registered for the component type named javax.faces.Input. Renderer classes are also registered under symbolic renderer type names; in order to associate the component with a renderer type, the setRendererType( ) is called with the renderer type name, i.e., javax.faces.Text in this example.

In addition to setting the renderer type, the tag handler also configures the component based on the custom action element attribute values. For instance, the tag handler for the <h:inputText> action element gets the size attribute value entered in the page and configures the component with this value. I've omitted the code for this here, but I describe it in detail in Chapters 13 and 14.

The component must also be added as a child of the component represented by the parent JSF action element. For components at the top level, the parent component is the UIViewRoot and, for nested components, it's some other component type, e.g., a form component. Here's a code snippet that shows how the tag handler deals with this:

```
public int doStartTag( ) {
    ...
    UIComponentTag parentTag = getParentUIComponentTag(pageContext);
```

```
            UIComponent parent = parentTag.getComponent( );
            parent.getChildren( ).add(comp);
            ...
        }
    }
```

As I mentioned earlier, all JSF tag handlers extend a class named javax.faces.webapp.UIComponentTag, which takes care of most of the grunt work. Its getParentUIComponentTag( ) method locates the tag handler for the parent JSF component action element. The component that tag handler represents can then be accessed through the getComponent( ) method. The return type for this method is javax.faces.component.UIComponent, which is the abstract class that all JSF component classes extend.

With access to the parent component, the tag handler asks it to include the new component as one of its children. JSF defines a very simple yet powerful API for working with the children of a component: a single method named getChildren( ) that returns a java.util.List. All manipulation of the children list is done through the List:

```
parent.getChildren( ).add(child);        // Add a child
parent.getChildren( ).add(index, child); // Add a child at an index
parent.getChildren( ).remove(child);     // Remove a child
parent.getChildren( ).remove(index);     // Remove a child at an index
parent.getChildren().clear( );           // Remove all children
parent.getChildren( ).contains(child);   // Look for a child
parent.getChildren( ).get(index);        // Get a child
parent.getChildren().size( );            // Count the children
parent.getChildren().iterator( );        // Iterate through the children
```

Because the getChildren( ) method is defined on the UIComponent class that all component classes extend, all JSF component types can have children.

In addition to the getChildren( ) method, there's also a getChildCount( ) method which is slightly more efficient than calling getChildren().size( ) when the component doesn't have any children, because no List needs to be created.

When you request the JSP page in Example 6-1, all JSF tag handlers are creating their corresponding component class instances and setting up the parent-child relationships as described in this section, resulting in the component tree shown in Figure 6-3

At the top of the tree, there's a UIViewRoot component with a UIForm component as its child. The UIForm component, in turn, has a UIInput, a UISelectMany, and a UICommand component as its children. The UISelectMany component has four UISelectItem components; one for each choice.

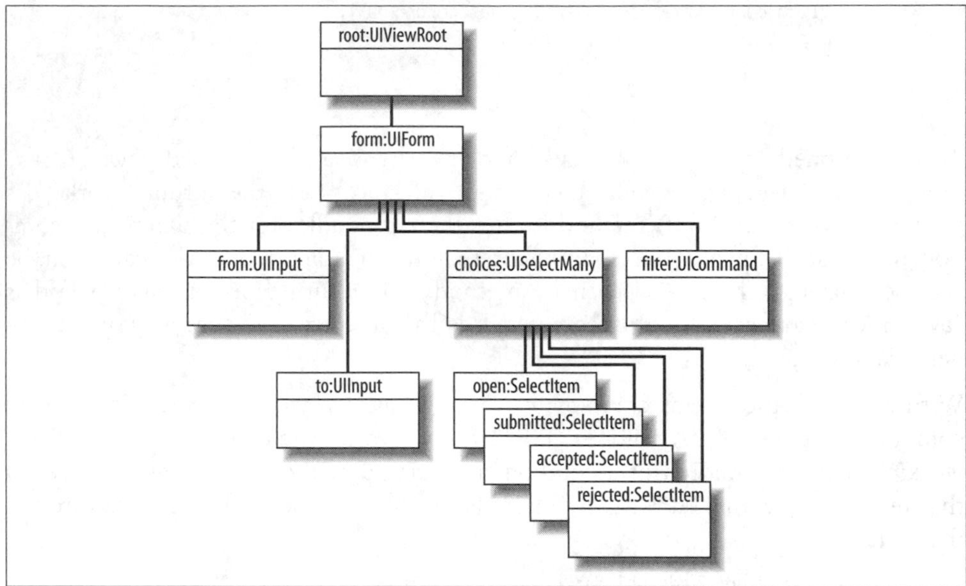

Figure 6-3. Component tree for the filter area components

Rendering the View

When JSP is used as the presentation layer technology, the JSP container processes the JSP page that defines the view as any JSP page so only the JSF custom action tag handlers can influence what happens. The part of the page that consists of template text and regular standard and custom actions is totally under the control of the JSP container, and JSF must play nice to render the markup for the components where it belongs relative to the other type of content.

Besides creating JSF components, the tag handlers also ask each component to render itself. Two rendering methods the tag handlers call for each component are named `encodeBegin( )` and `encodeEnd( )`. The `encodeBegin( )` method typically writes an opening tag (e.g., `<form>` for the form component), while `encodeEnd( )` writes a closing tag (e.g., `</form>`) or a single tag for a component that doesn't require separate opening and closing tags (e.g., an input component that generates a single HTML `<input>` tag). As you know by now, the component classes typically don't generate output directly. Instead, they delegate this task to a renderer. This is true for all components defined by the JSF specification, and it is the recommended behavior for custom components. The component rendering methods just obtain an instance of their renderer and call methods with the same name on the renderer:

```
package javax.faces.component;

import javax.faces.context.FacesContext;
import javax.faces.render.Renderer;
import javax.faces.webapp.UIComponentTag;
```

```
...
public class UIInput extends UIComponentBase {
    public void encodeBegin(FacesContext context) throws IOException {
        ...
        String rendererType = getRendererType( );
        if (rendererType != null) {
            getRenderer(context).encodeBegin(context, this);
        }
    }

    protected Renderer getRenderer(FacesContext context) {
        RenderKit rk = context.getRenderKit( );
        return rk.getRenderer(getFamily(), getRendererType( ));
    }
    ...
}
```

Related renderers are grouped together in *render kits*, represented by instances of the `javax.faces.render.RenderKit` class, and a specific render kit is associated with each view as a `UIViewRoot` property. The default render kit contains renderers for HTML, but you can develop render kits for other markup languages. The component classes obtain the current kit through a `FacesContext` method, and then ask the current kit for an instance of a renderer of the type the component is configured with.

Ignoring component data that should be represented by HTML element attributes, this is how the `encodeBegin( )` and `encodeEnd( )` methods for the default form renderer may generate the HTML elements for a form component:

```
import java.io.IOException;
import javax.faces.component.UIComponent;
import javax.faces.context.FacesContext;
import javax.faces.context.ResponseWriter;
import javax.faces.render.Renderer;
...
public class FormRenderer extends Renderer {
    ...
    public void encodeBegin(FacesContext context, UIComponent component)
        throws IOException {
        ResponseWriter out = context.getResponseWriter( );
        out.startElement("form", component);
        out.writeAttribute("method", "post", null);
        ...
    }

    public void encodeEnd(FacesContext context, UIComponent component)
        throws IOException {
        ResponseWriter out = context.getResponseWriter( );
        out.endElement("form");
    }
    ...
}
```

The rendering methods get a javax.faces.context.ResponseWriter from the context and use it to write their markup elements to the response. The ResponseWriter class is an extension of java.io.Writer, with methods that makes it easier to write markup language elements such as HTML and XML elements, e.g., the startElement( ), writeAttribute( ), and endElement( ) methods used in this example.

The tag handler calls the encodeBegin( ) method in its doStartTag( ) method and the encodeEnd( ) method in its doEndTag( ) method. In between these two calls, the JSP container may add template text and output from other JSF component tag handlers as well as non-JSF tag handlers to the response.

The third rendering method a JSF tag handler may call during rendering is named encodeChildren( ). The tag handler calls this method only if a component property named rendersChilden is set to true. This feature is used by complex components that must control in detail how their children are rendered, for instance, a component that generates an HTML table and uses its child components to generate the column values for each row. For a component with rendersChildren set to true, the tag handler calls encodeBegin( ), then encodeChildren( ), and finally encodeEnd( ) on the component, all in its doEndTag( ) method to ensure that all child components have been created before the component is rendered. The encodeChildren( ) method then calls encodeBegin( ) and encodeEnd( ) on the component children as often as needed.

Most component types don't need this kind of control over the layout of its children, so they set rendersChilden to false. An example is the form component. Because it doesn't layout its children, you can mix HTML elements for layout with JSF component action elements for its children that render themselves within the <h:form> element body.

The result of processing the JSP page containing component action elements and template text shown in Example 6-1 is an HTML response similar to this:

```
<form method="post" action="/jsfbook/expense/stage1/filterArea.faces">
  From: <input type="text" name="_id0:_id1">
  <br>
  To: <input type="submit" name="_id0:_id2">
  <br>
  Status:
  <input type="checkbox" name="_id0:_id3" value="1">Open<br>
  <input type="checkbox" name="_id0:_id3" value="2">Submitted<br>
  <input type="checkbox" name="_id0:_id3" value="3">Accepted<br>
  <input type="checkbox" name="_id0:_id3" value="4">Rejected<br>
  <p>
  <input type="submit" name="_id0:_id4" value="Filter">
  <input type="hidden" name="_id0">
</form>
```

The first point of interest here is the action attribute value for the <form> element. The form renderer generates a URL for this attribute, which ensures that the view that created the response containing the form also processes the form submit request. I'll cover how the request is processed in the next chapter.

Nested within the <form> element, there are <input> elements for each nested JSF component. The name attributes contain unique identifiers for all components. JSF generates component IDs automatically, unless you specify one explicitly:

```
From: <h:inputText id="from" size="8" />
```

You can specify explicit IDs for components that you must access from other code, e.g., in client-side scripting code and validators that need access to another component besides the one they're attached to. In most cases you don't need an explicit ID, though, because there are other means for linking a component to code, e.g., the component binding mechanisms described in Chapter 12.

Note also how the name attribute values hold values that combine the form's ID and the child components' IDs. This is because the form component is a *naming container*. You can read more about naming containers in Chapter 12 and Appendix C, but what this means to you is that component IDs need to be unique only within the closest parent component that is also a naming container, which simplifies application maintenance when a JSF view is created from multiple files containing shared parts (e.g., a search form that's included in every view).

In addition to the <input> elements for the input fields tied to the components nested within the form, there's also an <input> element of type hidden, representing the form component itself. When the form is submitted, JSF uses the corresponding request parameter with the form component's ID to identify the form that was submitted in cases where there is more than one form in the view.

Saving the View State

One of the key differences between JSF and a standalone application GUI framework like Swing is how component state is handled. In a standalone application, maintaining state is not an issue, because the user interface and the application logic is all part of the same operating system process, on the same machine—as long as the application is running, state is simply kept in memory. With JSF, on the other hand, the user interface is presented to a client (a browser) that is separated from the application logic by a network, communicating through a stateless protocol (HTTP). Unless special care is taken to handle state, the application forgets all about the client and its state as soon as it has sent the response to an individual request.

There are two ways to deal with this: save the state on the server and send back a state identifier with the response that the client returns for all new requests, or send back the complete state to the client and have it return the state with each request.

The Servlet and JSP specifications provide support for the first approach—passing and identifier back and forth, keeping the state on the server—and expose it as a *session scope*: a collection of named values on the server representing a specific client's state. The identifier is sent between the client and the server either in a cookie or encoded in the URLs. JSF hides all the details, but if you're curious, I recommend my

JavaServer Pages book (O'Reilly) or Jason Hunter and William Crawford's *Java Servlet Programming* (O'Reilly).

Saving state on the server can limit scalability due to high memory consumption for each user, while sending it back and forth between the client and server can increase the response times over a slow connection. JSF therefore supports both approaches for the component state and lets you decide which one to use per application by setting a context parameter in the application deployment descriptor (the *WEB-INF/web.xml* file):

```
...
  <context-param>
    <param-name>javax.faces.STATE_SAVING_METHOD</param-name>
    <param-value>server</param-value>
  </context-param>
...
```

The `javax.faces.STATE_SAVING_METHOD` init parameter can be set to either `server` or `client`. When saving state in the client, JSF collects the state that needs to be saved by calling a method named `saveState()` on all components in the view at some point during response rendering. In addition to saving the components' internal state (property values, etc.), the actual component tree structure is also saved, so that the tree can be rebuilt when the user sends a new request for the view. JSF gets this information by traversing the component tree and saving information about all top-level components and all parent/child relationships. How the state information is saved in the response depends on the response markup language and the JSF implementation. For HTML, it's saved typically in an encoded format in a hidden form field.

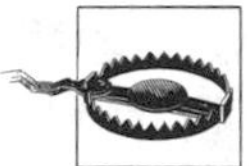

Note that the `saveState()` method and its peer-method `restoreState()`, for restoring the state, are not always called, so you mustn't use these methods for anything other than saving and restoring state (such as initializing temporary per-request state). The specification guarantees that they are called only as a pair: if one is called, the other must also be called. Typically, none of them are called when the state is saved on the server.

For most applications, saving state on the server should be your first choice for production use, because it cuts down on the bandwidth requirements. During development, client-side saving has the benefit that it makes it easier to create a new view for a modified JSP page, as explained in Chapter 12. Whether you pick server or client state initially, you can always switch to the other mode at any time because the application behaves in a similar manner either way.

Installing and Configuring a JSF Web Application

So far, we've looked at a very simple JSP page and how the tag handlers represented in the page use the JSF API to create JSF components behind the scene. Before we look at examples of other features, let's walk through how to install and run the simple page from Example 6-1.

The JSP page is part of a Java web application. As you may recall from Chapter 4, a Java web application consists of all the application files (JSP files, images, class files, and so on) plus a deployment descriptor (the *web.xml* file), arranged in a directory structure. A part of the directory structure for the book example application looks like this:

```
/index.html
/cover.gif
/expense/stage1/filterArea.jsp
...
/WEB-INF/web.xml
/WEB-INF/faces-config.xml
/WEB-INF/lib/jsf-api.jar
/WEB-INF/lib/jsf-impl.jar
...
```

At the top level, there's an *index.html* page with links to all examples in the book. The */expense/stage1/filterArea.jsp* file is one of them, containing the code for Example 6-1. So, a JSP page with JSF components is included in a web application just the same as a regular JSP page: as a file in the public part of the directory structure.

You must put at least these two declarations in the *WEB-INF/web.xml* file for a JSF application:

```
...
  <servlet>
    <servlet-name>FacesServlet</servlet-name>
    <servlet-class>javax.faces.webapp.FacesServlet</servlet-class>
  </servlet>

  <servlet-mapping>
    <servlet-name>FacesServlet</servlet-name>
    <url-pattern>*.faces</url-pattern>
  </servlet-mapping>
...
```

The `<servlet>` element declares a name for the servlet that processes all JSF requests and the `<servlet-mapping>` element maps requests with a path that ends with a *.faces* extension to this servlet. This is the recommended extension mapping. For each request, the `FacesServlet` replaces the *.faces* extension with a *.jsp* extension and uses the modified path to locate the JSP page that defines the corresponding view. If you have a very good reason for using another mapping, perhaps because you already use the *.faces* extension for other application resources, you can use any extension you want, or even a prefix mapping such as */faces/**, instead. See Appendix F for details about additional configuration needed for such alternative mappings.

If you have a JSF development tool and are using a JSP 2.0 web container, you may want to use a *.jsf* extension for your JSP pages instead of the standard *.jsp* extension.

The JSF specification reserves the *.jsf* extension so JSF development tools can take advantage of it and provide special support for JSP pages that contains JSF custom actions. Again, Appendix F describes what you must do to make this work. All JSP pages for the sample application use a *.jsp* extension, though.

The deployment descriptor may optionally include the context parameter described earlier to indicate whether to save state on the server or in the response and, of course, any other declarations your application needs. Appendix F contains a complete deployment descriptor reference.

JSF also uses a separate configuration file named *WEB-INF/faces-config.xml*, briefly introduced in Chapter 2. We'll look at the contents of this file when it's needed, but we'll ignore it for now.

The *WEB-INF/lib* directory for the example application contains the JSF reference implementation JAR files. Because JSF is such a new technology, few web containers provide native support for it, so the class files for a JSF implementation must be bundled with the application (along with any other class files the application need). Soon, all major web containers will likely offer native support for JSF, making it unnecessary for the application to bundle the JSF classes.

Running a JSP Page Containing JSF Components

If you have installed the example web application as described in Chapter 3, you've copied the whole directory structure to Tomcat's *webapps* directory as a subdirectory named *jsfbook*. If so, you can run the JSP page in Example 6-1 by typing the URL *http://localhost:8080/jsfbook/expense/stage1/filterArea.faces* in a browser. The result is shown in Figure 6-2.

There are a couple of things to note about the URL used to run the page. First, the path starts with a */jspbook* prefix. This is the application's *context path*. A Java web application is always associated with a context path when it's deployed to a web container, as you may recall from Chapter 4. When you use Tomcat, the context path is, by default, the name of the *webapps* subdirectory that holds the application. For other containers, you may be prompted for a name when you install the application. The second thing to note is that the URL ends with *.faces*. This is the extension we mapped to the JSF servlet in the deployment descriptor, so you must use this extension for all JSF page requests to have them processed by the JSF implementation. As I mentioned earlier, JSF replaces the extension with *.jsp* to get the context-relative path to the JSP page that creates the JSF components.

When you request this page the first time, JSF processes it as a regular JSP page. The tag handlers for the JSF actions in the page create their corresponding JSF components, configure them using the action element attributes, add them to the view, and ask them to render themselves, as illustrated in Figure 6-4.

Template text and content generated by non-JSF actions ends up in the response as a result of the regular JSP processing intermixed with the content rendered by the JSF components.

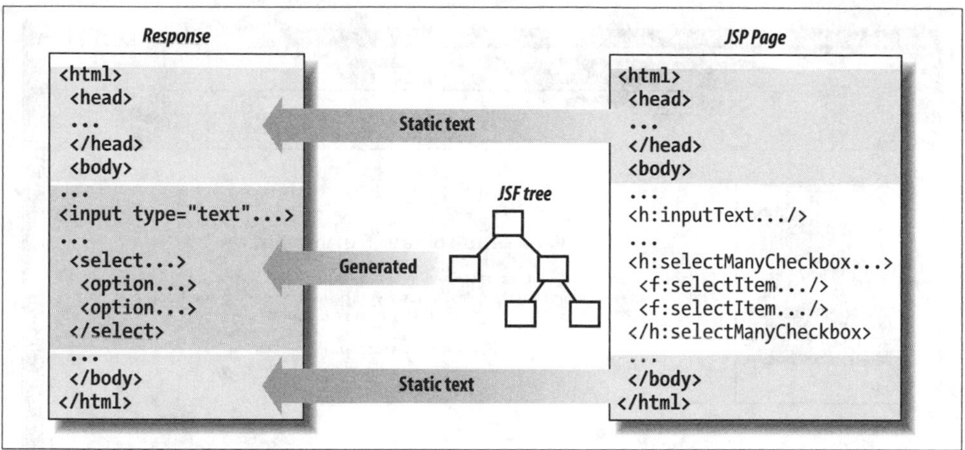

Figure 6-4. Processing a JSP page with JSF components

Go ahead and fill out some values, check off a checkbox or two, and click the button. Note how the values are sticky—whatever you enter is redisplayed when the page is reloaded. The JSF components take care of all the details so you don't have to, which is one of the main advantages of JSF over, say, plain JSP.

Instead of typing the URL for the example in a browser, you can use the book *index.html* page, shown in Figure 6-5, and simply click the links for each example.

The index page also contains links to the source for all JSP pages, so it's easy to look at as you experiment with the examples.

Binding Components to Model Properties

In Example 6-1, the components save their current value and redisplay it when the page is reloaded. That's great, but in order for the backend code to get the values, it would need to locate the corresponding user interface components and ask them for their values. That would introduce an undesirable dependency between the user interface and the backend code.

To solve this problem, JSF lets you bind components directly to JavaBeans properties of any application class as well as to elements of an array or `java.util.List`, or `java.util.Map`* entry. When the component is rendered, it reads the property or element value and renders it; when a request is processed, it sets the property or element value to the current component value. This way, the backend code doesn't need to know anything about the user interface—it just works with the properties of the application model classes.

* If you come from a Struts background, note that you can use a `Map` similarly to how a `DynaBean` is used in Struts.

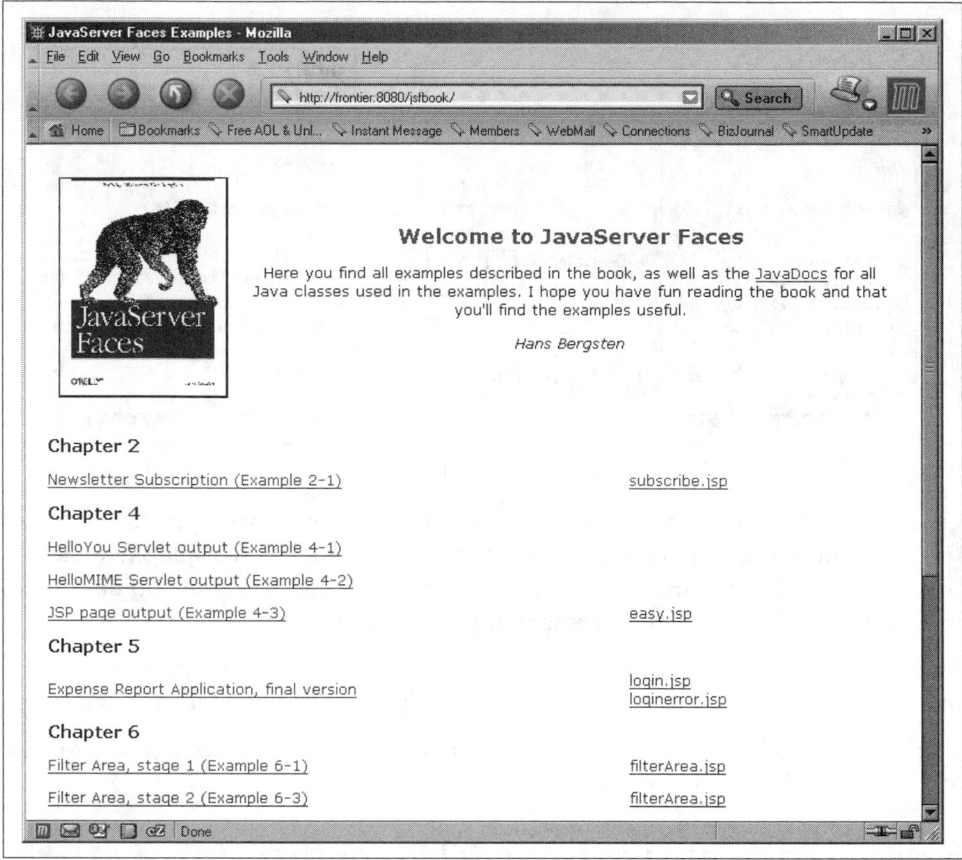

Figure 6-5. JSF book examples index page

A JSF application typically uses two types of classes with JavaBeans properties: the real application beans representing application concepts and what I call "glue beans," which sit between the real application beans and the user interface. Others call the latter a "backing bean" or "code-behind file," but it all means the same thing.

The `Report` class introduced in Chapter 5 is an example of a real application bean. The `ReportHandler` class is an example of a "glue bean," partly shown in Example 6-2.

Example 6-2. Parts of the ReportHandler class

```
package com.mycompany.expense;

import java.util.Date;
...

public class ReportHandler {
    ...
    private Date from;
```

Example 6-2. Parts of the ReportHandler class (continued)

```
    private Date to;
    private int[] status;

    ...
    public Date getFrom( ) {
        if (from == null) {
            from = getPreviousMonth(new Date( ));
        }
        return from;
    }

    public void setFrom(Date from) {
        this.from = from;
    }

    public Date getTo( ) {
        if (to == null) {
            to = new Date( );
        }
        return to;
    }

    public void setTo(Date to) {
        this.to = to;
    }

    public String[] getStatus( ) {
        if (status == null) {
            if (isManager) {
                status = new int[1];
                status[0] = Report.STATUS_SUBMITTED;
            }
            else {
                status = new int[4];
                status[0] = Report.STATUS_OPEN;
                status[1] = Report.STATUS_SUBMITTED;
                status[2] = Report.STATUS_ACCEPTED;
                status[3] = Report.STATUS_REJECTED;
            }
        }

        // Convert the int[] to a String[] to match the SelectItem type
        String[] stringStatus = new String[status.length];
        for (int i = 0; i < status.length; i++) {
            stringStatus[i] = String.valueOf(status[i]);
        }
        return stringStatus;
    }

    public void setStatus(String[] stringStatus) {
        status = null;
        if (stringStatus != null) {
```

Example 6-2. Parts of the ReportHandler class (continued)

```
            status = new int[stringStatus.length];
            for (int i = 0; i < status.length; i++) {
                status[i] = Integer.valueOf(stringStatus[i]).intValue( );
            }
        }
    }
    ...
}
```

The ReportHandler class contains JavaBeans accessor methods for properties corresponding to the user interface input fields in the filtering criteria form: from, to, and status.* When the JSF components are bound to these properties, the properties automatically provide default values when the components are rendered the first time and are set to the values the user enters when the form is submitted. Backend logic can then access the values easily without knowing anything about the user interface components. As you will see later, this type of "glue bean" also often implements event handler methods that invoke the real application beans with values captured by the user interface.

Using JSF EL Expressions

In Chapter 4, I introduced the JSP and the JSP 2.0 Expression Language (EL). JSP EL expressions are evaluated when the JSP page is processed—in other words, when the response is rendered.

JSF also supports an EL. Syntactically, the JSP 2.0 EL and the JSF EL are identical, but JSF may evaluate the EL expressions both when it processes input the user submitted (e.g., to update the application bean properties) and when it renders the response. This is the main difference between the JSF EL and the JSP EL.

To distinguish between a JSP EL expression and a JSF EL expression, you must use different delimiters for each type: a JSP EL expression is always written as ${*expression*}, while a JSF EL expression is written as #{*expression*}, i.e., with a #{ as the start delimiter instead of ${. None of the JSF custom action element attributes accept a JSP EL expression, only a JSF EL expression.

To bind a component's main value to a property of a bean or an element of another data structure, JSF uses a *value binding* expression. A value binding expression is the part of a JSF EL expression that evaluates to a bean property, a java.util.List or array element, or a java.util.Map entry. The entity a value binding points to can be

* The status property is declared as a String[] in the public API, because it must match the data type used for the choice values created by the <f:selectItem> elements, but internally the status values are held by an int[] to match the data type used in the business logic classes. We'll return to these details in Chapter 7.

both read and written. In programming lingo, this amounts to what's often called an *rvalue* (the right-hand side of an assignment expression) for read access and an *lvalue* (the left-hand side of an assignment expression) for write access.

Some components, such as an output component, represent a read-only value; there's no way a user can change the value. All components also have a number of properties in addition to their main value, for instance, the size of an input field and the number of rows and columns of a text area. You can use value binding expressions to set the value of a read-only component and component properties, but you can also use the complete JSF EL expression syntax, e.g., use a bean property value combined with an EL operator, like this: `#{report.status == 'open'}`. EL expressions mixed with text are also supported for this type of property:

```
<h:outputText value="#{report.startDate} to #{report.endDate}" />
```

As with the JSP EL, a JSF EL expression has access to a number of variables holding implicit objects. Compared to the variables exposed by the JSP EL, JSF removes `pageScope` and `pageContext` and adds two new variables for accessing JSF components present in a view and JSF context information: `view` and `facesContext`. All implicit object variables are listed in Table 6-2.

Table 6-2. Variables for implicit JSF EL objects

Variable name	Description
`requestScope`	A collection (a `java.util.Map`) of all request scope variables
`sessionScope`	A collection (a `java.util.Map`) of all session scope variables
`applicationScope`	A collection (a `java.util.Map`) of all application scope variables
`param`	A collection (a `java.util.Map`) of all request parameter values as a single `String` value per parameter
`paramValues`	A collection (a `java.util.Map`) of all request parameter values as a `String` array per parameter
`header`	A collection (a `java.util.Map`) of all request header values as a single `String` value per header
`headerValues`	A collection (a `java.util.Map`) of all request header values as a `String` array per header
`cookie`	A collection (a `java.util.Map`) of all request cookie values as a single `javax.servlet.http.Cookie` value per cookie
`initParam`	A collection (a `java.util.Map`) of all application initialization parameter values as a single `String` value per value
`facesContext`	An instance of the `javax.faces.context.FacesContext` class, providing access to various JSF context data
`view`	An instance of the `javax.faces.component.UIViewRoot` class, providing access to all components in the current view

The reason JSF excludes the `pageScope` and `pageContext` variables is that they exist only during processing of the JSP page, but JSF also needs to evaluate its EL expressions while processing user input, before any JSP page is processed. Another reason the variables are excluded is that JSF can be used with other presentation layer technologies besides JSP, in which there is no such thing as a page scope or a page context. The `facesContext` variable is basically a replacement for `pageContext`, providing access to the same information and more.

The implicit `view` variable holds a reference to the `UIViewRoot` component. Because all component classes follow the JavaBeans coding conventions, properties and children of a component can be accessed through this variable. For instance, a value binding expression for a property of the first child of the form in Example 6-1 looks like this:

```
#{view.children[0].children[0].valid}
```

Here, the first child (index 0) of the `view` is the form component, and its first child is the input component, which has a property named `valid`. JSF 1.0 doesn't provide any method that exposes the children by their ID, so you must access them by their numeric index.

You'll see plenty of examples of both complete JSF EL expression and value binding expressions later in this book so don't worry if it seems like magic at this point.

Using Value Binding Expressions

Let's improve the filtering criteria form by binding the fields to properties of the `ReportHandler` class. Example 6-3 shows the new filtering criteria page with the value binding expressions added.

Example 6-3. New filtering criteria form with value binding expressions added (expense/stage2/filterArea.jsp)

```
<%@ page contentType="text/html" %>
<%@ taglib uri="http://java.sun.com/jsf/html" prefix="h" %>
<%@ taglib uri="http://java.sun.com/jsf/core" prefix="f" %>

<f:view>
  <h:messages layout="table" />
  <h:form>
    From: <h:inputText size="8" value="#{reportHandler.from}" />
    <br>
    To: <h:inputText size="8" value="#{reportHandler.to}" />
    <br>
    Status:
    <h:selectManyCheckbox value="#{reportHandler.status}">
      <f:selectItem itemValue="1" itemLabel="Open" />
      <f:selectItem itemValue="2" itemLabel="Submitted" />
      <f:selectItem itemValue="3" itemLabel="Accepted" />
      <f:selectItem itemValue="4" itemLabel="Rejected" />
    </h:selectManyCheckbox>
    <p>
    <h:commandButton value="Filter" />
  </h:form>
</f:view>
```

The value attributes for the input components contain value binding expressions that point to the corresponding properties in a ReportHandler instance available through a variable named reportHandler. If you run this page, you'll see that the default dates returned by the getFrom( ) and getTo( ) methods shown in Example 6-2 end up in the input fields, and the same goes for the default choices returned by the getStatus( ) method.

Converting Between Model and View Data Formats

Adding the value binding expression takes us one step closer to a real application, but we're not done yet. First, note that the date fields are too short to show the dates in the format in which they are presented. Also, if you try to submit the form, error messages regarding the dates are displayed at the top of the page. The error messages are displayed by the <h:messages> action I added at the top in Example 6-3, which I'll get back to in the next chapter.

The reason for the error messages is that the value is sent to the application as a string (an HTTP request parameter is always a string), but the data type for the from and to properties is java.util.Date. JSF takes care of conversion between strings and simple data types—numbers and Booleans—all by itself, but a date can be written in many different ways, so we need to give JSF a clue about how to interpret a string representing a date. Example 6-4 shows you how this is done.

Example 6-4. Filtering criteria form with date converters (expense/stage3/filterArea.jsp)

```
<%@ page contentType="text/html" %>
<%@ taglib uri="http://java.sun.com/jsf/html" prefix="h" %>
<%@ taglib uri="http://java.sun.com/jsf/core" prefix="f" %>

<f:view>
  <h:messages layout="table"/>
  <h:form>
    From:
    <h:inputText size="8" value="#{reportHandler.from}">
      <f:convertDateTime dateStyle="short" />
    </h:inputText>
    <br>
    To:
    <h:inputText size="8" value="#{reportHandler.to}">
      <f:convertDateTime dateStyle="short" />
    </h:inputText>
    <br>
    Status:
    <h:selectManyCheckboxl value="#{reportHandler.status}">
      <f:selectItem itemValue="1" itemLabel="Open" />
      <f:selectItem itemValue="2" itemLabel="Submitted" />
      <f:selectItem itemValue="3" itemLabel="Accepted" />
      <f:selectItem itemValue="4" itemLabel="Rejected" />
    </h:selectManyCheckbox>
    <p>
```

Example 6-4. Filtering criteria form with date converters (expense/stage3/filterArea.jsp) (continued)

```
    <h:commandButton value="Filter" />
  </h:form>
</f:view>
```

The nested `<f:convertDateTime>` actions added for both `<h:inputText>` actions in Example 6-4 create and configure converters for conversion between `String` and `java.util.Date` values and link them to the corresponding components.

The converters can be configured in many ways using optional attributes. Here, I use the `dateStyle` attribute. It accepts the values `default`, `short`, `medium`, `long`, and `full`, corresponding to the formatting styles with the same names supported by the `java.text.DateFormat` class. If you want to show the time, you can optionally specify a style for the time portion with the `timeStyle` attribute, using the same values as for the date portion.

The exact format for the date and time styles depends on the locale used for the page (we'll get back to locales in Chapter 11), but here are samples of what they look like with the English locale.

```
default        Sep 9, 2003 5:41:15 PM
short          9/9/03 5:41 PM
medium         Sep 9, 2003 5:41:15 PM
long           September 9, 2003 5:41:15 PM PST
full           Tuesday, September 9, 2003 5:41:15 PM PST
```

As an alternative to the style attributes, you can use the `pattern` attribute. It accepts a symbol pattern of the same type as the `java.text.SimpleDateFormat` class, e.g., `yyyy-MM-dd` for `2003-09-09`.

JSF also provides an `<f:convertNumber>` action with similar attributes for precise interpretation and formatting of numbers (see Appendix A for details). In the rare event that you need to convert between strings and a type not supported out-of-the-box by JSF, you can create your own custom converter.

Creating Objects Automatically as They Are Needed

With the converters in place, Example 6-4 works great, but there's still a bit of magic left. You may be asking yourself how the `reportHandler` variable gets its value; it's actually done automatically by JSF when the variable is first needed. JSF creates and configures instances of classes defined in the JSF *faces-config.xml* file for variables that are referenced in a value expression. Let's take a closer look at this feature.

Example 6-5 shows the `reportHandler` variable declaration in the *faces-config.xml* file for the sample application, minus details that are not relevant for the examples in this chapter.

Example 6-5. ReportHandler declaration in faces-config.xml

```
<faces-config>
  ...
  <managed-bean>
    <managed-bean-name>reportHandler</managed-bean-name>
    <managed-bean-class>
      com.mycompany.expense.ReportHandler
    </managed-bean-class>
    <managed-bean-scope>session</managed-bean-scope>
    ...
  </managed-bean>
  ...
</faces-config>
```

The `<managed-bean>` element declares a variable that the application uses. The variable is mapped to a class that complies with the JavaBeans specification rules on naming conventions for accessor methods and has a public no-arguments constructor—hence, the *bean* reference in the element name.

All three subelements shown in Example 6-5 are mandatory: the `<managed-bean-name>` element declares the variable name used to refer to instances of the class; the `<managed-bean-class>` element declares the fully qualified class name; the `<managed-bean-scope>` element declares in which scope instances should be placed. The supported scopes values are `request`, `session`, `application`, and the special value `none`.

When JSF evaluates a value binding expression and encounters a variable that doesn't exist in one of the scopes, it consults the configuration file and creates an instance of the managed bean with a matching name. If the bean scope is declared as something other than `none`, JSF saves the instance in the specified scope. A bean declared with scope `none` is created every time the application asks for it, and it's not placed in any scope. This can be useful for beans with properties that have calculated values (e.g., the current time) and never need to be accessed by other application classes.

To recap what's going on in Example 6-4, when the JSP page is rendered for the first time, JSF evaluates the `#{reportHandler.from}` value binding expression for the first JSF component. It can't find the `reportHandler` variable in any scope, so it consults the *jsf-config.xml* file shown in Example 6-5. There, it finds a declaration for the `reportHandler` bean, so it creates an instance of the bean and saves it in the declared scope (the session scope, in this case). JSF then continues its evaluation of the value binding expression, getting the `from` property value of the newly created bean and using it as the value for the component. JSF then evaluates the `#{reportHandler.to}` value binding expression for the second component. Now the `reportHandler` variable is available in the session scope, so it gets the `to` property value and uses it for the second component, and so on for all components in the view.

Conditionally Render Components

So far, the components we've created are always shown to the user, but sometimes that's not what we want. The menu area in the sample application, for instance, contains buttons for accepting or rejecting a report only if the current user is a manager. Component properties may also depend on runtime conditions, e.g., the way the menu area buttons are enabled or disabled depending on the current report's status in the sample application.

Figure 6-6 shows the menu area as it appears to a regular user for a brand new report without entries, i.e., without the buttons available only to managers and with all buttons disabled.

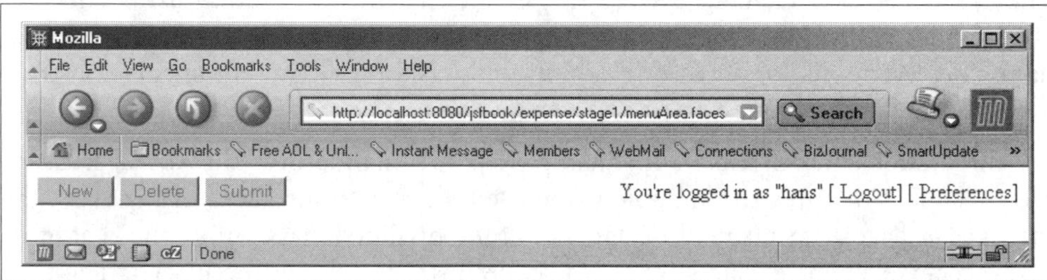

Figure 6-6. Menu area

If you come from a JSP background and have used JSTL a bit, your first impulse is likely to use the JSTL <c:if> or <c:choose> actions for conditional processing along these lines:

```
<%@ page contentType="text/html" %>
<%@ taglib uri="http://java.sun.com/jsf/html" prefix="h" %>
<%@ taglib uri="http://java.sun.com/jsf/core" prefix="f" %>
<%@ taglib uri="http://java.sun.com/jsp/jstl/core" prefix="c" %>

<f:view>
  <h:form>
    <table cellpadding="0" cellspacing="0" width="100%">
      <tr>
        <td>
          <h:commandButton value="New"
            disabled="#{reportHandler.currReport.status == 0}" />
          <h:commandButton value="Delete"
            disabled="#{reportHandler.currReport.status == 0 ||
              reportHandler.currReport.status == 2 ||
              reportHandler.currReport.status == 3}" />
          <h:commandButton value="Submit"
            disabled="#{reportHandler.currReport.status == 0 ||
              reportHandler.currReport.status == 2 ||
              reportHandler.currReport.status == 3}" />
         <c:if test="${reportHandler.manager}">
           <h:commandButton id="acceptButton" value="Accept"
```

```
              disabled="#{reportHandler.currReport.status == 0 ||
                ! reportHandler.currReport.status == 2}" />
            <h:commandButton id="rejectButton" value="Reject"
              disabled="#{reportHandler.currReport.status == 0 ||
                !reportHandler.currReport.status == 2}" />
          </c:if>
        </td>
        <td align="right">
          You're logged in as "${pageContext.request.remoteUser}"
          [<h:outputLink value="../../logout.jsp" />
             <h:outputText value="Logout" />
           </h:outputLink>]
          [<h:outputLink value="prefUser.faces" />
             <h:outputText value="Preferences" />
           </h:outputLink>]
        </td>
      </tr>
    </table>
  </h:form>
</f:view>
```

The `<c:if>` action in this example includes or excludes the manager buttons depending on a property of the `reportHandler` that tells whether the current user is a manager, and the components are disabled based on JSF EL expressions checking the current report's status.

I recommend that you fight the urge to implement the logic this way when you use JSF. There are a number of reasons:

- Using JSTL actions and JSF actions means using both JSP EL expressions and JSF EL expressions. Because of the subtle differences between these two expression types, it's not always obvious what's going on. For instance, all variables in a JSP EL expression must refer to existing beans, while beans for variables in a JSF value binding expression are created automatically if they don't exist, as I described earlier. Another difference is that a JSF EL expression can't access page scope variables.
- When you use `<c:if>` to conditionally include or exclude a JSF action, the corresponding component is physically added or removed from the view's component tree. This can lead to strange effects because the component loses its state when its removed from the view.
- The `<c:if>` action and the type of conditions used in the EL expressions represent application logic, and it's better kept out of the template altogether.

I suggest that you look at the JSP page as just a way to layout JSF components and static text on the screen, and forget that it can actually contain conditional code like the JSTL `<c:if>` and `<c:choose>` elements.

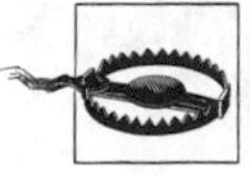

If you can't fight the urge to use JSTL actions to conditionally include or exclude JSF component action elements, you must use the id attribute to give these JSF components explicit IDs, as in the previous example. If you don't, all kinds of strange things can happen.

Conditionally Disable Components Using Bean Properties

A better approach to conditionally include and disable components is to externalize all details for these decisions to a Java class. Example 6-6 shows this approach.

Example 6-6. Menu area using value expressions for conditional rendering (expense/stage1/menuArea.jsp)

```
<%@ page contentType="text/html" %>
<%@ taglib uri="http://java.sun.com/jsf/html" prefix="h" %>
<%@ taglib uri="http://java.sun.com/jsf/core" prefix="f" %>

<f:view>
  <h:form>
    <table cellpadding="0" cellspacing="0" width="100%">
      <tr>
        <td>
          <h:commandButton value="New"
            disabled="#{reportHandler.newDisabled}" />
          <h:commandButton value="Delete"
            disabled="#{reportHandler.deleteDisabled}" />
          <h:commandButton value="Submit"
            disabled="#{reportHandler.submitDisabled}" />
          <h:commandButton value="Accept"
            rendered="#{reportHandler.acceptRendered}"
            disabled="#{reportHandler.acceptDisabled}" />
          <h:commandButton value="Reject"
            rendered="#{reportHandler.rejectRendered}"
           disabled="#{reportHandler.rejectDisabled}" />
        </td>
        <td align="right">
          You're logged in as "${pageContext.request.remoteUser}"
          [<h:outputLink value="../../logout.jsp" />
             <h:outputText value="Logout" />
           </h:outputLink>]
          [<h:outputLink value="prefUser.faces" />
             <h:outputText value="Preferences" />
           </h:outputLink>]
        </td>
      </tr>
    </table>
  </h:form>
</f:view>
```

All HTML form elements have an attribute named disabled. When set to true, the browser disables the corresponding user interface widget: a button can't be clicked, an input field doesn't accept input, and so on.

All JSF components that are rendered as HTML form elements also support the disabled attribute and, in Example 6-6, I use value binding expressions that point to reportHandler properties to calculate the appropriate value at runtime. Example 6-7 shows how the property getter methods are implemented in the ReportHandler class.

Example 6-7. ReportHandler methods for conditional rendering and disabling

```
package com.mycompany.expense;

...
public class ReportHandler {
    ...
    private Rules rules;
    private Report currentReport;
    private String currentUser;
    private boolean isManager;
    ...

    public boolean isNewDisabled( ) {
        return isReportNew( );
    }

    public boolean isDeleteDisabled( ) {
        return isReportNew( ) ||
            !rules.canDelete(currentUser, isManager, currentReport);
    }

    public boolean isSubmitDisabled( ) {
        return isReportNew( ) ||
            !rules.canSubmit(currentUser, isManager, currentReport);
    }

    public boolean isAcceptDisabled( ) {
        return isReportNew( ) ||
            !rules.canAccept(currentUser, isManager, currentReport);
    }

    public boolean isRejectDisabled( ) {
        return isReportNew( ) ||
            !rules.canReject(currentUser, isManager, currentReport);
    }

    ...
    private boolean isReportNew( ) {
        return currentReport.getStatus( ) == Report.STATUS_NEW;
    }
    ...
}
```

The methods simply return a Boolean value that reflects how the corresponding button should be handled in the page.

Most of these methods first check if the report has status New (i.e., it doesn't have any entries yet), and if not, call a method in a separate Rules class to see if the report can be deleted, submitted, and so on. These rules are used for other parts of the application that we haven't looked at yet, so it makes sense to put them in a separate class. Having them in a separate class makes it easy to change the rules, if necessary.

The Rules class is shown in Example 6-8.

Example 6-8. Report processing rules in the Rules class

```
package com.mycompany.expense;

public class Rules {
    public boolean canEdit(String user, boolean isManager, Report report) {
        return report.getOwner( ).equals(user) && !isLocked(report);
    }

    public boolean canDelete(String user, boolean isManager, Report report) {
        return report.getOwner( ).equals(user) && !isLocked(report);
    }

    public boolean canSubmit(String user, boolean isManager, Report report) {
        return report.getOwner( ).equals(user) && !isLocked(report);
    }

    public boolean canAccept(String user, boolean isManager, Report report) {
        return isManager && report.getStatus( ) == Report.STATUS_SUBMITTED;
    }

    public boolean canReject(String user, boolean isManager, Report report) {
        return isManager && report.getStatus( ) == Report.STATUS_SUBMITTED;
    }

    public boolean canView(String user, boolean isManager, Report report) {
        return isManager || report.getOwner( ).equals(user);
    }

    public boolean isLocked(Report report) {
        return report.getStatus( ) == Report.STATUS_SUBMITTED ||
          report.getStatus( ) == Report.STATUS_ACCEPTED;
    }
}
```

All Rules methods consider both the type of user and the report's status when deciding whether the operation can be performed.

An instance of the Rules class is created in the ReportHandler constructor, where the instance variables for the current user and the current report are also initialized, as shown in Example 6-9.

Example 6-9. Initialization of ReportHandler instance variables

```
public class ReportHandler {
    ...
    private Rules rules;
    private Report currentReport;
    private String currentUser;
    private boolean isManager;
    ...
    public ReportHandler( ) {
        rules = new Rules( );
        currentReport = getCurrentReport( );
        currentUser = getCurrentUser( );
        isManager = isManager( );
    }
    ...
    public Report getCurrentReport( ) {
        if (currentReport == null) {
            currentReport = createNewReport( );
        }
        return currentReport;
    }

    public boolean isManager( ) {
        FacesContext context = FacesContext.getCurrentInstance( );
        ExternalContext ec = context.getExternalContext( );
        return ec.isUserInRole("manager");
    }
    ...

    private String getCurrentUser( ) {
        FacesContext context = FacesContext.getCurrentInstance( );
        ExternalContext ec = context.getExternalContext( );
        return ec.getRemoteUser( );
    }

    private Report createNewReport( ) {
        Report report = new Report( );
        report.setOwner(getCurrentUser( ));
        ...
        return report;
    }
    ...
}
```

The `isManager( )` method deserves some explanation. As you may recall from Chapter 4, container-based security works in terms of roles assigned to real users when the web application is deployed. To test if the current user is playing a certain role, the servlet `HttpServletRequest` class has a method called `isUserInRole( )`. That's the method used by the `isManager( )` method, indirectly, through a JSF class called `javax.faces.context.ExternalContext`.

The isManager( ) method first gets a reference to the current FacesContext instance through the static getCurrentInstance( ) method. Methods about the runtime context that are not related directly to JSF are delegated to the ExternalContext class, available through the getExternalContext( ) method. The isUserInRole( ) is one such method, and the isManager( ) method calls it with the role name "manager" and returns the result.

The getCurrentUser( ) method uses the same technique to get a reference to the ExternalContext, and then uses the getRemoteUser( ) method to get the username of the authenticated user making the request.

Conditionally Include Components Using Bean Properties

All JSF action elements also have a rendered property. If you set it to false, the component (and all its children) remains in the view but it's never asked to render itself. In Example 6-6, the rendered attributes for the Accept and Reject buttons are set to value binding expressions that delegate the rendering decision to the reportHandler bean. Here's how the ReportHandler class implements the corresponding getter methods:

```
public boolean isAcceptRendered( ) {
    return isManager( );
}

public boolean isRejectRendered( ) {
    return isManager( );
}
```

The JSF <h:commandButton> action elements in Example 6-6 use value binding expressions that get the appropriate values from the reportHandler bean for the disabled and rendered attribute values, pushing all the detailed decisions to the bean. Placing this type of logic in a bean instead of in the page has clear maintenance advantages, so I recommend that you follow this pattern for your own applications.

In this chapter, we looked at how JSF components are created and how they generate the HTML elements for the browser in some detail. In the next chapter, we'll look at what happens when the user fills out a form and submits it to JSF for processing.

CHAPTER 7

Validating Input

There are two types of input validation you must consider in any application: *syntactic* and *semantic* validation. A form field value that represents a date, for instance, must be written in a certain format (i.e., be syntactically correct) in order to be interpreted by the application. It may also have to follow other rules (i.e., be semantically correct) to be accepted, e.g., be a date in the future or later than another date.

In JSF, components perform syntactic validation typically during the conversion from a request parameter string value to the native type of the business data property bound to the component. For semantic validation, you can attach validators to the components. JSF comes with a set of standard validators for the most common validation needs and lets you develop custom validators for more complex rules. We'll look at both alternatives in this chapter.

Dealing with Syntax Errors in User Input

In Chapter 6, we created a few components, arranged them as a component tree in a view, rendered them to the browser, and saved the view state either in the response itself or on the server. Presumably, there's a user sitting there admiring our nice form with an input field and a button. Let's see what happens when she submits the form.

First, JSF must figure out which view to use for processing the request. This information is encoded in the URI itself. As you may recall from Chapter 6, we've decided to use the default extension mapping for JSF requests, so the request paths always end with a *.faces* suffix. The view ID is the context relative path with *.faces* replaced by *.jsp*. So with a context-relative path like */test.faces*, the view ID is `/test.jsp`. JSF uses this ID to locate the state information on the server, or retrieve it from the request data if it was previously passed to the client with the response. It rebuilds the component tree, and then calls `restoreState()` on all components so they can get back their old internal state.

Next, each component is asked to look for its value in the request. JSF calls a method called `decode()` on each component to accomplish this task. As with rendering, components typically delegate this task to an associated renderer; if a renderer was used to render the component, it's the one most likely to know how to find the component's value in the request.

For HTML, component values are sent as HTTP request parameter String values, with names corresponding to the component IDs. The decode( ) method saves this raw parameter value as the submitted value for the component.

When all components have had a chance to read their values from the request, JSF asks them to validate the new value by calling the validate( ) method. If a component is bound to a model property (via a value binding) of a different type than String, the first part of validation is trying to convert the value to the model property's data type. I mentioned in Chapter 6 that JSF provides a set of standard converters for numbers, Boolean values, and time values, and you can also register custom converters for other data types. A converter is a subclass of the javax.faces.convert.Converter class and must provide implementations of two abstract methods:

```
public Object getAsObject(javax.faces.context.FacesContext,
    javax.faces.component.UIComponent component, String value);

public String getAsString(javax.faces.context.FacesContext,
    javax.faces.component.UIComponent component, Object value);
```

Converters are registered with JSF either under a symbolic name or for a specific data type (i.e., a fully qualified class or interface name). You rarely need a custom converter, but how to register one is described in Appendix E. JSF register the converters in Table 7-1 and 7-2 by default, and they are sufficient for most applications.

Table 7-1. Standard converters registered by name

Symbolic name	Class name
javax.faces.DateTime	javax.faces.convert.DateTimeConverter
javax.faces.Number	javax.faces.convert.NumberConverter

Table 7-2. Standard converters registered by type

Type	Symbolic name	Class name
Boolean and boolean	javax.faces.Boolean	javax.faces.convert.BooleanConverter
Byte and byte	javax.faces.Byte	javax.faces.convert.ByteConverter
Character and char	javax.faces.Character	javax.faces.convert.CharacterConverter
Double and double	javax.faces.Double	javax.faces.convert.DoubleConverter
Float and float	javax.faces.Float	javax.faces.convert.FloatConverter
Integer and int	javax.faces.Integer	javax.faces.convert.IntegerConverter
Long and long	javax.faces.Long	javax.faces.convert.LongConverter
Short and short	javax.faces.Short	javax.faces.convert.ShortConverter

The converters in Table 7-1 can be configured and attached to a component, with JSF converter action elements in a JSP page as shown in Chapter 6. Behind the scenes, the tag handlers call the `setConverter( )` method on a component, as shown in Example 7-1.

Example 7-1. Creating and configuring a converter

```
import javax.faces.application.Application;
import javax.faces.component.UIInput;
import javax.faces.context.FacesContext;
import javax.faces.convert.DateTimeConverter;
...
public class ConvertDateTimeTag extends TagSupport {
    private String dateStyle;
    ...

    public int doStartTag( ) throws JspException {
        ...
        FacesContext context = FacesContext.getCurrentInstance( )
        Application application = context.getApplication( );
        DateTimeConverter dateTimeConv = (DateTimeConverter)
            application.createConverter("javax.faces.DateTime");
        dateTimeConv.setDateStyle(dateStyle);
        input.setConverter(dateTimeConv);
        ...
    }
}
```

Pretty much everything in JSF is pluggable, with the concrete classes to use being declared in the *faces-config.xml* file (default classes are used if no replacements are defined). An abstract class named `javax.faces.application.Application` defines methods for getting hold of registered converters, among other things. The `getApplication( )` method on `FacesContext` provides access to an instance of a concrete `Application` subclass. With access to the `Application`, the code in Example 7-1 asks it to create an instance of the converter class registered under the symbolic name `javax.faces.DateTime`, and then sets the converter's `dateStyle` property and tells the component to use the converter.

When a component is equipped with a converter, the `validate( )` method* calls its `getAsObject( )` method to convert the request parameter `String` value. If the component doesn't have a converter, the `validate( )` method uses the data type of the property pointed to by the value binding to locate a matching converter, i.e., one of the standard converters in Table 7-2 or a custom converter registered for the type.

* The `validate( )` method actually delegates the conversion to the renderer, if any, which in turn calls the converter. This allows a fancy renderer that represents a single value as more than one user interface element (e.g., a date represented by three select lists for year, month, and day) to be in control of converting the submitted value (or values, in this example).

Things can go bad at this stage, of course: maybe there's no converter for the data type or the conversion fails due to syntax errors. In either case, the `validate()` method marks the submitted value as invalid and adds an error message to a list maintained by the `FacesContext`. That's where the `<h:messages>` action introduced in Chapter 6 finds the messages and displays them on the page. The same list is used for error messages produced by validators, so we'll return to what a message looks like and how you can define custom messages after we've looked at the validation process.

If the conversion is successful, and there are no validators registered for the component, the converted value is saved as the component's local value and is later used to update the model property value.

Using the Standard Validators

The expense report entry form part of the sample application contains a number of fields that require validation: all fields must have a value, a syntactically valid date must be entered in the Date field, and the Amount field must contain an amount larger than one. Figure 7-1 shows all these fields, with a couple of error messages, generated by the initial implementation of this form.

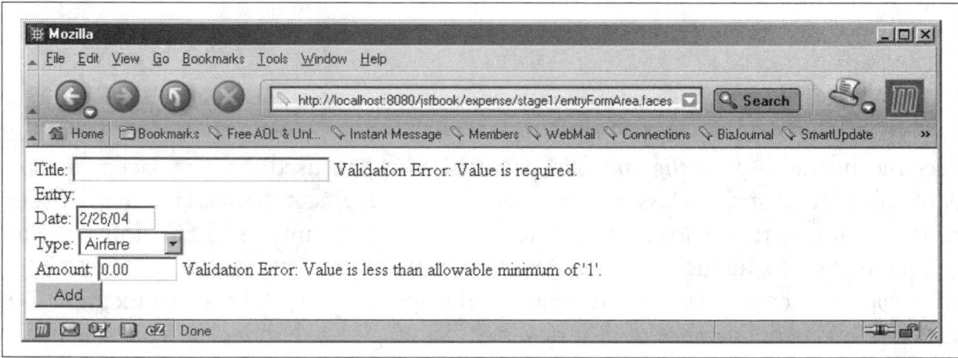

Figure 7-1. The first version of the report entry form area JSP page

The JSP file for this version of the form is shown in Example 7-2.

Example 7-2. Initial report entry form area JSP page (expense/stage1/entryFormArea.jsp)

```
<%@ page contentType="text/html" %>
<%@ taglib uri="http://java.sun.com/jsf/html" prefix="h" %>
<%@ taglib uri="http://java.sun.com/jsf/core" prefix="f" %>

<f:view>
  <h:form>
    Title:
    <h:inputText id="title" size="30" required="true"
      value="#{reportHandler.currentReport.title}" />
    <h:message for="title" />
```

Example 7-2. Initial report entry form area JSP page (expense/stage1/entryFormArea.jsp)

```
    <br>
    Entry:
    <br>
    Date:
    <h:inputText id="date" size="8" required="true"
      value="#{entryHandler.currentEntry.date}">
      <f:convertDateTime dateStyle="short" />
    </h:input_text>
    <h:message for="date" />
    <br>
    Type:
    <h:selectOneMenu id="type" required="true"
      value="#{entryHandler.currentEntry.type}">
      <f:selectItems value="#{entryHandler.expenseTypeChoices}"/>
    </h:selectOneMenu>
    <h:message for="type" />
    <br>
    Amount:
    <h:inputText id="amount" size="8" required="true"
      value="#{entryHandler.currentEntry.amount}">
      <f:convertNumber pattern="#,##0.00" />
      <f:validateDoubleRange minimum="1"/>
    </h:input_text>
    <h:message for="amount" />
    <br>
    <h:commandButton value="Add"
      disabled="#{reportHandler.addEntryDisabled}"/>
  </h:form>
</f:view>
```

The Title field input component is represented by an `<h:inputText>` action in Example 7-2. The only validation requirement for this component is that a value must be entered; the format of the value doesn't matter. This requirement is declared by setting the `required` attribute to `true`, causing the action's tag handler to call `setRequired(true)` on the corresponding `UIComponent` when the view is created.

When the user submits the form, JSF processes the request as described in the previous section. If the `validate()` method can successfully convert the submitted value to the native data type, it moves on to semantic validation. If the required property is set to `true`, the `validate()` method verifies that there's a submitted value. If there isn't, the method marks the component value as invalid and adds an error message to the `FacesContext` message list, just as when the value can't be converted.

This leads us to the next piece of the puzzle. Note that I assign an ID to the input component with the `id` attribute, and that this ID is also used as the value of the `for` attribute in the `<h:message>` action element that follows the Title `<h:inputText>` action. In Chapter 6, we used the `<h:messages>` (plural) action to display error messages for all components in one place. The `<h:message>` (singular) action displays messages for the single component specified by the `for` attribute, so a potential error message can be displayed next to the corresponding user interface widget.

The input component for the Date field is also declared as required and it is linked to an `<h:message>` action through a unique component ID. Additionally, a nested `<f:convertDateTime>` action configures the component with a `DateTime` converter. As described in the previous section, the converter ensures that the value the user enters is a syntactically correct date string. Otherwise, it adds an error message to the list, which the `<h:message>` action displays.

The Amount field input component is more interesting. Besides the required attribute and a number converter, a nested `<f:validateDoubleRange>` action configures this component with a `javax.faces.validator.DoubleRangeValidator`, a validator for testing if the value is a decimal number above or below certain values. In Example 7-2, only a minimum value is specified, but you can also specify a maximum value. Table 7-3 lists all standard validators. Appendix A describes the validator JSP actions in detail.

Table 7-3. Standard validators

JSP action	Default Class	Description
`<f:validateDoubleRange>`	`javax.faces.validator.DoubleRangeValidator`	Checks that a component value is a decimal above a minimum or a maximum
`<f:validateLength>`	`javax.faces.validator.LengthValidator`	Checks that the number of characters in the value is above a minimum or below a maximum.
`<f:validateLongRange>`	`javax.faces.validator.LongRangeValidator`	Checks that a component value is a nondecimal above a minimum or a maximum

When a component is configured to use a validator, the `validate()` method first checks if a value is submitted at all (if the `required` property is also set to `true`) and then asks the validator to validate the value. If the validator doesn't accept the value, the component value is marked as invalid and an error message is added to the `FacesContext` message list, just as for all other input validation errors.

You can configure a component with more than one validator. If there's more than one validator, they are called in the order they are added to the component.

Value Bindings for the Report Entry Fields

Besides the elements and attributes for conversion and validation, all JSF component action elements in Example 7-2 have `value` attributes that bind them to bean properties, in the same way as in the examples in Chapter 6.

The value binding expression for the Title is `reportHandler.currentReport.title`. The first part, `reportHandler`, is the variable for the `ReportHandler` we looked at in Chapter 6. This class has a property named `currentReport` that holds a reference to an instance of the Report class described in Chapter 5, which in turn has a property named title:

```
package com.mycompany.expense;
...
public class ReportHandler {
    private Report currentReport;
    ...
    public Report getCurrentReport( ) {
        if (currentReport == null) {
            currentReport = createNewReport( );
        }
        return currentReport;
    }
    ...
    private Report createNewReport( ) {
        Report report = new Report( );
        report.setOwner(getCurrentUser( ));
        ...
        return report;
    }
    ...
}
```

```
package com.mycompany.expense;
...
public class Report implements Serializable {
    private String title;
    ...
    public synchronized String getTitle( ) {
        return title;
    }

    public synchronized void setTitle(String title) {
        this.title = title;
    }
    ...
}
```

The value binding is used as an lvalue when the submitted form is processed, setting the title property of the current report to the value of the UIInput component. When the response is rendered, it's used as an rvalue, so the UIInput component reads its value from the title property.

The components for the Date, Type, and Amount fields all have value bindings that bind them to properties of an instance of the ReportEntry class (presented in Chapter 5), available through another glue class called EntryHandler:

```
package com.mycompany.expense;
...
public class EntryHandler {
    private ReportEntry currentEntry;
```

```
    ...
    public ReportEntry getCurrentEntry( ) {
        if (currentEntry == null) {
            currentEntry = new ReportEntry( );
        }
        return currentEntry;
    }
    ...
}
```

```
package com.mycompany.expense;

import java.io.Serializable;
import java.util.Date;

public class ReportEntry implements Serializable {
    private Date date;
    private int type;
    private double amount;
    ...
    public Date getDate( ) {
        if (date == null) {
            date = new Date( );
        }
        return date;
    }

    public void setDate(Date date) {
        this.date = date;
    }

    public int getType( ) {
        return type;
    }

    public void setType(int type) {
        this.type = type;
    }

    public double getAmount( ) {
        return amount;
    }

    public void setAmount(double amount) {
        this.amount = amount;
    }
    ...
}
```

The Type field is represented by a `UISelectOne` component, with a renderer that renders it as a selection list. The value binding expression binds it to the type property of the current ReportEntry instance, exactly the same as for all the other components, but how it gets its list of choices is new:

```
Type:
<h:selectOneMenu id="type" required="true"
  value="#{entryHandler.currentEntry.type}">
  <f:selectItems value="#{entryHandler.expenseTypeChoices}"/>
</h:selectOneMenu>
```

In Chapter 6, the choices for the Status checkboxes are listed right in the page, but here I use a `<f:selectItems>` action bound to an `EntryHandler` property named `expenseTypeChoices` instead. Using a value binding to pull in the choices makes it easy to customize the application. The `expenseTypeChoices` property has a `java.util.List` with `javax.faces.model.SelectItem` instances as its value:

```
package com.mycompany.expense;

import java.util.ArrayList;
import java.util.Iterator;
import java.util.List;
import java.util.Map;
import java.util.Map.Entry;
import javax.faces.model.SelectItem;
...
public class EntryHandler {
    private Map expenseTypes;
    private List expenseTypeChoices;
    ...
    public void setExpenseTypes(Map expenseTypes) {
        this.expenseTypes = expenseTypes;
    }

    public List getExpenseTypeChoices() {
        if (expenseTypeChoices == null) {
            expenseTypeChoices = new ArrayList();
            Iterator i = expenseTypes.entrySet().iterator();
            while (i.hasNext()) {
                Map.Entry me = (Map.Entry) i.next();
                expenseTypeChoices.add(new SelectItem(me.getValue(),
                        (String) me.getKey()));
            }
        }
        return expenseTypeChoices;
    }
    ...
}
```

`UISelectItem` or `UISelectItems` child components represent the choices handled by `UISelectOne` and `UISelectMany` components, and the value of a `UISelectItem` or `UISelectItems` component is one or more `SelectItem` instances.

`SelectItem` is a bean with three properties: `value`, `label`, and `description`. The `value` property is the value that is included in the request when the choice is selected, and the label is the descriptive text displayed to the user. The description property isn't used by any of the standard renderers, but a custom renderer can use it, e.g., to display a more detailed description as a "tool tip." The SelectItem class provides constructors that let you set one or more of the property values. Here, I use a constructor that sets the value and label properties, and leave the description undefined.

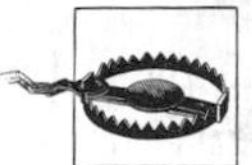

The basic data type for the SelectItem value property must be the same as for the value of the selection component the SelectItem instance belongs to. For instance, the value property of a SelectItem representing a choice for a UISelectOne component with a value of type Integer or int must be of type Integer. If the types don't match, the selection component's value isn't rendered or updated correctly.

The getExpenseTypeChoices( ) method creates and returns a List of SelectItem instances with the value and label taken from a java.util.Map, set by the setExpenseTypes( ) method. This design makes it easy to customize the available choices. The Map is declared and initialized as a managed bean in the *faces-config.xml* file:

```
<faces-config>
  ...
  <managed-bean>
    <managed-bean-name>expenseTypes</managed-bean-name>
    <managed-bean-class>java.util.TreeMap</managed-bean-class>
    <managed-bean-scope>application</managed-bean-scope>
    <map-entries>
      <value-class>java.lang.Integer</value-class>
      <map-entry>
        <key>Breakfast</key>
        <value>1</value>
      </map-entry>
      <map-entry>
        <key>Lunch</key>
        <value>2</value>
      </map-entry>
      <map-entry>
        <key>Dinner</key>
        <value>3</value>
      </map-entry>
      ...
    </map-entries>
  </managed-bean>
  ...
</faces-config>
```

In addition to the bean variable name and the class name, I declare the bean's scope as application, because the expense types are the same for all users of the application. I use a java.util.TreeMap class to get it automatically sorted by the key values.

The <map-entries> element contains a <value-class> element that says that the values should be created as Integer values, and then a <map-entry> element with nested <key> and <value> elements for each entry.

The entryHandler variable is also declared as a managed bean, with property declarations that tell JSF to initialize it with references to both the ReportHandler instance and the expense type Map instance:

```
<managed-bean>
  <managed-bean-name>entryHandler</managed-bean-name>
  <managed-bean-class>
    com.mycompany.expense.EntryHandler
  </managed-bean-class>
  <managed-bean-scope>session</managed-bean-scope>
  <managed-property>
    <property-name>reportHandler</property-name>
    <value>#{reportHandler}</value>
  </managed-property>
  <managed-property>
    <property-name>expenseTypes</property-name>
    <value>#{expenseTypes}</value>
  </managed-property>
  ...
</managed-bean>
```

Most of this should look familiar, because it's the same type of declaration that we looked at for the reportHandler in Chapter 6. The only difference is the <managed-property> element. This is how you tell JSF to initialize a bean's properties. Each element contains a <property-name> element that contains the property name and a <value> element that contains a JSF EL expression that evaluates to the value it should be set to. Instead of a JSF EL expression, you can use a static value string or a <map-entries> element to initialize a property of type Map, or <list-entries> to initialize a List or array property. I'll show you examples of some of these alternatives later. All options are described in Appendix E.

To tie it all together, when the #{entryHandler.expenseTypeChoices} expression is evaluated for the first time in a session, JSF looks up the entryHandler variable declaration in the *faces-config.xml* file and creates an instance of the EntryHandler class. It then tries to set all the declared properties and finds the reference to the expenseTypes variable. If this variable doesn't exist, it looks up its *faces-config.xml* declaration, creates an instance of the TreeMap, initializes it with all the declared entries, and saves a reference to the instance as an application scope variable. JSF then sets the EntryHandler instance's expenseType property to a reference to the TreeMap and saves the initialized EntryHandler instance as a session scoped variable named entryHandler. Now the evaluation moves on, resulting in a call to the getExpenseTypeChoices() method, which creates the List of SelectItem instances from the TreeMap entries and returns it. Voila! The UISelectOne now has access to its choices in the required format.

After all this, I must admit that the `getExpenseTypeChoices( )` method could return the `Map` with the choices directly instead of converting it to a `List` with `SelectItem` instances. If you use a `Map` as the value for a `UISelectItems` component, it converts it to `SelectItem` instances with the keys as labels and the values as values internally. I'm doing the conversion explicitly in the `EntryHandler` class in order to show you what's really going on and also because it makes other examples in this book easier to implement. Unless you need to set the description properties for the `SelectItem` instances, or deal with internationalization (as shown in Chapter 11), using a `Map` directly may be the better alternative.

Defining Custom Error Messages

As you can see in Figure 7-1, the default error messages that the JSF reference implementation produces are generic. Also, they might differ between JSF implementations, so you'll probably want to define your own messages.

All standard messages are defined as resources of a Java resource bundle, and you can create your own bundle and selectively override the standard messages with your own versions. Your own bundle must be declared in the *faces-config.xml* file, like this:

```
<faces-config>
  <application>
    <message-bundle>custMessages</message-bundle>
  </application>
  ...
</faces-config>
```

The value of the `<message-bundle>` element is the so-called bundle *base name*. If you're unfamiliar with resource bundles, don't worry. Even though there's more than one way to make a bundle (as well as to skin a cat), the easiest way is to create a text file that contains all the resources as text strings identified by keys. The name of the file is the base name followed by a *.properties* extension, and the file must be stored somewhere in the application's classpath. I recommend putting it in the application's *WEB-INF/classes* directory, because it's always included in the classpath. Here's the sample application's *custMessage.properties* file with the replacement text for the message generated by the `DoubleRangeValidator` when the value is below the specified minimum:

```
javax.faces.validator.DoubleRangeValidator.MINIMUM=Please enter a value greater \
than {0}.
```

Each message is declared as a key, an equal sign, and a text value. The keys for all standard messages are defined by the JSF specification. They use a long prefix to avoid clashes with other standard messages and application-specific message. For your own message keys, you can use whatever unique string you want, but some kind of prefix is often a good idea for a large application. The value in this case is so long that it doesn't fit on one line, so I use a backslash at the end of the first line to indicate that the value continues on the next line.

Messages often contain placeholders, such as the {0} placeholder in this example. The placeholders for standard message are replaced with real values at runtime, typically representing validator properties, the submitted value, or a component identifier. The placeholder used in this example is replaced with the minimum allowed value.

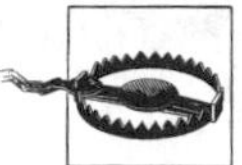

Be careful with messages that contain single quotes. If the message text contains both a single quote and at least one placeholder, you must double the single quote, e.g., "This value isn''t larger than {0}". For messages without placeholders, single quotes must *not* be duplicated, e.g., "Single quote usage isn't consistent".

Two texts can be defined for each message: a summary and a detailed description. The `<h:message>` and `<h:messages>` actions shows either one or both depending on which attributes you use, as described in Appendix A. To define the detailed description for a message, use the standard key plus the string "_detail":

```
javax.faces.validator.DoubleRangeValidator.MINIMUM=Please enter a value greater \
than {0}.
javax.faces.validator.DoubleRangeValidator.MINIMUM_detail=The value you entered \
is smaller than the smallest value allowed
```

Using a Custom Validator

The standard validators are sufficient for many applications, but sometimes you have to roll your own to get what you need. The filtering criteria form in the sample application, for instance, has two date fields for specifying a date range. With a custom validator, we can make sure that the date entered in the To field is in fact later than the date entered in the From field, so let's build one. Figure 7-2 shows the filtering criteria form with a validation message from the custom validator.

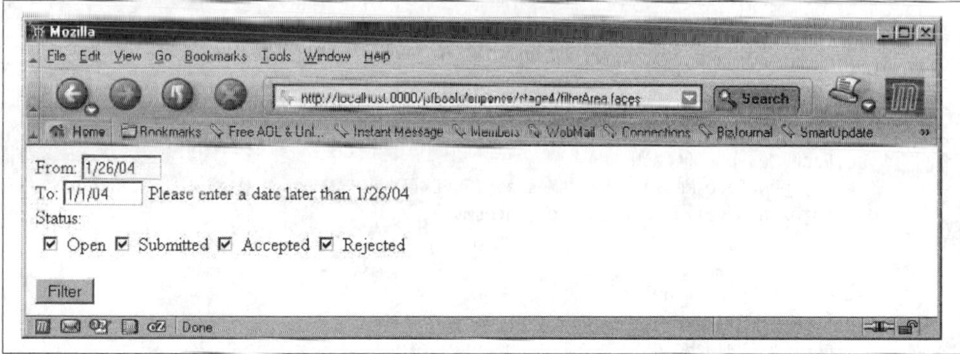

Figure 7-2. The filtering criteria form with a custom validator

Example 7-3 shows a custom validator class that compares the date values of two components to ensure that one is later than the other.

Example 7-3. The LaterThanValidator class

```
package com.mycompany.jsf.validator;

import java.text.MessageFormat;
import java.io.Serializable;
import java.util.Date;
import java.util.Locale;
import java.util.ResourceBundle;
import javax.faces.application.Application;
import javax.faces.application.FacesMessage;
import javax.faces.component.UIComponent;
import javax.faces.component.EditableValueHolder;
import javax.faces.component.ValueHolder;
import javax.faces.context.FacesContext;
import javax.faces.convert.Converter;
import javax.faces.validator.Validator;
import javax.faces.validator.ValidatorException;

public class LaterThanValidator implements Validator, Serializable {
    private String peerId;

    public void setPeerId(String peerId) {
        this.peerId = peerId;
    }

    public void validate(FacesContext context, UIComponent component,
        Object value) throws ValidatorException {

        Application application = context.getApplication( );

        String messageBundleName = application.getMessageBundle( );
        Locale locale = context.getViewRoot().getLocale( );
        ResourceBundle rb =
            ResourceBundle.getBundle(messageBundleName, locale);

        UIComponent peerComponent = component.findComponent(peerId);
        if (peerComponent == null) {
            String msg = rb.getString("peer_not_found");
            FacesMessage facesMsg =
                new FacesMessage(FacesMessage.SEVERITY_FATAL, msg, msg);
            throw new ValidatorException(facesMsg);
        }

        ValueHolder peer = null;
        try {
            peer = (ValueHolder) peerComponent;
        }
        catch (ClassCastException e) {
            String msg = rb.getString("invalid_component");
```

Example 7-3. The LaterThanValidator class (continued)

```
            FacesMessage facesMsg =
                new FacesMessage(FacesMessage.SEVERITY_FATAL, msg, msg);
            throw new ValidatorException(facesMsg);
        }

        if (peer instanceof EditableValueHolder &&
            !((EditableValueHolder) peer).isValid( )) {
            // No point in validating against an invalid value
            return;
        }

        Object peerValue = peer.getValue( );
        if (!(peerValue instanceof Date)) {
            String msg = rb.getString("invalid_peer");
            FacesMessage facesMsg =
                new FacesMessage(FacesMessage.SEVERITY_FATAL, msg, msg);
            throw new ValidatorException(facesMsg);
        }

        if (!(value instanceof Date) ||
            !((Date) value).after((Date) peerValue)) {
            String msg = rb.getString("not_later");
            String detailMsgPattern = rb.getString("not_later_detail");
            Object[] params =
                {formatDate((Date) peerValue, context, component)};
            String detailMsg =
                MessageFormat.format(detailMsgPattern, params);
            FacesMessage facesMsg =
                new FacesMessage(FacesMessage.SEVERITY_ERROR, msg, detailMsg);
            throw new ValidatorException(facesMsg);
        }
    }
    ...
```

A validator implements the `javax.faces.validator.Validator` interface, which defines a single method named `validate( )`. Regular JavaBeans property setter methods are often used to configure a validator. The `LaterThanValidator` needs to know about two values: the value to be validated and the value to compare it to. JSF passes the `LaterThanValidator` the value to validate as an argument to `validate( )`, and a property named `peerId` holds a reference to the component with the value to compare it to.

The `validate( )` method is where all the real work takes place. First, it needs to get the message bundle that holds the messages for this validator. The bundle name specified by the `<message-bundle>` element in the *faces-config.xml* file is returned by the `getMessageBundle( )` method of the `Application` class. The `LaterThanValidator` requires that all its messages be defined in this bundle, but you may want to provide default messages in a separate bundle bundled with the validator if you're developing validators to be used with many applications. If so, you should still look in the application's bundle first. Only use the default bundle if the message isn't defined in the application bundle. That's how all the JSF standard validators work.

Next, the `LaterThanValidator` tries to find the component with the value to compare to, defined by the `peerId` property. It does this by calling the `findComponent()` method on the component the validator is attached to. If it can't find the peer component, it gets the message with the key `peer_not_found` from the message bundle. For a reusable validator, you should use message keys that stand a chance of being unique in any application. Instead of using a short name like `peer_not_found`, include the same type of reversed domain name as is recommended for Java package names as a key prefix, e.g., `com.mycompany.peer_not_found`. If you're working for a large company, you may want to add additional parts to the prefix to avoid name clashes with messages created in other parts of the company.

The `validate()` method creates a `javax.faces.application.FacesMessage` instance to hold the message text. The `FacesMessage` class defines three properties: `severity`, `summary`, and `detail`. All of them can be set as constructor arguments, as they are here, or they can be set through setter methods. The severity must be set to one of four `FacesMessage` constants: `SEVERITY_INFO`, `SEVERITY_WARN`, `SEVERITY_ERROR`, or `SEVERITY_FATAL`. You can use `<h:message>` and `<h:messages>` attributes to ask for different style sheet classes to be used for messages of different severity, e.g., to render informational messages black and error messages red. For all `LaterThanValidator` messages that relate to errors a developer may make (i.e., an invalid peer component), I use the fatal severity level and the same text for both the summary and detail. I use the error severity for the error a user may make, i.e., enter a date that is not later than the first date.

To signal that the validation failed, the validator throws a `javax.faces.validator.ValidatorException` that contains the `FacesMessage` instance. The component that calls the `validate()` method catches the exception and adds it to the message queue so that it can be displayed to the user by a `<h:message>` or `<h:messages>` action when the response is rendered. It also marks the component value as invalid.

If the peer component is found, the `validate()` method tries to cast the component reference to the `javax.faces.component.ValueHolder` type. This is an interface implemented by all component types that hold a value, containing all methods for accessing the component value. With a few exceptions, most standard component types implement this interface. If the peer component reference can't be cast to this type, an exception holding a message with the `invalid_component` text is thrown, just as it was before.

The `EditableValueHolder` interface extends the `ValueHolder` interface, and all component types that let the user change the value it holds implement it (for example, the `UIInput` component). If the user can change the value, it's possible that she entered an incorrect value. The `LaterThanValidator` therefore checks if the peer component is marked as invalid, and stops the processing if it is. It doesn't throw an exception in this case, because there's already a message queued for the peer component that describes why it's invalid.

Next up is a test on the data type of the peer component value. If it's not a `java.util.Date`, an exception holding a message with the `invalid_peer` text is thrown.

Finally, the real test can be done: is the value of the component the validator is attached to a `Date` that's later than the `Date` value of the peer component? If the answer is "no," an exception holding a message with the `not_later` text is thrown. Compared to the other messages, this one is slightly different. Note how I get separate detail text from the bundle and use `java.text.MessageFormat` to format it. The `not_later` text contains a placeholder, as you will soon see, and formatting the text replaces it with the peer component's value.

Before replacing the placeholder in the detail text, I use the private `formatDate( )` method to convert the peer component's `Date` value to a formatted `String`:

```
        private String formatDate(Date date, FacesContext context,
            UIComponent component) {
            Converter converter = ((ValueHolder) component).getConverter( );
            if (converter != null) {
                return converter.getAsString(context, component, date);
            }
            return date.toString( );
        }
    }
```

The `formatDate( )` method tries to get the converter the component is equipped with. If it finds one, it uses it to convert the `Date` object; otherwise, it uses the `toString( )` method. Because this method is called to format the value shown in the error message, the value in the message is always formatted the way the component wants it, no matter how the converter is configured.

That's the code. Now we must create the messages. We created the application's message bundle properties file earlier (the *custMessage.properties* file), so all we have to do is add the keys and text that the `LaterThanValidator` uses:

```
invalid_component=The component to compare to is of a type that can't have a value
peer_not_found=The value to compare to can't be found
invalid_peer=Can only compare to a date value
not_later=Invalid date
not_later_detail=Please enter a date later than {0}
```

There's really nothing new here. The messages for the custom validator are declared the same way as the replaced standard message we looked at earlier was.

Registering a Custom Validator

Okay, so now we have a custom validator and all its messages are defined in the *custMessage.properties* file. How can we use it? In Java code, you could simply create an instance of the validator class, set the peerId property, and attach the validator to a component, like this:

```
import com.mycompany.jsf.validator.LaterThanValidator;
import javax.faces.component.UIInput;

    UIInput from = new UIInput( );
    from.setId("from");
    UIInput to = new UIInput( );
    LaterThanValidator validator = new LaterThanValidator( );
    validator.setPeerId("from");
    to.addValidator(validator);
    ...
```

But, as I mentioned earlier, JSF allows you to register pretty much every type of class under a symbolic name, so that you can replace implementations without changing all the code that uses it. Validators are no exception, and here's how you register the LaterThanValidator in the *faces-config.xml* file:

```
<faces-config>
  ...
  <validator>
    <validator-id>com.mycompany.jsf.validator.LATER_THAN</validator-id>
    <validator-class>
      com.mycompany.jsf.validator.LaterThanValidator
    </validator-class>
    <property>
      <property-name>peerId</property-name>
      <property-class>java.lang.String</property-class>
    </property>
  </validator>
  ...
</faces-config>
```

A top-level <validator> element contains a <validator-id> element with a unique identifier and a <validator-class> element with the fully qualified class name. The <property> element, with nested <property-name> and <property-class> elements, declares a supported property. A JSF development tool can use this information to help the user configure the validator.

With this declaration in place, the Java code can be changed (as shown in Example 7-4) to create the validator instance using the ID instead of creating an instance of a specific class.

Example 7-4. Getting a registered validator

```
import com.mycompany.jsf.validator.LaterThanValidator;
import javax.faces.application.Application;
import javax.faces.component.UIInput;
import javax.faces.context.FacesContext;

    UIInput from = new UIInput( );
    from.setId("from");
```

Example 7-4. Getting a registered validator (continued)

```
    UIInput to = new UIInput( );
    Application application = context.getApplication( );
    LaterThanValidator validator = (LaterThanValidator)
        application.createValidator("com.mycompany.jsf.validator.LATER_THAN");
    validator.setPeerId("from");
    to.addValidator(validator);
    ...
```

The call to the Application createValidator( ) method returns an instance of the validator class registered with the specified ID. In order to set the peerId property, I need to cast it to LaterThanValidator; in this example, the registered class must be either this class or a subclass. If a validator doesn't have any properties, any class that implements the Validator interface will do.

Using a Custom Validator in a JSP Page

To use a custom validator in a JSP page, you need a JSP custom action that configures the converter and attaches it to a component. Example 7-5 shows the version of the filtering criteria form from the JSP page that produces the screen in Figure 7-2.

Example 7-5. The filtering criteria form with a custom validator (expense/stage4/filterArea.jsp)

```
<%@ page contentType="text/html" %>
<%@ taglib uri="http://java.sun.com/jsf/html" prefix="h" %>
<%@ taglib uri="http://java.sun.com/jsf/core" prefix="f" %>
<%@ taglib uri="http://mycompany.com/jsftaglib" prefix="my" %>

<f:view>
  <h:form>
    From:
    <h:inputText id="from" size="8" required="true"
      value="#{reportHandler.from}">
      <f:convertDateTime dateStyle="short" />
    </h:inputText>
    <h:message for="from" />
    <br>
    To:
    <h:inputText id="to" size="8" required="true"
      value="#{reportHandler.to}">
      <f:convertDateTime dateStyle="short" />
      <my:validateLater than="from" />
    </h:inputText>
    <h:message for="to" />
    <br>
    Status:
    <h:selectManyCheckbox value="#{reportHandler.status}">
      <f:selectItem itemValue="1" itemLabel="Open" />
      <f:selectItem itemValue="2" itemLabel="Submitted" />
      <f:selectItem itemValue="3" itemLabel="Accepted" />
      <f:selectItem itemValue="4" itemLabel="Rejected" />
```

Example 7-5. The filtering criteria form with a custom validator (expense/stage4/filterArea.jsp)

```
    </h:selectManyCheckbox>
    <p>
    <h:commandButton value="Filter" />
  </h:form>
</f:view>
```

The custom action that configures the validator and attaches it to the component for the To field in Example 7-5 is called `<my:validateLater>` and belongs to the custom tag library declared by the `taglib` directive with the `uri` attribute set to `http://mycompany.com/jsftaglib` at the beginning of the page.

Developing a Validator Custom Action

If you're new to JSP, the concept of custom tag libraries and custom actions may seem like hocus pocus, so let's take it step by step.

You've already seen the JSF and JSTL tag libraries in action. The only thing that differs between them and a custom tag library developed in-house or by a third party is that they are defined by public specifications. Other than that, they are just tag libraries, developed using the same JSP API that you use to develop your own custom tag libraries.

The behavior of a custom action is implemented by a Java class called a tag handler, and linked to a tag name and rules for how it can be used declared in a Tag Library Descriptor (TLD). Related custom actions are declared in the same TLD, together making up the library. Besides custom action declarations, the TLD also contains information about the library itself. Example 7-8 shows the TLD for the library with the `<my:validateLater>` action.

Example 7-6. The TLD for the example tag library (taglib.tld)

```
<?xml version="1.0" encoding="ISO-8859-1" ?>
<!DOCTYPE taglib
  PUBLIC "-//Sun Microsystems, Inc.//DTD JSP Tag Library 1.2//EN"
  "http://java.sun.com/dtd/web-jsptaglibrary_1_2.dtd">

<taglib>
  <tlib-version>1.0</tlib-version>
  <jsp-version>1.2</jsp-version>
  <short-name>my</short-name>
  <uri>http://mycompany.com/jsftaglib</uri>

  <tag>
    <name>validateLater</name>
    <tag-class>com.mycompany.jsf.taglib.ValidateLaterThanTag</tag-class>
    <body-content>empty</body-content>

    <attribute>
      <name>than</name>
```

Example 7-6. The TLD for the example tag library (taglib.tld) (continued)

```
      <required>true</required>
      <rtexprvalue>false</rtexprvalue>
    </attribute>
  </tag>
</taglib>
```

The file must use the extension *.tld* to be recognized as a TLD and it is typically named *taglib.tld*.

At the beginning of the file, the `<tlib-version>` element specifies the tag library version, the `<jsp-version>` element identifies the version of the JSP specification the library complies with, and the `<short-name>` element provides a suggested namespace prefix for the custom action elements. The most interesting element at this level is the `<uri>` element. It declares the unique identifier for the library that's used as the `uri` attribute value of the `taglib` directive in JSP pages using the library. If you look at Example 7-5, you see how the `uri` attribute value used for the custom tag library matches the `<uri>` element value in Example 7-6.

Each custom action in the library is declared by a `<tag>` element. The nested `<name>` element gives the element name to use in the JSP page, the `<tag-class>` element identifies the tag handler Java class, and the `<body-content>` element declares how the element body should be processed. The `empty` value used here means that this action element must not have a body at all.

If the custom action supports any attributes, they must be declared by `<attribute>` elements. The attribute name is given by the `<name>` element, and the `<required>` element tells if the attribute is required or not. The `<rtexprvalue>` element value must be `true` if the attribute value can be set by a request-time attribute value, e.g., by an JSP EL expression. If it's `false`, only a static text value can be used as the attribute value. You should always disable request-time attribute values for JSF custom actions, to avoid potential clashes between the JSF EL values and JSP expression values.

The container locates the TLD based on the `taglib` directive's `uri` attribute when the JSP page is processed and then uses the information in the TLD to match custom action elements in the JSP page to the corresponding tag handler classes.

The tag handler class for the `<my:validate_later>` custom action is shown in Example 7-7.

Example 7-7. Validator tag handler class

```
package com.mycompany.jsf.taglib;

import com.mycompany.jsf.validator.LaterThanValidator;
import javax.faces.application.Application;
import javax.faces.context.FacesContext;
import javax.faces.validator.Validator;
import javax.faces.webapp.ValidatorTag;
```

Example 7-7. Validator tag handler class (continued)

```
public class ValidateLaterThanTag extends ValidatorTag {
    private String peerId;

    public void setThan(String peerId) {
     this.peerId = peerId;
    }

    protected Validator createValidator( ) {
        Application application =
            FacesContext.getCurrentInstance().getApplication( );
        LaterThanValidator validator = (LaterThanValidator)
            application.createValidator("com.mycompany.jsf.validator.LATER_THAN");
        validator.setPeerId(peerId);
        return validator;
    }
}
```

Because JSF provides a base class, `javax.faces.webapp.ValidatorTag`, it's very easy to develop this sort of tag handler. The `ValidateLaterThanTag` class extends the JSF base class and implements just two methods: the `setThan( )` method called by JSP with the `than` action element attribute value, and the `createValidator( )` method called by the base class to get the configured validator.

All we have to do in the `createValidator( )` method is get the validator instance from the `Application` and set its `peerId` to the `than` value, which is almost identical to the code in Example 7-4.

Deploying the Custom Tag Library

You can deploy the custom tag library two different ways: you can deploy it as separate files in the web application structure, or package all files in a JAR file and deploy the JAR file. During development, it's often convenient to deploy the files separately, because it makes it easier to replace updated class files or the TLD. Just place the TLD somewhere under the application's *WEB-INF* directory, for example, in a subdirectory named *WEB-INF/tlds*. Put the tag handler class files under *WEB-INF/classes* using a directory structure that matches the package structure, such as *WEB-INF/classes/com/mycompany/jsf/taglib* for the `ValidateLaterThanTag` in Example 7-7.

For production deployment, it's better to package all tag library files in a JAR file. The TLD goes in the JAR file's *META-INF* directory, and the class files in a directory structure mirroring the package structure: for example, *META-INF/taglib.tld* and *com/mycompany/jsf/taglib/ValidateLaterThanTag.class* for the example tag library. To deploy the library, put the JAR file in the application's *WEB-INF/lib* directory.

An Alternative for the Lazy

Creating a special custom action for your custom validators makes it easier for a page author to use them, but JSF actually provides a generic custom action that you can use to attach any validator to a component. It's named `<f:validator>`:

```
<h:inputText id="to" size="8" required="true"
  value="#{reportHandler.to}">
  <f:convertDateTime dateStyle="short" />
  <f:validator validatorId=" com.mycompany.jsf.validator.LATER_THAN" />
  <f:attribute name="peerId" value="from" />
</h:inputText>
```

The `validatorId` attribute value is the identifier the validator is registered with in the *faces-config.xml* file.

Because the generic `<f:validator>` action doesn't allow you to set validator-specific properties, you must provide the peer component ID through a generic component attribute instead, set by the `<f:attribute>` action. This means we must also modify the `LaterThanValidator` code slightly to get the peer ID from the generic attribute instead. This code in the `validate()` method replaces the `setPeerId()` method to deal with this difference:

```
...
    public void validate(FacesContext context, UIComponent component,
        Object value) throws ValidatorException {

    // Get the peer component ID
    String peerId = (String) component.getAttributes().get("peerId");
    ...
```

I recommend that you take the time to create a custom action, though. It's well worth the five minutes or so that it takes.

Other Ways to Validate Input

The converters and validators validate simple syntax and semantic rules, but many applications require more complex input validation. For instance, in a flight reservation application, verifying seat availability on the selected flight and validating the credit card information require access to external systems. It's common to defer this type of validation to the backend code, invoked through event handlers when all the simple tests succeed. We'll look at event handlers in the next chapter.

CHAPTER 8

Handling Events

When the user clicks a button or link, changes a value in a field, or makes a selection in a list, the application may need to react. JSF user interface components signal user actions by firing an event handled by application code that has registered itself to be notified of the event. It's a model borrowed from traditional GUI frameworks, making it easy to develop and maintain the code for each specific user action in a separate code module. You can even use multiple event handling modules for different aspects of the processing, such as one that logs the action and another that acts on it.

On the surface, the JSF model looks the same as the event model used for standalone applications, but there's a twist: with JSF, the user actions take place in a client (e.g., a browser) that has no permanent connection to the server, so the delivery of some types of event is delayed until a new connection is established (e.g., when the user submits a form). To deal with this difference, JSF defines a strict request processing lifecycle, where events are generated and handled in different phases.

In this chapter, we first look at the event model and how it relates to the request processing lifecycle to understand what's going on. We then implement event handling for parts of the sample application.

Understanding the JSF Event Model

The JSF event model is based on the event model defined by the JavaBeans specification. In this model, an event is represented by an instance of an event class. An event source object fires an event by calling an event notification method on event listener objects registered to receive the event, passing a reference to the event object as a notification method argument.

Let's look at what this means in more detail. All JSF event classes extend the `javax.faces.event.FacesEvent` class:

```
package javax.faces.event;

import java.util.EventObject;
import javax.faces.component.UIComponent;
```

```
...

public abstract class FacesEvent extends EventObject {
    public FacesEvent(UIComponent component) {
        super(component);
    }

    public UIComponent getComponent( ) {
        return ((UIComponent) getSource( ));
    }
    ...
}
```

The FacesEvent class extends the standard Java event superclass java.util.EventObject and has a constructor that takes the UIComponent event source object as an argument. It also implements a type-safe accessor method for the event source object.

When a user clicks a button, it triggers an event represented by the javax.faces.event.ActionEvent class:

```
package javax.faces.event;

import javax.faces.component.UIComponent;

public class ActionEvent extends FacesEvent {
    public ActionEvent(UIComponent component) {
        super(component);
    }
    ...
}
```

Other events are represented by similar concrete subclasses, such as the javax.faces.event.ValueChangeEvent, which signals a value change.

Along with the event classes, there are listener interfaces declaring the methods that the event source calls to notify listeners of the event. A listener interface can contain methods for many related events, but for the JSF component events, there's a separate interface per event. Here's the javax.faces.event.ActionListener interface:

```
package javax.faces.event;

import javax.faces.component.UIComponent;

public interface ActionListener extends FacesListener {
    public void processAction(ActionEvent event) throws AbortProcessingException;
}
```

The ActionListener interface extends the javax.faces.event.FacesListener interface and defines one method, taking an ActionEvent instance as the single argument.

Classes that want to be informed about events are called *event listeners*. They declare which events they are interested in by implementing the corresponding listener interfaces. Hence, an event listener that wants to deal with the ActionEvent fired by a command component declares its intent like this:

```
package com.mycompany.expense.ui;

import javax.faces.event.ActionListener;

public class ReportHandler implements ActionListener {
    ...
    public void processAction(ActionEvent e) throws AbortProcessingException {
        ...
    }
}
```

To prevent other listeners from seeing an event, all JSF event-processing methods can throw a javax.faces.event.AbortProcessingException. This is rarely needed, but can come in handy when serious problems occur while processing the event. If the event notification method throws this exception, JSF stops the event processing immediately.

Event source classes, like UICommand, declare the type of events they can fire by providing methods for registering and deregistering the corresponding event listeners:

```
    public void addActionListener(ActionListener listener) {
        addFacesListener(listener);
    }

    public void removeActionListener(ActionListener listener) {
        removeFacesListener(listener);
    }
```

The methods follow the JavaBeans conventions: the method names are made from the words add and remove followed by the listener interface name, and both methods take an instance of the listener as the single argument.

The addFacesListener( ) and removeFacesListener( ) methods called by the registration and deregistration methods are protected methods implemented by UIComponentBase, so that the task of maintaining the listener list doesn't have to be implemented by all subclasses.

When a component notices that a user event has happened, it creates an instance of the corresponding event class and adds it to an event list. Eventually, JSF tells the component to fire the event, i.e., loop through the list of listeners for that event and call the event notification method on each one.

The Request Processing Lifecycle Phases

So far, so good. If you've programmed with GUI frameworks or in other event-driven environments, the JSF event model should look familiar. But as I mentioned in the introduction, the fact that JSF operates with a disconnected client that only occasionally communicates with the server where the application runs requires a few twists to the model.

First of all, the application may declare that the component instances should not be saved on the server between requests, due to memory usage concerns. JSF must then save enough information somewhere (e.g., in the response) to be able to reconstruct the component tree and restore all component state when it receives the next request. In other words, component instances may come and go in a JSF application, as opposed to a GUI application where they remain in memory as long as the application runs.

JSF must also deal with the fact that value changes happen in the client and that the server can't detect the changes until it receives a new request with the new values. One possible work-around is to add client-side scripting to the mix, so that value changes causes an immediate request; unfortunately, that solution can make the application feel sluggish, and it doesn't work at all if the client doesn't support scripting.

Button and link clicks are a bit easier to deal with, because they cause a new request always to be sent. Events corresponding to these user actions can, however, be classified further into events that affect only the user interface (e.g., show the next set of rows in a table or change from a brief to a detailed display) and events that must be processed by backend code (e.g., permanently save the values entered in a form or finalize a reservation request). For user interface events, the backend typically shouldn't be bothered at all. An event that involves the backend, on the other hand, must not be processed until all model properties have been updated with the new values received with the request.

JSF deals with all these concerns by defining a request processing lifecycle with well-defined phases (shown in Figure 8-1), where different activities take place and events fire in an orderly manner at the appropriate time.

The phases are described in detail in Appendix C, but here's a quick rundown:

- In the Restore View phase, the components that make up the view are restored either from data in the request or from data saved on the server, as described in Chapter 6.
- Next, in the Apply Request Values phase, each component in the view looks for its own value in the request and saves it.
- The phase where the components may validate their new values is appropriately called the Process Validations phase. What happens in this phase, as well as in the Apply Request Values phase, is described in more detail in Chapter 7.
- Model properties bound to components through value bindings, as described in Chapter 6, are updated with the new values in the Update Model Values phase.
- When the model properties have been populated with the latest values, event listeners may call backend code to process the new data in the Invoke Application phase.
- Finally, a response to the request is sent, using the same view or a new one. This happens in the Render Response.

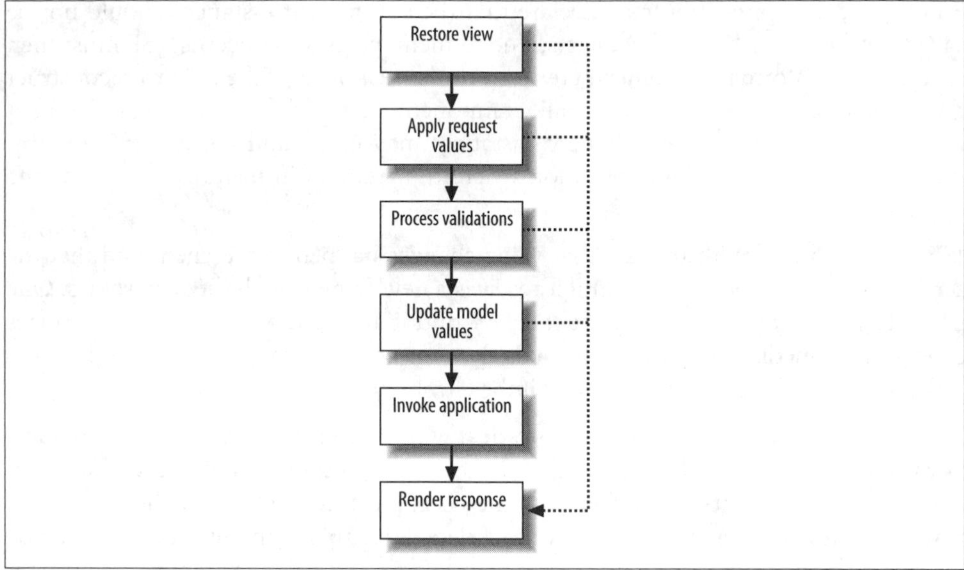

Figure 8-1. Request processing lifecycle phases

If the user triggered the request by clicking a button or a link, the corresponding `UICommand` component discovers this in the Apply Request Values phase when it finds a request parameter with a name that matches its ID. It creates an `ActionEvent` to represent the event, but doesn't notify the listeners immediately, because the rest of the components in the tree may not have picked up their values yet. Instead it adds it to a queue by calling its `queueEvent()` method.

At the end of the Apply Request Values phase, when all components know about their new values, it's safe to fire an `ActionEvent` that affects the user interface. JSF asks the `UICommand` that queued it to notify all listeners by calling its `broadcast()` method. But as you'll see soon, that's not the whole story: sometimes this event must not be broadcast until the Invoke Application phase.

Value change event handling happens in the Process Validations phase in a similar fashion, by default. A component that discovers that a value in the request is both valid and different from its previous value queues a `ValueChangeEvent`. Because the user may have changed a number of values since the previous request, it is likely that more than one event is queued in this phase. At the end of the phase, JSF scans the queue and calls the `broadcast()` method on the component that queued a `ValueChangeEvent`.

A listener processing an event may in turn do things that cause other events to be queued, so JSF continues to scan the queue at the end of a phase until the event queue is empty before moving on to the next phase.

Handling Application Backend Events

Separate the queuing from the firing of the event is the easy part. Dealing with the two subcategories of `ActionEvent` requires one more twist. From what I've said so far, it looks like an `ActionEvent` is always processed at the end of the Apply Request Values phase, but that's only appropriate for user interface events. As you may recall, an `ActionEvent` that requires backend processing must not be handled until the model properties are updated, i.e., after the Update Model Values phase at the earliest.

Let's look at some real examples of action handling using the report entry form in the sample application. We start with events that invoke backend logic in this section and look at user interface events in the next.

As you may recall, the report entry form has three fields for entering a date, an expense type and an amount for a report entry, and an Add button. Figure 8-2 shows the form produced by the version of the page we use in this section.

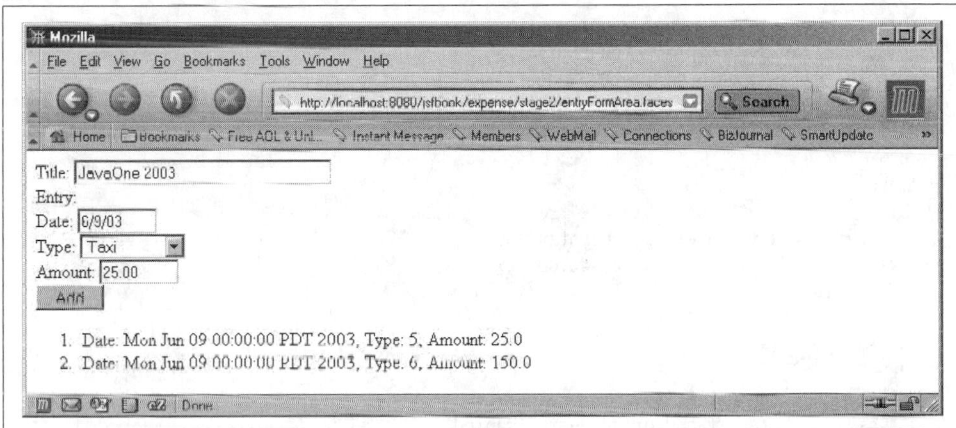

Figure 8-2. The report entry form area with a few entries

The Add button is a typical example of the most common type of event handling, namely a button that fires an event that requires processing by the application backend. When the user clicks this button, a new entry with the values entered in the fields is added to the current report.

Example 8-1 shows a version of the JSP page where the Add button is bound to an event handling method that invokes the backend code for adding the entry.

Example 8-1. Entry form area JSP page with an Add button action reference (expense/stage2/entryFormArea.jsp)

```
<%@ page contentType="text/html" %>
<%@ taglib uri="http://java.sun.com/jsf/html" prefix="h" %>
<%@ taglib uri="http://java.sun.com/jsf/core" prefix="f" %>
```

Example 8-1. Entry form area JSP page with an Add button action reference (expense/stage2/entryFormArea.jsp) (continued)

```
<f:view>
  <h:form>
    Title:
    <h:inputText id="title" size="30" required="true"
      value="#{reportHandler.currentReport.title}" />
    <h:message for="title" />
    <br>
    Entry:
    <br>
    Date:
    <h:inputText id="date" size="8" required="true"
      value="#{entryHandler.currentEntry.date}">
      <f:convertDateTime dateStyle="short" />
    </h:inputText>
    <h:message for="date" />
    <br>
    Type:
    <h:selectOneMenu id="type" required="true"
      value="#{entryHandler.currentEntry.type}">
      <f:selectItems value="#{entryHandler.expenseTypeChoices}"/>
    </h:selectOneMenu>
    <h:message for="type" />
    <br>
    Amount:
    <h:inputText id="amount" size="8" required="true"
      value="#{entryHandler.currentEntry.amount}">
      <f:convertNumber pattern="#,##0.00" />
      <f:validateDoubleRange minimum="1"/>
    </h:inputText>
    <h:message for="amount" />
    <br>
    <h:commandButton value="Add"
      disabled="#{reportHandler.addEntryDisabled}"
      action="#{entryHandler.add}" />
  </h:form>
  <h:messages globalOnly="true" />

  <%-- Loop to verify that it works --%>
  <%@ taglib uri="http://java.sun.com/jsp/jstl/core" prefix="c" %>
  <ol>
    <c:forEach items="${reportHandler.currentReportEntries}" var="e">
      <li>Date: ${e.date}, Type: ${e.type}, Amount: ${e.amount}</li>
    </c:forEach>
  </ol>
</f:view>
```

The only real difference compared to the version of the page we used in Chapter 7 is the action attribute for the Add button `<h:commandButton>` action element. Of less interest at this point is the JSTL `<c:forEach>` action that lists all entries in the current report at the end of the page. I added the loop just to verify that the Add button's event handler really does what it's supposed to do. This loop gets the report entries from the report handler we looked at in Chapter 6. I'm not showing you the details here, but I promise to return to them when we replace the plain list with a real report entries table in Chapter 10.

The `action` attribute contains a *method binding expression*. The method binding expression syntax is similar to that of a value binding expression. It's a subset of the JSF EL that evaluates to a bean method with a certain signature. In Example 8-1, the method binding expression points to a method named `add` in the `EntryHandler` instance available through the `entryHandler` variable. Before we look at the `add()` method, let's see how it relates to the event listeners and the request processing life-cycle we discussed earlier.

Using an Action Method and the Default ActionListener

The `UICommand` component supports method bindings for two types of methods: *action methods* and *action listener methods*. Either type can be used to process an `ActionEvent`, but the action method type is the most commonly used. An action method has no parameters and returns a `String` value called the *action outcome*. The outcome is typically "success" if everything went as planned, and "error" or "failure" if there was a problem. The outcome value can affect which view is displayed next, which we get back to in Chapter 9. In a JSP page, you can use the `action` attribute with a method binding expression to bind a `UICommand` component to an action method, as shown in Example 8-1.

As you know from the earlier discussions, an `ActionEvent` is handled by a listener that implements the `ActionListener` interface, so there must be something else going on to invoke the action method. The missing piece is called the default `ActionListener`. This is a listener that is provided by the JSF implementation* to make it easier to handle events. When a `UICommand` component is asked to fire an `ActionEvent`, it first notifies all regular listeners attached to the component, if any. Then it checks if it's been configured with an action method binding. If so, it creates an instance of the default `ActionListener` and asks it to handle the event. The default `ActionListener` evaluates the action method binding and invokes the method. As hinted at earlier, the default `ActionListener` uses the action outcome value to decide which view to use for the response. All of this happens behind the scenes, so you just have to write the action method and bind it to the component.

Example 8-2 shows the `add()` action method bound to the Add button in Example 8-1.

* As is true for pretty much everything in JSF, an application can define a customized default `ActionListener` if needed.

Example 8-2. The EntryHandler add action method

```
package com.mycompany.expense;
...

public class EntryHandler {
    private ReportHandler reportHandler;
    private ReportEntry currentEntry;
    ...

    public String add( ) {
        return reportHandler.addEntry(currentEntry);
    }
    ...
}
```

The `add( )` method is very simple: it just relays the call to the `ReportHandler`, which is in charge of accessing the current report, passing on the current entry as an argument to the `addEntry( )` method.

So the meat is in the `ReportHandler addEntry( )` method, shown in Example 8-3.

Example 8-3. The ReportHandler addEntry() method

```
package com.mycompany.expense;

import javax.faces.application.Application;
import javax.faces.application.FacesMessage;
import javax.faces.context.FacesContext;
...

public class ReportHandler {
    private ReportRegistry registry;
    private Rules rules;
    private Report currentReport;
    private String currentUser;
    private boolean isManager;

    ...
    public String addEntry(ReportEntry entry) {
        try {
            refreshCache( );
        }
        catch (RegistryException e) {
            addMessage("registry_error", e.getMessage( ));
            return "error";
        }

        if (!rules.canEdit(currentUser, isManager, currentReport)) {
            addMessage("report_no_edit_access", null);
            return "error";
        }
```

Example 8-3. The ReportHandler addEntry() method (continued)

```
        String outcome = "success";
        currentReport.addEntry(entry);
        try {
            saveReport( );
        }
        catch (RegistryException e) {
            currentReport.removeEntry(entry.getId( ));
            addMessage("registry_error", e.getMessage( ));
            outcome = "error";
        }
        return outcome;
    }
```

The addEntry( ) method first calls a method named refreshCache( ) to ensure it has the most recent copy of the current report, in case some other user has modified it:

```
    private void refreshCache( ) throws RegistryException {
        if (!isReportNew( )) {
            setCurrentReport(registry.getReport(currentReport.getId( )));
        }
    }

    private void setCurrentReport(Report report) {
        currentReport = report;
        entriesModel = null;
    }
```

If the refresh fails, the addEntry( ) method adds an error message to the JSF message list and returns "error" as the outcome. Next, it checks that the current user is allowed to edit the current report by calling the canEdit( ) method implemented by the Rules class we looked at in Chapter 6. If the answer is "no", it adds another error message to the list.

If the user has write access, the entry is added to the current report by calling the addEntry( ) method on the current Report instance and the updated report is saved in the registry by calling saveReport( ).

```
    private void saveReport( ) throws RegistryException {
        if (isReportNew( )) {
            currentReport.setStatus(Report.STATUS_OPEN);
            registry.addReport(currentReport);
        }
        else {
            registry.updateReport(currentReport);
        }
        entriesModel = null;
    }
```

The saveReport( ) method adds the report to the registry if it's new (i.e., it hasn't been saved yet) or updates the registry version of the report if it's already in the registry.

Saving the report may fail, and if it does, the addEntry( ) method restores the local copy of the current report to its previous state by removing the entry it just added, and adds an error message to the list as before.

All error messages are added to the JSF message list by the addMessage( ) method:

```
private void addMessage(String messageKey, Object param) {
    FacesContext context = FacesContext.getCurrentInstance( );
    Application application = context.getApplication( );
    String messageBundleName = application.getMessageBundle( );
    Locale locale = context.getViewRoot().getLocale( );
    ResourceBundle rb =
        ResourceBundle.getBundle(messageBundleName, locale);
    String msgPattern = rb.getString(messageKey);
    String msg = msgPattern;
    if (param != null) {
        Object[] params = {param};
        msg = MessageFormat.format(msgPattern, params);
    }
    FacesMessage facesMsg =
        new FacesMessage(FacesMessage.SEVERITY_ERROR, msg, msg);
    context.addMessage(null, facesMsg);
}
```

The only difference compared to the code we used in Chapter 7 is that instead of throwing an exception that contains the FacesMessage instance, and relying on the component to add it to the message queue, I use the FacesContext addMessage( ) method to queue the message myself. The first addMessage( ) argument takes a component's client ID. This must be used for a message that is associated with a specific component instance. Here I use a null value instead, which means that the message is an application-level message. If you look at Example 8-1, there's an <h:messages> action element at the bottom of the page, just before the entries loop, with a globalOnly attribute set to true. Configured this way, the action displays only application-level error messages. The component-specific messages are displayed by <h:message> actions for each component, just as before.

Using an Action Listener Method or Instance

In most cases, you don't need access to the actual ActionEvent in order to do the right thing, because each component can be bound to a separate action method that implements component-specific behavior. The exception is when one method needs to handle events fired by multiple components, but that turns out to be a very rare case. In fact, there's nothing in the sample application that requires this, and I'm hard pressed to come up with any good use case for it. Even so, the JSF specification supports two alternatives to the action method that provides access to the ActionEvent, in case you do need it.

The first alternative is the action listener method binding, defined by the actionListener attribute in a JSP page:

```
<h:commandButton value="Add"
  actionListener="#{entryHandler.handleAdd}" />
```

An action listener method has the exact same signature as the ActionListener processAction( ) method we looked at earlier; it takes an ActionEvent argument and has a void return type:

```
public void processAction(ActionEvent e) throws AbortProcessingException {
    UIComponent myCommand = e.getComponent( );
    // Do whatever you need to do depending on which component fired
    // the event
    ...
}
```

Any object available as a JSF EL expression variable can implement the action listener method, but you can bind a component only to one action listener method. If you need to use more than one listener to handle the same event—maybe one that logs the event and another that really acts on it—you can attach as many ActionListener instances as you want to the component. The JSF core tag library includes an action element that makes this easy to do in a JSP page:

```
<h:commandButton value="Add">
  <f:actionListener type="com.mycompany.LogEventListener" />
  <f:actionListener type="com.mycompany.HandleAddListener" />
</h:commandButton>
```

The <f:actionListener> action creates an instance of the class specified by the type attribute and calls the addActionListener( ) method on the UICommand component.

Specifying When to Fire an Event

So far, I've told you how to bind a component to an event handling method, but I haven't let you in yet on the secret of how an ActionEvent can be made to fire either at the end of the Apply Request Value phase or in the Invoke Application phase.

There are different ways to solve this problem, but the specification group decided to go with an approach in which the source component decides when the event should be processed, with a little bit of help from the application developer. Here's how it works. The FacesEvent class—which all JSF events must extend either directly or through one of the standard subclasses, such as ActionEvent—defines a property named phaseId:

```
package javax.faces.event;

import java.util.EventObject;
...
public abstract class FacesEvent extends EventObject {
    private PhaseId phaseId = PhaseId.ANY_PHASE;
```

```
        public PhaseId getPhaseId( ) {
            return phaseId;
        }

        public void setPhaseId(PhaseId phaseId) {
            this.phaseId = phaseId;
        }
        ...
    }
```

The phaseId property data type is PhaseId, which is a type-safe enumeration containing one value per request processing lifecycle phase: PhaseId.APPLY_REQUEST_VALUES, PhaseId.PROCESS_VALIDATIONS, PhaseId.UPDATE_MODEL_VALUES, PhaseId.INVOKE_APPLICATION, PhaseId.RENDER_RESPONSE, or PhaseId.ANY_PHASE. The PhaseId.ANY_PHASE value means "process the event in the phase where it was queued," and it's the default value for the phaseId property.

So even though UICommand always queues an ActionEvent in the Apply Request Values phase, it sets the phaseId to PhaseId.INVOKE_APPLICATION to delay the event handling unless you tell it that you want to process it immediately. You do so through a UICommand property called immediate. If immediate is true, the phaseId is left unchanged so the event is processed in the Apply Request Values phase. The default ActionListener also tells JSF to proceed directly to the Render Response phase after invoking the action method. The default value for immediate is false, because the ActionEvent is typically used to invoke backend code.

Most of the logic for keeping track of the phase in which an event is to be processed is implemented by the UIViewRoot component that sits at the top of the component tree. At the end of each phase, UIViewRoot goes through the event queue and calls the broadcast( ) method on all event source components. It starts with all events with phaseId set to PhaseId.ANY_PHASE and then the events queued for the current phase. It continues until there are no more events with these phaseId values in the queue, so if processing one event leads to a new event, the new event is also processed, as long as it's for a matching phase.

Handling User Interface Events

When the user clicks a button or a link, chances are good that backend code should be asked to do something, like adding a report entry to the current report when the Add button is clicked in the sample application. Occasionally, though, an event affects only the user interface. For instance, clicking a button or changing the value of an input control may expose additional options or display more information.

As an example of user interface changes triggered either by a button click or a value change, let's add a feature to the sample application, namely an extendable expense types list. Initially, only the most common expense types are listed, but the user can extend the list with more uncommon choices.

Triggering an Event by Clicking a Button or a Link

In the first version of the extendable expense types feature, I use a button to switch between the standard and the extended list. Figure 8-3 shows what it looks like.

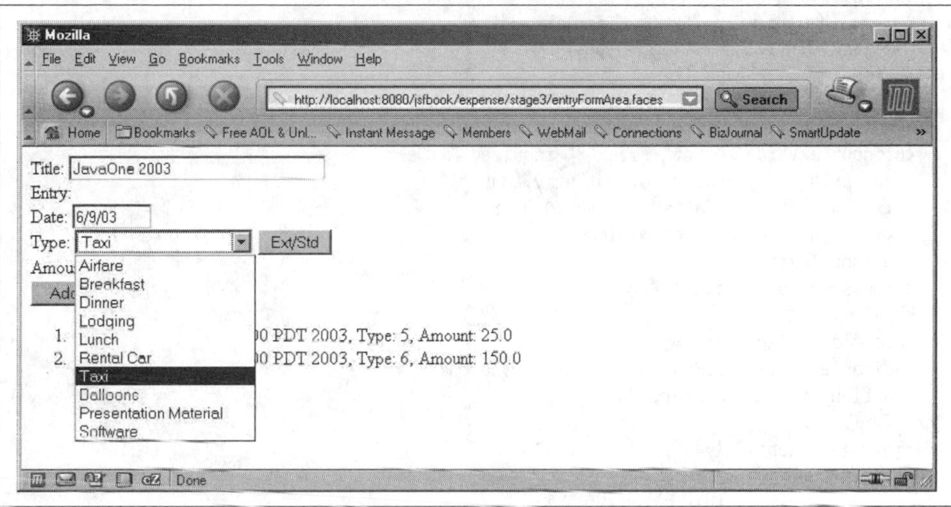

Figure 8-3. The report entry form area with a button for extending the type choices

The JSP page for this version of the entry form area is shown in Example 8-4.

Example 8-4. Entry form area JSP page with a button for extending the type choices (expense/stage3/entryFormArea.jsp)

```
<%@ page contentType="text/html" %>
<%@ taglib uri="http://java.sun.com/jsf/html" prefix="h" %>
<%@ taglib uri="http://java.sun.com/jsf/core" prefix="f" %>

<f:view>
  <h:form>
    Title:
    <h:inputText id="title" size="30" required="true"
      value="#{reportHandler.currentReport.title}" />
    <h:message for="title" />
    <br>
    Entry:
    <br>
    Date:
    <h:inputText id="date" size="8" required="true"
      value="#{entryHandler.currentEntry.date}">
      <f:convertDateTime  dateStyle="short" />
    </h:inputText>
    <h:message for="date" />
    <br>
    Type:
    <h:selectOneMenu id="type" required="true"
```

Example 8-4. Entry form area JSP page with a button for extending the type choices (expense/stage3/entryFormArea.jsp) (continued)

```
      value="#{entryHandler.currentEntry.type}">
      <f:selectItems value="#{entryHandler.currentChoices}"/>
    </h:selectOneMenu>
    <h:commandButton value="Ext/Std" immediate="true"
      action="#{entryHandler.toggleTypes}" />
    <h:message for="type" />
    <br>
    Amount:
    <h:inputText id="amount" size="8" required="true"
      value="#{entryHandler.currentEntry.amount}">
      <f:convertNumber pattern="#,##0.00" />
      <f:validateDoubleRange minimum="1"/>
    </h:inputText>
    <h:message for="amount" />
    <br>
    <h:commandButton value="Add"
      disabled="#{reportHandler.addEntryDisabled}"
      action="#{entryHandler.add}" />
  </h:form>
  <h:messages globalOnly="true" />

  <%-- Loop to verify that it works --%>
  <%@ taglib uri="http://java.sun.com/jsp/jstl/core" prefix="c" %>
  <ol>
    <c:forEach items="${reportHandler.currentReportEntries}" var="e">
      <li>Date: ${e.date}, Type: ${e.type}, Amount: ${e.amount}</li>
    </c:forEach>
  </ol>
</f:view>
```

As you can see in Example 8-4, I've added a button with the label "Ext/Std" for toggling between the standard choices list and the extended list. I've also replaced the value binding expression for the entry type list with one that gets the current choices, i.e., with or without the extension choices.

The one thing that's different about the `<h:commandButton>` element for the Ext/Std button compared to the one for the Add button is the `immediate` attribute. Setting this attribute to `true` means that the `ActionEvent` is processed in the Apply Request Values phase and that the processing then jumps directly to the Render Response phase, without doing any validation or updating model values. That's exactly how we want a pure user interface event to be handled, because we don't want error messages about missing or invalid values to be shown just because the user asks for more options.

The `action` attribute for the `<h:commandButton>` action element contains a method binding expression that points to the `toggleTypes()` method in the `entryHandler`. Example 8-5 shows how it's implemented in the corresponding `EntryHandler` class.

Example 8-5. Additions for extendable types in EntryHandler

```
package com.mycompany.expense;

import java.util.ArrayList;
import java.util.Iterator;
import java.util.List;
import java.util.Map.Entry;
import java.util.Map;
...
public class EntryHandler {
    private Map specialTypes;
    private List specialChoices;
    private boolean includeSpecial;
    ...
    public String toggleTypes( ) {
        includeSpecial = !includeSpecial;
        return "success";
    }
    ...
```

The `toggleTypes( )` method simply sets a variable named `includeSpecial` to the reverse of its previous value, alternating between `true` and `false`.

The other changes to the `EntryHandler` class that this new feature requires are pretty mundane: we need to configure it with the list of extension choices and implement a `getCurrentChoices( )` method that takes the `includeSpecial` flag into consideration. Both of these tasks are very similar to what we did in Chapter 7 for the list of standard choices.

The extension choices are defined in the *faces-config.xml* file as a new `Map` property named `specialTypes`:

```
<faces-config>
  <managed-bean>
    <managed-bean-name>specialTypes</managed-bean-name>
    <managed-bean-class>java.util.TreeMap</managed-bean-class>
    <managed-bean-scope>application</managed-bean-scope>
    <map-entries>
      <value-class>java.lang.Integer</value-class>
      <map-entry>
        <key>Presentation Material</key>
        <value>100</value>
      </map-entry>
      <map-entry>
        <key>Software</key>
        <value>101</value>
      </map-entry>
      <map-entry>
        <key>Balloons</key>
        <value>102</value>
      </map-entry>
    </map-entries>
  </managed-bean>
```

```
    <managed-bean>
      <managed-bean-name>entryHandler</managed-bean-name>
      <managed-bean-class>
        com.mycompany.expense.EntryHandler
      </managed-bean-class>
      <managed-bean-scope>session</managed-bean-scope>
      ...
      <managed-property>
        <property-name>specialTypes</property-name>
        <value>#{specialTypes}</value>
      </managed-property>
      ...
    </managed-bean>
    ...
  </faces-config>
```

No surprises here. The new specialTypes property is configured exactly like the expenseTypes property described in Chapter 7.

The third and final addition is a new method for getting the list of selection items. Note that the <h:selectItems> element in Example 8-4 is bound now to the currentChoices property instead of the expenseTypeChoices property:

```
      public List getCurrentChoices( ) {
          List choices = new ArrayList( );
          choices.addAll(getExpenseTypeChoices( ));
          if (includeSpecial) {
              choices.addAll(getSpecialChoices( ));
          }
          return choices;
      }
  }
```

The getCurrentChoices( ) method uses the getExpenseTypeChoices( ) method described in Chapter 7. If includeExtensions is true, it calls a similar method to include the extension types in the list along with the standard types.

Finally, we must implement the setter method for the specialTypes property and the getSpecialChoices( ) method that returns a List containing SelectItem instances for the extension types:

```
      public void setSpecialTypes(Map specialTypes) {
          this.specialTypes = specialTypes;
      }

      private List getSpecialChoices( ) {
          if (specialChoices == null) {
              specialChoices = new ArrayList( );
              if (specialTypes != null) {
                  Iterator i = specialTypes.entrySet().iterator( );
                  while (i.hasNext( )) {
                      Map.Entry me = (Map.Entry) i.next( );
                      specialChoices.add(new SelectItem(me.getValue( ),
                          (String) me.getKey( )));
```

```
                }
            }
        }
        return specialChoices;
    }
```

This should also look familiar from Chapter 7. JSF calls the `setSpecialTypes()` method with the `Map` created from the *faces-config.xml* managed bean declaration, and the `getSpecialChoices()` method creates a `List` with `SelectItem` instances based on the `Map` values and returns it.

The effect of all this is that when the user clicks the Ext/Std button, the default `ActionListener` associated with the button handles the event in the Apply Request Values phase (because the `immediate` attribute is set to `true`) by invoking the `toggleTypes()` method and asking JSF to redisplay the same page without going through the Process Validations and Update Model Values phases. When the `UISelectOne` component for the expense types list evaluates its value binding in the Render Response phase, it invokes the `getCurrentChoices()` method, which includes or excludes the extension types depending on the value of the `includeSpecial` flag.

Triggering an Event by Changing a Value

When the user changes the value of an input component, a `ValueChangeEvent` is fired when the form is submitted. You have similar options for handling a `ValueChangeEvent` as you have for an `ActionEvent`: use a value change listener method binding or attach one or more `ValueChangeListener` to the component:

```
<!-- Using a method binding expression -->
<h:selectBooleanCheckbox valueChangeListener="#{myBean.handleNewValue}" />

<!-- Using one or more listeners -->
<h:selectBooleanCheckbox>
  <f:valueChangeListener type="com.mycompany.LogEventListener" />
  <f:valueChangeListener type="com.mycompany.HandleNewValueListener" />
</h:selectBooleanCheckbox>
```

Two things make the JSF `ValueChangeEvent` less important than similar events in a traditional GUI framework: it fires only when the form is submitted (because that's when the server can detect the change), and JSF's mechanisms for validation and automatic model updates handle most of the typical use cases. That said, it's still useful for some features, especially if you know that your users use JavaScript-enabled browsers and are connected to the server via a high-speed connection so frequent requests don't cause performance problems.

In this section, we look at how to use a `ValueChangeEvent` triggered by a change in a checkbox value to switch between the standard and extended report entry type choices. Example 8-6 shows the entry form page modified for this purpose.

Example 8-6. Entry form area JSP page with a checkbox for extending the type choices (expense/stage4/entryFormArea.jsp)

```
<%@ page contentType="text/html" %>
<%@ taglib uri="http://java.sun.com/jsf/html" prefix="h" %>
<%@ taglib uri="http://java.sun.com/jsf/core" prefix="f" %>

<f:view>
  <h:form>
    Title:
    <h:inputText id="title" size="30" required="true"
      value="#{reportHandler.currentReport.title}" />
    <h:message for="title" />
    <br>
    Entry:
    <br>
    Date:
    <h:inputText id="date" size="8" required="true"
      value="#{entryHandler.currentEntry.date}">
      <f:convertDateTime  dateStyle="short" />
    </h:inputText>
    <h:message for="date" />
    <br>
    Type:
    <h:selectOneMenu id="type" required="true"
      value="#{entryHandler.currentEntry.type}">
      <f:selectItems value="#{entryHandler.currentChoices}"/>
    </h:selectOneMenu>
    Extended Choices:
    <h:selectBooleanCheckbox immediate="true" onchange="this.form.submit();"
     valueChangeListener="#{entryHandler.toggleTypes}" />
    <h:message for="type" />
    <br>
    Amount:
    <h:inputText id="amount" size="8" required="true"
      value="#{entryHandler.currentEntry.amount}">
      <f:convertNumber pattern="#,##0.00" />
      <f:validateDoubleRange minimum="1"/>
    </h:inputText>
    <h:message for="amount" />
    <br>
    <h:commandButton value="Add"
      disabled="#{reportHandler.addEntryDisabled}"
      action="#{entryHandler.add}" />
  </h:form>
  <h:messages layout="table" globalOnly="true" />

  <%-- Loop to verify that it works --%>
  <%@ taglib uri="http://java.sun.com/jsp/jstl/core" prefix="c" %>
  <ol>
    <c:forEach items="${reportHandler.currentReportEntries}" var="e">
      <li>Date: ${e.date}, Type: ${e.type}, Amount: ${e.amount}</li>
    </c:forEach>
  </ol>
</f:view>
```

The <h:commandButton> element is replaced with an <h:selectBooleanCheckbox> element in Example 8-6. Its immediate attribute is set to true, causing the ValueChangeEvent to fire in the Apply Request Values phase instead of in the Process Validations phase. This means that we can handle the event without causing any validation error messages to be displayed.

The onchange attribute contains JavaScript that submits the form the checkbox belongs to when its value is changed, so that the user doesn't have to click on any button for the change to take effect.

Finally, the valueChangeListener attribute binds the component to a value change listener method in the entryHandler bean. This method looks almost the same as the toggleTypes( ) method used for the Ext/Std button in Example 8-4, but it has a different signature:

```
package com.mycompany.expense;

import javax.faces.context.FacesContext;
import javax.faces.event.ValueChangeEvent;
...
public class EntryHandler {
    ...
    public void toggleTypes(ValueChangeEvent event) {
        includeSpecial = !includeSpecial;
        FacesContext.getCurrentInstance().renderResponse( );
    }
    ...
}
```

A value change listener method is a method with a ValueChangeEvent as its single parameter and a void return type. The toggleType( ) method used here doesn't use the event at all. It just flips the includeSpecial flag, the same as the method used in the previous section. What's different is that it also tells JSF to jump straight to the Render Response phase by calling the FacesContext renderResponse( ) method. For an action method, this happens automatically, but for all other method binding method types you must do so explicitly when needed. The rest remains the same as when we used a button to trigger the type list changes.

The event handling concepts and mechanisms that I've described in this chapter may take some time to truly understand, but when you do, they make sense given the nature of a web application with the client separated from the server. In the next chapter, we'll add to what you've learned here, looking at how to tell JSF to switch to a new view depending on the event-handling outcome.

CHAPTER 9

Controlling Navigation

In this book's sample application, all main functionality is handled through a single screen, but that's not always the case, of course. Moving between screens in a web application based on user actions is a common requirement. In this chapter, we look at how JSF supports moving between screens implemented as JSF views as well as moving to screens implemented with other web page technology, such as pure HTML pages, or responses generated by regular servlets or a plain JSP pages without JSF components.

Moving Between JSF Views

In addition to the main functionality, the sample application lets the user edit preferences through a separate set of screens. The application ignores all preference settings, but looking at how these preferences screens are implemented illustrates how JSF navigation works.

On a regular web site, links are used to navigate between different pages. A JSF web application may also use links, and there's a special action element that you should use to add a link to a page. It's the `<h:outputLink>` action element, and here's how it's used in the sample application's menu area:

```
...
  <h:outputLink value="prefUser.faces">
    <h:outputText value="Preferences" />
  </h:outputLink>
...
```

The action uses the `value` attribute to render the corresponding HTML `<a>` element's `href` value, with an encoded session ID if needed for cookie-less session tracking. Nested `<f:param>` action elements can be used to add query string parameters (see Appendix A for details). The link text is taken from the value of one or more child components, such as the output component represented by the `<h:outputText>` element in this example. Figure 9-1 shows the menu area with the generated link in a browser.

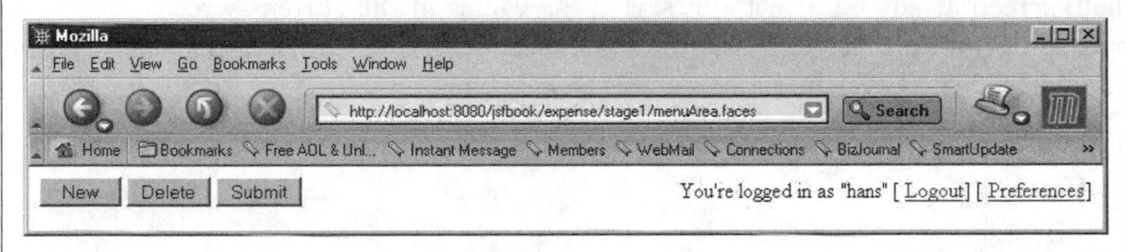

Figure 9-1. Menu area with link to the first preferences screen

Navigation through a direct link is simple and sufficient in many cases, but not when user input must be processed before moving on to the next screen. The User Preferences feature is implemented as three screens in which the user can enter his name and address on the first screen, select a language on the second, and select font style and size preferences on the third. Clicking the buttons in each screen either saves or ignores the input, and brings up a new screen. Figure 9-2 shows all three screens.

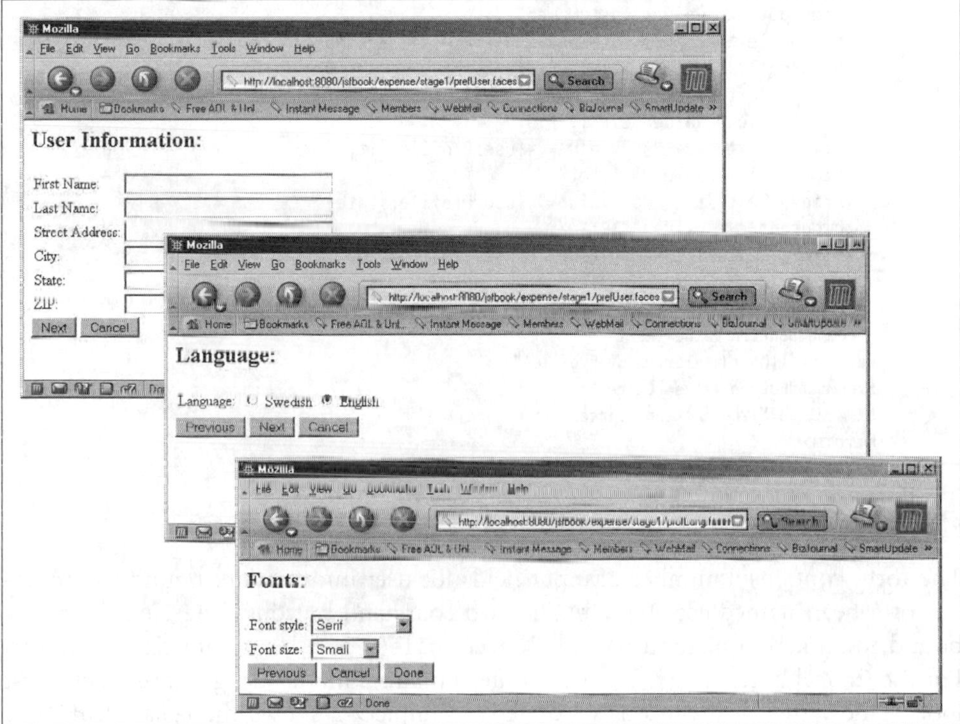

Figure 9-2. Preferences screens

The user enters the first screen through the Preferences link in the menu area of the main application screen. Clicking Next saves the values of the current screen and displays the next screen, while clicking Previous returns to the previous screen without saving the values. The Cancel buttons available in all screens let the user return to the main screen at any point without saving the values in the current screen. The Done button on the final screen saves the font selections and returns to the main screen. Example 9-1 shows the initial version of the JSP page for the user information screen.

Example 9-1. Initial version: user information page with Next and Cancel buttons (expense/stage1/prefUser.jsp)

```
<%@ page contentType="text/html" %>
<%@ taglib uri="http://java.sun.com/jsf/html" prefix="h" %>
<%@ taglib uri="http://java.sun.com/jsf/core" prefix="f" %>

<f:view>
  <html>
    <body>
      <h2>User Information:</h2>
      <h:form>
        <h:panelGrid columns="2">
          <h:outputText value="First Name:" />
          <h:inputText size="30" value="#{userProfile.firstName}" />
          <h:outputText value="Last Name:" />
          <h:inputText size="30" value="#{userProfile.lastName}" />
          <h:outputText value="Street Address:"/>
          <h:inputText size="30" value="#{userProfile.street}" />
          <h:outputText value="City:" />
          <h:inputText size="30" value="#{userProfile.city}" />
          <h:outputText value="State:" />
          <h:inputText size="30" value="#{userProfile.state}" />
          <h:outputText value="ZIP:" />
          <h:inputText size="30" value="#{userProfile.zip}" />
        </h:panelGrid>

        <h:commandButton value="Next"
          action="#{userHandler.updateProfile}" />
        <h:commandButton value="Cancel"
          immediate="true" action="cancel" />
      </h:form>
    </body>
  </html>
</f:view>
```

The form contains a number of input fields for user information, bound to properties of a bean named `userProfile`, and two command buttons. The Next button is bound to an action method named `updateProfile()` in a bean named `userHandler`. For the Cancel button, the `action` attribute contains a literal string: `cancel`. Let's first look at how the Next button is handled. Example 9-2 shows the `updateProfile()` method in the class used as the `userHandler` bean.

Example 9-2. The UserHandler class

```
package com.mycompany.expense;

...
public class UserHandler {
```

Example 9-2. The UserHandler class (continued)

```
    ...
    public String updateProfile() {
        return "success";
    }
    ...
}
```

As you may recall from Chapter 8, an action method must return a `String` value representing the outcome of the action. I'm cheating here and always return "success". In a real application, the values captured by the `userProfile` bean would be saved in a database and potential database errors would be handled by queuing a message and returning "error."

I allow myself to cheat here because what's important is how the outcome value affects navigation. Outcomes can be mapped to view identifiers by navigation rules declared in the *faces-config.xml* file, like this:

```
<faces-config>
  ...
  <navigation-rule>
    <from-view-id>/expense/stage1/prefUser.jsp</from-view-id>
    <navigation-case>
      <from-action>#{userHandler.updateProfile}</from-action>
      <from-outcome>success</from-outcome>
      <to-view-id>/expense/stage1/prefLang.jsp</to-view-id>
    </navigation-case>
  </navigation-rule>
  ...
</faces-config>
```

A `<navigation-rule>` element contains subelements that declare when the rule applies and which view to switch to when it does. The `<from-view-id>` element is optional. If it's specified, it must be either a complete view identifier (the context-relative path to the JSP page, when you use JSP) or a view identifier prefix ending with an asterisk, e.g., `/expense/stage1/*` to match all view identifiers that start with `/expense/stage1/`. If the `<from-view-id>` element is omitted, the rule matches all views identifiers. If more than one `<navigation-rule>` element has matching `<from-view-id>` elements, all of them are considered by the navigation handler.

One or more `<navigation-case>` elements declare how to deal with different cases within the matching view. The `<from-action>` element is optional and may be used to limit the rule to apply only to outcomes from the specified action method. The `<from-outcome>` element is also optional and limits the rule to the specified outcome value. The `<to-view-id>` element is mandatory, and JSF switches to the specified view when it finds a match.

So, when the Next button in Example 9-1 is clicked, the `updateProfile()` method is invoked and returns the "success" outcome value. This outcome matches the rule defined for this view in the *faces-config.xml* file, so JSF uses the `/expense/stage1/prefLang.jsp` view to render the response.

For the Cancel button, I specify a literal value of "cancel" instead of an action method. This comes in handy when you only want to switch to a new view, without processing any input. JSF uses the literal value just as it uses an outcome from an action method to look for a matching navigation rule. Here's the rule that matches the Cancel button's `action` attribute value:

```
<navigation-rule>
  <from-view-id>/expense/stage1/*</from-view-id>
  <navigation-case>
    <from-outcome>cancel</from-outcome>
    <to-view-id>/expense/stage1/menuArea.jsp</to-view-id>
    <redirect/>
  </navigation-case>
</navigation-rule>
```

Note that I use a prefix pattern for the `<from-view-id>` and no `<from-action>` element, so this rule applies to the Cancel button in all three preferences views.

The `<h:commandButton>` action elements for all Cancel buttons also have the `immediate` attribute described in Chapter 8 set to `true`, so no validation or model updates take place when the user clicks the Cancel button.

Choosing Between Redirect and Direct Rendering

I also use an empty `<redirect>` element within the `<navigation-case>` element for the Cancel button. This is an optional element that tells JSF to send a redirect response that asks the browser to request the specified view instead of rendering it as the response to the current request.

The visible difference between a redirect response and the direct rendering of a new view is that with a redirect, the browser adjusts its address field to show the URL for the new view, but with direct rendering, the address field remains unchanged. This, in turn, affects what happens if the user reloads or bookmarks the page: with the address in the browser unchanged, reloading and bookmarking applies to the old address.

So how do you decide if you should use a redirect? To a large extent, it's a matter of preference. I look at it like this: direct rendering is always faster, so it's the first choice. But because the URL in the browser continues to refer to the old view even though a new view is displayed, ask yourself what happens if the user decides to reload the page or bookmark it. If doing so can cause any kind of harm (e.g., submitting an order twice) or result in unexpected behavior (e.g., using a bookmark brings up the wrong page), use a redirect instead.

Using a Panel Component for Layout

The JSP pages for the other two views follow the same pattern as the first one, as shown in Example 9-3 and 9-4.

Example 9-3. Language selection page with Previous, Next and Cancel buttons (expense/stage1/prefLang.jsp)

```
<%@ page contentType="text/html" %>
<%@ taglib uri="http://java.sun.com/jsf/html" prefix="h" %>
<%@ taglib uri="http://java.sun.com/jsf/core" prefix="f" %>

<f:view>
  <html>
    <body>
      <h2>Language:</h2>
      <h:form>
        <h:panelGrid columns="2">
          <h:outputText value="Language:" />
          <h:selectOneRadio value="#{userProfile.locale}">
            <f:selectItem itemValue="sv" itemLabel="Swedish"/>
            <f:selectItem itemValue="en" itemLabel="English"/>
          </h:selectOneRadio>
        </h:panelGrid>

        <h:commandButton value="Previous"
          immediate="true" action="previous" />
        <h:commandButton value="Next"
          action="#{userHandler.updateProfile}" />
        <h:commandButton value="Cancel"
          immediate="true" action="cancel" />
      </h:form>
    </body>
  </html>
</f:view>
```

Example 9-4. Font selection page with Previous, Done and Cancel buttons (expense/stage1/prefFont.jsp)

```
<%@ page contentType="text/html" %>
<%@ taglib uri="http://java.sun.com/jsf/html" prefix="h" %>
<%@ taglib uri="http://java.sun.com/jsf/core" prefix="f" %>

<f:view>
  <html>
    <body>
      <h2>Fonts:</h2>
      <h:form>
        <h:panelGrid columns="2">
          <h:outputText value="Font style:" />
          <h:selectOneMenu value="#{userProfile.fontStyle}">
            <f:selectItem itemValue="serif" itemLabel="Serif"/>
            <f:selectItem itemValue="san-serif" itemLabel="San-Serif"/>
            <f:selectItem itemValue="mono" itemLabel="Monospaced"/>
          </h:selectOneMenu>
          <h:outputText value="Font size:" />
          <h:selectOneMenu value="#{userProfile.fontSize}">
            <f:selectItem itemValue="small" itemLabel="Small"/>
            <f:selectItem itemValue="normal" itemLabel="Normal"/>
```

Example 9-4. Font selection page with Previous, Done and Cancel buttons (expense/stage1/prefFont.jsp) (continued)

```
          <f:selectItem itemValue="large" itemLabel="Large"/>
        </h:selectOneMenu>
      </h:panelGrid>
      <h:commandButton value="Previous"
        immediate="true" action="previous" />
      <h:commandButton value="Cancel"
        immediate="true" action="cancel" />
      <h:commandButton value="Done"
        action="#{userHandler.updateProfile}" />
    </h:form>
  </body>
</html>
</f:view>
```

Navigation rules similar to the ones we looked at earlier take care of switching between the next and previous views and redirecting to the menu view when the Done button is clicked:

```
<navigation-rule>
  <from-view-id>/expense/stage1/prefLang.jsp</from-view-id>
  <navigation-case>
    <from-outcome>previous</from-outcome>
    <to-view-id>/expense/stage1/prefUser.jsp</to-view-id>
  </navigation-case>
  <navigation-case>
    <from-action>#{userHandler.updateProfile}</from-action>
    <from-outcome>success</from-outcome>
    <to-view-id>/expense/stage1/prefFont.jsp</to-view-id>
  </navigation-case>
</navigation-rule>

<navigation-rule>
  <from-view-id>/expense/stage1/prefFont.jsp</from-view-id>
  <navigation-case>
    <from-outcome>previous</from-outcome>
    <to-view-id>/expense/stage1/prefLang.jsp</to-view-id>
  </navigation-case>
  <navigation-case>
    <from-action>#{userHandler.updateProfile}</from-action>
    <from-outcome>success</from-outcome>
    <to-view-id>/expense/stage1/menuArea.jsp</to-view-id>
    <redirect/>
  </navigation-case>
</navigation-rule>
```

All three JSP pages also use a JSF custom action element we haven't talked about yet: the `<h:panelGrid>` element. This action element represents a panel component, acting as a container for any number of child components, with a grid renderer that renders the child components as an HTML table with the specified number of columns. In all three pages, the `columns` attribute is set to `2`, so the first child ends up in the first column, the second in the second column, the third in the first column of the next row, and so on. For the page in Example 9-4, the result looks something like this:

```
<table>
  <tr>
    <td>Font style:</td>
    <td>
      <select name="_id0:_id3">
        <option value="serif">Serif</option>
        <option value="san-serif">San-Serif</option>
        <option value="mono">Monospaced</option>
      </select>
    </td>
  </tr>
  <tr>
    <td>Font size:</td>
    <td>
      <select name="_id0:_id8">
        <option value="small">Small</option>
        <option value="normal">Normal</option>
        <option value="large">Large</option>
      </select>
    </td>
  </tr>
</table>
```

You can, of course, use the HTML table elements explicitly for layout in a JSP page instead of using the `<h:panelGrid>` custom action. As with so much else, it's mostly a matter of preference, but using the custom action means a little bit less typing—and therefore a slightly better chance that there are no errors—while using HTML elements gives you more control over the layout.

Returning a Non-JSF View Response

In most cases, links and submit buttons in a screen generated by a JSF view trigger a request back to the same view, so that user input can be processed by the same view as we discussed earlier. There are exceptions, though. Links may point directly to any type of resource, e.g., a regular JSP or HTML page. It's also possible that the response to a JSF view request must be generated by some other resource type than a JSF view.

Linking Non-JSF Resources

You've already seen an example of a link to a different resource than the JSF view that rendered the screen containing the view, namely the link to the first preferences view in the menu area view. The logout link is another example, and in links to a regular JSP page instead of a JSF view:

```
[<h:outputLink value="../../logout.jsp">
  <h:outputText value="Logout" />
</h:outputLink>]
```

The *logout.jsp* page is located in the top directory for the application, so that accessing this page doesn't trigger the authentication constraint declared for all resources in the *expense* directory; it wouldn't make sense to have to login if the session has timed out just to be able to logout. I therefore specify the path as a relative path to the file located two directories up from the file with the link. An alternative is to use a JSF EL expression that adds the context path for the application to a context-relative path so that it makes sense to the browser:

```
[<h:outputLink
  value="#{facesContext.externalContext.request.contextPath}/logout.jsp">
  <h:outputText value="Logout" />
</h:outputLink>]
```

The JSF EL expression evaluates to the application context path, e.g., */jsfbook* if you use the default for the sample application, so the HTML link's `href` attribute is rendered with the value */jsfbook/logout.jsp*. It would, of course, be better if the link renderer added the context-path automatically for a context-relative path, but it slipped through the cracks for the JSF 1.0 specification. Hopefully it will be corrected in a future release.

The logout JSP page simply invalidates (terminates) the session and redirects to the index page with links to all book examples:

```
<%@ taglib prefix="c" uri="http://java.sun.com/jsp/jstl/core" %>

<% session.invalidate(); %>
<c:redirect url="/index.html"/>
```

Processing JSF Input and Generating a Non-JSF Response

If user input must be processed before the response is rendered using some other type of resource than a JSF view, you can do so in a JSF action method or an action event listener. When the input is processed, render the response any way you like, and just tell JSF that a response has already been sent to prevent it from trying to generate a response from the view.

Let's say that you have a JSF view containing links to external resources, such as referral links to Amazon.com. When the user clicks a link, you want to log this fact before you redirect to the book details page on Amazon.com—maybe to make sure their click-count is accurate. The link may be represented by a `<h:commandLink>` action element, like this:

```
<h:form>
  <h:commandLink action="#{logger.logJSFBookClick}">
    <h:outputText value="JavaServer Faces, Hans Bergsten (O'Reilly)" />
  </h:commandLink>
</h:form>
```

The `<h:commandLink>` action element must be nested within an `<h:form>` element, and it generates an HTML link element with a JavaScript event handler that submits the form when the link is clicked. What's most important in this example is that it's bound to an action method that may look like this:

```
public String logJSFBookClick( ) {
    // Whatever is needed to log the event
    ...

    FacesContext context = FacesContext.getCurrentInstance( );
    ExternalContext ec = context.getExternalContext( );
    try {
        ec.redirect("http://www.amazon.com/exec/obidos/ASIN/0596005393");
    }
    catch (IOException ioe) {
        return "failure";
    }
    context.responseComplete( );
    return "success";
}
```

The action method first does whatever it needs to do to log the fact that the link was clicked. It then generates a redirect response by obtaining the `ExternalContext` and calling its `redirect( )` method. This is just one example of a possible non-JSF response. The method could generate a regular response by setting response headers and writing the body directly, or it could get hold of a `RequestDispatcher` and forward to a servlet or a JSP page. What really matters is that after the method has generated the response, it must call the `FacesContext responseComplete( )` method. After processing all events for a phase, the JSF implementation checks to see if anyone has called this method, and if so, it ends the processing of the request without generating a response.

Returning a JSF View Response to a Non-JSF Request

A less common scenario is that a request is first processed by a regular servlet, but a JSF view is used to generate the response. One example of where this approach is needed is for an application framework that needs to process the request before passing it on to a JSF view.

To let a JSF view generate a response to a non-JSF request, the servlet must create a `FacesContext` instance, configure it with the view, and ask JSF to render the response. Here's the code for doing this:

```
import javax.faces.FactoryFinder;
import javax.faces.application.Application;
import javax.faces.application.ViewHandler;
import javax.faces.component.UIViewRoot;
import javax.faces.context.FacesContext;
import javax.faces.context.FacesContextFactory;
import javax.faces.lifecycle.LifecycleFactory;
```

```
import javax.faces.lifecycle.Lifecycle;
...
public class MyServet extends HttpServlet {
    public void doPost(HttpServletRequest request,
        HttpServletResponse response) throws IOException {
        // Whatever processing is needed
        ...
        LifecycleFactory lFactory = (LifecycleFactory)
        FactoryFinder.getFactory(FactoryFinder.LIFECYCLE_FACTORY);
        Lifecycle lifecycle =
            lFactory.getLifecycle(LifecycleFactory.DEFAULT_LIFECYCLE);

        FacesContextFactory fcFactory = (FacesContextFactory)
        FactoryFinder.getFactory(FactoryFinder.FACES_CONTEXT_FACTORY);
        FacesContext context =
            fcFactory.getFacesContext(context, request, response, lifecycle);

        Application application = context.getApplication( );
        ViewHandler viewHandler = application.getViewHandler( );
        UIViewRoot view = viewHandler.createView(facesContext, "/myView.jsp");
        facesContext.setViewRoot(view);

        lifecycle.render( );
    }
```

A number of JSF factories and other internal classes are needed to make this work. The internal class that controls the request processing is called `javax.faces.lifecycle.Lifecycle`, and because an application or a tool can plug in its own, customized version, a factory named `javax.faces.lifecycle.LifecycleFactory` is responsible for creating instances of the `Lifecycle` class. `FacesContext` instances are also created by a factory—for example, in order to provide different implementations of `FacesContext` for a servlet and a portlet environment. Both of these factories are managed by yet another factory, called the `javax.faces.FactoryFinder`.

The factories are used to create a `Lifecycle` instance, which is then used to construct a `FacesContext` instance, along with the objects that represent the Servlet context, request and response. Next, a `ViewHandler` is retrieved from the `Application` class that you've seen earlier. The `ViewHandler` is also a pluggable class that can be replaced for an application if you prefer to use a different presentation technology than JSP. The `ViewHandler` is asked to create a `UIViewRoot` for the JSF view, and the returned instance is installed on the new `FacesContext` object. Finally, the `Lifecycle` is asked to render the view.

As you've seen in this chapter, the most common navigation needs are satisfied by the `<h:outputLink>` action and the combination of the `<h:commandButton>`, action methods, and navigation rules defined in the *faces-config.xml* file. For special cases, such as the ones described in the last section, you can drop down to the API level to do whatever is needed.

CHAPTER 10

Working with Tabular Data

Almost all applications deal with tabular data of some kind. An application management tool typically shows a list with statistics for installed applications and allows an operator to start and stop applications from the list, and a human resource application may display a list of employees and let an administrator select and edit the profile for any one of them. The sample application we develop in this book works with two sets of tabular data: the list of all expense reports and the list of entries for an individual report.

In this chapter, we look at different ways to display and manipulate tabular data, ranging from displaying a simple read-only listing to developing an editable table.

Displaying a Read-Only Table

With Java, you can represent tabular data in many different ways. Commonly, it's represented as a `java.util.List` or array with beans or `java.util.Map` instances representing the columns for each row. If the data is stored in a database, a `java.sql.ResultSet` or a JSTL `javax.servlet.jsp.jstl.sql.Result` object typically represents it.

The JSTL `<c:forEach>` action supports looping over all these data types, with the exception of `java.sql.ResultSet`, so if all you need is rendering a read-only list or table, you can use JSTL just as you would in a regular JSP page. I actually used this approach in Chapter 8, to verify that the entries added by the action method for the Add button in the report entry form actually were added to the list:

```
<%@ taglib uri="http://java.sun.com/jsp/jstl/core" prefix="c" %>
<ol>
  <c:forEach items="${reportHandler.currentReportEntries}" var="e">
    <li>Date: ${e.date}, Type: ${e.type}, Amount: ${e.amount}</li>
  </c:forEach>
</ol>
```

Here the JSP EL expression for the `items` attribute gets the `List` of `ReportEntry` instances returned by the `getCurrentReportEntries( )` method in the `ReportHandler` class:

```
package com.mycompany.expense;

import java.util.Collections;
import java.util.Comparator;
import java.util.Date;
import java.util.List;
...

public class ReportHandler {
    ...
    public List getCurrentReportEntries( ) {
        List currentList = currentReport.getEntries( );
        Collections.sort(currentList, new Comparator( ) {
                public int compare(Object o1, Object o2) {
                    Date d1 = ((ReportEntry) o1).getDate( );
                    Date d2 = ((ReportEntry) o2).getDate( );
                    return d1.compareTo(d2);
                }
        });
        return currentList;
    }
    ...
}
```

This method gets the entries from the current report and sorts them in ascending date order with the help of the `java.util.Collections` class's `sort( )` method and an anonymous `java.util.Comparator` class instance that compares the `ReportEntry` dates. The JSTL `<c:forEach>` action loops through the elements in the returned `List`, evaluating its body once for each element, with the current element exposed to the EL expressions in its body through the variable named by the `var` attribute.

It's important to understand that the `<c:forEach>` element body can't include any JSF component custom actions, such as `<h:outputText>`. The reason for this limitation has to do with the fact that the number of times the `<c:forEach>` action processes its body depends on the runtime value of the `items` attribute. The first time the page is processed it may loop over the body 10 times, adding new JSF components for the columns in the 10 rows to the view. The next time, it may loop over the body only five times. It would then have to remove the components for the last five rows that were added to the view the last time the page was processed. Part of this particular problem could be solved by letting the component IDs be set by an EL expression, and use the expression to make the IDs unique for the components in each row by appending the row number. It turns out that this opens up another can of worms, so the specification group decided that the best solution was to forbid JSF components actions within the body of a `<c:forEach>` action (as well as any other custom actions that loop over the element body) and provide a special component type to deal with tabular data instead.

The JSF component for tabular data is called `UIData`, and the JSF tag library includes an `<h:dataTable>` action that associates it with a table renderer for generating an HTML table. You can use it to display the current report entries as a read-only table:

```
<h:dataTable value="#{reportHandler.currentReportEntries}" var="e">
  <h:column>
    <f:facet name="header">
      <h:outputText value="Date" />
    </f:facet>
    <h:outputText value="#{e.date}" />
  </h:column>
  <h:column>
    <f:facet name="header">
      <h:outputText value="Type" />
    </f:facet>
    <h:outputText value="#{e.type}" />
  </h:column>
  <h:column>
    <f:facet name="header">
      <h:outputText value="Amount" />
    </f:facet>
    <h:outputText value="#{e.amount}" />
  </h:column>
</h:dataTable>
```

It's a lot more to type than the JSTL version, and probably not worth it for a plain read-only table, but it's also much more powerful. As you'll see soon, the `<h:dataTable>` action allows you to create tables with editable elements, buttons, and links very easily once you've learned the basics.

Let's look at the `<h:dataTable>` action in more detail. Its `value` attribute must be a value expression that evaluates to either a `List` or an array of objects that in turn have properties representing columns; a JDBC `java.sql.ResultSet` or a JSTL `javax.servlet.jsp.jstl.sql.Result` representing a database query result, or a JSF data type named `javax.faces.model.DataModel`. In this example, the `currentReportEntries` property getter method, shown earlier, returns a `List` of `ReportEntry` instances. The action creates a `UIData` component with the children defined within its body. The `UIData` component lets its children process the tabular data, once for each element in a `List` or array or for every row in a database query result, and makes the object that represents the current element or row available to the children through the variable named by the `<h:dataTable>` action element's `var` attribute.

Within `<h:dataTable>` action element's body, use an `<h:column>` element for each column that you want to display. In the simplest case, the `<h:column>` element contains just one JSF component action element, suitable for displaying the column's data.

For instance, in this example I use an `<h:outputText>` action element for each column, bound to a property of the `ReportEntry` bean representing the current row.

Using Facets

Some component types use facets. A *facet* is different from a regular child component in that it has a special purpose, specified by its name, but any component type can be used as a facet. In a JSP page, a facet is represented by the `<f:facet>` element. The `<h:column>` action supports two facets: `header` and `footer`. The `<h:dataTable>` action renders the `header` facet as a column header and, as you've probably guessed, it renders the `footer` facet as a column footer. You can specify `header` and `footer` facets for the table itself using `<f:facet>` elements as direct children of the `<h:dataTable>` element. It renders the table header and footer as rows with a single column spanning the whole table before and after the real table data.

A Word About JSF and Databases

I have already mentioned that the `<h:dataTable>` action supports values of type `java.sql.ResultSet` and `javax.servlet.jsp.jstl.sql.Result`, i.e., the JDBC and JSTL database query result data types. This means you can use the JSTL `<sql:query>` action to execute an SQL query directly in a JSP page or use JDBC in an action method and expose the `ResultSet` as a request, session or application scope variable and display the result with `<h:dataTable>`.

For a very simple application, either of those approaches typically works fine. But when you use JSF, you already have to do quite a bit of Java programming so I recommend that you go the extra mile and create bean classes to represent the database data instead. The `ReportEntry`, `Report`, and `ReportRegistry` classes used in the sample application illustrate one way to represent tabular data as beans. Using beans makes the application much more maintainable than direct database access from JSP or application logic code—if you need to change the database schema to improve performance, or change the SQL statements because you're moving to a different database vendor, the main application code remains the same and only the database abstraction classes need to be modified (in the sample application, all you need to do in a case like this is replace the `ReportRegistry` implementation).

That's all I'm going to say about JSF and databases, because that's all there is to say about databases that is JSF-specific. To learn more about how to use the JSTL `<sql:query>` action and JDBC in a web application, I recommend my *JavaServer Pages* book (O'Reilly), which describes JSTL in detail and includes a brief introduction to JDBC, or a book dedicated to JDBC such as George Reese's *Database Programming with JDBC and Java* (O'Reilly) or *Java Database Best Practices* (O'Reilly).

Processing Row-Specific Events

A very common application feature is to have one table with summary information (a master table) with each row linked to the details about the item in that row. The sample application uses this approach for selecting an individual report to work with. To implement this feature, you must figure out which master table row the user selected and make the corresponding details available for edit or display.

In the final version of the sample application, both the master table and the details are displayed on the same screen, but let's look at how to implement it using two screens first, so we can focus on one thing at the time. Figure 10-1 shows the first rough cut of the reports list screen, with the report titles as links to a report details screen.

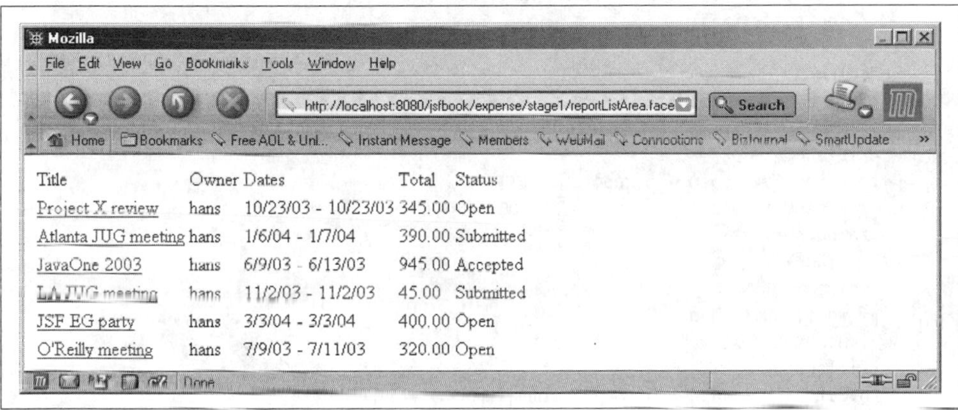

Figure 10-1. Simple reports list screen

Example 10-1 shows the JSP page for this initial version.

Example 10-1. Reports list with links (expense/stage1/reportListArea.jsp)

```
<%@ page contentType="text/html" %>
<%@ taglib uri="http://java.sun.com/jsf/html" prefix="h" %>
<%@ taglib uri="http://java.sun.com/jsf/core" prefix="f" %>

<f:view>
  <h:form>
    <h:dataTable value="#{reportHandler.reportsModel}" var="report">
      <h:column>
        <f:facet name="header">
          <h:outputText value="Title" />
        </f:facet>
        <h:commandLink action="#{reportHandler.select}" immediate="true">
          <h:outputText value="#{report.title}" />
        </h:commandLink>
      </h:column>
      <h:column>
```

Example 10-1. Reports list with links (expense/stage1/reportListArea.jsp) (continued)

```
        <f:facet name="header">
          <h:outputText value="Owner" />
        </f:facet>
        <h:outputText value="#{report.owner}" />
      </h:column>
      <h:column>
        <f:facet name="header">
          <h:outputText value="Dates" />
        </f:facet>
        <h:outputText value="#{report.startDate}">
          <f:convertDateTime datestyle="short" />
        </h:outputText>
        <h:outputText value=" - " />
        <h:outputText value="#{report.endDate}">
          <f:convertDateTime datestyle="short" />
        </h:outputText>
      </h:column>
      <h:column>
        <f:facet name="header">
          <h:outputText value="Total" />
        </f:facet>
        <h:outputText value="#{report.total}">
          <f:convertNumber pattern="#,###.00" />
        </h:outputText>
      </h:column>
      <h:column>
        <f:facet name="header">
          <h:outputText value="Status" />
        </f:facet>
        <h:outputText value="#{statusStrings[report.status]}"/>
      </h:column>
    </h:dataTable>
  </h:form>
</f:view>
```

Example 10-1 looks a lot like the read-only table example we saw earlier, but there are a number of important differences. The two most important differences are that the Title column uses an `<h:commandLink>` component for its value and that the `<h:dataTable>` action element's `value` attribute in Example 10-1 contains an expression that evaluates to an instance of `javax.faces.model.DataModel` instead of a `List`. These two differences are related.

As you may recall from Chapter 9, the `<h:commandLink>` action element creates a command component rendered as an HTML link. Clicking on the link submits the form it's contained in and fires an `ActionEvent` for the command component, just as with the `<h:commandButton>`. There are two things to be aware of, though: `<h:commandLink>` only works if the client supports JavaScript, and because it submits a form, it must be nested within an `<h:form>` element. The command component's children, often represented by one or more `<h:outputText>` action elements as in Example 10-1, render the link text.

The tricky part is how to determine which row the link is clicked for, when handling the `ActionEvent`. Theoretically, you could do it with elaborate use of a query string parameter or a hidden field to hold a row identifier value, but JSF offers a much easier way to deal with it through the `DataModel` class.* This is an abstract class representing tabular data, containing the properties described in Table 10-1.

Table 10-1. javax.faces.model.DataModel properties

Property name	Java type	Access	Description
`rowAvailable`	`boolean`	Read	`true` when the `rowIndex` property holds the index of an existing row.
`rowCount`	`int`	Read	The number of rows represented by this instance, or –1 if unknown.
`rowData`	`Object`	Read	The `Object` representing the row at `rowIndex`, or `null` if `rowIndex` is –1.
`rowIndex`	`int`	Read/write	The zero-based index for the currently selected row, or –1 if no row is selected.
`wrappedData`	`Object`	Read/write	The `Object` representing the table.

When the `UIData` component processes a request, it repeatedly increments the `rowIndex` property and gives the column components a chance to process each row represented by the `rowData` property, as long as `rowAvailable` is `true`. In other words, it doesn't create one component instance per column and row; it creates one component instance per column and lets that one instance process the column's values for all rows. It also fiddles with the component IDs so that the single component is rendered with a unique ID per row. When a link or a button in a certain row is clicked, this row-unique ID is sent to the server and `UIData` uses it to determine for which row it was clicked. The details are pretty hairy, but all you need to know in order to associate the event with the correct row is that when the event is processed, the `DataModel` `rowIndex` property is set to the appropriate index.

Let's use Example 10-1 to illustrate how it works, starting with the getter method for the `reportHandler` bean's `reportModel` property that the `<h:dataTable>` action uses as its data model:

```
package com.mycompany.expense;

import java.util.Date;
import java.util.List;
import javax.faces.model.DataModel;
```

* As well as lots of complex behavior implemented by the `javax.faces.component.UIData` class.

```
import javax.faces.model.ListDataModel;
...

public class ReportHandler {
    ...
    private DataModel reportsModel;
    private Date from;
    private Date to;
    private int[] status;
    ...
    public DataModel getReportsModel( ) {
        if (reportsModel == null) {
            reportsModel = new ListDataModel( );
        }
        reportsModel.setWrappedData(getReports( ));
        return reportsModel;
    }

    public List getReports( ) {
        String user = null;
        if (!isManager) {
            user = getCurrentUser( );
        }
        List l = null;
        try {
            l = registry.getReports(user, from, to, status);
        }
        catch (RegistryException e) {
            // Queue an error message
            ...
        }
        return l;
    }
```

The getReportsModel( ) method creates an instance of the javax.faces.model.ListDataModel class if it doesn't exist. The ListDataModel class is a standard concrete subclass of the abstract DataModel class that adapts a List so it can be used as the model. In addition to the ListDataModel, JSF provides concrete implementations for other common tabular data types: ArrayDataModel, ResultDataModel (for a JSTL Result), ResultSetDataModel (for a JDBC ResultSet), and ScalarDataModel (for any type, representing a one-row data model).

The getReportsModel( ) method then populates the ListDataModel with the List returned by the getReports( ) method. This List contains all reports from the registry that match the current filter criteria values held by the from, to, and status instance variables—limited to reports owned by the current user, unless it's a manager.

The <h:commandLink> for the Title column is bound to a ReportHandler action method named select( ). As I mentioned earlier, the UIData together with its renderer ensure that the DataModel is positioned at the row corresponding to the component that fired the ActionEvent when the action method is invoked, so we can use the DataModel to get the data for the selected row in the select( ) method:

```
        public String select( ) {
            Report selectedReport = (Report) reportsModel.getRowData( );
            if (!rules.canView(currentUser, isManager, selectedReport)) {
                // Queue error message
                ...
                return "error";
            }
            setCurrentReport(selectedReport);
            return "success";
        }
        ...
    }
```

The select( ) method calls the getRowData( ) method to get a reference to the Report instance representing the selected row. If the current user is allowed to see the report, the currentReport variable is updated so that when the details screen asks for the current report, it gets a reference to the selected report.

The last piece of the puzzle is to bring up the details screen. That's handled by a navigation rule in the *faces-config.xml* file:

```
<navigation-rule>
  <from-view-id>/expense/stage1/reportListArea.jsp</from-view-id>
  <navigation-case>
    <from-action>#{reportHandler.select}</from-action>
    <from-outcome>success</from-outcome>
    <to-view-id>/expense/stage1/entryListArea.jsp</to-view-id>
    <redirect/>
  </navigation-case>
</navigation-rule>
```

If the select( ) method returns "success", the browser is redirected to the details view, as described in Chapter 9; otherwise, the report list view is re-rendered.

There are a couple of other details in Example 10-1 that are noteworthy. First, look at the <h:column> element for the Dates column:

```
<h:column>
  <f:facet name="header">
    <h:outputText value="Dates" />
  </f:facet>
  <h:outputText value="#{report.startDate}">
    <f:convertDateTime datestyle="short" />
  </h:outputText>
  <h:outputText value=" - " />
  <h:outputText value="#{report.endDate}">
    <f:convertDateTime  datestyle="short" />
  </h:outputText>
</h:column>
```

As illustrated by this example, you're not limited to using one component per column. You can have as many component action elements within an <h:column> element as you need, e.g., to combine multiple column values in the underlying data model into one value in the rendered table as I do here to display the date range for each report. What you can't use within an <h:column> element, though, is plain template text or non-JSF component action elements. If a column should contain fixed text, use an <h:outputText> element with a static value or use an <f:verbatim> action element to wrap the non-JSF elements:

```
<h:column>
  <f:verbatim>
    This is some template text followed by a JSTL action.
    <x:out select="$doc/title" />
  </f:verbatim>
</h:column>
```

The <f:verbatim> action creates a JSF output component and sets its value to the body evaluation result.

The other interesting detail is how the Report bean's numeric status property value is converted into the corresponding text value.

```
<h:column>
  <f:facet name="header">
    <h:outputText value="Status" />
  </f:facet>
  <h:outputText value="#{statusStrings[report.status]}" />
</h:column>
```

I could have added a read-only statusText property to the Report bean and used it here to get the text value, but that would have meant mixing user interface concerns with business logic, and I want to avoid that as much as possible. A simple solution is to create a List populated with String values, where the index corresponds to a numeric status code. This *faces-config.xml* declaration does the trick:

```
<managed-bean>
  <managed-bean-name>statusStrings</managed-bean-name>
  <managed-bean-class>java.util.ArrayList</managed-bean-class>
  <managed-bean-scope>request</managed-bean-scope>
  <list-entries>
    <null-value/>
    <value>Open</value>
    <value>Submitted</value>
    <value>Accepted</value>
    <value>Rejected</value>
  </list-entries>
</managed-bean>
```

The status codes used by the Report class are 1 through 4, so I populate the first element (i.e., the element at index 0) with a null value, and then the rest with the appropriate String values. With a List declared like this, I can use a simple JSF EL expression for the value attribute, using the report status code as the index for the List element I want.

Dealing with Large Tables

When the tabular data potentially spans many rows, a nice application lets the user work with just a few rows at a time. Letting the user sort the data is another nice touch. With both these features added, the reports list area looks like Figure 10-2.

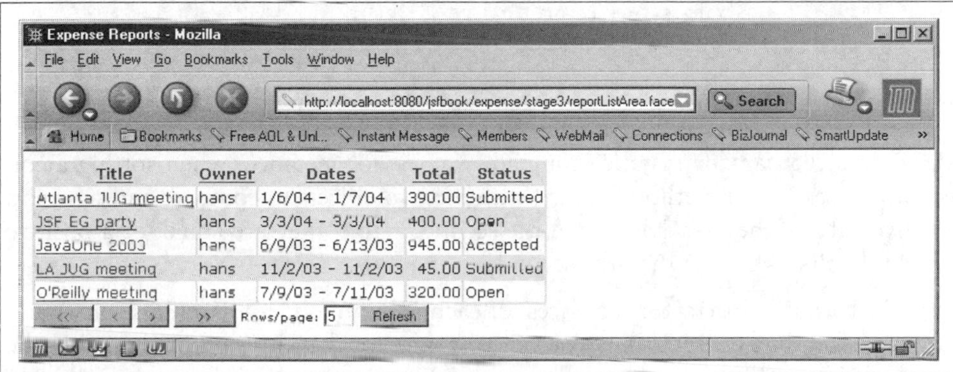

Figure 10-2. The reports list area with sorting and scrolling added

Each column header is now a link that the user clicks to sort the table on the values in that column. Clicking the same column header link twice reverses the order.

Below the table, I've added buttons and a field for scrolling through the data. The field holds the number of rows to show per page, and the scrolling buttons scroll to the first page, the previous page, the next page, and the last page, respectively. The user can click the Refresh button to refresh the screen after changing the rows per page value.

Another difference compared to the previous version of this page is the use of background colors for the table and its rows, the font styles, and the alignment of the column values. I'll tell you how to spice up the user interface like this at the end of this section.

Sorting the Data

To sort the data, we first need to add a few more things to the ReportHandler class:

```
package com.mycompany.expense;

import java.util.Collections;
import java.util.Comparator;
...
public class ReportHandler {
    ...
```

```
    private static final Comparator ASC_TITLE_COMPARATOR = new Comparator( ) {
            public int compare(Object o1, Object o2) {
                String s1 = ((Report) o1).getTitle( );
                String s2 = ((Report) o2).getTitle( );
                return s1.compareTo(s2);
            }
        };

    private static final Comparator DESC_TITLE_COMPARATOR = new Comparator( ) {
            public int compare(Object o1, Object o2) {
                String s1 = ((Report) o1).getTitle( );
                String s2 = ((Report) o2).getTitle( );
                return s2.compareTo(s1);
            }
        };
    ...
```

A `java.util.Comparator` instance compares values, for instance, when sorting a collection. Its `compare( )` method is called with the two objects to compare and returns a negative value if the first is less than the second, zero if they are equal, or a positive value if the first is greater than the second.

I create two static `Comparator` instances for each column: one for ascending order and one for descending order. I show you only the ones for the Title column here, but the others are identical (with the exception of which `Report` property they compare).

To sort the reports list, I add a `sortReports( )` method:

```
    private void sortReports(List reports) {
        switch (sortBy) {
            case SORT_BY_TITLE:
                Collections.sort(reports,
                    ascending ? ASC_TITLE_COMPARATOR : DESC_TITLE_COMPARATOR);
                break;
            case SORT_BY_OWNER:
                Collections.sort(reports,
                    ascending ? ASC_OWNER_COMPARATOR : DESC_OWNER_COMPARATOR);
                break;
            case SORT_BY_DATE:
                Collections.sort(reports,
                    ascending ? ASC_DATE_COMPARATOR : DESC_DATE_COMPARATOR);
                break;
            case SORT_BY_TOTAL:
                Collections.sort(reports,
                    ascending ? ASC_TOTAL_COMPARATOR : DESC_TOTAL_COMPARATOR);
                break;
            case SORT_BY_STATUS:
                Collections.sort(reports,
                    ascending ? ASC_STATUS_COMPARATOR : DESC_STATUS_COMPARATOR);
                break;
        }
    }
```

The method uses the java.util.Collections sort() method to sort a List of Report instances, picking one of the static Comparator instances depending on the values of a sortBy and an ascending variable:

```
private static final int SORT_BY_TITLE = 0;
private static final int SORT_BY_OWNER = 1;
private static final int SORT_BY_DATE = 2;
private static final int SORT_BY_TOTAL = 3;
private static final int SORT_BY_STATUS = 4;

private boolean ascending = false;
private int sortBy = SORT_BY_DATE;
...
public String sortByTitle() {
    if (sortBy == SORT_BY_TITLE) {
        ascending = !ascending;
    }
    else {
        sortBy = SORT_BY_TITLE;
        ascending = true;
    }
    return "success";
}
...
```

One action method per column sets the values of these variables. If the same request action method is called twice, it flips the value of the ascending variable; otherwise, it sets the sortBy variable to the selected column and the ascending variable to its initial value.

The final new method is called getSortedReportsModel():

```
public DataModel getSortedReportsModel() {
    if (reportsModel == null) {
        reportsModel = new ListDataModel();
    }
    List reports = getReports();
    sortReports(reports);
    reportsModel.setWrappedData(reports);
    return reportsModel;
}
```

The only difference—compared to the getReportsModel() method we used previously—is that this method sorts the list by calling the sortReports() method before it populates the DataModel wrapper.

Now we have all the code we need for sorting. Example 10-2 shows how the new methods are bound to components in the JSP page.

Example 10-2. Reports list with sortable columns (expense/stage2/reportListArea.jsp)

```
<%@ page contentType="text/html" %>
<%@ taglib uri="http://java.sun.com/jsf/html" prefix="h" %>
<%@ taglib uri="http://java.sun.com/jsf/core" prefix="f" %>
```

Example 10-2. Reports list with sortable columns (expense/stage2/reportListArea.jsp) (continued)

```
<f:view>
  <h:form>
    <h:dataTable value="#{reportHandler.sortedReportsModel}" var="report">
      <h:column>
        <f:facet name="header">
          <h:commandLink action="#{reportHandler.sortByTitle}"
            immediate="true">
            <h:outputText value="Title" />
          </h:commandLink>
        </f:facet>
        <h:commandLink action="#{reportHandler.select}" immediate="true">
          <h:outputText value="#{report.title}" />
        </h:commandLink>
      </h:column>
      ...
    </h:dataTable>
  </h:form>
</f:view>
```

The first change is the value binding expression for the `<h:dataTable>` action. It's now bound to the method that sorts the entries before it returns the `DataModel`.

Next, all column header facets now use an `<h:commandLink>` action bound to the sort request action methods, such as `sortByTitle( )`, with the `immediate` attribute set to `true` so sorting doesn't trigger validation and model updates. Example 10-2 shows only the Title column, because the others all follow the same pattern.

That's all there is to it, and I think this is a great example of the advantage JSF offers compared to plain JSP or similar template models—all the complex code is implemented by pure Java methods and only minimal changes are needed in the template to bind to them.

Scrolling Through the Data

Adding the ability to scroll through the data requires similar changes. The main pieces of information we need to control are the index of the first row to display and how many rows to display. The `<h:dataTable>` action element provides attributes for these values:

```
<h:dataTable value="#{reportHandler.sortedReportsModel}" var="report"
  first="#{reportHandler.firstRowIndex}"
  rows="#{reportHandler.noOfRows}">
  ...
</h:dataTable>
```

Binding these attributes to properties of the `ReportHandler` makes it easy to adjust their values programmatically when the scrolling buttons are clicked. Here's how the properties are implemented:

```
package com.mycompany.expense;
...
```

```
public class ReportHandler {
    private int noOfRows = 5;
    private int firstRowIndex = 0;
    ...
    public int getNoOfRows( ) {
        return noOfRows;
    }

    public void setNoOfRows(int noOfRows) {
        this.noOfRows = noOfRows;
    }

    public int getFirstRowIndex( ) {
        return firstRowIndex;
    }
```

The noOfRows property is implemented as a read/write property, i.e., with both a getter and a setter method, while the firstRowIndex property is implemented as a read-only property (its value can only be changed indirectly by clicking the scrolling buttons, not directly by the user).

Four action methods support scrolling through the rows:

```
    public String scrollFirst( ) {
        firstRowIndex = 0;
        return "success";
    }

    public String scrollPrevious( ) {
        firstRowIndex -= noOfRows;
        if (firstRowIndex < 0) {
            firstRowIndex = 0;
        }
        return "success";
    }

    public String scrollNext( ) {
        firstRowIndex += noOfRows;
        if (firstRowIndex >= reportsModel.getRowCount( )) {
            firstRowIndex = reportsModel.getRowCount( ) - noOfRows;
            if (firstRowIndex < 0) {
                firstRowIndex = 0;
            }
        }
        return "success";
    }

    public String scrollLast( ) {
        firstRowIndex = reportsModel.getRowCount( ) - noOfRows;
        if (firstRowIndex < 0) {
            firstRowIndex = 0;
        }
        return "success";
    }
```

The scrollFirst() method is simple; it just sets the row index to zero and returns "success". The scrollPrevious() method is almost as simple. It first subtracts the number of rows per page from the current index to get the next index. If this happens to result in a value less than zero, it adjusts it to zero.

The methods for scrolling forward are a little bit more complicated, because they need to ensure that the index stays within the bounds of the table. They use the DataModel getRowCount() method to get the total number of rows represented by the model. For the ListDataModel subclass I use here, this method always returns a valid value, but for the ResultSetDataModel it returns –1, signaling that the number of rows is unknown. The reason is that the only way to know how many rows a java.sql.ResultSet contains is to get them all, and that would be wasteful in many cases. If you use the ResultSetDataModel and want to implement forward scrolling, you must either find out how many rows it holds through other means (e.g., by running a SELECT COUNT(*) query before you run the real query) or use the DataModel isRowAvailable() method to decide when to stop scrolling forward.

The scrollNext() method first adds the number of rows per page to the current index, and then adjusts it if it ends up pointing beyond the table bounds. The scrollLast() method sets the first-row index for the last page by removing the number of rows per page from the total number of rows, adjusting it if the result is less that zero.

All scrolling methods—as well as the sorting methods described earlier—return "success" as the outcome, even though it's very unlikely that the outcome values ever will be used for navigation. The specification recommends returning null as the outcome from action methods that never drive navigation, but to me, that means putting logic in the action method that doesn't belong there. Whether to stay in the same view or display a new view is a decision that may change depending on the application's screen layout and is therefore better expressed as a navigation rule (or the lack of a rule) in the *faces-config.xml* file. An advantage of returning null, though, is that the rules aren't scanned at all, saving some processing time. Other than that, returning null or an outcome value that doesn't match a navigation rule has the same effect.

Another set of methods is needed to enable and disable the scrolling buttons appropriately:

```
public boolean isScrollFirstDisabled( ) {
    return firstRowIndex == 0;
}

public boolean isScrollLastDisabled( ) {
    return firstRowIndex >= reportsModel.getRowCount( ) - noOfRows;
}
```

```
    public boolean isScrollNextDisabled( ) {
        return firstRowIndex >= reportsModel.getRowCount( ) - noOfRows;
    }

    public boolean isScrollPreviousDisabled( ) {
        return firstRowIndex == 0;
    }
```

These methods return `false` if there are enough rows to scroll the requested amount of rows in the requested direction represented by each method.

Example 10-3 shows the report list JSP page modified to support scrolling, with the help of these new `ReportHandler` methods.

Example 10-3. Reports list with scrolling support (expense/stage3/reportListArea.jsp)

```
<%@ page contentType="text/html" %>
<%@ taglib uri="http://java.sun.com/jsf/html" prefix="h" %>
<%@ taglib uri="http://java.sun.com/jsf/core" prefix="f" %>
<html>
  <head>
    <title>Expense Reports</title>
    <link rel="stylesheet" type="text/css"
      href="${pageContext.request.contextPath}/style.css">
  </head>
  <body>
    <f:view>
      <h:form>
        <h:dataTable value="#{reportHandler.sortedReportsModel}" var="report"
          first="#{reportHandler.firstRowIndex}"
          rows="#{reportHandler.noOfRows}"
          styleClass="tablebg" rowClasses="oddRow, evenRow"
          columnClasses="left, left, left, right, left">
          ...
        </h:dataTable>
        <h:commandButton value="<<"
          disabled="#{reportHandler.scrollFirstDisabled}"
          action="#{reportHandler.scrollFirst}" />
        <h:commandButton value="<"
          disabled="#{reportHandler.scrollPreviousDisabled}"
          action="#{reportHandler.scrollPrevious}" />
        <h:commandButton value=">"
          disabled="#{reportHandler.scrollNextDisabled}"
          action="#{reportHandler.scrollNext}" />
        <h:commandButton value=">>"
          disabled="#{reportHandler.scrollLastDisabled}"
          action="#{reportHandler.scrollLast}" />
        Rows/page:
        <h:inputText value="#{reportHandler.noOfRows}" size="3"/>
        <h:commandButton value="Refresh" />
      </h:form>
    </f:view>
  </body>
</html>
```

I've omitted the <h:column> elements in Example 10-3, because they are identical to the ones in Example 10-2.

The first and rows attributes for the <h:dataTable> action are bound to the corresponding ReportHandler properties, as we discussed earlier. After the <h:dataTable> action element comes the four scrolling buttons, each with a disabled attribute and an action attribute, bound to the corresponding properties and action methods.

The <h:inputText> element for the number of rows per page field is bound to the noOfRows property so that the user can easily change the value. The Refresh button, finally, is represented by an <h:commandButton> action. Because all it needs to do is submit the form to set the new page per rows value, it's not bound to any method.

Giving the Table Some Style

Let's talk about style. The preferred way to describe the look of HTML documents nowadays is with Cascading Style Sheets (CSS), so JSF supports this mechanism. All of the HTML component action elements support one or more attributes that let you specify CSS classes that you then declare in a style sheet.

The <h:dataTable> element is a good example:

```
<h:dataTable value="#{reportHandler.sortedReportsModel}" var="report"
  first="#{reportHandler.firstRowIndex}"
  rows="#{reportHandler.noOfRows}"
  styleClass="tablebg" rowClasses="oddRow, evenRow"
  columnClasses="left, left, left, right, left">
  ...
</h:dataTable>
```

All JSF HTML components support the styleClass attribute. Its value is used as is as the value of the class attribute of the generated HTML element. When you specify it for the <h:dataTable> element, it ends up as the class attribute value of the HTML <table> element. For a component type that isn't rendered normally as an HTML element (such as a plain output component), specifying a styleClass value results in a <span> element with the class attribute, rendered around the component's value.

You can also specify classes to use for the <tr> and <td> elements the <h:dataTable> action generates. The rowClasses attribute takes a comma-separated list of class names that are used for the <tr> elements. If two classes are specified, for instance, the first one is used for the first row and the second one for the second row, then the first class is used again for the third row, and so on. The columnClasses attribute also takes a comma-separated list of class names, used in order for the <td> elements of each row. There are two more CSS attributes that I don't use in this example, namely the headerClass and footerClass attributes for specifying classes for the header and footer elements.

Just as for regular HTML, you can include the CSS declarations directly in the JSP page or write them in a separate file referenced by a `<link>` element in the page header section:

```
<link rel="stylesheet" type="text/css"
  href="${pageContext.request.contextPath}/style.css">
```

As I described in Chapter 4, I use a JSP 2.0 EL expression as part of the `href` attribute value to create an absolute path for the style sheet file. Details about CSS are out of the scope of this book, but here are the declarations for the style classes used in Example 10-3:

```
.tablebg {
  background-color: #EEF3FB;
}
.oddRow {
  background-color: #FFFFFF;
}
.evenRow {
  background-color: #EEF3FB;
}
.left {
  text-align: left;
}
.right {
  text-align: right;
}
```

If you want to learn about CSS, the specifications available at *http://www.w3c.org* are fairly easy to read. There are also books about CSS that show you practical applications of style sheets, such as Eric Meyer's *Cascading Style Sheets: The Definitive Guide* (O'Reilly).

As an alternative to CSS, the JSF HTML components also support all the HTML 4.01 attributes that affect the style directly, such as `bgcolor`, `border`, `cellpadding`, `cellspacing`, `frame`, `rules`, `style`, and `width` for the `<h:dataTable>` component element.

Editing Tabular Data

Figure 10-3 shows the version of the report entries list area that is displayed when you click a link in the reports list, where the user can edit the current entries of the selected report. Each entry is represented by editable fields and a selection list, plus buttons to delete or update the entry.

At the top of the screen, the report title is displayed along with a link for navigating back to the reports list page. It's always a good idea to provide explicit navigation features like this in a web application, because the standard Back button behavior is unreliable. For instance, if the user updates the report entries so the total amount changes and then clicks the browser's Back button, the browser may display a cached version of the reports list page with the old total. Different browsers also

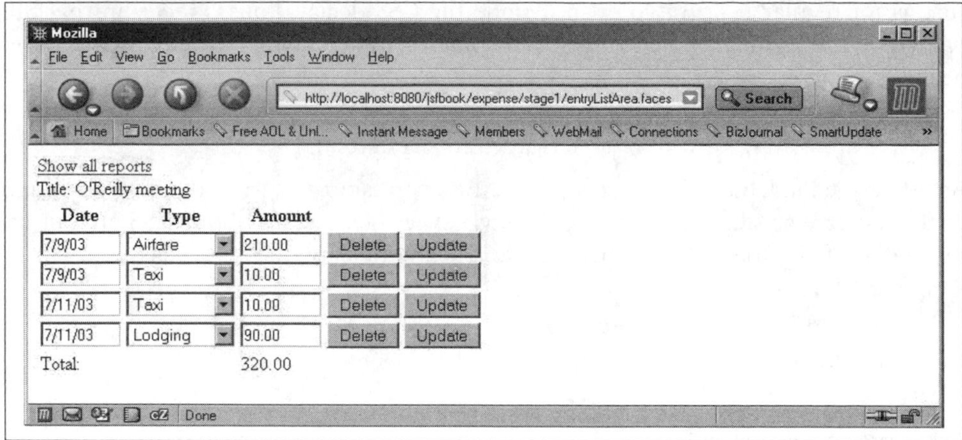

Figure 10-3. The report entries list area with editable columns

handle Back button clicks differently, especially when the previous page was generated by an HTTP POST request, as it always is in this example. Some redisplay a cached version, but others ask the user if a new POST request should be sent to the server. Various tricks can improve the situation, but none is foolproof, so I recommend designing the user interface with links and buttons for navigation and teach your users to use them instead of the Back button.

Example 10-4 shows the JSP page for the entries list.

Example 10-4. Entries list with editable fields (expense/stage1/entryListArea.jsp)

```
<%@ page contentType="text/html" %>
<%@ taglib uri="http://java.sun.com/jsf/html" prefix="h" %>
<%@ taglib uri="http://java.sun.com/jsf/core" prefix="f" %>

<f:view>
  <h:outputLink value="reportListArea.faces">
    <h:outputText value="Show all reports" />
  </h:outputLink>
  <h:form>
    Title:
    <h:outputText value="#{reportHandler.currentReport.title}" />
    <h:dataTable value="#{reportHandler.reportEntriesModel}" var="entry">
      <h:column>
        <f:facet name="header">
          <h:outputText value="Date" />
        </f:facet>
        <h:inputText size="8" required="true" value="#{entry.date}"
          disabled="#{reportHandler.editDisabled}">
          <f:convertDateTime datestyle="short" />
        </h:inputText>
        <f:facet name="footer">
          <h:outputText value="Total:" />
        </f:facet>
```

Example 10-4. Entries list with editable fields (expense/stage1/entryListArea.jsp) (continued)

```
      </h:column>
      <h:column>
        <f:facet name="header">
          <h:outputText value="Type" />
        </f:facet>
        <h:selectOneMenu id="type" required="true" value="#{entry.type}"
          disabled="#{reportHandler.editDisabled}">
          <f:selectItems value="#{entryHandler.currentChoices}"/>
        </h:selectOneMenu>
      </h:column>
      <h:column>
        <f:facet name="header">
          <h:outputText value="Amount" />
        </f:facet>
        <h:inputText size="8" required="true" value="#{entry.amount}"
          disabled="#{reportHandler.editDisabled}">
          <f:convertNumber pattern="#,###.00" />
          <f:validateDoubleRange minimum="1" />
        </h:inputText>
        <f:facet name="footer">
          <h:outputText value="#{reportHandler.currentReport.total}">
            <f:convertNumber pattern="#,###.00" />
          </h:outputText>
        </f:facet>
      </h:column>
      <h:column>
        <h:commandButton action="#{reportHandler.removeEntry}"
          value="Delete"
          disabled="#{reportHandler.editDisabled}" />
      </h:column>
      <h:column>
        <h:commandButton action="#{reportHandler.updateEntry}"
          value="Update"
          disabled="#{reportHandler.editDisabled}" />
      </h:column>
    </h:data_table>
  </h:form>
</f:view>
```

The columns holding editable values are represented by either an `<h:inputText>` or an `<h:selectOneMenu>` action element, bound to the properties of the bean representing the current row and configured with converters and validators as needed, just as for the read-only components in the previous examples.

In addition, each input component has a `disabled` attribute bound to a `ReportHandler` property named `editDisabled`. This property has the value `true` if the current user isn't allowed to edit the selected report, ensuring that the input elements are enabled only when the user is in fact allowed to change their values. The property getter method is implemented like this:

```
package com.mycompany.expense;
...
```

```
public class ReportHandler {
    private Rules rules;
    private Report currentReport;
    private String currentUser;
    private boolean isManager;
    ...
    public boolean isEditDisabled( ) {
        return !isReportNew( ) &&
            !rules.canEdit(currentUser, isManager, currentReport);
    }
    ...
}
```

You probably recognize it as the same type of method used in Chapter 6 to enable or disable the buttons in the menu area depending on the current report's status and the role associated with the current user. The `isEditDisabled( )` method returns `false` if the report is new (i.e., it has no entries) and if the current user is allowed to edit it. The `Rules` class implements the last part of the condition:

```
package com.mycompany.expense;

public class Rules {
    public boolean canEdit(String user, boolean isManager, Report report) {
        return report.getOwner( ).equals(user) && !isLocked(report);
    }
    ...
    public boolean isLocked(Report report) {
        return report.getStatus( ) == Report.STATUS_SUBMITTED ||
            report.getStatus( ) == Report.STATUS_ACCEPTED;
    }
}
```

The Delete and Update buttons in each row are represented by columns that have `<h:commandButton>` action elements as their values. Each button is bound to an action method that is very similar to the action method that selects a report in the reports list area:

```
package com.mycompany.expense;
...

public class ReportHandler {
    ...
    public String removeEntry( ) {
        ReportEntry selectedEntry =
            (ReportEntry) entriesModel.getRowData( );
        int entryId = selectedEntry.getId( );
        return removeEntry(entryId);
    }

    public String updateEntry( ) {
        ReportEntry selectedEntry =
            (ReportEntry) entriesModel.getRowData( );
        int entryId = selectedEntry.getId( );
        return updateEntry(selectedEntry);
    }
```

Both methods get the ReportEntry for the row in which the button was clicked and call methods to remove or update the entry in the current report:

```
public String removeEntry(int entryId) {
    try {
        refreshCache( );
    }
    catch (RegistryException e) {
        addMessage("registry_error", e.getMessage( ));
        return "error";
    }

    if (!rules.canEdit(currentUser, isManager, currentReport)) {
        addMessage("report_no_edit_access", null);
        return "error";
    }

    String outcome = "success";
    ReportEntry currentEntry = currentReport.getEntry(entryId);
    currentReport.removeEntry(entryId);
    try {
        saveReport( );
    }
    catch (RegistryException e) {
        addMessage("registry_error", e.getMessage( ));
        currentReport.addEntry(currentEntry);
        outcome = "error";
    }
    return outcome;
}

public String updateEntry(ReportEntry entry) {
    try {
        refreshCache( );
    }
    catch (RegistryException e) {
        addMessage("registry_error", e.getMessage( ));
        return "error";
    }

    if (!rules.canEdit(currentUser, isManager, currentReport)) {
        addMessage("report_no_edit_access", null);
        return "error";
    }

    String outcome = "success";
    ReportEntry currentEntry = currentReport.getEntry(entry.getId( ));
    currentReport.removeEntry(entry.getId( ));
    currentReport.addEntry(entry);
    try {
        saveReport( );
    }
    catch (RegistryException e) {
        addMessage("registry_error", e.getMessage( ));
```

```
                currentReport.removeEntry(entry.getId( ));
                currentReport.addEntry(currentEntry);
                outcome = "error";
            }
            return outcome;
        }
        ...
    }
```

These methods refresh the cached copy of the current report, check if the current user is allowed to edit the report, remove or update the entry in the cached copy, and then save the updated copy in the registry. If anything goes wrong, they add an appropriate error message, restore the cached copy to its previous state, and return an "error" outcome.

Besides the editable columns and buttons, a couple of columns in Example 10-4 also have footer facets. The Date column has a footer with an `<h:outputText>` element with the static value "Total:", and the Amount column has a footer with an `<h:outputText>` element bound to the `total` property of the current report. This results in the effect shown in Figure 10-3. I could have defined a `footer` facet for the `<h:dataTable>` itself instead, but I choose to do it this way to get the label aligned with the first column and the total amount aligned with the third column, as opposed to getting both the label and the total amount displayed unaligned with the columns.

The information in this chapter can be applied to many applications that deal with tabular data, whether the data is displayed on one or multiple screens, with columns containing a mixture of read-only, read/write, link, and button components. For tables that are more dynamic, you may have to combine these basics with other techniques we talked about earlier. For instance, if the component type for a column needs to be chosen based on the data of the current row, use the rendered attribute to pick the right type for each column:

```
<h:column>
  <h:inputText value="#{entry.amount}" rendered="#{not entry.editDisabled}" />
  <h:outputText value="#{entry.amount}" rendered="#{entry.editDisabled}" />
</h:column>
```

In this example, I assume that individual entries in the report may or may not be edited, and I use JSF EL expressions testing a property on the entry itself to set the `rendered` attribute to either `true` or `false`. The result is that the column values for different rows are represented by either an input or an output component. For some tables, you may also need to use `<h:panelGrid>` elements to get the layout you want, and maybe even nest one `<h:dataTable>` within another. For the really exceptional cases, a custom renderer or a custom component may be required, but the standard `<h:dataTable>` takes you a long way as you've seen in this chapter.

CHAPTER 11

Internationalization

Developing an application that caters to the needs of users from different parts of the world requires two related processes, known as internationalization and localization. *Internationalization* refers to preparing an application by identifying everything that will vary in different geographical regions and providing the means to use different versions of all these items, instead of hardcoded values. Examples of such items include labels and messages, online help texts, graphics, format of dates, times and numbers, currencies, measurements, and sometimes even the page layouts and colors. Many people use the abbreviation i18n for the word "internationalization," because the word is spelled with the letter I followed by 18 characters and an N—i18n is much easier to type.

An application that has been internationalized can be *localized* for different regions without changing any code. *Localization* means making the application messages, help texts, graphics, and so forth—as well as rules for formatting dates/times and numbers—for one or more regions available to the internationalized application. Localization is sometimes abbreviated l10n, following the same logic as the i18n abbreviation. Adding support for a new region is as simple as installing new localized resources.

The Java core libraries include a number of tools to make it easy to develop internationalized applications and create localized resources, and JSF builds on these features. In this chapter, we first look at how to use the core libraries and the JSF features to internationalize part of the sample application. Dealing with languages containing other characters than those used in Western languages can be a bit tricky, but I'll show you how to do it for JSF in the last section of the chapter.

Localizing Application Output

Remember the pages for setting user preferences from Chapter 9? One of the pages allows the user to select her preferred language; let's add what's needed for actually using the selected language. Figure 11-1 shows one of the preferences pages when Swedish is selected as the preferred language.

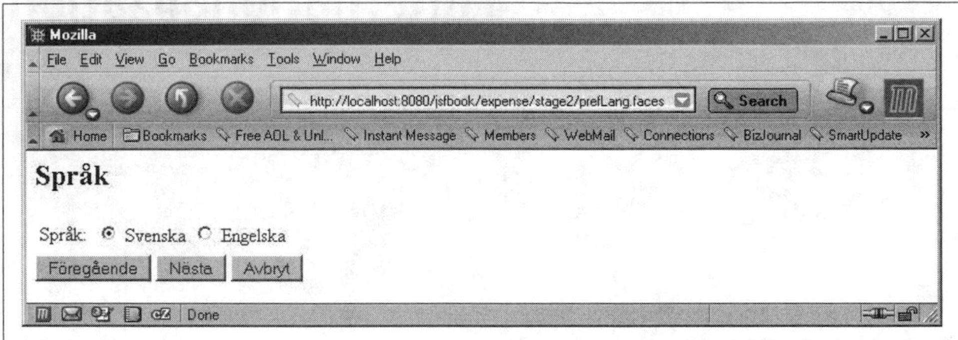

Figure 11-1. User information page with Swedish as the selected language

Java was designed with internationalization in mind and includes a number of classes to make the process as painless as possible. In i18n terminology, a *locale* represents a specific geographical region. In Java, a locale is represented by an instance of the `java.util.Locale` class. Java includes other classes for formatting dates and numbers according to the rules defined for a locale, and classes to help you include localized strings and other objects in an application.

You create a `Locale` instance using a constructor that takes a country code and language code as arguments:

```
java.util.Locale usLocale = new Locale("en", "US");
```

Here, a `Locale` for U.S. English is created. George Bernard Shaw (a famous Irish playwright) once observed, "England and America are two countries divided by a common language," so it's no surprise that both a language code and a country code are needed to describe some locales completely. The language code, a lowercase two-letter combination, is defined by the ISO 639 standard available at *http://www.ics.uci.edu/pub/ietf/http/related/iso639.txt*. The country code, an uppercase two-letter combination, is defined by the ISO 3166 standard, available at *http://www.chemie.fu-berlin.de/diverse/doc/ISO_3166.html*. Table 11-1 and Table 11-2 show some of these codes.

Table 11-1. ISO-639 language codes

Language code	Language
af	Afrikaans
da	Danish
de	German
el	Greek
en	English
es	Spanish

Table 11-1. ISO-639 language codes (continued)

Language code	Language
`fr`	French
`ja`	Japanese
`pl`	Polish
`ru`	Russian
`sv`	Swedish
`zh`	Chinese

Table 11-2. ISO-3166 country codes

Country code	Country
DK	Denmark
DE	Germany
GR	Greece
MX	Mexico
NZ	New Zealand
ZA	South Africa
GB	United Kingdom
US	United States

The country code is optional because it's redundant for some languages (like Swedish). Another optional item supported by the `Locale` class is called a *variant*. A variant can specify a locale that applies to a specific platform, in addition to a language and a country. One example is if you use a locale to select help texts, you may want to provide one set of descriptions for Internet Explorer and another for Netscape browsers.

In JSF, a view is associated with a specific locale through a `UIViewRoot` property named `locale` of the type `Locale`. If no locale is specified for a view, JSF uses information encoded in the request data to try to determine which locale the user prefers. Browsers may send this information in a request header called `Accept-Language`. The value of this header contains one or more codes for the user's preferred locales based on how the browser is configured. If you use a Netscape 6 or Mozilla browser, you can specify your preferred locales in the Edit → Preferences dialog, under the Navigator → Languages tab. In Internet Explorer 5, you find the same thing in Tools → Internet Options when you click the Languages button under the General tab. If you specify more than one language, they are included in the header as a comma-separated list:

```
Accept-Language: en-US, en, sv
```

The languages are listed in order of preference, with each language represented by just the language code or the language code and country code separated by a dash (-).

This example header specifies the first choice as U.S. English, followed by any type of English, and finally Swedish. The HTTP specification also allows an alternative to listing the codes in order of preference, namely, adding a so-called *q-value* to each code. The q-value is a value between 0.0 and 1.0, indicating the relative preference between the codes.

If the `locale` property for a view isn't set, e.g., because it's the first time the view is requested, JSF compares the locales specified by the `Accept-Language` header to the list of locales supported by the application, declared like this in the *faces-config.xml* file:

```
<faces-config>
  <application>
    <locale-config>
      <default-locale>en<default-locale>
      <supported-locale>sv</supported-locale>
      ...
    </locale-config>
    ...
  </application>
  ...
</faces-config>
```

Within the `<locale-config>` element, one `<default-locale>` element declares the default locale and zero or more `<supported-locales>` declare additional supported locales. The default locale is included automatically in the set of supported locales, so you shouldn't declare it twice.

For each locale from the `Accept-Language` header (in priority order), JSF first tries to find a supported locale that matches all parts of the preferred locale: language, country, and variant. If it doesn't find a perfect match, it drops the variant and tries again. If it still can't find a match, it drops the country. As soon as it finds a supported locale using this algorithm, it selects it and ignores the other locales. This means that with English, German, and Swedish as the available locales and an `Accept-Language` header containing the value "sv, en-US", the Swedish locale is selected (it's listed first, so it has higher priority). With an `Accept-Language` header such as "fr, en-US", the English locale is selected, since the highest priority locale (`fr`) is not available, and the closest match for the `en-US` locale is the `en` locale. If the application supports both the `en` and the `en-US` locale, the `en-US` locale is used because it's an exact match for the user's preferences. If the browser doesn't send an `Accept-Language` header or if none of its locales matches a supported locale, the application's default locale is selected. If no default locale is declared, the Java runtime's default locale is used instead.

Letting JSF pick a locale based on the `Accept-Language` header helps selecting the best initial locale for a user, but for a localized application you should always provide means for explicit locale selection. Many users aren't aware of the browser locale selection feature. Besides, providing a list of locales to pick from makes it clear to the user exactly which locales are supported. The sample application defaults to English but allows the user to pick one of the other supported locales through the preferences screen.

Example 11-1 shows the JSP page where the user selects the preferred language

Example 11-1. Internationalized language selection page (expense/stage2/prefLang.jsp)

```
<%@ page contentType="text/html" %>
<%@ taglib uri="http://java.sun.com/jsf/html" prefix="h" %>
<%@ taglib uri="http://java.sun.com/jsf/core" prefix="f" %>

<f:view locale="#{userProfile.locale}">
  <f:loadBundle basename="labels" var="labels" />
  <html>
    <body>
      <h2><h:outputText value="#{labels.prefLangHeader}" /></h2>
      <h:form>
        <h:panelGrid columns="2">
          <h:outputText value="#{labels.langSelectLabel}" />
          <h:selectOneRadio value="#{userProfile.locale}">
            <f:selectItem itemValue="sv" itemLabel="#{labels.svChoice}"/>
            <f:selectItem itemValue="en" itemLabel="#{labels.enChoice}"/>
          </h:selectOneRadio>
        </h:panelGrid>
        <h:commandButton value="#{labels.prevButtonLabel}"
          immediate="true" action="previous" />
        <h:commandButton value="#{labels.nextButtonLabel}"
          action="#{userHandler.updateProfile}" />
        <h:commandButton value="#{labels.cancelButtonLabel}"
          immediate="true" action="cancel" />
      </h:form>
    </body>
  </html>
</f:view>
```

The user selects the preferred language by clicking one of two radio buttons, represented by the `<h:selectOneRadio>` action element. The `value` attribute of this element binds it to the `locale` property of a `UserProfile` bean in the session scope. So far, it's the same as the version of this page that we looked at in Chapter 9.

What's different is that the selected locale is now actually used to pick the corresponding text for everything in the page. Note how I use a `locale` attribute for the `<f:view>` action, bound to the `UserProfile` bean's `locale` property. The first time a user requests the page, the `UserProfile` bean is created and added to the session scope under the name `userProfile` (when the value binding is evaluated, based on the managed bean declaration in the *faces-config.xml* file). The bean's `locale` property has the value "en" as default, so this is the value passed to the `<f:view>` action and used subsequently to set the `UIViewRoot` `locale` property value. If the user selects another locale and submits the form, the new locale is picked up the next time the JSP page is processed. All the preferences pages linked from the language selection page shown in Example 11-1 are internationalized in the same way, so you can click the Next button after changing the language selection to verify that it works.

The UIViewRoot locale property can also be set programmatically, for example, by an action method or an event listener, but you must be careful when you do so. The same locale that was used to render the response must also be used to process the input (if any) sent with the next request. The locale property must therefore be changed only after all input values have been processed (typically at the end of the Process Validations phase at the earliest) and before the first component is rendered (typically at the very beginning of the Render Response phase at the latest).

Selecting Localized Text

The next JSF action in Example 11-1 is the <f:loadBundle> action. This action loads the *resource bundle* specified by the basename attribute that corresponds to the locale identified by the locale property value in UIViewRoot. A resource bundle holds localized resources (such as text, images, and sounds) and is represented by an instance of the java.util.ResourceBundle class. This class is actually the abstract superclass for two subclasses that do the real work, ListResourceBundle and PropertyResourceBundle, but it provides methods that let you get an appropriate subclass instance, hiding the details about which subclass actually provides the resources. Details about the difference between these two subclasses are beyond the scope of this book. Suffice it to say that the <f:loadBundle> action can use resources provided through either one of them, or even custom subclasses.

For most web applications, an instance of the PropertyResourceBundle is used. A PropertyResourceBundle instance is associated with a named set of localized text resources. Keys identifying resources and their corresponding text values are stored in a regular text file, known as a *resource bundle file*:

```
prefLangHeader=Language
langSelectLabel=Language:
enChoice=English
svChoice=Swedish
```

This is the same kind of file we used in Chapter 7 when we defined error messages. This example shows four keys: prefLangHeader, langSelectLabel, enChoice, and svChoice. The key is a string, without space or other special characters, and the value is any text. If the value spans more than one line, the linebreak must be escaped with a backslash character (\):

```
multi_line_msg=This text value\
continues on the next line.
```

A resource bundle file must use a *.properties* file name extension, but there can be more than one file per bundle, with a locale code included in the filename. To localize an application, create a separate resource bundle file for each locale, all with the same main name (the *base name*) but with unique suffixes to identify the locale. For instance, a file named *lables_en_US.properties*, where en is the language code for English and US is the country code for U.S.A., can contain text for the US English locale. All resource bundle files must be located in the classpath used by the Java Virtual Machine (JVM). In the case of web applications, I suggest that you store the file in the application's *WEB-INF/classes* directory, because this directory is always included in the classpath. The sample application contains two resource bundle files, one for each supported locale (English and Swedish): *labels_en.properties* and *labels_sv.properties*.

In addition to loading a ResourceBundle instance that represents the specified base name and the current locale, the <f:loadBundle> wraps it in a java.util.Map and saves the Map in the request scope with the name specified by the var attribute. The Map implementation of the get( ) method calls through to the wrapped ResourceBundle instance's getObject( ) method. If the specified key matches a resource, its value is returned. Otherwise, the key embedded in questions marks, e.g., "???myKey???," is returned to make it easier to detect common problems, such as key name typos.

With localized resources exposed as a Map, you can use standard JSF EL expressions to access the localized values. For instance, this is how the main title of the language selection page is handled in Example 11-1:

```
<f:view locale="#{userProfile.locale}">
  <f:loadBundle basename="labels" var="labels" />
  <html>
    <body>
      <h2><h:outputText value="#{labels.prefLangHeader}" /></h2>
```

The <f:view> action sets the locale for the view to the currently selected locale held by the userProfile bean's locale property, and the <f:loadBundle> action exposes the labels resource bundle for this locale as a Map named labels in the request scope. The key for the localized page title is prefLangHeader, so picking up a localized value for this key is as easy as using an <h:outputText> action with the value attribute set to a JSF EL expression that receives the prefLangHeader property from the labels Map variable. If you look at all other JSF components in Example 11-1, you'll see that they all receive their value from the labels variable in the same way.

It's fairly common for resource bundle keys to be composed from multiple words separated by dots: for instance, "choice.en". A dot is a special character in the JSF EL, so trying to access a key from a bundle with an expression like #{labels.choice.en} always fails. If your resource bundle key names contain dots, you must use the array element operator instead, i.e., #{labels['choice.en']}.

Formatting Dates and Numbers

One thing the inhabitants of this planet have a hard time agreeing on is how to write dates and numbers. The order of the month, the day, and the year; if the numeric value or the name should be used for the month; what character to use to separate the fractional part of a number; all of these details differ between countries, even between countries that speak the same language. And even though these details may seem picky, using an unfamiliar format can cause a great deal of confusion. For instance, if you ask for something to be done by 5/2, an American thinks you mean May 2 while a Swede believes that it's due by February 5.

Java provides two classes, named `java.text.NumberFormat` and `java.text.DateFormat`, for formatting numbers and dates appropriately for a specific locale, and the standard JSF converters for date/time and numeric values use these classes.

Example 11-2 shows a localized version of the menu area page with an added feature: it displays the current date on the right.

Example 11-2. Internationalized menu area page (expense/stage2/menuArea.jsp)

```
<%@ page contentType="text/html" %>
<%@ taglib uri="http://java.sun.com/jsf/html" prefix="h" %>
<%@ taglib uri="http://java.sun.com/jsf/core" prefix="f" %>

<jsp:useBean id="now" scope="request" class="java.util.Date" />
<f:view locale="#{userProfile.locale}">
  <f:loadBundle basename="labels" var="labels" />
  <h:form>
    <table cellpadding="0" cellspacing="0" width="100%">
      <tr>
        <td>
          <h:commandButton value="#{labels.newButtonLabel}"
            disabled="#{reportHandler.newDisabled}" />
          <h:commandButton value="#{labels.deleteButtonLabel}"
            disabled="#{reportHandler.deleteDisabled}" />
          <h:commandButton value="#{labels.submitButtonLabel}"
            disabled="#{reportHandler.submitDisabled}" />
          <h:commandButton value="#{labels.acceptButtonLabel}"
            rendered="#{reportHandler.acceptRendered}"
            disabled="#{reportHandler.acceptDisabled}" />
          <h:commandButton value="#{labels.rejectButtonLabel}"
            rendered="#{reportHandler.rejectRendered}"
            disabled="#{reportHandler.rejectDisabled}" />
        </td>
        <td align="right">
          <h:outputText value="#{labels.loggedInAs}" />
          "${pageContext.request.remoteUser}"
          [<h:outputLink value="../../logout.jsp">
             <h:outputText value="#{labels.logoutLinkLabel}" />
           </h:outputLink>]
          [<h:outputLink value="prefUser.faces">
             <h:outputText value="#{labels.prefLinkLabel}" />
           </h:outputLink>]
         <h:outputText value="#{now}">
           <f:convertDateTime datestyle="long" />
         </h:outputText>
        </td>
```

Example 11-2. Internationalized menu area page (expense/stage2/menuArea.jsp) (continued)

```
      </tr>
    </table>
  </h:form>
</f:view>
```

The menu area page is internationalized in the same way as the language selection page we looked at earlier: the `<f:view>` action sets the locale and all text is picked up from the bundle loaded by the `<f:loadBundle>` action. The only new thing is the `<h:outputText>` element at the end, showing the value of the `now` variable created by the `<jsp:useBean>` standard JSP action at the top of the page. The `now` variable holds the current date and time and, because the output component is configured with a standard date/time converter, its value is formatted according to the current locale. Figure 11-2 shows this version of the menu area page with the date formatted according to the Swedish locale.

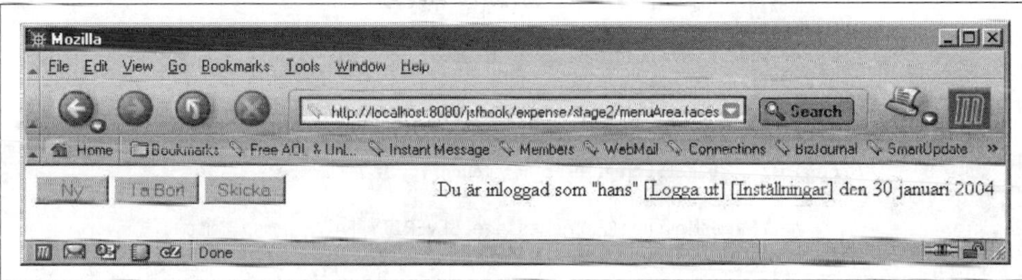

Figure 11-2. The menu area with a date formatted according to the Swedish locale

As I mentioned before, the format of a date or a time value can be controlled through various attributes supported by the `<f:convertDateTime>` action. In Example 11-2, I use only the `dateStyle` attribute, but Appendix A describes all available options. The standard number converter also formats the value of the component it's attached to according to the rules for the current locale, and it can be configured with similar attributes.

Localizing Messages

If your application supports more than one locale, you must be concerned also with the messages generated by the validators, the converters, and possibly your application code. The good news is that JSF is already internationalized with regards to how it handles messages—and if you follow the code samples for application-generated messages from Chapter 7, so is your application. This piece of code from the custom validator we developed in Chapter 7 shows what I mean:

```
package com.mycompany.jsf.validator;

import java.text.MessageFormat;
import java.util.Date;
```

```
import java.util.Locale;
import java.util.ResourceBundle;
import javax.faces.application.Application;
import javax.faces.application.FacesMessage;
import javax.faces.component.StateHolder;
import javax.faces.component.UIComponent;
import javax.faces.context.FacesContext;
import javax.faces.validator.Validator;
import javax.faces.validator.ValidatorException;
...
public class LaterThanValidator implements Validator, StateHolder {
    ...
    public void validate(FacesContext context, UIComponent component,
        Object value) throws ValidatorException {

        Application application = context.getApplication( );

        String messageBundleName = application.getMessageBundle( );
        Locale locale = context.getViewRoot( ).getLocale( );
        ResourceBundle rb =
            ResourceBundle.getBundle(messageBundleName, locale);

        UIComponent peerComponent = component.findComponent(peerId);
        if (peerComponent == null) {
            String msg = rb.getString("peer_not_found");
            FacesMessage facesMsg =
                new FacesMessage(FacesMessage.SEVERITY_FATAL, msg, msg);
            throw new ValidatorException(facesMsg);
        }
        ...
    }
}
```

The `validate( )` method obtains the current locale from the `UIViewRoot` and uses it to get a `ResourceBundle` for this locale. It then gets the localized message string from this bundle. This means that you just need to add message resource bundle files with localized error messages for all the locales you support. Here's what the custom messages file for the Swedish locale (*custMessages_sv.properties*) looks like:

```
javax.faces.validator.DoubleRangeValidator.MINIMUM=Ange ett värde större an {0}.

not_later=Ogiltigt datum
not_later_detail=Ange ett datum senare än {0}
```

There are a couple of important things to notice. The first is that all JSF validators and converters, and all other types of classes that generate messages, also use a locale-specific `ResourceBundle` instance to get the message text, so you can localize all standard messages as well. Here I also define a Swedish version of a `DoubleRangeValidator` message.

Second, note that I don't specify a value for the `peer_not_found` key used by the `LaterThanValidator` code. This illustrates a neat feature of the `ResourceBundle` class, namely, that an instance for a specific bundle—say, "en_US"—is linked to a parent instance for a less precise locale—say, "en"—all the way up to the default bundle (a bundle without a locale code appended to the base name). For the sample application, I have a default resource bundle file named *custMessages.properties* containing all messages in English and a *custMessages_sv.properties* file containing messages in Swedish, so when I ask the ResourceBundle for the *custMessages_sv.properties* file to give me the value for a key that's not defined there, it returns the value defined in *custMessages.properties* instead. I use this feature in the sample application to avoid translating all the messages that can only occur due to design errors, as opposed to user errors. It can also be a real time-saver when you deal with a language where only a few messages need to be customized for a specific country, while most of them are the same for all countries speaking the same language.

Handling Localized Application Input

The locale also plays a role when input is being processed. As I mentioned earlier, dates and numbers are written according to different rules in different parts of the world, so input must be parsed according to the rules for the current locale.

All JSF input components use the current locale when they parse input, so there's really nothing you need to do beyond what we've already covered. To verify this, let's use an internationalized version of the entry form area (Example 11-3) and see what happens.

Example 11-3. Internationalized version of the entry form area page (expense/stage5/entryFormArea.jsp)

```
<%@ page contentType="text/html" %>
<%@ taglib uri="http://java.sun.com/jsf/html" prefix="h" %>
<%@ taglib uri="http://java.sun.com/jsf/core" prefix="f" %>

<f:view locale="#{userProfile.locale}">
  <f:loadBundle basename="labels" var="labels" />
  <h:form>
    <h:outputText value="#{labels.reportTitleLabel}" />
    <h:inputText id="title" size="30" required="true"
      value="#{reportHandler.currentReport.title}" />
    <h:message for="title" />
    <br>
    <h:outputText value="#{labels.reportEntryLabel}" />
    <br>
    <h:outputText value="#{labels.entryDateLabel}" />
    <h:inputText id="date" size="10" required="true"
      value="#{entryHandler.currentEntry.date}">
      <f:convertDateTime datestyle="short" />
    </h:input_text>
    <h:message for="date" />
    <br>
    <h:outputText value="#{labels.entryTypeLabel}" />
```

Example 11-3. Internationalized version of the entry form area page (expense/stage5/entryFormArea.jsp) (continued)

```
    <h:selectOneMenu id="type" required="true"
      value="#{entryHandler.currentEntry.type}">
      <f:selectItems value="#{entryHandler.i18nChoices}"/>
    </h:selectOneMenu>
    <h:message for"type" />
    <br>
    <h:outputText value="#{labels.entryAmountLabel}" />
    <h:inputText id="amount" size="10" required="true"
      value="#{entryHandler.currentEntry.amount}">
      <f:convertNumber pattern="#,##0.00" />
      <f:validateDoubleRange minimum="1"/>
    </h:inputText>
    <h:message for="amount" />
    <br>
    <h:commandButton value="#{labels.addButtonLabel}"
      disabled="#{reportHandler.editDisabled}"
      action="#{entryHandler.add}" />
  </h:form>
  <h:messages globalOnly="true" />

  <%-- Loop to verify that it works --%>
  <%@ taglib uri="http://java.sun.com/jsp/jstl/core" prefix="c" %>
  <ol>
    <c:forEach items="${reportHandler.currentReportEntries}" var="e">
      <li>Date: ${e.date}, Type: ${e.type}, Amount: ${e.amount}</li>
    </c:forEach>
  </ol>
</f:view>
```

This entry form area page is internationalized in exactly the same way as the pages we've worked with earlier. The only difference is that it contains input components in addition to the output components. The input component for the Date field is configured with a date/time converter, and the input component for the Amount field with a number converter.

If you use the preferences pages to switch between the English and the Swedish locale and then load the entry form area page, you'll see that the default values for the Date and Amount are formatted differently. In the English locale, the date is formatted as 1/30/04, but in the Swedish locale it's 2004-01-30. The difference between the number formats is subtle, but it's there. In the English locale, a dot separates the integer part from the fractional part, but in the Swedish locale, a comma is used as the separator.

The real thrill comes when you submit an entry. Because the converters are locale-sensitive, they interpret the date and number strings correctly no matter which locale you use. The simple loop at the end of the page writes out all entry values with their native Java formatting, so you can see that they are interpreted correctly.

Maybe you're curious about the localized Type selection menu values. I fixed that by implementing a new method in the EntryHandler class for getting the available choices with localized labels:

```
public List getI18nChoices( ) {
    FacesContext context = FacesContext.getCurrentInstance( );
    Locale locale = context.getViewRoot( ).getLocale( );
    ResourceBundle bundle =
        ResourceBundle.getBundle("entryTypes", locale);
    List i18nChoices = new ArrayList( );
    Iterator i = expenseTypes.entrySet( ).iterator( );
    while (i.hasNext( )) {
        Map.Entry me = (Map.Entry) i.next( );
        i18nChoices.add(new SelectItem(me.getValue( ),
            getResource(bundle, (String) me.getKey( ))));
    }
    return i18nChoices;
}

private String getResource(ResourceBundle bundle, String key) {
    key = key.replaceAll(" ", "_");
    String resource = null;
    try {
        resource = bundle.getString(key);
    }
    catch (MissingResourceException e) {
        resource = "???" + key + "???";
    }
    return resource;
}
```

The getI18nChoices( ) method works the same as the other methods for getting the choices we've looked at earlier, except that it uses the Map keys as resource bundle keys to look up the localized value. Because the Map keys may contain spaces (e.g., "Rental Car") and spaces are not allowed in bundle keys, the getResource( ) helper method replaces all spaces in the key with underscore characters. It also catches the MissingResourceException and wraps the key with question marks if it's thrown, to mimic the behavior of the resource Map exposed by the <f:loadBundle> action.

Dealing with Non-Western Languages

Supporting locales with non-Western languages adds another dimension to the subject of localization—namely, the issue of character encoding. As you probably know, the characters displayed on your screen are really represented by sequences of bits. To know which character to display for a sequence of bits, applications (e.g., a browser) consult a mapping between the bit sequences and the characters they represent. ASCII is an early standard mapping; it maps 7 bits (the numerical values 0 through 127) to the characters in the English alphabet, the numbers 0 through 9, punctuation characters, and some control characters. That was all that was really needed in the early days of computing, because most computers were kept busy crunching numbers.

But as computers were given new tasks, often dealing with human-readable text, 7 bits didn't cut it. Adding one bit made it possible to represent all letters used in the Western European languages, but it was not enough to represent all characters used around the world. This problem was partly solved by defining a number of standards for using eight bits to represent different character subsets. Each of the 10 ISO-8859 standards defines what is called a *charset*: a mapping between eight bits (a byte) and a character. For instance, ISO-8859-1, also known as Latin-1, defines the subset used for Western European languages such as English, French, Italian, Spanish, German, and Swedish. ISO-8859-1 is the default charset for HTTP. Other standards in the same series are ISO-8859-2, covering Central and Eastern European languages such as Hungarian, Polish, and Romanian, and ISO-8859-5, with Cyrillic letters used in Russian, Bulgarian, and Macedonian. Chinese, Japanese and Korean contain thousands of characters but with 8 bits, you can only represent 256. A number of multibyte charsets have therefore been defined to handle these languages, such as Big5 for Chinese, Shift_JIS for Japanese, and EUC-KR for Korean.

As you can imagine, all these different standards make it hard to exchange information encoded in different ways. To solve this problem, companies such as Apple, IBM, Microsoft, Novell, Sun, and Xerox founded the Unicode Consortium in 1991, and defined the Unicode standard. Unicode uses 2 bytes (16 bits) to define unique codes for 49,194 characters in Version 3.0, covering most of the world's languages. Java uses Unicode for its internal representation of characters, and Unicode is also supported by many other technologies, like XML and LDAP. Unicode support is included in all modern browsers, e.g., Netscape and Internet Explorer since Version 4. To learn more about Unicode, visit *http://www.unicode.org/*.

What does this all mean to web application developers? Well, since ISO-8859-1 is the default charset for HTTP, you don't have to worry about character encoding at all when you work with Western languages. But if you provide content in another language, such as Japanese or Russian, you must tell the browser which charset you're using so it can interpret and render the characters correctly. If the files that you serve contain characters encoded with a charset other than ISO-8859-1, you must inform the web container.

We're using JSP pages to build the JSF responses, so let's focus on the JSP features that deal with character encoding. JSP is Java, so the web container uses Unicode internally, but the JSP page is typically stored using another encoding, and the response may need to be sent to the browser with yet another encoding. There are two JSP page directive attributes that specify these charsets. The `pageEncoding` attribute specifies the charset for the bytes in the JSP page itself, so the container can translate them to Unicode when it reads the file. The `contentType` attribute can contain a charset in addition to the MIME type, as shown in Figure 11-3. This charset tells the container to convert the Unicode characters used internally to the specified charset encoding when the response is sent to the browser. It also sets the charset attribute in the `Content-Type` response header that tells the browser how to interpret the response. If a `pageEncoding` is not specified, the charset specified by the `contentType` attribute is used to interpret the JSP file bytes as well, and vice versa (if a `pageEncoding` is specified but not a `contentType` charset). If a charset is not specified at all, ISO-8859-1 is used for both the file and the response.*

Enough theory. Figure 11-3 shows a simple JSP page that sends the text "Hello World" in Japanese to the browser. The Japanese characters are copied with permission from Jason Hunter's *Java Servlet Programming* (O'Reilly).

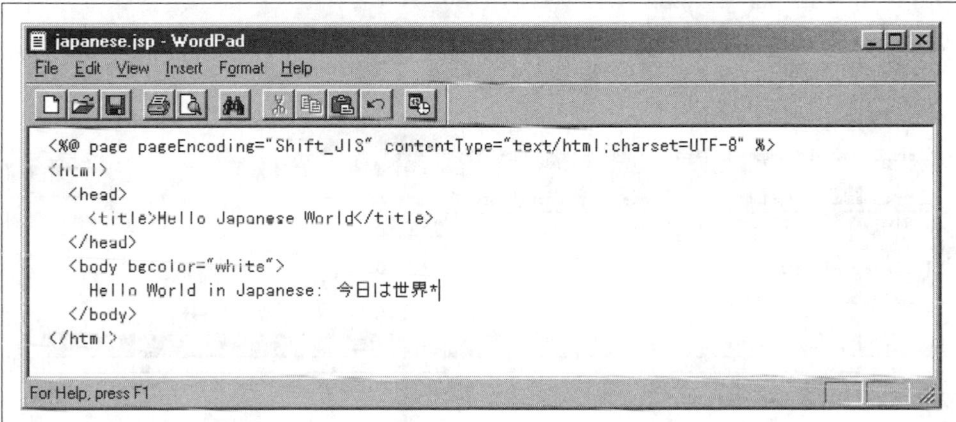

Figure 11-3. Japanese JSP page (japanese.jsp)

To create a file with Japanese or other non-Western European characters, you obviously need a text editor that can handle multibyte characters. The JSP page in Figure 11-3 was created with WordPad on a Windows system, using a Japanese font called MS Gothic, and saved as a file encoded with the Shift_JIS charset. Shift JIS is therefore the charset specified by the `pageEncoding` attribute, so the container knows how to read the file. The `contentType` attribute, using the `charset` attribute, specifies another charset called UTF-8 for the response. UTF-8 is an efficient charset that encodes Unicode characters as one, two, or three bytes, as needed, and is supported by all modern browsers (e.g., Netscape and Internet Explorer, Version 4 or later). It can be used for any language, assuming the browser has access to a font with the language character symbols.

Note the page directive that defines the charset for the file must appear as early as possible in the JSP page, before any characters that can be interpreted only when the charset is known. I recommend you insert it as the first line in the file to avoid problems.

* For a JSP Document (a JSP page in XML format), UTF-8 or UTF-16 is the default, as determined by the XML parser.

If you pull strings from a resource bundle file, you must also do a bit of work for non-Western languages. The resource bundle file itself must be ISO-8859-1–encoded, but there's a tool bundled with the Java 2 SDK called *native2ascii* that you can use to convert a file in any encoding to ISO-8859-1 encoding. See the Java SDK documentation for details (*http://java.sun.com/j2se/1.4.2/docs/tooldocs/windows/native2ascii.html*).

To illustrate how all this works, I developed a simple test page that displays the current date formatted according to the Japanese, Greek, and Russian locales. Figure 11-4 shows what it looks like.

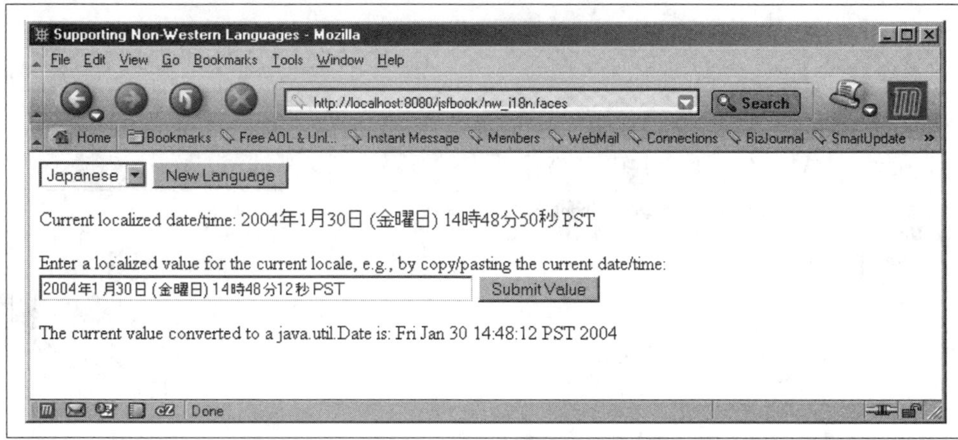

Figure 11-4. Test page for non-Western locales

You can switch between the locales by choosing one in the selection list and clicking the New Language button. The page also includes an input field for a date/time value in a format that corresponds to the currently selected locale and a button to submit it. If the value can be interpreted as a date/time value, it's printed in Java's standard format at the bottom of the page.

Example 11-4 shows the JSP page for the test page.

Example 11-4. Test page for non-Western languages (nw_i18n.jsp)

```
<%@ page contentType="text/html;charset=UTF-8" %>
<%@ taglib uri="http://java.sun.com/jsf/html" prefix="h" %>
<%@ taglib uri="http://java.sun.com/jsf/core" prefix="f" %>

<jsp:useBean id="now" scope="request" class="java.util.Date" />
<f:view locale="#{param['i18n:locale'] == null ? 'ja' : param['i18n:locale']}">
  <html>
    <head>
      <title>
        Non-Western Languages Localization
      </title>
    </head>
    <body bgcolor="white">
```

Example 11-4. Test page for non-Western languages (nw_i18n.jsp) (continued)

```
      <h:form id="i18n">
        <h:selectOneMenu id="locale" value="#{view.locale.language}">
          <f:selectItem itemValue="ja" itemLabel="Japanese" />
          <f:selectItem itemValue="el" itemLabel="Greek" />
          <f:selectItem itemValue="ru" itemLabel="Russian" />
        </h:selectOneMenu>
        <h:commandButton value="New Language" />
        <p>
        Current localized date/time:
        <h:outputText value="#{now}">
          <f:convertDateTime datestyle="full" timestyle="full" />
        </h:outputText>
        <p>
        Enter a localized value for the current locale, e.g., by copy/pasting
        the current date/time:<br>
        <h:inputText size="50" value="#{input}">
          <f:convertDateTime datestyle="full" timestyle="full"/>
        </h:inputText>
        <h:commandButton value="Submit Value" />
        <p>
        The current value converted to a java.util.Date is:
        ${input}
      </h:form>
    </body>
  </html>
</f:view>
```

A JSP page directive at the top of the page declares this page produces a UTF-8–encoded response. If you don't hardcode a response encoding, the container picks an encoding that can be used for the selected locale—but it may not be the one you want. A J2EE 1.4 (Servlet 2.4 and JSP 2.0) container provides a standardized way to map locales to encodings in the *web.xml* file (see Appendix F for details) so you have full control over the selection, but if you use a J2EE 1.3 (Servlet 2.3 and JSP 1.2) container, the mapping is implementation dependent. I recommend that you always hardcode UTF-8, unless you must support browsers without UTF-8 support (such browsers are very rare).

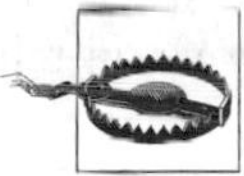

Be aware that the J2EE 1.3 specifications are vague regarding which encoding wins if you declare a hardcoded encoding with the page directive and then set the locale in the page body, so the container may choose a different locale than the one you declared. If at all possible, use a J2EE 1.4 container, for which this issue has been clarified (the hardcoded encoding always wins).

The locale is set by an `<f:view>` action as before, but Example 11-4 has a more complex JSF EL expression as the value. It uses the conditional operator to set the locale either to the value of a request parameter named `i18n:locale` or to "ja" (Japanese) if there is no parameter with that name. If you look further down in Example 11-4, you'll see there's an `<h:selectOneMenu>` action element with an `id` attribute set to `locale`, nested within an `<h:form>` action element with an `id` attribute set to `i18n`. The name of the request parameter that holds the value of an input component is made up from the ID of the form and the input component itself, separated by a colon, because a form is a naming container (I'll get back to what a naming container is in Chapter 12). Hence, the request parameter named `i18n:locale` holds the code for the selected locale and the `<f:view>` action element uses it to set the view locale. The first time the page is requested, the parameter isn't included, so Japanese is used as the default locale.

The `<h:selectOneMenu>` action element uses another funny-looking JSF EL expression as its value. It looks up the `locale` property value of the `UIViewRoot` component and then gets the value of the `Locale` instance's `language` property. The nested `<f:selectItem>` elements define choices with the language codes for Japanese, Greek, and Russian as their values; as a result, the previously selected locale is shown as the current choice for each new request.

An `<h:outputText>` action element with its nested `<f:convertDateTime>` element creates an output component that displays the current date and time, represented by a `java.util.Date` variable created by a JSP `<jsp:useBean>` action at the top of the page. Before we move on, you may want to switch between the locales and see how the current date/time value changes. Because the view's locale changes when you pick a new locale from the list, the output component's converter knows how to format the value correctly.

The character encoding also plays a crucial role when it comes to processing input. A regular HTTP request can only contain parameter values made up from the characters defined by the ISO-8859-1 charset, so the browser must encode all other characters entered in input fields in terms of the allowed characters. It encodes each nonstandard character as a string, starting with a percent sign followed by a hexadecimal value for the character, e.g., `%E4`. The problem is that the hexadecimal value only makes sense if you know which charset it comes from. And even though the HTTP specification says that the charset name must be sent in the `Content-Type` request header, most browsers don't. Luckily, all commonly used browsers use the charset of the response containing the form to encode the parameter values when the form is submitted. As long as you keep track of the response encoding, you can tell the container which charset to use to decode the parameter values. JSF hides this complexity as long as your application doesn't disable session tracking. At the end of the Render Response phase, JSF saves the character encoding used for the response in a session variable, and before reading any request parameters from the next request for the view, it tells the container to use the same encoding. If you run into problems in this area, first confirm that session tracking is working. Make sure all your users have cookies enabled, or that you use JSF components for all links so they include the session ID when cookies are disabled.

The JSP page in Example 4-1 contains an `<h:inputText>` action that creates an input component with a date/time converter so you can try this out. Enter a value that matches the currently selected locale, e.g., by copying the current date/time value, and submit the form. If the value can be interpreted as a valid date/time value, the JSP EL expression at the end of the page picks it up from where the input component saved it and adds it to the response in its native format. If the value is invalid, the invalid value remains in the input field (so you can correct it), but no value is stored for the JSP EL expression to pick up.

Internationalizing an application is a lot of work, as you've seen in this chapter, but if you're reasonably sure that you will have to do it sooner or later, I suggest that you do it up front. Retrofitting an application for internationalization later is boring and involves a lot more work than doing it from the start.

CHAPTER 12

Odds and Ends

At this point, we've developed most of the expense report application and discussed many JSF features along the way. But I've left out a few that don't fit the scope of the preceding chapters, and some that are not needed for the sample application but may be useful in other applications. I discuss most of these features in this chapter and cover the rest in the remaining chapters.

Building a View from Many JSP Files

In the preceding chapters, we've worked with the different areas of the sample application as separate pages. Besides making it easier to explain the features one by one without overwhelming you with unrelated details, this approach also make sense for developing a real application, because you can work with smaller files that are easier to grasp and debug. At some point, though, you need to put all the pieces together. There are two ways to build up a JSF view from multiple JSP files: statically include all pieces into one file when the JSP page is transformed into a servlet and compiled, or dynamically include the files each time the main file is requested.

The JSP include directive (`<%@ include file="..." %>`) supports the static include option. It includes the contents of the specified file, whether it's a file with just plain markup elements or a file with JSP elements. Because the include is processed when the page is transformed into a servlet, the name of the file to include must be entered as a static value. When a JSP file is included this way, it shares the page scope (and all other scopes) and all scripting variables with the including file. The included file is rarely a syntactically complete JSP or HTML page; I recommend that you use a different file extension to highlight this fact. Any extension will do, but *.jspf* and *.htmlf* are good choices ("f" stands for "fractional" or "fragment"). The container is not required to detect changes in a file included by the include directive and, therefore, may not recompile the including file when the included file is changed. Most modern containers, such as Tomcat 5, do detect these changes, however.

The include action (<jsp:include page="..." />) as well as the JSTL import action (<c:import url="..." />) support dynamic includes. They both include the response produced by executing the specified resource (e.g., a JSP page or a servlet), which can be named by a JSP EL or Java expression evaluated at runtime. The included resource has access to the same scopes as the including file except for the page scope, and the container always detects when it's changed and recompiles it when needed. The standard include action only includes the content produced by a resource in the same web application, while the JSTL import action includes content from resources either in the same web application, a separate web application in the same container, or an external server accessible through a supported protocol (e.g., HTTP or FTP). For a resource in the same web application, it works exactly like the standard include action.

Note that a dynamically included page can't set response headers or status codes for things like cookies or redirect requests. With JSF, that's rarely a problem because each request is always processed by a servlet (which can set these things before the JSP page is processed), but if you mix regular JSP pages and JSP pages containing JSF components, it may be an issue to consider.

The following general JSP rules of thumb will help you pick the most appropriate include mechanism:

- Use the include directive (<% include ... %>) for files that rarely change and are known at development time, e.g., headers and footers. The including and included files are merged in the translation phase, so there's no runtime overhead. Be aware, though, that including large files may cause the generated _jspService() method to run into the size limit for a Java method (64 KB) in some containers. Even in a container with a more sophisticated code generation algorithm, using the include directive means the file is replicated in the class files for all JSP pages that include it, increasing the overall memory requirements for the application.
- Use the include directive (<% include ... %>) if the included file must set response headers, or redesign the application so that included pages never have to do this.
- You may want to use either the standard include action (<jsp:include>) or the JSTL import action (<c:import>) for a file that is likely to change, for instance, a navigation menu or a file containing a shared part with lots of layout and style options (such as a "news flash" box), and you must use one of these actions when the file to include isn't known until runtime. Of the two, the JSTL import action is more flexible, as it can include both local and external resources. It's also more strictly defined in terms of what happens when the include fails, so it can safely be combined with JSTL <c:catch> for finely grained error handling. Due to its flexibility, it may be slightly less efficient than the standard include action, but not enough to matter in most cases.

For pages containing JSF components, there are additional concerns to be aware of when you use dynamic includes, described later in this chapter. Unless you have to use dynamic includes (say, because the page to include isn't known until runtime), I recommend that you use static includes for all pages containing JSF component action elements.

Using Static Includes for Pages with JSF Components

Static includes for JSP pages containing JSF component actions work the same as for regular JSP pages. I use static includes to piece together the sample application, because the main reason for splitting it up in the first place is maintainability. All filenames are known at development time and using static includes avoid the runtime penalty and other issues, as described earlier.

Example 12-1 shows the top level JSP page, i.e., the one the pulls in all the other ones.

Example 12-1. The top-level page for the sample application (expense/final/reports.jsp)

```
<%@ page contentType="text/html" %>
<%@ taglib uri="http://java.sun.com/jsf/html" prefix="h" %>
<%@ taglib uri="http://java.sun.com/jsf/core" prefix="f" %>
<%@ taglib uri="http://mycompany.com/jsftaglib" prefix="my" %>

<html>
  <head>
    <title>Expense Reports</title>
    <link rel="stylesheet" type="text/css"
      href="${pageContext.request.contextPath}/style.css">
  </head>
  <body bgcolor="white">
    <f:view locale="#{userProfile.locale}">
      <f:loadBundle basename="labels" var="labels" />
      <table width="95%" align="center">
        <tr>
          <td colspan="2">
            <!-- Title -->
            <h:outputText value="#{labels.applicationTitle}"
              styleClass="title" />
          </td>
        </tr>
        <tr>
          <td colspan="2" class="toolbar">
            <!-- Menu -->
            <h:form>
              <%@ include file="menuArea.jspf" %>
            </h:form>
          </td>
        </tr>
        <tr>
          <td valign="top" width="60%">
            <!-- Reports -->
```

Example 12-1. The top-level page for the sample application (expense/final/reports.jsp) (continued)

```
          <h:form>
            <%@ include file="reportsArea.jspf" %>
          </h:form>
        </td>
        <td valign="top">
          <!-- Details -->
          <%@ include file="detailsArea.jspf" %>
        </td>
      </tr>
    </table>
    <h:messages globalOnly="true" />
  </f:view>
 </body>
</html>
```

At the top of the page, there's a JSP page directive that declares the content type for the response generated by the page and `taglib` directives for all tag libraries used in this page, as well as in the included pages for the different screen areas. Because this is the top-level page, it contains the `<html>`, `<head>`, and `<body>` HTML elements, including a link to the stylesheet for the application in the same way as for the styled page we looked at in Chapter 10. It also contains the `<f:view>` action element and an `<f:loadBundle>` action element, setting the locale for the view to the one selected in the preferences page and loading the localized resource bundle as I described in Chapter 11. At the bottom of the page, there's an `<h:message>` action for displaying possible error messages not associated with specific components, such as messages about problems accessing the report registry.

Other than that, this page uses HTML table elements for the layout of the different areas and `<%@ include file="..." %>` directives to include each area. Note that all the included files have a *.jspf* extension. As I described earlier, this means they are incomplete JSP pages, e.g., they don't have the `taglib` directives so they don't work if you request them directly.

Using one or multiple forms

In Example 12-1, two of the files (*menuArea.jspf* and *reportsArea.jspf*) are included within `<h:form>` elements, and the third (*detailsArea.jspf*) in turn includes two other files within `<h:form>` elements. Using more than one form per JSF view may cause some unwanted side effects. Forget about JSF for a bit and imagine a plain HTML page with two forms. If the user enters values in both forms and then submits one of them, the browser sends a request to the server with request parameters for all input fields in the form that was submitted. The input added in the other form isn't sent to the server at all, so it's lost. This behavior is expected in HTML because the response to the request is usually a brand new page, generated based on the data in the submitted form. With JSF, however, the same page is often redisplayed, so it's more likely that the lost input is noticeable and may cause confusion. Another thing to be aware of is that when view state is saved in the client, it's typically included as a hidden field in each form. Using multiple forms therefore increases the response size, which may be a concern for low bandwidth connections.

Sometimes using more than one form for a JSF view is preferable in order to avoid other confusing side effects related to using just one form. When you submit a form, JSF runs through the request processing lifecycle phases for all components that belong to the submitted form, including validation. Normally, this is what you want, but consider the different screen areas in the sample application. If all components belong to the same form, trying to submit a report or delete a report entry may fail due to validation errors if an unrelated value in, say, the entry form area is missing or invalid. That's why I use multiple forms in the sample application: one for the menu area, one for the whole reports area, and one each for the entry form and the entry list.

There's no right or wrong choice here. In general, though, I suggest that you try to stick to just one form to keep it simple. Use multiple forms only when the risk for failure due to unrelated validation errors outweighs the potential confusion caused by potential loss of input in the nonsubmitted forms.

The included files

Let's look at some of the files included by the top-level page. The first one is *menuArea.jspf*, shown in Example 12-2.

Example 12-2. The final menu area page (expense/final/menuArea.jspf)

```
<table cellpadding="0" cellspacing="0" width="100%">
  <tr>
    <td>
      <h:commandButton value="#{labels.newButtonLabel}"
        disabled="#{reportHandler.newDisabled}"
        action="#{reportHandler.create}" />
      <h:commandButton value="#{labels.deleteButtonLabel}"
        disabled="#{reportHandler.deleteDisabled}"
        action="#{reportHandler.delete}" />
      <h:commandButton value="#{labels.submitButtonLabel}"
        disabled="#{reportHandler.submitDisabled}"
        action="#{reportHandler.submit}" />
      <h:commandButton value="#{labels.acceptButtonLabel}"
        rendered="#{reportHandler.acceptRendered}"
        disabled="#{reportHandler.acceptDisabled}"
        action="#{reportHandler.accept}" />
      <h:commandButton value="#{labels.rejectButtonLabel}"
        rendered="#{reportHandler.rejectRendered}"
        disabled="#{reportHandler.rejectDisabled}"
        action="#{reportHandler.reject}" />
    </td>
    <td align="right">
      <span class="small">
        <h:outputText value="#{labels.loggedInAs}" />
```

Example 12-2. The final menu area page (expense/final/menuArea.jspf) (continued)

```
        "${pageContext.request.remoteUser}"
        [<h:outputLink value="../../logout.jsp">
           <h:outputText value="#{labels.logoutLinkLabel}" />
         </h:outputLink>]
        [<h:outputLink value="prefUser.faces">
           <h:outputText value="#{labels.prefLinkLabel}" />
         </h:outputLink>]
      </span>
    </td>
  </tr>
</table>
```

This should look familiar; it's the internationalized version of the page that we developed in Chapter 11, minus the tag library declarations, the `<f:view>` action, the `<f:loadBundle>` action, and the `<h:form>` action, which are now inherited from the *reports.jsp* page.

Example 12-3 shows the *detailsArea.jspf* page.

Example 12-3. The details area page (expense/final/detailsArea.jspf)

```
<table class="box" width="100%">
  <tr>
    <td>
      <h:outputText value="#{labels.detailsAreaTitle}"
        styleClass="smalltitle" />
    </td>
  </tr>
  <tr>
    <td>
      <!-- Entry form -->
      <h:form>
        <%@ include file="entryFormArea.jspf" %>
      </h:form>
    </td>
  </tr>
  <tr>
    <td>
      <!-- Entry list -->
      <h:form>
        <%@ include file="entryListArea.jspf" %>
      </h:form>
    </td>
  </tr>
</table>
```

It's similar to the top-level page in that it uses HTML table elements layout and includes the entry form and entry list subareas from separate files.

The *reportsArea.jspf* file is almost identical to the *detailsArea.jspf* file, and the files these two include in turn are the final versions of the pages we worked with in the preceding chapters, minus the stuff inherited from the top-level page (just as for the *menuArea.jspf* file). Instead of wasting trees by printing them here, I suggest that you look at them at your leisure. The end result is shown in Figure 12-1.

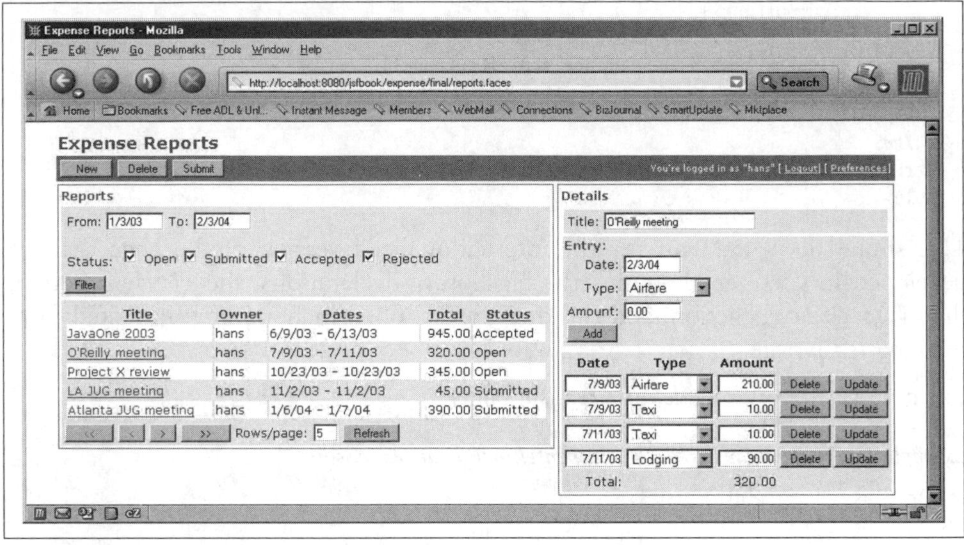

Figure 12-1. The complete expense report screen

Using Dynamic Includes for Pages with JSF Components

Dynamically including JSP pages containing JSF components works almost the same as dynamically including regular JSP pages, but there are a couple of important issues you need to be aware of. When you dynamically include a regular JSP page, the included page is processed and the content it produces is added to the including page's response. The same is true when you dynamically include a JSP page containing JSF components, but only for content that is *not* generated by JSF components. JSF component actions in the included page add components to the component tree created by the including page, and then immediately ask each component to render itself. The result is often not what you expected. Example 12-4 and 12-5 show two pages that illustrate what's happening.

Example 12-4. Top-level page dynamically including another (main.jsp)

```
<%@ page contentType="text/html" %>
<%@ taglib uri="http://java.sun.com/jsf/html" prefix="h" %>
<%@ taglib uri="http://java.sun.com/jsf/core" prefix="f" %>
<html>
  <body>
    <f:view>
      Template text at the top of the main page.
      <br>
      <h:outputText value="Text from a JSF component in the main page" />
      <br>
```

Example 12-4. Top-level page dynamically including another (main.jsp) (continued)

```
      <f:subview id="sv1">
        <jsp:include page="included.jsp" />
      </f:subview>
    </f:view>
  </body>
</html>
```

Example 12-5. Dynamically included page with template data (included.jsp)

```
<%@ taglib uri="http://java.sun.com/jsf/html" prefix="h" %>
<%@ taglib uri="http://java.sun.com/jsf/core" prefix="f" %>
Template text at the top of the included page.
<br>
<h:outputText value="Text from a JSF component in the included page" />
```

When you request the page in Example 12-4, it includes the page in Example 12-5, producing the response shown in Figure 12-2.

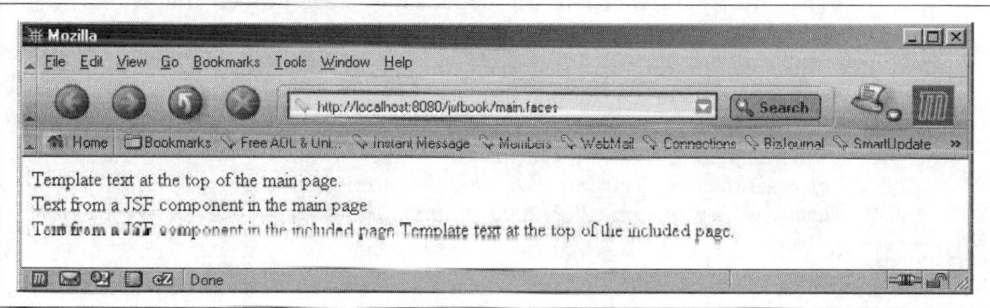

Figure 12-2. Template text out of order

If you look closely, you'll see that the template text from the included page comes *after* the text from the output component in the same page, even though the template text appears *at the top* of the included page in Example 12-5.

What's going on here is caused by a difference in semantics between JSF and JSP. The JSP <jsp:include> action processes the included page, buffers all content the page produces, and then adds it to the response generated by the including page. While processing the included page, however, it invokes the JSF <h:outputText> action, which creates an output component, adds it to the component tree owned by the including page, and asks the component to render itself. And here's the twist: the component renders itself to the response of the *including* page, before the buffered non-JSF content from the included page is added.

To avoid this reordering of content, you must get rid of all non-JSF content in the included page. You can minimize non-JSF content by using JSF action elements like <h:panelGrid> instead of HTML tables for layout and <h:outputText> for all text. For the remainder, you must use the <f:verbatim> action element, as shown in Example 12-6.

Example 12-6. Dynamically included page with <f:verbatim> (included2.jsp)

```
<%@ taglib uri="http://java.sun.com/jsf/html" prefix="h" %>
<%@ taglib uri="http://java.sun.com/jsf/core" prefix="f" %>
<f:verbatim>
  Template text at the top of the included page.
  <br>
</f:verbatim>
<h:outputText value="Text from a JSF component in the included page" />
```

The modified version of the included page wraps the template text within the body of an `<f:verbatim>` action. This action creates an output component with the value set to the content produced by non-JSF actions and template text in its body.

By default, the `<f:verbatim>` action leaves all text alone, but you can use the escape attribute with the value `true` to tell it to convert characters with special meaning (such as the less-than and greater-than signs in HTML) to the corresponding character entity code (`<` and `>`). The `<h:outputText>` action also supports the escape attribute, but with `true` as the default.

This type of escaping is important to minimize the risk for *cross-site scripting* attacks on a site that displays content entered by site visitors. A cross-site scripting attack means that a visitors enters content that, when rendered, creates problems for another visitor, e.g., causing the browser to close. You can read more about this vulnerability at *http://www.cert.org/advisories/CA-2000-02.html*.

With the included file modified as in Example 12-6, the content is generated in the expected order, as shown in Figure 12-3.

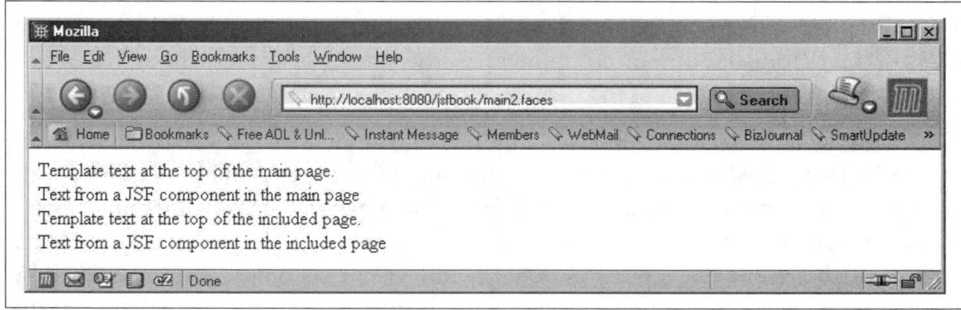

Figure 12-3. Template text wrapped within an <f:verbatim> element

Having to wrap all non-JSF content in `<f:verbatim>` elements is clearly not an elegant solution, and hopefully a better JSF/JSP integration strategy will be defined by future versions of the specifications. Until then, I recommend that you use static includes whenever possible.

Naming containers for included content

You must also use <f:subview> elements when dynamically including JSP pages containing JSF component actions from another JSP page with JSF component actions. In Example 12-4, the <f:subview> is used like this:

```
<f:subview id="sv1">
  <jsp:include page="included.jsp" />
</f:subview>
```

Alternatively, you can put the <f:subview> element in the included page, wrapping all the other elements.

The <f:subview> element creates a naming container component to hold all the included components. You must use an id attribute value that is unique among all component IDs used for components nested within the same <f:view> element. A naming container is a component type that adjusts the markup IDs (e.g., HTML id and name attributes) generated for its children by combining its own component ID with the children's ID. For instance, the HTML name attribute value generated for an <h:inputComponent> with the id attribute value input nested within a naming container component with the id attribute value sv1 is sv1:input. The combined ID is referred to as a client ID in the specification.

Using <f:subview> elements for included components ensures that the markup elements generated for the included components have ID values that are unique within the view, even if you include the same page more than once in the same view or use the same component ID for two components in different included files.

Combining JSF Views with Other Content

In the previous section, I described how to build a JSF view from multiple JSP pages, but sometimes you need to combine the content generated by a JSF view with content generated by other technologies, such as regular JSP pages and static HTML files.

Most web sites use a common layout for all pages, typically with a header at the top, a menu to the left, and footer at the bottom. To simplify maintenance and make it easy to change the site's look, large sites often use tools that pull together each page based on a layout template at runtime. For JSP-based sites, a tool called *Tiles* is commonly used. Tiles is distributed as part of Apache Struts,* but it can also be used independently. Tiles has a lot of features, but the main principle is pretty simple: each page directly requested by the user calls on a layout template to generate the response from the data the page tells the template to use. Example 12-7 shows a simple Tiles layout template.

* Struts is available at *http://jakarta.apache.org/struts/*.

Example 12-7. Tiles layout template (tilesLayout.jsp)

```
<%@ taglib uri="http://jakarta.apache.org/struts/tags-tiles" prefix="tiles" %>
<html>
  <body bgcolor="white">
    <table width="100%">
      <tr>
        <td colspan="2" align="center">
         <tiles:insert attribute="header" />
        </td>
      </tr>
      <tr>
        <td width="20%">
         <tiles:insert attribute="menu" />
        </td>
        <td>
         <tiles:insert attribute="body" />
        </td>
        <td>
         <tiles:insert page="poll.jsp" />
        </td>
      </tr>
    </table>
  </body>
</html>
```

The template is a JSP page. At the top, there's a `taglib` declaration for the Tiles tag library bundled with Struts. The rest of the page consists of HTML table elements defining the layout and `<tiles:insert>` action elements inserting the content from named sources. The action supports many different kinds of content sources. In Example 12-7, I use the `attribute` attribute to pull the content from an attribute provided by each page and the `page` attribute to explicitly name a JSP page, but there are many other options.

The last `<tiles:insert>` element inserts a page named *poll.jsp*, which is a JSP page with JSF components. It's shown in Example 12-8.

Example 12-8. A JSF-based poll page (poll.jsp)

```
<%@ taglib uri="http://java.sun.com/jsf/html" prefix="h" %>
<%@ taglib uri="http://java.sun.com/jsf/core" prefix="f" %>

<f:view>
  <h3>Quick Poll</h3>
  What do you think of JSF?
  <h:form>
    <h:panelGrid columns="1">
      <h:commandLink action="#{poll.vote1}">
        <h:outputText value="It rocks!" />
      </h:commandLink>
      <h:commandLink action="#{poll.vote2}">
        <h:outputText value="It seems okay" />
      </h:commandLink>
```

Example 12-8. A JSF-based poll page (poll.jsp) (continued)

```
      <h:commandLink action="#{poll.vote3}">
        <h:outputText value="It sucks!" />
      </h:commandLink>
    </h:panelGrid>
  </h:form>
  <h:panelGrid columns="2" rendered="#{poll.showScore}">
    <h:outputText value="Total votes:" />
    <h:outputText value="#{poll.total}" />
    <h:outputText value="It rocks!" />
    <h:outputText value="#{poll.vote1Score}%" />
    <h:outputText value="It seems okay" />
    <h:outputText value="#{poll.vote2Score}%" />
    <h:outputText value="It sucks!" />
    <h:outputText value="#{poll.vote3Score}%" />
  </h:panelGrid>
</f:view>
```

The details aren't really the point of this example, but the *poll.jsp* page is a JSP page with JSF components for displaying three alternative answers as links—bound to action methods counting the votes—and other components for displaying the current score. What is important is that it's a page with JSF components.

Example 12-9 shows one of the pages applying the template.

Example 12-9. A page applying the template (page1.jsp)

```
<%@ page contentType="text/html" %>
<%@ taglib uri="http://jakarta.apache.org/struts/tags-tiles" prefix="tiles" %>

<tiles:insert page="tilesLayout.jsp">
  <tiles:put name="header" value="header.html" />
  <tiles:put name="menu" value="menu.html" />
  <tiles:put name="body" value="body1.html" />
</tiles:insert>
```

It's also a JSP page with the Tiles tag library declaration at the top. The rest of the page contains just Tiles action elements. The `<tiles:insert>` element tells Tiles to use the layout template in Example 12-7 with the attribute values defined by the `<tiles:put>` elements. These elements define the files to use as the header, menu, and body of the final, laid-out page. For this simple example, all files are simple HTML files, but they could just as well be JSP pages or even servlets or pages for some other presentation technology.

Two more files, named *page2.jsp* and *page3.jsp* (which are identical to the one in Example 12-9, except for the body filename), complete the example. Requesting *page1.jsp* and clicking on the poll answers a few times results in a response like the one shown in Figure 12-4.

The response contains the content from the shared header and menu HTML files, the page-specific HTML file, and the shared JSP page with the poll JSF components,

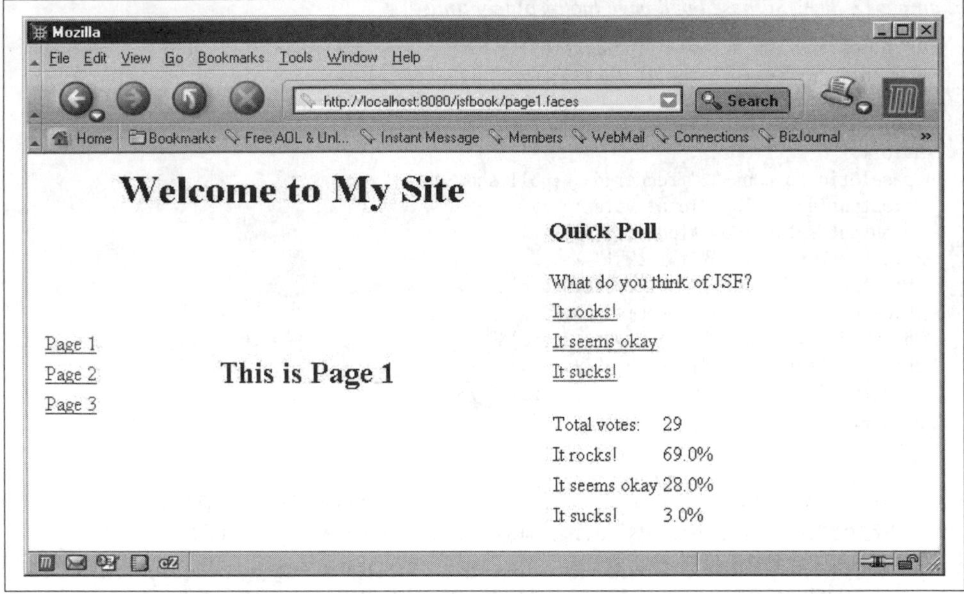

Figure 12-4. Response combining JSF content with other content

as expected. The crucial piece of the puzzle, though, is the URL used to request the *page1.jsp* file. It must be a URL that matches the pattern used for JSF requests, i.e., ending in *.faces* when you use the standard extension mapping. Requesting the page as a regular JSP page, i.e., with a *.jsp* extension, doesn't work because it doesn't invoke JSF. Trying to work around this and invoke JSF through the include mechanism instead (for example, by using *poll.faces* as the URL in the Tiles action elements) also fails, because the JSF 1.0 servlet only works if it's invoked directly, not when it's included by another resource. It's possible that some of this may be improved in a future version of the JSF specification.

If the template refers to more than one page containing JSF components, you must also apply the techniques described in the previous section regarding dynamic includes. Specifically, the page that includes the others (e.g., the layout page) must have the `<f:view>` element and the included pages must be wrapped in `<f:subview>` elements and must only contain JSF actions—no template text or non-JSF action elements, unless they are wrapped within `<f:verbatim>` elements.

Dealing with Struts Applications and JSF

The Apache Struts framework is probably the web application framework most widely used today; many people wonder how JSF and Struts fit together, or if JSF in fact replaces Struts. I like to look at it from two different angels: how JSF may be used for existing Struts applications and which technologies to pick for a new project.

Before we look at the different options, a brief review of the main differences in how the two technologies separate application logic and presentation logic makes it easier to come to an informed decision. Figure 12-5 illustrates the main interactions.

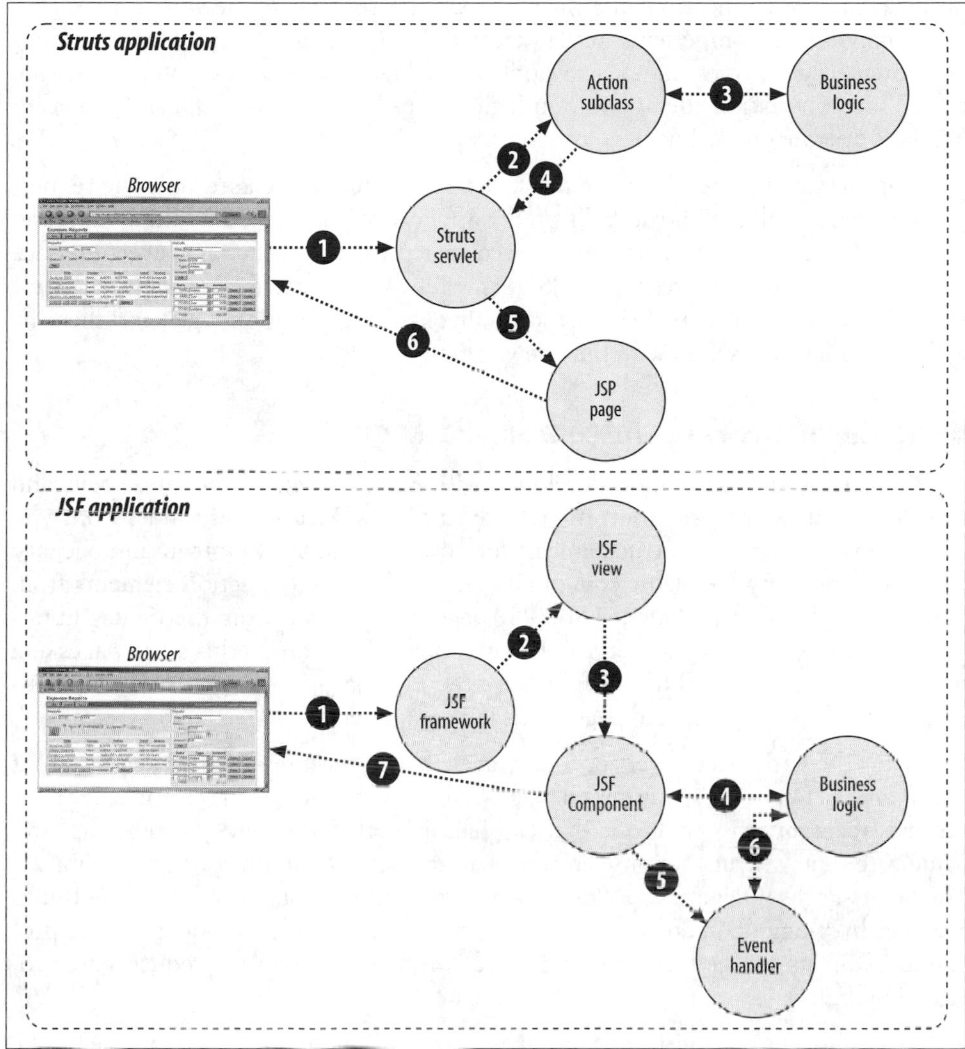

Figure 12-5. Architecture of Struts versus architecture of JSF

The main components in a typical Struts application are the Struts servlet, application logic implemented as Struts `Action` subclasses accessing business logic objects implemented as regular Java classes, and JSP pages for presentation. All requests are targeted to the Struts servlet, which delegates to a specific `Action` subclass identified by parts of the URL. The `Action` subclass does its thing by pulling input from the request data and saving objects representing the result in the request or session scope. It then returns a value that tells the Struts servlet which JSP page to use for the response. The Struts servlet invokes the selected JSP page, which renders a response based on the result objects.

In a typical JSF application, the main players are the JSF framework classes, JSF views containing components (often created by JSP pages), and event handlers implemented as action methods in application logic classes. The components are bound to properties in the application logic or business logic objects, and the event handlers operate on the business logic objects.

Ignoring the details, the difference that takes some time to get used to is the request processing control flow. Struts calls on the application logic to do its thing first, and then invokes a separate presentation piece that turns the result into user interface widgets (i.e., renders the response). JSF first calls on user interface widgets (the view components) to fire events. Event handlers invoke the application logic, and then the widgets render themselves with their new values.

Using the Struts-Faces Integration Package

If you have a large application developed with Struts, using all the latest bells and whistles, such as the validation framework, modules, Struts-Tiles, and so on, you probably want to stick to Struts, at least for now. A Struts-Faces integration package being developed by the Struts community lets you replace the action elements from the Struts and JSTL tag libraries in the JSP pages with actions from the JSF tag libraries representing the more powerful JSF components. You can do this a few pages at a time if you can't do it all at once, because the integration package supports a mixture of the old-style pages and pages with JSF components.

Based on the early access version that's available at the time of this writing, all it takes are a few configuration changes, such as replacing the standard Struts `RequestProcessor` class with one that can handle both Struts and JSF requests, and using a few new Struts action elements that are part of the integration tag library. The Struts-Faces integration package takes care of all the details needed to tie things together by plugging in custom versions of a few JSF classes, so requests to be processed by Struts `Action` subclasses are passed on to Struts, and JSF requests are processed by JSF.

For more information about the Struts-Faces integration package, keep an eye on the Struts home page at *http://www.Jakarta.apache.org/struts/*.

Migrating a Struts Application to JSF

Struts 1.1 and JSF 1.0 are definitely not equivalent in terms of features, and they aren't intended to be. Struts focuses on the Controller part of the MVC triage, with features like declarative navigation and validation, which are more sophisticated than what you find in JSF 1.0. JSF, on the other hand, focuses on the user interface, providing an event-driven component model similar to what's commonly used for standalone GUI applications, while Struts is more or less ignorant about how the user interface is developed.

That said, there's a lot of overlap between the two; converting a Struts application that doesn't use the more advanced Struts features to a pure JSF application is an option to consider. To get a feel for what it takes to convert a Struts application to JSF, let's look at a Struts application that I developed for my book *JavaServer Pages* (O'Reilly). It's a simple billboard service, where employees can post messages related to different projects they are involved with. An employee can customize the application to show only messages about the projects she's interested in. Figure 12-6 shows the three application screens.

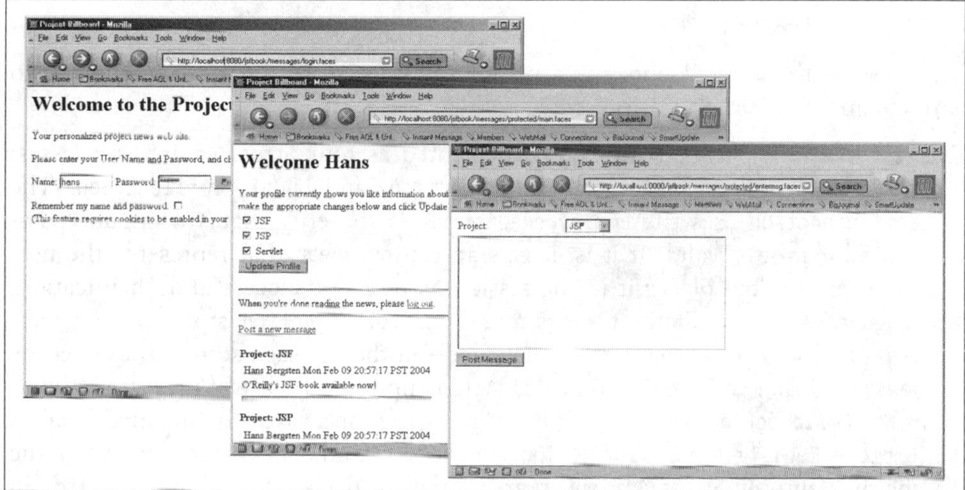

Figure 12-6. Billboard application screens

This application uses application-controlled authentication with a custom login page. The main screen has a form where the user can select projects of interest and a list of matching messages. It also has a link to the third screen, where new messages can be posted, and a logout link.

Figure 12-7 shows all application classes.

Access control is implemented by an `AccessControlFilter` class, which is a filter that processes requests for URLs with */protected* as a path element, which is true for all requests except for authentication and the logout requests. The filter looks for an object in the session scope that serves as proof for successful user authentication. If it finds the object, the filter lets the request pass through to the requested resource; otherwise, it forwards the request to the login screen. A context listener creates an instance of an `EmployeeRegistryBean` that interfaces a database with user information

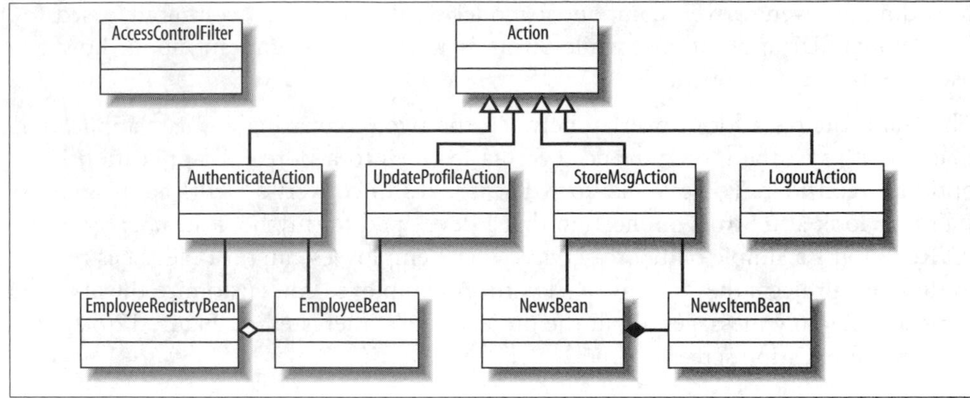

Figure 12-7. Billboard application classes

and a NewsBean that represents an in-memory message store, and saves references to both instances in the application scope.

The rest of the application logic is implemented as four Struts Action subclasses: AuthenticateAction, LogoutAction, StoreMsgAction, and UpdateProfileAction. The AuthenticateAction uses the EmployeeRegistryBean to verify that a username/password combination is valid. If it is, it gets an EmployeeBean that represents the user from the registry and places it in the session as proof of successful authentication. The LogoutAction invalidates the session. The StoreMsgAction stores a new message—represented by a NewsItemBean instance—in the message store represented by the NewsBean instance. The UpdateProfileAction updates the list of projects of interest in the EmployeeBean representing the current user and saves the updated bean in the EmployeeRegistryBean. The Action subclasses handle navigation between the screens by returning Struts ActionForward instances, declared as global forwards in the Struts configuration file.

All source code for the Struts version of this application is included with the examples for *JavaServer Pages*, available at *http://www.hansbergsten.com/*, in case you want to compare it to the JSF version.

To convert an application like this to JSF, you must do three things: convert the Struts Action subclasses to beans with action methods and properties, update the JSP pages to use JSF components bound to properties in the beans, and define JSF navigation rules matching the Struts global forward declarations. In this particular case, I also replaced the context listener with managed bean declarations, but whether that makes sense depends on the application. You should be able to reuse all model beans without modification.

I also modified the EmployeeRegistryBean to use a Map as its data source instead of a real database, to keep things simple. The content of the registry is configured in the *faces-config.xml* file, and the examples application defines one employee with the username hans and the password secret, in case you want to try it out.

Converting the Struts Action subclasses is by far the most time consuming activity, but it's very straightforward. Example 12-10 shows the original Struts StoreMsgAction class and Example 12-11 shows the JSF version of the same class.

Example 12-10. Struts StoreMsgAction class

```
package com.ora.jsp.servlets;

import java.io.*;
import java.sql.*;
import javax.servlet.*;
import javax.servlet.http.*;
import com.ora.jsp.beans.emp.*;
import org.apache.struts.action.*;

public class UpdateProfileAction extends Action {

    public ActionForward perform(ActionMapping mapping,
        ActionForm form, HttpServletRequest request,
        HttpServletResponse response) throws IOException, ServletException {

        if (request.getMethod( ).equals("POST")) {
            String[] projects = request.getParameterValues("projects");
            if (projects == null) {
                projects = new String[0];
            }
            HttpSession session = request.getSession( );
            EmployeeBean emp =
                (EmployeeBean) session.getAttribute("validUser");
            emp.setProjects(projects);
            EmployeeRegistryBean empReg = (EmployeeRegistryBean)
                getServlet( ).getServletContext( ).getAttribute("empReg");
            try {
                empReg.saveEmployee(emp);
            }
            catch (SQLException e) {
                throw new ServletException("Database error", e);
            }
        }
        ActionForward nextPage = mapping.findForward("main");
        return nextPage;
    }
}
```

Example 12-11. JSF StoreMsgAction class

```
package com.mycompany.messages;

public class StoreMsgAction {
    private NewsBean newsBean;
    private EmployeeBean validUser;
    private String category;
    private String msg;
```

Example 12-11. JSF StoreMsgAction class (continued)

```
    private String requestMethod;

    public void setNewsBean(NewsBean newsBean) {
        this.newsBean = newsBean;
    }

    public void setValidUser(EmployeeBean validUser) {
        this.validUser = validUser;
    }

    public String getCategory( ) {
        return category;
    }

    public void setCategory(String category) {
        this.category = category;
    }

    public String getMsg( ) {
        return msg;
    }

    public void setMsg(String msg) {
        this.msg = msg;
    }

    public void setRequestMethod(String requestMethod) {
        this.requestMethod = requestMethod;
    }

    public String store( ) {
        if ("POST".equals(requestMethod)) {
            NewsItemBean item = new NewsItemBean( );
            item.setCategory(category);
            item.setMsg(msg);
            item.setPostedBy(validUser.getFirstName( ) + " " +
                validUser.getLastName( ));
            newsBean.setNewsItem(item);
        }
        return "success";
    }
}
```

The main difference between the two versions is that properties are used to provide all data needed to perform the action for the JSF version, while the Struts version gets references to what it needs through servlet API calls. Real Struts applications often use an `ActionForm` to capture the form input and let the `Action` read its properties instead of using the servlet API. If you're used to this approach, you may recognize the JSF bean as a combination of the Struts `ActionForm` and `Action` classes. Another difference is that the JSF version doesn't extend any framework class or implement any framework interface.

The JSF version is declared as a request scope managed bean with the newsBean, validUser, and requestMethod properties initialized from value binding expressions in the bean declaration:

```
<faces-config>
  ...
  <managed-bean>
    <managed-bean-name>storeMsgAction</managed-bean-name>
    <managed-bean-class>
      com.mycompany.messages.StoreMsgAction
    </managed-bean-class>
    <managed-bean-scope>request</managed-bean-scope>
    <managed-property>
      <property-name>newsBean</property-name>
      <value>#{newsRegistry}</value>
    </managed-property>
    <managed-property>
      <property-name>validUser</property-name>
      <value>#{validUser}</value>
    </managed-property>
    <managed-property>
      <property-name>requestMethod</property-name>
      <value>#{facesContext.externalContext.request.method}</value>
    </managed-property>
  </managed-bean>
  ...
</faces-config>
```

The category and msg properties are bound to JSF components in the JSP page:

```
<%@ page contentType="text/html" %>
<%@ taglib uri="http://java.sun.com/jsf/html" prefix="h" %>
<%@ taglib uri="http://java.sun.com/jsf/core" prefix="f" %>

<f:view>
  <html>
    <head>
      <title>Project Billboard</title>
    </head>
    <body bgcolor="white">

      <h:form>
        <table>
          <tr>
            <td>Project:</td>
            <td>
              <h:selectOneMenu value="#{storeMsgAction.category}">
                <f:selectItem itemLabel="JSF" itemValue="JSF" />
                <f:selectItem itemLabel="JSP" itemValue="JSP" />
                <f:selectItem itemLabel="Servlet" itemValue="Servlet" />
              </h:selectOneMenu>
            </td>
          </tr>
          <tr>
```

```
            <td colspan=2>
              <h:inputTextarea value="#{storeMsgAction.msg}"
                cols="50" rows="10" />
            </td>
          </tr>
        </table>
        <h:commandButton value="Post Message"
          action="#{storeMsgAction.store}" />
      </h:form>
    </body>
  </html>
</f:view>
```

You can find the source code for all the other classes in the example download, but all action classes follow the same pattern.

The other two types of changes—updating the JSP pages to use JSF components bound to properties in the beans and defining JSF navigation rules—are less dramatic and they are no different from what we've already discussed in the this book. If you're interested in the details for the billboard application, I suggest that you look at the JSP pages and the *faces-config.xml* file in the example download.

Picking the Right Technology for a New Application

If you're about to start the development of a new application, you may feel torn between all the possibilities. I don't have a crystal ball so I can't tell you what the future holds (and even if I did, I doubt it would help much), but based on what has happened with other Java web application technologies over the years, I'm pretty confident that JSF will continue to evolve and incorporate more of the features found in frameworks like Struts. It's also clear that there's broad industry support for JSF, so we're likely to see a lot of JSF implementations, development tools, component kits and add-ons, and training classes and books entering the market in 2004 and beyond.

I suggest that you look primarily for what you need from a framework for the first version of the application. If JSF covers those needs, I recommend that you go for a pure JSF application. If there are Struts features that you know you need for the first version, consider using the Struts-Faces integration package and pick the best parts from each technology.

Programmatically Modifying Components

In all examples you've seen so far, component property values are pulled in from a bean, like here:

```
<h:commandButton value="New" disabled="#{reportHandler.newDisabled}" />
```

I personally like this model, because it provides a clean separation between application logic and user interface components, but it's not the only model supported by

JSF. Some people are used to manipulating component properties programmatically instead. For instance, say you want to highlight an invalid value by turning the text in an input field red and adding a custom error message next to the field. To do so programmatically, you need references to the input component and the output component that holds the error message. Then you need to call the appropriate property setter method on the components.

The most convenient and easiest way to get a reference to a JSF component is using a *component binding*. A component binding is a special type of value binding that JSF uses to bind a component instance to a property in a bean. Here's an example:

```
<%@ page contentType="text/html" %>
<%@ taglib uri="http://java.sun.com/jsf/html" prefix="h" %>
<%@ taglib uri="http://java.sun.com/jsf/core" prefix="f" %>
<f:view>
  <html>
    <body bgcolor="white">
      <h:form>
        Everything but "the kitchen sink":
        <h:inputText validator="#{myBean.validateText}" />
        <h:outputText binding="#{myBean.errorComp}" />
        <br>
        <h:commandButton value="Test" />
      </h:form>
    </body>
  </html>
</f:view>
```

This page contains a form with an input component, an output component, and a command button. If you enter the value "the kitchen sink" as the input value and click the button, a custom validator calls property setter methods on the input and output components to display an error message and turn the input red.

The `binding` attribute for the `<h:outputText>` action element contains a component binding expression pointing to the errorComp property in a managed bean named `myBean`:

```
package com.mycompany.beans;

import javax.faces.component.UIComponent;
import javax.faces.component.html.HtmlOutputText;
import javax.faces.context.FacesContext;

public class MyBean {
    private HtmlOutputText errorComp;

    public void setErrorComp(HtmlOutputText errorComp) {
        this.errorComp = errorComp;
    }

    public HtmlOutputText getErrorComp( ) {
        return errorComp;
    }
    ...
```

JSF calls the setter method when the component is first created and during the Restore View phase for all subsequent request. The reference is therefore always initialized when the bean methods are invoked.

The getter method is more controversial. It may return a component instance created by the bean, possibly preconfigured, depending on runtime conditions. The JSF actions call the getter method when the component is about to be created; if it returns a component instance instead of `null`, the returned instance is added to the component tree. This can be handy for complex configuration cases. One example is a `UIData` component that needs to be configured with different `UIColumn` children depending on runtime conditions, say, for an application that supports ad-hoc database queries. But the getter method can also cause confusion if misused—the returned component may be a different type of component than what the action element represents. I recommend that you use this feature only if you absolutely have to.

With the component binding in place, any method in the same bean (such as the validator method, used in this example) has easy access to the component. The `validator` attribute lets you bind a component to a validator method in a bean instead of using a separate validator instance attached to the component, as we did in Chapter 7. It's an alternative that makes sense when the validation rules apply only to a specific component instance:*

```
        public void validateText(FacesContext context, UIComponent comp,
          Object value) {
          if ("the kitchen sink".equals(value)) {
              errorComp.setValue("I said everything but!");
              errorComp.setStyle("color: red");
              comp.getAttributes( ).put("style", "color: red");
          }
          else {
              errorComp.setValue(null);
              errorComp.setStyle(null);
              comp.getAttributes( ).put("style", null);
          }
        }
    }
```

The validator method takes a `FacesContext`, a `UIComponent`, and an `Object` containing the value as arguments, and it has a `void` return type.

The `validateText( )` method compares the component's value to the string "the kitchen sink". If it's a match, the method sets the value of the output component to an error message and the `style` property to a CSS style that turns the text red.

* Because the `validator` attribute is easier to use than the `<f:validator>` action element, you may want to use it even for common validation needs. One way to do this is to create a managed bean that contains only validation methods that you can bind to from any component.

Note that the data type of the errorComp property in this example is javax.faces.component.html.HtmlOutputText. This is a subclass of the generic UIOutput component class, providing type-safe property accessor methods for all HTML-specific properties the text renderer in the default HTML render kit supports. As you may recall, JSF components can be used with different renderers, so the generic component classes don't have property accessor methods for render-dependent things like CSS styles or field width. To make it slightly easier to work with the combinations of generic components and the HTML renderers defined by JSF, the specification defines a concrete component class for each combination and requires that the JSP component actions create instances of the corresponding concrete class. This makes it possible to use the concrete HTMLOutputText class as the component binding property type and, hence, to set the CSS style for the output component by calling the setStyle( ) method.

Contrast this with how the CSS style for the input component is set in the validateText( ) method. The input component reference is one of the method arguments, so no component binding is needed, but the argument type is the generic UIComponent class. For a generic component class, render-dependent things are set as generic attributes that the renderer then reads. In this example, we know that the input component is in fact an instance of the concrete HtmlInputText class, so an alternative to setting the style as an attribute is to cast the argument to this type and call the type-safe setStyle( ) method instead.

Attribute-Property Transparency

To make life more interesting, and also easier on renderers, JSF provides what's called *attribute-property transparency* in the specification. The transparency is achieved by giving the java.util.Map returned by the getAttributes( ) method special qualities—if the key passed to the get( ) and put( ) methods matches the name of a bean-style property of the component class, the Map uses the property accessor method to read or write the value; otherwise the value is handled as a regular Map entry. You can therefore access both render-dependent attributes (such as style attributes) and render-independent properties (such as a component's value) as if they were all generic attributes, which avoids a lot of typecasting in renderers.

As an example, a renderer can get the value of the submittedValue property from a UIComponent reference without casting the reference to EditableValueHolder (which is the interface that defines the accessor methods for the submittedValue property), like this:

```
public void encodeBegin(FacesContext context,
    UIComponent component) throws IOException {
    ...
    Object submittedValue =
        component.getAttributes( ).get("submittedValue");
    ...
}
```

As an alternative to using a component binding to get hold of a component, there's a findComponent( ) method you can use if you know the component's ID. The bean can be rewritten like this to use this approach instead:

```
package com.mycompany.beans;

import javax.faces.component.UIComponent;
import javax.faces.component.html.HtmlOutputText;
import javax.faces.context.FacesContext;

public class MyBean {
    public void validateText(FacesContext context, UIComponent comp,
      Object value) {

      HtmlOutputText errorComp = (HtmlOutputText)
          comp.findComponent(comp.getId( ) + "Error");

      if ("the kitchen sink".equals(value)) {
          errorComp.setValue("I said everything but!");
          errorComp.setStyle("color: red");
          comp.getAttributes( ).put("style", "color: red");
      }
      else {
          errorComp.setValue(null);
          errorComp.setStyle(null);
          comp.getAttributes( ).put("style", null);
      }
    }
}
```

Here I assume that the ID for the output component is the same as for the input component plus "Error", so you must add the corresponding id attributes for both components in the JSP page.

The findComponent( ) argument value is a string that identifies a component. In the simplest case, it's just a component ID. This works fine if the component you're looking for is part of the same naming container as the component that you call the method on (or the naming container itself). Otherwise, you need to use either a relative or an absolute path, where a colon serves as a path element separator.

An absolute path starts with a colon; for example, ":myForm:myOutput" means "start at the component tree root and locate a naming container with the ID myForm, and then locate a component with the ID myOutput in that naming container." A relative path doesn't start with a colon; for example, "myForm:myOutput" means "unless the component I'm calling this method on is a naming container, search for a parent that is or the view root is found. Using the root or the naming container as the starting point, locate a naming container with the ID myForm, and then locate a component with the ID myOutput in that naming container."

Only three of the standard component classes implement the NamingContainer interface (act as naming containers): UIForm, UIData, and UINamingContainer (created by the <f:subview> action); it's only for children of these component types that you need to worry about the more complex findComponent( ) argument syntax.

Whether to use component bindings or the findComponent( ) method is a matter of taste. I prefer to avoid the whole issue and configure the components in the JSP page by pulling values from a bean instead, as shown in most of the other examples in this book.

Using a PhaseListener

There's an event type we haven't talked about so far, namely the javax.faces.event.PhaseEvent. This is an event that fires before and after each request processing lifecycle phase, invoking all javax.faces.event.PhaseListener instances registered with the javax.faces.lifecycle.Lifecycle infrastructure object responsible for coordinating the request processing.

A very simple application probably doesn't have any use for this event, but it can come in handy in some scenarios. For instance, say that your application relies on an external resource (such as a database). Instead of dealing with the (hopefully rare) situation that the database is unavailable in all component event handlers, you can use a PhaseListener that checks the resource status and navigates to an error page if it's not available. Here's an outline for such a listener:

```
package com.mycompany.event;

import javax.faces.application.NavigationHandler;
import javax.faces.context.FacesContext;
import javax.faces.event.PhaseEvent;
import javax.faces.event.PhaseId;
import javax.faces.event.PhaseListener;

public class CheckResourceListener implements PhaseListener {
    public PhaseId getPhaseId( ) {
        return PhaseId.RESTORE_VIEW;
    }

    public void beforePhase(PhaseEvent event) {
    }

    public void afterPhase(PhaseEvent event) {
        FacesContext context = event.getFacesContext( );
        if (!isEverythingOkay(context)) {
            NavigationHandler nh =
                context.getApplication( ).getNavigationHandler( );
            nh.handleNavigation(context, null, "unavailable");
        }
    }

    private boolean isEverythingOkay(FacesContext context) {
        ...
```

```
            return result;
        }
    }
```

The PhaseListener interface has three methods. The getPhaseId( ) method returns the PhaseId value for the phase the listener wants to be notified in or the PhaseId.ANY_PHASE value in order to be notified in all phases. Here I return PhaseId.RESTORE_VIEW to be notified as early as possible.

The listener is notified by a call to the beforePhase( ) method before the regular processing for the phase begins and by a call to the afterPhase( ) method when the regular phase processing is completed. I've chosen to use another JSF infrastructure class called the javax.faces.application.NavigationHandler to navigate to the error page and, because it relies on having access to a view, I implement all logic in the afterPhase( ) method. If I had implemented the navigation by some other means, e.g., by calling the FacesContext redirect( ) method with a hardcoded path, I could have done it in the beforePhase( ) method instead.

The NavigationHandler is a pluggable class. The default implementation reads the navigation rules in the *faces-config.xml* file and acts accordingly when the handleNavigation( ) method is called. In this example, I call it with a null value for the argument that holds the action method binding expression when the navigation is initiated by the default ActionListener class, because there is no action binding in this case. The outcome argument is set to "unavailable", matching this navigation rule:

```
<navigation-rule>
  <navigation-case>
    <from-outcome>unavailable</from-outcome>
    <to-view-id>/unavailable.jsp</to-view-id>
    <redirect/>
  </navigation-case>
</navigation-rule>
```

Because I've left out the <from-view-id> element, the rule applies to all views in the application, redirecting to a view represented by the *unavailable.jsp* page. This page can display an explanation of what's going on and ask the user to come back later.

The easiest way to register your PhaseListener is by adding a declaration in the *faces-config.xml* file:

```
<faces-config>
  ...
  <lifecycle>
    <phase-listener>
      com.mycompany.event.CheckResourceListener
    </phase-listener>
  </lifecycle>
  ...
</faces-config>
```

Checking the status of an external resource is just one example of how you can use a PhaseListener. Another example is letting a listener handle custom access control as an alternative to the access control filter used for the billboard application we looked at earlier. In the next section, I show you a PhaseListener that captures state information that can then be used for debugging.

Debugging and Error Handling Ideas

JSF is such a new technology that very few best practices for debugging and error handling have emerged yet, but let's look at some possibilities.

Using Standard Java Debugging Techniques

Because JSF lends itself to a design where application logic is implemented as plain Java classes, all the usual techniques—such as Java debuggers and JUnit* test cases—can be used for a large part of the application.

Using Standard Web Application Error Handling

A JSF application is also a servlet-based application, so truly exceptional runtime exceptions can be trapped and handled by error handlers declared in the *web.xml* file:

```
<web-xml>
  ...
  <error-page>
    <exception-type>java.lang.Throwable</exception-type>
    <location>/errorpage.jsp</location>
  </error-page>
  ...
</web-xml>
```

The <error-page> element contains an <exception-type> element that names an exception type and a <location> element with a context-relative path for the resource to invoke if the exception is thrown by any request. The resource can be a JSP page or servlet that displays a friendly message instead of the stack trace most web containers show by default. It can also log information about the error, available as request scope attributes as well as through the implicit pageContext variable in a JSP page. If you need to deal with different types of exceptions in different ways, you can declare more than one error handler. The web container picks the one with an exception type that most closely matches the thrown exception. For more on all of this, I recommend my book *JavaServer Pages* (O'Reilly).

* JUnit is available at *http://www.junit.org/*.

Using Client-Side State Saving During Development

A JSF-specific suggestion is to use client-side state saving during development; in other words, include this declaration in the *web.xml* file:

```
<faces-config>
  ...
  <context-param>
    <param-name>javax.faces.STATE_SAVING_METHOD</param-name>
    <param-value>client</param-value>
  </context-param>
  ...
</faces-config>
```

The first time JSF processes a JSP page with JSF component actions, it creates the components and configures them based on the action element attributes' values. It then saves the whole component tree, either on the server or in the response sent back to the client. When the next request for the same view arrives, JSF restores the saved component tree and does not reconfigure it based on action element attributes in the JSP page. This means that if you change an attribute value in the JSP page, or add or remove an attribute, the changes are ignored as long as the saved state is available.

If you use server-side state saving, one way to get rid of the view state is to kill the session, but this method is not guaranteed to work in all JSF implementations because the specification doesn't say where on the server the state must be saved. While most implementations probably save the state in the session, there are other implementation options.

When you use client-side state saving, the state is always part of the response (typically encoded in hidden form fields in the response) so it can be sent back with the next POST request. But a GET request doesn't include the state, so JSF must recreate the view from the JSP page. You can trigger a GET request in many ways; for example, by selecting the URL in the browser's history list, clicking a link to the page, or typing the URL in the browser's address field. A request without the saved state is guaranteed to create a view from scratch, so all changes you've made in the JSP page are considered in this case.

Capturing State with a PhaseListener

An interesting use of the `PhaseListener` class we discussed in the previous section is to capture data about the request and all components in each phase and save the data where it can be picked up and displayed later. The captured data can be used to better understand what happens in the different phases and to figure out why things don't work as expected.

I developed a `PhaseListener` that captures most data of interest, including the component tree structure, all component attributes and properties, and all variables in the request, session and application scopes, before and after each phase. Figure 12-8 shows an example of a response rendered by a servlet where you can analyze the captured data.

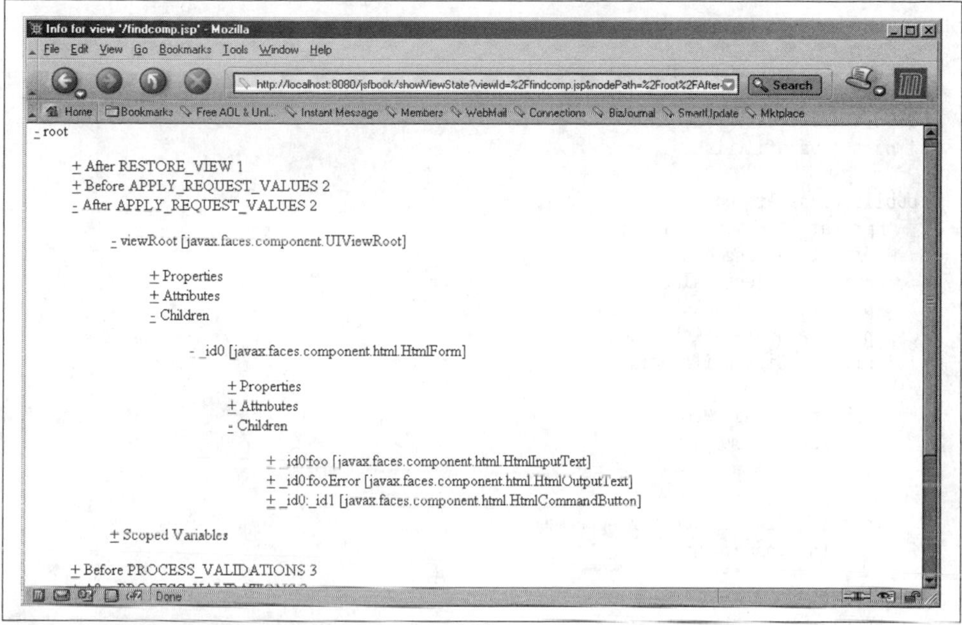

Figure 12-8. Analyzing captured data

The data is displayed as a tree. The first level of the tree has one node for each point in the lifecycle. For each such node, there's a node that holds the component tree and another that holds the scoped variables. You can compare a component's property values in different phases and see when they change. For instance, if you look at an input component, you see how the submitted value migrates from the `submittedValue` property to the `localValue` and `value` properties.

I've commented out the registration elements for this listener in the example application's *faces-config.file* because there's a fair amount of processing overhead when it's used. To try it out, remove the comment, restart the web container (or just the application, if your container allows that), and run a few examples to capture data:

```
<faces-config>
  ...
<!--
  <lifecycle>
    <phase-listener>
      com.mycompany.jsf.event.CaptureStatePhaseListener
    </phase-listener>
  </lifecycle>
-->
  ...
</faces-config>
```

The source code for the listener and the servlet is included in the examples download, so you can look at the details at your leisure and modify the listener to capture additional data that I left out. All captured data is represented as instances of a simple TreeNode class arranged as a tree:

```
package com.mycompany.jsf.model;

import java.util.ArrayList;
import java.util.List;

public class TreeNode {
    private TreeNode parent;
    private String name;
    private Object value;
    private boolean isExpanded;
    private boolean isLeafNode;
    private List children;

    public String getName( ) {
        return name;
    }

    public void setName(String name) {
        this.name = name;
    }

    public Object getValue( ) {
        return value;
    }

    public void setValue(Object value) {
        this.value = value;
    }

    public boolean isExpanded( ) {
        return isExpanded;
    }

    public void setExpanded(boolean isExpanded) {
        this.isExpanded = isExpanded;
    }

    public boolean isLeafNode( ) {
        return isLeafNode;
    }

    public void setLeafNode(boolean isLeafNode) {
        this.isLeafNode = isLeafNode;
    }

    public List getChildren( ) {
        if (children == null) {
            children = new ArrayList( );
```

```
        }
        return children;
    }

    public void addChild(TreeNode child) {
        if (children == null) {
            children = new ArrayList( );
        }
        child.setParent(this);
        children.add(child);
    }

    public String getPath( ) {
        List chain = new ArrayList( );
        chain.add(getName( ));
        TreeNode parent = getParent( );
        while (parent != null) {
            chain.add(parent.getName( ));
            parent = parent.getParent( );
        }
        StringBuffer sb = new StringBuffer( );
        for (int i = chain.size( ) - 1; i >= 0; i--) {
            sb.append("/").append(chain.get(i));
        }
        return sb.toString( );
    }

    private TreeNode getParent( ) {
        return parent;
    }

    private void setParent(TreeNode parent) {
        this.parent = parent;
    }
}
```

The TreeNode class is a bean with five public properties: name, value, isExpanded, isLeafNode, and children. The children property is populated through the addChild( ) method, which also establishes a parent-child relationship used by the getPath( ) method to return a slash-separated absolute path for a node.

The listener creates a tree per view, with subtrees for the before and after data for each phase. For instance, this is how it captures the application scope variables values:

```
package com.mycompany.jsf.event;

import java.util.Map;
import java.util.Map.Entry;
import javax.faces.context.FacesContext;
import javax.faces.event.PhaseEvent;
import javax.faces.event.PhaseId;
import javax.faces.event.PhaseListener;
import com.mycompany.jsf.model.TreeNode;
...
```

```
public class CaptureStatePhaseListener implements PhaseListener {
    ...
    public void beforePhase(PhaseEvent event) {
        String phaseName = event.getPhaseId( ).toString( );
        if (event.getPhaseId( ) != PhaseId.RESTORE_VIEW) {
            capturePhaseData("Before " + phaseName, event.getFacesContext( ));
        }
    }

    public void afterPhase(PhaseEvent event) {
        String phaseName = event.getPhaseId( ).toString( );
        capturePhaseData("After " + phaseName, event.getFacesContext( ));

        if (event.getPhaseId( ) == PhaseId.RENDER_RESPONSE) {
            captureRequestData(event.getFacesContext( ));
        }
    }
    ...
    private void capturePhaseData(String phaseName, FacesContext context) {
        TreeNode root = getRoot(context);

        TreeNode phaseNode = new TreeNode( );
        phaseNode.setName(phaseName);
        root.addChild(phaseNode);
        ...
        TreeNode varNode = new TreeNode( );
        varNode.setName("Scoped Variables");
        phaseNode.addChild(varNode);

        TreeNode appNode = new TreeNode( );
        appNode.setName("applicationMap");
        Map appMap = context.getExternalContext( ).getApplicationMap( );
        addLeafNodes(appNode, appMap);
        varNode.addChild(appNode);
        ...
    }

    private void addLeafNodes(TreeNode parent, Map map) {
        Iterator i = map.entrySet( ).iterator( );
        while (i.hasNext( )) {
            Map.Entry me = (Map.Entry) i.next( );
            TreeNode leaf = new TreeNode( );
            leaf.setLeafNode(true);
            leaf.setName(me.getKey( ).toString( ));
            leaf.setValue(toString(me.getValue( )));
            parent.addChild(leaf);
        }
    }
    ...
}
```

The listener calls the capturePhaseData( ) from the beforePhase( ) and afterPhase( ) methods. The getRoot( ) method creates a new root TreeNode instance for the view or picks up an existing one for the view from a `Map` stored as a session variable. It then creates one `TreeNode` to hold all data for this call and a child `TreeNode` to hold all scoped variables and chains the nodes together with the root node.

Next, the `capturePhaseData( )` method gets a `Map` with all application scope variables from the `ExternalContext` and calls the `addLeafNodes( )` method. The `addLeafNode( )` method loops through the `Map` and creates one leaf node for each variable, with the variable name and value as the node name and value. It then adds the leaf node to the application scope node. The rest of the `CaptureStatePhaseListener` class captures the other data in a very similar way.

The servlet, called `com.mycompany.jsf.servlets.ShowViewStateServlet` and mapped to the URL pattern */showViewState/**, lists all available view state trees if it's called without any parameters or the tree for the view identified by the `viewId` parameter. We won't look at the code here because we're going to replace it with a custom JSF component in Chapter 14.

CHAPTER 13

Developing Custom Renderers and Other Pluggable Classes

The JSF specification includes the basic components most applications need: simple input and output, selection lists, menus and checkboxes, links and buttons, a data grid, and panels for layout. When the provided set of components isn't enough, I recommend that you first look around to see if someone else has developed the component you need. At the time of this writing there are already open source components for the Proposed Final Draft specification version, and when the final specification version is released and JSF gains in popularity, I'm sure there will be plenty of both free and commercial components to pick from. Keep an eye on Sun's JSF site at *http://java.sun.com/j2ee/javaserverfaces* for references to ready-made components.

If you can't find what you're looking for, you need to roll up your sleeves and develop your own components. As you probably recall, JSF uses separate classes for a component's behavior and for component rendering. The component classes implement render-independent behavior, such as pushing and pulling the component value to and from a model property, validating an input value, and firing events. The standard components delegate the tasks of generating content to represent the component in a form suitable for a client device (e.g., as HTML elements for a browser) and figuring out how to decode the request data to get the submitted value for the component to a renderer.

In many cases, you only need to develop a custom renderer for one of the standard components to get the custom behavior you want. For instance, whether you want your users to enter a date by picking it from a calendar, selecting a year, month, and day from three menus, or to write it as a complete date string, the component's behavior—pushing the entered value to the model on submit and pulling it from the model for display—remains the same, so there's no need to develop a custom component. All that's needed is a renderer that generates the content to represent the component value in the desired format. The same is true for more complex components, such as alternative displays of tabular data. Only when you need a component with render-independent behavior not provided by the standard components do you need to implement a custom component class. We will look at examples of custom renderers in this chapter and custom components in Chapter 14.

Besides custom component and renderer classes, JSF allows you to replace most of the infrastructure classes, such as the classes used for evaluation of JSF EL expressions and for navigation. At the end of this chapter, we take a brief look at when you may want to replace some of these classes and how to do it.

Developing Custom Renderers

Developing a custom renderer is relatively simple. All renderers extend an abstract class called `javax.faces.render.Renderer`. Subclasses of this class are attached to components and are responsible for rendering (or *encoding*, as it's called in the specification) the component and, if it's an input component, for decoding the submitted value to the component's internal representation.

A component is equipped with a renderer of a specific type by calling the component's `setRendererType()` method. The renderer type is an identifier that's unique per *component family*. Each component belongs to a component family, which identifies the basic nature of a component, e.g., that it's an output component or a command component. Which renderer class to use for a component is determined by the combination of the renderer type the component is equipped with and the family it belongs to. Picking a renderer class based on the combination of the two IDs makes it possible to use the same, intuitive renderer type IDs for renderer classes with widely different behavior, each class registered for a different component family. For instance, the renderer type ID `javax.faces.Link` combined with the `javax.faces.Output` family can identify a renderer class that renders a regular HTML link element with the component's value as the URL, and the same renderer type ID combined with the `javax.faces.Command` family can identify another renderer class that renders an HTML link element with JavaScript code for submitting the form the component belongs to and with the component's value as the link text. Without the component family concept, one renderer class would have to support both types of components or renderer type IDs would have to include something similar to a family ID in their names, which would lead to namespace scalability problems in the long run.

For the JSP layer, a custom action represents the combination of a component type and a renderer type, so you must implement a custom action tag handler for the combination of a standard component and your custom renderer as well if you want it to be easy to use in a JSP page.

A Renderer for Encoding Only

Let's start with a renderer that only deals with encoding—no decoding. The only standard renderer for the `UIData` component (i.e., the component that represents tabular data) is a renderer that represents the component as an HTML table. Quite often, though, an application needs to render tabular data horizontally: for instance, as a navigation bar with page number links to individual pages in a large query result, as shown in Figure 13-1.

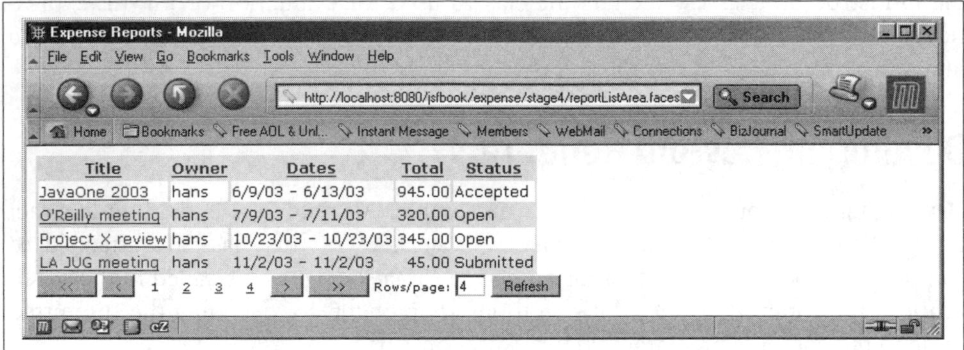

Figure 13-1. Reports lists area with page navigation links

Figure 13-1 shows a new version of the reports list area from the sample application with a page links bar in addition to the first, previous, next, and last page button we used earlier.

To develop and use this custom renderer, there are three things you must do: implement the renderer class, register the renderer class with JSF, and implement a JSP custom action that represents a `UIData` component equipped with the custom renderer.

The new component/renderer combination bound to a data model containing beans representing each report list page can then be added to the original report list area page to renderer the page links bar. Let's take it step by step, starting with the renderer class.

The Renderer class

The links in Figure 13-1 are generated with a custom renderer for the `UIData` component named `com.mycompany.jsf.render.BarRenderer`. Just as for the standard table renderer, the bar renderer uses `UIColumn` children components to represent columns of the tabular data, often a single column child containing a command component with a link renderer for processing a single table column. The bar renderer iterates through the model rows and renders its column children. Unlike the standard table renderer, which nests its children within a `<tr>` element for each row and `<td>` elements for each column, the bar renderer doesn't add any markup elements on its own, so you have full control over the generated content.

The `BarRenderer` class declaration and the first public method look like this:

```
package com.mycompany.jsf.renderer;

import java.io.IOException;
import java.util.Iterator;
import java.util.List;
```

```
import javax.faces.context.FacesContext;
import javax.faces.context.ResponseWriter;
import javax.faces.component.UIColumn;
import javax.faces.component.UIComponent;
import javax.faces.component.UIData;
import javax.faces.component.UIViewRoot;
import javax.faces.render.Renderer;

public class BarRenderer extends Renderer {

    public boolean getRendersChildren( ) {
        return true;
    }
```

The BarRenderer class extends the abstract javax.faces.render.Renderer class and overrides the inherited implementation of the getRendersChildren( ) method to return true instead of false. This is a requirement for a renderer that controls in detail how its children are rendered. The same method exists in the UIComponent class, but a component configured with a renderer delegates the getRendersChildren( ) method call to its renderer by default.

Let's pause for a moment and discuss why getRendersChildren( ) method is needed. If the response to a JSF request was composed solely from JSF components, it could be created simply by asking the root component to recursively render the complete tree. What complicates matters is the fact that, with the JSP layer, the response is composed by combining JSF-generated content with template text and non-JSF action content from the JSP page. Consider this JSP page snippet:

```
<h:form>
  Label: <h:inputText value="#{myBean.myProperty}" />
</h:form>
```

When the JSP container processes this page, it invokes the doStartTag( ) method on the tag handler for the <h:form> action, writes the "Label:" template text to the response, invokes the doStartTag( ) and the doEndTag( ) methods on the tag handler for the <h:inputText> action, and invokes the doEndTag( ) method on the tag handler for the <h:form> action. Unless we're careful here, the template text ends up before the <form> and <input> elements generated by the JSF components. To avoid this, the JSF rendering API defines both an encodeBegin( ) method and an encodeEnd( ) method. For a component that doesn't render its children, like the UIForm component, the tag handler's doStartTag( ) method calls encodeBegin( ), which writes the <form> start tag to the response. The start tag therefore comes before the template text added to the response by the JSP container. The doStartTag( ) method for the <h:inputText> action then writes the single tag for the <input> element, and the doEndTag( ) method for the <h:form> action adds the end tag for the <form> element.

So far so good, but this doesn't work for a component that needs full control over how its children are rendered, like the UIData component. Besides calling the encode methods of the component, a tag handler also creates the component it represents and adds it as a child of the component represented by its parent tag handler. The table renderer for the UIData component uses the children's facets to render the table header and footer elements, and then the children's children to render columns for each row in its data model. Hence, all children must be available already when the UIData encodeBegin( ) method is called, and the tag handlers for the children must not invoke any encode methods on the children. The bar renderer we develop in this section is simpler, but it also need to control how the children are rendered.

To tell the tag handlers when to call the encode methods and which methods to call, the component or its renderer returns true or false from the getRendersChildren( ) method. The tag handler must first call the getRendersChildren( ) method to decide which of the rendering methods to call. If the method return true, it must call encodeBegin( ), encodeChildren( ), and encodeEnd( ) in the doEndTag( ) method and it must not call any encoding methods on the component's children; the component does that itself in its encodeChildren( ) method instead. If getRendersChildren( ) returns false, only encodeBegin( ) and encodeEnd( ) must be called (in doStartTag( ) and doEndTag( ), respectively) and all child components must be asked to render themselves individually.* As with the getRendersChildren( ) method, all encoding methods are part of the UIComponent interface, but a component configured with a renderer delegates the calls to its renderer.

A renderer may split its work between the three rendering methods, as I mentioned. For instance, a renderer that renders a markup element for itself with the children rendered as nested elements may render the start tag in encodeBegin( ) and the end tag in encodeEnd( ), and if it renders its children, render the children's elements in encodeChildren( ). For the BarRenderer, I decided to implement all rendering in the encodeChildren( ) method, which looks like this:

```
public void encodeChildren(FacesContext context, UIComponent component)
    throws IOException {

    if (!component.isRendered( )) {
        return;
    }

    String clientId = null;
    if (component.getId( ) != null &&
        !component.getId( ).startsWith(UIViewRoot.UNIQUE_ID_PREFIX)) {
        clientId = component.getClientId(context);
    }

    ResponseWriter out = context.getResponseWriter( );
    if (clientId != null) {
        out.startElement("span", component);
```

* The same rules applies to any type of class that asks a component to render itself, such as those used with a custom ViewHandler, as described in Chapter 15.

```
            out.writeAttribute("id", clientId, "id");
        }

        UIData data = (UIData) component;

        int first = data.getFirst( );
        int rows = data.getRows( );
        for (int i = first, n = 0; n < rows; i++, n++) {
            data.setRowIndex(i);
            if (!data.isRowAvailable( )) {
                break;
            }

            Iterator j = data.getChildren( ).iterator( );
            while (j.hasNext( )) {
                UIComponent column = (UIComponent) j.next( );
                if (!(column instanceof UIColumn)) {
                    continue;
                }
                encodeRecursive(context, column);
            }
        }

        if (clientId != null) {
            out.endElement("span");
        }
    }
```

The encodeChildren( ) method first checks the value of the component's rendered property. All components have this property, and it can be set to false to temporarily hide a component without removing it from the view. If the rendered property is false, the encodeChildren( ) method returns immediately.

Next comes a bit of code for figuring out if the component has an ID, and if so, whether it's assigned by the page author or automatically assigned. If the ID starts with a character defined by the UIViewRoot.UNIQUE_ID_PREFIX constant (an underline character), it must be automatically assigned, because the JSP component actions are required to assign an ID with this prefix for components without an id attribute, and the id attribute value a page author assigns is not allowed to start with this character. The point of these rules is to ensure that an explicitly assigned IDs is always reflected in the generated markup so it can be used by client side scripting code to access the markup element for the component.

The encodeChildren( ) method calls the component's getClientId( ) method to get an ID value suitable for use in the generated markup if the ID is explicitly assigned. The client ID may be exactly the same as the component ID, but if the component belongs to a naming container, the ID is adjusted by prepending the component IDs for all parent naming containers, with colons separating the individual IDs. For instance, the client ID for a component with the ID input in a form with the ID myForm is myForm:input, because the form component is a naming container. The renderer also gets a chance to convert the client ID in other ways, e.g., encode special characters, so the only sure way to know what the client ID happens to be for a component is to call the getClientId( ) method.

The convention established by the standard JSF HTML renderers is to generate a <span> element with an id attribute when the page author has explicitly assigned an ID. The exception is if there's another HTML element that represents the complete component, such as a <table> element, in which case, the HTML element is used for the ID instead of a <span> element. The encodeChildren( ) method uses the javax.faces.context.ResponseWriter class to generate the <span> element. As you may recall from Chapter 6, the ResponseWriter is an extension of java.io.Writer with methods for writing markup language elements, such as HTML and XML elements. The encodeChildren( ) method calls the startsElement( ) and writeAttribute( ) methods to write the <span> element start tag with the id attribute with the client ID as the value. Both of these methods take an extra argument over what's absolutely needed to write the start tag and the attribute: the startElement( ) method takes a reference to the component the element is generated for and the writeAttribute( ) method takes the name of the component property or attribute the markup element attribute value comes from. These values can be used by a custom ResponseWriter provided by a JSF development tool to keep track of how the generated markup corresponds to the components in the view. The default ResponseWriter doesn't do anything with this information, but you should still provide it to help tools that do.

After writing the <span> element, it's time to generate the HTML elements for the children. Two UIData properties controls which rows to render. The first property holds the index of the first row to render and the rows property holds the number of rows to render. The encodeChildren( ) method loops over the rows from the UIData component's model using these property values as the initial loop variable value and in the loop end condition, respectively. For each processed row, encodeChildren( ) calls the UIData setRowIndex( ) method with the current index to position the model at the current row and expose it to the component's children through the variable named by the var property. The isRowAvailable( ) returns true if there's a row that corresponds to the current index. If isRowAvailable( ) returns false, there are less rows in the table model than the maximum specified by the rows property, so the encodeChildren( ) method exits the loop.

As long as a row is available, all the UIData children are asked to render themselves. The children are bound typically to properties of the current row object exposed through the var variable so the result is different for each row. Just as for the standard table renderer, the bar renderer processes children only of type UIColumn. The actual rendering is handled by the private encodeRecursive( ) method, which we'll look at in a bit. Finally, if a <span> element start tag was rendered earlier, the end tag is generated after rendering all children.

The encodeRecursive( ) method looks like this:

```
        private void encodeRecursive(FacesContext context, UIComponent component)
            throws IOException {

            if (!component.isRendered( )) {
                return;
            }

            component.encodeBegin(context);
            if (component.getRendersChildren( )) {
                component.encodeChildren(context);
            } else {
                Iterator i = component.getChildren( ).iterator( );
                while (i.hasNext( )) {
                    UIComponent child = (UIComponent) i.next( );
                    encodeRecursive(context, child);
                }
            }
            component.encodeEnd(context);
        }
    }
```

First, encodeRecursive( ) checks if the child component should be rendered at all and returns if not. It then calls the encodeBegin( ) method. If the component renders its children, it calls the encodeChildren( ) method. Otherwise, the encodeRecursive( ) method iterates through all the component's children and calls itself recursively for each child. Finally, it calls the encodeEnd( ) method.

When the encodeChildren( ) method returns, a <span> element with the UIData component's client ID has been rendered if an explicit ID is specified, containing whatever the UIData child components render for each row in the table. With a single UIColumn child containing a command component with a link renderer, the result is a list of HTML <a> elements with JavaScript code for submitting the form the UIData component belongs to, as shown in Figure 13-1.

Registering the renderer

All pluggable classes in JSF must be registered under a unique name in the *faces-config.xml* class, so that other classes can create instances of these classes. A renderer is a pluggable class, and here's how you register it:

```
<faces-config>
  ...
  <render-kit>
    <renderer>
      <component-family>javax.faces.Data</component-family>
      <renderer-type>com.mycompany.Bar</renderer-type>
      <renderer-class>
        com.mycompany.jsf.renderer.BarRenderer
      </renderer-class>
    </renderer>
```

```
    ...
  </render-kit>
  ...
</faces-config>
```

Renderers are grouped into render kits declared by a <render-kit> element. Within this element, you can optionally have a <render-kit-id> element that gives the render kit a unique ID within the application. An application can then use a <default-render-kit-id> element (see Appendix E for details) to say that it wants to use the custom kit with this ID instead of the default HTML kit. An example is a render kit with WML renderers if you're developing an application for WAP clients. If you omit the <render-kit-id> element, as I do here, the renderer is added instead to the default HTML render kit.

Within the kit, each renderer is identified by two pieces of information: a component family and a renderer type, declared by the <component-family> and <renderer-type> elements. As I mentioned earlier, a component family identifies the type of component the renderer belongs to, such as a command component or an input component. All standard JSF classes use component family names composed from the javax.faces prefix followed by the component class name minus the "UI" class name prefix, e.g., javax.faces.Data for the UIData component. The renderer type ID must be unique per component family. All standard JSF renderer type IDs are also prefixed with javax.faces. I follow the same convention for the custom bar renderer, giving it the renderer type ID com.mycompany.Bar, but you can use any name as long as it's unique within the component family.

The JSP tag handler class

In order to use a UIData component with the custom renderer in a JSP page, you must develop a JSP tag handler that creates and configures an instance of the component and tells it to use the BarRenderer class for rendering. It's easier than it sounds, because a base class called javax.faces.webapp.UIComponentTag handles most of the tricky details. Here's the complete com.mycompany.jsf.taglib.DataBarTag class:

```
package com.mycompany.jsf.taglib;

import javax.faces.webapp.UIComponentTag;
import javax.faces.component.UIComponent;
import javax.faces.component.UIData;
import javax.faces.context.FacesContext;
import javax.faces.el.ValueBinding;

public class DataBarTag extends UIComponentTag {

    private String first;
    private String rows;
    private String value;
    private String var;
```

```
public void setFirst(String first) {
    this.first = first;
}

public void setRows(String rows) {
    this.rows = rows;
}

public void setValue(String value) {
    this.value = value;
}

public void setVar(String var) {
    this.var = var;
}

public String getComponentType( ) {
 return "javax.faces.Data";
}

public String getRendererType( ) {
 return "com.mycompany.Bar";
}

protected void setProperties(UIComponent component) {
    super.setProperties(component);

 FacesContext context = getFacesContext( );
    if (first != null) {
        if (isValueReference(first)) {
            ValueBinding vb =
                context.getApplication( ).createValueBinding(first)
            component.setValueBinding("first", vb);
        } else {
            ((UIData) component).setFirst(Integer.parseInt(first));
        }
    }

    if (rows != null) {
        if (isValueReference(rows)) {
            ValueBinding vb =
                context.getApplication( ).createValueBinding(rows)
            component.setValueBinding("rows", vb);
        } else {
            ((UIData) component).setRows(Integer.parseInt(rows));
        }
    }

    if (value != null) {
        ValueBinding vb =
            context.getApplication( ).createValueBinding(value)
        component.setValueBinding("value", vb);
    }
```

```
            if (var != null) {
                ((UIData) component).setVar(var);
            }
        }
    }
```

The class is called DataBarTag, following the standard JSF convention of using the combination of the component type and the renderer type IDs as the custom action name, and the JSP convention of using the action name plus a "Tag" suffix for the tag handler class. The tag handler class extends UIComponentTag and supports four custom action attributes: first, rows, value, and var. Each attribute is backed by a private instance variable and a setter method, called by the JSP container when it processes the page.

The UIComponentTag calls the getComponentType( ) and getRendererType( ) methods to know which type of JSF component to create and which type of renderer to configure it with. All you need to do is ensure that these two methods return the desired type IDs. The DataBarTag class returns javax.faces.Data as the component type and com.mycompany.Bar as the renderer type. The UIComponentTag creates an instance of the class mapped to the returned component type and adds it to the component tree for the view when the JSP page with this custom action is processed the first time.

The UIComponentTag then calls the setProperties( ) method. The implementation of this method in the DataBarTag class calls super.setProperties( ) to let the parent class do the default processing, which includes configuring the component with the renderer type returned by the getRendererType( ) method. The UIComponentTag class implementation of the setProperties( ) method also sets the component properties supported by all components—id, binding, and rendered—and provides the tag handler setter methods for these properties; all you need to do to support these properties is declare that your subclass accepts them in the Tag Library Descriptor, as you'll see soon.

The rest of the setProperties( ) method configures the component based on the attributes that are unique for this custom action. For the DataBarTag, this means the first, rows, value, and var attributes. The page author may set the first two either to static values or to JSF EL expressions, so the tag handler needs to figure out which is which. It does so with the help of the isValueReference( ) method implemented by the UIComponentTag. This method returns true if the value is delimited by the #{ and } delimiters. If so, the setProperties( ) method converts the expression string into an instance of the javax.faces.el.ValueBinding class representing the value binding and calls the component's setValueBinding( ) method with the ValueBinding as an argument. The component evaluates the value binding as needed during the different request processing lifecycles, as described in the previous chapters. If the attribute value isn't a value binding expression, the setProperties( ) method casts the component reference to UIData and calls the corresponding type-safe property setter method.

The two remaining action attributes are handled slightly different. The `value` attribute must be set to a value binding expression, because the model can't be expressed as a static value in a meaningful way. The `setProperties()` method therefore assumes it's a value binding expression without checking the syntax first. The `var` attribute, on the other hand, must be a static value. This is a convention established by JSTL and JSP to make it possible to add more translation-time checking for variables in future versions of the specifications. The `var` attribute value is therefore always set as a static component property value.

As with any JSP tag handler class, it must also be declared in a TLD. I add the declaration to the same *taglib.tld* file as we created for the custom validation action in Chapter 7, like this:

```
<taglib>
  ...
  <tag>
    <name>dataBar</name>
    <tag-class>com.mycompany.jsf.taglib.DataBarTag</tag-class>
    <body-content>JSP</body-content>

    <attribute>
      <name>id</name>
      <required>false</required>
      <rtexprvalue>false</rtexprvalue>
    </attribute>

    <attribute>
      <name>binding</name>
      <required>false</required>
      <rtexprvalue>false</rtexprvalue>
    </attribute>

    <attribute>
      <name>rendered</name>
      <required>false</required>
      <rtexprvalue>false</rtexprvalue>
    </attribute>

    <attribute>
      <name>first</name>
      <required>false</required>
      <rtexprvalue>false</rtexprvalue>
    </attribute>

    <attribute>
      <name>rows</name>
      <required>false</required>
      <rtexprvalue>false</rtexprvalue>
    </attribute>

    <attribute>
      <name>value</name>
```

```
      <required>true</required>
      <rtexprvalue>false</rtexprvalue>
    </attribute>

    <attribute>
      <name>var</name>
      <required>false</required>
      <rtexprvalue>false</rtexprvalue>
    </attribute>
  </tag>
  ...
</taglib>
```

The tag handler is declared with the `<tag>` element, with its name and implementation class defined by the nested `<name>` and `<tag-class>` elements. The `<body-content>` element for a JSF component tag handler must be set to `JSP` to tell the JSP container to evaluate action elements in the body, e.g., action elements that represent child components, validators, or converters.

Each action attribute is described by an `<attribute>` element. The nested `<name>` element contains the attribute name and the `<required>` element tells if the attribute is required or not. The `<rtexprvalue>` element declares if the attribute can be set as a so-called *request time attribute value*, which is either a Java or a JSP EL expression. You must set this element value to `false` for JSF custom actions in order to prevent clashes and potential security issues caused by mixing a JSP EL or Java expression with a JSF EL expression. To the JSP container, a JSF EL expression is just a plain string, not a request-time attribute value; the tag handler is responsible for turning it into `ValueBinding` instances, as described earlier.

For the `dataBar` action, I declare the standard attributes implemented by the `UIComponentTag` class (`id`, `binding`, and `rendered`) plus the attributes added by the custom action tag handler.

Using the custom renderer

We now have a custom renderer for the `UIData` component and a JSP custom action for the combination. Example 13-1 shows the part of the modified reports list area JSP page that produces the screen in Figure 13-1 with the page links added by the bar renderer. The parts not shown are identical to the final version we looked at in Chapter 10.

Example 13-1. Navigation bar that is created by the Bar renderer (expense/stage4/reportListArea.jsp)

```
<%@ page contentType="text/html" %>
<%@ taglib uri="http://java.sun.com/jsf/html" prefix="h" %>
<%@ taglib uri="http://java.sun.com/jsf/core" prefix="f" %>
<%@ taglib uri="http://mycompany.com/jsftaglib" prefix="my" %>
```

Example 13-1. Navigation bar that is created by the Bar renderer (expense/stage4/reportListArea.jsp) (continued)

```
<html>
  <head>
    <title>Expense Reports</title>
    <link rel="stylesheet" type="text/css"
      href="${pageContext.request.contextPath}/style.css">
  </head>
  <body>
    <f:view>
      <h:form>
        <h:dataTable value="#{reportHandler.sortedReportsModel}" var="report"
          rows="#{reportHandler.noOfRows}"
          first="#{reportHandler.firstRowIndex}"
          styleClass="tablebg" rowClasses="oddRow, evenRow"
          columnClasses="left, left, left, right, left">
          ...
        </h:dataTable>

        <h:commandButton value="<<"
          disabled="#{reportHandler.scrollFirstDisabled}"
          action="#{reportHandler.scrollFirst}" />
        <h:commandButton value="<"
          disabled="#{reportHandler.scrollPreviousDisabled}"
          action="#{reportHandler.scrollPrevious}" />
        <my:dataBar value="#{reportHandler.pages}" var="page"
          rows="#{reportHandler.noOfPageLinks}"
          first="#{reportHandler.firstPageIndex}">
          <h:column>
            <h:commandLink action="#{page.select}"
              immediate="true"
              rendered="#{page.number != reportHandler.currentPage}">
              <h:outputText value="#{page.number}" style="padding: 1em" />
            </h:commandLink>
            <h:outputText value="#{page.number}" style="padding: 1em"
              rendered="#{page.number == reportHandler.currentPage}" />
          </h:column>
        </my:dataBar>
        <h:commandButton value=">"
          disabled="#{reportHandler.scrollNextDisabled}"
          action="#{reportHandler.scrollNext}" />
        <h:commandButton value=">>"
          disabled="#{reportHandler.scrollLastDisabled}"
          action="#{reportHandler.scrollLast}" />
        Rows/page:
        <h:inputText value="#{reportHandler.noOfRows}" size="3"/>
        <h:commandButton value="Refresh" />
      </h:form>
    </f:view>
  </body>
</html>
```

I've added the taglib directive for the custom tag library holding the custom action and inserted the <my:dataBar> custom action between the command buttons for scrolling.

In order to use the <my:dataBar> custom action, we need to provide the UIData component it represents with a model with one row per page of expense reports and properties for the first and rows attributes. We also need an action method that selects a specific page and adjusts the row index for the model used by the <h:dataTable> action in the same page that displays the expense reports table. Because of the tight interaction between the two models used in this page, I've added all these things to the ReportHandler class we used in the previous chapters to control the expense reports list.

The <my:dataBar> attributes values bind the component to the new ReportHandler properties. The value attribute is bound to a getter method that returns a model suitable for the page navigation bar component, implemented like this:

```
package com.mycompany.expense;

import java.util.ArrayList;
import java.util.List;
...
public class ReportHandler {

    private int noOfRows = 5;
    private int firstRowIndex = 0;
    private int noOfPageLinks = 5;
    ...

    public List getPages( ) {
        int totalNoOfRows = getSortedReportsModel( ).getRowCount( );
        int noOfPages =  totalNoOfRows / noOfRows;
        if (totalNoOfRows % noOfRows > 0) {
            noOfPages += 1;
        }

        List pages = new ArrayList(noOfPages);
        for (int i = 0; i < noOfPages; i++) {
            pages.add(new Page(i + 1, this));
        }
        return pages;
    }
```

The getPages( ) method first finds out how many rows there are in the reports table model and divides that number with the number of rows shown per page to get the total number of pages. If it doesn't divide evenly, it adds one to the number of pages to account for the incomplete last page. Next, getPages( ) creates a List with a Page instance per page and returns it. The Page class is an inner class that looks like this:

```
public static class Page {
    private int number;
    private ReportHandler handler;
```

```
    public Page(int number, ReportHandler handler) {
        this.number = number;
        this.handler = handler;
    }

    public int getNumber( ) {
        return number;
    }

    public String select( ) {
        handler.setCurrentPage(number);
        return null;
    }
}
```

It holds the number for the page it represents and a reference to the ReportHandler class it belongs to. A getNumber( ) method returns the page number and a select( ) method tells the ReportHandler that the page has been selected. We'll look at how the select( ) method is used shortly.

The rows attribute tells how many rows to process per page. When the UIData component is used with the bar renderer to generate page navigation links, rows is the number of page links to render at the most. The attribute is bound to a property named noOfPageLinks, implemented like this in the ReportHandler class:

```
public int getNoOfPageLinks( ) {
    return noOfPageLinks;
}
```

The property getter method just returns the value of the corresponding instance variable. Nothing prevents you from adding a setter method and binding it to an input component so the user can change the value, but the number of links to render is most likely fixed. The only reason for defining this value as a property instead of setting it as a static attribute value in the JSP page is that I need the value in the bean to calculate other information later.

The first attribute is bound to a property named firstPageIndex. As the name implies, it tells the component which row in the model to start at for each page. The property getter method looks like this:

```
public int getFirstPageIndex( ) {
    int noOfPages = getPages( ).size( );
    if (noOfPages <= noOfPageLinks) {
        return 0;
    }

    int firstPageIndex = (firstRowIndex / noOfRows) - 1;
    if (firstPageIndex < 0) {
        firstPageIndex = 0;
    }
    else if (noOfPages - firstPageIndex < noOfPageLinks) {
        firstPageIndex = noOfPages - noOfPageLinks;
```

```
    }
    return firstPageIndex;
}
```

This one is a bit more complex because it must ensure that the rendered page links are synchronized with the reports rendered in the reports table. The getFirstPageIndex( ) method first figures out how many pages there are by checking the size of the List returned by the getPages( ) method. If the number of pages is less than the maximum number of links to render, getFirstPageIndex( ) returns 0 so that links for all pages are rendered. If there are more pages than links that should be rendered, the index is set to the index of the first report that's currently rendered divided by the number of reports displayed per page, minus one. This value is then adjusted to 0 if it happens to result in a negative value, or to an index that ensures that the maximum number of links can be rendered even if the current page is one of the last few pages. This algorithm ensures that the maximum number of links is always rendered and there's always a link to the previous page, if any. If you find it hard to visualize, experiment with the sample page shown in Example 13-1.

The body of the <my:dataBar> action element contains one <h:column> action element, representing the single column component child element. This element in turn contains two JSF action elements for rendering a page reference per row in the model. The first action element is <h:commandLink> with an action attribute that binds it to a method named select( ) in the bean exposed through the variable named by the <my:dataBar> var attribute. The model for the <my:dataBar> action is a List of Page instances, so when the user clicks the link, the select( ) method in the Page instance represented by the link is invoked. As you saw earlier, the Page select( ) method calls the setCurrentPage( ) on the ReportHandler with its own page number as the argument. The setCurrentPage( ) method is implemented like this:

```
private void setCurrentPage(int currentPage) {
    firstRowIndex = (currentPage - 1) * noOfRows;
}
```

It sets the instance variable that holds the index for the first row in the reports table to the provided page number minus one and multiplied by the number of rows displayed per page, resulting in the index for the top row of the selected page. The <h:dataTable> for the reports table is bound to the firstRowIndex property, so when the page is rendered, the reports on the selected page are rendered.

The rendered attribute for the <h:commandLink> element contains a JSF EL expression that compares the page number represented by the current Page instance with the value of the currentPage property of the ReportHandler. The expression evaluates to true if they are different, so the link is rendered for all pages except the current one. The currentPage property getter method looks like this:

```
public int getCurrentPage( ) {
    return (firstRowIndex / noOfRows) + 1;
}
```

It calculates the number for the current page by dividing the index for the current first row in the reports table with the number of reports displayed per page plus one.

The second column action child is an output component that is represented by an `<h:outputText>` action element. This element has a JSF expression as the `rendered` attribute value that evaluates to the opposite result: `true` if the current page is the same as that represented by the `Page` instance. The effect is that the value for the current page is rendered as text instead of as a link.

For both the `<h:commandLink>` element and the `<h:outputText>` element, a `style` attribute defines padding for the text they generate so that the page numbers are separated by a bit of space in the browser.

A Renderer for Encoding and Decoding

To customize the way the value for an input component is entered, we must develop a custom renderer that implements the decoding behavior in addition to the encoding behavior. An example is a custom renderer for the `UIInput` component that lets the user pick a date by selecting the year, month, and day from three selection lists, as shown in Figure 13-2.

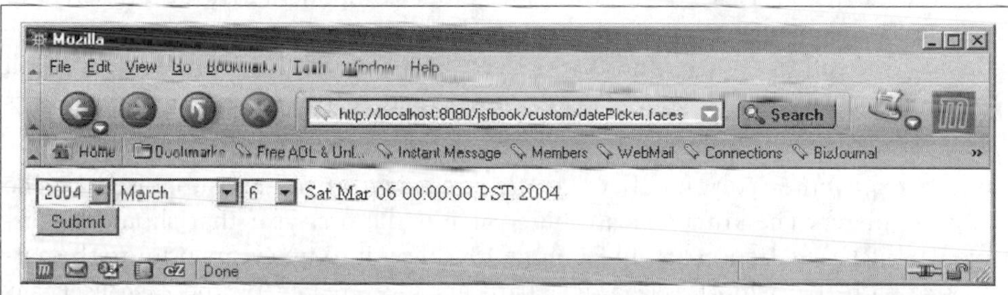

Figure 13-2. Date selection lists rendered by a custom renderer for an input component

Because the date value is rendered as three selection lists, it's sent to the server as three separate parameters. The custom renderer reads all three and creates a single `java.util.Date` value that the input component can handle.

Before we dig into the code, let's see how the custom renderer can be used. Example 13-2 shows the JSP page using the custom action element that ties together the custom renderer and the input component.

Example 13-2. Using the date picker (custom/datePicker.jsp)

```
<%@ page contentType="text/html" %>
<%@ taglib uri="http://java.sun.com/jsf/html" prefix="h" %>
<%@ taglib uri="http://java.sun.com/jsf/core" prefix="f" %>
<%@ taglib uri="http://mycompany.com/jsftaglib" prefix="my" %>

<jsp:useBean id="now" scope="request" class="java.util.Date" />
```

Example 13-2. Using the date picker (custom/datePicker.jsp) (continued)

```
<f:view>
  <html>
    <body>
      <h:form>
        <my:inputDatePicker value="#{myDate}"
          startYear="#{now.year + 1900 - 2}" years="10" />
        <h:outputText value="#{myDate}" />
        <br>
        <h:commandButton value="Submit" />
      </h:form>
    </body>
  </html>
</f:view>
```

As for the bar renderer described in the previous section, the date-picker renderer is backed by a custom action in the sample tag library, so the JSP page contains a `taglib` directive for this library.

The `<my:inputDatePicker>` custom action creates an input component and configures it to use the custom date-picker renderer we'll develop in this section. The action supports four attributes: `value`, `startYear`, `years`, and `styleClass`. The tag handler uses the `value` attribute to set the input component's `value` property. In Example 13-2, I bind it to a simple name, which JSF evaluates to a request scope variable. You can of course bind it to a bean property, in the same way as for all other components. I use a request scope variable here just to show you that it works and to keep the example simple.

The other attributes correspond to render-dependent attributes supported by the custom renderer. The `startYear` attribute value is the first year that should be displayed in the year selection list. In Example 13-2, I set it to two years prior to the current year with the help of a `java.util.Date` instance created by the `<jsp:useBean>` standard action. The year property of a `Date` is the year minus 1900, so I first add 1900 and then subtract two from this value. The `years` attribute is for the number of years to show in the year selection list. The final supported attribute is `styleClass`. I don't use it in this example, but it can be used to assign a CSS class name to the generated HTML element, just as for all the standard JSF action elements.

All attributes accept JSF EL expressions and they are all optional. If `value` isn't set or evaluates to `null`, the current date is used. The default for `startYear` is the current year and the default for `years` is five years.

Just as we did for the bar renderer described in the previous section, we must develop the custom renderer class, register the renderer class with JSF, and implement a JSP custom action that represents a `UIInput` component equipped with the custom renderer.

The Renderer class

The custom renderer is implemented as a class called `com.mycompany.jsf.renderer.DatePickerRenderer`. Compared to the bar renderer from the previous section, the primary difference in this renderer is that it implements decoding and conversion behavior in addition to its encoding behavior. The decoding and conversion logic is implemented like this:

```
package com.mycompany.jsf.renderer;

import java.io.IOException;
import java.text.DateFormatSymbols;
import java.util.ArrayList;
import java.util.Date;
import java.util.HashMap;
import java.util.Iterator;
import java.util.List;
import java.util.Map;

import javax.faces.context.FacesContext;
import javax.faces.context.ResponseWriter;
import javax.faces.component.EditableValueHolder;
import javax.faces.component.ValueHolder;
import javax.faces.component.UIComponent;
import javax.faces.model.SelectItem;
import javax.faces.render.Renderer;

public class DatePickerRenderer extends Renderer {

    public void decode(FacesContext context, UIComponent component) {

        if (isDisabledOrReadOnly(component)) {
            return;
        }

        String clientId = component.getClientId(context);
        Map params = context.getExternalContext().getRequestParameterMap();
        String year = (String) params.get(clientId + "_year");
        if (year != null) {
            Map dateParts = new HashMap();
            dateParts.put("year", year);
            dateParts.put("month", params.get(clientId + "_month"));
            dateParts.put("day", params.get(clientId + "_day"));
            ((EditableValueHolder) component).setSubmittedValue(dateParts);
        }
    }
```

JSF calls the `decode()` method of each `UIComponent` instance with a rendered property set to `true` during the Apply Request Values phase, and a component configured with a renderer delegates the call to its renderer. The `UIForm` component modifies this behavior so that the `decode()` method is invoked on its children only if the form is submitted. Hence, if you have more than one form in the same view, only the components in the submitted form are decoded.

The decode( ) method should always check if the component is marked as disabled or read-only before proceeding, to prevent the component's value from being set in these cases. If a component is rendered as disabled, the browser doesn't send a parameter for the corresponding field; unless the decoding processes is aborted, the normal decoding logic sets the value to null. The browser may send a value for a read-only field, but the component still shouldn't be decoded because a component marked as read-only shouldn't be updated. To keep this example simple, the DatePickerRenderer doesn't support the readonly and disabled attributes, but I included this piece of logic in the decode( ) method anyway, because it's an important requirement for renderers that do support these attributes and it isn't obvious that the test is needed. The isDisabledOrReadOnly( ) method returns true if one or both of these attributes are enabled:

```
private boolean isDisabledOrReadOnly(UIComponent component) {
    boolean disabled = false;
    boolean readOnly = false;

    Object disabledAttr = component.getAttributes( ).get("disabled");
    if (disabledAttr != null) {
        disabled = disabledAttr.equals(Boolean.TRUE);
    }
    Object readOnlyAttr = component.getAttributes( ).get("readonly");
    if (readOnlyAttr != null) {
        readOnly = readOnlyAttr.equals(Boolean.TRUE);
    }
    return disabled || readOnly;
}
```

Both attributes are render-dependent, so they are included in the component's list of generic attributes accessible through the getAttributes( ) method if they are set. The isDisabledOrReadOnly( ) method tries to get the attributes from the list and returns true if one or both are set to Boolean.TRUE.

If it's okay to proceed, the decode( ) method gets a Map containing all request parameters from the ExternalContext and looks for the parameter that holds the year value. The parameter name for the year is the component's client ID plus the string _year. If it finds this parameter, it creates a Map and populates it with the year plus the month and day values from similarly named parameters. It saves the Map as the submittedValue property of the component after casting the component reference to the EditableValueHolder type. This is an interface that all input components implement, containing the methods related to the component's editable value, such as the submittedValue property setter method.

When all of the components in the component tree have been decoded, the request processing lifecycle enters the Process Validations phase, as you may recall from Chapter 8. The first thing that takes place in this phase is the conversion of the submitted value into the data type that the component needs. Because only the renderer knows the form in which the submitted value is saved, the component asks its renderer to perform the conversion by calling the getConvertedValue( ) method:

```
public Object getConvertedValue(FacesContext context,
    UIComponent component, Object submittedValue) {

    Map dateParts = (Map) submittedValue;
    int year = Integer.parseInt((String) dateParts.get("year"));
    int month = Integer.parseInt((String) dateParts.get("month"));
    int day = Integer.parseInt((String) dateParts.get("day"));
    return new Date(year - 1900, month - 1, day);
}
```

For the DatePickerRenderer, this method extracts the year, month, and day values from the Map passed as the submitted value and converts them into a Date instance that it returns. The component saves the returned value as its local value and resets the submitted value.

In other renderers, this method may instead get a Converter instance from the component by casting the component reference to ValueHolder and calling its getConverter( ) method, or locate a Converter for the data type of the property the component is bound to, and use the Converter to convert the value as discussed in Chapter 7. In this case, the conversion may fail, so the getConvertedValue( ) method may throw a ConverterException. If that happens, the component keeps its submitted value so it can be displayed when the component is rendered again along with an error message.

All rendering logic for the DatePickerRenderer is implemented in the encodeBegin( ) method:

```
public void encodeBegin(FacesContext context, UIComponent component)
        throws IOException {

    if (!component.isRendered( )) {
        return;
    }

    Date date = null;
    Map submittedValue = (Map)
        ((EditableValueHolder) component).getSubmittedValue( );
    if (submittedValue != null) {
        date = (Date) getConvertedValue(context, component, submittedValue);
    }
    else {
        Object value = ((ValueHolder) component).getValue( );
        date = value instanceof Date ? (Date) value : new Date( );
    }

    String styleClass =
        (String) component.getAttributes( ).get("styleClass");
    int startYear = date.getYear( ) + 1900;
```

```
        Object startYearAttr = component.getAttributes( ).get("startYear");
        if (startYearAttr != null) {
            startYear = ((Number) startYearAttr).intValue( );
        }
        int years = 5;
        Object yearsAttr = component.getAttributes( ).get("years");
        if (yearsAttr != null) {
            years = ((Number) yearsAttr).intValue( );
        }

        String clientId = component.getClientId(context);
        ResponseWriter out = context.getResponseWriter( );
        renderMenu(out, getYears(startYear, years), date.getYear( ) + 1900,
            clientId + "_year", styleClass, component);
        renderMenu(out, getMonths( ), date.getMonth( ) + 1,
            clientId + "_month", styleClass, component);
        renderMenu(out, getDays( ), date.getDate( ),
            clientId + "_day", styleClass, component);
    }
```

The encodeBegin( ) method returns immediately if the component's rendered property is set to false, just as for the BarRenderer we looked at earlier.

A renderer for an input component must render the submitted value if it's set, and use the local value only if there's no submitted value. This rule handles the case where the user has entered a value that doesn't pass conversion or validation rules. If so, the component's submitted value remains; otherwise, it's reset at the same time as the validated value is saved as the local value. The encodeBegin( ) method first tries to get the submitted value and converts it to a java.util.Date by calling the getConvertedValue( ) method if it's set. If no submitted value is available, the local value is used as is or a new Date instance is created as a default value. The encodeBegin( ) method also obtains all supported render-dependent attribute values, or establishes defaults for the attributes that aren't set.

Next, it gets the client ID for the component. Because this is an input component, the client ID must be used as an attribute of the generated HTML element—whether it's set explicitly by the page author—in order for the renderer to figure out which parameter holds the component value when the form it belongs to is submitted.

It then renders the three selection lists by calling the private renderMenu( ) method for each list:

```
    private void renderMenu(ResponseWriter out, List items, int selected,
        String clientId, String styleClass, UIComponent component)
        throws IOException {

        out.startElement("select", component);
        out.writeAttribute("name", clientId, "id");
        if (styleClass != null) {
            out.writeAttribute("class", styleClass, "styleClass");
        }
```

```
        Iterator i = items.iterator( );
        while (i.hasNext( )) {
            SelectItem si = (SelectItem) i.next( );
            Integer value = (Integer) si.getValue( );
            String label = si.getLabel( );
            out.startElement("option", component);
            out.writeAttribute("value", value, null);
            if (value.intValue( ) == selected) {
                out.writeAttribute("selected", "selected", null);
            }
            out.writeText(label, null);
        }
        out.endElement("select");
    }
```

The renderMenu( ) method is called with references to the ResponseWriter, a List of SelectItem instances for the selection list, the value for the choice that should be selected, the client ID, a CSS class, and the component. The method renders a <select> element with the client ID as the name attribute and a class attribute with the CSS class if one is specified.

The method then iterates through the List of SelectItem instances and generates an <option> element for each, adding the selected attribute for the element represented by a SelectItem with a value that matches the selected method argument.

Three private methods provide a List with SelectItem instances for each selection list:

```
    private List getYears(int startYear, int noOfyears) {
        List years = new ArrayList( );
        for (int i = startYear; i < startYear + noOfyears; i++) {
            Integer year = new Integer(i);
            years.add(new SelectItem(year, year.toString( )));
        }
        return years;
    }

    private List getMonths( ) {
        DateFormatSymbols dfs = new DateFormatSymbols( );
        String[] names = dfs.getMonths( );
        List months = new ArrayList( );
        for (int i = 0; i < 12; i++) {
            Integer key = new Integer(i + 1);
            String label = names[i];
            months.add(new SelectItem(key, label));
        }
        return months;
    }

    private List getDays( ) {
        List days = new ArrayList( );
        for (int i = 1; i < 32; i++) {
            Integer day = new Integer(i);
```

```
            days.add(new SelectItem(day, day.toString( )));
        }
        return days;
    }
```

The getYears( ) and getDays( ) methods simply create SelectItem instances with numeric key and label values. The getMonths( ) method uses the java.text.DateFormatSymbols class to get the month names and uses them as labels.

Registering the renderer

As before, we must register the date-picker renderer in the *faces-config.xml* file:

```
<faces-config>
    ...
    <renderer>
      <component-family>javax.faces.Input</component-family>
      <renderer-type>com.mycompany.DatePicker</renderer-type>
      <renderer-class>
        com.mycompany.jsf.renderer.DatePickerRenderer
      </renderer-class>
    </renderer>
    ...
</faces-config>
```

This is a renderer for a UIInput component, so we set the <component-family> element value to javax.faces.Input. For the <renderer-type> element, we use the value com.mycompany.DatePicker, following the same convention as for the bar custom renderer.

The JSP tag handler class

The JSP tag handler class for the <my:inputDatePicker> action follows the same pattern as the tag handler for the <my:dataBar> action:

```
package com.mycompany.jsf.taglib;

import javax.faces.webapp.UIComponentTag;
import javax.faces.component.UIComponent;
import javax.faces.context.FacesContext;
import javax.faces.el.ValueBinding;

public class InputDatePickerTag extends UIComponentTag {

    private String startYear;
    private String years;
    private String value;
    private String styleClass;

    public void setStartYear(String startYear) {
        this.startYear = startYear;
    }

    public void setYears(String years) {
```

```
        this.years = years;
    }

    public void setValue(String value) {
        this.value = value;
    }

    public void setStyleClass(String styleClass) {
        this.styleClass = styleClass;
    }

    public String getComponentType( ) {
        return "javax.faces.Input";
    }

    public String getRendererType( ) {
        return "com.mycompany.DatePicker";
    }

    protected void setProperties(UIComponent component) {
        super.setProperties(component);

        FacesContext context = getFacesContext( );
        if (startYear != null) {
            if (isValueReference(startYear)) {
                ValueBinding vb =
                    context.getApplication( ).createValueBinding(startYear);
                component.setValueBinding("startYear", vb);
            } else {
                component.getAttributes( ).put("startYear",
                    new Integer(startYear));
            }
        }

        if (years != null) {
            if (isValueReference(years)) {
                ValueBinding vb =
                    context.getApplication( ).createValueBinding(years);
                component.setValueBinding("years", vb);
            } else {
                component.getAttributes( ).put("years", new Integer(years));
            }
        }

        if (value != null) {
            if (isValueReference(value)) {
                ValueBinding vb =
                    context.getApplication( ).createValueBinding(value);
                component.setValueBinding("value", vb);
            } else {
                component.getAttributes( ).put("value", value);
            }
        }
```

```
            if (styleClass != null) {
                if (isValueReference(styleClass)) {
                    ValueBinding vb =
                        context.getApplication( ).createValueBinding(styleClass);
                    component.setValueBinding("styleClass", vb);
                } else {
                    component.getAttributes( ).put("styleClass", styleClass);
                }
            }
        }
    }
```

The InputDatePickerTag class extends the UIComponentTag and provides setter methods for all the supported attributes: value, startYear, years, and styleClass.

The getComponentType( ) method returns javax.faces.Input and the getRendererType( ) method returns com.mycompany.DatePicker. The UIComponentTag uses these values to create an input component and configure it to use the custom renderer. The setProperties( ) method sets the component properties and generic attributes corresponding to the custom action attributes, just as for the DataBarTag class described in the previous section.

In order to focus on the most important aspects of a renderer for an input component, I've left out a number of attributes that you would most likely want to support in a production version of this type of custom action and custom renderer. For instance, the JSF <h:inputText> action supports the immediate and valueChangeListener attributes. To support them for the date picker custom action, just add tag handler setter methods and code in the setProperties( ) method for setting the values on the component, either as generic attributes or by casting the component reference to EditableValueHolder and calling the type-safe setter methods.

Similarly, the <h:inputText> action supports a number of render-dependent attributes in addition to the styleClass attribute, such as style, disabled, readonly, onchange, and so on. To add support for render-dependent attributes like this, add a setter method in the tag handler class and code for setting the attributes as generic attributes in the setProperties( ) method, plus the same kind of code that the DatePickerRenderer uses to render the styleClass attribute value for all the additional attributes.

Using Other Custom Classes

In the next chapter, we'll look at how to develop custom components in addition to custom renderers. Custom renderers and components are, however, not the only types of classes that you can plug into JSF. As I've mentioned before, pretty much everything in JSF is pluggable. You can replace the default ActionListener, NavigationHandler, VariableResolver, PropertyResolver, ViewHandler, and StateManager implementation classes. If a custom version of any of these classes has a constructor that takes an argument of the same type, JSF uses that constructor and passes in the previously registered instance as the argument. This makes it easy to provide a custom class that implements only some of the methods and delegates the rest to the previous instance. I'll show you an example of how to do this for a custom `ViewHandler` in Chapter 15.

A custom `VariableResolver` can be used to add implicit EL variables, such as an implicit variable named `now` that holds a `java.util.Date` instance for the current time. A custom `PropertyResolver` can add support for custom properties or data types not supported out of the box, such as a pseudo-property named `ids` for objects of type `UIComponent` to hold a `java.util.Map` with all children keyed by their IDs. This would make it easy to access components by their ID in a JSF EL expression, e.g., `#{view.ids.form.ids.input}` would access a component with the ID `input` nested within a component with the ID `form`.

Custom `ActionListener` and `NavigationHandler` classes can implement more sophisticated strategies than the default versions, which may be useful for integration with an application framework like Struts. A custom `StateManager` can fine-tune the state saving mechanism specifically for your application. We'll look at how to provide alternatives to JSP for creating views with custom `ViewHandler` classes in Chapter 15. The APIs for all these classes are straightforward, so if you need to use a custom version, you can read up on what to do in Appendix D.

You can even replace all factory classes, to provide replacements for all the core infrastructure classes, i.e., `FacesContext`, `Application`, `Lifecycle`, and `RenderKit`, and all standard components, validators, and converters. See Appendix D and E for details.

Packaging Custom Classes

JSF merges the definitions found in multiple *faces-config.xml* files. When a JSF application starts, the implementation looks for *faces-config.xml* files in this order:

1. All JAR file resources in the web application's `ServletContext` resource paths (in the reverse order of which they are returned by the `ServletContext getResourcePaths()` method) are scanned for files named *META-INF/faces-config.xml*.
2. A comma-separated list of context-relative paths defined by the `javax.faces.CONFIG_FILES` context parameter in the *web.xml* file.
3. The *WEB-INF/faces-config.xml* file.

This algorithm allows developers of custom classes to bundle them in JAR files with their declarations, making installation as easy as dropping the JAR file into the *WEB-INF/lib* directory. Because the *WEB-INF/faces-config.xml* file is considered last, you can override all configuration setting for a specific application in this file. Factory classes can be declared in additional files. See Appendix D for details.

CHAPTER 14

Developing Custom Components

In the previous chapter, we looked at how a custom renderer can be developed for an existing component to change how the component is represented and how the user can enter a value for it. A custom renderer is often all that's needed to get the customized behavior you want for your application, but occasionally you must also develop a custom component. Before you do, remember to look to see if someone else has already developed what you need, for instance among the resources listed at *http://java.sun.com/j2ee/javaserverfaces*.

If you can't find an existing component that fits your needs, this chapter describes how to develop a custom component, either by extending an existing standard component or developing a brand new component type.

Extending an Existing Component

The preferences screens for the sample application we developed in Chapter 9 are not all that user friendly. For instance, you can see the different setting only by navigating through the screens in a fixed order; you can't jump simply from one setting to another. This type of data is better presented as tabs on one screen, as shown in Figure 14-1.

Much of what is needed for this design can be done with existing components. The contents of each tab can be represented by a panel component, e.g., with the `<h:panelGroup>` or `<h:panelGrid>` action elements. Yet another panel can hold the whole set of tabs together, but it needs a custom panel renderer that ensures that only the currently selected tab panel is rendered. The same custom renderer can also create the tab control bar, and pick up the tab label texts or images from facets attached to each tab panel.

The part of the design that makes sense to implement as a custom component is the tab label. Clicking on the label should result in the rendering of the corresponding tab panel's content, so the label component must act as a command component with built-in event handling behavior, toggling the `rendered` attribute for the panels that make up the individual tabs.

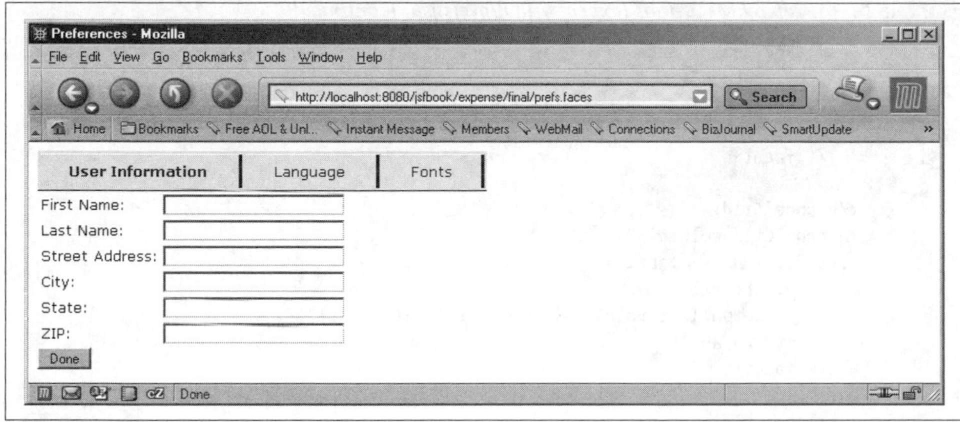

Figure 14-1. User preferences as tabs

Example 14-1 shows parts of the JSP page that creates a view based on this design with panels, a custom renderer, and a custom component for the labels.

Example 14-1. Preferences as tabs (expense/final/prefs.jsp)

```
<%@ page contentType="text/html" %>
<%@ taglib uri="http://java.sun.com/jsf/html" prefix="h" %>
<%@ taglib uri="http://java.sun.com/jsf/core" prefix="f" %>
<%@ taglib uri="http://mycompany.com/jsftaglib" prefix="my" %>

<f:view locale="#{userProfile.locale}">
  <f:loadBundle basename="labels" var="labels" />
  <html>
    <head>
      <title><h:outputText value="#{labels.prefLinkLabel}" /></title>
      <link rel="stylesheet" type="text/css"
        href="${pageContext.request.contextPath}/style.css">
    </head>
    <body>
      <h:form>
        <my:panelTabbed labelAreaClass="labels"
          selectedLabelClass="selected-tab" unselectedLabelClass="tab">
          <h:panelGrid columns="2">
            <f:facet name="label">
              <my:tabLabel>
                <h:outputText value="#{labels.prefUserHeader}" />
              </my:tabLabel>
            </f:facet>
            <h:outputText value="#{labels.firstNameLabel}" />
            <h:inputText size="30" value="#{userProfile.firstName}" />
            <h:outputText value="#{labels.lastNameLabel}" />
            <h:inputText size="30" value="#{userProfile.lastName}" />
            ...
          </h:panelGrid>
          <h:panelGrid columns="2">
```

Example 14-1. Preferences as tabs (expense/final/prefs.jsp) (continued)

```
          <f:facet name="label">
            <my:tabLabel>
              <h:outputText value="#{labels.prefLangHeader}" />
            </my:tabLabel>
          </f:facet>
          ...
        </h:panelGrid>
        <h:panelGrid columns="2">
          <f:facet name="label">
            <my:tabLabel>
              <h:outputText value="#{labels.prefFontHeader}" />
            </my:tabLabel>
          </f:facet>
          ...
        </h:panelGrid>
      </my:panelTabbed>
      <h:commandButton value="#{labels.doneButtonLabel}"
        action="#{userHandler.updateProfile}" />
    </h:form>
  </body>
</html>
</f:view>
```

The `<my:panelTabbed>` action element creates the main panel with a custom renderer. Within this element, there's one `<h:panelGrid>` element per preference type (user information, language, and font selections). Each such panel is configured with a facet named `label`, consisting of a custom component created by a `<my:tabLabel>` action element. The custom tab label component uses the output generated by its children as the content of a link it renders as the tab label. Here I use a simple output component, but you can use `<h:graphicImage>` instead if you want to use an image as the label.

All in all, we need to develop a custom renderer for the outer panel, a custom component and a renderer for the tab control label, and custom actions for both component/renderer combinations. We must also register the custom component and the two custom renderers.

The TabbedRenderer Class

Let's look at the custom renderer for the panel that contains all the tabs first. It's a class called `com.mycompany.renderer.TabbedRenderer`:

```
package com.mycompany.jsf.renderer;

import com.mycompany.jsf.component.UITabLabel;

import java.io.IOException;
import java.util.Iterator;
import java.util.List;
```

```java
import javax.faces.context.FacesContext;
import javax.faces.context.ResponseWriter;
import javax.faces.component.UIComponent;
import javax.faces.component.UIViewRoot;
import javax.faces.render.Renderer;

public class TabbedRenderer extends Renderer {

    public boolean getRendersChildren( ) {
        return true;
    }

    public void decode(FacesContext context, UIComponent component) {
        Iterator i = component.getChildren( ).iterator( );
        while (i.hasNext( )) {
            UIComponent child = (UIComponent) i.next( );
            if (!child.isRendered( )) {
                UITabLabel tabLabel = (UITabLabel) child.getFacet("label");
                if (tabLabel != null) {
                    tabLabel.processDecodes(context);
                }
            }
        }
    }

    public void encodeBegin(FacesContext context, UIComponent component)
        throws IOException {

        if (!component.isRendered( )) {
            return;
        }

        int selected = 0;
        List children = component.getChildren( );
        boolean pickedSelected = false;
        for (int i = 0; i < children.size( ); i++) {
            UIComponent child = (UIComponent) children.get(i);
            if (child.isRendered( ) && !pickedSelected) {
                selected = i;
                pickedSelected = true;
            }
            else {
                child.setRendered(false);
            }
        }

        String labelAreaClass =
            (String) component.getAttributes( ).get("labelAreaClass");
        String selectedLabelClass =
            (String) component.getAttributes( ).get("selectedLabelClass");
        String unselectedLabelClass =
            (String) component.getAttributes( ).get("unselectedLabelClass");

        ResponseWriter out = context.getResponseWriter( );
```

```
    out.startElement("table", component);
    if (component.getId( ) != null &&
        !component.getId( ).startsWith(UIViewRoot.UNIQUE_ID_PREFIX)) {
            out.writeAttribute("id", component.getClientId(context),
                "id");
    }
    if (labelAreaClass != null) {
        out.writeAttribute("class", labelAreaClass, "labelAreaClass");
    }

    out.startElement("tr", component);
    for (int i = 0; i < children.size( ); i++) {
        UIComponent child = (UIComponent) children.get(i);
        UITabLabel tabLabel = (UITabLabel) child.getFacet("label");
        if (tabLabel != null) {
            String styleClass = i == selected ?
                selectedLabelClass : unselectedLabelClass;
            out.startElement("td", component);
            if (styleClass != null) {
                out.writeAttribute("class", styleClass,
                    i == selected ?
                        "selectedLabelClass" : "unselectedLabelClass");
            }
            encodeRecursive(context, tabLabel);
            out.endElement("td");
        }
    }
    out.endElement("tr");
    out.endElement("table");
}

public void encodeChildren(FacesContext context, UIComponent component)
    throws IOException {

    Iterator i = component.getChildren( ).iterator( );
    while (i.hasNext( )) {
        UIComponent child = (UIComponent) i.next( );
        if (child.isRendered( )) {
            child.encodeBegin(context);
            if (child.getRendersChildren( )) {
                child.encodeChildren(context);
            }
            child.encodeEnd(context);
        }
    }
}

private void encodeRecursive(FacesContext context, UIComponent component)
    throws IOException {

    if (!component.isRendered( )) {
        return;
    }
```

```
            component.encodeBegin(context);
            if (component.getRendersChildren()) {
                component.encodeChildren(context);
            } else {
                Iterator i = component.getChildren().iterator();
                while (i.hasNext()) {
                    UIComponent child = (UIComponent) i.next();
                    encodeRecursive(context, child);
                }
            }
            component.encodeEnd(context);
        }
    }
```

This class should look familiar. It's very similar to the renderer classes we developed in Chapter 13.

The `decode()` method is needed to override the default behavior of decoding only components that has the `rendered` property set to `true`. Only the tabbed panel child representing the currently selected tag has `rendered` set to `true`, but the tab label facets for all children must still be decoded in order to react when the user selects a new tab. The custom `decode()` method therefore decodes the facets for all children with `rendered` set to `false`; the default behavior ensures that the facet for the currently selected tab is decoded.

The `encodeBegin()` method figures out which child tab component to render by iterating through all children and selecting the first one with `rendered` set to `true`. It then sets `rendered` to `false` for all the others. I do this to ensure that only one tab panel is rendered the first time the view is rendered, even if the page author has used the default value of `true` for the `rendered` attribute on all tab panels.

With one of the tab panels selected as the current tab, it's time to render the tab labels. The `TabbedRenderer` uses different CSS classes: one for the selected tab label and one for the other tab labels, specified by the `selectedLabelClass` and `unselectedLabelClass` attributes. The page author can use different styles to give the user a visual cue about which one is currently selected—for instance, a bold font for the selected tab. The renderer also supports a `labelAreaClass` attribute for a CSS class applied to the whole label area. It can be used for setting a background color or border properties. The `encodeBegin()` method writes a `<table>` element with the `labelAreaClass` as the `class` attribute value. It then writes one row (a `<tr>` element) with one `<td>` element per tab with either the `selectedLabelClass` or the `unselectedLabelClass` as the class attribute value. It renders the tab panel's `label` facet as the content of the `<td>` element by calling the `encodeRecursive()` method, which is implemented the same way as it is in the examples in Chapter 13.

The `encodeChildren()` method just iterates through all children and renders the one with rendered set to `true`.

The TabbedRender must also be registered in the *faces-config.xml* file, as described in Chapter 13: the component family name is javax.faces.Panel and the renderer type is com.mycompany.Tabbed. A tag handler for the <my:panelTabbed> custom action is also needed. It's implemented as a class named com.mycompany.jsf.taglib.PanelTabbedTag. The tag handler class follows the same pattern as the tag handlers we looked at in Chapter 13 and it's included with the source code for all examples, so I suggest that you look at it on your own.

The UITabLabel Class

With the custom renderer out of the way, let's see how to develop a custom component. The custom component needed for the tab labels is implemented as a class named UITabLabel:

```
package com.mycompany.jsf.component;

import java.util.Iterator;
import javax.faces.component.UICommand;
import javax.faces.component.UIComponent;
import javax.faces.el.MethodBinding;
import javax.faces.event.ActionEvent;
import javax.faces.event.ActionListener
import javax.faces.event.FacesEvent;

public class UITabLabel extends UICommand {

    public static final String COMPONENT_TYPE = "com.mycompany.TabLabel";
    public static final String COMPONENT_FAMILY = "javax.faces.Command";

    public UITabLabel( ) {
        super( );
        setRendererType("javax.faces.Link");
    }

    public String getFamily( ) {
        return COMPONENT_FAMILY;
    }
```

All JSF components must extend the abstract UIComponent class, either directly or indirectly by extending a subclass. A subclass with default implementations for all methods is called UIComponentBase, and all top-level standard components extend this class instead of UIComponent. The custom UITabLabel class extends the UICommand class because its behavior is the same as the standard command component with just a few twists.

The COMPONENT_TYPE and COMPONENT_FAMILY constants are not required, but they are defined by convention in all standard JSF component classes, so I do the same for the custom component. They hold the component type and component family identifiers for the component.

The constructor sets the renderer type for the component to javax.faces.Link. Combined with a getFamily( ) method that returns javax.faces.Command, this means that the custom component is associated with the standard link renderer for a command component. UIComponentBase methods call the getFamily( ) and the getRendererType( ) methods when a renderer is needed and use the returned values to get an instance of the renderer class registered for the combination of the renderer type and component family.

A standard link renderer is exactly what I want for this custom component, because it should behave exactly as a command link except that the custom component should handle the ActionEvent fired when the user clicks the link in a custom way. This custom behavior is achieved by overriding the broadcast( ) method:

```
public void broadcast(FacesEvent event) {
    if (event instanceof ActionEvent) {
        processAction((ActionEvent) event);
    }
}
```

JSF calls the broadcast( ) method of a component for which an event is queued to let the component notify all its listeners. The default implementation of broadcast( ) in UIComponentBase notifies all registered listeners of the event, and the UICommand specialization of this method also invokes the methods defined by the action and actionListener properties. For the tab label custom component, however, I want to prevent the developer from using listeners or action methods to process the event, because the component represents a special-purpose command. The broadcast( ) method in UITabLabel therefore calls the private processAction( ) method to handle the event itself instead:

```
private void processAction(ActionEvent event) {
    UIComponent parent = getParent( );
    UIComponent panelTabbed = parent.getParent( );
    Iterator i = panelTabbed.getChildren( ).iterator( );
    while (i.hasNext( )) {
        UIComponent tab = (UIComponent) i.next( );
        if (tab.equals(parent)) {
            tab.setRendered(true);
        }
        else {
            tab.setRendered(false);
        }
    }
}
```

The processAction( ) method locates the component's parent (the tab panel) and then the tab panel's parent (the outer panel with the tabbed renderer). It then asks the outer panel for all its children and iterates through them. When it encounters its own parent, it sets the parent's rendered property to true. For all other panels, it sets the rendered property to false. The effect is that when the outer panel next renders its children, it renders only the panel selected by the tab label custom component.

The rest of the UITabLabel class consists of overridden methods inherited from the UICommand class, changed to prevent the developer from defining action and actionListener method bindings and registering action listeners for the component:

```
    public MethodBinding getAction( ) {
        return null;
    }

    public void setAction(MethodBinding action) {
        throw new UnsupportedOperationException( );
    }

    public MethodBinding getActionListener( ) {
        return null;
    }

    public void setActionListener(MethodBinding actionListener) {
        throw new UnsupportedOperationException( );
    }

    public void addActionListener(ActionListener listener) {
        throw new UnsupportedOperationException( );
    }

    public ActionListener[] getActionListeners( ) {
        return new ActionListener[0];
    }

    public void removeActionListener(ActionListener listener) {
        throw new UnsupportedOperationException( );
    }
}
```

These methods return null or an empty array, or throw an UnsupportedOperationException in case someone calls them. It's not an absolute requirement to implement these methods, because all listeners and action methods are ignored anyway. However, it may save someone from wondering why additional event handlers are not invoked, so it's worth the extra bytes.

Registering the Component

All custom components must be registered in the *faces-config.xml* file. Here's how you register the UITabLabel component:

```
<faces-config>
  ...
  <component>
    <component-type>
      com.mycompany.TabLabel
    </component-type>
    <component-class>
      com.mycompany.jsf.component.UITabLabel
```

```
      </component-class>
    </component>
    ...
  </faces-config>
```

The <component> element contains two mandatory nested elements. The <component-type> element assigns the component a unique identifier and the <component-class> holds the fully qualified component class name. As you may recall from Chapter 6, the code that creates components does so by calling the Application createComponent( ) method. It takes the component type identifier as the argument and returns an instance of the class mapped to the identifier.

The JSP Tag Handler Class

Finally, we need a tag handler for the <my:tabLabel> custom action. It's a very simple class:

```
package com.mycompany.jsf.taglib;

import javax.faces.webapp.UIComponentTag;

public class TabLabelTag extends UIComponentTag {

    public String getComponentType( ) {
        return "com.mycompany.TabLabel";
    }

    public String getRendererType( ) {
        return "javax.faces.Link";
    }
}
```

The TabLabelTag class extends UIComponentTag, the same way as the tag handler classes we developed in Chapter 13. It implements the getComponentType( ) and getRendererType( ) methods to return the values needed by the superclass to create and configure the component. That's all, because this custom action doesn't provide any attributes for customization of the component or the renderer.

Developing a New Component from Scratch

In Chapter 13 and the previous section of this chapter, you've seen how custom renderers can be used to customize the presentation of a standard component, and if that's not enough, how to extend an existing component to get a component with a slightly different behavior. These options cover most possibilities, and you very rarely need to develop a brand new component class. In fact, I had a hard time coming up with an example for this section. I wanted to develop a fairly simple component to illustrate the main points, but it turns out that all the simple components are provided already as standard JSF components, and almost any customization is better done with a custom renderer.

The only component I could think of that must be implemented from scratch (except for the basic behavior inherited from `UIComponentBase`) is a tree control, where nodes in a tree structure can be expanded or collapsed. It's a far more complex example than what I first had in mind, but I believe it's still a good one. Be aware, though, that this is not for the faint of heart so hold on tight as we dig deep into the intricacies of the JSF component API and its interaction with other JSF classes and the request processing lifecycle.

Figure 14-2 shows the tree control in action, exploring the component state information captured by the `CaptureStatePhaseListener` discussed in Chapter 12.

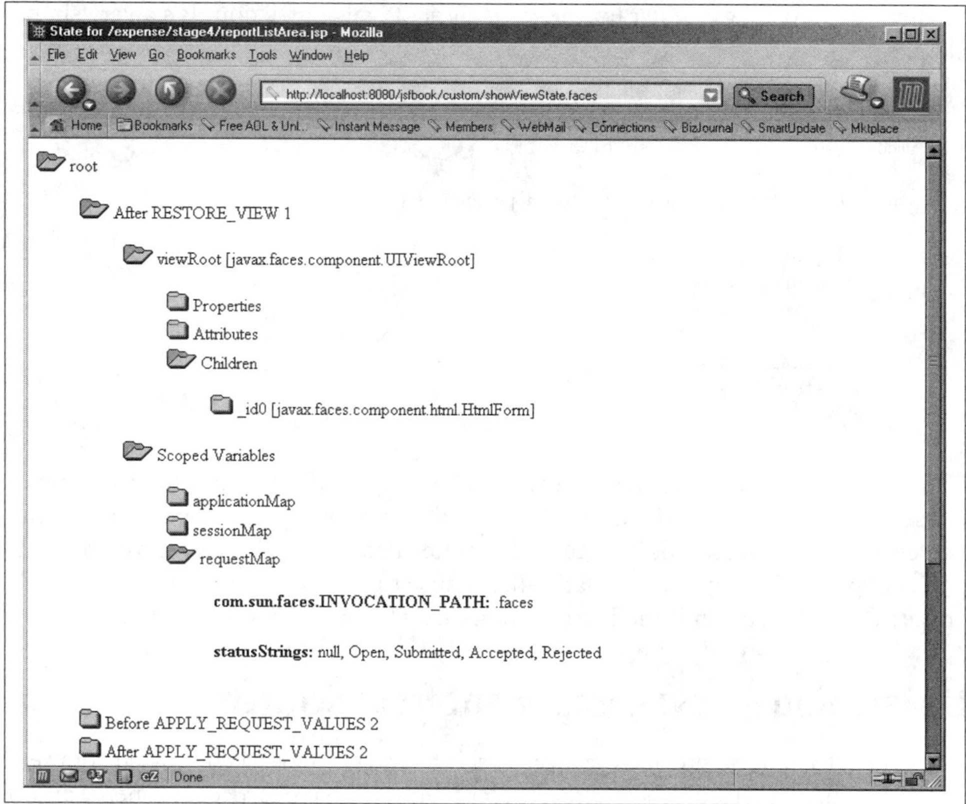

Figure 14-2. Tree control with captured component state nodes

In Figure 14-2, I use folder icons to represent all nodes in the tree that have children. Clicking an open folder collapses the node, while clicking on a closed folder expands the node. The leaf nodes are displayed as plain text, with the node name in bold. All of this is, of course, configurable. You can easily use input components to represent the nodes in order to let their values be edited instead of just displayed.

Example 14-2 shows the JSP page that creates the view shown in Figure 14-2.

Example 14-2. Using the tree control to show view state (custom/showViewState.jsp)

```
<%@ page contentType="text/html" %>
<%@ taglib uri="http://java.sun.com/jsf/html" prefix="h" %>
<%@ taglib uri="http://java.sun.com/jsf/core" prefix="f" %>
<%@ taglib uri="http://mycompany.com/jsftaglib" prefix="my" %>

<f:view>
  <html>
    <head>
      <title><h:outputText value="State for #{param.viewId}" /></title>
    </head>
    <body>
      <h:form>
        <my:tree value="#{sessionScope['com.mycompany.debug'][param.viewId]}"
          var="node" varNodeToggler="t">
          <f:facet name="openNode">
            <h:panelGroup>
              <h:commandLink action="#{t.toggleExpanded}">
                <h:graphicImage value="/images/folder-open.gif"
                  style="border: none" />
                <f:param name="viewId" value="#{param.viewId}" />
              </h:commandLink>
              <h:outputText value=" #{node.name}" />
            </h:panelGroup>
          </f:facet>
          <f:facet name="closedNode">
            <h:panelGroup>
              <h:commandLink action="#{t.toggleExpanded}">
                <h:graphicImage value="/images/folder-closed.gif"
                  style="border: none" />
                <f:param name="viewId" value="#{param.viewId}" />
              </h:commandLink>
              <h:outputText value=" #{node.name}" />
            </h:panelGroup>
          </f:facet>
          <f:facet name="leafNode">
            <h:panelGrid columns="2">
              <h:outputText value="#{node.name}: " style="font-weight: bold" />
              <h:outputText value="#{node.value}" />
            </h:panelGrid>
          </f:facet>
        </my:tree>
      </h:form>
    </body>
  </html>
</f:view>
```

The tree control consists of three pieces: a custom component, a custom renderer, and a custom model; additionally, for use in a JSP page, there's a custom action.

The `<my:tree>` custom action creates the tree component and associates it with the tree renderer. The `value` attribute in Example 14-2 contains a value binding expression that evaluates to an instance of the `TreeNode` class we looked at in Chapter 12. The tree component accepts an instance of this type as its model but creates an instance of its real model class (`TreeModel`) around it, as you'll soon see. In this particular example, the `TreeNode` value is the root node for the data saved by the `CaptureStatePhaseListener` for the view specified by the `viewId` request parameter.

Three facets named `openNode`, `closedNode`, and `leafNode` contain components for handling the different types of nodes. For the first two, I use `<h:commandLink>` action elements with a nested `<h:graphicImage>` action element to render the folder images the user can click on, plus an `<h:outputText>` action element to render the node name. For the leaf node, I use a couple of `<h:outputText>` actions to render the node name and value. The components used as facets have access to the current `TreeNode` instance through the variable defined by the `var` attribute of the `<my:tree>` action element. They also have access to a convenient action method implemented by a bean exposed through the `varNodeToggler` attribute. The bean provides an action method that expands the node if it's collapsed or collapses it if it's expanded. We'll take a closer look at this bean when we go through the custom component code.

The TreeModel Class

The `com.mycompany.jsf.model.TreeModel` class is the model class for the tree component. It provides random access to nodes in a tree made up of instances of the `TreeNode` class we looked at in Chapter 12:

```
package com.mycompany.jsf.model;

import java.util.StringTokenizer;
import javax.faces.component.NamingContainer;

public class TreeModel {
    private final static String SEPARATOR =
        String.valueOf(NamingContainer.SEPARATOR_CHAR);

    private TreeNode root;
    private TreeNode currentNode;

    public TreeModel(TreeNode root) {
        this.root = root;
    }

    public TreeNode getNode( ) {
        return currentNode;
    }
```

```
        public void setNodeId(String nodeId) {
            if (nodeId == null) {
                currentNode = null;
                return;
            }

            TreeNode node = root;
            StringBuffer sb = new StringBuffer( );
            StringTokenizer st =
                new StringTokenizer(nodeId, SEPARATOR);

            sb.append(st.nextToken( )).append(SEPARATOR);
            while (st.hasMoreTokens( )) {
                int nodeIndex = Integer.parseInt(st.nextToken( ));
                sb.append(nodeIndex);
                try {
                    node = (TreeNode) node.getChildren( ).get(nodeIndex);
                }
                catch (IndexOutOfBoundsException e) {
                    String msg = "Node node with ID " + sb.toString( ) +
                        ". Failed to parse " + nodeId;
                    throw new IllegalArgumentException(msg);
                }
                sb.append(SEPARATOR);
            }
            currentNode = node;
        }
    }
```

The TreeModel constructor takes the root TreeNode reference as its single argument and saves it in an instance variable. The setNodeId( ) method sets the current node to the specified node ID, which is a colon-separated list of node indexes. For instance, "0:0:1" means "the second child node of the first child node under the root node." The getNode( ) method returns the current node or null if no node ID is selected.

The UITree Component Class

The com.mycompany.jsf.component.UITree class is the implementation of the tree component. It's quite similar to the standard UIData component. It uses a set of component instances defined as facets to render all objects in the model. It repeatedly calls the setNodeId( ) method as it traverses the tree in all request processing lifecycle phases and exposes the current node through a request scope variable, and then asks the appropriate facet for the current node to process it. The main difference is that the UITree component works with a tree structure model, while UIData works with a model of rows and columns.

The first part of the class should look familiar from the previous section:

```
package com.mycompany.jsf.component;

import java.io.IOException;
import java.io.Serializable;
```

```
import java.util.HashMap;
import java.util.Iterator;
import java.util.List;
import java.util.Map;

import javax.faces.application.FacesMessage;
import javax.faces.context.FacesContext;
import javax.faces.component.EditableValueHolder;
import javax.faces.component.NamingContainer;
import javax.faces.component.UIComponent;
import javax.faces.component.UIComponentBase;

import javax.faces.el.ValueBinding;
import javax.faces.event.AbortProcessingException;
import javax.faces.event.FacesEvent;
import javax.faces.event.FacesListener;
import javax.faces.event.PhaseId;

import com.mycompany.jsf.model.TreeNode;
import com.mycompany.jsf.model.TreeModel;

public class UITree extends UIComponentBase implements NamingContainer {


    public static final String COMPONENT_TYPE = "com.mycompany.Tree";
    public static final String COMPONENT_FAMILY = "com.mycompany.Tree";

    public UITree( ) {
        super( );
        setRendererType("com.mycompany.Tree");
    }

    public String getFamily( ) {
        return (COMPONENT_FAMILY);
    }
```

The UITree class extends the UIComponentBase class (the class with default implementations of all UIComponent methods). It also implements the NamingContainer interface, giving it a say in the generation of client IDs for its children. I'll show you how this comes into play later. Just like the UITabLabel component we looked at earlier, UITree declares COMPONENT_TYPE and COMPONENT_FAMILY constants, sets its default renderer type in the constructor, and returns the family name from the getFamily( ) method.

The component-specific properties are implemented as standard bean accessor methods:

```
private Object value = null;
private String var = null;
private String varNodeToggler = null;
private TreeModel model = null;

public Object getValue( ) {
    if (value != null) {
        return value;
    }
```

```
        ValueBinding vb = getValueBinding("value");
        if (vb != null) {
            return (vb.getValue(getFacesContext( )));
        } else {
            return null;
        }
    }

    public void setValue(Object value) {
        model = null;
        this.value = value;
    }

    public void setValueBinding(String name, ValueBinding binding) {
        if ("value".equals(name)) {
            model = null;
        } else if ("var".equals(name) || "nodeId".equals(name) ||
                   "varNodeToggler".equals(name)) {
            throw new IllegalArgumentException( );
        }
        super.setValueBinding(name, binding);
    }

    public String getVar( ) {
        return var;
    }

    public void setVar(String var) {
        this.var = var;
    }

    public String getVarNodeToggler( ) {
        return varNodeToggler;
    }

    public void setVarNodeToggler(String varNodeToggler) {
        this.varNodeToggler = varNodeToggler;
    }

    private TreeModel getDataModel( ) {
        if (model != null) {
            return model;
        }

        Object value = getValue( );
        if (value != null) {
            if (value instanceof TreeModel) {
                model = (TreeModel) value;
            } else if (value instanceof TreeNode) {
                model = new TreeModel((TreeNode) value);
            }
        }
        return model;
    }
```

The value (i.e., the model) can be set by calling `setValue( )` with an instance of either `TreeModel` or `TreeNode` or by calling `setValueBinding( )` with a `ValueBinding` instance that evaluates to an object of one of these two types. The `getValue( )` method returns the value set by the `setValue( )` method or the evaluation result of the value binding if an explicit value hasn't been set. This is standard behavior for all properties that can be set either explicitly or through a value binding; setting an explicit value in effect shadows a value binding.

The `setValueBinding( )` method specializes the default behavior by throwing an exception if it's called with value bindings for the properties `var`, `varNodeToggler`, or `nodeId`, because these properties must only be set to explicit values: `var` and `varNodeToggler` hold variables names and must be explicit to allow better type-checking in future versions of the JSF and JSP specifications, and `nodeId` is used to traverse through the tree in a controlled manner, so a value binding wouldn't be useful for this property. The accessor methods for `var` and `varNodeToggler` follow the standard pattern of setting and returning the corresponding instance variable value.

The `getDataModel( )` method returns a previously cached model, if any, or sets the cache variable to either the current value (if it's a `TreeModel`) or to a new instance of `TreeModel` (if it's a `TreeNode`) with the provided value object as the root node. Deciding when to reset the cache is an issue that contributes to the complexity for this type of component. A cache is needed in the first place because the model is used frequently and performance would suffer if a value binding had to be evaluated for every access—causing a new `TreeModel` instance to be created when a `TreeNode` is used as the value. On the other hand, not resetting the cache at certain points leads to old data being processed. The `UITree` component (as well as the `UIData` component) resets the cache when `setValue( )` or `setValueBinding( )` is called to set a new value, before decoding (in case the model has changed since the response was sent), and before rendering (in case the model has been changed by event processing).

Another set of methods provide type-safe accessors for the facets:

```
public UIComponent getOpenNode( ) {
    return getFacet("openNode");
}

public void setOpenNode(UIComponent openNode) {
    getFacets( ).put("openNode", openNode);
}

public UIComponent getClosedNode( ) {
    return getFacet("closedNode");
}

public void setClosedNode(UIComponent closedNode) {
    getFacets( ).put("closedNode", closedNode);
}

public UIComponent getLeafNode( ) {
```

```
        return getFacet("leafNode");
    }

    public void setLeafNode(UIComponent closedNode) {
        getFacets( ).put("leafNode", closedNode);
    }
```

All these methods call through to the getFacet( ) method implemented by UIComponentBase to save or get the corresponding facet.

The next set of methods provide access to the nodes in the model:

```
    ...
    private String nodeId;
    ...
    public TreeNode getNode( ) {
        if (getDataModel( ) == null) {
            return null;
        }
        return (getDataModel( ).getNode( ));
    }

    public String getNodeId( ) {
        return nodeId;
    }

    public void setNodeId(String nodeId) {
        saveDescendantState( );

        this.nodeId = nodeId;
        TreeModel model = getDataModel( );
        if (model == null) {
            return;
        }
        model.setNodeId(nodeId);

        restoreDescendantState( );

        Map requestMap =
            getFacesContext().getExternalContext( ).getRequestMap( );
        if (var != null) {
            if (nodeId == null) {
                requestMap.remove(var);
            } else {
                requestMap.put(var, getNode( ));
            }
        }
        if (varNodeToggler != null) {
            if (nodeId == null) {
                requestMap.remove(varNodeToggler);
            } else {
                requestMap.put(varNodeToggler, getNodeToggler( ));
            }
        }
    }
```

The getNode( ) method just calls through to the model and returns the current node or null. The getNodeId( ) simply returns the corresponding instance variable value.

The setNodeId( ) method is a hardworking method. To support using input components for the nodes (e.g., input fields, checkboxes, and selections lists) while still using only one set of components for all nodes, the state held by the components for the current node must be saved before a new node is selected. This is handled by the saveDescendantState( ) method. After saving the state, it's safe to tell the model to select the new node and then call the restoreDescendantState( ) method to configure the components with the state saved previously for the new node.

The model's current node is exposed to the facets through the variable defined by the var property. The setNodeId( ) method obtains a Map with all request scope variables and saves the current node under the var variable name, or removes the variable if the current node ID is set to null. It then does the same for the varNodeToggler variable, setting or removing an instance of the bean containing the node-toggler action method.

The saveDescendantState( ) method and its helper method look like this:

```
...
private Map saved = new HashMap( );
...
private void saveDescendantState( ) {
    FacesContext context = getFacesContext( );
    Iterator i = getFacets().values( ).iterator( );
    while (i.hasNext( )) {
        UIComponent facet = (UIComponent) i.next( );
        saveDescendantState(facet, context);
    }
}

private void saveDescendantState(UIComponent component,
    FacesContext context) {

    if (component instanceof EditableValueHolder) {
        EditableValueHolder input = (EditableValueHolder) component;
        String clientId = component.getClientId(context);
        SavedState state = (SavedState) saved.get(clientId);
        if (state == null) {
            state = new SavedState( );
            saved.put(clientId, state);
        }
        state.setValue(input.getLocalValue( ));
        state.setValid(input.isValid( ));
        state.setSubmittedValue(input.getSubmittedValue( ));
        state.setLocalValueSet(input.isLocalValueSet( ));
    }

    Iterator kids = component.getChildren( ).iterator( );
    while (kids.hasNext( )) {
        saveDescendantState((UIComponent) kids.next( ), context);
    }
}
```

The main saveDescendantState() method iterates through all facets and calls the helper method with the same name for each facet. The helper method checks if the facet implements the EditableValueHolder interface, designating it as an input component. If the facet does implement the interface, the helper method saves the component's local value, submitted value, and the flag indicating if the submitted value is valid or not in a Map with the client ID as the key. The method then iterates through the facet's children and calls itself recursively for each one.

The saved state for each input component is held by an instance of an inner class named SavedState:

```
private static class SavedState implements Serializable {

    private Object submittedValue;
    private boolean valid = true;
    private Object value;
    private boolean localValueSet;

    Object getSubmittedValue( ) {
        return submittedValue;
    }

    void setSubmittedValue(Object submittedValue) {
        this.submittedValue = submittedValue;
    }

    boolean isValid( ) {
        return valid;
    }

    void setValid(boolean valid) {
        this.valid = valid;
    }

    Object getValue( ) {
        return value;
    }

    public void setValue(Object value) {
        this.value = value;
    }

    boolean isLocalValueSet( ) {
        return localValueSet;
    }

    public void setLocalValueSet(boolean localValueSet) {
        this.localValueSet = localValueSet;
    }
}
```

The SavedState class is a regular bean with accessor methods for all state variables.

The restoreDescendantState( ) method and its helper method look like this:

```
private void restoreDescendantState( ) {
    FacesContext context = getFacesContext( );
    Iterator i = getFacets().values( ).iterator( );
    while (i.hasNext( )) {
        UIComponent facet = (UIComponent) i.next( );
     restoreDescendantState(facet, context);
    }
}

private void restoreDescendantState(UIComponent component,
    FacesContext context) {

    String id = component.getId( );
    component.setId(id); // Forces the client ID to be reset

    if (component instanceof EditableValueHolder) {
        EditableValueHolder input = (EditableValueHolder) component;
        String clientId = component.getClientId(context);
        SavedState state = (SavedState) saved.get(clientId);
        if (state == null) {
            state = new SavedState( );
        }
        input.setValue(state.getValue( ));
        input.setValid(state.isValid( ));
        input.setSubmittedValue(state.getSubmittedValue( ));
        input.setLocalValueSet(state.isLocalValueSet( ));
    }

    Iterator kids = component.getChildren( ).iterator( );
    while (kids.hasNext( )) {
        restoreDescendantState((UIComponent) kids.next( ), context);
    }
}
```

These methods are the reverse of the saveDescendantState( ) methods, setting the state of the facets represented by input components to the state saved previously.

The saved state is kept in a Map with the client ID as the key, as I mentioned earlier, so let's look at how the UITree manipulates the client IDs to ensure that a unique ID is used for each node. The UITree class implements the NamingContainer interface. The getClientId( ) method in the UIComponentBase checks if the component has a parent or grandparent that implements this interface. If so, it calls the naming container's getClientId( ) method and concatenates the component's component ID to the value returned by the naming container's getClientId( ) method, separated by a colon. The UITree class—which is a naming container—implements getClientId( ) like this:

```
public String getClientId(FacesContext context) {
    String ownClientId = super.getClientId(context);
    if (nodeId != null) {
        return ownClientId + NamingContainer.SEPARATOR_CHAR + nodeId;
```

```
        } else {
            return ownClientId;
        }
    }
```

It returns the client ID for the UITree concatenated with the current node ID value separated by the value of the NamingContainer.SEPARATOR_CHAR constant, which is a colon. Every time a facet's getClientId( ) method is called, the UITree getClientId( ) method is also called, resulting in a unique client ID for each node in the model. The getClientId( ) implementation in UIComponentBase caches the client ID, so for this to work, the cache must also be reset by calling setId( ) on the facet component in the restoreDescendantState( ) method.

A JSF request goes through a number of phases defined by a request processing lifecycle, as you may recall from Chapter 8 (Appendix C describes them in more detail). The UITree component specializes the behavior of the request processing lifecycle methods for the Apply Request Values, Process Validations, and Update Model Values phases:

```
    public void processDecodes(FacesContext context) {
        if (!isRendered( )) {
            return;
        }

        model = null;
        saved = new HashMap( );

        processNodes(context, PhaseId.APPLY_REQUEST_VALUES, null, 0);
        setNodeId(null);
        decode(context);
    }

    public void processValidators(FacesContext context) {
        if (!isRendered( )) {
            return;
        }

        processNodes(context, PhaseId.PROCESS_VALIDATIONS, null, 0);
        setNodeId(null);
    }

    public void processUpdates(FacesContext context) {
        if (!isRendered( )) {
            return;
        }

        processNodes(context, PhaseId.UPDATE_MODEL_VALUES, null, 0);
        setNodeId(null);
    }
```

The JSF Lifecycle class calls these methods on the root component in the view's component tree, and the default behavior implemented by the UIComponentBase class is to iterate through all facets and children and call the same method on each. Because the UITree component uses one set of facets to process all nodes in its tree model, it must modify this behavior and instead invoke each facet once for each node.

The processDecodes( ) method resets the model cache, as I mentioned earlier, and also removes the saved state to start fresh for a potentially new model. With exception for resetting the cache, all the phase processing methods follow the same pattern. They call a method called processNodes( ) with a PhaseId instance that identifies the phase each method is responsible for. During the processing of the nodes, the current node ID is manipulated, so all methods reset it to null when processNodes( ) returns.

The processNodes( ) method looks like this:

```
private void processNodes(FacesContext context, PhaseId phaseId,
    String parentId, int childLevel) {

    UIComponent facet = null;
    setNodeId(parentId != null ?
        parentId + NamingContainer.SEPARATOR_CHAR + childLevel :
        "0");
    TreeNode node = getNode( );
    if (node.isLeafNode( )) {
        facet = getLeafNode( );
    }
    else if (node.isExpanded( )) {
        facet = getOpenNode( );
    }
    else {
        facet = getClosedNode( );
    }

    if (phaseId == PhaseId.APPLY_REQUEST_VALUES) {
        facet.processDecodes(context);
    } else if (phaseId == PhaseId.PROCESS_VALIDATIONS) {
        facet.processValidators(context);
    } else {
        facet.processUpdates(context);
    }

    if (node.isExpanded( )) {
        int kidId = 0;
        String currId = getNodeId( );
        Iterator i = node.getChildren( ).iterator( );
        while (i.hasNext( )) {
            TreeNode kid = (TreeNode) i.next( );
            processNodes(context, phaseId, currId, kidId++);
        }
    }
}
```

In addition to the PhaseId and the FacesContext, the processNodes( ) method has one parameter containing the node ID for the parent node or null for the root node, and one parameter containing the index for the child node to process. The two parameters are used to construct and set the node ID for the node to process. Then the processNodes( ) method retrieves the facet matching the current node's type and invokes the appropriate phase processing method on the facet. This means that a submitted value (if any) is saved in the facet, events may be queued, and the current node in the model is updated with the submitted value if it passes validation. Finally, if the node is expanded, the processNodes( ) method calls itself recursively for each child node, adjusting the parent node ID and the child node index for each call.

The facets may queue events during the Apply Request Values and the Process Validations phases, and the UITree component must modify the default event processing behavior to ensure that the model's current node matches the node for which the event was fired before the event listeners are invoked. The first piece of this puzzle is the queueEvent( ) method:

```
public void queueEvent(FacesEvent event) {
    super.queueEvent(new ChildEvent(this, event, getNodeId( )));
}
```

The facets call this method to queue an event, and the UIComponentBase implementation they inherit calls the same method on the component's parent. Usually this means that the implementation in UIViewRoot is called, adding the event to the queue, but for UITree children, the UITree implementation intercepts the call. It wraps the event in an instance of an inner class named ChildEvent and saves the current node ID along with the original event, and then calls the queueEvent( ) method on its parent to add the wrapped event to the event queue with itself as the source.

Eventually, JSF calls the broadcast( ) method on the event source component so it can notify its event listeners of the event. The UITree class provides a customized version of this method as well:

```
public void broadcast(FacesEvent event) throws AbortProcessingException {

    if (!(event instanceof ChildEvent)) {
        super.broadcast(event);
        return;
    }

    ChildEvent childEvent = (ChildEvent) event;
    String currNodeId = getNodeId( );
    setNodeId(childEvent.getNodeId( ));
    FacesEvent nodeEvent = childEvent.getFacesEvent( );
    nodeEvent.getComponent( ).broadcast(nodeEvent);
    setNodeId(currNodeId);
    return;
}
```

If the event is an instance of the ChildEvent class, the broadcast( ) method sets the current node for the model to the node ID saved in the event, unwraps the original event, and asks the real source component to broadcast the original event to its listeners.

The ChildEvent class looks like this:

```
private static class ChildEvent extends FacesEvent {
    private FacesEvent event;
    private String nodeId;

    public ChildEvent(UIComponent component, FacesEvent event,
        String nodeId) {
        super(component);
        this.event = event;
        this.nodeId = nodeId;
    }

    public FacesEvent getFacesEvent( ) {
        return event;
    }

    public String getNodeId( ) {
        return nodeId;
    }

    public PhaseId getPhaseId( ) {
        return event.getPhaseId( );
    }

    public void setPhaseId(PhaseId phaseId) {
        event.setPhaseId(phaseId);
    }

    public boolean isAppropriateListener(FacesListener listener) {
        return false;
    }

    public void processListener(FacesListener listener) {
        throw new IllegalStateException( );
    }
}
```

It extends the FacesEvent class, like all JSF event classes must, but implements the isAppropriateListener( ) and processListener( ) methods to return false and throw an exception because this event type is intended only for wrapping a real event. It also provides accessor methods for the wrapped event and the node ID, and accessor methods for the phaseId property that delegate to the wrapped event.

The tree renderer that we'll look at next performs the actual rendering, but the UITree class prepares for the rendering with a customized encodeBegin( ) method:

```
public void encodeBegin(FacesContext context) throws IOException {
    model = null;
```

```
        if (!keepSaved(context)) {
            saved = new HashMap( );
        }
        super.encodeBegin(context);
    }

    private boolean keepSaved(FacesContext context) {
        Iterator clientIds = saved.keySet( ).iterator( );
        while (clientIds.hasNext( )) {
            String clientId = (String) clientIds.next( );
            Iterator messages = context.getMessages(clientId);
            while (messages.hasNext( )) {
                FacesMessage message = (FacesMessage) messages.next( );
                if (message.getSeverity( ).compareTo(FacesMessage.SEVERITY_ERROR)
                    >= 0) {
                    return true;
                }
            }
        }
        return false;
    }
```

It resets the model cache, as I mentioned earlier, so that a possible value binding is reevaluated in case a new model has been created while processing the events. Depending on the result of validation and event processing, it may also reset the saved component values. The keepSaved( ) method returns true if there's an error message queued for at least one of the nodes. If so, the saved state is kept in order to render the node with the invalid value; otherwise, the saved state is dropped so that the new values are rendered.

Only two things remain: the mysterious NodeToggler, and how to save and restore the state for the UITree itself. Let's start with the NodeToggler. It's implemented as an inner class.

```
    public static class NodeToggler {
        private UITree tree;

        public NodeToggler(UITree tree) {
            this.tree = tree;
    }

        public String toggleExpanded( ) {
            TreeNode node = tree.getDataModel( ).getNode( );
            node.setExpanded(!node.isExpanded( ));
            return "toggledExpanded";
        }
    }
```

The NodeToggler class provides a method named toggleExpand( ) that gets the current node from the UITree and reverses the value of the node's expanded property. This is the behavior most developers using a tree control want when the user clicks on a node, so making it available as part of the component itself saves them from implementing it over and over. The setNodeId( ) method we looked at earlier makes an instance of the NodeToggler available through a request scope variable named by the varNodeToggler property. The setNodeId( ) method gets hold of the bean instance by calling getNodeToggler( ):

```
private NodeToggler getNodeToggler( ) {
    if (nodeToggler == null) {
        nodeToggler = new NodeToggler(this);
    }
    return nodeToggler;
}
```

The method creates an instance the first time it's called and returns the same instance from then on.

That takes care of the components fundamental behavior. The only thing I haven't showed you yet is saving and restoring the component's state, so let's do that now. The saveState( ) and restoreState( ) methods look like this:

```
public Object saveState(FacesContext context) {
    Object values[] = new Object[4];
    values[0] = super.saveState(context);
    values[1] = value;
    values[2] = var;
    values[3] = varNodeToggler;
    return (values);
}

public void restoreState(FacesContext context, Object state) {
    Object values[] = (Object[]) state;
    super.restoreState(context, values[0]);
    value = values[1];
    var = (String) values[2];
    varNodeToggler = (String) values[3];
}
```

Both these methods are defined by an interface called StateHolder that all JSF components implement indirectly because the UIComponent class implements it. JSF may call the saveState( ) method sometime during the Render Response phase. Exactly when depends on which presentation layer technology and JSF implementation you use. The only requirement is that the method must return an object containing the values that need to be saved in order to restore a new instance of the component class to the same state as the current instance. All standard components in the JSF reference implementation return an Object array, but a Map or a List would work fine as well. The first element in the array is the object returned by the superclass implementation and it holds all generic state, such as value bindings, listeners, converters, validators, and the id property value. The next three elements hold the only properties that are unique to the UITree class: value, var, and varNodeToggler.

The restoreState( ) method is called during the Restore View State phase with the object returned by saveState( ) during the previous request. It simply unpacks the data and assigns it to the appropriate instance variables.

There's no guarantee that any of these methods is called, so you should never count on it—for instance, to reset some per-request state variables. The only specification requirement is that if one of these methods is called, the other must also be called. The JSF reference implementation calls them only when the view state is saved on the client. When the state is saved on the server, the reference implementation keeps the whole tree in the session as is instead. Other implementations may use different strategies, e.g., call these methods even when the state is saved on the server to minimize the memory needs.

The TreeRenderer Class

The com.mycompany.jsf.renderer.TreeRenderer class is similar to the renderers we've looked at earlier:

```
package com.mycompany.jsf.renderer;

import java.io.IOException;
import java.util.Iterator;
import java.util.List;

import javax.faces.context.FacesContext;
import javax.faces.context.ResponseWriter;
import javax.faces.component.NamingContainer;
import javax.faces.component.UIComponent;
import javax.faces.component.UIViewRoot;
import javax.faces.render.Renderer;

import com.mycompany.jsf.component.UITree;
import com.mycompany.jsf.model.TreeNode;

public class TreeRenderer extends Renderer {

    public boolean getRendersChildren( ) {
        return true;
    }

    public void encodeChildren(FacesContext context, UIComponent component)
        throws IOException {

        if (!component.isRendered( )) {
            return;
        }

        if (((UITree) component).getValue( ) == null) {
            return;
        }
```

```
        ResponseWriter out = context.getResponseWriter( );
        String clientId = null;
        if (component.getId( ) != null &&
            !component.getId( ).startsWith(UIViewRoot.UNIQUE_ID_PREFIX)) {
            clientId = component.getClientId(context);
        }

        boolean isOuterSpanUsed = false;
        if (clientId != null) {
            isOuterSpanUsed = true;
            out.startElement("span", component);
            out.writeAttribute("id", clientId, "id");
        }
        encodeNodes(context, out, (UITree) component, null, 0);
        ((UITree) component).setNodeId(null);
        if (isOuterSpanUsed) {
            out.endElement("span");
        }
    }
```

It extends the Renderer class and returns true from the getRendersChildren( ) method because it controls the rendering of the UITree component's children.

The encodeChildren( ) method renders the whole tree. It generates a <span> element with an id attribute if the component has been given an explicit ID (just like the BarRenderer we developed in Chapter 13). The model nodes are rendered recursively by the encodeNodes( ) method:

```
    private void encodeNodes(FacesContext context, ResponseWriter out,
        UITree tree, String parentId, int childLevel) throws IOException {

        UIComponent facet = null;
        tree.setNodeId(parentId != null ?
            parentId + NamingContainer.SEPARATOR_CHAR + childLevel : "0");
        TreeNode node = tree.getNode( );
        if (node.isLeafNode( )) {
            facet = tree.getLeafNode( );
        }
        else if (node.isExpanded( )) {
            facet = tree.getOpenNode( );
        }
        else {
            facet = tree.getClosedNode( );
        }

        encodeRecursive(context, facet);
        out.startElement("br", tree);
        out.endElement("br");
        if (node.isExpanded( )) {
            out.startElement("blockquote", tree);
            int kidId = 0;
            String currId = tree.getNodeId( );
            Iterator i = node.getChildren( ).iterator( );
            while (i.hasNext( )) {
```

```
                TreeNode kid = (TreeNode) i.next( );
                encodeNodes(context, out, tree, currId, kidId++);
            }
            out.endElement("blockquote");
        }
    }
```

The encodeNodes( ) method is similar to the processNodes( ) method in the UITree class. It first calls the setNodeId( ) method on the UITree component to set the current node based on the parent node ID and the child node index. It then gets the current node and the facet that corresponds to the current node's type, and lets the facet render the node followed by a <br> element. If the node is expanded, encodeNodes( ) renders the current node's child nodes recursively within a <blockquote> element.

The facets and all their children are rendered recursively by the encodeRecursive( ) method:

```
        private void encodeRecursive(FacesContext context, UIComponent component)
            throws IOException {

            if (!component.isRendered( )) {
                return;
            }

            component.encodeBegin(context);
            if (component.getRendersChildren( )) {
                component.encodeChildren(context);
            } else {
                Iterator i = component.getChildren( ).iterator( );
                while (i.hasNext( )) {
                    UIComponent child = (UIComponent) i.next( );
                    encodeRecursive(context, child);
                }
            }
            component.encodeEnd(context);
        }
    }
```

This method is identical to the one with the same name in the renderers we developed in Chapter 13, so if you develop many renderers, it's a good idea to put this method in a base class that all other custom renderers extend.

Registering the Component and the Renderer

The components and its renderer are registered like this in the *faces-config.xml* file:

```
    <faces-config>
      ...
      <component>
        <component-type>
          com.mycompany.Tree
        </component-type>
        <component-class>
```

```
        com.mycompany.jsf.component.UITree
      </component-class>
    </component>
    ...
    <render-kit>
      <renderer>
        <component-family>com.mycompany.Tree</component-family>
        <renderer-type>com.mycompany.Tree</renderer-type>
        <renderer-class>
          com.mycompany.jsf.renderer.TreeRenderer
        </renderer-class>
      </renderer>
    </render-kit>
    ...
  </faces-config>
```

This is the same kind of declarations as you've seen earlier, with a <component> element for mapping the component type identifier to the component implementation class and a <renderer> element for mapping the combination of a component family and a renderer type to the renderer implementation class.

The JSP Tag Handler Class

As usual, we also need a custom action tag handler class for the component/renderer combination:

```
package com.mycompany.jsf.taglib;

import javax.faces.webapp.UIComponentTag;
import javax.faces.component.UIComponent;
import javax.faces.context.FacesContext;
import javax.faces.el.ValueBinding;
import com.mycompany.jsf.component.UITree;

public class TreeTag extends UIComponentTag {
    private String value;
    private String var;
    private String varNodeToggler;

    public void setValue(String value) {
        this.value = value;
    }

    public void setVar(String var) {
        this.var = var;
    }

    public void setVarNodeToggler(String varNodeToggler) {
        this.varNodeToggler = varNodeToggler;
    }

    public String getComponentType( ) {
        return "com.mycompany.Tree";
    }
```

```
        public String getRendererType( ) {
            return "com.mycompany.Tree";
        }

        protected void setProperties(UIComponent component) {
            super.setProperties(component);

            FacesContext context = getFacesContext( );
            if (value != null) {
                ValueBinding vb =
                    context.getApplication( ).createValueBinding(value);
                component.setValueBinding("value", vb);
            }

            if (var != null) {
                ((UITree) component).setVar(var);
            }

            if (varNodeToggler != null) {
                ((UITree) component).setVarNodeToggler(varNodeToggler);
            }
        }
    }
```

The com.mycompany.jsf.taglib.TreeTag follows the same pattern as all other component tag handlers, with setter methods for all action attributes, getComponentType( ) and getRendererType( ) methods returning the appropriate values, and a setProperties( ) method that sets the component properties and attributes to the custom action attribute values. It must be declared also in the TLD for the tag library, just as you've seen for the other tag handlers.

The tag handler class completes the set of classes for the tree control. This custom component implementation is a complex as it gets, so if you managed to follow along through all twists and turns, you should be able to tackle any type of component. Even if you never need to implement a custom component, I hope the example showed you how flexible the component API is and how you can accomplish even complex features—such as preprocessing of child events—by specializing just a few methods.

CHAPTER 15

Developing a Custom Presentation Layer

The sample application used for the examples in the previous chapters is developed with the JSP custom tag libraries defined by JSF, but as I mentioned in Chapter 1, JSF allows you to plug in other presentation layer technologies besides JSP. In this chapter, I sketch out two alternatives: JSF views defined by pure Java code and JSF views defined in XML files tied to pure HTML templates. In a real application, the implementation of these alternative presentation layers must be fleshed out, but this chapter illustrates what's possible by plugging a few custom classes into the JSF framework.

The ViewHandler Class

The `javax.faces.application.ViewHandler` class is responsible for making JSF views available to the rest of the JSF framework. It's a fairly simple class, with three primary methods: `createView( )`, `renderView( )`, and `restoreView( )`.

The `createView( )` method creates a component tree corresponding to a view identifier with at least a `UIViewRoot` component as the root, and returns it initialized with render kit and locale information. The `renderView( )` method renders the specified view and saves the view state, and the `restoreView( )` method restores a view from the saved state information. Both of these methods cooperate with a `javax.faces.application.StateManager` for handling the details about how and where the view state is saved. A custom `ViewHandler` can support pretty much any type of view representation by implementing these three methods.

Declare that an application uses a custom `ViewHandler` in the *faces-config.xml* file:

```
<faces-config>
  ...
  <application>
    <view-handler>
      com.mycompany.jsf.pl.ClassViewHandlerImpl
    </view-handler>
  </application>
  ...
</faces-config>
```

Because only one ViewHandler can be used at a time, I have commented out the declarations for the custom handlers we develop in this chapter in the book examples *faces-config.xml* file. To run the examples from this chapter, you must first remove the comments around one declaration at a time and restart the web container.

Using Java Classes as Views

As you've seen, JSF components are implemented as regular Java classes extending the javax.faces.component.UIComponent class, and can be instantiated and manipulated programmatically. The JSF component actions you use in the JSP pages create instances of these classes and configure them based on the custom action attributes, as discussed in Chapter 13 and 14.

If you come from a standalone GUI development background, working directly with instances of component classes may feel more familiar than messing around with special elements in a JSP page. The first custom ViewHandler we look at supports this development model with JSF views implemented as regular Java classes, similar to the classes used for a Java Swing interface.

Developing the View Class

Before we look at the custom ViewHandler, let's look at a class that creates a view. The com.mycompany.newsservice.views.SubscribeView class creates a view that's identical to the newsletter subscription example in Chapter 2:

```
package com.mycompany.newsservice.views;

import javax.faces.application.Application;
import javax.faces.component.UICommand;
import javax.faces.component.UIForm;
import javax.faces.component.UIInput;
import javax.faces.component.UIOutput;
import javax.faces.component.UIPanel;
import javax.faces.component.UISelectItems;
import javax.faces.component.UISelectMany;
import javax.faces.component.UIViewRoot;
import javax.faces.context.FacesContext;
import javax.faces.model.SelectItem;
import javax.faces.el.MethodBinding;
import javax.faces.el.ValueBinding;

import java.util.ArrayList;
import java.util.HashMap;
import java.util.List;
import java.util.Map;

import com.mycompany.jsf.pl.View;
```

```
public class SubscribeView implements View {
    public UIViewRoot createView(FacesContext context) {
        Application application = context.getApplication( );
        UIViewRoot viewRoot = new UIViewRoot( );

        UIForm form = new UIForm( );
        viewRoot.getChildren( ).add(form);

        UIPanel grid = new UIPanel( );
        grid.setRendererType("javax.faces.Grid");
        grid.getAttributes( ).put("columns", "2");

        UIOutput emailLabel = new UIOutput( );
        emailLabel.setValue("Email Address:");
        grid.getChildren( ).add(emailLabel);
        UIInput email = new UIInput( );
        ValueBinding emailAddr =
            application.createValueBinding("#{subscr.emailAddr}");
        email.setValueBinding("value", emailAddr);
        grid.getChildren( ).add(email);

        UIOutput subsLabel = new UIOutput( );
        subsLabel.setValue("Newsletters:");
        grid.getChildren( ).add(subsLabel);
        UISelectMany subs = new UISelectMany( );
        subs.setRendererType("javax.faces.Checkbox");
        UISelectItems sis = new UISelectItems( );
        List choices = new ArrayList( );
        choices.add(new SelectItem("1", "JSF News"));
        choices.add(new SelectItem("2", "IT Industry News"));
        choices.add(new SelectItem("3", "Company News"));
        sis.setValue(choices);
        subs.getChildren( ).add(sis);
        grid.getChildren( ).add(subs);
        form.getChildren( ).add(grid);

        UICommand command = new UICommand( );
        command.setValue("Save");
        MethodBinding action =
            application.createMethodBinding("#{subscrHandler.saveSubscriber}",
                null);
        command.setAction(action);
        form.getChildren( ).add(command);
        viewRoot.getChildren( ).add(form);

        return viewRoot;
    }
}
```

The SubscribeView class implements an interface named com.mycompany.jsf.pl.View, which declares a single method named createView( ). This method creates and returns an instance of UIViewRoot with components of other types as its children.

Declaring the method in an interface that all view classes must implement makes it possible for the `ViewHandler` to work with any view class without knowing its name.

The `createView( )` method in the `SubscribeView` class creates a `UIForm` component containing a `UIPanel` component configured with a grid renderer for layout. Children of type `UIOutput` for text labels, a `UIInput` component for the email address, and a `UISelectMany` component with a checkbox renderer for the list of newsletters are added as children of the `UIPanel` component. The child component created for the `UISelectMany` component is a `UISelectItems` component with `SelectItem` instances for each newsletter choices. The final `UIForm` child is a `UICommand` component for submitting the form.

The `UIInput` and `UISelectMany` components are bound to the same managed bean properties as we used for the JSP version of this view in Chapter 2. The `ValueBinding` objects are created by calling the `Application` `createValueBinding( )` method with the same kind of JSF value binding expressions as for the JSP layer. The `UICommand` component is bound to an action method in a similar manner, with a `MethodBinding` object created by the `Application` `createMethodBinding( )` method.

Rendering the view created by the `SubscribeView` class results in the screen shown in Figure 15-1.

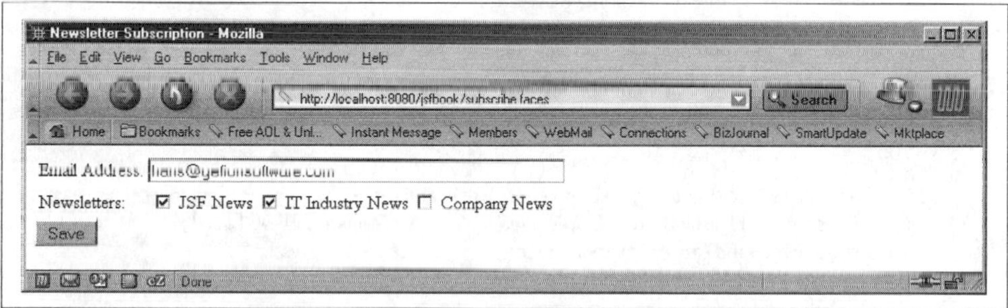

Figure 15-1. The screen generated from the SubscribeView

It works just like its JSP counterpart, so run the example, add a value in the email field, select a few checkboxes, click the button, and verify that the method in the `SubscriberHandler` class is invoked just as in Chapter 2, writing the email address and the current selections to the shell where the web container runs.

In this example, I don't use any converters or validators, but such objects can of course be added to the components using the methods you've seen in the previous chapters. For some applications it may even make sense to handle events with listeners implemented as anonymous inner classes, as is common in a Java Swing application, instead of binding the components to managed bean methods.

Developing the ViewHandler

Let's move on to the custom ViewHandler that supports views represented by regular Java classes like the SubscribeView class. The class declaration and the constructor look like this:

```
package com.mycompany.jsf.pl;

import java.io.IOException;
import java.io.InputStream;
import java.io.OutputStream;
import java.io.OutputStreamWriter;
import java.util.HashMap;
import java.util.Iterator;
import java.util.Locale;
import java.util.Map;
import javax.faces.FactoryFinder;
import javax.faces.application.StateManager;
import javax.faces.application.StateManager.SerializedView;
import javax.faces.application.ViewHandler;
import javax.faces.component.UIComponent;
import javax.faces.component.UIViewRoot;
import javax.faces.context.ExternalContext;
import javax.faces.context.FacesContext;
import javax.faces.context.ResponseWriter;
import javax.faces.render.RenderKit;
import javax.faces.render.RenderKitFactory;
import javax.servlet.ServletRequest;
import javax.servlet.ServletResponse;
import com.mycompany.newsservice.views.SubscribeView;

public class ClassViewHandlerImpl extends ViewHandler {
    private static final String STATE_VAR = "com.mycompany.viewState";
    protected ViewHandler origViewHandler;
    private Map views = new HashMap( );

    public ClassViewHandlerImpl(ViewHandler origViewHandler) {
        this.origViewHandler = origViewHandler;
    }
```

The com.mycompany.jsf.pl.ClassViewHandlerImpl extends the abstract ViewHandler class. The constructor takes an argument of type ViewHandler and saves a reference to it in an instance variable. When a pluggable class, such as a ViewHandler implementation, has a constructor with an argument of the same type as the object it replaces, JSF uses this constructor to give it a reference to the previously registered object. This makes it easy for a custom class to delegate most of the implementation to the previously registered object. I use this feature to delegate the processing of a number of methods in the ClassViewHandlerImpl:

```
public Locale calculateLocale(FacesContext context) {
    return origViewHandler.calculateLocale(context);
}
```

```
public String calculateRenderKitId(FacesContext context) {
    return origViewHandler.calculateRenderKitId(context);
}

public String getActionURL(FacesContext context, String viewId) {
    return origViewHandler.getActionURL(context, viewId);
}

public String getResourceURL(FacesContext context, String path) {
    return origViewHandler.getResourceURL(context, path);
}
```

The custom class doesn't modify the behavior for these methods, so I let the previous ViewHandler implementation handle them instead. You can look at the description of these methods in Appendix D for details, but briefly, the default calculateLocale( ) determines the locale based on the Accept-Language header as described in Chapter 11, calculateRenderKitId( ) returns either the ID for the JSF default render kit or the render kit ID specified in the *faces-config.xml* file, getActionURL( ) returns a URL for invoking the specified view, and getResourceURL( ) returns a URL for a resource within the web application (e.g., an image file).

The first customized method is the createView( ) method:

```
public UIViewRoot createView(FacesContext context, String viewId) {
    String realViewId = viewId;
    if (viewId.indexOf(".") != -1) {
        realViewId = viewId.substring(0, viewId.indexOf("."));
    }
    UIViewRoot viewRoot = createViewRoot(context, realViewId);
    if (viewRoot != null) {
        if (context.getViewRoot( ) != null) {
            UIViewRoot oldRoot = context.getViewRoot( );
            viewRoot.setLocale(oldRoot.getLocale( ));
            viewRoot.setRenderKitId(oldRoot.getRenderKitId( ));
        }
        else {
            ViewHandler activeVH =
                context.getApplication( ).getViewHandler( );
            viewRoot.setLocale(activeVH.calculateLocale(context));
            viewRoot.setRenderKitId(activeVH.calculateRenderKitId(context));
        }
    }
    return viewRoot;
}
```

JSF calls this method to create a new view when it can't find a previously saved view state for the requested view or when the processing of a navigation rule results in the selection of a new view.

The viewId parameter identifies the view to create. The ViewHandler implementation defines exactly what a view ID is, but it's typically a part of the request URI path, possibly modified to be the same independent of whether JSF is mapped to a URI prefix (e.g., */faces/**) or an extension (e.g., **.faces*). To use a concrete example, the ViewHandler for the JSP layer uses the context-relative path for the JSP page as the view ID. Because the JSF specification doesn't define a public method for converting a request path to a view ID, the createView( ) method is invoked with the context-relative path instead (despite the parameter name) and it's up to the createView( ) method to do the conversion between a path and a view ID. The JSP layer ViewHandler converts the request path to a context-relative JSP page path by either appending the JSP extension (when prefix mapping is used) or replacing the request path extension with the JSP extension (when extension mapping is used). The custom ClassViewHandlerImpl class simply drops the extension if there is one and uses the rest of the path as the view ID.

After adjusting the path to a viewId value, the createView( ) method calls the createViewRoot( ) method to create the view and then sets the locale and render-kit ID for the returned UIViewRoot. This information is copied from the previous view, if any, or calculated by calling the calculateLocale( ) and calculateRenderKitId( ) methods on the ViewHandler returned by the Application instance It's important to delegate to the handler returned by the Application instance, because it's the one most recently registered and it may customize the implementation of these methods but delegate the rest of the processing to the previously registered handler.

The createViewRoot( ) method uses a View implementation like the SubscribeView class to create the component tree for the view:

```
protected UIViewRoot createViewRoot(FacesContext context, String viewId) {
    UIViewRoot viewRoot = null;
    View view = (View) views.get(viewId);
    if (view == null) {
        if ("/subscribe".equals(viewId)) {
            view = new SubscribeView( );
            views.put(viewId, view);
        }
    }
    if (view != null) {
        viewRoot = view.createView(context);
        viewRoot.setViewId(viewId);
    }
    return viewRoot;
}
```

The ClassViewHandlerImpl class uses a java.util.Map as a cache for View instances, so the createViewRoot( ) method first tries to get hold of an instance from the cache. If it can't find one, it creates an instance of the View class registered for the view ID and puts it in the cache. In this example ViewHandler implementation, I have hardcoded the class name for the one View class it supports, but a real implementation could be configured with mappings between view IDs and implementation classes instead. With a reference to a cached or newly created View instance, the createViewRoot( ) method calls the createView( ) method on the View, sets the viewId property on the returned UIViewRoot, and returns it.

JSF calls the renderView( ) method when it's time to render the view:

```
public void renderView(FacesContext context, UIViewRoot viewToRender)
    throws IOException {

    setupResponseWriter(context);

    StateManager sm = context.getApplication( ).getStateManager( );
    SerializedView state = sm.saveSerializedView(context);
    context.getExternalContext( ).getRequestMap( ).put(STATE_VAR, state);

    context.getResponseWriter( ).startDocument( );
    renderResponse(context, viewToRender);
    context.getResponseWriter( ).endDocument( );
}
```

The ResponseWriter all renderers use to generate the markup for the components is created and configured by a call to the setupResponseWriter( ) method:

```
private void setupResponseWriter(FacesContext context)
    throws IOException {

    ServletResponse response = (ServletResponse)
        context.getExternalContext( ).getResponse( );
    OutputStream os = response.getOutputStream( );
    Map headers = context.getExternalContext( ).getRequestHeaderMap( );
    String acceptHeader = (String) headers.get("Accept");

    RenderKitFactory renderFactory = (RenderKitFactory)
        FactoryFinder.getFactory(FactoryFinder.RENDER_KIT_FACTORY);
    RenderKit renderKit =
        renderFactory.getRenderKit(context,
             context.getViewRoot( ).getRenderKitId( ));
    ResponseWriter writer =
        renderKit.createResponseWriter(new OutputStreamWriter(os),
            acceptHeader, response.getCharacterEncoding( ));
    context.setResponseWriter(writer);
    response.setContentType(writer.getContentType( ));
}
```

A web container uses the ServletResponse object returned by the ExternalContext getResponse( ) method to generate the response. The setupResponseWriter( ) method gets hold of the ServletResponse object and retrieves the java.io.OutputStream for the response body. It then extracts the value of the Accept request header, containing a comma-separated list of the content MIME types (e.g., "text/html, text/plain") the client accepts.

The ResponseWriter writes markup elements, so different implementation classes may be needed for different markup languages (e.g., one for XML languages and one for HTML). The JSF class that knows the details about a specific markup language is the RenderKit, so the setupResponseWriter( ) method creates an appropriate ResponseWriter by retrieving the RenderKit for the view and calling its createResponseWriter( ) method with the Accept header value and a java.io.OutputStreamWriter wrapped around the response body output stream. A fancy render kit implementation may use the Accept header value to return a ResponseWriter instance configured to produce slightly different element syntax depending on the header value, e.g., use strict XML syntax if the header value contains "application/xhtml+xml" (the MIME type for XHTML) or use plain old HTML syntax if it contains only "text/html". The ResponseWriter getContentType( ) always returns the MIME type it's compliant with, so the setupResponseWriter( ) method uses this value to set the content type for the ServletResponse object.

Returning to the renderView( ) method, the view state is collected and returned as an instance of the SerializedView class by the StateManager saveSerializedView( ) method. This method collects the state for all components by calling their saveState( ) methods (as I described in Chapter 14) and traverses the component tree to figure out parent-child relationships for all components. It encodes this information in an implementation-dependent way and returns it as an instance of the ServializedView class. The renderView( ) method saves the state as a request scope variable for later and calls the protected renderResponse( ) method to render the components:

```
protected void renderResponse(FacesContext context, UIComponent component)
    throws IOException {

    component.encodeBegin(context);
    if (component.getRendersChildren( )) {
        component.encodeChildren(context);
    }
    else {
        Iterator i = component.getChildren( ).iterator( );
        while (i.hasNext( )) {
            renderView(context, (UIComponent) i.next( ), state);
        }
    }
    component.encodeEnd(context);
}
```

The renderResponse( ) method calls encodeBegin( ), encodeChildren( ) for components that render their own children, and encodeEnd( ) recursively on all components in the component tree.

Renderers for the UIForm component call the ViewHandler writeState( ) method just before they render the end tag for the form:

```
public void writeState(FacesContext context) {
    SerializedView state = (SerializedView)
        context.getExternalContext( ).getRequestMap( ).get(STATE_VAR);
    if (state != null) {
        StateManager sm = context.getApplication( ).getStateManager( );
        sm.writeState(context, state);
    }
}
```

For ClassViewHandler, this method calls the StateManager writeState( ) method with the state saved as a request scope attribute value by the renderView( ) method. The writeState( ) method in the JSF reference implementation's default StateManager writes a complete HTML element for a hidden field containing the state if client-side state is enabled, which works fine for this example custom ViewHandler. Other JSF implementations may implement the writeState( ) method differently, e.g., writing just the encoded state value to a previously created element, because the JSF spec leaves these details up to each vendor. To be on the safe side, it's a good idea to implement a custom StateManager along with the custom ViewHandler, to ensure that they are in sync, but I rely on the reference implementation behavior for this example.

This roundabout way of getting the state added to the response is needed primarily for the JSP layer. When the JSP presentation layer is used, the component tree is created at the same time as it's rendered, so the state can't be collected until at the end of the rendering phase. The JSP layer's ViewHandler therefore buffers the response and writes a marker in the buffered response* every time the writeState( ) method is called. When the whole tree has been created and rendered to the buffer, it asks the StateManager to collect the state and then goes back and replaces the markers with the hidden fields for the state by calling the StateManager writeState( ) method.

The restoreView( ) method is called to restore a view from the state information included with the request for client-side state or available somewhere on the server for server-side state:

```
public UIViewRoot restoreView(FacesContext context, String viewId) {
    String realViewId = viewId;
    if (viewId.indexOf(".") != -1) {
        realViewId = viewId.substring(0, viewId.indexOf("."));
    }

    String renderKitId =
        context.getApplication().getViewHandler().
        calculateRenderKitId(context);

    StateManager sm = context.getApplication().getStateManager();
    return sm.restoreView(context, realViewId, renderKitId);
}
```

The viewId parameter may hold either a URI path or a real viewId, so it's adjusted the same way as in the createView( ) method.

With client-side state, only the render kit knows how the state was encoded in the response† and, therefore, how to pick it up from the request data, so the

* Instead of writing a marker, an implementation can make a note about where in the buffer the state should be inserted.

† The StateManager cooperates with a class named javax.faces.render.ResponseStateManager that belongs to the render kit for encoding the state in a response, as well as for extracting it from request data.

restoreView( ) method must first figure out which render kit the application uses. It does so by calling the calculateRenderKit( ) method of the most recently registered ViewHandler instance, just as in the createView( ) method shown earlier. If the application doesn't specify a render kit, the default JSF HTML render kit is used.

The restoreView( ) method asks the StateManager to restore the view, potentially with the help from the render kit, and returns the UIViewRoot for the view or null if no state is available for the view. The JSF implementation then processes the returned view as we've talked about in previous chapters.

Using Pure HTML Templates with XML View Definition Files

When you use JSP pages to create JSF views, you must use special elements (the JSF custom action elements as well as standard JSP directives and action elements). To look at the result, you need to let a web container process the page first instead of just opening the page in a browser. In addition, plain HTML–based development tools are not always able to deal with the special elements. Developing the views as regular Java classes—as described in the previous section—may be familiar to old GUI application gurus, but it doesn't work well when nonprogrammers develop the user interface layout.

The Apache Tapestry (*http://jakarta.apache.org/tapestry/*) open source web interface framework uses an approach in which each page is described by a combination of a page specification file, a Java class similar to a JSF "glue class" or "backing bean," and a plain HTML template file. The page specification file defines Tapestry components and binds them to elements in the HTML template identified by special ID attributes and to properties of the Java page class. This means that people skilled in user interface design and experienced with HTML, CSS, and so on, can develop the user interface with standard HTML development tools—they don't have to learn another set of special markup elements or worry about EL expressions and request processing lifecycles. Java programmers develop the page classes and the business logic classes, and tie the whole thing together through the page specification file.

With a custom ViewHandler, JSF can support this development model as well. In this section, we look at an embryo for such a ViewHandler implementation. I'm not making any claims that this example supports all the same features as Tapestry, just that it's similar in spirit. The custom ViewHandler can provide the base for a JSF environment on par with Tapestry, but to reach that point it needs to be extended with more code than I can describe in this book and it may also require custom versions of additional JSF classes.

Developing the HTML Template and the View Specification

This custom ViewHandler works with views described by a combination of an HTML template and a view specification file. The HTML template for the newsletter subscription view looks like this:

```
<html>
  <head>
    <title>Newsletter Subscription</title>
  </head>
  <body>
    <form id="form">
      <table>
        <tr>
          <td>Email Address:</td>
          <td><input id="form:emailAddr" size="50" /></td>
        </tr>
        <tr>
          <td>Newsletters:</td>
          <td>
            <span id="form:subs">
              <input type="checkbox" value="1">foo</input>
              <input type="checkbox" value="2">bar</input>
            </span>
          </td>
        </tr>
      </table>
      <input id="form:save" type="submit" value="Save" />
    </form>
  </body>
</html>
```

It's a plain XHTML file with id attributes for the elements that represent JSF components. To keep the example simple, I've used id attribute values with the JSF naming container syntax, but a more sophisticated implementation would make it possible to use plain values instead. The reason for using XHTML instead of HTML is also to keep the implementation simple. There are parsers that can parse HTML and present it to an application as XML, so a real implementation can support both HTML and XHTML without too many modifications.

For the checkboxes, I'm using a <span> element to give the whole group one id attribute, because the whole group is handled by one JSF component. The <input> elements within the <span> element are ignored when the view is rendered, but serves a purpose during the template design to see how the page looks like in a browser.

The view specification file is an XML file that looks like this for the newsletter view:

```
<view-specification>
  <component id="form" type="javax.faces.Form">
    <component id="emailAddr" type="javax.faces.Input"
      value="#{subscr.emailAddr}" />
    <component id="subs" type="javax.faces.SelectMany"
```

```
      rendererType="javax.faces.Checkbox" value="#{subscr.subscriptionIds}">
      <component type="javax.faces.SelectItem" itemValue="1"
        itemLabel="JSF News" />
      <component type="javax.faces.SelectItem" itemValue="2"
        itemLabel="IT Industry News" />
      <component type="javax.faces.SelectItem" itemValue="3"
        itemLabel="Company News" />
    </component>
    <component id="save" type="javax.faces.Command" value="Save"
      action="#{subscrHandler.saveSubscriber}" />
  </component>
</view-specification>
```

A <view-specification> element encloses all the other elements. Each component is described by a <component> element. All <component> elements must have a type attribute with a JSF component type identifier as the value. An id attribute must be provided for components tied to elements in the template file, such as the form, input field, and checkbox list components in this example. For <component> elements representing child components not tied directly to the template, such as the javax.faces.SelectItem components providing the list of choices for the javax.faces.SelectMany component, the id attribute is optional.

All attributes other than id and type must correspond to properties of the specified component type or to attributes recognized by the component's renderer. The ViewHandler configures the components based on the attributes in the view specification file when it creates the view. When it renders the view, it uses the attributes defined for the corresponding elements in the template file to further configure the components. This means that you can specify all render-dependent attributes, such as CSS class and field size, in the template file so the template can be debugged by opening it directly in a browser.

The input components are bound to managed bean properties through JSF value binding expressions and the command component is bound to an action method by a method binding expression, the same as in a JSP page with JSF custom actions. Rendering the view results in the same screen as for the example in the previous section, shown in Figure 15-1.

Developing the ViewHandler

The com.mycompany.jsf.pl.XMLViewHandlerImlp supports this type of view, defined by the combination of a view specification class and an HTML template:

```
package com.mycompany.jsf.pl;

import java.io.IOException;
import java.io.InputStream;
import java.io.OutputStream;
import java.io.OutputStreamWriter;
import java.util.Iterator;
import java.util.Stack;
```

```
import javax.faces.application.Application;
import javax.faces.application.ViewHandler;
import javax.faces.component.ActionSource;
import javax.faces.component.UIComponent;
import javax.faces.component.UISelectMany;
import javax.faces.component.UISelectOne;
import javax.faces.component.UIViewRoot;
import javax.faces.context.ExternalContext;
import javax.faces.context.FacesContext;
import javax.faces.context.ResponseWriter;
import javax.faces.el.PropertyNotFoundException;
import javax.faces.el.ValueBinding;
import javax.faces.el.MethodBinding;

import org.xml.sax.Attributes;
import org.xml.sax.SAXException;
import org.xml.sax.SAXParseException;
import org.xml.sax.helpers.DefaultHandler;
import javax.xml.parsers.SAXParserFactory;
import javax.xml.parsers.ParserConfigurationException;
import javax.xml.parsers.SAXParser;

public class XMLViewHandlerImpl extends ViewHandlerImpl {

    public XMLViewHandlerImpl(ViewHandler origViewHandler) {
        super(origViewHandler);
    }
```

The `XMLViewHandlerImpl` class extends the `ClassViewHandlerImpl` class we developed in the previous section and inherits all its public methods. The differences between the two are in the protected methods.

The protected `createViewRoot( )` method looks like this:

```
protected UIViewRoot createViewRoot(FacesContext context, String viewId) {

    SAXParserFactory factory = SAXParserFactory.newInstance( );
    SAXParser saxParser = null;
    try {
        saxParser = factory.newSAXParser( );
    }
    catch (SAXException e) {
        throw new IllegalArgumentException(e.getMessage( ));
    }
    catch (ParserConfigurationException e) {
        throw new IllegalArgumentException(e.getMessage( ));
    }

    UIViewRoot viewRoot = new UIViewRoot( );
    viewRoot.setViewId(viewId);
    ExternalContext ec = context.getExternalContext( );
    InputStream viewSpecIS = null;

    DefaultHandler handler =
        new ViewSpecHandler(context.getApplication( ), viewRoot);
```

```
        try {
            viewSpecIS = context.getExternalContext( ).
                getResourceAsStream(viewId + ".view");
            saxParser.parse(viewSpecIS, handler);

        } catch (SAXParseException e) {
            String msg = "View spec parsing error: " + e.getMessage( ) +
                " at line=" + e.getLineNumber( ) +
                " col=" + e.getColumnNumber( );
            throw new IllegalArgumentException(msg);
        } catch (Exception e) {
            String msg = "View spec parsing error: " + e.getMessage( );
            throw new IllegalArgumentException(msg);
        } finally {
            try {
                if (viewSpecIS != null) {
                    viewSpecIS.close( );
                }
            } catch (IOException e) {}
        }
        return viewRoot;
    }
```

The `createViewRoot( )` method creates the view by parsing the view specification file, creating the components defined by the `<component>` elements, configuring them based on the attribute values, and arranging them in a tree structure based on the element nesting. It uses the standard Java XML parser API (JAXP) to create a SAX parser. Next, it creates a `UIViewRoot` for the view and passes it along with a reference to the JSF `Application` object to a new instance of the `ViewSpecHandler` inner class. This class is an extension of the `org.xml.sax.helpers.DefaultHandler` class, which is a class for handling SAX parser events.

The view specification must be stored in a file with a path corresponding to the view ID plus the *.view* extension. The `createView( )` method obtains an input stream for this file from the `ExternalContext` and then asks the SAX parser to parse the file.

If you've never used a SAX parser before, you may wonder how all this works, but it's fairly straightforward. The SAX parser calls methods on its `DefaultHandler` instance when it encounters things like the start tag or end tag for an element, characters, or whitespace. The `DefaultHandler` provides default implementations for all methods, so an application specific subclass only needs to implement the methods for the events of interest.

The `ViewSpecHandler` class is just interested in start and end tags, so it implements only the `startElement( )` and `endElement( )` methods:

```
    private static class ViewSpecHandler extends DefaultHandler {
        private Stack stack;
        private Application application;

        public ViewSpecHandler(Application application, UIComponent root) {
            this.application = application;
```

```
        stack = new Stack( );
        stack.push(root);
    }

    public void startElement(String namespaceURI, String lName,
        String qName, Attributes attrs) throws SAXException {

        if ("component".equals(qName)) {
            UIComponent component = createComponent(application, attrs);
            ((UIComponent) stack.peek( )).getChildren( ).add(component);
            stack.push(component);
        }
    }

    public void endElement(String namespaceURI, String lName,
        String qName) throws SAXException {

        if ("component".equals(qName)) {
            stack.pop( );
        }
    }
```

The `ViewSpecHandler` constructor saves a reference to the `Application` objects, creates a `java.util.Stack`, and pushes the root component onto the stack.

The `startElement( )` method checks if the element is a `<component>` element. If it is, `startElement( )` calls `createComponent( )` to create an instance, which it then adds as a child of the component at the top of the stack and then pushes onto the stack. A real implementation would also support other element types for attaching validators, converters, and listeners to the components. The `endElement( )` method simply pops the top object off the stack.

The `createComponent( )` method is doing the grunt work in the `ViewSpecHandler` class:

```
private UIComponent createComponent(Application application,
    Attributes attrs) {

    if (attrs == null || attrs.getValue("type") == null) {
        String msg =
            "'component' element without 'type' attribute found";
        throw new IllegalArgumentException(msg);
    }

    String type = attrs.getValue("type");
    UIComponent component = application.createComponent(type);
    if (component == null) {
        String msg = "No component class registered for 'type' " +
            type;
        throw new IllegalArgumentException(msg);
    }

    for (int i = 0; i < attrs.getLength( ); i++) {
        String name = attrs.getLocalName(i);
```

```
            if ("".equals(name)) {
                name = attrs.getQName(i);
            }
            if ("type".equals(name)) {
                continue;
            }
            String value = attrs.getValue(i);
            if (value.startsWith("#{")) {
                if ("action".equals(name)) {
                    MethodBinding mb =
                        Application.createMethodBinding(value, null);
                    ((ActionSource) component).setAction(mb);
                }
                else {
                    ValueBinding vb =
                        application.createValueBinding(value);
                    component.setValueBinding(name, vb);
                }
            }
            else {
                component.getAttributes( ).put(name, value);
            }
        }
        return component;
    }
```

It first verifies that there's a type attribute for the <component> element and calls the Application createComponent( ) method to create a component of the specified type. It then uses the remainder of the attributes to configure the component.

If the attribute value starts with the JSF EL #{ delimiter, it creates either a MethodBinding or a ValueBinding and calls the appropriate component methods to set it. In this example, I only recognize the action attribute as an attribute that takes a MethodBinding, but a real implementation should instead use introspection to figure out if the expression is for a method or value binding. Attributes that don't have a JSF EL expression value are set through the component's generic attributes list. When all <component> element attributes have been processed, the configured component is returned.

The protected renderResponse( ) method is almost identical to the createViewRoot( ) method:

```
    protected void renderResponse(FacesContext context, UIComponent component)
        throws IOException {

        SAXParserFactory factory = SAXParserFactory.newInstance( );
        SAXParser saxParser = null;
        try {
            saxParser = factory.newSAXParser( );
        }
        catch (SAXException e) {
            throw new IllegalArgumentException(e.getMessage( ));
        }
```

```
        catch (ParserConfigurationException e) {
            throw new IllegalArgumentException(e.getMessage( ));
        }

        UIViewRoot root = (UIViewRoot) component;
        String viewId = root.getViewId( );
        ExternalContext ec = context.getExternalContext( );
        InputStream templIS = null;

        DefaultHandler handler = new TemplateHandler(context, root);
        try {
            templIS = context.getExternalContext( ).
                getResourceAsStream(viewId + ".html");
            saxParser.parse(templIS, handler);

        } catch (SAXParseException e) {
            String msg = "Template parsing error: " + e.getMessage( ) +
                " at line=" + e.getLineNumber( ) +
                " col=" + e.getColumnNumber( );
            throw new IllegalArgumentException(msg);
        } catch (Exception e) {
            String msg = "Template parsing error: " + e.getMessage( );
            throw new IllegalArgumentException(msg);
        } finally {
            try {
                if (templIS != null) {
                    templIS.close( );
                }
            } catch (IOException e) {}
        }
    }
```

The differences are that it parses the template file—stored with a path corresponding to the view ID plus the *.html* extension—with an instance of the `TemplateHandler` class, and that it uses the existing component tree instead of creating it.

The `TemplateHandler` class handles the start and end tag events for all elements in the template file, plus the events for characters in template element bodies.

```
    private static class TemplateHandler extends DefaultHandler {
        private StringBuffer textBuff = null;
        private FacesContext context;
        private ResponseWriter out;
        private UIViewRoot root;
        private Stack stack;
        private boolean suppressTemplate;

        public TemplateHandler(FacesContext context, UIViewRoot root) {

            this.context = context;
            this.root = root;
            out = context.getResponseWriter( );
            stack = new Stack( );
            stack.push(root);
        }
```

The constructor saves references to the FacesContext and the view's UIViewRoot, and gets a reference to the ResponseWriter. It also creates a Stack and pushes the root component onto the top.

The SAX parser calls a handler method named characters( ) when it encounters characters in element bodies:

```
        public void characters(char buf[], int offset, int len)
            throws SAXException {

            if (suppressTemplate) {
                return;
            }

            if (textBuff == null) {
                textBuff = new StringBuffer(len * 2);
            }
            textBuff.append(buf, offset, len);
        }

        private void handleTextIfNeeded( ) {
            if (textBuff != null) {
                String value = textBuff.toString( ).trim( );
                textBuff = null;
                if (value.length( ) == 0) {
                    return;
                }
                try {
                    out.writeText(value, null);
                }
                catch (IOException ioe) {}
            }
        }
    }
```

The characters( ) method saves the characters in a StringBuffer, unless the template content is currently suppressed (a situation I'll talk more about in a bit). The other event handling methods call the private handleTextIfNeeded( ) method to add buffered characters to the response.

The startElement( ) method looks like this:

```
    public void startElement(String namespaceURI, String lName,
        String qName, Attributes attrs) throws SAXException {

        handleTextIfNeeded( );

        String id = attrs.getValue("id");
        if (id != null && root.findComponent(id) != null) {
            UIComponent comp = findAndConfigure(id, attrs);
            stack.push(comp);
            try {
                comp.encodeBegin(context);
            }
```

```
            catch (IOException ioe) {}
            suppressTemplate = suppressTemplate(comp);
        }
        else {
            stack.push(qName);
            if (!suppressTemplate) {
                try {
                    out.startElement(qName, null);
                    for (int i = 0; i < attrs.getLength( ); i++) {
                        out.writeAttribute(attrs.getQName(i),
                             attrs.getValue(i), null);
                    }
                }
                catch (IOException ioe) {}
            }
        }
    }
```

The `startElement( )` method calls the `handleTextIfNeeded( )` method to add buffered text to the response, if any. Next, it looks for an `id` attribute. If it finds one, the template element may be bound to a component with this ID. The `startElement( )` calls the `findComponent( )` method on the root component method with the ID to locate the component, and if it finds one, it calls the `findAndConfigure( )` method to configure it based on the template element attributes. It then pushes the component onto the stack and calls its `encodeBegin( )` method to let it render itself.

The `findAndConfigure( )` method looks like this:

```
    private UIComponent findAndConfigure(String id, Attributes attrs) {
        UIComponent comp = root.findComponent(id);
        for (int i = 0; i < attrs.getLength( ); i++) {
            // Don't overwrite "id"
            if ("id".equals(attrs.getQName(i))) {
                continue;
            }
            comp.getAttributes( ).put(attrs.getQName(i), attrs.getValue(i));
        }
        return comp;
    }
```

It locates the component and sets all attributes from the template element, except the `id` attribute. The `id` attributes in the template have values with the naming container client ID syntax, so they must not be used to override the components' real IDs.

After calling the `encodeBegin( )` on the component, the `startElement( )` method sets a `suppressTemplate` variable to the value returned by the `suppressTemplate( )` method:

```
    private boolean suppressTemplate(UIComponent comp) {
        return comp.getRendersChildren( ) ||
            comp instanceof UISelectMany || comp instanceof UISelectOne;
    }
```

This method returns true if the component renders its children. A call to getRendersChildren( ) should be enough, but (possibly due to a specification bug) this method returns false for components of type UISelectMany and UISelectOne, even though they in fact do render their own children.

The example ViewHandler ignores all of the content of a template element bound to a component that renders its children; for instance, the template <input> elements in the body of the <span> element for the UISelectMany component in the newsletter subscription template file. A more sophisticated implementation could possibly use the template element body to configure the main component, e.g., decide which type of renderer it should use.

The remainder of the startElement( ) method deals with template elements without id attributes and elements with id attributes that don't match a component in the view. For these elements, the element name is pushed onto the stack and if suppressTemplate is false, the element and all its attributes are copied as is to the response.

The endElement( ) method takes care of the rest of the rendering requirements:

```
        public void endElement(String namespaceURI, String lName,
            String qName) throws SAXException {

            handleTextIfNeeded( );

            Object o = stack.pop( );
            if (o instanceof String) {
                try {
                    out.endElement(qName);
                    out.writeText("\n", null);
                }
                catch (IOException ioe) {}
            }
            else {
                UIComponent comp = (UIComponent) o;
                try {
                    if (comp.getRendersChildren( )) {
                        comp.encodeChildren(context);
                    }
                    comp.encodeEnd(context);
                    out.writeText("\n", null);
                }
                catch (IOException ioe) {}
                if (suppressTemplate) {
                    suppressTemplate = false;
                }
            }
        }
    }
}
```

It first calls the handleTextIfNeeded( ) method and then pops the top object off the stack. If the object is a String, the end tag must be for a template element, not bound to a component, so it's just added to the response.

If it's not a String, it must be a component. The endElement( ) method calls its encodeChildren( ) method if the component's getRenderersChildren( ) method returns true. Then the encodeEnd( ) method is called to finish the rendering of the component. When the component has been rendered, the suppressTemplate flag is reset if it was set to start processing content from the template again.

The XMLViewHandlerImpl class described in this section provides the basic functionality needed to support the use of pure HTML templates with the component configuration in separate view specification files. A number of enhancements must be made before it can be used for real products; for instance, more thorough error handling is needed, view specification elements for facets, validators, converters, and listeners must be added and supported by the SAX parser handlers, and elements for including pieces from an external view specification and template file combination àla Tapestry's component specification files is essential. A special render kit and a slightly different rendering model may also be needed to match some of Tapestry's features (such as clean support for generation of client-side validation code). Performance enhancements, e.g., in the form of cached templates, are also possible.

The ClassViewHandlerImpl class described in the first section of this chapter can also be improved, but these two examples illustrate the possibilities and I hope might inspire someone to pick up where I left off and develop a useful alternative to the JSP layer that may get the official blessing in a future version of the JSF specification.

APPENDIX A

Standard JSF Tag Libraries

This appendix contains reference material for the custom action elements in the standard JSF tag libraries that you can use in JSP pages.

Each action element is described with an overview, a syntax reference, an attribute table, and an example. The syntax reference shows all supported attributes, with optional attributes embedded in square brackets ([ ]). Mutually exclusive attributes are separated with vertical bars (|). For attributes that accept predefined values, all values are listed separated with vertical bars; the default value (if any) is in boldface. Italics are used for attribute values that don't have a fixed set of accepted values.

The attributes table has an EL expression type column, with the values None, Any, VB, or MB. None means that a static attribute value must be used. Any means that a static value or any type of JSF EL expression can be used, including EL expressions containing any of the EL operators. VB means that the value can be a static value (unless otherwise noted) or a value binding expression, i.e., the EL subset that identifies a read/write bean property, a `java.util.List` or array element, a `java.util.Map` value, or a simple scoped variable. MB means that the value must be a method binding, with the method signature described in the description column.

JSF Tag Libraries URIs and Default Prefixes

The URIs and default prefixes for the JSF tag libraries are listed in Table A-1.

Table A-1. URIs and prefixes for the JSTL libraries

Library	URI	Prefix
Core	`http://java.sun.com/jsf/core`	f
HTML	`http://java.sun.com/jsf/html`	h

HTML Tag Library Actions

The HTML library contains action elements that represent JSF components associated with renderers for rendering them as HTML elements. Most of the actions in this library represent the standard concrete HTML component classes, which provide an interface with accessor method for the combination of the generic component type's properties and the attributes supported by the associated renderer.

Supported HTML 4.01 Attributes

The JSP actions in the JSF HTML tag library support most attributes that the HTML 4.01 specification declares for the corresponding HTML elements. The individual action descriptions include the supported HTML 4.01 attributes in the syntax section but not in the attributes table. These attributes are instead described in Table A-2. All these attributes are optional and can be set to static values or using any type of JSF EL expression.

Table A-2. Supported HTML 4.01 attributes

Attribute name	Java type	Description
`accept`	`String`	A comma-separated list of content types the server that processes the form handles correctly.
`acceptcharset`	`String`	Corresponds to the HTML `accept-charset` attribute (with a dash as a separator). A space- and/or comma-separated list of character encodings accepted by the server processing the form.
`alt`	`String`	Alternative text that may be used by a browser that can't show the element (e.g., text-to-speech browser).
`bgcolor`	`String`	Deprecated. The background color for the document body or table cells.
`border`	`String`	The number of pixels for the frame around a table.
`cellpadding`	`String`	The amount of space between cell borders and the cell content, in pixels or a percentage of the space available.
`cellspacing`	`String`	The amount of space between cells and the table frame, in pixels or a percentage of the space available.
`charset`	`String`	The character encoding of the target resource.
`coords`	`String`	A comma-separated list of values that specifies the position of the element on the screen.
`dir`	`String`	The text direction, one of `ltr` (left-to-right) or `rtl` (right-to-left).
`disabled`	`boolean`	If set to `true`, the element is disabled: it can't receive focus, it's skipped in tabbing navigation, and it can't be "successful" (e.g., a button can't submit a form).
`enctype`	`String`	The content type used for the form data in a POST request.
`frame`	`String`	One of `void`, `above`, `below`, `hsides`, `lhs`, `rhs`, `vsides`, `box`, or `border`. Specifies the visible sides of a table frame.

Table A-2. Supported HTML 4.01 attributes (continued)

Attribute name	Java type	Description
hreflang	String	Must be used together only with the href attribute. Specifies the language of the referenced resource.
lang	String	The base language.
longdesc	String	A description of an image.
onblur	String	Client-side event handler code to execute when the element loses focus. Only valid for the same elements as onfocus.
onchange	String	Client-side event handler code to execute when the element loses focus and its value has been changed since it got focus. Only valid for <input>, <select>, and <textarea>.
onclick	String	Client-side event handler code to execute when the element is clicked.
ondblclick	String	Client-side event handler code to execute when the element is double-clicked.
onfocus	String	Client-side event handler code to execute when the element gets focus. Only valid for <a>, <area>, <label>, <input>, <select>, <textarea>, and <button>.
onkeydown	String	Client-side event handler code to execute when a key is pressed down over the element.
onkeypress	String	Client-side event handler code to execute when a key is pressed and released over the element.
onkeyup	String	Client-side event handler code to execute when a key is released over the element.
onmousedown	String	Client-side event handler code to execute when a mouse button is pressed over the element.
onmousemove	String	Client-side event handler code to execute when the mouse is moved while over the element.
onmouseout	String	Client-side event handler code to execute when the mouse button is moved away from the element.
onmouseover	String	Client-side event handler code to execute when the mouse is moved onto the element.
onmouseup	String	Client-side event handler code to execute when a mouse button is released over the element.
onreset	String	Client-side event handler code to execute when a form is reset. Only valid for <form>.
onselect	String	Client-side event handler code to execute when text is selected. Only valid for <input> and <textarea>.
onsubmit	String	Client-side event handler code to execute when a form is submitted. Only valid for <form>.
readonly	boolean	If set to true, the element is read-only: it can't receive focus, it's skipped in tabbing navigation.
rel	String	A space-separated list of link types, describing the relationship from the current document and the referenced document.

Table A-2. Supported HTML 4.01 attributes (continued)

Attribute name	Java type	Description
rev	String	A space-separated list of link types, describing the reverse link for the referenced document.
rules	String	One of none, groups, rows, cols, or all. Specifies the visible rules between cells within a table.
shape	String	One of default, rect, circle, or poly. Specifies the shape of a region.
size	String	The width of an input field in number of characters or the number visible options in a selection list.
style	String	Explicit CSS style information. This attribute is rendered on the main element (e.g., <table>) representing the component or on a <span> element for a component that isn't represented by a main element.
styleClass	String	One or more space-separated class names that can be used in stylesheets. The HTML 4.01 attribute name for the same purpose is class, but unfortunately that name can't be used as a JSP custom action attribute name (because of a name clash with the class property implemented by the Object class). The class attribute is rendered on the same type of element as the style attribute.
summary	String	A summary of a table's purpose.
tabindex	String	The element's position in the tabbing ordering, a number between 0 and 32767.
target	String	The name of the frame that should display the response resulting from the request triggered by the element.
title	String	An advisory title for the element, e.g., used as a tool-tip.
type	String	When used for an <a> element, an advisory hint about the content type of the referenced resource.
width	String	The desired width of a table, in pixels or a percentage of the space available.

<h:column>

This action represents an instance of the component type registered with the type ID javax.faces.Column (by default, an instance of the javax.faces.component.UIColumn class). A component of this type is rendered by its parent so the action doesn't associate the component with a renderer.

A column component is used typically as a child of a javax.faces.component.UIData component and represents a single column of tabular data. It can be equipped with a header and a footer facet for a column header and footer. Its children are used to process the column's data.

Syntax

```
<h:column [id="id"] [binding="componentBinding"] [rendered="true|false"] >
  [<f:facet name="header">...</facet>]
  [<f:facet name="footer">...</facet>]
  JSF component action elements
</h:column>
```

Attributes

Attribute name	Java type	EL expression type	Description
binding	String	VB	Must be a value binding expression for a property the component is bound to.
id	String	None	The component ID.
rendered	boolean	Any	If set to `false`, the component isn't rendered and doesn't participate in any request processing.

Example

```
<h:dataTable value="#{reportHandler.currentReports}" var="report">
  <h:column rendered="#{reportHandler.showDate}">
    <f:facet name="header">
      <h:outputText value="Date" />
    </f:facet>
    <h:outputText value="#{report.date}" />
  </h:column>
  ...
</h:dataTable>
```

<h:commandButton>

This action represents an instance of the component type registered with the type ID `javax.faces.HtmlCommandButton` (by default, an instance of the `javax.faces.component.html.HtmlCommandButton` class), combined with a renderer registered with the renderer type ID `javax.faces.Button`.

The component is rendered as an HTML `<input>` element with the type attribute set to `submit`, `reset`, or `image` (depending on the value of this action element's `type` and `image` attribute values), the `name` attribute set to the component's client ID, and the `value` attribute set to the component's value. Clicking the rendered button submits the form it belongs to and triggers a `javax.faces.event.ActionEvent`.

Syntax

```
<h:commandButton [id="id"] [binding="componentBinding"] [rendered="true|false"]
  [value="value"] [type="submit|reset" | image="imageURL"]
  [action="actionMethodBinding"] [actionListener="actionListenerBinding"]
  [immediate="true|false"]
  <!-- HTML attributes -->
  [accesskey="accessKey"] [alt="altText"] [dir="ltr|rtl"] [disabled="true|false"]
  [lang="lang"]
  [onblur="code"] [onchange="code"] [onclick="code"] [ondblclick="code"]
  [onfocus="code"] [onkeydown="code"] [onkeypress="code"] [onkeyup="code"]
  [onmousedown="code"] [onmousemove="code"] [onmouseout="code"]
  [onmouseover="code"] [onmouseup="code"] [onselect="code"]
  [readonly="true|false"] [style="style"] [styleClass="styleClass"]
  [tabindex="tabIndex"] [title="title"]
/>
```

Attributes

Attribute name	Java type	EL expression type	Description
action	String	MB	A method binding for a method with a String return type and an empty parameter list. Invoked to process the component's ActionEvent.
actionListener	String	MB	A method binding for a method with a void return type and an ActionEvent parameter. Invoked to process the component's ActionEvent.
binding	String	VB	Must be a value binding expression for a property the component is bound to.
id	String	None	The component ID.
image	String	Any	An absolute or relative URL for an image. If set, the type attribute for the <input> element is set to image.
immediate	boolean	Any	If set to true, the ActionEvent is processed in the Apply Request Values phase; if false, the event is processed in the Invoke Application phase.
rendered	boolean	Any	If set to false, the component isn't rendered and doesn't participate in any request processing.
type	String	Any	The button type, one of submit or reset. Ignored if image is set.
value	Object	Any	The component value.

Example

```
<h:form>
  <h:commandButton value="Save" action="#{formHandler.save}" />
</h:form>
```

<h:commandLink>

This action represents an instance of the component type registered with the type ID javax.faces.html.HtmlCommandLink (by default, an instance of the javax.faces.component.html.HtmlCommandLink class), combined with a renderer registered with the renderer type ID javax.faces.Link.

The component is rendered as an HTML <a> element, an href attribute containing "#", and an onclick attribute containing JavaScript code for submitting the form the component belongs to with the component's client ID as a request parameter. If the component has UIParameter component children, the generated JavaScript code also ensures that each parameter is included as request parameters when the form is submitted, with both the name and value URL encoded. The component's children that are not UIParameter components are rendered as the content of the <a> element, i.e., as the link text or image. Clicking the rendered link submits the form it belongs to and triggers a javax.faces.event.ActionEvent.

Syntax

```
<h:commandLink [id="id"] [binding="componentBinding"] [rendered="true|false"]
  [value="value"]
  [action="actionMethodBinding"] [actionListener="actionListenerBinding"]
  [immediate="true|false"]
  <!-- HTML attributes -->
  [accesskey="accessKey"] [charset="charset"] [coords="coords"] [dir="ltr|rtl"]
  [hreflang="lang"] [lang="lang"]
  [onblur="code"] [ondblclick="code"] [onfocus="code"]
  [onkeydown="code"] [onkeypress="code"] [onkeyup="code"]
  [onmousedown="code"] [onmousemove="code"] [onmouseout="code"]
  [onmouseover="code"] [onmouseup="code"]
  [rel="rel"] [rev="rev"] [shape="shape"] [style="style"]
  [styleClass="styleClass"] [tabindex="tabIndex"] [target="target"]
  [title="title"] [type="contentType"]
>
  [<f:param name="name" value="value" />]
  JSF component action elements
</h:commandLink>
```

Attributes

Attribute name	Java type	EL expression type	Description
`action`	`String`	MB	A method binding for a method with a `String` return type and an empty parameter list. Invoked to process the component's `ActionEvent`.
`actionListener`	`String`	MB	A method binding for a method with a `void` return type and an `ActionEvent` parameter. Invoked to process the component's `ActionEvent`.
`binding`	`String`	VB	Must be a value binding expression for a property the component is bound to.
`id`	`String`	None	The component ID.
`immediate`	`boolean`	Any	If set to `true`, the `ActionEvent` is processed in the Apply Request Values phase; if `false`, the event is processed in the Invoke Application phase.
`rendered`	`boolean`	Any	If set to `false`, the component isn't rendered and doesn't participate in any request processing.
`value`	`Object`	Any	The component value.

Example

```
<h:form>
  <h:commandLink action="#{formHandler.save}">
    <h:outputText value="Save" />
  </h:commandLink>
</h:form>
```

<h:dataTable>

This action represents an instance of the component type registered with the type ID `javax.faces.HtmlDataTable` (by default, an instance of the `javax.faces.component.html.HtmlDataTable` class), combined with a renderer registered with the renderer type ID `javax.faces.Table`.

The component is rendered as an HTML `<table>` element. `UIColumn` child components are responsible for rendering the table columns. The columns can hold any type of component, including input components and command components. The `value` attribute value can be of any type, but the primary model type is the `javax.faces.model.DataModel` class (see Appendix B). A value of type `Object[]` is wrapped automatically in an instance of `ArrayDataModel`, a `java.util.List` in a `ListDataModel`, a `javax.servlet.jsp.jstl.sql.Result` in a `ResultDataModel`, a `java.sql.ResultSet` in a `ResultSetDataModel`, and any other type in a `ScalarDataModel`.

Both the data table component and its column children may be equipped with `header` and `footer` facets. The table's `header` facet is rendered as one `<th>` element (with a `colspan` attribute set to the number of children) within a `<tr>` element, and column `header` facets are rendered as `<th>` elements within a separate `<tr>` element. A `<thead>` element encloses both header `<tr>` elements. The `footer` facets, if any, are rendered in a similar manner, but with `<td>` elements instead of `<th>` and a `<tfoot>` element instead of the `<thead>` element. CSS style classes for the header and footer cells can be specified by the `headerClass` and `footerClass` attributes.

The table rows are rendered within a `<tbody>` element, with a `<tr>` element for each row and a `<td>` element for each column child. The first row to render and how many rows to render can be specified by the `first` and `rows` attributes, and CSS style classes for the rows and cells can be specified by the `rowClasses` and `columnClasses` attributes.

Syntax

```
<h:dataTable [id="id"] [binding="componentBinding"] [rendered="true|false"]
  [value="value"] [var="var"] [first="first"] [rows="rows"]
  [headerClass="styleClass"] [footerClass="styleClass"]
  [rowClasses="styleClasses"] [columnClasses="styleClasses"]
  <!-- HTML attributes -->
  [bgcolor="color"] [border="border"] [cellpadding="padding"]
  [cellspacing="spacing"] [dir="ltr|rtl"] [frame="frame"] [lang="lang"]
  [onclick="code"] [ondblclick="code"]
  [onkeydown="code"] [onkeypress="code"] [onkeyup="code"]
  [onmousedown="code"] [onmousemove="code"] [onmouseout="code"]
  [onmouseover="code"] [onmouseup="code"]
  [rules="rules"] [style="style"] [styleClass="styleClass"] [summary="summary"]
  [title="title"] [width="width"]
>
  [<f:facet name="header">...</facet>]
  [<f:facet name="footer">...</facet>]
  <h:column>
    JSF component action elements
  </h:column>
</h:dataTable>
```

Attributes

Attribute name	Java type	EL expression type	Description
binding	String	VB	Must be a value binding expression for a property the component is bound to.
columnClasses	String	Any	A comma-separated list of CSS class names for the table body `<td>` elements. If there are fewer classes than columns, no `class` attribute is rendered for the last columns. If there are more classes than columns, the overflow classes are ignored.
first	int	Any	The zero-based index of the first row in the model to process.
footerClass	String	Any	The CSS class for footer cells.
headerClass	String	Any	The CSS class for header cells.
id	String	None	The component ID.
rendered	boolean	Any	If set to `false`, the component isn't rendered and doesn't participate in any request processing.
rowClasses	String	Any	A comma-separated list of CSS class names for the table rows. The classes are used for the `<tr>` elements in the order they are listed, repeating the list over all rows in the table.
rows	int	Any	The number of rows to process.
value	Object	VB	The component value.
var	String	No	The name of the request scope variable that holds the current row object.

Example

```
<h:dataTable value="#{reportHandler.currentReports}" var="report">
  <f:facet name="header">
    <h:outputText value="Expense Reports" />
  </f:facet>
  <h:column rendered="#{reportHandler.showDate}">
    <f:facet name="header">
      <h:outputText value="Date" />
    </f:facet>
    <h:outputText value="#{report.date}" />
  </h:column>
  ...
</h:dataTable>
```

<h:form>

This action represents an instance of the component type registered with the type ID `javax.faces.HtmlForm` (by default, an instance of the `javax.faces.component.html.HtmlForm` class), combined with a renderer registered with the renderer type ID `javax.faces.Form`.

The component is rendered as an HTML <form> element with an action attribute set to a URL that identifies the view containing the form and a method attribute set to post. When the form is submitted, only components that are children of the submitted form are processed.

Syntax

```
<h:form [id="id"] [binding="componentBinding"] [rendered="true|false"]
  <!-- HTML attributes -->
  [accept="contentTypes"] [acceptcharset="charEncodings"] [enctype="encType"]
  [dir="ltr|rtl"] [lang="lang"]
  [onclick="code"] [ondblclick="code"]
  [onkeydown="code"] [onkeypress="code"] [onkeyup="code"]
  [onmousedown="code"] [onmousemove="code"] [onmouseout="code"]
  [onmouseover="code"] [onmouseup="code"] [onreset="code"] [onsubmit="code"]
  [style="style"] [styleClass="styleClass"] [target="target"] [title="title"]
>
   JSF component action elements
</h:form>
```

Attributes

Attribute name	Java type	EL expression type	Description
binding	String	VB	Must be a value binding expression for a property the component is bound to.
id	String	None	The component ID.
rendered	boolean	Any	If set to false, the component isn't rendered and doesn't participate in any request processing.

Example

```
<h:form>
  <h:panelGrid columns="2">
    <h:outputText value="First name:" />
    <h:inputText value="#{user.firstName}" />
    <h:outputText value="Last name:" />
    <h:inputText value="#{user.lastName}" />
  </h:panelGrid>
</h:form>
```

<h:graphicImage>

This action represents an instance of the component type registered with the type ID javax.faces.HtmlGraphicImage (by default, an instance of the javax.faces.component.html.HtmlGraphicImage class), combined with a renderer registered with the renderer type ID javax.faces.Image.

The component is rendered as an HTML <img> element with a src attribute holding the component's value or the url attribute value, adjusted to a context-relative path if it starts with a slash and with encoded session ID information if necessary.

Syntax

```
<h:graphicImage [id="id"] [binding="componentBinding"] [rendered="true|false"]
  [value="value" | url="imageURL"]
  <!-- HTML attributes -->
  [alt="altText"] [dir="ltr|rtl"] [height="height"] [ismap="true|false"]
  [lang="lang"] [longdesc="descURI"]
  [onclick="code"] [ondblclick="code"]
  [onkeydown="code"] [onkeypress="code"] [onkeyup="code"]
  [onmousedown="code"] [onmousemove="code"] [onmouseout="code"]
  [onmouseover="code"] [onmouseup="code"]
  [style="style"] [styleClass="styleClass"] [title="title"] [usemap="mapName"]
  [width="width"]
/>
```

Attributes

Attribute name	Java type	EL expression type	Description
binding	String	VB	Must be a value binding expression for a property the component is bound to.
id	String	None	The component ID.
rendered	boolean	Any	If set to false, the component isn't rendered and doesn't participate in any request processing.
url	String	Any	The image resource URL. An alias for the value attribute.
value	Object	Any	The component value.

Example

```
<h:graphicImage value="/images/folder-open.gif" />
```

<h:inputHidden>

This action represents an instance of the component type registered with the type ID javax.faces.HtmlInputHidden (by default, an instance of the javax.faces.component.html.HtmlInputHidden class), combined with a renderer registered with the renderer type ID javax.faces.Hidden.

The component is rendered as an HTML <input> element with a type attribute set to hidden, a name attribute set to the component's client ID and a value attribute set to the component's value.

Syntax

```
<h:inputHidden [id="id"] [binding="componentBinding"] [rendered="true|false"]
  [value="value"] [converter="converter"]
  [required="true|false"] [validator="validatorMethod"]
  [valueChangeListener="listenerMethod"] [immediate="true|false"]
/>
```

Attributes

Attribute name	Java type	EL expression type	Description
binding	String	VB	Must be a value binding expression for a property the component is bound to.
converter	String *or* javax.faces.convert.Converter	VB	If set as a static value, a registered converter ID. If set as a value binding expression, an instance of an object that implements Converter.
id	String	None	The component ID.
immediate	boolean	Any	If set to true, the ValueChangeEvent is processed in the Apply Request Values phase; if false, the event is processed in the Process Validations phase.
rendered	boolean	Any	If set to false, the component isn't rendered and doesn't participate in any request processing.
required	boolean	Any	If true, JSF verifies that a value is submitted for this component and marks it as invalid and queues an error message if not.
validator	String	MB	A method binding for a method with a void return type and FacesContext, UIComponent, and Object parameters. Invoked to validate the component's local value (the Object parameter).
value	Object	VB	The component value.
valueChangeListener	String	MB	A method binding for a method with a void return type and an ValueChangeEvent parameter. Invoked to process the component's ValueChangeEvent.

Example

```
<h:form>
  <h:inputHidden value="#{user.type}" />
</h:form>
```

<h:inputSecret>

This action represents an instance of the component type registered with the type ID javax.faces.HtmlInputSecret (by default, an instance of the javax.faces.component.html.HtmlInputSecret class), combined with a renderer registered with the renderer type ID javax.faces.Secret.

The component is rendered as an HTML <input> element with a type attribute set to password, a name attribute set to the component's client ID and a value attribute set to the component's value only if the action's redisplay attribute is set to true.

Syntax

```
<h:inputSecret [id="id"] [binding="componentBinding"] [rendered="true|false"]
  [value="value"] [redisplay="true|false"] [converter="converter"]
  [required="true|false"] [validator="validatorMethod"]
  [valueChangeListener="listenerMethod"] [immediate="true|false"]
  <!-- HTML attributes -->
  [accesskey="accessKey"] [alt="altText"] [dir="ltr|rtl"]
  [disabled="true|false"] [lang="lang"] [maxlength="maxLength"]
  [onblur="code"] [onchange="code"] [onclick="code"] [ondblclick="code"]
  [onfocus="code"] [onkeydown="code"] [onkeypress="code"] [onkeyup="code"]
  [onmousedown="code"] [onmousemove="code"] [onmouseout="code"]
  [onmouseover="code"] [onmouseup="code"] [onselect="code"]
  [readonly="true|false"] [size="size"] [style="style"] [styleClass="styleClass"]
  [tabindex="tabIndex"] [title="title"]
/>
```

Attributes

Attribute name	Java type	EL expression type	Description
binding	String	VB	Must be a value binding expression for a property the component is bound to.
converter	String *or* javax.faces.convert.Converter	VB	If set as a static value, a registered converter ID. If set as a value binding expression, an instance of an object that implements Converter.
id	String	None	The component ID.
immediate	boolean	Any	If set to true, the ValueChangeEvent is processed in the Apply Request Values phase; if false, the event is processed in the Process Validations phase.
redisplay	boolean	Any	If set to true, render the component's value as the <input> element value attribute value.
rendered	boolean	Any	If set to false, the component isn't rendered and doesn't participate in any request processing.
required	boolean	Any	If true, JSF verifies that a value is submitted for this component and marks it as invalid and queues an error message if not.

Attribute name	Java type	EL expression type	Description
validator	String	MB	A method binding for a method with a void return type and FacesContext, UIComponent, and Object parameters. Invoked to validate the component's local value (the Object parameter).
value	Object	VB	The component value.
valueChangeListener	String	MB	A method binding for a method with a void return type and an ValueChangeEvent parameter. Invoked to process the component's ValueChangeEvent.

Example

```
<h:form>
  <h:inputSecret value="#{user.password}" />
</h:form>
```

<h:inputText>

This action represents an instance of the component type registered with the type ID javax.faces.HtmlInputText (by default, an instance of the javax.faces.component.html.HtmlInputText class), combined with a renderer registered with the renderer type ID javax.faces.Text.

The component is rendered as an HTML <input> element with a type attribute set to text, a name attribute set to the component's client ID, and a value attribute set to the component's value.

Syntax

```
<h:inputText [id="id"] [binding="componentBinding"] [rendered="true|false"]
  [value="value"] [converter="converter"]
  [required="true|false"] [validator="validatorMethod"]
  [valueChangeListener="listenerMethod"] [immediate="true|false"]
  <!-- HTML attributes -->
  [accesskey="accessKey"] [alt="altText"] [dir="ltr|rtl"]
  [disabled="true|false"] [lang="lang"] [maxlength="maxLength"]
  [onblur="code"] [onchange="code"] [onclick="code"] [ondblclick="code"]
  [onfocus="code"] [onkeydown="code"] [onkeypress="code"] [onkeyup="code"]
  [onmousedown="code"] [onmousemove="code"] [onmouseout="code"]
  [onmouseover="code"] [onmouseup="code"] [onselect="code"]
  [readonly="true|false"] [size="size"] [style="style"] [styleClass="styleClass"]
  [tabindex="tabIndex"] [title="title"]
/>
```

Attributes

Attribute name	Java type	EL expression type	Description
binding	String	VB	Must be a value binding expression for a property the component is bound to.
converter	String *or* javax.faces.convert.Converter	VB	If set as a static value, a registered converter ID. If set as a value binding expression, an instance of an object that implements Converter.
id	String	None	The component ID.
immediate	boolean	Any	If set to true, the ValueChangeEvent is processed in the Apply Request Values phase; if false, the event is processed in the Process Validations phase.
rendered	boolean	Any	If set to false, the component isn't rendered and doesn't participate in any request processing.
required	boolean	Any	If true, JSF verifies that a value is submitted for this component and marks it as invalid and queues an error message if not.
validator	String	MB	A method binding for a method with a void return type and FacesContext, UIComponent, and Object parameters. Invoked to validate the component's local value (the Object parameter).
value	Object	VB	The component value.
valueChangeListener	String	MB	A method binding for a method with a void return type and an ValueChangeEvent parameter. Invoked to process the component's ValueChangeEvent.

Example

```
<h:form>
  <h:inputText value="#{user.email}" />
</h:form>
```

<h:inputTextarea>

This action represents an instance of the component type registered with the type ID javax.faces.HtmlInputTextarea (by default, an instance of the javax.faces.component.html.HtmlInputTextarea class), combined with a renderer registered with the renderer type ID javax.faces.Textarea.

The component is rendered as an HTML <textarea> element with a name attribute set to the component's client ID and a body holding the component's value.

Syntax

```
<h:inputTextarea [id="id"] [binding="componentBinding"] [rendered="true|false"]
  [value="value"] [converter="converter"]
  [required="true|false"] [validator="validatorMethod"]
  [valueChangeListener="listenerMethod"] [immediate="true|false"]
  <!-- HTML attributes -->
  [accesskey="accessKey"] [cols="noOfCols"] [dir="ltr|rtl"]
  [disabled="true|false"] [lang="lang"]
  [onblur="code"] [onchange="code"] [onclick="code"] [ondblclick="code"]
  [onfocus="code"] [onkeydown="code"] [onkeypress="code"] [onkeyup="code"]
  [onmousedown="code"] [onmousemove="code"] [onmouseout="code"]
  [onmouseover="code"] [onmouseup="code"] [onselect="code"]
  [readonly="true|false"] [rows="noOfRows"] [style="style"]
  [styleClass="styleClass"] [tabindex="tabIndex"] [title="title"]
/>
```

Attributes

Attribute name	Java type	EL expression type	Description
`binding`	`String`	VB	Must be a value binding expression for a property the component is bound to.
`converter`	`String` *or* `javax.faces.convert.Converter`	VB	If set as a static value, a registered converter ID. If set as a value binding expression, an instance of an object that implements `Converter`.
`id`	`String`	None	The component ID.
`immediate`	`boolean`	Any	If set to `true`, the `ValueChangeEvent` is processed in the Apply Request Values phase; if `false`, the event is processed in the Process Validations phase.
`rendered`	`boolean`	Any	If set to `false`, the component isn't rendered and doesn't participate in any request processing.
`required`	`boolean`	Any	If `true`, JSF verifies that a value is submitted for this component and marks it as invalid and queues an error message if not.
`validator`	`String`	MB	A method binding for a method with a `void` return type and `FacesContext`, `UIComponent`, and `Object` parameters. Invoked to validate the component's local value (the `Object` parameter).
`value`	`Object`	VB	The component value.
`valueChangeListener`	`String`	MB	A method binding for a method with a `void` return type and an `ValueChangeEvent` parameter. Invoked to process the component's `ValueChangeEvent`.

Example

```
<h:form>
  <h:inputTextarea value="#{user.bio}" />
</h:form>
```

<h:message>

This action represents an instance of the component type registered with the type ID javax.faces.HtmlMessage (by default, an instance of the javax.faces.component.html. HtmlMessage class), combined with a renderer registered with the renderer type ID javax. faces.Message.

The component gets the first message queued for the component identified by the for attribute. The message properties identified by the showDetail and showSummary attributes for this message are rendered as text, within an HTML <span> element if any of the CSS style attributes apply or the id attribute is set. If the tooltip attribute is set to true and both the summary and the detailed text are rendered, the message summary is rendered as the value of the <span> element's title attribute.

Syntax

```
<h:message for="componentId"
  [id="id"] [binding="componentBinding"] [rendered="true|false"]
  [showDetail="true|false"] [showSummary="true|false"] [tooltip="true|false"]
  [errorClass="styleClass"] [errorStyle="style"]
  [fatalClass="styleClass"] [fatalStyle="style"]
  [infoClass="styleClass"] [infoStyle="style"]
  [warnClass="styleClass"] [warnStyle="style"]
  <!-- HTML attributes -->
  [style="style"] [styleClass="styleClass"] [title="title"]
/>
```

Attributes

Attribute name	Java type	EL expression type	Description
binding	String	VB	Must be a value binding expression for a property the component is bound to.
errorClass	String	Any	One or more space-separated CSS class names used as a <span> element's class attribute if the message is of ERROR severity.
errorStyle	String	Any	Explicit CSS style information used as a <span> element's style attribute if the message is of ERROR severity.
fatalClass	String	Any	One or more space-separated CSS class names used as a <span> element's class attribute if the message is of FATAL severity.
fatalStyle	String	Any	Explicit CSS style information used as a <span> element's style attribute if the message is of FATAL severity.

Attribute name	Java type	EL expression type	Description
for	String	Any	A string for locating the component for which the message is rendered in the same format as for the UIComponent findComponent( ) method (see Appendix C for details).
id	String	None	The component ID.
infoClass	String	Any	One or more space-separated CSS class names used as a <span> element's class attribute if the message is of INFO severity.
infoStyle	String	Any	Explicit CSS style information used as a <span> element's style attribute if the message is of INFO severity.
rendered	boolean	Any	If set to false, the component isn't rendered and doesn't participate in any request processing.
showDetail	boolean	Any	If true, renders the message details text.
showSummary	boolean	Any	If true, renders the message summary text.
tooltip	boolean	Any	If true, renders the message summary as the value of a <span> element's title attribute.
warnClass	String	Any	One or more space-separated CSS class names used as a <span> element's class attribute if the message is of WARN severity.
warnStyle	String	Any	Explicit CSS style information used as a <span> element's style attribute if the message is of WARN severity.

Example

```
<h:form>
  <h:inputText id="firstName" value="#{user.firstName}" />
  <h:message for="firstName" errorStyle="color: red" />
</h:form>
```

<h:messages>

This action represents an instance of the component type registered with the type ID javax.faces.HtmlMessages (by default, an instance of the javax.faces.component.html.HtmlMessages class), combined with a renderer registered with the renderer type ID javax.faces.Messages.

The component receives all queued messages or only those queued without a component identifier if the globalOnly attribute is set to true. The message properties identified by the showDetail and showSummary attributes are rendered as cells in an HTML table if the layout attribute is set to table; otherwise within an HTML <span> element if any of the CSS style attributes apply or the id attribute is set. If the tooltip attribute is set to true and both the summary and the detailed text are rendered, the message summary is rendered as the value of the <td> or <span> element's title attribute.

Syntax

```
<h:messages [id="id"] [binding="componentBinding"] [rendered="true|false"]
  [globalOnly="true|false"] [layout="list|table"]
  [showDetail="true|false"] [showSummary="true|false"] [tooltip="true|false"]
  [errorClass="styleClass"] [errorStyle="style"]
  [fatalClass="styleClass"] [fatalStyle="style"]
  [infoClass="styleClass"] [infoStyle="style"]
  [warnClass="styleClass"] [warnStyle="style"]
  <!-- HTML attributes -->
  [style="style"] [styleClass="styleClass"] [title="title"]
/>
```

Attributes

Attribute name	Java type	EL expression type	Description
binding	String	VB	Must be a value binding expression for a property the component is bound to.
errorClass	String	Any	One or more space-separated CSS class names used as a <span> element's class attribute if the message is of ERROR severity.
errorStyle	String	Any	Explicit CSS style information used as a <span> element's style attribute if the message is of ERROR severity.
fatalClass	String	Any	One or more space-separated CSS class names used as a <span> element's class attribute if the message is of FATAL severity.
fatalStyle	String	Any	Explicit CSS style information used as a <span> element's style attribute if the message is of FATAL severity.
globalOnly	boolean	Any	If true, render only messages without a component ID.
id	String	None	The component ID.
infoClass	String	Any	One or more space-separated CSS class names used as a <span> element's class attribute if the message is of INFO severity.
infoStyle	String	Any	Explicit CSS style information used as a <span> element's style attribute if the message is of INFO severity.
layout	String	Any	One of list or table. If set to table, render the messages as an HTML table with one row per message.
rendered	boolean	Any	If set to false, the component isn't rendered and doesn't participate in any request processing.
showDetail	boolean	Any	If true, render the message details text.
showSummary	boolean	Any	If true, render the message summary text.
tooltip	boolean	Any	If true, render the message summary as the value of a <span> element's title attribute.

Attribute name	Java type	EL expression type	Description
warnClass	String	Any	One or more space-separated CSS class names used as a <span> element's class attribute if the message is of WARN severity.
warnStyle	String	Any	Explicit CSS style information used as a <span> element's style attribute if the message is of WARN severity.

Example

```
<!-- Render summaries for all messages at the top of the page -->
<h:messages/>
<h:form>
  <h:inputText id="firstName" value="#{user.firstName}" />
  <!-- Render details per component next to the field -->
  <h:message for="firstName" errorStyle="color: red" />
</h:form>
```

<h:outputFormat>

This action represents an instance of the component type registered with the type ID javax.faces.HtmlOutputFormat (by default, an instance of the javax.faces.component.html.HtmlOutputFormat class), combined with a renderer registered with the renderer type ID javax.faces.Format.

The component is rendered as text, within an HTML <span> element if any of the CSS style attributes apply or the id attribute is set. The component's value should be a parameterized message string. An Object[] is created from the component's UIParameter children and passed along with the components value as arguments to the java.text.MessageFormat format( ) method to format a message, which is rendered.

Syntax

```
<h:outputFormat [id="id"] [binding="componentBinding"] [rendered="true|false"]
  [value="value"] [converter="converter"] [escape="true|false"]
  <!-- HTML attributes -->
  [style="style"] [styleClass="styleClass"] [title="title"]
>
  <f:param value="value" />
</h:outputFormat>
```

Attributes

Attribute name	Java type	EL expression type	Description
binding	String	VB	Must be a value binding expression for a property the component is bound to.
converter	String *or* javax.faces.convert.Converter	VB	If set as a static value, a registered converter ID. If set as a value binding expression, an instance of an object that implements Converter.

Attribute name	Java type	EL expression type	Description
escape	boolean	Any	If true, render special HTML and XML characters as character entity codes, e.g., < as <.
id	String	None	The component ID.
rendered	boolean	Any	If set to false, the component isn't rendered and doesn't participate in any request processing.
value	Object	No	The component value.

Example

```
<f:loadBundle basename="messages" var="msgs" />
<h:outputFormat value="#{msgs.sunRiseAndSetText}">
  <f:param value="#{city.sunRiseTime}" />
  <f:param value="#{city.sunSetTime}" />
</h:outputFormat>
```

<h:outputLabel>

This action represents an instance of the component type registered with the type ID javax.faces.HtmlOutputLabel (by default, an instance of the javax.faces.component.html.HtmlOutputLabel class), combined with a renderer registered with the renderer type ID javax.faces.Label.

The component is rendered as an HTML <label> element with a for attribute set to the client ID for the component identified by the action element's for attribute value. The <label> element body is generated from the <h:outputLabel> element's body. While the <h:outputLabel> element supports a value attribute, it's ignored by the JSF 1.0 reference implementation, but other implementations may respect it and use it as the <label> body.

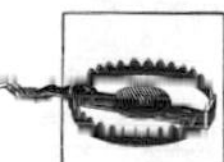

With the JSF 1.0 reference implementation, the action element that represents the component identified by the for attribute value must appear before the <h:outputLabel> element in the JSP page or both action elements must be nested within an action element for a component that renders its children, e.g., <h:panelGrid> or <h:panelGroup>. This is because the label renderer requires that the referenced component exists when the output component is rendered. The specification is not clear enough to tell if this is a bug or not, so other implementations may be less restrictive about the ordering and nesting.

Syntax

```
<h:outputLabel for="componentId"
  [id="id"] [binding="componentBinding"] [rendered="true|false"]
  [value="value"] [converter="converter"]
  <!-- HTML attributes -->
  [accesskey="accessKey"] [dir="ltr|rtl"] [lang="lang"]
```

```
    [onblur="code"] [onchange="code"] [onclick="code"] [ondblclick="code"]
    [onfocus="code"] [onkeydown="code"] [onkeypress="code"] [onkeyup="code"]
    [onmousedown="code"] [onmousemove="code"] [onmouseout="code"]
    [onmouseover="code"] [onmouseup="code"]
    [style="style"] [styleClass="styleClass"] [tabindex="tabIndex"] [title="title"]
  >
    JSF component action elements or non-JSF content
  </h:outputLabel>
```

Attributes

Attribute name	Java type	EL expression type	Description
binding	String	VB	Must be a value binding expression for a property the component is bound to.
converter	String *or* javax.faces.convert.Converter	VB	If set as a static value, a registered converter ID. If set as a value binding expression, an instance of an object that implements Converter.
for	String	Any	A string for locating the component for which the message is rendered in the same format as for the UIComponent findComponent( ) method (see Appendix B for details).
id	String	None	The component ID.
rendered	boolean	Any	If set to false, the component isn't rendered and doesn't participate in any request processing.
value	Object	No	The component value. Note that the JSF 1.0 reference implementation ignores the value.

Example

```
  <h:inputText id="firstName" value="#{user.firstName}" />
  <h:outputLabel for="firstName" />
```

<h:outputLink>

This action represents an instance of the component type registered with the type ID javax.faces.HtmlOutputLink (by default, an instance of the javax.faces.component.html.HtmlOutputLink class), combined with a renderer registered with the renderer type ID javax.faces.Link.

The component is rendered as an HTML <a> element with an href attribute set to the component's value. If the component has UIParameter component children, their name and value properties are added as query string parameters to the href attribute value, with both the name and value URL encoded. The component's children that are not UIParameter components are rendered as the content of the <a> element, i.e., as the link text or image.

Syntax

```
<h:outputLink [id="id"] [binding="componentBinding"] [rendered="true|false"]
  [value="value"] [converter="converter"]
  <!-- HTML attributes -->
  [accesskey="accessKey"] [charset="charset"] [coords="coords"] [dir="ltr|rtl"]
  [hreflang="lang"] [lang="lang"]
  [onblur="code"] [onclick="code"] [ondblclick="code"] [onfocus="code"]
  [onkeydown="code"] [onkeypress="code"] [onkeyup="code"]
  [onmousedown="code"] [onmousemove="code"] [onmouseout="code"]
  [onmouseover="code"] [onmouseup="code"]
  [rel="rel"] [rev="rev"] [shape="shape"] [style="style"]
  [styleClass="styleClass"] [tabindex="tabIndex"] [target="target"]
  [title="title"] [type="contentType"]
>
  [<f:param name="name" value="value" />]
  JSF component action elements
</h:outputLink>
```

Attributes

Attribute name	Java type	EL expression type	Description
binding	String	VB	Must be a value binding expression for a property the component is bound to.
converter	String *or* javax.faces.convert.Converter	VB	If set as a static value, a registered converter ID. If set as a value binding expression, an instance of an object that implements Converter.
id	String	None	The component ID.
rendered	boolean	Any	If set to false, the component isn't rendered and doesn't participate in any request processing.
value	Object	No	The component value.

Example

```
<h:outputLink value="../../logout.jsp" />
```

<h:outputText>

This action represents an instance of the component type registered with the type ID javax.faces.HtmlOutputText (by default, an instance of the javax.faces.component.html.HtmlOutputText class), combined with a renderer registered with the renderer type ID javax.faces.Text.

The component is rendered as text, within an HTML <span> element if any of the HTML attributes or the id attribute is set.

Syntax

```
<h:outputText [id="id"] [binding="componentBinding"] [rendered="true|false"]
  [value="value"] [converter="converter"] [escape="true|false"]
  <!-- HTML attributes -->
  [style="style"] [styleClass="styleClass"] [title="title"]
/>
```

Attributes

Attribute name	Java type	EL expression type	Description
binding	String	VB	Must be a value binding expression for a property the component is bound to.
converter	String *or* javax.faces.convert.Converter	VB	If set as a static value, a registered converter ID. If set as a value binding expression, an instance of an object that implements Converter.
escape	boolean	Any	If true, render special HTML and XML characters as character entity codes, e.g., < as <.
id	String	None	The component ID.
rendered	boolean	Any	If set to false, the component isn't rendered and doesn't participate in any request processing.
value	Object	No	The component value.

Example

```
<h:outputText value="#{user.name}" />
```

<h:panelGrid>

This action represents an instance of the component type registered with the type ID javax.faces.HtmlPanelGrid (by default, an instance of the javax.faces.component.html.HtmlPanelGrid class), combined with a renderer registered with the renderer type ID javax.faces.Grid.

The component is rendered as an HTML table with the number of columns specified by the columns attribute. The component's children are used to render the table cells, with new rows as the number of columns is reached.

The panel component may be equipped with a header and a footer facet. The table's header facet is rendered as one <th> element (with a colspan attribute set to the value of the columns attribute) within a <tr> element, enclosed within an <thead> element. The footer facet is rendered in a similar manner, but with a <td> element instead of <th> and a <tfoot> element instead of the <thead> element. CSS style classes for the header and footer cells can be specified by the headerClass and footerClass attributes.

The table rows are rendered within a <tbody> element, with a <tr> element for each row and a <td> element for each column. CSS style classes for the rows and cells can be specified by the rowClasses and columnClasses attributes.

Syntax

```
<h:panelGrid [id="id"] [binding="componentBinding"] [rendered="true|false"]
  [columns="noOfColumns"]
  [headerClass="styleClass"] [footerClass="styleClass"]
  [rowClasses="styleClasses"] [columnClasses="styleClasses"]
  <!-- HTML attributes -->
  [bgcolor="color"] [border="border"] [cellpadding="padding"]
  [cellspacing="spacing"] [dir="ltr|rtl"] [frame="frame"] [lang="lang"]
  [onclick="code"] [ondblclick="code"]
  [onkeydown="code"] [onkeypress="code"] [onkeyup="code"]
  [onmousedown="code"] [onmousemove="code"] [onmouseout="code"]
  [onmouseover="code"] [onmouseup="code"]
  [rules="rules"] [style="style"] [styleClass="styleClass"] [summary="summary"]
  [title="title"] [width="width"]
>
  [<f:facet name="header">...</facet>]
  [<f:facet name="footer">...</facet>]
  JSF component action elements
</h:panelGrid>
```

Attributes

Attribute name	Java type	EL expression type	Description
binding	String	VB	Must be a value binding expression for a property the component is bound to.
columnClasses	String	Any	A comma-separated list of CSS class names for the table body <td> elements. If there are fewer classes than columns, no class attribute is rendered for the last columns. If there are more classes than columns, the overflow classes are ignored.
columns	int	Any	The number of columns to render.
footerClass	String	Any	The CSS class for footer cells.
headerClass	String	Any	The CSS class for header cells.
id	String	None	The component ID.
rendered	boolean	Any	If set to false, the component isn't rendered and doesn't participate in any request processing.
rowClasses	String	Any	A comma-separated list of CSS class names for the table rows. The classes are used for the <tr> elements in the order they are listed, repeating the list over all rows in the table.

Example

```
<h:form>
  <h:panelGrid columns="2">
    <h:outputText value="First name:" />
```

```
    <h:inputText value="#{user.firstName}" />
    <h:outputText value="Last name:" />
    <h:inputText value="#{user.lastName}" />
  </h:panelGrid>
</h:form>
```

<h:panelGroup>

This action represents an instance of the component type registered with the type ID `javax.faces.HtmlPanelGroup` (by default, an instance of the `javax.faces.component.html.HtmlPanelGroup` class), combined with a renderer registered with the renderer type ID `javax.faces.Group`.

The component acts as a container for other components in situations where only one component is allowed, e.g., when a group of components is used as a facet. It renders its children, within an HTML <span> element if any of the HTML attributes or the `id` attribute is set.

Syntax

```
<h:panelGroup [id="id"] [binding="componentBinding"] [rendered="true|false"]
  <!-- HTML attributes -->
  [style="style"] [styleClass="styleClass"]
>
  JSF component action elements
</h:panelGroup>
```

Attributes

Attribute name	Java type	EL expression type	Description
`binding`	`String`	VB	Must be a value binding expression for a property the component is bound to.
`id`	`String`	None	The component ID.
`rendered`	`boolean`	Any	If set to `false`, the component isn't rendered and doesn't participate in any request processing.

Example

```
<h:form>
  <h:panelGrid columns="2">
    <f:facet name="header">
      <h:panelGroup>
        <h:outputText value="Sales stats for " />
        </h:outputText value="#{sales.region}" style="font-weight: bold" />
      </h:panelGroup>
    </f:facet>
    <h:outputText value="January" />
    <h:inputText value="#{sales.jan}" />
    <h:outputText value="February" />
    <h:inputText value="#{sales.feb}" />
    ...
  </h:panelGrid>
</h:form>
```

<h:selectBooleanCheckbox>

This action represents an instance of the component type registered with the type ID javax.faces.HtmlSelectBooleanCheckbox (by default, an instance of the javax.faces.component.html.HtmlSelectBooleanCheckbox class), combined with a renderer registered with the renderer type ID javax.faces.Checkbox.

The component is rendered as an HTML <input> element with a type attribute set to checkbox and a name attribute set to the component's client ID. If the component's value is true, a checked attribute is rendered as well.

Syntax

```
<h:selectBooleanCheckbox [id="id"] [binding="componentBinding"]
  [rendered="true|false"] [value="value"] [converter="converter"]
  [required="true|false"] [validator="validatorMethod"]
  [valueChangeListener="listenerMethod"] [immediate="true|false"]
  <!-- HTML attributes -->
  [accesskey="accessKey"] [dir="ltr|rtl"] [disabled="true|false"] [lang="lang"]
  [onblur="code"] [onchange="code"] [onclick="code"] [ondblclick="code"]
  [onfocus="code"] [onkeydown="code"] [onkeypress="code"] [onkeyup="code"]
  [onmousedown="code"] [onmousemove="code"] [onmouseout="code"]
  [onmouseover="code"] [onmouseup="code"] [onselect="code"]
  [readonly="true|false"] [style="style"] [styleClass="styleClass"]
  [tabindex="tabIndex"] [title="title"]
/>
```

Attributes

Attribute name	Java type	EL expression type	Description
binding	String	VB	Must be a value binding expression for a property the component is bound to.
converter	String *or* javax.faces.convert.Converter	VB	If set as a static value, a registered converter ID. If set as a value binding expression, an instance of an object that implements Converter.
id	String	None	The component ID.
immediate	boolean	Any	If set to true, the ValueChangeEvent is processed in the Apply Request Values phase; if false, the event is processed in the Process Validations phase.
rendered	boolean	Any	If set to false, the component isn't rendered and doesn't participate in any request processing.

Attribute name	Java type	EL expression type	Description
required	boolean	Any	If true, JSF verifies that a value is submitted for this component and marks it as invalid and queues an error message if not.
validator	String	MB	A method binding for a method with a void return type and FacesContext, UIComponent and Object parameters. Invoked to validate the component's local value (the Object parameter).
value	Object	VB	The component value.
valueChangeListener	String	MB	A method binding for a method with a void return type and an ValueChangeEvent parameter. Invoked to process the component's ValueChangeEvent.

Example

```
<h:form>
  <h:selectBooleanCheckbox value="#{user.vip}" />
</h:form>
```

<h:selectManyCheckbox>

This action represents an instance of the component type registered with the type ID javax.faces.HtmlSelectManyCheckbox (by default, an instance of the javax.faces.component.html.HtmlSelectManyCheckbox class), combined with a renderer registered with the renderer type ID javax.faces.Checkbox.

The component is rendered as an HTML <table> element with an <input> element for each choice represented by its children (one or more UISelectItem and UISelectItems components) as the table cells. If the layout attribute is set to pageDirection, each cell is rendered in a separate table row; otherwise all cells are rendered in one row. A UISelectItemGroup child component is rendered as a nested table within the corresponding outer table cell. If the id attribute is set, a <span> element with an id attribute containing the component's client ID is rendered around the outer table.

The <input> elements are rendered with a type attribute set to checkbox and a name attribute set to the component's client ID. Each <input> element is nested also within a <label> elements with a for attribute set to the component's client ID. For all choices that match one of the component's values, the checked attribute is set for the corresponding <input> element.

Syntax

```
<h:selectManyCheckbox [id="id"] [binding="componentBinding"]
  [rendered="true|false"] [value="value"] [converter="converter"]
```

```
    [required="true|false"] [validator="validatorMethod"]
    [valueChangeListener="listenerMethod"] [immediate="true|false"]
    [disabledClass="styleClass"] [enabledClass="styleClass"]
    [layout="lineDirection|pageDirection"]
    <!-- HTML attributes -->
    [accesskey="accessKey"] [border="border"] [dir="ltr|rtl"]
    [disabled="true|false"] [lang="lang"]
    [onblur="code"] [onchange="code"] [onclick="code"] [ondblclick="code"]
    [onfocus="code"] [onkeydown="code"] [onkeypress="code"] [onkeyup="code"]
    [onmousedown="code"] [onmousemove="code"] [onmouseout="code"]
    [onmouseover="code"] [onmouseup="code"] [onselect="code"]
    [readonly="true|false"] [style="style"] [styleClass="styleClass"]
    [tabindex="tabIndex"] [title="title"]
  >
    <f:selectItem> and/or <f:selectItems> action elements
  </h:selectManyCheckbox>
```

Attributes

Attribute name	Java type	EL expression type	Description
binding	String	VB	Must be a value binding expression for a property the component is bound to.
converter	String *or* javax.faces.convert.Converter	VB	If set as a static value, a registered converter ID. If set as a value binding expression, an instance of an object that implements Converter.
disabledClass	String	Any	The CSS class used for the <label> element around disabled choices.
enabledClass	String	Any	The CSS class used for the <label> element around enabled choices.
id	String	None	The component ID.
immediate	boolean	Any	If set to true, the ValueChangeEvent is processed in the Apply Request Values phase; if false, the event is processed in the Process Validations phase.
layout	String	Any	If set to lineDirection, the checkboxes are rendered horizontally. If set to pageDirection, the checkboxes are rendered vertically.
rendered	boolean	Any	If set to false, the component isn't rendered and doesn't participate in any request processing.

Attribute name	Java type	EL expression type	Description
required	boolean	Any	If true, JSF verifies that a value is submitted for this component and marks it as invalid and queues an error message if not.
validator	String	MB	A method binding for a method with a void return type and FacesContext, UIComponent and Object parameters. Invoked to validate the component's local value (the Object parameter).
value	Object	VB	The component value.
valueChangeListener	String	MB	A method binding for a method with a void return type and an ValueChangeEvent parameter. Invoked to process the component's ValueChangeEvent.

Example

```
<h:form>
  <h:selectManyCheckbox value="#{user.projects}">
    <f:selectItems value="#{allProjects}" />
  </h:selectManyCheckbox>
</h:form>
```

<h:selectManyListbox>

This action represents an instance of the component type registered with the type ID javax.faces.HtmlSelectManyListbox (by default, an instance of the javax.faces.component.html.HtmlSelectManyListbox class), combined with a renderer registered with the renderer type ID javax.faces.Listbox.

The component is rendered as an HTML <select> element with a name attribute set to the component's client ID and a multiple attribute. If the size attribute is set, it is added to the <select> element with the specified value; otherwise a size attribute with the number of choices as the value is added. Each choice represented by the component's children (one or more UISelectItem and UISelectItems components) is rendered as an <option> element or as an <optgroup> element if the child is of the UISelectItemGroup subtype. For all choices that match one of the component's values, the selected attribute is set for the corresponding <option> element. If a choice is marked as disabled, the disabled attribute is also added.

Syntax

```
<h:selectManyListbox [id="id"] [binding="componentBinding"]
  [rendered="true|false"] [value="value"] [converter="converter"]
  [required="true|false"] [validator="validatorMethod"]
```

```
    [valueChangeListener="listenerMethod"] [immediate="true|false"]
    <!-- HTML attributes -->
    [accesskey="accessKey"] [dir="ltr|rtl"] [disabled="true|false"] [lang="lang"]
    [onblur="code"] [onchange="code"] [onclick="code"] [ondblclick="code"]
    [onfocus="code"] [onkeydown="code"] [onkeypress="code"] [onkeyup="code"]
    [onmousedown="code"] [onmousemove="code"] [onmouseout="code"]
    [onmouseover="code"] [onmouseup="code"] [onselect="code"]
    [readonly="true|false"] [size="size"] [style="style"] [styleClass="styleClass"]
    [tabindex="tabIndex"] [title="title"]
  >
    <f:selectItem> and/or <f:selectItems> action elements
  </h:selectManyListbox>
```

Attributes

Attribute name	Java type	EL expression type	Description
`binding`	`String`	VB	Must be a value binding expression for a property the component is bound to.
`converter`	`String` *or* `javax.faces.convert.Converter`	VB	If set as a static value, a registered converter ID. If set as a value binding expression, an instance of an object that implements `Converter`.
`id`	`String`	None	The component ID.
`immediate`	`boolean`	Any	If set to `true`, the `ValueChangeEvent` is processed in the Apply Request Values phase; if `false`, the event is processed in the Process Validations phase.
`rendered`	`boolean`	Any	If set to `false`, the component isn't rendered and doesn't participate in any request processing.
`required`	`boolean`	Any	If `true`, JSF verifies that a value is submitted for this component and marks it as invalid and queues an error message if not.
`validator`	`String`	MB	A method binding for a method with a `void` return type and `FacesContext`, `UIComponent` and `Object` parameters. Invoked to validate the component's local value (the `Object` parameter).
`value`	`Object`	VB	The component value.
`valueChangeListener`	`String`	MB	A method binding for a method with a `void` return type and an `ValueChangeEvent` parameter. Invoked to process the component's `ValueChangeEvent`.

Example

```
<h:form>
  <h:selectManyListbox value="#{user.projects}">
    <f:selectItems value="#{allProjects}" />
  </h:selectManyListbox>
</h:form>
```

<h:selectManyMenu>

This action represents an instance of the component type registered with the type ID `javax.faces.HtmlSelectManyMenu` (by default, an instance of the `javax.faces.component.html.HtmlSelectManyMenu` class), combined with a renderer registered with the renderer type ID `javax.faces.Menu`. The component is rendered as an HTML `<select>` element with a `name` attribute set to the component's client ID and a `multiple` attribute and a `size` attribute with `1` as the value. Each choice represented by the component's children (one or more `UISelectItem` and `UISelectItems` components) is rendered as an `<option>` element or as an `<optgroup>` element if the child is of the `UISelectItemGroup` subtype. For all choices that match one of the component's values, the `selected` attribute is set for the corresponding `<option>` element. If a choice is marked as disabled, the `disabled` attribute is also added.

Syntax

```
<h:selectManyMenu [id="id"] [binding="componentBinding"] rendered="true|false"]
  [value="value"] [converter="converter"]
  [required="true|false"] [validator="validatorMethod"]
  [valueChangeListener="listenerMethod"] [immediate="true|false"]
  <!-- HTML attributes -->
  [accesskey="accessKey"] [dir="ltr|rtl"] [disabled="true|false"] [lang="lang"]
  [onblur="code"] [onchange="code"] [onclick="code"] [ondblclick="code"]
  [onfocus="code"] [onkeydown="code"] [onkeypress="code"] [onkeyup="code"]
  [onmousedown="code"] [onmousemove="code"] [onmouseout="code"]
  [onmouseover="code"] [onmouseup="code"] [onselect="code"]
  [readonly="true|false"] [style="style"] [styleClass="styleClass"]
  [tabindex="tabIndex"] [title="title"]
>
  <f:selectItem> and/or <f:selectItems> action elements
</h:selectManyMenu>
```

Attributes

Attribute name	Java type	EL expression type	Description
binding	String	VB	Must be a value binding expression for a property the component is bound to.
converter	String *or* javax.faces.convert.Converter	VB	If set as a static value, a registered converter ID. If set as a value binding expression, an instance of an object that implements Converter.
id	String	None	The component ID.

Attribute name	Java type	EL expression type	Description
immediate	boolean	Any	If set to true, the ValueChangeEvent is processed in the Apply Request Values phase; if false, the event is processed in the Process Validations phase.
rendered	boolean	Any	If set to false, the component isn't rendered and doesn't participate in any request processing.
required	boolean	Any	If true, JSF verifies that a value is submitted for this component and marks it as invalid and queues an error message if not.
validator	String	MB	A method binding for a method with a void return type and FacesContext, UIComponent and Object parameters. Invoked to validate the component's local value (the Object parameter).
value	Object	VB	The component value.
valueChangeListener	String	MB	A method binding for a method with a void return type and an ValueChangeEvent parameter. Invoked to process the component's ValueChangeEvent.

Example

```
<h:form>
  <h:selectManyMenu value="#{user.projects}">
    <f:selectItems value="#{allProjects}" />
  </h:selectManyMenu>
</h:form>
```

<h:selectOneListbox>

This action represents an instance of the component type registered with the type ID javax.faces.HtmlSelectOneListbox (by default, an instance of the javax.faces.component.html.HtmlSelectOneListbox class), combined with a renderer registered with the renderer type ID javax.faces.Listbox.

The component is rendered as an HTML <select> element with a name attribute set to the component's client ID. If the size attribute is set, it is added to the <select> element with the specified value; otherwise a size attribute with the number of choices as the value is added. Each choice represented by the component's children (one or more UISelectItem and UISelectItems components) is rendered as an <option> element or as an <optgroup> element if the child is of the UISelectItemGroup subtype. For all choices that match one of the component's values, the selected attribute is set for the corresponding <option> element. If a choice is marked as disabled, the disabled attribute is also added.

Syntax

```
<h:selectOneListbox [id="id"] [binding="componentBinding"]
  [rendered="true|false"] [value="value"] [converter="converter"]
  [required="true|false"] [validator="validatorMethod"]
  [valueChangeListener="listenerMethod"] [immediate="true|false"]
  <!-- HTML attributes -->
  [accesskey="accessKey"] [dir="ltr|rtl"] [disabled="true|false"] [lang="lang"]
  [onblur="code"] [onchange="code"] [onclick="code"] [ondblclick="code"]
  [onfocus="code"] [onkeydown="code"] [onkeypress="code"] [onkeyup="code"]
  [onmousedown="code"] [onmousemove="code"] [onmouseout="code"]
  [onmouseover="code"] [onmouseup="code"] [onselect="code"]
  [readonly="true|false"] [size="size"] [style="style"] [styleClass="styleClass"]
  [tabindex="tabIndex"] [title="title"]
>
  <f:selectItem> and/or <f:selectItems> action elements
</h:selectOneListbox>
```

Attributes

Attribute name	Java type	EL expression type	Description
binding	String	VB	Must be a value binding expression for a property the component is bound to.
converter	String *or* javax.faces.convert.Converter	VB	If set as a static value, a registered converter ID. If set as a value binding expression, an instance of an object that implements Converter.
id	String	None	The component ID.
immediate	boolean	Any	If set to true, the ValueChangeEvent is processed in the Apply Request Values phase; if false, the event is processed in the Process Validations phase.
rendered	boolean	Any	If set to false, the component isn't rendered and doesn't participate in any request processing.
required	boolean	Any	If true, JSF verifies that a value is submitted for this component and marks it as invalid and queues an error message if not.
validator	String	MB	A method binding for a method with a void return type and FacesContext, UIComponent and Object parameters. Invoked to validate the component's local value (the Object parameter).

Attribute name	Java type	EL expression type	Description
value	Object	VB	The component value.
valueChangeListener	String	MB	A method binding for a method with a void return type and an ValueChangeEvent parameter. Invoked to process the component's ValueChangeEvent.

Example

```
<h:form>
  <h:selectOneListbox value="#{user.country}">
    <f:selectItems value="#{allCountries}" />
  </h:selectOneListbox>
</h:form>
```

<h:selectOneMenu>

This action represents an instance of the component type registered with the type ID javax.faces.HtmlSelectOneMenu (by default, an instance of the javax.faces.component.html.HtmlSelectOneMenu class), combined with a renderer registered with the renderer type ID javax.faces.Menu.

The component is rendered as an HTML <select> element with a name attribute set to the component's client ID, and a multiple attribute and a size attribute with 1 as the value. Each choice represented by the component's children (one or more UISelectItem and UISelectItems components) is rendered as an <option> element or as an <optgroup> element if the child is of the UISelectItemGroup subtype. For all choices that match one of the component's values, the selected attribute is set for the corresponding <option> element. If a choice is marked as disabled, the disabled attribute is also added.

Syntax

```
<h:selectOneMenu [id="id"] [binding="componentBinding"]
  [rendered="true|false"] [value="value"] [converter="converter"]
  [required="true|false"] [validator="validatorMethod"]
  [valueChangeListener="listenerMethod"] [immediate="true|false"]
  <!-- HTML attributes -->
  [accesskey="accessKey"] [dir="ltr|rtl"] [disabled="true|false"] [lang="lang"]
  [onblur="code"] [onchange="code"] [onclick="code"] [ondblclick="code"]
  [onfocus="code"] [onkeydown="code"] [onkeypress="code"] [onkeyup="code"]
  [onmousedown="code"] [onmousemove="code"] [onmouseout="code"]
  [onmouseover="code"] [onmouseup="code"] [onselect="code"]
  [readonly="true|false"] [style="style"] [styleClass="styleClass"]
  [tabindex="tabIndex"] [title="title"]
>
  <f:selectItem> and/or <f:selectItems> action elements
</h:selectOneMenu>
```

Attributes

Attribute name	Java type	EL expression type	Description
binding	String	VB	Must be a value binding expression for a property the component is bound to.
converter	String *or* javax.faces.convert.Converter	VB	If set as a static value, a registered converter ID. If set as a value binding expression, an instance of an object that implements Converter.
id	String	None	The component ID.
immediate	boolean	Any	If set to true, the ValueChangeEvent is processed in the Apply Request Values phase; if false, the event is processed in the Process Validations phase.
rendered	boolean	Any	If set to false, the component isn't rendered and doesn't participate in any request processing.
required	boolean	Any	If true, JSF verifies that a value is submitted for this component and marks it as invalid and queues an error message if not.
validator	String	MB	A method binding for a method with a void return type and FacesContext, UIComponent and Object parameters. Invoked to validate the component's local value (the Object parameter).
value	Object	VB	The component value.
valueChangeListener	String	MB	A method binding for a method with a void return type and an ValueChangeEvent parameter. Invoked to process the component's ValueChangeEvent.

Example

```
<h:form>
  <h:selectOneMenu value="#{user.country}">
    <f:selectItems value="#{allCountries}" />
  </h:selectOneMenu>
</h:form>
```

<h:selectOneRadio>

This action represents an instance of the component type registered with the type ID `javax.faces.HtmlSelectOneRadio` (by default, an instance of the `javax.faces.component.html.HtmlSelectOneRadio` class), combined with a renderer registered with the renderer type ID `javax.faces.Radio`.

The component is rendered as an HTML `<table>` element with an `<input>` element for each choice represented by its children (one or more `UISelectItem` and `UISelectItems` components) as the table cells. If the `layout` attribute is set to `pageDirection`, each cell is rendered in a separate table row; otherwise all cells are rendered in one row. A `UISelectItemGroup` child component is rendered as a nested table within the corresponding outer table cell. If the `id` attribute is set, a `<span>` element with an `id` attribute containing the component's client ID is rendered around the outer table.

The `<input>` elements are rendered with a `type` attribute set to `radio` and a `name` attribute set to the component's client ID. Each `<input>` element is also nested within a `<label>` elements with a `for` attribute set to the component's client ID. For all choices that match one of the component's values, the `checked` attribute is set for the corresponding `<input>` element.

Syntax

```
<h:selectOneRadio [id="id"] [binding="componentBinding"]
  [rendered="true|false"] [value="value"] [converter="converter"]
  [required="true|false"] [validator="validatorMethod"]
  [valueChangeListener="listenerMethod"] [immediate="true|false"]
  [disabledClass="styleClass"] [enabledClass="styleClass"]
  [layout="lineDirection|pageDirection"]
  <!-- HTML attributes -->
  [accesskey="accessKey"] [border="border"] [dir="ltr|rtl"]
  [disabled="true|false"] [lang="lang"]
  [onblur="code"] [onchange="code"] [onclick="code"] [ondblclick="code"]
  [onfocus="code"] [onkeydown="code"] [onkeypress="code"] [onkeyup="code"]
  [onmousedown="code"] [onmousemove="code"] [onmouseout="code"]
  [onmouseover="code"] [onmouseup="code"] [onselect="code"]
  [readonly="true|false"] [style="style"] [styleClass="styleClass"]
  [tabindex="tabIndex"] [title="title"]
>
  <f:selectItem> and/or <f:selectItems> action elements
</h:selectOneRadio>
```

Attributes

Attribute name	Java type	EL expression type	Description
`binding`	`String`	VB	Must be a value binding expression for a property the component is bound to.
`converter`	`String` *or* `javax.faces.convert.Converter`	VB	If set as a static value, a registered converter ID. If set as a value binding expression, an instance of an object that implements `Converter`.

Attribute name	Java type	EL expression type	Description
disabledClass	String	Any	The CSS class used for the <label> element around disabled choices.
enabledClass	String	Any	The CSS class used for the <label> element around enabled choices.
id	String	None	The component ID.
immediate	boolean	Any	If set to true, the ValueChangeEvent is processed in the Apply Request Values phase; if false, the event is processed in the Process Validations phase.
layout	String	Any	If set to lineDirection, the checkboxes are rendered horizontally. If set to pageDirection, the checkboxes are rendered vertically.
rendered	boolean	Any	If set to false, the component isn't rendered and doesn't participate in any request processing.
required	boolean	Any	If true, JSF verifies that a value is submitted for this component and marks it as invalid and queues an error message if not.
validator	String	MB	A method binding for a method with a void return type and FacesContext, UIComponent and Object parameters. Invoked to validate the component's local value (the Object parameter).
value	Object	VB	The component value.
valueChangeListener	String	MB	A method binding for a method with a void return type and an ValueChangeEvent parameter. Invoked to process the component's ValueChangeEvent.

Example

```
<h:form>
  <h:selectOneRadio value="#{user.country}">
    <f:selectItems value="#{allCountries}" />
  </h:selectOneRadio>
</h:form>
```

Core Library Actions

The core library contains action elements that represent JSF artifacts that are independent of the page markup language, such as converters and validators.

<f:actionListener>

This action creates an instance of the class defined by the type attribute, which must implement the javax.faces.event.ActionListener interface, and adds it to the component represented by the closest JSF component parent action element.

For an alternative, see the action and actionListener attributes for the HTML library <h:commandButton> and <h:commandLink> actions.

Syntax

```
<f:actionListener type="className" />
```

Attributes

Attribute name	Java type	EL expression type	Description
type	String	Any	The fully qualified class name for a class implementing the ActionListener interface.

Example

```
<h:form>
  <h:commandButton value="Save">
    <f:actionListener type="com.mycompany.SaveListener" />
  </h:commandButton>
</h:form>
```

<f:attribute>

This action sets a generic attribute for the component represented by the closest JSF component parent action element.

Syntax

```
<f:attribute name="name" value="value" />
```

Attributes

Attribute name	Java type	EL expression type	Description
name	String	Any	The attribute name.
value	Object	Any	The attribute value.

Example

```
<h:form>
  <h:inputText id="from" value="#{filter.from}" />
  <h:inputText value="#{filter.to}">
    <f:validator validatorId="com.mycompany.laterThanValidator" />
    <f:attribute name="compareToComp" value="from" />
  </h:inputText>
</h:form>
```

<f:convertDateTime>

This action creates an instance of the converter registered with the ID `javax.faces.DateTime`, configures it based on the action attributes and associates the converter instance with the component represented by the closest JSF component parent action element.

Syntax

```
<f:convertDateTime
  [dateStyle="default|short|medium|long|full"]
  [timeStyle="default|short|medium|long|full"]
  [pattern="pattern"]
  [type="time|date|both"]
  [locale="locale"]
  [timeZone="timeZone"]
/>
```

Attributes

Attribute name	Java type	EL expression type	Description
`dateStyle`	`String`	Any	One of the predefined locale-dependent date patterns.
`locale`	`String` *or* `java.util.Locale`	Any	A locale to be used instead of the default.
`pattern`	`String`	Any	A custom pattern in the form accepted by `java.text.SimpleDateFormat` (see the next table).
`timeStyle`	`String`	Any	One of the predefined locale-dependent time patterns.
`timeZone`	`String` *or* `java.util.TimeZone`	Any	The time zone to use instead of the default.
`type`	`String`	Any	Which portions to format or parse. Defaults to `time` if `timeStyle` is set, to `date` if `dateStyle` is set, or to `both` if both style attributes are set.

The symbols that can be used in a custom pattern, set by the `pattern` attribute, are the same as those supported by the `java.text.SimpleDateFormat`:

Symbol	Description	Presentation format	Example
`G`	Era designator	Text	AD
`y`	Year	Number	2002
`M`	Month in year	Text or number	May or 05
`d`	Day in month	Number	16
`h`	Hour in AM/PM (1-12)	Number	4
`H`	Hour in day (0-23)	Number	16
`m`	Minute in hour	Number	18

Symbol	Description	Presentation format	Example
s	Second in minute	Number	23
S	Millisecond	Number	678
E	Day in week	Text	Thursday
D	Day in year	Number	144
F	Day of week in month	Number	3
w	Week in year	Number	20
W	Week in month	Number	3
a	AM/PM marker	Text	PM
k	Hour in day (1-24)	Number	17
K	Hour in AM/PM (0-11)	Number	3
z	Time zone	Text	GMT
'	Escape for text	Delimiter	
''	Single quote in text	Literal	'

The number of symbols in the pattern determines the presentation format. For Text, four or more symbols means that the full form is used (e.g., "Thursday"), while less than four means that an abbreviation is used (e.g., "Thu"). For Number, the number of symbols sets the minimum number of digits. For Text or Number values, three or more symbols mean that the text format is used, otherwise the number format is used.

Example

```
<h:form>
  <h:inputText value="#{user.birthDate}">
    <f:convertDateTime dateStyle="short" />
  </h:inputText>
</h:form>
```

<f:convertNumber>

This action creates an instance of the converter registered with the ID `javax.faces.Number`, configures it based on the action attributes and associates the converter instance with the component represented by the closest JSF component parent action element.

Syntax

```
<f:convertNumber
  [pattern="pattern"]
  [minIntegerDigits="min"] [maxIntegerDigits="max"]
  [minFractionDigits="min"] [maxFractionDigits="max"]
  [groupingUsed="true|false"] [integerOnly="true|false"]
  [type="number|currency|percent"]
  [currencyCode="currencyCode"] [currencySymbol="currencySymbol"]
  [locale="locale"]
/>
```

Attributes

Attribute name	Java type	EL expression type	Description
currencyCode	String	Any	An ISO-4217 currency code.
currencySymbol	String	Any	A Java string to use as the currency symbol.
groupingUsed	boolean	Any	Set to `true` to include grouping separators in the result.
integerOnly	boolean	Any	Set to `true` to only parse the integer portion.
locale	String *or* java.util.Locale	Any	A locale to be used instead of the default.
maxFractionDigits	int	Any	The maximum number of digits in the fractional portion.
maxIntegerDigits	int	Any	The maximum number of digits in the integer portion.
minFractionDigits	int	Any	The minimum number of digits in the fractional portion.
minIntegerDigits	int	Any	The minimum number of digits in the integer portion.
pattern	String	Any	A custom pattern in the form accepted by `java.text.DecimalFormat` (see the next table).
type	String	Any	The name of one of the predefined locale-dependent patterns.

The symbols that can be used in a custom pattern, set by the `pattern` attribute, are the same as those supported by the `java.text.DecimalFormat`:

Symbol	Description	Location
0	Required digit	Number
#	Digit, zero is not displayed	Number
.	Decimal separator	Number
-	Minus sign	Number
,	Grouping separator	Number
E	Separates mantissa and exponent in scientific notation	Number
%	Multiply by 100 and show as percentage	Prefix or suffix
\u2030	Multiply by 1000 and shows as mille	Prefix or suffix
¤ *or* \u00A4	Currency sign	Prefix or suffix
'	Escape for text	Prefix or suffix
''	Single quote in text	Prefix or suffix

Example

```
<h:form>
  <h:inputText value="#{user.salary}">
    <f:convertNumber integerOnly="true" />
  </h:inputText>
</h:form>
```

<f:converter>

This action creates an instance of the class registered with the specified converter ID, which must implement the `javax.faces.convert.Converter` interface, and associates it with the component represented by the closest JSF component parent action element.

For an alternative, see the `converter` attribute for HTML library actions that represents JSF components with a `value` property.

Syntax

```
<f:converter converterId="converterId" />
```

Attributes

Attribute name	Java type	EL expression type	Description
`converterId`	`String`	Any	The ID used to register a class implementing the `Converter` interface.

Example

```
<h:form>
  <h:inputText value="#{user.ssn}">
    <f:converter converterId="ssnConverter" />
  </h:inputText>
</h:form>
```

<f:facet>

This action adds the component represented by the JSF action in its body as a facet with the specified name to the component represented by closest JSF component parent action element. To use a number of components as a facet, create them as children of a simple container component, e.g., by nesting the corresponding HTML library component actions within the body of an `<h:panelGroup>` action element.

Syntax

```
<f:facet name="facetName">
  JSF component action elements
</f:facet>
```

Attributes

Attribute name	Java type	EL expression type	Description
name	String	None	The facet name.

Example

```
<h:dataTable value="#{reportHandler.reports}" var="report">
  <f:facet name="header">
    <h:outputText value="Reports" />
  </f:facet>
  ...
</h:dataTable>
```

<f:loadBundle>

This action creates an instance of class implementing the `java.util.Map` interface with a `get()` method that returns the value of the corresponding resource in the specified resource bundle and saves the instance as a variable in the request scope. Localized resources from the bundle can then be accessed through the `Map` with regular JSF EL expressions, e.g., as `#{mapVar.resourceName}`. The resource bundle must be available in the web application's classpath, e.g., as a properties file in the *WEB-INF/classes* directory. For keys that don't match a resource, the `Map` returns the key embedded in question marks, e.g., "???myKey???".

Syntax

```
<f:loadBundle basename="baseName" var="var" />
```

Attributes

Attribute name	Java type	EL expression type	Description
basename	String	Any	The resource bundle name.
var	String	None	The variable name.

Example

```
<f:loadBundle basename="messages" var="msgs" />
<h:outputText value="#{msgs.title}" />
```

<f:param>

This action represents an instance of the component type registered with the type ID `javax.faces.Parameter` (by default, an instance of the `javax.faces.component.UIParameter` class). The action creates an instance of the component class, configures it with the name and value from the action attributes and adds it as a child to the component represented by closest JSF component parent action element.

Syntax

```
<f:param [id="id"] [binding="componentBinding"] [name="name"] value="value" />
```

Attributes

Attribute name	Java type	EL expression type	Description
binding	String	VB	Must be a value binding expression for a property the component is bound to.
id	String	None	The component ID.
name	String	Any	The parameter name.
value	String	Any	The parameter value.

Example

```
<f:loadBundle basename="messages" var="msgs" />
<h:outputFormat value="#{msgs.sunRiseAndSetText}">
  <f:param value="#{city.sunRiseTime}" />
  <f:param value="#{city.sunSetTime}" />
</h:outputFormat>
```

<f:selectItem>

This action represents an instance of the component type registered with the type ID javax.faces.SelectItem (by default, an instance of the javax.faces.component.UISelectItem class). The action creates an instance of the component class, configures it based on the action attributes and adds it as a child to the component represented by closest JSF component parent action element.

Syntax

```
<f:selectItem [id="id"] [binding="componentBinding"]
  [value="value" |
    itemValue="itemValue" itemLabel="itemLabel" [itemDisabled="true|false"]
    [itemDescription="itemDescription"]
  ]
/>
```

Attributes

Attribute name	Java type	EL expression type	Description
binding	String	VB	Must be a value binding expression for a property the component is bound to.
id	String	None	The component ID.
itemDescription	String	Any	The item description.

Attribute name	Java type	EL expression type	Description
itemDisabled	boolean	Any	Set to true if the item is disabled.
itemLabel	String	Any	The item label.
itemValue	Object	Any	The item value.
value	javax.faces.model.SelectItem	VB	A SelectItem instance containing all model properties.

Example

```
<h:form>
  <h:selectManyCheckbox value="#{user.projects}">
    <f:selectItem itemValue="JSF" itemValue="1" />
    <f:selectItem itemValue="JSP" itemValue="2" />
    <f:selectItem itemValue="Servlets" itemValue="3" />
  </h:selectManyCheckbox>
</h:form>
```

<f:selectItems>

This action represents an instance of the component type registered with the type ID javax.faces.SelectItems (by default, an instance of the javax.faces.component.UISelectItems class). The action creates an instance of the component class, configures it based on the action attributes and adds it as a child to the component represented by closest JSF component parent action element.

If the value is set to an instance of a class implementing the java.util.Map interface, the keys are used as select item labels and the values as select item values.

Syntax

```
<f:selectItems [id="id"] [binding="componentBinding"] value="value" />
```

Attributes

Attribute name	Java type	EL expression type	Description
binding	String	VB	Must be a value binding expression for a property the component is bound to.
id	String	None	The component ID.
value	javax.faces.model.SelectItem, an array or Collection with javax.faces.model.SelectItem elements, or a java.util.Map.	VB	One or more SelectItem instances.

Example

```
<h:form>
  <h:selectManyCheckbox value="#{user.projects}">
```

```
    <f:selectItems value="#{allProjects}" />
  </h:selectManyCheckbox>
</h:form>
```

<f:subView>

This action represents an instance of the component type registered with the type ID `javax.faces.NamingContainer` (by default, an instance of the `javax.faces.component.UINamingContainer` class).

The action creates an instance of the component class to hold all components defined in an included subview, configures it based on the action attributes and adds it as a child to the component represented by closest JSF component parent action element. For details on how to use this action, see Chapter 12.

Syntax

```
<f:subView id="id" [binding="componentBinding"] [rendered="true|false"]>
  JSF component action elements
</f:subView>
```

Attributes

Attribute name	Java type	EL expression type	Description
`binding`	`String`	VB	Must be a value binding expression for a property the component is bound to.
`id`	`String`	None	The component ID.
`rendered`	`boolean`	Any	If set to `false`, the component isn't rendered and doesn't participate in any request processing.

Example

```
<f:view>
  <f:subview id="header">
    <jsp:include page="header.jsp" />
  </f:subview>
  ...
  <f:subview id="footer">
    <jsp:include page="footer.jsp" />
  </f:subview>
</f:view>
```

<f:validateDoubleRange>

This action creates an instance of the validator registered with the ID `javax.faces.DoubleRange`, configures it based on the action attributes and associates the validator instance with the component represented by the closest JSF component parent action element.

Syntax

```
<f:validateDoubleRange [maximum="max"] [minimum="min"] />
```

Attributes

Attribute name	Java type	EL expression type	Description
maximum	double	Any	The maximum allowed value.
minimum	double	Any	The minimum allowed value.

Example

```
<h:inputText value="#{product.price}">
  <f:convertNumber type="currency" />
  <f:validateDoubleRange minimum="0.0" />
</h:inputText>
```

<f:validateLength>

This action creates an instance of the validator registered with the ID `javax.faces.Length`, configures it based on the action attributes and associates the validator instance with the component represented by the closest JSF component parent action element.

Syntax

```
<f:validateLength [maximum="max"] [minimum="min"] />
```

Attributes

Attribute name	Java type	EL expression type	Description
maximum	int	Any	The maximum length (number of characters) allowed value.
minimum	int	Any	The minimum length (number of characters) allowed value.

Example

```
<h:inputText value="#{user.zipCode}">
  <f:validateLength minimum="5" maximum="5" />
</h:inputText>
```

<f:validateLongRange>

This action creates an instance of the validator registered with the ID `javax.faces.LongRange`, configures it based on the action attributes and associates the validator instance with the component represented by the closest JSF component parent action element.

Syntax

```
<f:validateLongRange [maximum="max"] [minimum="min"] />
```

Attributes

Attribute name	Java type	EL expression type	Description
maximum	long	Any	The maximum allowed value.
minimum	long	Any	The minimum allowed value.

Example

```
<h:inputText value="#{employee.salary}">
  <f:convertNumber type="currency" />
  <f:validateLongRange minimum="50000" maximum="150000" />
</h:inputText>
```

<f:validator>

This action creates an instance of the class registered with the specified validator ID, which must implement the `javax.faces.validator.Validator` interface, and associates it with the component represented by the closest JSF component parent action element.

For an alternative, see the `validator` attribute for HTML library actions that represents JSF input components.

Syntax

```
<f:validator validatorId="validatorId" />
```

Attributes

Attribute name	Java type	EL expression type	Description
validatorId	String	Any	The ID used to register a class implementing the `Validator` interface.

Example

```
<h:form>
  <h:inputText value="#{user.ssn}">
    <f:validator validatorId="ssnValidator" />
  </h:inputText>
</h:form>
```

<f:valueChangeListener>

This action creates an instance of the class defined by the type attribute, which must implement the `javax.faces.event.ValueChangeListener` interface, and adds it to the component represented by the closest JSF component parent action element.

For an alternative, see the valueChangeListener attributes for the HTML library that represents JSF input components.

Syntax

```
<f:valueChangeListener type="className" />
```

Attributes

Attribute name	Java type	EL expression type	Description
type	String	Any	The fully qualified class name for a class implementing the ValueChangeListener interface.

Example

```
<h:form>
  <h:selectBooleanCheckbox value="Details" immediate="true">
    <f:valueChangeListener type="com.mycompany.DescrLevelListener" />
  </h:selectBooleanCheckbox>
</h:form>
```

<f:verbatim>

This action represents an instance of the component type registered with the type ID javax.faces.Output (by default, an instance of the javax.faces.component.UIOutput class), combined with a renderer registered with the renderer type ID javax.faces.Text.

The action creates an instance of the component class, sets its value to the evaluation result of the element body, sets the transient property to true and the escape property to the value set by the action attribute with the same name, and adds the component as a child of the component represented by the closest JSF component parent action element.

Syntax

```
<f:verbatim [escape="true|false">
  Template text and/or non-JSF action elements
</f:verbatim>
```

Attributes

Attribute Name	Java Type	Dynamic Value Accepted	Description
escape	boolean	Any	If true, render special HTML and XML characters as character entity codes, e.g., < as <.

Example

```
<f:subview id="header">
  <f:verbatim>
    <html>
      <head>
        <title>Welcome to my site!</title>
      </head>
  </f:verbatim>
</f:subview>
```

<f:view>

This action represents an instance of the component type registered with the type ID `javax.faces.ViewRoot` (by default, an instance of the `javax.faces.component.UIViewRoot` class).

The action creates an instance of the component class to hold all components that are part of the view and sets the view's locale to the specified value.

Syntax

```
<f:view [locale="locale"]>
  JSF component action elements, template text and/or non-JSF action elements
</f:view>
```

Attributes

Attribute Name	Java Type	Dynamic Value Accepted	Description
`locale`	`String` *or* `java.util.Locale`	Any	A locale to be used instead of the default.

Example

```
<f:view locale="#{user.locale}">
  ...
</f:view>
```

APPENDIX B

JSF Expression Language Reference

This appendix contains a reference to the JSF Expression Language (EL). EL expressions can be used in JSF action element attribute values in a JSP page for all attributes declared to accept EL attribute values in Appendix A.

JSF EL expression can be used also to create instances of the `javax.faces.el.MethodBinding` and `javax.faces.el.ValueBinding` classes used in the component APIs for other presentation layer technologies. See the `javax.faces.application.Application createMethodBinding( )` and `createValueBinding( )` methods in Appendix D for details.

Syntax

A JSF EL expression starts with the #{ delimiter (a hash mark plus a left curly brace) and ends with } (a right curly brace):

```
#{anExpression}
```

When used in an attribute value for a standard JSF custom action, any number of EL expressions and static text parts can be combined. Such an expression is read-only, with the evaluation result of each expression converted to a `String` and then concatenated with the text parts:

```
<h:outputText value="The result of 1 + 2 + 3 is #{1 + 2 + 3}" />
```

The language is case-sensitive. All keywords are in lowercase, and identifiers must be written with correct capitalization.

Literals

Literals represent strings, numbers, Boolean values, and the `null` value.

Literal type	Description
String	Enclosed with single or double quotes. A quote of the same type within the string must be escaped with backslash: \' in a string enclosed with single quotes, \" in a string enclosed with double quotes. The backslash character must be escaped as \\ in both cases.
Integer	An optional sign (+ or -) followed by digits between 0 and 9.
Floating point	The same as an Integer literal, except that a dot is used as the separator for the fractional part and that an exponent can be specified as e or E followed by an Integer literal.
Boolean	`true` or `false`
Null	`null`

Keywords and Reserved Words

The following words are keywords or reserved for potential use in a future version:

```
and or not eq ne lt gt le ge true false null instanceof empty div mod
```

They can't be used as property names or variable names, unless they are quoted.

Variables

Variables are named references to data (objects) that are created by the application or declared as managed beans in the *faces-config.xml* file, and implicitly created by the EL. Every object that is available as a request, session or application attribute can be used as an EL variable

```
#{aVariable}
```

Implicit Variables

All information about a request and other data can be accessed through the EL implicit variables:

Variable name	Description
`requestScope`	A collection (a `java.util.Map`) of all request scope variables.
`sessionScope`	A collection (a `java.util.Map`) of all session scope variables.
`applicationScope`	A collection (a `java.util.Map`) of all application scope variables.
`param`	A collection (a `java.util.Map`) of all request parameter values as a single `String` value per parameter.
`paramValues`	A collection (a `java.util.Map`) of all request parameter values as a `String` array per parameter.
`header`	A collection (a `java.util.Map`) of all request header values as a single `String` value per header.

Variable name	Description
headerValues	A collection (a java.util.Map) of all request header values as a String array per header.
cookie	A collection (a java.util.Map) of all request cookie values as a single javax.servlet.http.Cookie value per cookie. See Appendix D for a list of properties for the Cookie class.
initParam	A collection (a java.util.Map) of all application initialization parameter values as a single String value per parameter.
facesContext	An instance of the javax.faces.context.FacesContext class, providing access to various JSF context data.
view	An instance of the javax.faces.component.UIViewRoot class, providing access to all components in the current view.

Support for additional implicit variables can be implemented through a custom javax.faces.el.VariableResolver class. See Appendix D for details.

Data Types

A variable is always of a specific Java type. Besides the standard Java types for numeric, Boolean, and text values, the EL provides special support for custom classes developed according to the JavaBeans guidelines, java.util.Map objects, java.util.List objects, and arrays.

Bean properties can be accessed using the special property accessor operator (a dot), and be nested to any length:

```
#{aBean.aProperty.aPropertyOfTheProperty.andSoOn}
```

Map entries can be accessed the same way:

```
#{aMap.aKey}
```

List and array elements can be accessed using the array accessor operator (square brackets):

```
#{aList[0]}
#{anArray[0]}
#{anArrayOrList[anExressionWithANumbericValue]}
```

The array accessor operator can also access bean properties and Map entries. It *must* be used when the property name is determined by a subexpression, the property name is a reserved word or contains characters used for operators, such as a dot:

```
#{aMap[param.customerName]}
#{aBean['empty']}
#{aMap['com.mycomp.logo']}
```

A custom javax.faces.el.PropertyResolver class can extend or modify how the property and element accessor operators behave. See Appendix D for details.

Coercion Rules

The EL automatically converts, or *coerces*, variable values and the result of an expression to the type required by an operator:

To Java type	Conversion rule
`String`	`null`: to empty string (`""`).
	All other types: to the corresponding `String` value.
`Primitive number` or `Number`	`null` or empty string: 0.
	`Character` or `char`: to the value represented by the character code.
	`String`: parse as an Integer or Floating point literal.
	Numeric types: coerce to the requested precision.
`boolean` *or* `Boolean`	`null`: to `false`.
	`String`: to `true` if the value is "true", ignoring case, otherwise `false`.
Other type	`null`: keep as `null`.
	String: use the `PropertyEditor` for the requested type, if any, otherwise `null` if the string is empty.
	Other: type cast, if possible.

In all cases, the EL evaluator throws an exception for attempts to convert between types not defined in the table or if the defined conversion rule fails.

Expressions and Operators

The combination of literal values, variables, and the following operators form an EL expression:

Operator	Precedence	Operation performed
`.`	1	Access a bean property or `Map` entry.
`[]`	1	Access an array or `List` element.
`()`	2	Group a subexpression to change the evaluation order.
`? :`	10	Conditional test: *condition ? ifTrue : ifFalse*.
`+`	5	Addition.
`-`	5	Subtraction.
`-`	3	Negation of a value.
`*`	4	Multiplication.
`/ or div`	4	Division.
`% or mod`	4	Modulo (remainder).
`== or eq`	7	Test for equality.
`!= or ne`	7	Test for inequality.
`< or lt`	6	Test for less than.

Operator	Precedence	Operation performed
`>` or `gt`	6	Test for greater than.
`<=` or `le`	6	Test for less than or equal.
`>=` or `ge`	6	Test for greater than or equal.
`&&` or `and`	8	Test for logical AND.
`||` or `or`	9	Test for logical OR.
`!` or `not`	3	Unary Boolean complement.
`empty`	3	Test for empty variable values (`null` or an empty `String`, array, `Map` or `Collection`).

Expressions are evaluated in the order defined by the operator precedence and left to right for operators of the same precedence.

Operand Evaluation and Coercing Rules

Before the operator is applied, the EL evaluator coerces the types of the operand values. An exception is thrown if no rule matches, the coercing fails, or applying the operator leads to an exception.

Property and array accessor operators

An expression of the form `#{exprA.identifierB}` is evaluated the same way as `#{exprA['identifierB']}`. When used as value binding expression to bind an input component's value to a property of an application bean, the expression is used both to read and write the property value.

When read, an expression of the form `#{exprA[exprB]}` is evaluated according to the following rules by default:

1. If `exprA` is `null`, return `null`
2. If `exprB` is `null`, return `null`
3. If `exprA` is a `Map` with a key matching `exprB`, return the value
4. If `exprA` is a `List` or array with an index matching `exprB` coerced to an `int`, return the value
5. If `exprA` is a bean with a property matching `exprB` coerced to a `String`, return the value.

When written, an expression of the form `#{exprA[exprB]}` is evaluated according to the following rules by default:

1. If `exprA` is `null`, throw a `PropertyNotFoundException`
2. If `exprB` is `null`, throw a `PropertyNotFoundException`
3. If `exprA` is a `Map`, call its `put()` method with the evaluation result of `exprB` as the key and the component's value as the value

4. If exprA is a List or array, call its set( ) method or the java.lang.reflect.Array.set( ) method with an index matching exprB coerced to an int and the component's value. If an exception is thrown, rethrow it wrapped in a PropertyNotFoundException
5. If exprA is a bean with a writeable property matching exprB coerced to a String, call the setter method with the component's value. If an exception is thrown, rethrow it wrapped in a ReferenceSyntaxException. If exprB doesn't match a writable property name, throw a PropertyNotFoundException

When written, an expression containing a single identifier is evaluated according to the following rules by default:

1. If the identifier matches an implicit variable name, throw a ReferenceSyntaxException
2. If the identifier matches a variable in the request, session, or application scope, replace the variable value with the component's value
3. Otherwise, create a new request scope variable with the component's value.

An expression may also be used as a method binding, binding an application bean method to a component. Such an expression must be of the form #{exprA.identifierB} or #{exprA['identifierB']}, where identifierB must be the name of a method with the appropriate signature, as defined per attribute that accepts a method binding expression.

Arithmetic operators

For addition, subtraction and multiplication, if any operand is null, the result is 0. Otherwise both operands are coerced to numbers (to BigDecimal if one of them is BigDecimal or if one is BigInteger and the other is Float, Double, or a String with floating-point syntax, to double if one of them is Float, Double, or a String with floating-point syntax, to BigInteger if one of them is BigInteger, to long otherwise), and the result of applying the operator is returned.

For division, if any operand is null, the result is 0. Otherwise both operands are coerced to numbers (to BigDecimal if one of them is BigInteger or BigDecimal, to double otherwise), and the result of applying the operator is returned.

For modulo, if any operand is null, the result is 0. Otherwise both operands are coerced to numbers (to double if one of them is BigDecimal, Float, Double, or a String with floating-point syntax, to BigInteger if one of them is BigInteger, to long otherwise), and the result of applying the operator is returned.

For negation, if the operand is null, the result is 0. Otherwise if the operand is a String, it's coerced to a number (to double if it represents a floating-point value, to long otherwise), and the result of applying the operator is returned. For numeric types, the operator is applied without coercing the value and the result is returned.

Relational operators

For "less than," "greater than," "less than or equal," and "greater than or equal," if the operands are equal, true is returned for "less than or equal" and "greater than or equal"; false otherwise. If the operands are not equal and one of them is null, false is returned. If one of the operands is a BigDecimal, the other is coerced to BigDecimal and the result of compareTo( ) is returned. If one of the operands is a Float or a Double, both are coerced to Double, and the result of applying the operator is returned. If one of the operands is a BigInteger, the other is coerced to BigInteger and the result of compareTo( ) is returned. If one of the operands is a Byte, Short, Character, Integer, or Long, both are coerced to long, and the result of applying the operator is returned. If one operand is a String, the other is coerced to a String, and the result of compareTo( ) is returned. Otherwise, if one of the operands is a Comparable, the result of comparing it to the other with the compareTo( ) method is returned.

For "equal" and "not equal," if the operands are equal, the operator is applied and the result is returned. If one of the operands is null, false is returned for "equal" and true for "not equal." If one of the operands is a BigDecimal, the other is coerced to BigDecimal and the result of equals( ) is used, negated for "not equal." If one of the operands is a Float or a Double, both are coerced to double, and the result of applying the operator is returned. If one of the operands is a BigInteger, the other is coerced to BigInteger and the result of equals( ) is used, negated for "not equal." If one of the operands is a Byte, Short, Character, Integer, or Long, both are coerced to long, and the result of applying the operator is returned. If one of the operands is a Boolean, both are coerced to boolean, and the result of applying the operator is returned. Otherwise, the result of comparing the values with the equals( ) method is returned, negated for "not equal."

Logical operators

For "and" and "or," both operands are coerced to boolean, and the result of applying the operator is returned. The evaluation stops as soon as the result can be determined, i.e., for the expression #{a && b && c && d}, only #{a && b} is evaluated if b is false.

For "not," the operand is coerced to boolean and the result of applying the operator is returned.

Empty operator

The "empty" operator returns true if the operand is null or an empty string, an empty array, an empty Map, or an empty Collection; otherwise it returns false.

APPENDIX C

Standard JSF Components and Render Kits

This appendix contains reference material for all standard JSF component classes and the standard render kit, as well as a description of the request processing lifecycle and how it relates to the component classes.

The first section contains an overview of the different component class categories and the standard HTML render kit. The middle sections each describe a specific JSF component class in detail, followed by sections describing each standard HTML renderer.

Component Class Categories

The primary JSF component classes implement render-independent behavior and must be combined with a renderer that knows how to represent them in a particular markup language, such as one of the renderers in the standard HTML render kit. Figure C-1 shows all render-independent component classes.

Each component class belongs to a *component family*, which identifies the basic nature of a component, for example, that it's an output component or a command component. More than one component class may belong to the same family, e.g., both the base class and its subclasses, which specialize the behavior of the base class. All standard component family names starts with a `javax.faces` prefix followed by descriptive name, e.g., `javax.faces.Output` for the `javax.faces.component.UIOutput` class. A component instance is associated with a renderer type that may be set programmatically by the developer. The *renderer type* tells in general terms how to represent the component, e.g., as a link or a button. The standard renderer type IDs also have a `javax.faces` prefix followed by a descriptive name, e.g., `javax.faces.Link` for a link renderer.

The specific renderer class to use for a component is determined by the combination of the renderer type it's configured to use and the family it belongs to. This makes it possible to use the same renderer type IDs for renderer classes with widely different behavior. For instance, the renderer type ID `javax.faces.Link` can be used for one

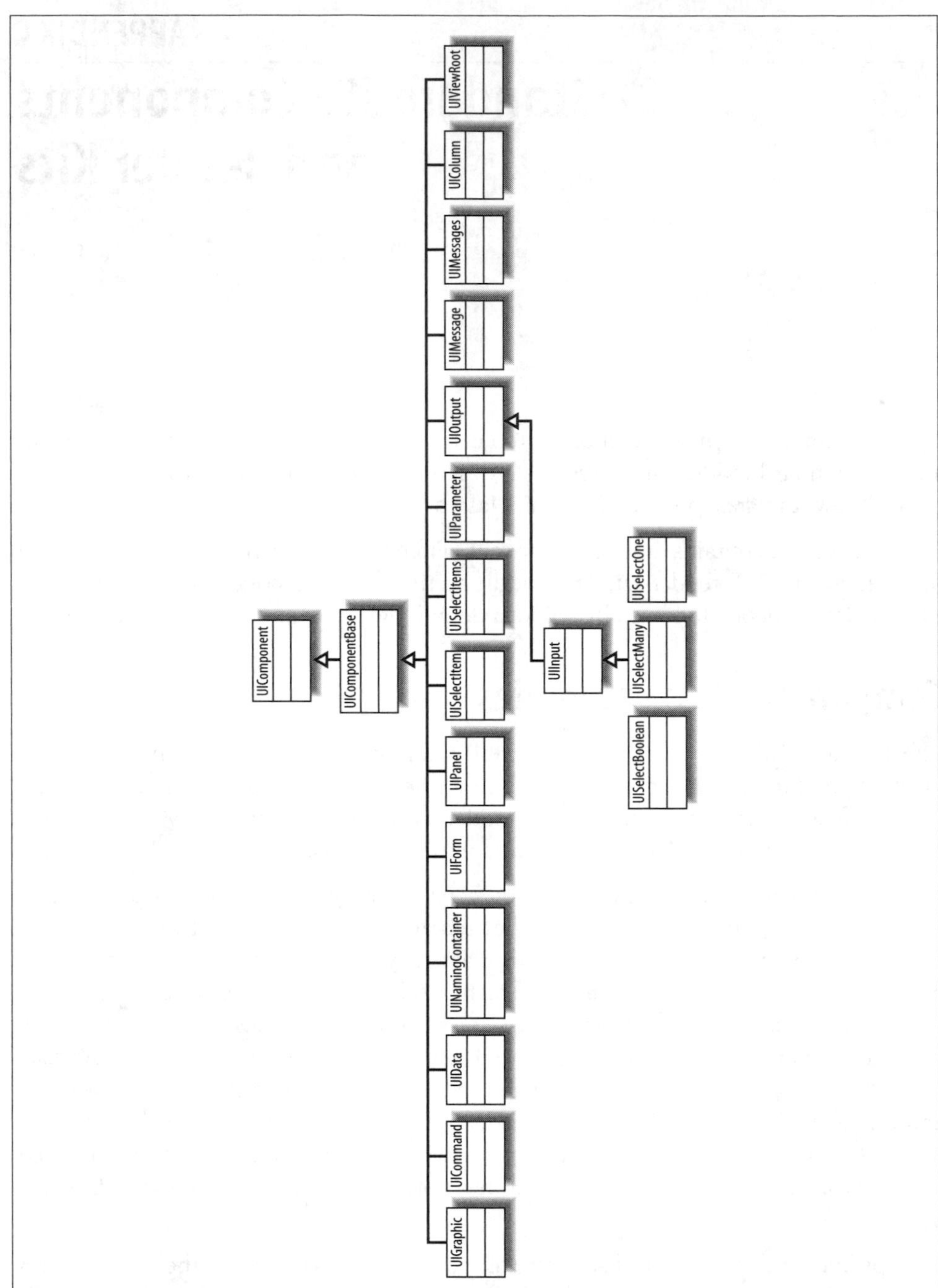

Figure C-1. Render-independent component classes

renderer class used with a component in the `javax.faces.Output` family to render a regular HTML link element with the components value as the URL, and also for another renderer class used with a component in the `javax.faces.Command` family to render an HTML link element with JavaScript code for submitting the form it belongs to and with the component's value as the link text. Without the component family concept, one renderer class would have to support both types of components, or renderer type IDs would have to include the something similar to a family ID in their names, which would lead to namespace scalability problems in the long run. Table C-1 lists all renderer type/component family combinations a JSF implementation must include in the HTML renderer kit. The renderer classes themselves are not defined by the JSF specification, only their behavior.

Table C-1. HTML Renderers

Component family	Renderer type
javax.faces.Command	javax.faces.Button
javax.faces.Command	javax.faces.Link
javax.faces.Data	javax.faces.Table
javax.faces.Form	javax.faces.Form
javax.faces.Graphic	javax.faces.Image
javax.faces.Input	javax.faces.Hidden
javax.faces.Input	javax.faces.Secret
javax.faces.Input	javax.faces.Text
javax.faces.Input	javax.faces.Textare
javax.faces.Message	javax.faces.Message
javax.faces.Messages	javax.faces.Messages
javax.faces.Output	javax.faces.Format
javax.faces.Output	javax.faces.Label
javax.faces.Output	javax.faces.Link
javax.faces.Output	javax.faces.Text
javax.faces.Panel	javax.faces.Grid
javax.faces.Panel	javax.faces.Group
javax.faces.SelectBoolean	javax.faces.Checkbox
javax.faces.SelectMany	javax.faces.Checkbox
javax.faces.SelectMany	javax.faces.Listbox
javax.faces.SelectMany	javax.faces.Menu
javax.faces.SelectOne	javax.faces.Listbox
javax.faces.SelectOne	javax.faces.Menu
javax.faces.SelectOne	javax.faces.Radio

The separation of component and renderer classes is what makes JSF so flexible and useful in many different scenarios, but it also makes it tedious to manipulate components programmatically. You must be aware of the distinction between render-independent properties and render-dependent attributes. The render-independent properties are represented by JavaBeans-style accessor methods in the component classes, and render-dependent attributes used by the renderers are set as generic component attributes, accessed with the `get( )` and `put( )` methods on the `java.util.Map` returned by the component `getAttributes( )` method. Because HTML is by far the most common rendering language, JSF defines classes that combine the render-independent properties and render-dependent attributes for all combinations of components and renderers in the HTML render kit, allowing you to manipulate both groups as regular JavaBeans properties. Table C-2 lists all these HTML-specific component classes.

Table C-2. HTML-specific component classes

Class name
javax.faces.component.html.HtmlCommandButton
javax.faces.component.html.HtmlCommandLink
javax.faces.component.html.HtmlDataTable
javax.faces.component.html.HtmlForm
javax.faces.component.html.HtmlGraphicImage
javax.faces.component.html.HtmlInputHidden
javax.faces.component.html.HtmlInputSecret
javax.faces.component.html.HtmlInputText
javax.faces.component.html.HtmlInputTextarea
javax.faces.component.html.HtmlMessage
javax.faces.component.html.HtmlMessages
javax.faces.component.html.HtmlOutputFormat
javax.faces.component.html.HtmlOutputFormat
javax.faces.component.html.HtmlOutputLabel
javax.faces.component.html.HtmlOutputText
javax.faces.component.html.HtmlPanelGrid
javax.faces.component.html.HtmlPanelGroup
javax.faces.component.html.HtmlSelectBooleanCheckbox
javax.faces.component.html.HtmlSelectManyCheckbox
javax.faces.component.html.HtmlSelectManyListbox
javax.faces.component.html.HtmlSelectManyMenu
javax.faces.component.html.HtmlSelectOneListbox
javax.faces.component.html.HtmlSelectOneMenu
javax.faces.component.html.HtmlSelectRadio

Render-Independent Components

JSF defines a number of interfaces for behavior that can be applied to component classes independent of their place in the class hierarchy and a class hierarchy containing classes for the standard render-independent components. It also defines a few model classes used as values for the standard component classes.

This section described the interfaces first and then the classes. Each interface or class section contains a brief description of the type, a table with information about the fully qualified type name and inheritance information, and a list of field, constructor, and method descriptions.

Component Interfaces

ActionSource

This interface contains all methods related to firing and handling a `javax.faces.event.ActionEvent`. All component classes that fire this event, such as command components, must implement this interface.

Synopsis

Interface name:	`javax.faces.component.ActionSource`
Extends:	None
Implemented by:	`javax.faces.component.UICommand`

Methods

`public void addActionListener(javax.faces.event.ActionListener l)`
: Adds the `ActionListener` to the list of listeners for the `ActionEvent` this component fires.

`public javax.faces.el.MethodBinding getAction()`
: Returns the `MethodBinding` for the action method that should be invoked to handle the `ActionEvent` this component fires or `null` if no method is bound.

`public javax.faces.el.MethodBinding getActionListener()`
: Returns the `MethodBinding` for the action listener method that should be invoked to handle the `ActionEvent` this component fires or `null` if no method is bound.

`public javax.faces.event.ActionListener[] getActionListeners()`
: Returns all `ActionListener` instances registered with this component or an empty array if none is registered.

`public boolean isImmediate()`
: Returns `true` if the `ActionEvent` should be processed in the Apply Request Values phase or `false` if it should be processed in the Invoke Application Phase.

`public void removeActionListener(javax.faces.event.ActionListener l)`
Removes the `ActionListener` from the list of listeners for the `ActionEvent` this component fires.

`public void setAction(javax.faces.el.MethodBinding action)`
Sets the `MethodBinding` for the action method that should be invoked to handle the `ActionEvent` this component fires.

`public void setActionListener(javax.faces.el.MethodBinding almb)`
Sets the `MethodBinding` for the action listener method that should be invoked to handle the `ActionEvent` this component fires.

`public void setImmediate(boolean immediate)`
Sets the phase where the `ActionEvent` should be processed: `true` for the Apply Request Values phase or `false` for the Invoke Application Phase.

EditableValueHolder

This interface contains all methods related to processing of a component value that can be set by an application user, including firing and handling a `javax.faces.event.ValueChangeEvent`. All classes that have an editable value and fire this event must implement this interface.

Synopsis

Interface name:	`javax.faces.component.EditableValueHolder`
Extends:	`javax.faces.component.ValueHolder`
Implemented by:	`javax.faces.component.UIInput`

Methods

`public void addValidator(javax.faces.validator.Validator validator)`
Adds the `Validator` to the list of validator for this component's value.

`public void addValueChangeListener(javax.faces.event.ValueChangeListener l)`
Adds the `ValueChangeListener` to the list of listeners for the `ValueChangeEvent` this component fires.

`public Object getSubmittedValue( )`
Returns the submitted value for this component, i.e., the unconverted value extracted from the request data or a value in a format known only to the component or its renderer.

`public javax.faces.el.MethodBinding getValidator( )`
Returns the `MethodBinding` for the validator method that should be invoked to validate this component's value or `null` if no method is bound.

`public javax.faces.validator.Validator[] getValidators( )`
Returns all `Validator` instances registered with this component or an empty array if none is registered.

`public javax.faces.el.MethodBinding getValueChangeListener( )`
Returns the `MethodBinding` for the value change method that should be invoked to handle the `ValueChangeEvent` this component fires or `null` if no method is bound.

`public javax.faces.event.ValueChangeListener[] getValueChangeListeners()`
: Returns all `ValueChangeListener` instances registered with this component or an empty array if none is registered.

`public boolean isImmediate()`
: Returns `true` if the `ValueChangeEvent` should be processed in the Apply Request Values phase or `false` if it should be processed in the Process Validations phase.

`public boolean isLocalValueSet()`
: Returns `true` if the local value for this component has been set, either explicitly by application code or implicitly after successful validation of the submitted value.

`public boolean isRequired()`
: Returns `true` if a value must be submitted for this component.

`public boolean isValid()`
: Returns `true` if the submitted value has been successfully converted and validated.

`public void removeValidator(javax.faces.validator.Validator validator)`
: Removes the `Validator` from the list of validator for this component's value.

`public void removeValueChangeListener(javax.faces.event.ValueChangeListener l)`
: Removes the `ValueChangeListener` from the list of listeners for the `ValueChangeEvent` this component fires.

`public void setImmediate(boolean immediate)`
: Sets the phase where the `ValueChangeEvent` should be processed: `true` for the Apply Request Values phase or `false` for the Process Validations phase.

`public void setLocalValueSet(boolean isLocalValueSet)`
: Sets the `localValueSet` property value.

`public void setRequired(boolean isRequired)`
: Sets the `required` property value.

`public void setSubmittedValue(Object submittedValue)`
: Sets the submitted value for this component, i.e., the unconverted value extracted from the request data or a value in a format known only to the component or its renderer.

`public void setValid(boolean isValid)`
: Sets the `valid` property value.

`public void setValidator(javax.faces.el.MethodBinding validator)`
: Sets the `MethodBinding` for the validator method that should be invoked to validate this component's value.

`public void setValueChangeListener(javax.faces.el.MethodBinding vclmb)`
: Sets the `MethodBinding` for the value change method that should be invoked to handle the `ValueChangeEvent` this component fires.

NamingContainer

This is an empty interface that marks a component class as a naming container. The `javax.faces.component.UIComponent findComponent()` and `getClientId()` methods use naming container parents in their processing. See these methods for details.

Synopsis

Interface name:	`javax.faces.component.NamingContainer`
Extends:	None
Implemented by:	`javax.faces.component.UIData`, `javax.faces.component.UIForm`, `javax.faces.component.UINamingContainer`

Fields

`public static char SEPARATOR_CHAR`

The component ID separator character; a colon.

StateHolder

This interface contains all methods related to saving and restoring view state for a component or an instance attached to a component. All component classes must implement this interface.

Synopsis

Interface name:	`javax.faces.component.StateHolder`
Extends:	None
Implemented by:	`javax.faces.component.UIComponent`, `javax.faces.convert.DateTimeConverter`, `javax.faces.convert.NumberConverter`, `javax.faces.validator.DoubleRangeValidator`, `javax.faces.validator.LengthValidator`, `javax.faces.validator.LongRangeValidator`

Methods

`public boolean isTransient( )`

Returns `true` if no state should be saved and restored for this instance.

`public void restoreState(javax.faces.context.FacesContext context, Object state)`

Restores the state for this instance from the provided value; an `Object` previously returned by the `saveState( )` method.

`public Object saveState(javax.faces.context.FacesContext context)`

Returns the state for this instance as an `Object` to be passed to the `restoreState( )` method when the instance is restored for the next request.

`public void setTransient(boolean isTransient)`

Sets the `transient` property value.

ValueHolder

This interface contains all methods related to processing of a component value that cannot be set by an application user, only by an application developer. All classes that have a value that can be converted must implement this interface.

Synopsis

Interface name:	`javax.faces.component.ValueHolder`
Extends:	None
Implemented by:	`javax.faces.component.UIInput`, `javax.faces.component.UIOutput`

Methods

`public javax.faces.convert.Converter getConverter( )`
Returns the `Converter` used to convert this component's value or `null` if none is registered.

`public Object getLocalValue( )`
Returns the local value of this component, without evaluating the value `javax.faces.el.ValueBinding` if set, or `null` if the component doesn't have a local value.

`public Object getValue( )`
Returns the value of this component, from the local value or by evaluating the value `javax.faces.el.ValueBinding` if it doesn't have a local value, or `null` if the component doesn't have a value at all.

`public void setConverter(javax.faces.convert.Converter converter)`
Sets the `Converter` used to convert this component's value.

`public void setValue(Object localValue)`
Sets the local value of this component.

Component Classes

UIColumn

This class represents a column component that may be used as a child of a `javax.faces.component.UIData` component or a custom component. A column component acts as a container for other components used to represent the column data. It can be equipped with header and footer facets. A component of this type is rendered by its parent.

Synopsis

Class name:	`javax.faces.component.UIColumn`
Extends:	`javax.faces.component.UIComponentBase`
Implements:	`javax.faces.component.StateHolder`

Fields

`public static String COMPONENT_FAMILY`
The component family: `javax.faces.Column`.

`public static String COMPONENT_TYPE`
The component family: `javax.faces.Column`.

Constructor

`public UIColumn( )`
Creates a new instance.

Methods

`public String getFamily( )`
Returns the component family ID.

`public javax.faces.component.UIComponent getFooter( )`
Returns the footer facet or `null` if none is set.

`public javax.faces.component.UIComponent getHeader( )`
Returns the header facet or `null` if none is set.

`public void setFooter(javax.faces.component.UIComponent footer)`
Sets the footer facet.

`public void setHeader(javax.faces.component.UIComponent header)`
Sets the header facet.

UICommand

This class represents a command component. A command component lets the user issue a command to the application, either to adjust the view or initiate backend processing. It's often rendered as button or a link, and it must be a child component of a form component, directly or indirectly. The default `rendererType` is `javax.faces.Button`.

When triggered by a user, the command component fires an `ActionEvent`, which can be handled by the application through an action method or one or more listeners, in the order: `javax.faces.event.ActionListener` instances (in the order they are registered), the action listener method, and then the action method.

Synopsis

Class name:	`javax.faces.component.UICommand`
Extends:	`javax.faces.component.UIComponentBase`
Implements:	`javax.faces.component.ActionSource`, `javax.faces.component.StateHolder`

Fields

`public static String COMPONENT_FAMILY`
The component family: `javax.faces.Command`.

`public static String COMPONENT_TYPE`
The component family: `javax.faces.Command`.

Constructor

`public UICommand( )`
Creates a new instance.

Methods

public void addActionListener(javax.faces.event.ActionListener l)
Adds the ActionListener to the list of listeners for the ActionEvent this component fires.

public void broadcast(javax.faces.event.FacesEvent event)
throws javax.faces.event.AbortProcessingException
Extends the inherited behavior by passing an ActionEvent to the action listener method (if any) and to the default ActionListener registered for the application to invoke the action method (if any).

public javax.faces.el.MethodBinding getAction()
Returns the MethodBinding for the action method that should be invoked to handle the ActionEvent this component fires or null if no method is bound.

public javax.faces.el.MethodBinding getActionListener()
Returns the MethodBinding for the action listener method that should be invoked to handle the ActionEvent this component fires or null if no method is bound.

public javax.faces.event.ActionListener[] getActionListeners()
Returns all ActionListener instances registered with this component or an empty array if none is registered.

public String getFamily()
Returns the component family ID.

public Object getValue()
Returns the component value.

public boolean isImmediate()
Returns true if the ActionEvent should be processed in the Apply Request Values phase or false if it should be processed in the Invoke Application Phase.

public void queueEvent(javax.faces.event.FacesEvent event)
Specializes the inherited behavior by setting the PhaseId for an ActionEvent to PhaseId.APPLY_REQUEST_VALUES if the immediate property is set to true and to PhaseId.INVOKE_APPLICATION if it's set to false before letting the superclass handle the method call.

public void removeActionListener(javax.faces.event.ActionListener l)
Removes the ActionListener from the list of listeners for the ActionEvent this component fires.

public void restoreState(javax.faces.context.FacesContext context, Object state)
Restores the state for this instance from the provided value; an Object previously returned by the saveState() method.

public Object saveState(javax.faces.context.FacesContext context)
Returns the state for this instance as an Object to be passed to the restoreState() method when the instance is restored for the next request.

public void setAction(javax.faces.el.MethodBinding action)
Sets the MethodBinding for the action method that should be invoked to handle the ActionEvent this component fires.

public void setActionListener(javax.faces.el.MethodBinding almb)
Sets the MethodBinding for the action listener method that should be invoked to handle the ActionEvent this component fires.

public void setImmediate(boolean immediate)
: Sets the phase where the ActionEvent should be processed: true for the Apply Request Values phase or false for the Invoke Application Phase.

public void setValue(Object localValue)
: Sets the local value of this component.

UIComponent and UIComponentBase

The UIComponent class is an abstract class that defines all methods shared by all JSF components. The UIComponentBase class is a concrete subclass of UIComponent that provides default implementations for all methods. It's used as the base class for all other JSF standard component classes and can also be used as the base class for custom classes.

Synopsis

Class name:	javax.faces.component.UIComponent
Extends:	None
Implements:	javax.faces.component.StateHolder
Class name:	javax.faces.component.UIComponentBase
Extends:	javax.faces.component.UIComponent
Implements:	javax.faces.component.StateHolder

Constructor

public UIComponentBase( )
: Creates a new UIComponentBase instance.

Methods

protected void addFacesListener(javax.faces.event.FacesListener l)
: Adds the FacesListener subclass to the list of listeners for the FacesEvent subclasses this component fires. This method is used by all subclasses to register specific event listeners.

public boolean broadcast(javax.faces.event.FacesEvent event)
 throws javax.faces.event.AbortProcessingException
: Invokes all registered event listeners for the specific FacesEvent subclass in the order they were registered.

public void decode(javax.faces.context.FacesContext context)
: Reads the submitted value for the component from the request information available through the FacesContext.

public void encodeBegin(javax.faces.context.FacesContext context)
 throws java.io.IOException
: If the rendered property is set to true, delegates the call to the registered renderer if any.

public void encodeChildren(javax.faces.context.FacesContext context)
 throws java.io.IOException
: If the rendered property is set to true, delegates the call to the registered renderer if any.

```
public void encodeEnd(javax.faces.context.FacesContext context)
  throws java.io.IOException
```

If the rendered property is set to `true`, delegates the call to the registered renderer if any.

```
public javax.faces.component.UIComponent findComponent(String expr)
```

Returns the component with an ID matching the search expression, or `null` if not found. The search expression is one component ID or a colon-separated list of component IDs expressing a naming container path, which may start with a colon representing the component tree root. The component to use as the starting point for the search is the root component if the expression starts with a colon; otherwise it's the closest parent component (or this component) that implements the `NamingContainer` interface or the root if no such component is found. The component is then located by calling `findComponent()` on the starting point component with the first part of the expression, and then recursively through the component tree as long as `findComponent()` returns a naming container, removing parts of the expression until only a single expression part remains, which is the component ID for the requested component.

```
public java.util.Map getAttributes()
```

Returns a mutable `Map` representing all generic attributes and all component properties. The `Map get()` and `put()` methods uses the property accessor methods for a key matching a property name, and reads or writes the value the same way as a regular `Map` for all other keys.

```
public int getChildCount()
```

Returns the number of children without creating a `List` for the children if it doesn't exists already.

```
public java.util.List getChildren()
```

Returns a mutable `List` for child references. Only elements of type `UIComponent` can be added, and the child's parent property is set or reset when a child is added or removed.

```
public String getClientId(javax.faces.context.FacesContext context)
```

Returns an ID value suitable for unique identification of the component in the generated markup. The ID is composed by concatenating the value returned from the closest parent that implements the `NamingContainer` interface (if any) with the value returned by the `getId()` method, separated by a colon. If the component has a renderer, its `convertClientId()` method is called to adjust the ID value based on the markup to be rendered if needed.

```
protected javax.faces.context.FacesContext getFacesContext()
```

Returns the `FacesContext` instance for the current request.

```
protected javax.faces.event.FacesListener[] getFacesListeners(Class c)
```

Returns all `FacesListener` subclass instances registered for the `FacesEvent` subclasses this component fires. This method is used by all subclasses to get its specific event listeners.

```
public javax.faces.component.UIComponent getFacet(String name)
```

Returns the named facet (or `null` if it doesn't exist) without creating a `Map` for the facets if it doesn't exists already.

`public java.util.Map getFacets()`
: Returns a mutable `Map` for facet references, with the facet names as keys and the components as values. Only elements of type `UIComponent` can be added, and the facet's `parent` property is set or reset when a child is added or removed.

`public java.util.Iterator getFacetsAndChildren()`
: Returns an `Iterator` for all facets and child components, with the facets in an undefined order followed by the child components in the order they were added.

`abstract public String getFamily()`
: Returns the component family ID.

`public String getId()`
: Returns the component ID.

`public javax.faces.component.UIComponent getParent()`
: Returns the component's parent or `null` if none.

`protected javax.faces.render.Renderer getRenderer(javax.faces.context.FacesContext context)`
: Returns the component's renderer or `null` if none.

`public String getRendererType()`
: Returns the component's renderer type or `null` if none.

`public boolean getRendersChildren()`
: If the component has a renderer, delegates the call to the renderer; otherwise, returns `false`.

`public javax.faces.el.ValueBinding getValueBinding(String name)`
: Returns the `ValueBinding` for the named property or `null` if none is registered.

`public boolean isRendered()`
: Returns `true` if the component (and its children) should be rendered.

`public boolean isTransient()`
: Returns `true` if no state should be saved and restored for this instance.

`public void processDecodes(javax.faces.context.FacesContext context)`
: If the `rendered` property is set to `true`, calls `getFacetsAndChildren()` and then calls the `processDecodes()` method on each returned facet and component, followed by a call to the `decode()` method for this component. If any exception is thrown by a facet or component, calls the `FacesContext renderResponse()` method to continue the request processing in the Render Response phase and rethrows the exception.

`public void processRestoreState(javax.faces.context.FacesContext context, Object state)`
: If the application is configured to save state in the client, calls `getFacetsAndChildren()` and then calls the `processRestoreState()` method on each returned facet and component, followed by a call to the `restoreState()` method for this component.

`public Object processSaveState(javax.faces.context.FacesContext context)`
: If the application is configured to save state in the client and the `transient` property is set to `false`, calls `getFacetsAndChildren()` and then calls the `processSaveState()` method on each returned facet and component, followed by a call to the `saveState()` method for this component. Returns an `Object` representing the child state combined with the component's own state.

`public void processUpdates(javax.faces.context.FacesContext context)`
: If the rendered property is set to `true`, calls `getFacetsAndChildren()` and then calls the `processUpdates()` method on each returned facet and component.

`public void processValidators(javax.faces.context.FacesContext context)`
: If the rendered property is set to `true`, calls `getFacetsAndChildren()` and then calls the `processValidators()` method on each returned facet and component.

`public void queueEvent(javax.faces.event.FacesEvent event)`
: Delegates the call to the parent component, eventually reaching the `UIViewRoot` component.

`protected void removeFacesListener(javax.faces.event.FacesListener l)`
: Removes the `FacesListener` subclass from the list of listeners for the `FacesEvent` subclasses this component fires. This method is used by all subclasses to deregister specific event listeners.

`public static Object restoreAttachedState(javax.faces.context.FacesContext context, Object objectsState);`
: Returns an `Object` for which the state was previously saved by `saveAttachedState()`.

`public void restoreState(javax.faces.context.FacesContext context, Object state)`
: Restores the state for this instance from the provided value; an `Object` previously returned by the `saveState()` method.

`public static Object saveAttachedState(javax.faces.context.FacesContext context, Object object);`
: Returns an `Object` representing the state of the provided `Object`. The state for the provided object is retrieved by calling the `saveState()` method if it implements the `StateHolder` interface or enough information needed to restore the object later (e.g., the class name or the serialized state). If the provided object is a `List`, the state for all elements is saved.

`public Object saveState(javax.faces.context.FacesContext context)`
: Returns the state for this instance as an `Object` to be passed to the `restoreState()` method when the instance is restored for the next request.

`public void setId(String id)`
: Sets the `id` property value. The ID must start with a letter other than underscore and may be followed by letters, digits, underscores, and dashes. The ID must be unique among all components within the view or among the children of the closest parent that implements the `NamingContainer` interface.

`public void setParent(javax.faces.component.UIComponent parent)`
: Sets the parent for this component.

`public void setRendered(boolean isRendered)`
: Sets the rendered property value.

`public void setRendererType(String rendererType)`
: Sets the renderer type for the component.

`public void setTransient(boolean isTransient)`
: Sets the `transient` property value.

`public void setValueBinding(String name, javax.faces.el.ValueBinding vb)`
: Sets the names property to a `ValueBinding` instance, to be evaluated when the value is needed, or if it's for the `value` property, needs to be written during the Update Model phase. Unless otherwise stated for a subclass, all component properties except `id` and `parent` can be set to a value binding instead of an explicit value.

UIData

This class represents a component that iterates through tabular data, letting its `javax.faces.component.UIColumn` component children process the data for each row. It can be equipped with header and footer facets. The default `rendererType` is `javax.faces.Table`.

Class name:	`javax.faces.component.UIData`
Extends:	`javax.faces.component.UIComponentBase`
Implements:	`javax.faces.component.NamingContainer`, `javax.faces.component.StateHolder`

Fields

`public static String COMPONENT_FAMILY`
: The component family: `javax.faces.Data`.

`public static String COMPONENT_TYPE`
: The component family: `javax.faces.Data`.

Constructor

`public UIData( )`
: Creates a new instance.

Methods

`public boolean broadcast(javax.faces.event.FacesEvent event)`
`  throws javax.faces.event.AbortProcessingException`
: Unwraps the event, calls `setRowIndex( )` with the index embedded in the wrapped event, and delegates the unwrapped event broadcasting to the real source component. See also `queueEvent( )`.

`public void encodeBegin(javax.faces.context.FacesContext context)`
`  throws java.io.IOException`
: Before delegating to the superclass, resets the cached child component per-row values unless an error message is queued for one of them.

`public String getClientId(javax.faces.context.FacesContext context)`
: Returns a client ID that includes the current value of the `rowIndex` property, unless it's –1. This ensures that the child components get a unique client ID per row.

`public String getFamily( )`
: Returns the component family ID.

`public int getFirst( )`
: Returns the zero-based index for the first row to process.

public javax.faces.component.UIComponent getFooter( )
: Returns the footer facet or null if none is set.

public javax.faces.component.UIComponent getHeader( )
: Returns the header facet or null if none is set.

public int getRowCount( )
: Returns the number of rows in the component's data model or –1 if the number of rows is unknown.

public Object getRowData( )
: Returns the Object representing the row at the current rowIndex or null if the index is –1.

public int getRowIndex( )
: Returns the zero-based index for the current row or –1 if no row is currently processed.

public Object getValue( )
: Returns the Object representing all rows.

public String getVar( )
: Returns the name of the request scope variable holding the current row object while the row is processed.

public boolean isRowAvailable( )
: Returns true if the current rowIndex value represents a row in the data model.

public void processDecodes(javax.faces.context.FacesContext context)
: If the rendered property is set to true, calls setRowIndex( ) with the value –1, calls the processDecodes( ) method on all facets in the order they are returned by getFacets().keySet().iterator( ), and then the processDecodes( ) method on all UIColumn children's facets. For the number of rows defined by the rows property, starting with row defined by the first property, calls setRowIndex( ) with the index for the row, and if isRowAvailable( ) returns true, calls getChildren( ) and then the processDecodes( ) method on each returned UIColumn component, followed by a call to the decode( ) method for this component. Calls setRowIndex( ) with the value –1. If any exception is thrown by a facet or component, calls the FacesContext renderResponse( ) method to continue the request processing in the Render Response phase and rethrows the exception.

public void processUpdates(javax.faces.context.FacesContext context)
: If the rendered property is set to true, calls setRowIndex( ) with the value –1, calls the processUpdates( ) method on all facets in the order they are returned by getFacets().keySet().iterator( ), and then calls the processUpdates( ) method on all UIColumn children's facets. For the number of rows defined by the rows property, starting with row defined by the first property, calls setRowIndex( ) with the index for the row, and if isRowAvailable( ) returns true, calls getChildren( ) and then the processUpdates( ) method on each returned UIColumn component. Calls setRowIndex( ) with the value –1.

public void processValidators(javax.faces.context.FacesContext context)
: If the rendered property is set to true, calls setRowIndex( ) with the value –1, calls the processValidator( ) method on all facets in the order they are returned by getFacets().keySet().iterator( ), and then calls the processValidators( ) method on all UIColumn children's facets. For the number of rows defined by the rows property, starting with row defined by the first property, calls setRowIndex( ) with the index for the row, and if isRowAvailable( ) returns true, calls getChildren( ) and then the

processValidators( ) method on each returned UIColumn component. Calls setRowIndex( ) with the value –1.

pubic void queueEvent(javax.faces.event.FacesEvent event)
: Before delegating the call to the parent component, wraps the event along with the current rowIndex value and itself as the event source in an instance of an inner class that extends FacesEvent.

public void restoreState(javax.faces.context.FacesContext context, Object state)
: Restores the state for this instance from the provided value; an Object previously returned by the saveState( ) method.

public Object saveState(javax.faces.context.FacesContext context)
: Returns the state for this instance as an Object to be passed to the restoreState( ) method when the instance is restored for the next request.

public void setFirst(int first)
: Sets the zero-based index of the first row to process.

public void setFooter(javax.faces.component.UIComponent footer)
: Sets the footer facet.

public void setHeader(javax.faces.component.UIComponent header)
: Sets the header facet.

public void setRowIndex(int rowIndex)
: Sets the zero-based index of the currently processed row or –1 if no row is processed.

public void setRows(int rows)
: Sets the number of rows to process or 0 if all rows should be processed.

public void setValue(Object value)
: Sets the data model representing the tabular data. If the object isn't of type DataModel, creates a wrapper of an appropriate type around it, one of ArrayDataModel, ListDataModel, ResultDataModel, ResultSetDataModel, or ScalarDataModel.

public void setValueBinding(String name, javax.faces.el.ValueBinding vb)
: Throws an IllegalArgumentException if the name is var or rowIndex before delegating the processing to the superclass.

public void setVar(String var)
: Sets the name of the request scope variable holding the current row object while the row is processed.

UIForm

This class represents a form component. A form component acts as a container for other components, typically input components, and ensures that input component children process input only when the form they belong to is the submitted form. The default rendererType is javax.faces.Form.

Class name:	javax.faces.component.UIForm
Extends:	javax.faces.component.UIComponentBase
Implements:	javax.faces.component.NamingContainer, javax.faces.component.StateHolder

Fields

public static String COMPONENT_FAMILY

The component family: javax.faces.Form.

public static String COMPONENT_TYPE

The component family: javax.faces.Form.

Constructor

public UIForm( )

Creates a new instance.

Methods

public String getFamily( )

Returns the component family ID.

public boolean isSubmitted( )

Returns true if submitting this form triggered the current request.

public void processDecodes(javax.faces.context.FacesContext context)

Call to the decode( ) method for this component to ensure that the submitted property is set before decoding the children. If the submitted property is set to true, calls getFacetsAndChildren( ) and then calls the processDecodes( ) method on each returned facet and component.

public void processUpdates(javax.faces.context.FacesContext context)

If the submitted property is set to true, calls getFacetsAndChildren( ) and then calls the processUpdates( ) method on each returned facet and component.

public void processValidators(javax.faces.context.FacesContext context)

If the submitted property is set to true, calls getFacetsAndChildren( ) and then calls the processValidators( ) method on each returned facet and component.

public void setSubmitted(boolean submitted)

Sets the submitted property value. This method must be called by the component's renderer during the Apply Request Values phase.

UIGraphic

This class represents a graphic image component. A graphic image component can be used standalone or as a child of a component with a link renderer, to render a clickable link image. The default rendererType is javax.faces.Image.

Class name:	javax.faces.component.UIGraphic
Extends:	javax.faces.component.UIComponentBase
Implements:	javax.faces.component.StateHolder

Fields

public static String COMPONENT_FAMILY

The component family: javax.faces.Graphic.

public static String COMPONENT_TYPE

The component family: javax.faces.Graphic.

Constructor

`public UIGraphic( )`
: Creates a new instance.

Methods

`public String getFamily( )`
: Returns the component family ID.

`public String getUrl( )`
: Returns the image URL.

`public Object getValue( )`
: Returns the component's value (the image URL).

`public javax.faces.el.ValueBinding getValueBinding(String name)`
: If the name is `url`, calls the superclass with the name `value` instead. Delegates request for all other properties to the superclass directly.

`public void restoreState(javax.faces.context.FacesContext context, Object state)`
: Restores the state for this instance from the provided value; an `Object` previously returned by the `saveState( )` method.

`public Object saveState(javax.faces.context.FacesContext context)`
: Returns the state for this instance as an `Object` to be passed to the `restoreState( )` method when the instance is restored for the next request.

`public void setUrl(String url)`
: Sets the image URL.

`public void setValue(Object value)`
: Sets the component's value (the image URL).

`public void setValueBinding(String name, javax.faces.el.ValueBinding vb)`
: If the name is `url`, calls the superclass with the name `value` instead. Delegates request for all other properties to the superclass directly.

UIInput

This class represents an input component. The user can enter a value for an input component, which is then saved as a property of an application class after conversion and validation. The default `rendererType` is `javax.faces.Text`.

When the value entered by a user is different than the previous value, the input component fires a `ValueChangeEvent`, which can be handled by the application through a value changed event method or one or more listeners, in the order: `javax.faces.event.ValueChangeListener` instances (in the order they are registered), and then the value change listener method.

Class name:	`javax.faces.component.UIInput`
Extends:	`javax.faces.component.UIOutput`
Implements:	`javax.faces.component.EditableValueHolder`, `javax.faces.component.StateHolder`

Fields

`public static String COMPONENT_FAMILY`
: The component family: `javax.faces.Input`.

`public static String COMPONENT_TYPE`
: The component family: `javax.faces.Input`.

`public static String CONVERSION_MESSAGE_ID`
: The ID for the conversion error message: `javax.faces.component.UIInput.CONVERSION`.

`public static String REQUIRED_MESSAGE_ID`
: The ID for the required value error message: `javax.faces.component.UIInput.REQUIRED`.

Constructor

`public UIInput()`
: Creates a new instance.

Methods

`public void addValidator(javax.faces.validator.Validator validator)`
: Adds the `Validator` to the list of validator for this component's value.

`public void addValueChangeListener(javax.faces.event.ValueChangeListener l)`
: Adds the `ValueChangeListener` to the list of listeners for the `ValueChangeEvent` this component fires.

`public void broadcast(javax.faces.event.FacesEvent event)`
`throws javax.faces.event.AbortProcessingException`
: Extends the inherited behavior by passing a `ValueChangeEvent` to the value change listener method (if any).

`protected boolean compareValues(Object previous, Object value)`
: Returns `true` if the new value differs from the previous value, taking `null` values into consideration; returns `false` if both values are `null` and `true` if only one of them is `null`.

`public void decode()`
: Sets the `valid` property to `true` before delegating the call to the superclass.

`public String getFamily()`
: Returns the component family ID.

`public Object getSubmittedValue()`
: Returns the submitted value for this component, i.e., the unconverted value extracted from the request data or a value in a format known only to the component or its renderer.

`public javax.faces.el.MethodBinding getValidator()`
: Returns the `MethodBinding` for the validator method that should be invoked to validate this component's value, or `null` if no method is bound.

`public javax.faces.validator.Validator[] getValidators()`
: Returns all `Validator` instances registered with this component or an empty array if none is registered.

`public javax.faces.el.MethodBinding getValueChangeListener()`
: Returns the `MethodBinding` for the value change method that should be invoked to handle the `ValueChangeEvent` this component fires or `null` if no method is bound.

`public javax.faces.event.ValueChangeListener[] getValueChangeListeners()`
: Returns all `ValueChangeListener` instances registered with this component or an empty array if none is registered.

`public boolean isImmediate()`
: Returns `true` if the `ValueChangeEvent` should be processed in the Apply Request Values phase, or `false` if it should be processed in the Process Validations phase.

`public boolean isLocalValueSet()`
: Returns `true` if the local value for this component has been set, either explicitly by application code or implicitly after successful validation of the submitted value.

`public boolean isRequired()`
: Returns `true` if a value must be submitted for this component.

`public boolean isValid()`
: Returns `true` if the submitted value has been successfully converted and validated.

`public void processDecodes(javax.faces.context.FacesContext context)`
: Extends the inherited behavior by calling `validate()` if the `immediate` property is set to `true`. If the validation fails, calls the `FacesContext` `renserResponse()` method.

`public void processUpdates(javax.faces.context.FacesContext context)`
: Extends the inherited behavior by calling `updateModel()`. If updating the model fails, calls the `FacesContext` `renserResponse()` method.

`public void processValidators(javax.faces.context.FacesContext context)`
: Extends the inherited behavior by calling `validate()` if the `immediate` property is set to `false`. If the validation fails, calls the `FacesContext` `renderResponse()` method.

`public void removeValidator(javax.faces.validator.Validator validator)`
: Removes the `Validator` from the list of validator for this component's value.

`public void removeValueChangeListener(javax.faces.event.ValueChangeListener l)`
: Removes the `ValueChangeListener` from the list of listeners for the `ValueChangeEvent` this component fires.

`public void restoreState(javax.faces.context.FacesContext context, Object state)`
: Restores the state for this instance from the provided value; an `Object` previously returned by the saveState( ) method.

`public Object saveState(javax.faces.context.FacesContext context)`
: Returns the state for this instance as an `Object` to be passed to the `restoreState()` method when the instance is restored for the next request.

`public void setImmediate(boolean immediate)`
: Sets the phase where the `ValueChangeEvent` should be processed: `true` for the Apply Request Values phase or `false` for the Process Validations phase.

`public void setLocalValueSet(boolean isLocalValueSet)`
: Sets the `localValueSet` property value.

`public void setRequired(boolean isRequired)`
: Sets the `required` property value.

`public void setSubmittedValue(Object submittedValue)`
: Sets the submitted value for this component, i.e., the unconverted value extracted from the request data or a value in a format known only to the component or its renderer.

`public void setValid(boolean isValid)`
: Sets the valid property value.

`public void setValidator(javax.faces.el.MethodBinding validator)`
: Sets the `MethodBinding` for the validator method that should be invoked to validate this component's value.

`public void setValue(Object value)`
: Extends the inherited behavior by calling `setLocalValueSet( )` with the value `true`.

`public void setValueChangeListener(javax.faces.el.MethodBinding vclmb)`
: Sets the `MethodBinding` for the value change method that should be invoked to handle the `ValueChangeEvent` this component fires.

`public void updateModel(javax.faces.context.FacesContext context)`
: If the `valid` and the `localValueSet` properties are set to `true` and there's a `ValueBinding` set for the `value` property, calls the `setValue( )` method on the `ValueBinding`. If the `setValue( )` call is successful, clears the local value and calls `setLocalValueSet( )` with the value `false`. If the `setValue( )` call fails, calls the `addMessage( )` method on the current `FacesContext` with a `CONVERSION_MESSAGE_ID` message, and calls `setValid( )` with the value `false`.

`public void validate(javax.faces.context.FacesContext context)`
: If `getSubmittedValue( )` returns a non-`null` value, convert the value to the data type for the local value by calling `getConvertedValue( )` on the renderer (if any) or `getAsObject( )` on the `Converter` returned by `getConverter( )` (if any), or the `Converter` returned by the `Application createConverter( )` method for data type of the `ValueBinding` (if any). If the conversion fails, calls the `addMessage( )` method on the current `FacesContext` with a `CONVERSION_MESSAGE_ID` message, and calls `setValid( )` with the value `false`. If the conversion is successful or no `Converter` was found, verifies that the local value isn't `null` or an empty `String` if the `required` property is set to `true`, and calls `addMessage( )` with a `REQUIRED_MESSAGE_ID` message if it is. Otherwise, calls the `validate( )` method on each registered `Validator`, followed by a call to the validator method binding (if any), catching any `ValidatorException` and calling `addMessage( )` with the message from the exception and `setValid( )` with the value `false` if one is thrown. If the validation is successful, stores the new value, and sets the submitted value to `null`, and if `compareValues( )` returns `true`, queues a `ValueChangeEvent`.

UIMessage

This class represents a message component. A message component renders the first message queued for a specific component, if any. The default rendererType is `javax.faces.Message`.

Class name:	`javax.faces.component.UIMessage`
Extends:	`javax.faces.component.UIComponentBase`
Implements:	`javax.faces.component.StateHolder`

Fields

`public static String COMPONENT_FAMILY`
: The component family: `javax.faces.Message`.

`public static String COMPONENT_TYPE`
: The component family: `javax.faces.Message`.

Constructor

`public UIMessage( )`
: Creates a new instance.

Methods

`public String getFamily( )`
: Returns the component family ID.

`public String getFor( )`
: Returns the client ID of the component to render a message for.

`public boolean isShowDetail( )`
: Returns `true` if the message details are rendered.

`public boolean isShowSummary( )`
: Returns `true` if the message summary are rendered.

`public void restoreState(javax.faces.context.FacesContext context, Object state)`
: Restores the state for this instance from the provided value; an `Object` previously returned by the saveState( ) method.

`public Object saveState(javax.faces.context.FacesContext context)`
: Returns the state for this instance as an `Object` to be passed to the `restoreState( )` method when the instance is restored for the next request.

`public void setFor(String clientID)`
: Sets the client ID of the component to render a message for.

`public void setShowDetail(boolean showDetail)`
: Sets the `showDetail` property. The default is `true`.

`public void setShowSummary(boolean showSummary)`
: Sets the `showSummary` property. The default is `false`.

UIMessages

This class represents a messages component. A messages component renders message queued for a specific component as well as "global messages" (messages queued without a component ID). The default `rendererType` is `javax.faces.Messages`.

Class name:	`javax.faces.component.UIMessages`
Extends:	`javax.faces.component.UIComponentBase`
Implements:	`javax.faces.component.StateHolder`

Fields

`public static String COMPONENT_FAMILY`
: The component family: `javax.faces.Messages`.

`public static String COMPONENT_TYPE`
: The component family: `javax.faces.Messages`.

Constructor

`public UIMessages( );`
: Creates a new instance.

Methods

`public String getFamily( )`
: Returns the component family ID.

`public boolean isGlobalOnly( )`
: Returns `true` if only global messages are rendered.

`public boolean isShowDetail( )`
: Returns `true` if the message details are rendered.

`public boolean isShowSummary( )`
: Returns `true` if the message summary are rendered.

`public void restoreState(javax.faces.context.FacesContext context, Object state)`
: Restores the state for this instance from the provided value; an `Object` previously returned by the `saveState( )` method.

`public Object saveState(javax.faces.context.FacesContext context)`
: Returns the state for this instance as an `Object` to be passed to the `restoreState( )` method when the instance is restored for the next request.

`public void setGlobalOnly(boolean globalOnly)`
: Sets the `globalOnly` property. The default is `false`.

`public void setShowDetail(boolean showDetail)`
: Sets the `showDetail` property. The default is `false`.

`public void setShowSummary(boolean showSummary)`
: Sets the `showSummary` property. The default is `true`.

UINamingContainer

This class represents a naming container component. A naming container component is used as a container for child components to ensure that their client IDs are unique in a view by combining the naming container's component ID with the child components' IDs. An instance of this class represents a JSF subview and it can also be used as a base class for other components that need to be naming containers. It doesn't have a default `rendererType`.

Class name:	`javax.faces.component.UINamingContainer`
Extends:	`javax.faces.component.UIComponentBase`
Implements:	`javax.faces.component.NamingContainer`, `javax.faces.component.StateHolder`

Fields

`public static String COMPONENT_FAMILY`
: The component family: `javax.faces.NamingContainer`.

`public static String COMPONENT_TYPE`
: The component family: `javax.faces.NamingContainer`.

Constructor

`public UINamingContainer( )`
: Creates a new instance.

Methods

`public String getFamily( )`
: Returns the component family ID.

UIOutput

This class represents an output component. An output component renderers its value, which may be bound to a property of an application class, possibly converted to a different data type. The default `rendererType` is `javax.faces.Text`.

Class name:	`javax.faces.component.UIOutput`
Extends:	`javax.faces.component.UIComponentBase`
Implements:	`javax.faces.component.StateHolder`, `javax.faces.component.ValueHolder`

Fields

`public static String COMPONENT_FAMILY`
: The component family: `javax.faces.Output`.

`public static String COMPONENT_TYPE`
: The component family: `javax.faces.Output`.

Constructor

`public UIOutput( )`
: Creates a new instance.

Methods

`public javax.faces.convert.Converter getConverter( )`
: Returns the `Converter` used to convert this component's value or `null` if none is registered.

`public String getFamily( )`
: Returns the component family ID.

`public Object getLocalValue( )`
: Returns the local value of this component, without evaluating the value `javax.faces.el.ValueBinding` if set, or `null` if the component doesn't have a local value.

public Object getValue( )
: Returns the value of this component, from the local value or by evaluating the value javax.faces.el.ValueBinding if it doesn't have a local value, or null if the component doesn't have a value at all.

public void restoreState(javax.faces.context.FacesContext context, Object state)
: Restores the state for this instance from the provided value; an Object previously returned by the saveState( ) method.

public Object saveState(javax.faces.context.FacesContext context)
: Returns the state for this instance as an Object to be passed to the restoreState( ) method when the instance is restored for the next request.

public void setConverter(javax.faces.convert.Converter converter)
: Sets the Converter used to convert this component's value.

public void setValue(Object localValue)
: Sets the local value of this component.

UIPanel

This class represents a panel component. A panel component is a container for other components. It doesn't have a default rendererType.

Class name:	javax.faces.component.UIPanel
Extends:	javax.faces.component.UIComponentBase
Implements:	javax.faces.component.StateHolder

Fields

public static String COMPONENT_FAMILY
: The component family: javax.faces.Panel.

public static String COMPONENT_TYPE
: The component family: javax.faces.Panel.

Constructor

public UIPanel( )
: Creates a new instance.

Methods

public String getFamily( )
: Returns the component family ID.

UIParameter

This class represents a parameter component. A parameter component provides a, possibly named, parameter value to its parent, such as a link component. The parameter component's value is rendered by its parent.

Class name:	javax.faces.component.UIParameter
Extends:	javax.faces.component.UIComponentBase
Implements:	javax.faces.component.StateHolder

Fields

`public static String COMPONENT_FAMILY`
: The component family: `javax.faces.Parameter`.

`public static String COMPONENT_TYPE`
: The component family: `javax.faces.Parameter`.

Constructor

`public UIParameter()`
: Creates a new instance.

Methods

`public String getFamily()`
: Returns the component family ID.

`public String getName()`
: Returns the parameter name or `null` if it doesn't have a name.

`public Object getValue()`
: Returns the parameter value.

`public void restoreState(javax.faces.context.FacesContext context, Object state)`
: Restores the state for this instance from the provided value; an `Object` previously returned by the `saveState()` method.

`public Object saveState(javax.faces.context.FacesContext context)`
: Returns the state for this instance as an `Object` to be passed to the `restoreState()` method when the instance is restored for the next request.

`public void setName(String name)`
: Sets the parameter name.

`public void setValue(Object value)`
: Sets the parameter value.

UISelectBoolean

This class represents a select boolean component. A select Boolean component lets the user set its value to `true` or `false`, which is then saved as a property of an application class after conversion and validation. The default `rendererType` is `javax.faces.Checkbox`.

When the value entered by a user is different than the previous value, the input component fires a `ValueChangeEvent`, which can be handled by the application through a value changed event method or one or more listeners, in the order: `javax.faces.event.ValueChangeListener` instances (in the order they are registered), and then the value change listener method.

Class name:	`javax.faces.component.UISelectBoolean`
Extends:	`javax.faces.component.UIInput`
Implements:	`javax.faces.component.EditableValueHolder`, `javax.faces.component.StateHolder`

Fields

`public static String COMPONENT_FAMILY`
: The component family: `javax.faces.SelectBoolean`.

`public static String COMPONENT_TYPE`
: The component family: `javax.faces.SelectBoolean`.

Constructor

`public UISelectBoolean()`
: Creates a new instance.

Methods

`public String getFamily()`
: Returns the component family ID.

`public javax.faces.el.ValueBinding getValueBinding(String name)`
: If the name is selected, calls the superclass with the name `value` instead. Delegates request for all other properties to the superclass directly.

`public boolean isSelected()`
: Returns the component's value converted to a `boolean`.

`public void setSelected(boolean selected)`
: Sets the component's value.

`public void setValueBinding(String name, javax.faces.el.ValueBinding vb)`
: If the name is selected, calls the superclass with the name `value` instead. Delegates request for all other properties to the superclass directly.

UISelectItem

This class represents a select items component. A select item component represents a choice for its parent (which must be a component that lets the user select among a number of choices), either as a `SelectItem` instance or through the `itemDescription`, `itemDisabled`, `itemLabel`, and `itemValue` properties. The select item component's value is rendered by its parent.

Class name:	`javax.faces.component.UISelectItem`
Extends:	`javax.faces.component.UIComponentBase`
Implements:	`javax.faces.component.StateHolder`

Fields

`public static String COMPONENT_FAMILY`
: The component family: `javax.faces.SelectItem`.

`public static String COMPONENT_TYPE`
: The component family: `javax.faces.SelectItem`.

Constructor

`public UISelectItem( )`
: Creates a new instance.

Methods

`public String getFamily( )`
: Returns the component family ID.

`public String getItemDescription( )`
: Returns the item description.

`public String getItemLabel( )`
: Returns the item label.

`public Object getItemValue( )`
: Returns the item value.

`public Object getValue( )`
: Returns the component value, an explicitly set `SelectItem` instance.

`public boolean isItemDisabled( )`
: Returns `true` if the item is disabled.

`public void restoreState(javax.faces.context.FacesContext context, Object state)`
: Restores the state for this instance from the provided value; an `Object` previously returned by the `saveState( )` method.

`public Object saveState(javax.faces.context.FacesContext context)`
: Returns the state for this instance as an `Object` to be passed to the `restoreState( )` method when the instance is restored for the next request.

`public void setItemDescription(String itemDescription)`
: Sets the item description.

`public void setItemDisabled(boolean itemDisabled)`
: Sets the `itemDisabled` property value.

`public void setItemLabel(String itemLabel)`
: Sets the item label.

`public void setItemValue(Object value)`
: Returns the item value.

`public void setValue(Object value)`
: Sets the component value, a `SelectItem` instance.

UISelectItems

This class represents a select items component. A select item component represents one or more choices for its parent (which must be a component that lets the user select among a number of choices), either as a `SelectItem` instance, a `SelectItem[]`, a `java.util.Collection` with `SelectItem` instances, or a `java.util.Map` with keys to use as item labels and values to use as item values. The select items component's value is rendered by its parent.

Class name:	`javax.faces.component.UISelectItems`
Extends:	`javax.faces.component.UIComponentBase`
Implements:	`javax.faces.component.StateHolder`

Fields

`public static String COMPONENT_FAMILY`
: The component family: `javax.faces.UISelectItems`.

`public static String COMPONENT_TYPE`
: The component family: `javax.faces.UISelectItems`.

Constructor

`public UISelectItems()`
: Creates a new instance.

Methods

`public String getFamily()`
: Returns the component family ID.

`public Object getValue()`
: Returns the component value.

`public void restoreState(javax.faces.context.FacesContext context, Object state)`
: Restores the state for this instance from the provided value; an `Object` previously returned by the `saveState()` method.

`public Object saveState(javax.faces.context.FacesContext context)`
: Returns the state for this instance as an `Object` to be passed to the `restoreState()` method when the instance is restored for the next request.

`public void setValue(Object value)`
: Sets the component value, a `SelectItem` instance, a `SelectItem[]`, a `java.util.Collection` with `SelectItem` instances, or a `java.util.Map` with keys to use as item labels and values to use as item values.

UISelectMany

This class represents a select-many component. A select-many component lets the user select one or more items among a set of items represented by `UISelectItem` and `UISelectItems` components, which is then saved as a property of an application class after conversion and validation. If the component is bound to a property, the data type for the select items must be the same basic type (either a primitive type or the corresponding boxed type) as the property data type. The default `rendererType` is `javax.faces.Listbox`.

When the selections made by a user is different than the previous selection, the component fires a `ValueChangeEvent`, which can be handled by the application through a value changed event method or one or more listeners, in the order: `javax.faces.event.ValueChangeListener` instances (in the order they are registered), and then the value change listener method.

Class name:	`javax.faces.component.UISelectMany`
Extends:	`javax.faces.component.UIInput`
Implements:	`javax.faces.component.EditableValueHolder`, `javax.faces.component.StateHolder`

Fields

`public static String COMPONENT_FAMILY`
: The component family: `javax.faces.SelectMany`.

`public static String COMPONENT_TYPE`
: The component family: `javax.faces.SelectMany`.

`public static String INVALID_MESSAGE_ID`
: The ID for the invalid value error message: `javax.faces.component.UISelectMany.INVALID`.

Constructor

`public UISelectMany( )`
: Creates a new instance.

Methods

`protected boolean compareValues(Object previous, Object value)`
: Returns `true` if the new selection differs from the previous selection, regardless of the elements order.

`public String getFamily( )`
: Returns the component family ID.

`public Object[] getSelectedValues( )`
: Returns the selected values.

`public javax.faces.el.ValueBinding getValueBinding(String name)`
: If the name is `selectedValues`, calls the superclass with the name `value` instead. Delegates request for all other properties to the superclass directly.

`public void setSelectedValues(Object[] selectedValues)`
: Sets the selected values.

`public void setValueBinding(String name, javax.faces.el.ValueBinding vb)`
: If the name is `selectedValues`, calls the superclass with the name `value` instead. Delegates request for all other properties to the superclass directly.

`public void validate(javax.faces.context.FacesContext context)`
: Extends the inherited behavior by verifying that all selected values match the available choices. If not, calls the `addMessage( )` method on the current `FacesContext` with a `INVALID_MESSAGE_ID` message and calls `setValid( )` with the value `false`.

UISelectOne

This class represents a select-one component. A select-one component lets the user select one item among a set of items represented by `UISelectItem` and `UISelectItems` components, which is then saved as a property of an application class after conversion and validation. If the component is bound to a property, the data type for the select items must be the same basic type (either a primitive type or the corresponding boxed type) as the property data type. The default `rendererType` is `javax.faces.Menu`.

When the selections made by a user is different than the previous selection, the component fires a `ValueChangeEvent`, which can be handled by the application through a value changed event method or one or more listeners, in the order: javax.faces.event.ValueChangeListener instances (in the order they are registered), and then the value change listener method.

Class name:	javax.faces.component.UISelectOne
Extends:	javax.faces.component.UIInput
Implements:	javax.faces.component.EditableValueHolder, javax.faces.component.StateHolder

Fields

public static String COMPONENT_FAMILY
    The component family: javax.faces.SelectOne.

public static String COMPONENT_TYPE
    The component family: javax.faces.SelectOne.

public static String INVALID_MESSAGE_ID
    The ID for the invalid value error message: javax.faces.component.UISelectOne.INVALID.

Constructor

public UISelectOne()
    Creates a new instance.

Methods

public String getFamily()
    Returns the component family ID.

public void validate(javax.faces.context.FacesContext context)
    Extends the inherited behavior by verifying that the selected value matches one of the available choices. If not, calls the addMessage() method on the current FacesContext with a INVALID_MESSAGE_ID message and calls setValid() with the value false.

UIViewRoot

This class represents a view root component. A view root component sits at the top of the component tree and acts as the container for all the other components in the view. It's not rendered.

Class name:	javax.faces.component.UIViewRoot
Extends:	javax.faces.component.UIComponentBase
Implements:	javax.faces.component.StateHolder

Fields

public static String COMPONENT_FAMILY
    The component family: javax.faces.ViewRoot.

public static String COMPONENT_TYPE
    The component family: javax.faces.View.

`public static String UNIQUE_ID_PREFIX`
: The prefix used for automatically created component IDs: `_id`.

Constructor

`public UIViewRoot( )`
: Creates a new instance.

Methods

`public String createUniqueId( )`
: Returns an automatically generated component ID that is unique within the view, prefixed with `UNIQUE_ID_PREFIX`.

`public void encodeBegin( )`
: Resets the state used by `createUniqueId( )`.

`public String getFamily( )`
: Returns the component family ID.

`public java.util.Locale getLocale( )`
: Returns the view's `Locale`, calculated by `ViewHandler calculateLocale( )` if not set.

`public String getRenderKitId( )`
: Returns the view's render kit ID or `RenderKitFactory.HTML_BASIC_RENDER_KIT` if not set.

`public String getViewId( )`
: Returns the view ID.

`public void processApplication(javax.faces.context.FacesContext context)`
: Iterates over all events queued for any phase and call the `broadcast( )` method on the source component for each, and then does the same for all events queued for the Invoke Application phase. Returns when there are no more events for these phases.

`public void processDecodes(javax.faces.context.FacesContext context)`
: Extends the inherited behavior by iterating over all events queued for any phase and calling the `broadcast( )` method on the source component for each, and then does the same for all events queued for the Apply Request Values phase. Clears the event queue if broadcasting the events caused the `FacesContext renderResponse( )` method to be called. Returns when there are no more events for these phases.

`public void processUpdates(javax.faces.context.FacesContext context)`
: Extends the inherited behavior by iterating over all events queued for any phase and calling the `broadcast( )` method on the source component for each, and then does the same for all events queued for the Update Model Values phase. Returns when there are no more events for these phases.

`public void processValidators(javax.faces.context.FacesContext context)`
: Extends the inherited behavior by iterating over all events queued for any phase and calling the `broadcast( )` method on the source component for each, and then does the same for all events queued for the Process Validations phase. Clears the event queue if broadcasting the events caused the `FacesContext renderResponse( )` method to be called. Returns when there are no more events for these phases.

`public void queueEvent(javax.faces.event.FacesEvent event)`
: Adds the event to the event queue.

`public void restoreState(javax.faces.context.FacesContext context, Object state)`
: Restores the state for this instance from the provided value; an `Object` previously returned by the `saveState()` method.

`public Object saveState(javax.faces.context.FacesContext context)`
: Returns the state for this instance as an `Object` to be passed to the `restoreState()` method when the instance is restored for the next request.

`public void setLocale(java.util.Locale locale)`
: Sets the view's `Locale`.

`public void setRenderKitId(String renderKitId)`
: Sets the view's render kit ID.

`public void setViewId(String viewId)`
: Sets the view ID.

Model Classes and Interfaces

ArrayDataModel

This class wraps an array to expose it as a `DataModel` for a `UIData` component.

Class name:	`javax.faces.model.ArrayDataModel`
Extends:	`javax.faces.model.DataModel`
Implements:	None

Constructors

`public ArrayDataModel()`
: Creates a new, empty instance.

`public ArrayDataModel(Object[] array)`
: Creates a new instance wrapping an array.

Methods

`public int getRowCount()`
: Returns the number of elements in the array or –1 if the array isn't set.

`public Object getRowData()`
: Returns the array element for the current row index or `null` if the array isn't set or there's no such element.

`public int getRowIndex()`
: Returns the zero-based index for the current row or –1 if no row is selected.

`public Object getWrappedData()`
: Returns the array, or `null` if the array isn't set.

`public boolean isRowAvailable()`
: Returns `true` if the array is set and the current row index is between 0 and the last index of the array.

`public void setRowIndex(int index)`
: Sets the zero-based index for the current row or to –1 if no row is selected.

`public void setWrappedData(Object data)`
: Sets the array.

DataModel

This abstract class represents the model for a `UIData` component.

Class name:	`javax.faces.model.DataModel`
Extends:	None
Implements:	None

Constructor

`public DataModel( )`
: Creates a new, empty instance.

Methods

`public void addDataModelListener(javax.faces.model.DataModelListener l)`
: Adds the `DataModelListener` to the list of listeners for the `DataModelEvent` this model fires.

`public javax.faces.model.DataModelListener[] getDataModelListeners( )`
: Returns all `DataModelListener` instances registered for the model.

`public abstract int getRowCount( )`
: Returns the number of rows represented by the model or –1 if unknown.

`public abstract Object getRowData( )`
: Returns an object representing the current row index or `null` if there is no row data for the row index.

`public abstract int getRowIndex( )`
: Returns the zero-based index for the current row or –1 if no row is selected.

`public abstract Object getWrappedData( )`
: Returns the raw data wrapped by this model or `null` if the data isn't set.

`public abstract boolean isRowAvailable( )`
: Returns `true` if the current row index matches an existing row.

`public void removeDataModelListener(javax.faces.model.DataModelListener l)`
: Removes the `DataModelListener` from the list of listeners for the `DataModelEvent` this model fires.

`public abstract void setRowIndex(int index)`
: Sets the zero-based index for the current row or to –1 if no row is selected.

`public abstract void setWrappedData(Object data)`
: Sets the data containing rows.

DataModelEvent

This class represents an event fired by the `DataModel` class.

Class name:	`javax.faces.model.DataModelEvent`
Extends:	`java.util.EventObject`
Implements:	`java.io.Serializable`

Constructor

`public DataModelEvent(javax.faces.model.DataModel, int index, Object data)`

Creates a new instance for the specified model, row index, and row data.

Methods

`public javax.faces.model.DataModel getDataModel( )`

Returns the `DataModel` that fired the event.

`public Object getRowData( )`

Returns the `Object` holding the data for the row the event refers to or `null` if it doesn't refer to a row.

`public int getRowIndex( )`

Returns the index for the row the event refers to or –1 if it doesn't refer to a row.

DataModelListener

This interface is implemented by listeners interested in the `DataModelEvent` fired by instances of the `DataModel` class.

Synopsis

Interface name:	`javax.faces.model.DataModelListener`
Extends:	None
Implemented by:	Application classes

Methods

`public void rowSelected(javax.faces.model.DataModelEvent event)`

Handles the event signaling that a row in the model has been selected.

ListDataModel

This class wraps a `java.util.List` to expose it as a `DataModel` for a `UIData` component.

Class name:	`javax.faces.model.ListDataModel`
Extends:	`javax.faces.model.DataModel`
Implements:	None

Constructors

`public ListDataModel()`
: Creates a new, empty instance.

`public ListDataModel(java.util.List list)`
: Creates a new instance wrapping a `List` instance.

Methods

`public int getRowCount()`
: Returns the size of the list, or –1 if the list isn't set.

`public Object getRowData()`
: Returns the list element for the current row index or `null` if the list isn't set or there's no such element.

`public int getRowIndex()`
: Returns the zero-based index for the current row or –1 if no row is selected.

`public Object getWrappedData()`
: Returns the `List` object or `null` if the list isn't set.

`public boolean isRowAvailable()`
: Returns `true` if the list is set and the current row index is between 0 and the last index of the list.

`public void setRowIndex(int index)`
: Sets the zero-based index for the current row or to –1 if no row is selected.

`public void setWrappedData(Object data)`
: Sets the `List` instance.

ResultDataModel

This class wraps a `javax.servlet.jsp.jstl.sql.Result` to expose it as a `DataModel` for a `UIData` component.

Class name:	`javax.faces.model.ResultDataModel`
Extends:	`javax.faces.model.DataModel`
Implements:	None

Constructors

`public ResultDataModel()`
: Creates a new, empty instance.

`public ResultDataModel(javax.servlet.jsp.jstl.sql.Result result)`
: Creates a new instance wrapping a `Result` instance.

Methods

`public int getRowCount()`
: Returns the size of the array returned by the `Result getRows()` method or –1 if the result isn't set.

public Object getRowData()

Returns the element for the current row index in the array returned by the Result getRows() method, or null if the result isn't set or there's no such element.

public int getRowIndex()

Returns the zero-based index for the current row or –1 if no row is selected.

public Object getWrappedData()

Returns the Result instance or null if the result isn't set.

public boolean isRowAvailable()

Returns true if the list is set and the current row index is between 0 and the last index of the array returned by the Result getRows() method.

public void setRowIndex(int index)

Sets the zero-based index for the current row or to –1 if no row is selected.

public void setWrappedData(Object data)

Sets the Result instance.

ResultSetDataModel

This class wraps a java.sql.ResultSet to expose it as a DataModel for a UIData component. The ResultSet must be scrollable, and if the UIData component has input components bound to columns in this model, it must be updatable.

Class name:	javax.faces.model.ResultSetDataModel
Extends:	javax.faces.model.DataModel
Implements:	None

Constructors

public ResultSetDataModel()

Creates a new, empty instance.

public ResultSetDataModel(java.sql.ResultSet resultSet)

Creates a new instance wrapping a ResultSet instance.

Methods

public int getRowCount()

Returns –1 because the number of rows is unknown until all rows have been retrieved.

public Object getRowData()

Returns a java.util.Map with the column values for the columns in the current row, with the column names as case-insensitive keys, or null if the result set isn't set or there's no such row.

public int getRowIndex()

Returns the zero-based index for the current row or –1 if no row is selected.

public Object getWrappedData()

Returns the ResultSet instance or null if the result set isn't set.

public boolean isRowAvailable()

Returns true if the result set is set and if calling the ResultSet absolute() method with current row index plus one returns true.

public void setRowIndex(int index)
: Sets the zero-based index for the current row or to –1 if no row is selected.

public void setWrappedData(Object data)
: Sets the ResultSet instance.

ScalarDataModel

This class wraps any Object to expose it as a DataModel with one row for a UIData component.

Class name:	javax.faces.model.ScalarDataModel
Extends:	javax.faces.model.DataModel
Implements:	None

Constructors

public ScalarDataModel( )
: Creates a new, empty instance.

public ScalarDataModel(Object object)
: Creates a new instance wrapping as Object instance.

Methods

public int getRowCount( )
: Returns 1, or –1 if the object isn't set.

public Object getRowData( )
: Returns the object or null if the object isn't set.

public int getRowIndex( )
: Returns the zero-based index for the current row or –1 if no row is selected.

public Object getWrappedData( )
: Returns the object or null if the object isn't set.

public boolean isRowAvailable( )
: Returns true if the object is set and the current row index is 0.

public void setRowIndex(int index)
: Sets the zero-based index for the current row or to –1 if no row is selected.

public void setWrappedData(Object data)
: Sets the Object instance.

SelectItem

This class represents a selectable item for UISelectOne and UISelectMany components.

Class name:	javax.faces.model.SelectItem
Extends:	None
Implements:	java.io.Serializable

Constructors

`public SelectItem()`
: Creates a new, empty instance.

`public SelectItem(Object value)`
: Creates a new instance with the specified item value.

`public SelectItem(Object value, String label)`
: Creates a new instance with the specified item value and label.

`public SelectItem(Object value, String label, String description)`
: Creates a new instance with the specified item value, label, and description.

`public SelectItem(Object value, String label, String description,boolean disabled)`
: Creates a new instance with the specified item value, label, description, and disabled flag.

Methods

`public String getDescription()`
: Returns the description or `null` if not set.

`public String getLabel()`
: Returns the label or `null` if not set.

`public Object getValue()`
: Returns the value or `null` if not set.

`public boolean isDisabled()`
: Returns the disabled flag.

`public void setDescription(String description)`
: Sets the description.

`public void setDisabled(boolean isDisabled)`
: Sets the disabled flag.

`public void setLabel(String label)`
: Sets the label.

`public void setValue(Object value)`
: Sets the value.

SelectItemGroup

This class represents a grouping of selectable items for `UISelectOne` and `UISelectMany` components, typically rendered as a submenu. The standard renderers use the `label` property value as the submenu label and ignore the value. While instances of this class can be included in the `selectItems` property value, forming nested groups, the standard renderers support only one-level grouping.

Class name:	`javax.faces.model.SelectItemGroup`
Extends:	`javax.faces.model.SelectItem`
Implements:	`java.io.Serializable`

Constructors

`public SelectItemGroup( )`
: Creates a new, empty instance.

`public SelectItem(String label)`
: Creates a new instance with the specified label.

`public SelectItem(String label, String description, boolean disabled javax.faces.model.SelectItem[] selectItems)`
: Creates a new instance with the specified label, description, disabled flag, and `SelectItem` instances.

Methods

`public javax.faces.model.SelectItem[] getSelectItems( )`
: Returns the `SelectItem` instances in the group or `null` if not set.

`public setSelectItems(javax.faces.model.SelectItem[] selectItems)`
: Sets the `SelectItem` instances in the group.

HTML Render Kit Classes

A renderer attached to a component is responsible for generating a representation of the component suitable for the specific device type the renderer represents, such as one or more HTML elements for a browser device. It is also responsible for extracting submitted values and configuring the component instance with the values or queue an event signaling that the component was activated. A renderer instance must be threadsafe, because a single instance of each type may be used for multiple, parallel requests.

The specification defines only the abstract `Renderer` class that all renderers must extend. The concrete renderers are defined in terms of their behavior only. This section describes the `Renderer` class, followed by descriptions of each concrete renderer in the standard HTML render kit.

Renderer Class

Renderer

This abstract class defines all methods that concrete renderer subclasses implement.

Class name:	`javax.faces.render.Renderer`
Extends:	None
Implements:	None

Constructor

`public Renderer( )`

Creates a new instance.

Methods

`public String convertClientId(javax.faces.context.FacesContext, String clientId)`

Returns a converted version of the client ID, if needed. This implementation returns the client ID unchanged.

`public void decode(javax.faces.context.FacesContext, javax.faces.component.UIComponent component)`

Extracts the value for the component from the request, and configures the component with the submitted value or queues an event for the component. This implementation does nothing.

`public void encodeBegin(javax.faces.context.FacesContext, javax.faces.component.UIComponent component)throws java.io.IOException`

Renders the beginning of the component value, such as a start tag. This implementation does nothing.

`public void encodeChildren(javax.faces.context.FacesContext, javax.faces.component.UIComponent component) throws java.io.IOException`

Renders all component children, called only if the component returns `true` from `getRendersChildren( )`. This implementation does nothing.

`public void encodeEnd(javax.faces.context.FacesContext, javax.faces.component.UIComponent component)throws java.io.IOException`

Renders the end of the component value, such as an element value and the end tag. This implementation does nothing.

`public Object getConvertedValue(javax.faces.context.FacesContext, javax.faces.component.UIComponent component, Object submittedValue) throws javax.faces.convert.ConverterException`

Returns the submitted value converted to the appropriate data type, possibly using a `Converter` attached to the component. This implementation does nothing.

`public boolean getRenderChildren( )`

Returns true if the renderer renders the components children. This implementation returns `false`.

Standard Renderer Behavior

This section describes all implementation-dependent standard renderer classes. Each renderer is described by the component family/renderer type it's registered for, its encode and decode behavior, and the component attributes it supports in the same format as in Appendix A. For descriptions of the attributes, see the description of the corresponding JSF tag library custom action in Appendix A.

If a component ID is explicitly set, the client ID for the component is rendered either as the `id` attribute on the main element representing the component, or as the `id` attribute of a `<span>` element around the text or element representation. All supported attributes may also be rendered on the main element or on a <span> element, and most of them are just passed through to the client, without any validation of their value.

As general rules, a component with the rendered property set to true isn't rendered at all, and an input component with either the disabled or the readonly attributes set to true isn't decoded.

Command/Button

This renderer represents a command component as a button.

Component family:	javax.faces.Command
Renderer type:	javax.faces.Button
Renders children:	No

Encode behavior

Renders the component as an HTML <input> element with the type attribute set to submit, reset or image (depending on the value of this action element's type and image attribute values), the name attribute set to the component's client ID, and the value attribute set to the component's value.

Decode behavior

Looks for a request parameter with the component's client ID as the name (possibly with a .x or .y suffix). If it finds the parameter and the type attribute isn't reset, the renderer creates a javax.faces.event.ActionEvent and passes it to the component's enqueueEvent() method.

Attributes

```
[type="submit|reset" | image="imageURL"]
[accesskey="accessKey"] [alt="altText"] [dir="ltr|rtl"]
[disabled="true|false"] [lang="lang"]
[onblur="code"] [onchange="code"] [onclick="code"] [ondblclick="code"]
[onfocus="code"] [onkeydown="code"] [onkeypress="code"] [onkeyup="code"]
[onmousedown="code"] [onmousemove="code"] [onmouseout="code"]
[onmouseover="code"] [onmouseup="code"] [onselect="code"]
[readonly="true|false"] [style="style"] [styleClass="styleClass"]
[tabindex="tabIndex"] [title="title"]
```

Command/Link

This renderer represents a command component as a link.

Component family:	javax.faces.Command
Renderer type:	javax.faces.Link
Renders children:	No

Encode behavior

Renders the component as an HTML <a> element an href attribute containing "#" and an onclick attribute containing JavaScript code for submitting the form the component belongs to with the component's client ID as a request parameter. If the component has UIParameter component children, the generated JavaScript code also ensures that each parameter is included as request parameters when the form is submitted, with both the name and value URL encoded. The component's children that are not UIParameter components are rendered as the content of the <a> element, i.e., as the link text or image.

Decode behavior

Looks for a request parameter with the component's client ID as the name. If it finds the parameter and the type attribute isn't reset, the renderer creates a javax.faces.event.ActionEvent and passes it to the component's enqueueEvent() method.

Attributes

```
[accesskey="accessKey"] [charset="charset"] [coords="coords"]
[dir="ltr|rtl"] [hreflang="lang"] [lang="lang"]
[onblur="code"] [ondblclick="code"] [onfocus="code"]
[onkeydown="code"] [onkeypress="code"] [onkeyup="code"]
[onmousedown="code"] [onmousemove="code"] [onmouseout="code"]
[onmouseover="code"] [onmouseup="code"]
[rel="rel"] [rev="rev"] [shape="shape"] [style="style"]
[styleClass="styleClass"] [tabindex="tabIndex"] [target="target"]
[title="title"] [type="contentType"]
```

Data/Table

This renderer represents a data component as a table.

Component family:	javax.faces.Data
Renderer type:	javax.faces.Table
Renders children:	Yes

Encode behavior

Renders the component an HTML <table> element. UIColumn child components are responsible for rendering the table columns. The columns can hold any type of component, including input components and command components.

Both the data table component and its column children may be equipped with header and footer facets. The table's header facet is rendered as one <th> element (with a colspan attribute set to the number of children) within a <tr> element, and column header facets are rendered as <th> elements within a separate <tr> element. A <thead> element encloses both header <tr> elements. The footer facets, if any, are rendered in a similar manner, but with <td> elements instead of <th> and a <tfoot> element instead of the <thead> element. CSS style classes for the header and footer cells can be specified by the headerClass and footerClass attributes.

The table rows are rendered within a <tbody> element, with a <tr> element for each row and a <td> element for each column child. The first row to render and how many rows to render can be specified by the `first` and `row` attributes, and CSS style classes for the rows and cells can be specified by the `rowClasses` and `columnClasses` attributes.

Decode behavior

None.

Attributes

```
[bgcolor="color"] [border="border"] [cellpadding="padding"]
[cellspacing="spacing"] [columnClasses="styleClasses"] [dir="ltr|rtl"]
[footerClass="styleClass"] [frame="frame"] [headerClass="styleClass"]
[lang="lang"] [onclick="code"] [ondblclick="code"]
[onkeydown="code"] [onkeypress="code"] [onkeyup="code"]
[onmousedown="code"] [onmousemove="code"] [onmouseout="code"]
[onmouseover="code"] [onmouseup="code"] [rowClasses="styleClasses"]
[rules="rules"] [style="style"] [styleClass="styleClass"]
[summary="summary"] [title="title"] [width="width"]
```

Form/Form

This renderer represents a form component as a form.

Component family:	`javax.faces.Form`
Renderer type:	`javax.faces.Form`
Renders children:	No

Encode behavior

Renders the component as an HTML <form> element with an `action` attribute set to a URL that identifies the view containing the form (obtained by passing the view ID to the `ViewHandler getActionURL()` method, and passing the returned value to the `ExternalContext encodeActionURL()` method) and a `method` attribute set to `post`. Also renders hidden fields for all command link components in the form and implementation-dependent markup for including the component's client ID as a request parameter when the form is submitted.

Decode behavior

Looks for a request parameter with the component's client ID as the name. If it finds the parameter, the renderer calls the component's `setSubmitted()` method with the value `true`; otherwise it calls the same method with the value `false`.

Attributes

None.

Graphic/Image

This renderer represents a graphic component as an image.

Component family:	`javax.faces.Graphic`
Renderer type:	`javax.faces.Image`
Renders children:	No

Encode behavior

Renders the component as an HTML `<img>` element with a `src` attribute holding the component's value after passing through the `ViewHandler` `getResourceURL( )` method and passing the returned value through the `ExternalContext` `encodeResourceURL( )` method.

Decode behavior

None.

Attributes

```
[alt="altText"] [dir="ltr|rtl"] [height="height"] [ismap="true|false"]
[lang="lang"] [longdesc="descURI"] [onclick="code"] [ondblclick="code"]
[onkeydown="code"] [onkeypress="code"] [onkeyup="code"]
[onmousedown="code"] [onmousemove="code"] [onmouseout="code"]
[onmouseover="code"] [onmouseup="code"]
[style="style"] [styleClass="styleClass"] [title="title"]
[usemap="mapName"] [width="width"]
```

Input/Hidden

This renderer represents an input component as a hidden field.

Component family:	`javax.faces.Input`
Renderer type:	`javax.faces.Hidden`
Renders children:	No

Encode behavior

Renders the component as an HTML `<input>` element with a `type` attribute set to `hidden`, a `name` attribute set to the component's client ID, and a `value` attribute set to the component's value.

Decode behavior

Looks for a request parameter with the component's client ID as the name. If it finds the parameter, the renderer passes the parameter value to the component's `setSubmittedValue( )` method.

Attributes

None.

Input/Secret

This renderer represents an input component as a password field.

Component family:	`javax.faces.Input`
Renderer type:	`javax.faces.Secret`
Renders children:	No

Encode behavior

Renders the component as an HTML `<input>` element with a `type` attribute set to `password`, a `name` attribute set to the component's client ID, and a `value` attribute set to the component's value only if the action's `redisplay` attribute is set to `true`.

Decode behavior

Looks for a request parameter with the component's client ID as the name. If it finds the parameter, the renderer passes the parameter value to the component's `setSubmittedValue()` method.

Attributes

```
[accesskey="accessKey"] [alt="altText"] [dir="ltr|rtl"]
[disabled="true|false"] [lang="lang"] [maxlength="maxLength"]
[onblur="code"] [onchange="code"] [onclick="code"] [ondblclick="code"]
[onfocus="code"] [onkeydown="code"] [onkeypress="code"] [onkeyup="code"]
[onmousedown="code"] [onmousemove="code"] [onmouseout="code"]
[onmouseover="code"] [onmouseup="code"] [onselect="code"]
[readonly="true|false"] [redisplay="true|false"] [size="size"]
[style="style"] [styleClass="styleClass"] [tabindex="tabIndex"]
[title="title"]
```

Input/Text

This renderer represents an input component as a text field.

Component family:	`javax.faces.Input`
Renderer type:	`javax.faces.Text`
Renders children:	No

Encode behavior

Renders the component as an HTML `<input>` element with a `type` attribute set to `text`, a `name` attribute set to the component's client ID, and a `value` attribute set to the component's value.

Decode behavior

Looks for a request parameter with the component's client ID as the name. If it finds the parameter, the renderer passes the parameter value to the component's `setSubmittedValue()` method.

Attributes

```
[accesskey="accessKey"] [alt="altText"] [dir="ltr|rtl"]
[disabled="true|false"] [lang="lang"] [maxlength="maxLength"]
[onblur="code"] [onchange="code"] [onclick="code"] [ondblclick="code"]
[onfocus="code"] [onkeydown="code"] [onkeypress="code"] [onkeyup="code"]
[onmousedown="code"] [onmousemove="code"] [onmouseout="code"]
[onmouseover="code"] [onmouseup="code"] [onselect="code"]
[readonly="true|false"] [size="size"] [style="style"]
[styleClass="styleClass"] [tabindex="tabIndex"] [title="title"]
```

Input/Textarea

This renderer represents an input component as a text area.

Component family:	`javax.faces.Input`
Renderer type:	`javax.faces.Textarea`
Renders children:	No

Encode behavior

The component is rendered as an HTML `<textarea>` element with a `name` attribute set to the component's client ID and a body holding the component's value.

Decode behavior

Looks for a request parameter with the component's client ID as the name. If it finds the parameter, the renderer passes the parameter value to the component's `setSubmittedValue()` method.

Attributes

```
[accesskey="accessKey"] [cols="noOfCols"] [dir="ltr|rtl"]
[disabled="true|false"] [lang="lang"]
[onblur="code"] [onchange="code"] [onclick="code"] [ondblclick="code"]
[onfocus="code"] [onkeydown="code"] [onkeypress="code"] [onkeyup="code"]
[onmousedown="code"] [onmousemove="code"] [onmouseout="code"]
[onmouseover="code"] [onmouseup="code"] [onselect="code"]
[readonly="true|false"] [rows="noOfRows"] [style="style"]
[styleClass="styleClass"] [tabindex="tabIndex"] [title="title"]
```

Message/Message

This renderer represents a message component as text.

Component family:	`javax.faces.Message`
Renderer type:	`javax.faces.Message`
Renders children:	No

Encode behavior

Renders the first message queued for the component identified by the component's `for` property. The message properties identified by the `showDetail` and `showSummary` component properties are rendered as text, within an HTML `<span>` element if any of the CSS style attributes apply or the component ID is set. If the `tooltip` attribute is set to `true` and both the summary and the detailed text are rendered, the message summary is rendered as the value of the `<span>` element's `title` attribute.

Decode behavior

None.

Attributes

```
[errorClass="styleClass"] [errorStyle="style"]
[fatalClass="styleClass"] [fatalStyle="style"]
[infoClass="styleClass"] [infoStyle="style"]
[style="style"] [styleClass="styleClass"]
[title="title"] [tooltip="true|false"]
[warnClass="styleClass"] [warnStyle="style"]
```

Messages/Messages

This renderer represents a message component as text or a table.

Component family:	`javax.faces.Messages`
Renderer type:	`javax.faces.Messages`
Renders children:	No

Encode behavior

Renders all queued messages or only those queued without a component identifier if the component's `globalOnly` property is set to `true`. The message properties identified by the `showDetail` and `showSummary` component properties are rendered as cells in an HTML table if the `layout` attribute is set to `table`; otherwise within an HTML `<span>` element if any of the CSS style attributes apply or the component ID is set. If the `tooltip` attribute is set to `true` and both the summary and the detailed text are rendered, the message summary is rendered as the value of the `<td>` or `<span>` element's `title` attribute.

Decode behavior

None.

Attributes

```
[errorClass="styleClass"] [errorStyle="style"]
[fatalClass="styleClass"] [fatalStyle="style"]
[infoClass="styleClass"] [infoStyle="style"]
[layout="list|table"]
[style="style"] [styleClass="styleClass"]
[title="title"] [tooltip="true|false"]
[warnClass="styleClass"] [warnStyle="style"]
```

Output/Format

This renderer represents an output component as a formatted message, with parameter component children providing the parameter values.

Component family:	`javax.faces.Output`
Renderer type:	`javax.faces.Format`
Renders children:	No

Encode behavior

Renders the component as text, within an HTML `<span>` element if any of the CSS style attributes apply or the component ID is set. The component's value should be a parameterized message string. An `Object[]` is created from the component's `UIParameter` children and passed along with the component's value as arguments to the `java.text.MessageFormat` `format()` method to format a message, which is then rendered, with all special characters converted to their character entity equivalents if escape is set to `true`.

Decode behavior

None.

Attributes

```
[escape="true|false"]
[style="style"] [styleClass="styleClass"] [title="title"]
```

Output/Label

This renderer represents an output component as a label for another component.

Component family:	`javax.faces.Output`
Renderer type:	`javax.faces.Label`
Renders children:	No

Encode behavior

Renders the component as an HTML `<label>` element with a `for` attribute set to the client ID for the component identified by the `for` attribute value.

Decode behavior

None.

Attributes

```
[accesskey="accessKey"] [dir="ltr|rtl"] for="componentId" [lang="lang"]
[onblur="code"] [onchange="code"] [onclick="code"] [ondblclick="code"]
[onfocus="code"] [onkeydown="code"] [onkeypress="code"] [onkeyup="code"]
[onmousedown="code"] [onmousemove="code"] [onmouseout="code"]
[onmouseover="code"] [onmouseup="code"] [style="style"]
[styleClass="styleClass"] [tabindex="tabIndex"] [title="title"]
```

Output/Link

This renderer represents an output component as a link.

Component family:	`javax.faces.Output`
Renderer type:	`javax.faces.Link`
Renders children:	No

Encode behavior

Renders the component as an HTML <a> element with an `href` attribute set to the component's value. If the component has `UIParameter` component children, their name and value properties are added as query string parameters to the `href` attribute value, with both the name and value URL-encoded. The component's children that are not `UIParameter` components are rendered as the content of the <a> element, i.e., as the link text or image.

Decode behavior

None.

Attributes

```
[accesskey="accessKey"] [charset="charset"] [coords="coords"]
[dir="ltr|rtl"] [hreflang="lang"] [lang="lang"]
[onblur="code"] [onclick="code"] [ondblclick="code"] [onfocus="code"]
[onkeydown="code"] [onkeypress="code"] [onkeyup="code"]
[onmousedown="code"] [onmousemove="code"] [onmouseout="code"]
[onmouseover="code"] [onmouseup="code"]
[rel="rel"] [rev="rev"] [shape="shape"] [style="style"]
[styleClass="styleClass"] [tabindex="tabIndex"] [target="target"]
[title="title"] [type="contentType"]
```

Output/Text

This renderer represents an output component as a text.

Component family:	`javax.faces.Output`
Renderer type:	`javax.faces.Text`
Renders children:	No

Encode behavior

The component is rendered as text, with all special characters converted to their character entity equivalents if escape is set to `true`, within an HTML <span> element if any of the HTML attributes or the component ID is set.

Decode behavior

None.

Attributes

```
[escape="true|false"] [style="style"] [styleClass="styleClass"]
[title="title"]
```

Panel/Grid

This renderer represents a panel component as a table.

Component family:	`javax.faces.Panel`
Renderer type:	`javax.faces.Grid`
Renders children:	Yes

Encode behavior

Renders the component as an HTML table with the number of columns specified by the `columns` attribute. The renderer uses the component's children to render the table cells, with new rows as the number of columns is reached.

The panel component may be equipped with a `header` and a `footer` facet. The table's `header` facet is rendered as one `<th>` element (with a `colspan` attribute set to the value of the `columns` attribute) within a `<tr>` element, enclosed within an `<thead>` element. The `footer` facet is rendered in a similar manner, but with a `<td>` element instead of `<th>` and a `<tfoot>` element instead of the `<thead>` element. CSS style classes for the header and footer cells can be specified by the `headerClass` and `footerClass` attributes.

The table rows are rendered within a `<tbody>` element, with a `<tr>` element for each row and a `<td>` element for each column. CSS style classes for the rows and cells can be specified by the `rowClasses` and `columnClasses` attributes.

Decode behavior

None.

Attributes

```
[bgcolor="color"] [border="border"] [cellpadding="padding"]
[cellspacing="spacing"] [columnClasses="styleClasses"]
[columns="noOfColumns"] [dir="ltr|rtl"] [footerClass="styleClass"]
[frame="frame"] [headerClass="styleClass"] [lang="lang"]
[onclick="code"] [ondblclick="code"] [onkeydown="code"]
[onkeypress="code"] [onkeyup="code"] [onmousedown="code"]
[onmousemove="code"] [onmouseout="code"] [onmouseover="code"]
[onmouseup="code"] [rowClasses="styleClasses"] [rules="rules"]
[style="style"] [styleClass="styleClass"] [summary="summary"]
[title="title"] [width="width"]
```

Panel/Group

This renderer represents a panel component as a container.

Component family:	`javax.faces.Panel`
Renderer type:	`javax.faces.Group`
Renders children:	Yes

Encode behavior

Renders the component's children, within an HTML <span> element if any of the HTML attributes or the component ID is set.

Decode behavior

None.

Attributes

```
[style="style"] [styleClass="styleClass"]
```

SelectBoolean/Checkbox

This renderer represents a select-boolean component as a checkbox.

Component family:	javax.faces.SelectBoolean
Renderer type:	javax.faces.Checkbox
Renders children:	No

Encode behavior

Renders the component as an HTML <input> element with a type attribute set to checkbox, a name attribute set to the component's client ID. If the component's value is true, a checked attribute is rendered as well.

Decode behavior

Looks for a request parameter with the component's client ID as the name. If it finds the parameter and its value is "yes" or "true," ignoring case, the renderer calls the component's setSubmittedValue( ) method with the value true; otherwise it calls the same method with the value false.

Attributes

```
[accesskey="accessKey"] [dir="ltr|rtl"] [disabled="true|false"]
[lang="lang"] [onblur="code"] [onchange="code"] [onclick="code"]
[ondblclick="code"] [onfocus="code"] [onkeydown="code"]
[onkeypress="code"] [onkeyup="code"] [onmousedown="code"]
[onmousemove="code"] [onmouseout="code"] [onmouseover="code"]
[onmouseup="code"] [onselect="code"] [readonly="true|false"]
[style="style"] [styleClass="styleClass"] [tabindex="tabIndex"]
[title="title"]
```

SelectMany/Checkbox

This renderer represents a select-many component as a group of checkboxes.

Component family:	javax.faces.SelectMany
Renderer type:	javax.faces.Checkbox
Renders children:	No

Encode behavior

Renders the component as an HTML `<table>` element with an `<input>` element for each choice represented by its children (one or more `UISelectItem` and `UISelectItems` components) as the table cells. If the `layout` attribute is set to `pageDirection`, each cell is rendered in a separate table row; otherwise all cells are rendered in one row. A `UISelectItemGroup` child component is rendered as a nested table within the corresponding outer table cell. If the component ID is set, a `<span>` element with an `id` attribute containing the component's client ID is rendered around the outer table.

The `<input>` elements are rendered with a `type` attribute set to `checkbox` and a `name` attribute set to the component's client ID. Each `<input>` element is also nested within a `<label>` elements with a `for` attribute set to the component's client ID. For all choices that match one of the component's values, the `checked` attribute is set for the corresponding `<input>` element.

Decode behavior

Looks for request parameters with the component's client ID as the name. If it finds parameters, the renderer the calls component's `setSubmittedValue()` method with a `String[]` holding all parameter values as the value; otherwise it calls the same method with an empty `String[]` as the value.

Attributes

```
[accesskey="accessKey"] [border="border"] [dir="ltr|rtl"]
[disabled="true|false"] [disabledClass="styleClass"]
[enabledClass="styleClass"] [lang="lang"]
[layout="lineDirection|pageDirection"] [onblur="code"]
[onchange="code"] [onclick="code"] [ondblclick="code"] [onfocus="code"]
[onkeydown="code"] [onkeypress="code"] [onkeyup="code"]
[onmousedown="code"] [onmousemove="code"] [onmouseout="code"]
[onmouseover="code"] [onmouseup="code"] [onselect="code"]
[readonly="true|false"] [style="style"] [styleClass="styleClass"]
[tabindex="tabIndex"] [title="title"]
```

SelectMany/Listbox

This renderer represents a select-many component as a selection list.

Component family:	`javax.faces.SelectMany`
Renderer type:	`javax.faces.Listbox`
Renders children:	No

Encode behavior

Renders the component as an HTML `<select>` element with a `name` attribute set to the component's client ID and a `multiple` attribute. If the `size` attribute is set, it is added to the `<select>` element with the specified value; otherwise a `size` attribute with the number of choices as the value is added. Each choice represented by the component's children (one or more `UISelectItem` and `UISelectItems` components) is rendered as an `<option>` element or as an `<optgroup>` element if the child is of the `UISelectItemGroup` subtype. For all choices that match one of the component's values, the selected attribute is set for the corresponding <option> element. If a choice is marked as disabled, the disabled attribute is also added.

Decode behavior

Looks for request parameters with the component's client ID as the name. If it finds parameters, the renderer the calls component's setSubmittedValue() method with a String[] holding all parameter values as the value; otherwise it calls the same method with an empty String[] as the value.

Attributes

```
[accesskey="accessKey"] [dir="ltr|rtl"] [disabled="true|false"]
[lang="lang"] [onblur="code"] [onchange="code"] [onclick="code"]
[ondblclick="code"] [onfocus="code"] [onkeydown="code"]
[onkeypress="code"] [onkeyup="code"] [onmousedown="code"]
[onmousemove="code"] [onmouseout="code"] [onmouseover="code"]
[onmouseup="code"] [onselect="code"] [readonly="true|false"]
[size="size"] [style="style"] [styleClass="styleClass"]
[tabindex-"tabIndex"] [title="title"]
```

SelectMany/Menu

This renderer represents a select-many component as a selection list drop-down menu.

Component family:	javax.faces.SelectMany
Renderer type:	javax.faces.Menu
Renders children:	No

Encode behavior

Renders the component as an HTML <select> element with a name attribute set to the component's client ID and a multiple attribute and a size attribute with 1 as the value. Each choice represented by the component's children (one or more UISelectItem and UISelectItems components) is rendered as an <option> element or as an <optgroup> element if the child is of the UISelectItemGroup subtype. For all choices that match one of the component's values, the selected attribute is set for the corresponding <option> element. If a choice is marked as disabled, the disabled attribute is also added.

Decode behavior

Looks for request parameters with the component's client ID as the name. If it finds parameters, the renderer the calls component's setSubmittedValue() method with a String[] holding all parameter values as the value; otherwise it calls the same method with an empty String[] as the value.

Attributes

```
[accesskey="accessKey"] [dir="ltr|rtl"] [disabled="true|false"]
[lang="lang"] [onblur="code"] [onchange="code"] [onclick="code"]
[ondblclick="code"] [onfocus="code"] [onkeydown="code"]
```

```
[onkeypress="code"] [onkeyup="code"] [onmousedown="code"]
[onmousemove="code"] [onmouseout="code"] [onmouseover="code"]
[onmouseup="code"] [onselect="code"] [readonly="true|false"]
[style="style"] [styleClass="styleClass"] [tabindex="tabIndex"]
[title="title"]
```

SelectOne/Listbox

This renderer represents a select-one component as a selection list.

Component family:	javax.faces.SelectOne
Renderer type:	javax.faces.Listbox
Renders children:	No

Encode behavior

Renders the component as an HTML <select> element with a name attribute set to the component's client ID. If the size attribute is set, it is added to the <select> element with the specified value; otherwise a size attribute with the number of choices as the value is added. Each choice represented by the component's children (one or more UISelectItem and UISelectItems components) is rendered as an <option> element or as an <optgroup> element if the child is of the UISelectItemGroup subtype. For the choice that matches the component's value, the selected attribute is set for the corresponding <option> element. If a choice is marked as disabled, the disabled attribute is also added.

Decode behavior

Looks for a request parameter with the component's client ID as the name. If it finds the parameter, the renderer passes the parameter value to the component's setSubmittedValue( ) method.

Attributes

```
[accesskey="accessKey"] [dir="ltr|rtl"] [disabled="true|false"]
[lang="lang"] [onblur="code"] [onchange="code"] [onclick="code"]
[ondblclick="code"] [onfocus="code"] [onkeydown="code"]
[onkeypress="code"] [onkeyup="code"] [onmousedown="code"]
[onmousemove="code"] [onmouseout="code"] [onmouseover="code"]
[onmouseup="code"] [onselect="code"] [readonly="true|false"]
[size="size"] [style="style"] [styleClass="styleClass"]
[tabindex="tabIndex"] [title="title"]
```

SelectOne/Menu

This renderer represents a select-one component as a selection list drop-down menu.

Component family:	javax.faces.SelectOne
Renderer type:	javax.faces.Menu
Renders children:	No

Encode behavior

Renders the component as an HTML <select> element with a name attribute set to the component's client ID and a multiple attribute and a size attribute with 1 as the value. Each choice represented by the component's children (one or more UISelectItem and UISelectItems components) is rendered as an <option> element or as an <optgroup> element if the child is of the UISelectItemGroup subtype. For the choice that matches the component's value, the selected attribute is set for the corresponding <option> element. If a choice is marked as disabled, the disabled attribute is also added.

Decode behavior

Looks for a request parameter with the component's client ID as the name. If it finds the parameter, the renderer passes the parameter value to the component's setSubmittedValue( ) method.

Attributes

```
[accesskey="accessKey"] [dir="ltr|rtl"] [disabled="true|false"]
[lang="lang"] [onblur="code"] [onchange="code"] [onclick="code"]
[ondblclick="code"] [onfocus="code"] [onkeydown="code"]
[onkeypress="code"] [onkeyup="code"] [onmousedown="code"]
[onmousemove="code"] [onmouseout="code"] [onmouseover="code"]
[onmouseup="code"] [onselect="code"] [readonly="true|false"]
[style="style"] [styleClass="styleClass"] [tabindex="tabIndex"]
[title="title"]
```

SelectOne/Radio

This renderer represents a select-one component as a radio button group.

Component family:	javax.faces.SelectOne
Renderer type:	javax.faces.Radio
Renders children:	No

Encode behavior

Renders the component as an HTML <table> element with an <input> element for each choice represented by the component's children (one or more UISelectItem and UISelectItems components) as the table cells. If the layout attribute is set to pageDirection, each cell is rendered in a separate table row; otherwise all cells are rendered in one row. A UISelectItemGroup child component is rendered as a nested table within the corresponding outer table cell. If the component ID is set, a <span> element with an id attribute containing the component's client ID is rendered around the outer table.

The <input> elements are rendered with a type attribute set to radio and a name attribute set to the component's client ID. Each <input> element is also nested within a <label> elements with a for attribute set to the component's client ID. For all the choice that matches the component's value, the checked attribute is set for the corresponding <input> element.

Decode behavior

Looks for a request parameter with the component's client ID as the name. If it finds the parameter, the renderer passes the parameter value to the component's `setSubmittedValue()` method.

Attributes

```
[accesskey="accessKey"] [border="border"] [dir="ltr|rtl"]
[disabled="true|false"] [disabledClass="styleClass"]
[enabledClass="styleClass"] [lang="lang"]
[layout="lineDirection|pageDirection"] [onblur="code"] [onchange="code"]
[onclick="code"] [ondblclick="code"] [onfocus="code"] [onkeydown="code"]
[onkeypress="code"] [onkeyup="code"] [onmousedown="code"]
[onmousemove="code"] [onmouseout="code"] [onmouseover="code"]
[onmouseup="code"] [onselect="code"] [readonly="true|false"]
[style="style"] [styleClass="styleClass"] [tabindex="tabIndex"]
[title="title"]
```

HTML-Specific Component Classes

The HTML-specific classes extend the generic component classes and provide property accessor methods for all render-dependent attributes, with one class defined for each combination of generic components and renderer in the HTML render kit. This section lists all methods for each class. For a description of each property, please see the corresponding render-dependent attribute description in Appendix A.

HtmlCommandButton

The `HtmlCommandButton` class is the HTML rendering-dependent class representing the `UICommand` component with a `javax.faces.Button` renderer.

Synopsis

Class name:	`javax.faces.component.html.HtmlCommandButton`
Extends:	`javax.faces.component.UICommand`
Implements:	`javax.faces.component.ActionSource`, `javax.faces.component.StateHolder`

Fields

`public static String COMPONENT_TYPE`

The component family: `javax.faces.HtmlCommandButton`.

Constructor

`public HtmlCommandButton()`

Creates a new instance.

Methods

```
public String getAccesskey( )
public String getAlt( )
public String getDir( )
public String getImage( )
public String getLang( )
public String getOnblur( )
public String getOnchange( )
public String getOnclick( )
public String getOndblclick( )
public String getOnfocus( )
public String getOnkeydown( )
public String getOnkeypress( )
public String getOnkeyup( )
public String getOnmousedown( )
public String getOnmousemove( )
public String getOnmouseout( )
public String getOnmouseover( )
public String getOnmouseup( )
public String getStyle( )
public String getStyleClass( )
public String getTabindex( )
public String getTitle( )
public String getType( )
public boolean isDisabled( )
public boolean isReadonly( )
public void restoreState(javax.faces.context.FacesContext context, Object state)
public Object saveState(javax.faces.context.FacesContext context)
public void setAccesskey(String accesskey)
public void setAlt(String alt)
public void setDir(String dir)
public void setDisabled(boolean disabled)
public void setImage(String image)
public void setLang(String lang)
public void setOnblur(String onblur)
public void setOnchange(String onchange)
public void setOnclick(String onclick)
public void setOndblclick(String ondblclick)
public void setOnfocus(String onfocus)
public void setOnkeydown(String onkeydown)
public void setOnkeypress(String onkeypress)
public void setOnkeyup(String onkeyup)
public void setOnmousedown(String onmousedown)
public void setOnmousemove(String onmousemove)
public void setOnmouseout(String onmouseout)
public void setOnmouseover(String onmouseover)
public void setOnmouseup(String onmouseup)
public void setReadonly(boolean readonly)
public void setStyle(String style)
public void setStyleClass(String styleClass)
public void setTabindex(String tabindex)
public void setTitle(String title)
public void setType(String type)
```

HtmlCommandLink

The `HtmlCommandLink` class is the HTML rendering-dependent class representing the `UICommand` component with a `javax.faces.Link` renderer.

Synopsis

Class name:	`javax.faces.component.html.HtmlCommandLink`
Extends:	`javax.faces.component.UICommand`
Implements:	`javax.faces.component.ActionSource`, `javax.faces.component.StateHolder`

Fields

`public static String COMPONENT_TYPE`

The component family: `javax.faces.HtmlCommandLink`.

Constructor

`public HtmlCommandLink( )`

Creates a new instance.

Methods

```
public String getAccesskey( )
public String getCharset( )
public String getCoords( )
public String getDir( )
public String getHreflang( )
public String getLang( )
public String getOnblur( )
public String getOnchange( )
public String getOnclick( )
public String getOndblclick( )
public String getOnfocus( )
public String getOnkeydown( )
public String getOnkeypress( )
public String getOnkeyup( )
public String getOnmousedown( )
public String getOnmousemove( )
public String getOnmouseout( )
public String getOnmouseover( )
public String getOnmouseup( )
public String getRel( )
public String getRev( )
public String getShape( )
public String getStyle( )
public String getStyleClass( )
public String getTabindex( )
public String getTarget( )
public String getTitle( )
public String getType( )
public void restoreState(javax.faces.context.FacesContext context, Object state)
```

```
public Object saveState(javax.faces.context.FacesContext context)
public void setAccesskey(String accesskey)
public void setCharset(String charset)
public void setCoords(String coords)
public void setDir(String dir)
public void setHreflang(String hreflang)
public void setLang(String lang)
public void setOnblur(String onblur)
public void setOnchange(String onchange)
public void setOnclick(String onclick)
public void setOndblclick(String ondblclick)
public void setOnfocus(String onfocus)
public void setOnkeydown(String onkeydown)
public void setOnkeypress(String onkeypress)
public void setOnkeyup(String onkeyup)
public void setOnmousedown(String onmousedown)
public void setOnmousemove(String onmousemove)
public void setOnmouseout(String onmouseout)
public void setOnmouseover(String onmouseover)
public void setOnmouseup(String onmouseup)
public void setRel(String rel)
public void setRev(String rev)
public void setShape(String shape)
public void setStyle(String style)
public void setStyleClass(String styleClass)
public void setTabindex(String tabindex)
public void setTarget(String target)
public void setTitle(String title)
public void setType(String type)
```

HtmlDataTable

The `HtmlDataTable` class is the HTML rendering-dependent class representing the `UIData` component with a `javax.faces.Table` renderer.

Synopsis

Class name:	`javax.faces.component.html.HtmlDataTable`
Extends:	`javax.faces.component.UIData`
Implements:	`javax.faces.component.StateHolder`, `javax.faces.component.NamingContainer`

Fields

`public static String COMPONENT_TYPE`

The component family: `javax.faces.HtmlDataTable`.

Constructor

`public HtmlDataTable( )`

Creates a new instance.

Methods

```
public String getBgcolor( )
public String getBorder( )
public String getCellpadding( )
public String getCellspacing( )
public String getColumnClasses( )
public String getDir( )
public String getFooterClass( )
public String getFrame( )
public String getHeaderClass( )
public String getLang( )
public String getOnclick( )
public String getOndblclick( )
public String getOnkeydown( )
public String getOnkeypress( )
public String getOnkeyup( )
public String getOnmousedown( )
public String getOnmousemove( )
public String getOnmouseout( )
public String getOnmouseover( )
public String getOnmouseup( )
public String getRowClasses( )
public String getRules( )
public String getStyle( )
public String getStyleClass( )
public String getSummary( )
public String getTitle( )
public String getWidth( )
public void restoreState(javax.faces.context.FacesContext context, Object state)
public Object saveState(javax.faces.context.FacesContext context)
public void setBgcolor(String bgcolor)
public void setBorder(String border)
public void setCellpadding(String cellpadding)
public void setCellspacing(String cellspacing)
public void setColumnClasses(String columnClasses)
public void setDir(String dir)
public void setFooterClass(String footerClass)
public void setFrame(String frame)
public void setHeaderClass(String headerClass)
public void setLang(String lang)
public void setOnclick(String onclick)
public void setOndblclick(String ondblclick)
public void setOnfocus(String onfocus)
public void setOnkeydown(String onkeydown)
public void setOnkeypress(String onkeypress)
public void setOnkeyup(String onkeyup)
public void setOnmousedown(String onmousedown)
public void setOnmousemove(String onmousemove)
public void setOnmouseout(String onmouseout)
public void setOnmouseover(String onmouseover)
public void setOnmouseup(String onmouseup)
public void setRowClasses(String rowClasses)
public void setRules(String rules)
```

```
public void setStyle(String style)
public void setStyleClass(String styleClass)
public void setSummary(String summary)
public void setTitle(String title)
public void setWidth(String width)
```

HtmlForm

The `HtmlForm` class is the HTML rendering-dependent class representing the `UIForm` component with a `javax.faces.Form` renderer.

Synopsis

Class name:	`javax.faces.component.html.HtmlForm`
Extends:	`javax.faces.component.UIForm`
Implements:	`javax.faces.component.StateHolder,` `javax.faces.component.NamingContainer`

Fields

`public static String COMPONENT_TYPE`
: The component family: `javax.faces.HtmlForm`.

Constructor

`public HtmlForm( )`
: Creates a new instance.

Methods

```
public String getAccept( )
public String getAcceptcharset( )
public String getDir( )
public String getEnctype( )
public String getLang( )
public String getOnclick( )
public String getOndblclick( )
public String getOnkeydown( )
public String getOnkeypress( )
public String getOnkeyup( )
public String getOnmousedown( )
public String getOnmousemove( )
public String getOnmouseout( )
public String getOnmouseover( )
public String getOnmouseup( )
public String getOnreset( )
public String getOnsubmit( )
public String getStyle( )
public String getStyleClass( )
public String getTarget( )
public String getTitle( )
public void restoreState(javax.faces.context.FacesContext context, Object state)
```

```
public Object saveState(javax.faces.context.FacesContext context)
public void setAccept(String accept)
public void setAcceptcharset(String acceptcharset)
public void setDir(String dir)
public void setEnctype(String enctype)
public void setLang(String lang)
public void setOnclick(String onclick)
public void setOndblclick(String ondblclick)
public void setOnkeydown(String onkeydown)
public void setOnkeypress(String onkeypress)
public void setOnkeyup(String onkeyup)
public void setOnmousedown(String onmousedown)
public void setOnmousemove(String onmousemove)
public void setOnmouseout(String onmouseout)
public void setOnmouseover(String onmouseover)
public void setOnmouseup(String onmouseup)
public void setOnreset(String onreset)
public void setOnsubmit(String onsubmit)
public void setStyle(String style)
public void setStyleClass(String styleClass)
public void setTarget(String target)
public void setTitle(String title)
```

HtmlGraphicImage

The `HtmlGraphicImage` class is the HTML rendering-dependent class representing the `UIGraphic` component with a `javax.faces.Image` renderer.

Synopsis

Class name:	`javax.faces.component.html.HtmlGraphicImage`
Extends:	`javax.faces.component.UIGraphic`
Implements:	`javax.faces.component.StateHolder`

Fields

`public static String COMPONENT TYPE`

The component family: `javax.faces.HtmlGraphicImage`.

Constructor

`public HtmlGraphicImage( )`

Creates a new instance.

Methods

```
public String getAlt( )
public String getDir( )
public String getHeight( )
public String getLang( )
public String getLongdesc( )
public String getOnclick( )
```

```
public String getOndblclick( )
public String getOnkeydown( )
public String getOnkeypress( )
public String getOnkeyup( )
public String getOnmousedown( )
public String getOnmousemove( )
public String getOnmouseout( )
public String getOnmouseover( )
public String getOnmouseup( )
public String getStyle( )
public String getStyleClass( )
public String getTitle( )
public String getUsemap( )
public String getWidth( )
public boolean isIsmap( )
public void restoreState(javax.faces.context.FacesContext context, Object state)
public Object saveState(javax.faces.context.FacesContext context)
public void setAlt(String alt)
public void setDir(String dir)
public void setHeight(String height)
public void setIsmap(boolean ismap)
public void setLang(String lang)
public void setLongdesc(String longdesc)
public void setOnclick(String onclick)
public void setOndblclick(String ondblclick)
public void setOnkeydown(String onkeydown)
public void setOnkeypress(String onkeypress)
public void setOnkeyup(String onkeyup)
public void setOnmousedown(String onmousedown)
public void setOnmousemove(String onmousemove)
public void setOnmouseout(String onmouseout)
public void setOnmouseover(String onmouseover)
public void setOnmouseup(String onmouseup)
public void setStyle(String style)
public void setStyleClass(String styleClass)
public void setTitle(String title)
public void setUsemap(String usemap)
public void setWidth(String width)
```

HtmlInputHidden

The `HtmlInputHidden` class is the HTML rendering-dependent class representing the `UIInput` component with a `javax.faces.Hidden` renderer.

Synopsis

Class name:	`javax.faces.component.html.HtmlInputHidden`
Extends:	`javax.faces.component.UIInput`
Implements:	`javax.faces.component.EditableValueHolder,` `javax.faces.component.StateHolder`

Fields

public static String COMPONENT_TYPE

The component family: javax.faces.HtmlInputHidden.

Constructor

public HtmlInputHidden( )

Creates a new instance.

Methods

```
public void restoreState(javax.faces.context.FacesContext context, Object state)
public Object saveState(javax.faces.context.FacesContext context)
```

HtmlInputSecret

The HtmlInputSecret class is the HTML rendering-dependent class representing the UIInput component with a javax.faces.Secret renderer.

Synopsis

Class name:	javax.faces.component.html.HtmlInputSecret
Extends:	javax.faces.component.UIInput
Implements:	javax.faces.component.EditableValueHolder, avax.faces.component.StateHolder

Fields

public static String COMPONENT_TYPE

The component family: javax.faces.HtmlInputHidden.

Constructor

public HtmlInputSecret( )

Creates a new instance.

Methods

```
public String getAccesskey( )
public String getAlt( )
public String getDir( )
public String getLang( )
public String getMaxlength( )
public String getOnblur( )
public String getOnchange( )
public String getOnclick( )
public String getOndblclick( )
public String getOnfocus( )
public String getOnkeydown( )
public String getOnkeypress( )
public String getOnkeyup( )
public String getOnmousedown( )
public String getOnmousemove( )
public String getOnmouseout( )
```

```
public String getOnmouseover( )
public String getOnmouseup( )
public String getOnselect( )
public String getSize( )
public String getStyle( )
public String getStyleClass( )
public String getTabindex( )
public String getTitle( )
public boolean isDisabled( )
public boolean isReadonly( )
public boolean isRedisplay( )
public void restoreState(javax.faces.context.FacesContext context, Object state)
public Object saveState(javax.faces.context.FacesContext context)
public void setAccesskey(String accesskey)
public void setAlt(String alt)
public void setDir(String dir)
public void setDisabled(boolean disabled)
public void setLang(String lang)
public void setMaxlength(String maxlength)
public void setOnblur(String onblur)
public void setOnchange(String onchange)
public void setOnclick(String onclick)
public void setOndblclick(String ondblclick)
public void setOnfocus(String onfocus)
public void setOnkeydown(String onkeydown)
public void setOnkeypress(String onkeypress)
public void setOnkeyup(String onkeyup)
public void setOnmousedown(String onmousedown)
public void setOnmousemove(String onmousemove)
public void setOnmouseout(String onmouseout)
public void setOnmouseover(String onmouseover)
public void setOnmouseup(String onmouseup)
public void setOnselect(String onselect)
public void setReadonly(boolean readonly)
public void setRedisplay(boolean redisplay)
public void setSize(String size)
public void setStyle(String style)
public void setStyleClass(String styleClass)
public void setTabindex(String tabindex)
public void setTitle(String title)
```

HtmlInputText

The `HtmlInputText` class is the HTML rendering-dependent class representing the `UIInput` component with a `javax.faces.Text` renderer.

Synopsis

Class name:	`javax.faces.component.html.HtmlInputText`
Extends:	`javax.faces.component.UIInput`
Implements:	`javax.faces.component.EditableValueHolder,` `javax.faces.component.StateHolder`

Fields

`public static String COMPONENT_TYPE`

The component family: `javax.faces.HtmlInputText`.

Constructor

`public HtmlInputText( )`

Creates a new instance.

Methods

```
public String getAccesskey( )
public String getAlt( )
public String getDir( )
public String getLang( )
public String getMaxlength( )
public String getOnblur( )
public String getOnchange( )
public String getOnclick( )
public String getOndblclick( )
public String getOnfocus( )
public String getOnkeydown( )
public String getOnkeypress( )
public String getOnkeyup( )
public String getOnmousedown( )
public String getOnmousemove( )
public String getOnmouseout( )
public String getOnmouseover( )
public String getOnmouseup( )
public String getOnselect( )
public String getSize( )
public String getStyle( )
public String getStyleClass( )
public String getTabindex( )
public String getTitle( )
public boolean isDisabled( )
public boolean isReadonly( )
public void restoreState(javax.faces.context.FacesContext context, Object state)
public Object saveState(javax.faces.context.FacesContext context)
public void setAccesskey(String accesskey)
public void setAlt(String alt)
public void setDir(String dir)
public void setDisabled(boolean disabled)
public void setLang(String lang)
public void setMaxlength(String maxlength)
public void setOnblur(String onblur)
public void setOnchange(String onchange)
public void setOnclick(String onclick)
public void setOndblclick(String ondblclick)
public void setOnfocus(String onfocus)
public void setOnkeydown(String onkeydown)
public void setOnkeypress(String onkeypress)
public void setOnkeyup(String onkeyup)
```

```
public void setOnmousedown(String onmousedown)
public void setOnmousemove(String onmousemove)
public void setOnmouseout(String onmouseout)
public void setOnmouseover(String onmouseover)
public void setOnmouseup(String onmouseup)
public void setOnselect(String onselect)
public void setReadonly(boolean readonly)
public void setSize(String size)
public void setStyle(String style)
public void setStyleClass(String styleClass)
public void setTabindex(String tabindex)
public void setTitle(String title)
```

HtmlInputTextarea

The `HtmlInputTextare` class is the HTML rendering-dependent class representing the `UIInput` component with a `javax.faces.Textare` renderer.

Synopsis

Class name:	`javax.faces.component.html.HtmlInputTextarea`
Extends:	`javax.faces.component.UIInput`
Implements:	`javax.faces.component.EditableValueHolder`, `javax.faces.component.StateHolder`

Fields

`public static String COMPONENT_TYPE`

The component family: `javax.faces.HtmlInputTextarea`.

Constructor

`public HtmlInputTextarea( )`

Creates a new instance.

Methods

```
public String getAccesskey( )
public String getCols( )
public String getDir( )
public String getLang( )
public String getOnblur( )
public String getOnchange( )
public String getOnclick( )
public String getOndblclick( )
public String getOnfocus( )
public String getOnkeydown( )
public String getOnkeypress( )
public String getOnkeyup( )
public String getOnmousedown( )
public String getOnmousemove( )
public String getOnmouseout( )
```

```
public String getOnmouseover( )
public String getOnmouseup( )
public String getOnselect( )
public String getRows( )
public String getStyle( )
public String getStyleClass( )
public String getTabindex( )
public String getTitle( )
public boolean isDisabled( )
public boolean isReadonly( )
public void restoreState(javax.faces.context.FacesContext context, Object state)
public Object saveState(javax.faces.context.FacesContext context)
public void setAccesskey(String accesskey)
public void setCols(String alt)
public void setDir(String dir)
public void setDisabled(boolean disabled)
public void setLang(String lang)
public void setOnblur(String onblur)
public void setOnchange(String onchange)
public void setOnclick(String onclick)
public void setOndblclick(String ondblclick)
public void setOnfocus(String onfocus)
public void setOnkeydown(String onkeydown)
public void setOnkeypress(String onkeypress)
public void setOnkeyup(String onkeyup)
public void setOnmousedown(String onmousedown)
public void setOnmousemove(String onmousemove)
public void setOnmouseout(String onmouseout)
public void setOnmouseover(String onmouseover)
public void setOnmouseup(String onmouseup)
public void setOnselect(String onselect)
public void setReadonly(boolean readonly)
public void setRows(String size)
public void setStyle(String style)
public void setStyleClass(String styleClass)
public void setTabindex(String tabindex)
public void setTitle(String title)
```

HtmlMessage

The `HtmlMessage` class is the HTML rendering-dependent class representing the `UIMessage` component with a `javax.faces.Message` renderer.

Synopsis

Class name:	`javax.faces.component.html.HtmlMessage`
Extends:	`javax.faces.component.UIMessage`
Implements:	`javax.faces.component.StateHolder`

Fields

`public static String COMPONENT_TYPE`

The component family: `javax.faces.HtmlMessage`.

Constructor

`public HtmlMessage( )`

Creates a new instance.

Methods

```
public String getErrorClass( )
public String getErrorStyle( )
public String getFatalClass( )
public String getFatalStyle( )
public String getInfoClass( )
public String getInfoStyle( )
public String getStyle( )
public String getStyleClass( )
public String getTitle( )
public String getWarnClass( )
public String getWarnStyle( )
public boolean isTooltip( )
public void restoreState(javax.faces.context.FacesContext context, Object state)
public Object saveState(javax.faces.context.FacesContext context)
public void setErrorClass(String errorClass)
public void setErrorStyle(String errorStyle)
public void setFatalClass(String fatalClass)
public void setFatalStyle(String fatalStyle)
public void setInfoClass(String infoClass)
public void setInfoStyle(String infoStyle)
public void setStyle(String style)
public void setStyleClass(String styleClass)
public void setTitle(String title)
public void setTooltip(boolean tooltip)
public void setWarnClass(String warnClass)
public void setWarnStyle(String warnStyle)
```

HtmlMessages

The `HtmlMessages` class is the HTML rendering-dependent class representing the `UIMessages` component with a `javax.faces.Messages` renderer.

Synopsis

Class name:	`javax.faces.component.html.HtmlMessages`
Extends:	`javax.faces.component.UIMessages`
Implements:	`javax.faces.component.StateHolder`

Fields

```
public static String COMPONENT_TYPE
```

The component family: `javax.faces.HtmlMessages`.

Constructor

```
public HtmlMessages( )
```

Creates a new instance.

Methods

```
public String getErrorClass( )
public String getErrorStyle( )
public String getFatalClass( )
public String getFatalStyle( )
public String getInfoClass( )
public String getInfoStyle( )
public String getLayout( )
public String getStyle( )
public String getStyleClass( )
public String getTitle( )
public String getWarnClass( )
public String getWarnStyle( )
public boolean isTooltip( )
public void restoreState(javax.faces.context.FacesContext context, Object state)
public Object saveState(javax.faces.context.FacesContext context)
public void setErrorClass(String errorClass)
public void setErrorStyle(String errorStyle)
public void setFatalClass(String fatalClass)
public void setFatalStyle(String fatalStyle)
public void setInfoClass(String infoClass)
public void setInfoStyle(String infoStyle)
public void setLayout(String layout)
public void setStyle(String style)
public void setStyleClass(String styleClass)
public void setTitle(String title)
public void setTooltip(boolean tooltip)
public void setWarnClass(String warnClass)
public void setWarnStyle(String warnStyle)
```

HtmlOutputFormat

The `HtmlOutputFormat` class is the HTML rendering-dependent class representing the `UIOutput` component with a `javax.faces.Format` renderer.

Synopsis

Class name:	`javax.faces.component.html.HtmlOutputFormat`
Extends:	`javax.faces.component.UIOutput`
Implements:	`javax.faces.component.StateHolder`, `javax.faces.component.ValueHolder`

Fields

`public static String COMPONENT_TYPE`
The component family: `javax.faces.HtmlOutputFormat`.

Constructor

`public HtmlOutputFormat( )`
Creates a new instance.

Methods

```
public String getStyle( )
public String getStyleClass( )
public String getTitle( )
public boolean isEscape( )
public void restoreState(javax.faces.context.FacesContext context, Object state)
public Object saveState(javax.faces.context.FacesContext context)
public void setEscape(boolean escape)
public void setStyle(String style)
public void setStyleClass(String styleClass)
public void setTitle(String title)
```

HtmlOutputLabel

The `HtmlOutputLabel` class is the HTML rendering-dependent class representing the `UIOutput` component with a `javax.faces.Label` renderer.

Synopsis

Class name:	`javax.faces.component.html.HtmlOutputLabel`
Extends:	`javax.faces.component.UIOutput`
Implements:	`javax.faces.component.StateHolder`, `javax.faces.component.ValueHolder`

Fields

`public static String COMPONENT_TYPE`
The component family: `javax.faces.HtmlOutputFormat`.

Constructor

`public HtmlOutputLabel( )`
Creates a new instance.

Methods

```
public String getAccesskey( )
public String getDir( )
public String getFor( )
public String getLang( )
public String getOnblur( )
public String getOnchange( )
```

```
public String getOnclick()
public String getOndblclick()
public String getOnfocus()
public String getOnkeydown()
public String getOnkeypress()
public String getOnkeyup()
public String getOnmousedown()
public String getOnmousemove()
public String getOnmouseout()
public String getOnmouseover()
public String getOnmouseup()
public String getStyle()
public String getStyleClass()
public String getTabindex()
public String getTitle()
public void restoreState(javax.faces.context.FacesContext context, Object state)
public Object saveState(javax.faces.context.FacesContext context)
public void setAccesskey(String accesskey)
public void setDir(String dir)
public void setFor(String for)
public void setLang(String lang)
public void setOnblur(String onblur)
public void setOnchange(String onchange)
public void setOnclick(String onclick)
public void setOndblclick(String ondblclick)
public void setOnfocus(String onfocus)
public void setOnkeydown(String onkeydown)
public void setOnkeypress(String onkeypress)
public void setOnkeyup(String onkeyup)
public void setOnmousedown(String onmousedown)
public void setOnmousemove(String onmousemove)
public void setOnmouseout(String onmouseout)
public void setOnmouseover(String onmouseover)
public void setOnmouseup(String onmouseup)
public void setStyle(String style)
public void setStyleClass(String styleClass)
public void setTabindex(String tabindex)
public void setTitle(String title)
```

HtmlOutputLink

The `HtmlOutputLink` class is the HTML rendering-dependent class representing the `UIOutput` component with a `javax.faces.Link` renderer.

Synopsis

Class name:	`javax.faces.component.html.HtmlOutputLink`
Extends:	`javax.faces.component.UIOutput`
Implements:	`javax.faces.component.StateHolder`, `javax.faces.component.ValueHolder`

Fields

`public static String COMPONENT_TYPE`

The component family: `javax.faces.HtmlOutputLink`.

Constructor

`public HtmlOutputLink( )`

Creates a new instance.

Methods

```
public String getAccesskey( )
public String getCharset( )
public String getCoords( )
public String getDir( )
public String getHreflang( )
public String getLang( )
public String getOnblur( )
public String getOnchange( )
public String getOnclick( )
public String getOndblclick( )
public String getOnfocus( )
public String getOnkeydown( )
public String getOnkeypress( )
public String getOnkeyup( )
public String getOnmousedown( )
public String getOnmousemove( )
public String getOnmouseout( )
public String getOnmouseover( )
public String getOnmouseup( )
public String getRel( )
public String getRev( )
public String getShape( )
public String getStyle( )
public String getStyleClass( )
public String getTabindex( )
public String getTarget( )
public String getTitle( )
public String getType( )
public void restoreState(javax.faces.context.FacesContext context, Object state)
public Object saveState(javax.faces.context.FacesContext context)
public void setAccesskey(String accesskey)
public void setCharset(String charset)
public void setCoords(String coords)
public void setDir(String dir)
public void setHreflang(String hreflang)
public void setLang(String lang)
public void setOnblur(String onblur)
public void setOnchange(String onchange)
public void setOnclick(String onclick)
public void setOndblclick(String ondblclick)
public void setOnfocus(String onfocus)
public void setOnkeydown(String onkeydown)
```

```
public void setOnkeypress(String onkeypress)
public void setOnkeyup(String onkeyup)
public void setOnmousedown(String onmousedown)
public void setOnmousemove(String onmousemove)
public void setOnmouseout(String onmouseout)
public void setOnmouseover(String onmouseover)
public void setOnmouseup(String onmouseup)
public void setRel(String rel)
public void setRev(String rev)
public void setShape(String shape)
public void setStyle(String style)
public void setStyleClass(String styleClass)
public void setTabindex(String tabindex)
public void setTarget(String target)
public void setTitle(String title)
public void setType(String type)
```

HtmlOutputText

The `HtmlOutputText` class is the HTML rendering-dependent class representing the `UIOutput` component with a `javax.faces.Text` renderer.

Synopsis

Class name:	`javax.faces.component.html.HtmlOutputText`
Extends:	`javax.faces.component.UIOutput`
Implements:	`javax.faces.component.StateHolder`, `javax.faces.component.ValueHolder`

Fields

`public static String COMPONENT_TYPE`

The component family: `javax.faces.HtmlOutputText`.

Constructor

`public HtmlOutputText( )`

Creates a new instance.

Methods

```
public String getStyle( )
public String getStyleClass( )
public String getTitle( )
public boolean isEscape( )
public void restoreState(javax.faces.context.FacesContext context, Object state)
public Object saveState(javax.faces.context.FacesContext context)
public void setEscape(boolean escape)
public void setStyle(String style)
public void setStyleClass(String styleClass)
public void setTitle(String title)
```

HtmlPanelGrid

The `HtmlPanelGrid` class is the HTML rendering-dependent class representing the `UIPanel` component with a `javax.faces.Grid` renderer.

Synopsis

Class name:	`javax.faces.component.html.HtmlPanelGrid`
Extends:	`javax.faces.component.UIPanel`
Implements:	`javax.faces.component.StateHolder`

Fields

`public static String COMPONENT_TYPE`

The component family: `javax.faces.HtmlPanelGrid`.

Constructor

`public HtmlPanelGrid( )`

Creates a new instance.

Methods

```
public String getBgcolor( )
public String getBorder( )
public String getCellpadding( )
public String getCellspacing( )
public String getColumnClasses( )
public int getColumns( )
public String getDir( )
public String getFooterClass( )
public String getFrame( )
public String getHeaderClass( )
public String getLang( )
public String getOnclick( )
public String getOndblclick( )
public String getOnkeydown( )
public String getOnkeypress( )
public String getOnkeyup( )
public String getOnmousedown( )
public String getOnmousemove( )
public String getOnmouseout( )
public String getOnmouseover( )
public String getOnmouseup( )
public String getRowClasses( )
public String getRules( )
public String getStyle( )
public String getStyleClass( )
public String getSummary( )
public String getTitle( )
public String getWidth( )
public void restoreState(javax.faces.context.FacesContext context, Object state)
public Object saveState(javax.faces.context.FacesContext context)
```

```
public void setBgcolor(String bgcolor)
public void setBorder(String border)
public void setCellpadding(String cellpadding)
public void setCellspacing(String cellspacing)
public void setColumnClasses(String columnClasses)
public void setColumns(int columns)
public void setDir(String dir)
public void setFooterClass(String footerClass)
public void setFrame(String frame)
public void setHeaderClass(String headerClass)
public void setLang(String lang)
public void setOnclick(String onclick)
public void setOndblclick(String ondblclick)
public void setOnfocus(String onfocus)
public void setOnkeydown(String onkeydown)
public void setOnkeypress(String onkeypress)
public void setOnkeyup(String onkeyup)
public void setOnmousedown(String onmousedown)
public void setOnmousemove(String onmousemove)
public void setOnmouseout(String onmouseout)
public void setOnmouseover(String onmouseover)
public void setOnmouseup(String onmouseup)
public void setRowClasses(String rowClasses)
public void setRules(String rules)
public void setStyle(String style)
public void setStyleClass(String styleClass)
public void setSummary(String summary)
public void setTitle(String title)
public void setWidth(String width)
```

HtmlPanelGroup

The `HtmlPanelGroup` class is the HTML rendering-dependent class representing the `UIPanel` component with a `javax.faces.Group` renderer.

Synopsis

Class name:	`javax.faces.component.html.HtmlPanelGroup`
Extends:	`javax.faces.component.UIPanel`
Implements:	`javax.faces.component.StateHolder`

Fields

`public static String COMPONENT_TYPE`

The component family: `javax.faces.HtmlPanelGroup`.

Constructor

`public HtmlPanelGroup()`

Creates a new instance.

Methods

```
public String getStyle()
public String getStyleClass()
public void restoreState(javax.faces.context.FacesContext context, Object state)
public Object saveState(javax.faces.context.FacesContext context)
public void setStyle(String style)
public void setStyleClass(String styleClass)
```

HtmlSelectBooleanCheckbox

The `HtmlSelectBooleanCheckbox` class is the HTML rendering-dependent class representing the `UISelectBoolean` component with a `javax.faces.Checkbox` renderer.

Synopsis

Class name:	`javax.faces.component.html.HtmlSelectBooleanCheckbox`
Extends:	`javax.faces.component.UISelectBoolean`
Implements:	`javax.faces.component.EditableValueHolder`, `javax.faces.component.StateHolder`

Fields

`public static String COMPONENT_TYPE`

The component family: `javax.faces.HtmlSelectBooleanCheckbox`.

Constructor

`public HtmlSelectBooleanCheckbox()`

Creates a new instance.

Methods

```
public String getAccesskey()
public String getDir()
public String getLang()
public String getOnblur()
public String getOnchange()
public String getOnclick()
public String getOndblclick()
public String getOnfocus()
public String getOnkeydown()
public String getOnkeypress()
public String getOnkeyup()
public String getOnmousedown()
public String getOnmousemove()
public String getOnmouseout()
public String getOnmouseover()
public String getOnmouseup()
public String getOnselect()
public String getStyle()
public String getStyleClass()
public String getTabindex()
```

```
public String getTitle( )
public boolean isDisabled( )
public boolean isReadonly( )
public void restoreState(javax.faces.context.FacesContext context, Object state)
public Object saveState(javax.faces.context.FacesContext context)
public void setAccesskey(String accesskey)
public void setDir(String dir)
public void setDisabled(boolean disabled)
public void setLang(String lang)
public void setOnblur(String onblur)
public void setOnchange(String onchange)
public void setOnclick(String onclick)
public void setOndblclick(String ondblclick)
public void setOnfocus(String onfocus)
public void setOnkeydown(String onkeydown)
public void setOnkeypress(String onkeypress)
public void setOnkeyup(String onkeyup)
public void setOnmousedown(String onmousedown)
public void setOnmousemove(String onmousemove)
public void setOnmouseout(String onmouseout)
public void setOnmouseover(String onmouseover)
public void setOnmouseup(String onmouseup)
public void setOnselect(String onselect)
public void setReadonly(boolean readonly)
public void setStyle(String style)
public void setStyleClass(String styleClass)
public void setTabindex(String tabindex)
public void setTitle(String title)
```

HtmlSelectManyCheckbox

The `HtmlSelectManyCheckbox` class is the HTML rendering-dependent class representing the `UISelectMany` component with a `javax.faces.Checkbox` renderer.

Synopsis

Class name:	`javax.faces.component.html.HtmlSelectManyCheckbox`
Extends:	`javax.faces.component.UISelectMany`
Implements:	`javax.faces.component.EditableValueHolder`, `javax.faces.component.StateHolder`

Fields

`public static String COMPONENT_TYPE`

The component family: `javax.faces.HtmlSelectManyCheckbox`.

Constructor

`public HtmlSelectManyCheckbox( )`

Creates a new instance.

Methods

```
public String getAccesskey( )
public String getBorder( )
public String getDir( )
public String getDisabledClass( )
public String getEnabledClass( )
public String getLang( )
public String getLayout( )
public String getOnblur( )
public String getOnchange( )
public String getOnclick( )
public String getOndblclick( )
public String getOnfocus( )
public String getOnkeydown( )
public String getOnkeypress( )
public String getOnkeyup( )
public String getOnmousedown( )
public String getOnmousemove( )
public String getOnmouseout( )
public String getOnmouseover( )
public String getOnmouseup( )
public String getOnselect( )
public String getStyle( )
public String getStyleClass( )
public String getTabindex( )
public String getTitle( )
public boolean isDisabled( )
public boolean isReadonly( )
public void restoreState(javax.faces.context.FacesContext context, Object state)
public Object saveState(javax.faces.context.FacesContext context)
public void setAccesskey(String accesskey)
public void setBorder(String border)
public void setDir(String dir)
public void setDisabled(boolean disabled)
public void setDisabledClass(String disabledClass)
public void setEnabledClass(String enabledClass)
public void setLang(String lang)
public void setLayout(String layout)
public void setOnblur(String onblur)
public void setOnchange(String onchange)
public void setOnclick(String onclick)
public void setOndblclick(String ondblclick)
public void setOnfocus(String onfocus)
public void setOnkeydown(String onkeydown)
public void setOnkeypress(String onkeypress)
public void setOnkeyup(String onkeyup)
public void setOnmousedown(String onmousedown)
public void setOnmousemove(String onmousemove)
public void setOnmouseout(String onmouseout)
public void setOnmouseover(String onmouseover)
public void setOnmouseup(String onmouseup)
public void setOnselect(String onselect)
public void setReadonly(boolean readonly)
```

```
public void setStyle(String style)
public void setStyleClass(String styleClass)
public void setTabindex(String tabindex)
public void setTitle(String title)
```

HtmlSelectManyListbox

The `HtmlSelectManyListbox` class is the HTML rendering-dependent class representing the `UISelectMany` component with a `javax.faces.Listbox` renderer.

Synopsis

Class name:	`javax.faces.component.html.HtmlSelectManyListbox`
Extends:	`javax.faces.component.UISelectMany`
Implements:	`javax.faces.component.EditableValueHolder`, `javax.faces.component.StateHolder`

Fields

`public static String COMPONENT_TYPE`

The component family: `javax.faces.HtmlSelectManyListbox`.

Constructor

`public HtmlSelectManyListbox( )`

Creates a new instance.

Methods

```
public String getAccesskey( )
public String getDir( )
public String getLang( )
public String getOnblur( )
public String getOnchange( )
public String getOnclick( )
public String getOndblclick( )
public String getOnfocus( )
public String getOnkeydown( )
public String getOnkeypress( )
public String getOnkeyup( )
public String getOnmousedown( )
public String getOnmousemove( )
public String getOnmouseout( )
public String getOnmouseover( )
public String getOnmouseup( )
public String getOnselect( )
public int getSize( )
public String getStyle( )
public String getStyleClass( )
public String getTabindex( )
public String getTitle( )
public boolean isDisabled( )
```

```
public boolean isReadonly( )
public void restoreState(javax.faces.context.FacesContext context, Object state)
public Object saveState(javax.faces.context.FacesContext context)
public void setAccesskey(String accesskey)
public void setDir(String dir)
public void setDisabled(boolean disabled)
public void setLang(String lang)
public void setOnblur(String onblur)
public void setOnchange(String onchange)
public void setOnclick(String onclick)
public void setOndblclick(String ondblclick)
public void setOnfocus(String onfocus)
public void setOnkeydown(String onkeydown)
public void setOnkeypress(String onkeypress)
public void setOnkeyup(String onkeyup)
public void setOnmousedown(String onmousedown)
public void setOnmousemove(String onmousemove)
public void setOnmouseout(String onmouseout)
public void setOnmouseover(String onmouseover)
public void setOnmouseup(String onmouseup)
public void setOnselect(String onselect)
public void setReadonly(boolean readonly)
public void setSize(int size)
public void setStyle(String style)
public void setStyleClass(String styleClass)
public void setTabindex(String tabindex)
public void setTitle(String title)
```

HtmlSelectManyMenu

The `HtmlSelectManyMenu` class is the HTML rendering-dependent class representing the `UISelectMany` component with a `javax.faces.Menu` renderer.

Synopsis

Class name:	`javax.faces.component.html.HtmlSelectManyMenu`
Extends:	`javax.faces.component.UISelectMany`
Implements:	`javax.faces.component.EditableValueHolder,` `javax.faces.component.StateHolder`

Fields

`public static String COMPONENT_TYPE`

The component family: `javax.faces.HtmlSelectManyMenu`.

Constructor

`public HtmlSelectManyMenu( )`

Creates a new instance.

Methods

```
public String getAccesskey( )
public String getDir( )
public String getLang( )
public String getOnblur( )
public String getOnchange( )
public String getOnclick( )
public String getOndblclick( )
public String getOnfocus( )
public String getOnkeydown( )
public String getOnkeypress( )
public String getOnkeyup( )
public String getOnmousedown( )
public String getOnmousemove( )
public String getOnmouseout( )
public String getOnmouseover( )
public String getOnmouseup( )
public String getOnselect( )
public String getStyle( )
public String getStyleClass( )
public String getTabindex( )
public String getTitle( )
public boolean isDisabled( )
public boolean isReadonly( )
public void restoreState(javax.faces.context.FacesContext context, Object state)
public Object saveState(javax.faces.context.FacesContext context)
public void setAccesskey(String accesskey)
public void setDir(String dir)
public void setDisabled(boolean disabled)
public void setLang(String lang)
public void setOnblur(String onblur)
public void setOnchange(String onchange)
public void setOnclick(String onclick)
public void setOndblclick(String ondblclick)
public void setOnfocus(String onfocus)
public void setOnkeydown(String onkeydown)
public void setOnkeypress(String onkeypress)
public void setOnkeyup(String onkeyup)
public void setOnmousedown(String onmousedown)
public void setOnmousemove(String onmousemove)
public void setOnmouseout(String onmouseout)
public void setOnmouseover(String onmouseover)
public void setOnmouseup(String onmouseup)
public void setOnselect(String onselect)
public void setReadonly(boolean readonly)
public void setStyle(String style)
public void setStyleClass(String styleClass)
public void setTabindex(String tabindex)
public void setTitle(String title)
```

HtmlSelectOneListbox

The `HtmlSelectOneListbox` class is the HTML rendering-dependent class representing the `UISelectOne` component with a `javax.faces.Listbox` renderer.

Synopsis

Class name:	`javax.faces.component.html.HtmlSelectOneListbox`
Extends:	`javax.faces.component.UISelectOne`
Implements:	`javax.faces.component.EditableValueHolder,` `javax.faces.component.StateHolder`

Fields

`public static String COMPONENT_TYPE`

The component family: `javax.faces.HtmlSelectOneListbox`.

Constructor

`public HtmlSelectOneListbox( )`

Creates a new instance.

Methods

```
public String getAccesskey( )
public String getDir( )
public String getLang( )
public String getOnblur( )
public String getOnchange( )
public String getOnclick( )
public String getOndblclick( )
public String getOnfocus( )
public String getOnkeydown( )
public String getOnkeypress( )
public String getOnkeyup( )
public String getOnmousedown( )
public String getOnmousemove( )
public String getOnmouseout( )
public String getOnmouseover( )
public String getOnmouseup( )
public String getOnselect( )
public int getSize( )
public String getStyle( )
public String getStyleClass( )
public String getTabindex( )
public String getTitle( )
public boolean isDisabled( )
public boolean isReadonly( )
public void restoreState(javax.faces.context.FacesContext context, Object state)
public Object saveState(javax.faces.context.FacesContext context)
public void setAccesskey(String accesskey)
public void setDir(String dir)
public void setDisabled(boolean disabled)
public void setLang(String lang)
```

```
public void setOnblur(String onblur)
public void setOnchange(String onchange)
public void setOnclick(String onclick)
public void setOndblclick(String ondblclick)
public void setOnfocus(String onfocus)
public void setOnkeydown(String onkeydown)
public void setOnkeypress(String onkeypress)
public void setOnkeyup(String onkeyup)
public void setOnmousedown(String onmousedown)
public void setOnmousemove(String onmousemove)
public void setOnmouseout(String onmouseout)
public void setOnmouseover(String onmouseover)
public void setOnmouseup(String onmouseup)
public void setOnselect(String onselect)
public void setReadonly(boolean readonly)
public void setSize(int size)
public void setStyle(String style)
public void setStyleClass(String styleClass)
public void setTabindex(String tabindex)
public void setTitle(String title)
```

HtmlSelectOneMenu

The `HtmlSelectOneMenu` class is the HTML rendering-dependent class representing the `UISelectOne` component with a `javax.faces.Menu` renderer.

Synopsis

Class name:	`javax.faces.component.html.HtmlSelectOneMenu`
Extends:	`javax.faces.component.UISelectOne`
Implements:	`javax.faces.component.EditableValueHolder`, `javax.faces.component.StateHolder`

Fields

`public static String COMPONENT_TYPE`

The component family: `javax.faces.HtmlSelectoneMenu`.

Constructor

`public HtmlSelectOneMenu()`

Creates a new instance.

Methods

```
public String getAccesskey()
public String getDir()
public String getLang()
public String getOnblur()
public String getOnchange()
public String getOnclick()
public String getOndblclick()
public String getOnfocus()
```

```
public String getOnkeydown( )
public String getOnkeypress( )
public String getOnkeyup( )
public String getOnmousedown( )
public String getOnmousemove( )
public String getOnmouseout( )
public String getOnmouseover( )
public String getOnmouseup( )
public String getOnselect( )
public String getStyle( )
public String getStyleClass( )
public String getTabindex( )
public String getTitle( )
public boolean isDisabled( )
public boolean isReadonly( )
public void restoreState(javax.faces.context.FacesContext context, Object state)
public Object saveState(javax.faces.context.FacesContext context)
public void setAccesskey(String accesskey)
public void setDir(String dir)
public void setDisabled(boolean disabled)
public void setLang(String lang)
public void setOnblur(String onblur)
public void setOnchange(String onchange)
public void setOnclick(String onclick)
public void setOndblclick(String ondblclick)
public void setOnfocus(String onfocus)
public void setOnkeydown(String onkeydown)
public void setOnkeypress(String onkeypress)
public void setOnkeyup(String onkeyup)
public void setOnmousedown(String onmousedown)
public void setOnmousemove(String onmousemove)
public void setOnmouseout(String onmouseout)
public void setOnmouseover(String onmouseover)
public void setOnmouseup(String onmouseup)
public void setOnselect(String onselect)
public void setReadonly(boolean readonly)
public void setStyle(String style)
public void setStyleClass(String styleClass)
public void setTabindex(String tabindex)
public void setTitle(String title)
```

HtmlSelectOneRadio

The `HtmlSelectOneRadio` class is the HTML rendering-dependent class representing the `UISelectOne` component with a `javax.faces.Radio` renderer.

Synopsis

Class name:	`javax.faces.component.html.HtmlSelectOneRadio`
Extends:	`javax.faces.component.UISelectOne`
Implements:	`javax.faces.component.EditableValueHolder`, `javax.faces.component.StateHolder`

Fields

`public static String COMPONENT_TYPE`

The component family: `javax.faces.HtmlSelectOneRadio`.

Constructor

`public HtmlSelectOneRadio( )`

Creates a new instance.

Methods

```
public String getAccesskey( )
public String getBorder( )
public String getDir( )
public String getDisabledClass( )
public String getEnabledClass( )
public String getLang( )
public String getLayout( )
public String getOnblur( )
public String getOnchange( )
public String getOnclick( )
public String getOndblclick( )
public String getOnfocus( )
public String getOnkeydown( )
public String getOnkeypress( )
public String getOnkeyup( )
public String getOnmousedown( )
public String getOnmousemove( )
public String getOnmouseout( )
public String getOnmouseover( )
public String getOnmouseup( )
public String getOnselect( )
public String getStyle( )
public String getStyleClass( )
public String getTabindex( )
public String getTitle( )
public boolean isDisabled( )
public boolean isReadonly( )
public void restoreState(javax.faces.context.FacesContext context, Object state)
public Object saveState(javax.faces.context.FacesContext context)
public void setAccesskey(String accesskey)
public void setBorder(String border)
public void setDir(String dir)
public void setDisabled(boolean disabled)
public void setDisabledClass(String disabledClass)
public void setEnabledClass(String enabledClass)
public void setLang(String lang)
public void setLayout(String layout)
public void setOnblur(String onblur)
public void setOnchange(String onchange)
public void setOnclick(String onclick)
public void setOndblclick(String ondblclick)
public void setOnfocus(String onfocus)
```

```
public void setOnkeydown(String onkeydown)
public void setOnkeypress(String onkeypress)
public void setOnkeyup(String onkeyup)
public void setOnmousedown(String onmousedown)
public void setOnmousemove(String onmousemove)
public void setOnmouseout(String onmouseout)
public void setOnmouseover(String onmouseover)
public void setOnmouseup(String onmouseup)
public void setOnselect(String onselect)
public void setReadonly(boolean readonly)
public void setStyle(String style)
public void setStyleClass(String styleClass)
public void setTabindex(String tabindex)
public void setTitle(String title)
```

Request Processing Lifecycle

When JSF view is requested, the components in the view are asked to perform tasks in a certain order, defined as phases of a request processing lifecycle. This section describes the main events for each phase.

Restore View

The requested view is restored from state sent with the request or available on the server, or created if no view state is available. The specification leaves the details up to the implementation, but the components' `restoreState( )` method is called in this phase if the `saveState( )` method was called earlier to save the state. If a new view is created in this phase, at least the `UIViewRoot` component is created and the processing continues in the Render Response phase.

Apply Request Values

The `processDecodes( )` method is called on the `UIViewRoot` component, causing the same method to be called recursively on all components in the component tree with the `rendered` property set to `true`, which in turn calls the `decode( )` method on the component (or its renderer). The `decode( )` method for an input component sets the `submittedValue` property for the component. For input components with the `immediate` property set to `true`, the submitted value is also converted and validated in this phase by calling the `validate( )` method, causing a `ValueChangeEvent` to be queued if the validated value differs from the previous value and the local value to be set to the converted, validated submitted value. If the submitted value is invalid, an error message is queued and the `FacesContext` `renderResponse( )` method is called. For a command component, the `decode( )` method queues an `ActionEvent` if the component triggered the request.

At the end of this phase, the `broadcast()` method of the source components for all events marked to be processed in any phase or in the Apply Request Values phase is called to notify the event handlers. The event handlers may call the `FacesContext` `renderResponse()` method, possibly after selecting a new view. If so, the processing continues in the Render Response phase. Alternatively, an event handler may render a response itself and call the `FacesContext` `responseComplete()` method, in which case the request processing is terminated.

Process Validations

The `processValidators()` method is called on the `UIViewRoot` component, causing the same method to be called recursively on all components in the component tree with the `rendered` property set to `true` and that were not validated during the Apply Request Values phase, which in turn calls the `validate()` method on the component if its an input component. Calling the `validate()` method causes a `ValueChangeEvent` to be queued if the validated value differs from the previous value and the local value to be set to the converted, validated submitted value. If the submitted value is invalid, an error message is queued and the `FacesContext` `renderResponse()` method is called.

At the end of this phase, the `broadcast()` method of the source components for all events marked to be processed in any phase or in the Process Validations phase is called to notify the event handlers. The event handlers may call the `FacesContext` `renderResponse()` method, possibly after selecting a new view. If so, the processing continues in the Render Response phase. Alternatively, an event handler may render a response itself and call the `FacesContext` `responseComplete()` method, in which case the request processing is terminated.

Update Model Values

When this phase is reached, all submitted values have been validated and converted to the appropriate local value data type. The `processUpdates()` method is called on the `UIViewRoot` component, causing the same method to be called recursively on all components in the component tree with the `rendered` property set to `true`, which in turn calls the `updateModel()` method on the component if its an input component. Calling the `updateModel()` method sets the property of the application object the component is bound to, if any, to the component's local value. If the property can't be set, an error message is queued and the `FacesContext` `renderResponse()` method is called.

At the end of this phase, the `broadcast()` method of the source components for all events marked to be processed in any phase or in the Update Model Values phase is called to notify the event handlers. The event handlers may call the `FacesContext` `renderResponse()` method, possibly after selecting a new view. If so, the processing continues in the Render Response phase. Alternatively, an event handler may render a response itself and call the FacesContext responseComplete( ) method, in which case the request processing is terminated.

Invoke Application

When this phase is reached, all application bean properties bound to input components have been set. The processApplication( ) method is called on the UIViewRoot component, causing the broadcast( ) method of the source components for all events marked to be processed in any phase or in the Invoke Application phase to be called to notify the event handlers. The event handlers may call the FacesContext renderResponse( ) method, possibly after selecting a new view. If so, the processing continues in the Render Response phase. Alternatively, an event handler may render a response itself and call the FacesContext responseComplete( ) method, in which case the request processing is terminated.

Render Response

In the phase, the component tree is rendered. The specification only defines the behavior for the JSP presentation layer an leaves the details up to the implementation for other presentation layer technologies. For the JSP layer, the JSP page is processed. If this is the first time the view is rendered, the JSF action elements in the page creates and configures the components they represent and ask them to render themselves by calling the encoding methods; otherwise the components are just asked to render themselves. The components' saveState( ) method may be called in this phase and the state for the complete tree included in the response—for example, as hidden fields in each HTML form.

APPENDIX D

Infrastructure API Reference

This appendix contains reference material for the JSF classes and interfaces other than the component, model and renderer classes described in Appendix C. All JSF implementations must provide default versions of all of these types, but an application can be configured to use customized versions of most of them.

Package javax.faces

FacesException

This class is extended by all other JSF exception classes.

Synopsis

Class name:	`javax.faces.FacesException`
Extends:	`java.lang.RuntimeException`
Implements:	`java.io.Serializable`

Constructors

`public FacesException()`
: Creates an empty instance.

`public FacesException(String message)`
: Creates an instance with the specified message.

`public FacesException(String message, Throwable rootCause)`
: Creates an instance with the specified message and root cause.

`public FacesException(Throwable rootCause)`
: Creates an instance with the specified root cause.

Methods

`public Throwable getCause()`
: Returns the root cause or null if none is set.

FactoryFinder

This class represents the registry for all JSF factory classes: `javax.faces.application.ApplicationFactory`, `javax.faces.context.FacesContextFactory`, `javax.faces.lifecycle.LifeCycleFactory` and `javax.faces.render.RenderKitFactory`. An application can be configured to use customized versions of all the factory classes, which in turn can create instances of customized versions of the classes they are responsible for.

The `FactoryFinder` returns instances of factory classes declared in one of these locations, listed in decreasing precedence order:

1. The factory class declared in the application's *WEB-INF/faces-config.xml* file.
2. The factory class declared in the last JSF configuration file declared by the `javax.faces.CONFIG_FILE` context initialization parameter.
3. The factory class declared in the JSF configuration file by a *META-INF/faces-config.xml* file in the last JAR file found in the application's resource path, e.g., the JAR files in the *WEB-INF/lib* directory.
4. The factory class named on the first line of a *META-INF/services/{factory-class-name}* resource available to the application's class loader.
5. The JSF implementation's default class.

Synopsis

Class name:	`javax.faces.FactoryFinder`
Extends:	None
Implements:	None

Fields

`public static String APPLICATION_FACTORY`
The factory name for the `ApplicationFactory` class: `javax.faces.application.ApplicationFacory`.

`public static String FACES_CONTEXT_FACTORY`
The factory name for the `FacesContextFactory` class: `javax.faces.context.FacesContextFacory`.

`public static String LIFECYCLE_FACTORY`
The factory name for the `LifecycleFactory` class: `javax.faces.lifecycle.LifecycleFacory`.

`public static String RENDER_KIT_FACTORY`
The factory name for the `RenderKitFactory` class: `javax.faces.render.RenderKitFacory`.

Methods

`public static Object getFactory(String factoryName)`
Returns the per-application single instance of the class registered for the named factory.

`public static void releaseFactories()`
Releases all references to the factory class instances. This method should be called only by the JSF implementation when the web application is shut down.

public static void setFactory(String factoryName, String factoryClassName)

Creates a mapping between the factory name and an implementation class, unless the named factory has already been looked up by a previous call to the getFactory() method. This method should be called only by the JSF implementation to create mappings corresponding to the precedence rules.

Package javax.faces.application

Application

A single instance of a subclass of this abstract class per application creates instances of pluggable application classes or the default class if no customized version is registered.

Synopsis

Class name:	javax.faces.application.Application
Extends:	None
Implements:	None

Constructors

public Application()

Creates an instance.

Methods

public abstract void addComponent(String componentType, String componentClassName)

Registers a mapping between a component type ID and a component implementation class name.

public abstract void addConverter(Class targetClass, String converterClassName)

Registers a mapping between a Class and a Converter implementation class name.

public abstract void addConverter(String converterId, String converterClassName)

Registers a mapping between a converter ID and a Converter implementation class name.

public abstract void addValidator(String validatorId, String converterClassName)

Registers a mapping between a validator ID and a Validator implementation class name.

public abstract javax.faces.component.UIComponent
createComponent(String componentType) throws javax.faces.FacesException

Returns a new instance of the UIComponent class registered for the component type ID.

public abstract javax.faces.component.UIComponent
createComponent(javax.faces.el.ValueBinding componentBinding,
javax.faces.context.FacesContext context, String componentType)
throws javax.faces.el.FacesException

Calls the ValueBinding getValue() method. If it returns a UIComponent instance, returns it. Otherwise, creates an instance of the class registered for the component type ID, calls the ValueBinding setValue() with the component instance, and returns the component instance.

`public abstract javax.faces.convert.Converter createConverter(Class targetClass) throws javax.faces.el.FacesException`

Returns a new instance of the `Converter` class registered for the target `Class`.

`public abstract javax.faces.convert.Converter createConverter(String converterId) throws javax.faces.el.FacesException`

Returns a new instance of the `Converter` class registered for the converter ID.

`public abstract javax.faces.el.MethodBinding createMethodBinding(String expr, Class[] params) throws javax.faces.el.ReferenceSyntaxException`

Returns a new `MethodBinding` instance for a method represented by the method binding expression with a signature matching the provided parameter list or that takes no parameters if the parameter list is `null` or an empty array.

`public abstract javax.faces.validator.Validator createValidator(String validatorId)`

Returns a new instance of the `Validator` class registered for the validator ID.

`public abstract javax.faces.el.ValueBinding createValueBinding(String expr) throws javax.faces.el.ReferenceSyntaxException`

Returns a new `ValueBinding` instance for representing the EL expression.

`public abstract javax.faces.event.ActionListener getActionListener()`

Returns an instance of the default `ActionListener` instance used for `ActionSource` components within the application. If no custom version is registered, returns an instance that invokes the component's action `MethodBinding` `invoke()` method, the applications `NavigationHandler` `handleNavigation()` method with the action methods outcome, and the `FacesContext` `renderResponse()` method.

`public abstract java.util.Iterator getComponentTypes()`

Returns an `Iterator` over all registered component type IDs.

`public abstract java.util.Iterator getConverterIds()`

Returns an `Iterator` over all registered converter IDs.

`public abstract java.util.Iterator getConverterTypes()`

Returns an `Iterator` over all `Class` instances for which a `Converter` is registered.

`public abstract java.util.Locale getDefaultLocale()`

Returns the default `Locale` for this application.

`public abstract String getDefaultRenderKitId()`

Returns the default render kit ID for this application.

`public abstract String getMessageBundle()`

Returns the base name for the custom message bundle for this application.

`public abstract javax.faces.application.NavigationHandler getNavigationHandler()`

Returns the `NavigationHandler` for this application.

`public abstract javax.faces.el.PropertyResolver getPropertyResolver()`

Returns the `PropertyResolver` for this application.

`public abstract javax.faces.application.StateManager getStateManager()`

Returns the `StateManager` for this application.

`public abstract java.util.Iterator getSupportedLocales()`

Returns an `Iterator` over the supported `Locales` registered for the application.

`public abstract java.util.Iterator getValidatorIds( )`
: Returns an `Iterator` over all registered validator IDs.

`public abstract javax.faces.el.VariableResolver getVariableResolver( )`
: Returns the `VariableResolver` for this application.

`public abstract javax.faces.application.ViewHandler getViewHandler( )`
: Returns the `ViewHandler` for this application.

`public abstract setActionListener(javax.faces.event.ActionListener listener)`
: Registers the default `ActionListener` to use for all `ActionSource` components within this application.

`public abstract setDefaultLocale(java.util.Locale locale)`
: Registers the default `Locale` for this application.

`public abstract setDefaultRenderKitId(String renderKitId)`
: Registers the default render kit ID for this application.

`public abstract setMessageBundle(String baseName)`
: Registers the base name for the resource bundle that must be consulted in addition to the implementation's message resource bundle for this application.

`public abstract setNavigationHandler(javax.faces.application.NavigationHandler nh)`
: Registers a custom `NavigationHandler` for this application.

`public abstract setPropertyResolver(javax.faces.el.PropertyResolver pr)`
: Registers a custom `PropertyResolver` for this application.

`public abstract setStateManager(javax.faces.application.StateManager sm)`
: Registers a custom `StateManager` for this application.

`public abstract setSupportedLocales(java.util.Collection locales)`
: Registers all `Locale` instances supported in addition to the default locale for this application.

`public abstract setVariableResolver(javax.faces.el.VariableResolver vr)`
: Registers a custom `VariableResolver` for this application.

`public abstract setViewHandler(javax.faces.application.ViewHandler vh)`
: Registers a custom `ViewHandler` for this application.

ApplicationFactory

An instance of a subclass of this abstract class is a factory for the `Application` instance for an application.

Synopsis

Class name:	`javax.faces.application.ApplicationFactory`
Extends:	None
Implements:	None

Constructors

`public ApplicationFactory( )`
: Creates an instance.

Methods

`public abstract javax.faces.application.Application getApplication()`

Returns the `Application` instance for this application, which is either an explicitly registered instance or an instance of the default class.

`public abstract setApplication(javax.faces.application.Application)`

Registers an `Application` instance for this application.

FacesMessage

This class is the base class for all specific message subclasses. The messages created by a JSF implementation contain localized text for the `Locale` returned by the `UIViewRoot getLocale()` method from the resource bundle with the base name returned by the `Application getMessageBundle()` or the bundle with the base name defined by the `FACES_MESSAGES` constant, searched in that order.

Synopsis

Class name:	`javax.faces.application.FacesMessage`
Extends:	None
Implements:	`java.io.Serializable`

Fields

`public static final String FACES_MESSAGES`

The base name for the standard messages resource bundle: `javax.faces.Messages`.

`public static final FacesMessage.Serverity SEVERITY_ERROR`

The severity level value for error messages.

`public static final FacesMessage.Serverity SEVERITY_FATAL`

The severity level value for fatal error messages.

`public static final FacesMessage.Serverity SEVERITY_INFO`

The severity level value for informational messages.

`public static final FacesMessage.Serverity SEVERITY_WARN`

The severity level value for warning messages.

Constructors

`public FacesMessage()`

Creates an empty instance.

`public FacesMessage(FacesMessage.Severity severity, String summary, String detail)`

Creates an instance with the specified severity, summary, and detail texts.

`public FacesMessage(String summary)`

Creates an instance with the specified summary text.

`public FacesMessage(String summary, String detail)`

Creates an instance with the specified summary and detail texts.

Methods

`public String getDetail( )`
: Returns the detail text or the summary text if no detail text is defined.

`public FacesMessage.Severity getSeverity( )`
: Returns the severity level.

`public String getSummary( )`
: Returns the summary text or `null` if no summary text is defined.

`public void setDetail(String detail)`
: Sets the detail text.

`public void setSeverity(FacesMessage.Severity severity)`
: Sets the severity level.

`public void setSummary(String summary)`
: Sets the summary text.

FacesMessage.Severity

Instances of this nested class represent severity levels for `FacesMessage` instances. All instances are created by the `FacesMessage` class and made available through public final static fields, with ordinal values in the order `SEVERITY_INFO`, `SEVERITY_WARN`, `SEVERITY_ERROR`, and `SEVERITY_FATAL`.

Synopsis

Class name:	`javax.faces.application.FacesMessage.Severity`
Extends:	None
Implements:	`java.lang.Comparable`

Methods

`public int compareTo(Object other)`
: Returns a negative integer, zero, or a positive integer if this object is less than, equal to, or greater than the specified object.

`public int getOrdinal( )`
: Returns the ordinal value for this instance.

`public String toString( )`
: Returns a `String` representation of this instance.

NavigationHandler

An instance of a subclass of this abstract class is invoked to handle navigation to different view based on the outcome of an action method. The default implementation behavior is described in Chapter 9.

Synopsis

Class name:	`javax.faces.application.NavigationHandler`
Extends:	None
Implements:	None

Constructors

`public NavigationHandler( )`

Creates an instance.

Methods

`public abstract void handleNavigation(javax.faces.context.FacesContext context, String fromAction, String outcome)`

Selects a new view (or sends a response and calls the `FacesContext` `responseComplete( )` method) based on the provided information about the method binding expression for the action method and the action outcome.

StateManager

An instance of a subclass of this abstract class is invoked to save and restore the state for a view, typically in cooperation with an instance of the `javax.faces.render.ResponseStateManager` for client-side state saving.

Synopsis

Class name:	`javax.faces.application.StateManager`
Extends:	None
Implements:	None

Fields

`public static final String STATE_SAVING_METHOD_CLIENT`

The client-side choice value for the state-saving method selection context initialization parameter: `client`.

`public static final String STATE_SAVING_METHOD_PARAM`

The name of the state-saving selection context initialization parameter: `javax.faces.STATE_SAVING_METHOD`.

`public static final String STATE_SAVING_METHOD_SERVER`

The server-side choice value for the state-saving method selection context initialization parameter: `server`.

Constructors

`public StateManager( )`

Creates an instance.

Methods

`protected abstract Object`
`getComponentStateToSave(javax.faces.context.FacesContext context)`

Returns a `Serializable` object representing the state of all components and their attached objects.

`protected abstract Object`
`getTreeStructureToSave(javax.faces.context.FacesContext context)`

Returns a `Serializable` object representing the component tree structure, i.e., the parent-child relationship for all components and facets in the view.

`public boolean isSavingStateInClient()`

Returns true if the `STATE_SAVING_METHOD_PARAM` context initialization parameter has the value `STATE_SAVING_METHOD_CLIENT`.

`protected abstract void`
`restoreComponentState(javax.faces.context.FacesContext context,`
`javax.faces.component.UIViewRoot viewRoot, String renderKitId)`

Restores the state of all components in the view being restored.

`protected abstract void`
`restoreView(javax.faces.context.FacesContext context,`
`String viewId, String renderKitId)`

Restores the view by calling the `restoreTreeStructure()` and `restoreComponentState()` methods.

`public abstract javax.faces.component.UIViewRoot`
`restoreTreeStructure(javax.faces.context.FacesContext context,`
`String viewId, String renderKitId)`

Restores the component tree structure for the view being restored.

`public abstract StateManager.SerializedView`
`saveSerializedView(javax.faces.context.FacesContext context)`

Returns the `StateManager.SerializedView` for the view, created from the objects created by the `getComponentStateToSave()` and `getTreeStructureToSave()` methods.

`public abstract void writeState(javax.faces.context.FacesContext context,`
`StateManager.SerializedView state)`

Saves the view state, by calling the `ResponseStateManager writeState()` method if `isSavingStateInClient()` returns true; otherwise in any manner that allows the state to be restored by the `restoreView()` method.

StateManager.SerializedView

An instance of this nested class represents the saved state for a view.

Synopsis

Class name:	`javax.faces.application.StateManager.SerializedView`
Extends:	None
Implements:	None

Methods

`public Object getState( )`
: Returns the state for the components in the view.

`public Object getStructure( )`
: Returns the component tree structure for the view.

ViewHandler

An instance of a subclass of this abstract class is invoked to create a view for a view ID, render the view and save and restore the state for a view, typically in cooperation with an instance of the `javax.faces.application.StateManager`. It's the main class for a presentation layer technology. See Chapter 15 for details.

Synopsis

Class name:	`javax.faces.application.ViewHandler`
Extends:	None
Implements:	None

Fields

`public static final String CHARACTER_ENCODING_KEY`
: The name of a session scope variable that holds the character encoding used for the previous response: `javax.faces.request.charset`.

`public static final String DEFAULT_SUFFIX`
: The default suffix for the resource that represents a view, used together with extension mapping for the `FacesServlet`: `.jsp`.

`public static final String DEFAULT_SUFFIX_PARAM_NAME`
: The name of the default suffix declaration context initialization parameter: `javax.faces.DEFAULT_SUFFIX`.

Constructors

`public ViewHandler( )`
: Creates an instance.

Methods

`public abstract java.util.Locale calculateLocale(javax.faces.context.FacesContext context)`
: Returns the `Locale` to use for this view. The default implementation returns the first supported locale (including the default locale) that best matches the locales in the `Accept-Language` header or the default locale if none matches. If no default locale is defined, it returns the default locale for the Java environment.

public abstract String
  calculateRenderKitId(javax.faces.context.FacesContext context)

Returns the render kit ID to use for this view. The default implementation returns the value returned by Application getDefaultRenderKitId( ) or the value defined by the RenderKitFactory.HTML_BASIC_RENDER_KIT field if there's no default render kit defined for the applications.

public abstract javax.faces.component.UIViewRoot
  createView(javax.faces.context.FacesContext context, String viewId)

Returns the UIViewRoot for the identified view, possibly populated with a complete component tree, with the UIViewRoot locale and renderKitId properties initialized.

public abstract String
  getActionURL(javax.faces.context.FacesContext context, String viewId)

Returns the URL matching the specified view ID, encoded by calling ExternalContext encodeActionURL( ).

public abstract String
  getResourceURL(javax.faces.context.FacesContext context, String path)

Returns the URL matching the specified path, encoded by calling ExternalContext encodeResourceURL( ). The default implementation prepends the context path to the specified path if it starts with a slash, i.e., converting a context-relative path to the absolute path a browser needs to locate the resource.

public abstract void renderView(javax.faces.context.FacesContext context,
  javax.faces.component.UIViewRoot viewRoot)

Renders the components in the specified view.

public abstract void renderView(javax.faces.context.FacesContext context,
  javax.faces.component.UIViewRoot viewRoot)

Renders the components in the specified view.

public abstract javax.faces.component.UIViewRoot
  restoreView(javax.faces.context.FacesContext context, String viewId)

Returns the restored UIViewRoot for the identified view or null if there's no state available for the view.

public abstract void writeState(javax.faces.context.FacesContext context)

Writes the state to the response with the help from the StateManager writeState( ) method or mark where the state needs to be written later.

Package javax.faces.context

ExternalContext

An instance of a subclass of this abstract class is available through the FacesContext and provides access to context objects that may vary between environments, such as a servlet and a portlet environment, in an environment-independent way. Classes using the methods only in this class to access the environment should be portable between different container environments.

Synopsis

Class name: javax.faces.context.ExternalContext
Extends: None
Implements: None

Fields

`public static final String BASIC_AUTH`
The identifier for the basic authentication scheme: BASIC.

`public static final String CLIENT_CERT_AUTH`
The identifier for the client certification authentication scheme: CLIENT_CERT.

`public static final String DIGEST_AUTH`
The identifier for the digest authentication scheme: DIGEST.

`public static final String FORM_AUTH`
The identifier for the form-based authentication scheme: FORM.

Constructors

`public ExternalContext()`
Creates an instance.

Methods

`public abstract void dispatch(String path) throws java.io.IOException`
Dispatchs the request to the resource at the specified path to let it generate the response.

`public abstract String encodeActionURL(String url)`
Returns the provided URL, possibly modified to ensure that it correctly identifies a JSF view. In a servlet environment, the URL is passed through the javax.servlet.http.HttpServletResponse encodeURL() method, which encodes it to include a session ID if needed.

`public abstract String encodeNamespace(String name)`
Returns the provided name, possibly prefixed with a namespace to ensure it's unique within the context of a particular page. In a servlet environment, the name is returned unmodified.

`public abstract String encodeResourceURL(String url)`
Returns the provided URL, possibly modified to ensure that it correctly identifies an application resource, such as an image. In a servlet environment, the URL is passed through the javax.servlet.http.HttpServletResponse encodeURL() method, which encodes it to include a session ID if needed.

`public abstract java.util.Map getApplicationMap()`
Returns a mutable Map representing the application scope, keyed by variable name with Object values.

`public abstract String getAuthType()`
Returns the name of the authentication scheme used for the current user, or null if the current user isn't authenticated by the container. One of BASIC_AUTH, CLIENT_CERT_AUTH, DIGEST_AUTH, or FORM_AUTH for the standard schemes.

public abstract Object getContext()
: Returns the native object representing the environment-specific context. In servlet environment, this is a javax.servlet.ServletContext instance.

public abstract String getInitParameter(String name)
: Returns the value of the named application context initialization parameter or null if not found.

public abstract java.util.Map getInitParameterMap()
: Returns an immutable Map with all application context initialization parameters, keyed by name with String values.

public abstract String getRemoteUser()
: Returns the name of the authenticated user or null if the current user isn't authenticated by the container.

public abstract Object getRequest()
: Returns the native object representing the environment-specific request data. In servlet environment, this is a javax.servlet.http.HttpServletRequest instance.

public abstract String getRequestContextPath()
: Returns the portion of the request URI that identifies the application context.

public abstract java.util.Map getRequestCookieMap()
: Returns an immutable Map with cookies received with the current request, keyed by name with javax.servlet.http.Cookie values.

public abstract java.util.Map getRequestHeaderMap()
: Returns an immutable Map with headers for the current request, keyed by name with String values.

public abstract java.util.Map getRequestHeaderValuesMap()
: Returns an immutable Map with headers for the current request, keyed by name with String[] values (holding all values for a header).

public abstract java.util.Locale getRequestLocale()
: Returns the Locale with the highest preference according to the request data.

public abstract java.util.Iterator getRequestLocales()
: Returns an Iterator over all Locale instances in preference order based on the request data.

public abstract java.util.Map getRequestMap()
: Returns a mutable Map representing the request scope, keyed by variable name with Object values.

public abstract java.util.Map getRequestParameterMap()
: Returns an immutable Map with parameters for the current request, keyed by name with String values.

public abstract java.util.Iterator getRequestParameterNames()
: Returns an Iterator over all request parameter names.

public abstract java.util.Map getRequestParameterValuesMap()
: Returns an immutable Map with parameters for the current request, keyed by name with String[] values (holding all values for a parameter).

`public abstract String getRequestPathInfo( )`

Returns the portion of the request URI path that follows the portion that identifies the servlet processing the request or `null` if there's no extra path info.

`public abstract String getRequestServletPath( )`

Returns the portion of the request URI path that identifies the servlet processing the request.

`public abstract java.net.URL getResource(String path)`
`throws java.net.MalformedURLException`

Returns a `URL` for reading the resource at the specified path or `null` if it doesn't exist.

`public abstract java.io.InputStream getResourceAsStream(String path)`

Returns an `InputStream` for reading the resource at the specified path or `null` if it doesn't exist.

`public abstract java.util.Set getResourcePaths(String path)`

Returns a `Set` of all resource paths that starts with the specified path.

`public abstract Object getResponse( )`

Returns the native object representing the environment-specific response data. In servlet environment, this is a `javax.servlet.http.HttpServletResponse` instance.

`public abstract Object getSession(boolean create)`

Returns the native object representing the environment-specific session data, creating one if it doesn't exist and `create` is `true`. In servlet environment, this is a `javax.servlet.http.HttpSession` instance.

`public abstract java.util.Map getSessionMap( )`

Returns a mutable `Map` representing the session scope, keyed by variable name with `Object` values.

`public abstract java.security.Principal getUserPrincipal( )`

Returns the `Principal` for the authenticated user or `null` if the current user isn't authenticated by the container.

`public abstract boolean isUserInRole(String role)`

Returns the true if the authenticated user is associated with the specified role.

`public abstract void log(String message)`

Writes the specified message to the application log.

`public abstract void log(String message, Throwable exception)`

Writes the specified message and exception to the application log.

`public abstract void redirect(String path) throws java.io.IOException`

Sends a redirect response to redirect the client to the resource at the specified path.

FacesContext

An instance of a subclass of this abstract class provides access to JSF-specific context information and methods. Note that an instance of this class and the objects it provides access to are associated with the thread processing a request, and references to any of these instances must not be passed to another thread.

Synopsis

Class name:	javax.faces.context.FacesContext
Extends:	None
Implements:	None

Constructors

`public FacesContext( )`

Creates an instance.

Methods

`public abstract void addMessage(String clientId, javax.faces.application.FacesMessage message)`

Adds the specified message to the message queue, for the specified component or as a global message if the client ID is null.

`public abstract javax.faces.application.Application getApplication( )`

Returns the Application this request belongs to.

`public abstract java.util.Iterator getClientIdsWithMessages( )`

Returns an Iterator over all client IDs for which at least one message is queued.

`public static javax.faces.context.FacesContext getCurrentInstance( )`

Returns the FacesContext instance for the current request.

`public abstract javax.faces.context.ExternalContext getExternalContext( )`

Returns the ExternalContext instance for the current request.

`public abstract javax.faces.application.FacesMessage.Severity getMaximumSeverity( )`

Returns the maximum severity of all queued messages.

`public abstract java.util.Iterator getMessages( )`

Returns an Iterator over all queued FacesMessage instances.

`public abstract java.util.Iterator getMessages(String clientId)`

Returns an Iterator over all queued FacesMessage instances for the specified client ID or over all global messages if clientId is null.

`public abstract javax.faces.render.RenderKit getRenderKit( )`

Returns the RenderKit for the current view, or null if there's no render kit ID defined for the view or it doesn't match a registered RenderKit.

`public abstract boolean getRenderResponse( )`

Returns true if renderResponse( ) has been called for the current request.

`public abstract boolean getResponseComplete( )`

Returns true if responseComplete( ) has been called for the current request.

`public abstract javax.faces.context.ResponseStream getResponseStream( )`

Returns the ResponseStream the context has been configured with for rendering a binary response or null if not set.

`public abstract javax.faces.context.ResponseWriter getResponseWriter( )`

Returns the ResponseWriter the context has been configured with for rendering a textual response or null if not set.

`public abstract javax.faces.component.UIViewRoot getViewRoot( )`
Returns the root component for the view's component tree or `null` if not set.

`public abstract void release( )`
Releases all resources associated with this context.

`public abstract void renderResponse( )`
Marks that the request processing must continue in the Render Response phase as soon as the current phase is completed.

`public abstract void responseComplete( )`
Marks that a response has already been sent and that the request processing must be terminated as soon as the current phase is completed.

`protected static void setCurrentInstance(javax.faces.context.FacesContext context)`
Sets the `FacesContext` for the current thread or to `null` if the thread is no longer processing a JSF request.

`public abstract void setResponseStream(javax.faces.context.ResponseStream rs)`
Sets the `ResponseStream` for rendering a binary response.

`public abstract void setResponseWriter(javax.faces.context.ResponseWriter rw)`
Sets the `ResponseWriter` for rendering a textual response.

`public abstract void setViewRoot(javax.faces.component.UIViewRoot viewRoot)`
Sets the root component for the view's component tree.

FacesContextFactory

An instance of a subclass of this abstract class is a factory for the `FacesContext` instance for a request. An implementation may use a pool of context instances and recycle them for new requests.

Synopsis

Class name:	`javax.faces.context.FacesContextFactory`
Extends:	None
Implements:	None

Constructors

`public FacesContextFactory( )`
Creates an instance.

Methods

`public abstract javax.faces.application.Application getFacesContext(Object context, Object request, Object response, javax.faces.lifecycle.Lifecycle lifecycle)`
Returns a `FacesContext` instance for handling a request, initialized with all the provided references.

ResponseStream

An instance of a subclass of this abstract class provides a stream for rendering a binary response.

Synopsis

Class name:	`javax.faces.context.ResponseStream`
Extends:	`java.io.OutputStream`
Implements:	None

Constructors

`public ResponseStream( )`

Creates an instance.

ResponseWriter

An instance of a subclass of this abstract class provides methods for rendering a textual response, with special methods for writing markup elements.

Synopsis

Class name:	`javax.faces.context.ResponseWriter`
Extends:	`java.io.Writer`
Implements:	None

Constructors

`public ResponseWriter( )`

Creates an instance.

Methods

`public abstract javax.faces.context.ResponseWriter cloneWithWriter(java.io.Writer writer)`

Returns a new instance wrapped around the provided `Writer`.

`public abstract void endDocument( ) throws java.io.IOException`

Closes any open tag (if any) and writes what is needed to end the document (if anything).

`public abstract void endElement(String name) throws java.io.IOException`

Closes any open tag (if any) and writes what is needed to close the named element.

`public abstract void flush( ) throws java.io.IOException`

Closes any open tag (if any) and flushes any buffered output (if any) to the underlying `Writer` or `OutputStream`, but does not flush the underlying output object.

`public abstract String getCharacterEncoding( )`

Returns the character encoding this instance is configured to use.

`public abstract String getContentType()`
: Returns the content MIME type this instance is configured to use.

`public abstract void startDocument() throws java.io.IOException`
: Writes what is needed to start the document (if anything).

`public abstract void startElement(String name, javax.faces.component.UIComponent component) throws java.io.IOException`
: Writes beginning of the start tag for the named element, up to and including the element name. Attributes can then be added by calls to the `writeAttribute()` and `writeURIAttribute()` methods, and the start tag closed by calls to `endElement()`, `endDocument()`, `startElement()`, `writeComment()`, `writeText()`, `close()`, `flush()`, or `write()`. The component reference may be used to associate the element with the component it's rendered for.

`public abstract void writeAttribute(String name, Object value, String property) throws java.io.IOException`
: Writes the specified attribute name with the specified value for the currently open element, after appropriate escaping of special characters for the content type being generated. The property name may be used to associate the attribute with the component property or attribute it corresponds to.

`public abstract void writeComment(Object comment) throws java.io.IOException`
: Closes any open tag (if any) and writes the comment in a format appropriate for the content type being generated.

`public abstract void writeText(Object text, java.lang.String property) throws java.io.IOException`
: Closes any open tag (if any) and writes the specified text, after appropriate escaping of special characters for the content type being generated. The property name may be used to associate the attribute with the component property or attribute it corresponds to.

`public abstract void writeURIAttribute(String name, Object value, String property) throws java.io.IOException`
: Writes the specified attribute name with the specified URI value for the currently open element, after appropriate escaping of special characters for the content type being generated. The property name may be used to associate the attribute with the component property or attribute it corresponds to.

Package javax.faces.convert

BigDecimalConverter

An instance of this class is used as a `Converter` for `java.math.BigDecimal` values.

Synopsis

Class name:	`javax.faces.convert.BigDecimalConverter`
Extends:	None
Implements:	`javax.faces.convert.Converter`

Fields

`public static final String CONVERTER_ID`

The identifier for this converter: `javax.faces.BigDecimal`.

Constructors

`public BigDecimalConverter( )`

Creates an instance.

Methods

`public Object getAsObject(javax.faces.context.FacesContext context, javax.faces.component.UIComponent component, String value)`

Converts the provided `String` value (which can be `null`) to a `BigDecimal` instance and returns the new instance. Throws a `ConverterException` if the conversion fails.

`public String getAsString(javax.faces.context.FacesContext context, javax.faces.component.UIComponent component, Object value)`

Converts the provided `BigDecimal` value (which can be `null`) to a `String` instance and returns the new instance. Throws a `ConverterException` if the conversion fails.

BigIntegerConverter

An instance of this class is used as a `Converter` for `java.math.BigInteger` values.

Synopsis

Class name:	`javax.faces.convert.BigIntegerConverter`
Extends:	None
Implements:	`javax.faces.convert.Converter`

Fields

`public static final String CONVERTER_ID`

The identifier for this converter: `javax.faces.BigInteger`.

Constructors

`public BigIntegerConverter( )`

Creates an instance.

Methods

`public Object getAsObject(javax.faces.context.FacesContext context, javax.faces.component.UIComponent component, String value)`

Converts the provided `String` value (which can be `null`) to a `BigInteger` instance and returns the new instance. Throws a `ConverterException` if the conversion fails.

`public String getAsString(javax.faces.context.FacesContext context, javax.faces.component.UIComponent component, Object value)`

Converts the provided `BigInteger` value (which can be `null`) to a `String` instance and returns the new instance. Throws a `ConverterException` if the conversion fails.

BooleanConverter

An instance of this class is used as a `Converter` for `Boolean` values.

Synopsis

Class name:	`javax.faces.convert.BooleanConverter`
Extends:	None
Implements:	`javax.faces.convert.Converter`

Fields

`public static final String CONVERTER_ID`
The identifier for this converter: `javax.faces.Boolean`.

Constructors

`public BooleanConverter( )`
Creates an instance.

Methods

`public Object getAsObject(javax.faces.context.FacesContext context, javax.faces.component.UIComponent component, String value)`
Converts the provided `String` value (which can be `null`) to a `Boolean` instance and returns the new instance. Throws a `ConverterException` if the conversion fails.

`public String getAsString(javax.faces.context.FacesContext context, javax.faces.component.UIComponent component, Object value)`
Converts the provided `Boolean` value (which can be `null`) to a `String` instance and returns the new instance. Throws a `ConverterException` if the conversion fails.

ByteConverter

An instance of this class is used as a `Converter` for `Byte` values.

Synopsis

Class name:	`javax.faces.convert.ByteConverter`
Extends:	None
Implements:	`javax.faces.convert.Converter`

Fields

`public static final String CONVERTER_ID`
The identifier for this converter: `javax.faces.Byte`.

Constructors

`public ByteConverter( )`
Creates an instance.

Methods

public Object getAsObject(javax.faces.context.FacesContext context, javax.faces.component.UIComponent component, String value)
: Converts the provided String value (which can be null) to a Byte instance and returns the new instance. Throws a ConverterException if the conversion fails.

public String getAsString(javax.faces.context.FacesContext context, javax.faces.component.UIComponent component, Object value)
: Converts the provided Byte value (which can be null) to a String instance and returns the new instance. Throws a ConverterException if the conversion fails.

CharacterConverter

An instance of this class is used as a Converter for Character values.

Synopsis

Class name:	javax.faces.convert.CharacterConverter
Extends:	None
Implements:	javax.faces.convert.Converter

Fields

public static final String CONVERTER_ID
: The identifier for this converter: javax.faces.Character.

Constructors

public CharacterConverter()
: Creates an instance.

Methods

public Object getAsObject(javax.faces.context.FacesContext context, javax.faces.component.UIComponent component, String value)
: Converts the provided String value (which can be null) to a Character instance and returns the new instance. Throws a ConverterException if the conversion fails.

public String getAsString(javax.faces.context.FacesContext context, javax.faces.component.UIComponent component, Object value)
: Converts the provided Character value (which can be null) to a String instance and returns the new instance. Throws a ConverterException if the conversion fails.

Converter

This interface is implemented by all converter classes, converting between a String value and a data type supported by the class.

Synopsis

Interface name:	`javax.faces.convert.Converter`
Extends:	None
Implemented by:	All standard and custom converters.

Methods

```
public Object getAsObject(javax.faces.context.FacesContext context,
  javax.faces.component.UIComponent component, String value)
```

Converts the provided `String` value (which can be `null`) to an instance of the supported type and returns the new instance. Throws a `ConverterException` if the conversion fails.

```
public String getAsString(javax.faces.context.FacesContext context,
  javax.faces.component.UIComponent component, Object value)
```

Converts the provided value of the supported type (which can be `null`) to a `String` instance and returns the new instance. Throws a `ConverterException` if the conversion fails.

ConverterException

An instance of this class is thrown by a `Converter` implementation to signal a conversion error.

Synopsis

Class name:	`javax.faces.convert.ConverterException`
Extends:	`javax.faces.FacesException`
Implements:	`java.io.Serializable`

Constructors

```
public ConverterException()
```

Creates an empty instance.

```
public ConverterException(java.faces.application.FacesMessage message)
```

Creates an instance with the specified message.

```
public ConverterException(java.faces.application.FacesMessage message,
  Throwable rootCause)
```

Creates an instance with the specified message and root cause.

```
public ConverterException(String message)
```

Creates an instance with the specified message text.

```
public ConverterException(String message, Throwable rootCause)
```

Creates an instance with the specified message text and root cause.

```
public ConverterException(Throwable rootCause)
```

Creates an instance with the specified root cause.

Methods

`public java.faces.application.FacesMessage getFacesMessage()`
: Returns the `FacesMessage` instance or `null` if none is set.

DateTimeConverter

An instance of this class is used as a `Converter` for `java.util.Date` values.

Synopsis

Class name:	`javax.faces.convert.DateTimeConverter`
Extends:	None
Implements:	`javax.faces.convert.Converter`, `javax.faces.component.StateHolder`

Fields

`public static final String CONVERTER_ID`
: The identifier for this converter: `javax.faces.DateTime`.

Constructors

`public DateTimeConverter()`
: Creates an instance.

Methods

`public Object getAsObject(javax.faces.context.FacesContext context, javax.faces.component.UIComponent component, String value)`
: Converts the provided `String` value (which can be `null`) to a `Date` instance and returns the new instance. Returns `null` if the value is `null` or an empty string (after trimming); otherwise, parses the value in the same way as `java.text.SimpleDateFormat` in nonlenient mode, guided by the `dateStyle`, `pattern`, `timeStyle`, `timeZone` and `type` property value for the `Locale` specified by the `locale` property or the view's `Locale`. Throws a `ConverterException` if the conversion fails.

`public String getAsString(javax.faces.context.FacesContext context, javax.faces.component.UIComponent component, Object value)`
: Converts the provided `Date` value (which can be `null`) to a `String` instance and returns the new instance, formatted in the same way as by `java.text.SimpleDateFormat`, guided by the `dateStyle`, `pattern`, `timeStyle`, `timeZone`, and `type` properties for the `Locale` specified by the `locale` property or the view's `Locale`. Throws a `ConverterException` if the conversion fails.

`public String getDateStyle()`
: Returns the `dateStyle` property value.

`public java.util.Locale getLocale()`
: Returns the `locale` property value.

`public String getPattern()`
: Returns the `pattern` property value.

`public String getTimeStyle( )`
: Returns the `timeStyle` property value.

`public java.util.TimeZone getTimeZone( )`
: Returns the `timeZone` property value.

`public String getType( )`
: Returns the type property value.

`public boolean isTransient( )`
: Returns `true` if no state should be saved and restored for this instance.

`public void restoreState(javax.faces.context.FacesContext context, Object state)`
: Restores the state for this instance from the provided value; an `Object` previously returned by the `saveState( )` method.

`public Object saveState(javax.faces.context.FacesContext context)`
: Returns the state for this instance as an `Object` to be passed to the `restoreState( )` method when the instance is restored for the next request.

`public void setDateStyle(String dateStyle)`
: Sets the `dateStyle` property value.

`public void setLocale(java.util.Locale locale)`
: Sets the `locale` property value.

`public void setPattern(String pattern)`
: Sets the `pattern` property value.

`public void setTimeStyle(String timeStyle)`
: Sets the `timeStyle` property value.

`public void setTimeZone(java.util.TimeZone timeZone)`
: Sets the `timeZone` property value.

`public void setTransient(boolean isTransient)`
: Sets the `transient` property value.

`public void setType(String type)`
: Sets the `type` property value.

DoubleConverter

An instance of this class is used as a `Converter` for `Double` values.

Synopsis

Class name:	`javax.faces.convert.DoubleConverter`
Extends:	None
Implements:	`javax.faces.convert.Converter`

Fields

`public static final String CONVERTER_ID`
: The identifier for this converter: `javax.faces.Double`.

Constructors

`public DoubleConverter()`

Creates an instance.

Methods

`public Object getAsObject(javax.faces.context.FacesContext context, javax.faces.component.UIComponent component, String value)`

Converts the provided `String` value (which can be `null`) to a `Double` instance and returns the new instance. Throws a `ConverterException` if the conversion fails.

`public String getAsString(javax.faces.context.FacesContext context, javax.faces.component.UIComponent component, Object value)`

Converts the provided `Double` value (which can be `null`) to a `String` instance and returns the new instance. Throws a `ConverterException` if the conversion fails.

FloatConverter

An instance of this class is used as a `Converter` for `Float` values.

Synopsis

Class name:	`javax.faces.convert.FloatConverter`
Extends:	None
Implements:	`javax.faces.convert.Converter`

Fields

`public static final String CONVERTER_ID`

The identifier for this converter: `javax.faces.Float`.

Constructors

`public FloatConverter()`

Creates an instance.

Methods

`public Object getAsObject(javax.faces.context.FacesContext context, javax.faces.component.UIComponent component, String value)`

Converts the provided `String` value (which can be `null`) to a `Float` instance and returns the new instance. Throws a `ConverterException` if the conversion fails.

`public String getAsString(javax.faces.context.FacesContext context, javax.faces.component.UIComponent component, Object value)`

Converts the provided `Float` value (which can be `null`) to a `String` instance and returns the new instance. Throws a `ConverterException` if the conversion fails.

IntegerConverter

An instance of this class is used as a `Converter` for `Integer` values.

Synopsis

Class name:	`javax.faces.convert.IntegerConverter`
Extends:	None
Implements:	`javax.faces.convert.Converter`

Fields

`public static final String CONVERTER_ID`

The identifier for this converter: `javax.faces.Integer`.

Constructors

`public IntegerConverter( )`

Creates an instance.

Methods

`public Object getAsObject(javax.faces.context.FacesContext context, javax.faces.component.UIComponent component, String value)`

Converts the provided `String` value (which can be `null`) to an `Integer` instance and returns the new instance. Throws a `ConverterException` if the conversion fails.

`public String getAsString(javax.faces.context.FacesContext context, javax.faces.component.UIComponent component, Object value)`

Converts the provided `Integer` value (which can be `null`) to a `String` instance and returns the new instance. Throws a `ConverterException` if the conversion fails.

LongConverter

An instance of this class is used as a `Converter` for `Long` values.

Synopsis

Class name:	`javax.faces.convert.LongConverter`
Extends:	None
Implements:	`javax.faces.convert.Converter`

Fields

`public static final String CONVERTER_ID`

The identifier for this converter: `javax.faces.Long`.

Constructors

`public LongConverter( )`

Creates an instance.

Methods

`public Object getAsObject(javax.faces.context.FacesContext context, javax.faces.component.UIComponent component, String value)`

Converts the provided String value (which can be null) to a Long instance and returns the new instance. Throws a ConverterException if the conversion fails.

`public String getAsString(javax.faces.context.FacesContext context, javax.faces.component.UIComponent component, Object value)`

Converts the provided Long value (which can be null) to a String instance and returns the new instance. Throws a ConverterException if the conversion fails.

NumberConverter

An instance of this class is used as a Converter for Double and Long values.

Synopsis

Class name:	javax.faces.convert.NumberConverter
Extends:	None
Implements:	javax.faces.convert.Converter, javax.faces.component.StateHolder

Fields

`public static final String CONVERTER_ID`

The identifier for this converter: javax.faces.Number.

Constructors

`public NumberConverter( )`

Creates an instance.

Methods

`public Object getAsObject(javax.faces.context.FacesContext context, javax.faces.component.UIComponent component, String value)`

Converts the provided String value (which can be null) to a Number instance and returns the new instance. Returns null if the value is null or an empty string (after trimming); otherwise, parses the value in the same way as java.text.DecimalFormat, guided by the component's pattern, integerOnly and type attributes for the Locale specified by the component's locale attribute or the view's Locale. Throws a ConverterException if the conversion fails.

`public String getAsString(javax.faces.context.FacesContext context, javax.faces.component.UIComponent component, Object value)`

Converts the provided Number value (which can be null) to a String instance and returns the new instance, formatted in the same way as by java.text.DecimalFormat, guided by the component's pattern, currencyCode, currencySymbol, groupingUsed, maxIntegerDigits, minIntegerDisgits, maxFractionDigits, minFractionDigits, and type attributes for the Locale specified by the component's locale attribute or the view's Locale. Throws a ConverterException if the conversion fails.

`public String getCurrencyCode( )`
: Returns the `currencyCode` property value.

`public String getCurrencySymbol( )`
: Returns the `currencySymbol` property value.

`public java.util.Locale getLocale( )`
: Returns the `locale` property value.

`public int getMaxFractionDigits( )`
: Returns the `maxFractionDigits` property value.

`public int getMaxIntegerDigits( )`
: Returns the `maxIntegerDigits` property value.

`public int getMinFractionDigits( )`
: Returns the `minFractionDigits` property value.

`public int getMinIntegerDigits( )`
: Returns the `minIntegerDigits` property value.

`public String getPattern( )`
: Returns the `pattern` property value.

`public String getType( )`
: Returns the `type` property value.

`public boolean isGroupingUsed( )`
: Returns the `groupingUsed` property value.

`public boolean isIntegerOnly( )`
: Returns the `isIntegerOnly` property value.

`public boolean isTransient( )`
: Returns `true` if no state should be saved and restored for this instance.

`public void restoreState(javax.faces.context.FacesContext context, Object state)`
: Restores the state for this instance from the provided value; an `Object` previously returned by the `saveState( )` method.

`public Object saveState(javax.faces.context.FacesContext context)`
: Returns the state for this instance as an `Object` to be passed to the `restoreState( )` method when the instance is restored for the next request.

`public void setCurrencyCode(String currencyCode)`
: Sets the `currencyCode` property value.

`public void setCurrencySymbol(String currencySymbol)`
: Sets the `currencySymbol` property value.

`public void setGroupingUsed(boolean groupingUsed)`
: Sets the `groupingUsed` property value.

`public void setIntegerOnly(boolean integerOnly)`
: Sets the `isIntegerOnly` property value.

`public void setLocale(java.util.Locale locale)`
: Sets the `locale` property value.

`public void setMaxFractionDigits(int maxFractionDigits)`
: Sets the `maxFractionDigits` property value.

public void setMaxIntegerDigits(int maxIntegerDigits)
Sets the maxIntegerDigits property value.

public void setMinFractionDigits(int minFractionDigits)
Sets the minFractionDigits property value.

public void setMinIntegerDigits(int minIntegerDigits)
Sets the minIntegerDigits property value.

public void setPattern(String pattern)
Sets the pattern property value.

public void setTransient(boolean isTransient)
Sets the transient property value.

public void setType(String type)
Sets the type property value.

ShortConverter

An instance of this class is used as a Converter for Short values.

Synopsis

Class name:	javax.faces.convert.ShortConverter
Extends:	None
Implements:	javax.faces.convert.Converter

Fields

public static final String CONVERTER_ID
The identifier for this converter: javax.faces.Short.

Constructors

public ShortConverter()
Creates an instance.

Methods

public Object getAsObject(javax.faces.context.FacesContext context, javax.faces.component.UIComponent component, String value)
Converts the provided String value (which can be null) to a Short instance and returns the new instance. Throws a ConverterException if the conversion fails.

public String getAsString(javax.faces.context.FacesContext context, javax.faces.component.UIComponent component, Object value)
Converts the provided Short value (which can be null) to a String instance and returns the new instance. Throws a ConverterException if the conversion fails.

Package javax.faces.el

EvaluationException

This is the base class for all more specific evaluation exception classes.

Synopsis

Class name:	`javax.faces.el.EvaluationException`
Extends:	`javax.faces.FacesException`
Implements:	`java.io.Serializable`

Constructors

`public EvaluationException( )`
Creates an empty instance.

`public EvaluationException(String message)`
Creates an instance with the specified message.

`public EvaluationException(String message, Throwable rootCause)`
Creates an instance with the specified message and root cause.

`public EvaluationException(Throwable rootCause)`
Creates an instance with the specified root cause.

MethodBinding

An instance of a subclass of this abstract class represents a dynamic binding to a method, typically created from a method binding expression.

Synopsis

Class name:	`javax.faces.el.MethodBinding`
Extends:	None
Implements:	None

Constructors

`public MethodBinding( )`
Creates an instance.

Methods

`public String getExpressionString( )`
Returns the method binding expression used to create this instance or `null` if none.

`public abstract Class getType(javax.faces.context.FacesContext context)`
Returns the `Class` representing the return type for the method this instance is bound to or `null` if `void`. Throws `MethodNotFoundException` if the method isn't found.

```
public abstract Object invoke(javax.faces.context.FacesContext context,
  Object[] params)
```
Invokes the method this instance is bound to and returns its return value. Throws `MethodNotFoundException` if the method isn't found or `EvaluationException` wrapped around an exception thrown by the method.

MethodNotFoundException

An instance of this class is thrown to signal that the method referenced by a method binding expression can't be found.

Synopsis

Class name:	`javax.faces.el.MethodNotFoundException`
Extends:	`javax.faces.el.EvaluationException`
Implements:	`java.io.Serializable`

Constructors

`public MethodNotFoundException()`
Creates an empty instance.

`public MethodNotFoundException(String message)`
Creates an instance with the specified message.

`public MethodNotFoundException(String message, Throwable rootCause)`
Creates an instance with the specified message and root cause.

`public MethodNotFoundException(Throwable rootCause)`
Creates an instance with the specified root cause.

PropertyNotFoundException

An instance of this class is thrown to signal that the property referenced by a value binding expression can't be found.

Synopsis

Class name:	`javax.faces.el.PropertyNotFoundException`
Extends:	`javax.faces.el.EvaluationException`
Implements:	`java.io.Serializable`

Constructors

`public PropertyNotFoundException()`
Creates an empty instance.

`public PropertyNotFoundException(String message)`
Creates an instance with the specified message.

`public PropertyNotFoundException(String message, Throwable rootCause)`
Creates an instance with the specified message and root cause.

public PropertyNotFoundException(Throwable rootCause)
Creates an instance with the specified root cause.

PropertyResolver

An instance of a subclass of this abstract class resolves property and element accessor operators in a JSF EL expression. See Appendix B for details about the default resolver.

Synopsis

Class name:	javax.faces.el.PropertyResolver
Extends:	None
Implements:	None

Constructors

public PropertyResolver()
Creates an instance.

Methods

public abstract Class getType(Object base, int index)
Returns the Class representing the type of the element of the base object at the specified index or null if unknown. Throws PropertyNotFoundException if the base object is null or the index is out of bounds, or EvaluationException wrapping any exception thrown while getting the type.

public abstract Class getType(Object base, Object property)
Returns the Class representing the type of the property of the base object (after coercing the property to a String if the base object is a bean) or null if unknown. Throws PropertyNotFoundException if the base object is a bean and the property doesn't exist or if the base object or the property is null, or EvaluationException wrapping any exception thrown while getting the type.

public abstract Object getValue(Object base, int index)
Returns the Object represented by the element of the base object at the specified index. Throws PropertyNotFoundException if the base object is null or the index is out of bounds, or EvaluationException wrapping any exception thrown while getting the value.

public abstract Object getValue(Object base, Object property)
Returns the Object represented by the property of the base object (after coercing the property to a String if the base object is a bean), or null if the base object or the property is null, or if the base object is a Map and the property doesn't match a key. Throws PropertyNotFoundException if the base object is a bean and the property doesn't exist or isn't readable, or EvaluationException wrapping any exception thrown while getting the type.

public abstract boolean isReadOnly(Object base, int index)
Returns true if the Object represented by the element of the base object at the specified index is known to be immutable; otherwise false. Throws

PropertyNotFoundException if the base object is null or the index is out of bounds, or EvaluationException wrapping any exception thrown while getting the value.

`public abstract boolean isReadOnly(Object base, Object property)`
: Returns true if the Object represented by the property of the base object, (after coercing the property to a String if the base object is a bean) is known to be immutable; otherwise false. Throws PropertyNotFoundException if the base object is a bean and the property doesn't exist or if the base object or the property is null, or EvaluationException wrapping any exception thrown while getting the type.

`public abstract void setValue(Object base, int index, Object value)`
: Sets the element of the base object at the specified index to the provide value. Throws PropertyNotFoundException if the base object is null or the index is out of bounds, or EvaluationException wrapping any exception thrown while getting the value.

`public abstract void setValue(Object base, Object property, Object value)`
: Sets the property of the base object, (after coercing the property to a String if the base object is a bean) to the provided value. Throws PropertyNotFoundException if the base object is a bean and the property doesn't exist or isn't writable or if the base object or the property is null, or EvaluationException wrapping any exception thrown while getting the type.

ReferenceSyntaxException

An instance of this class is thrown to signal a syntax error in a value or method binding expression.

Synopsis

Class name:	javax.faces.el.ReferenceSyntaxException
Extends:	javax.faces.el.EvaluationException
Implements:	java.io.Serializable

Constructors

`public ReferenceSyntaxException()`
: Creates an empty instance.

`public ReferenceSyntaxException(String message)`
: Creates an instance with the specified message.

`public ReferenceSyntaxException(String message, Throwable rootCause)`
: Creates an instance with the specified message and root cause.

`public ReferenceSyntaxException(Throwable rootCause)`
: Creates an instance with the specified root cause.

ValueBinding

An instance of a subclass of this abstract class represents a dynamic binding to a property or a read-only JSF EL expression, typically created from a value binding expression.

Synopsis

Class name:	`javax.faces.el.ValueBinding`
Extends:	None
Implements:	None

Constructors

`public ValueBinding( )`

Creates an instance.

Methods

`public String getExpressionString( )`

Returns the method binding expression used to create this instance or `null` if none.

`public abstract Class getType(javax.faces.context.FacesContext context)`

Returns the `Class` representing the data type for the evaluation result of this binding. Throws `PropertyNotFoundException` if the value binding refers to a property that isn't found or `EvaluationException` wrapped around an exception thrown while evaluating the value binding.

`public abstract Object getValue(javax.faces.context.FacesContext context)`

Returns the evaluation result for the binding. Throws `PropertyNotFoundException` if the value binding refers to a property that isn't found or readable, or `EvaluationException` wrapped around an exception thrown while evaluating the value binding.

`public abstract boolean isReadOnly(javax.faces.context.FacesContext context)`

Returns `true` if the binding represents a read-only property or JSF EL expression. Throws `PropertyNotFoundException` if the value binding refers to a property that isn't found or readable, or `EvaluationException` wrapped around an exception thrown while evaluating the value binding.

`public abstract void setValue(javax.faces.context.FacesContext context, Object value)`

Evaluates the binding and sets the property it refers to to the provide value. Throws `PropertyNotFoundException` if the value binding refers to a property that isn't found or writable, or `EvaluationException` wrapped around an exception thrown while evaluating the value binding.

VariableResolver

An instance of a subclass of this abstract class resolves variables in a JSF EL expression. See Appendix B for details about the default resolver.

Synopsis

Class name:	`javax.faces.el.VariableResolver`
Extends:	None
Implements:	None

Constructors

public VariableResolver()

Creates an instance.

Methods

public abstract Object resolveVariable(javax.faces.context.FacesContext context, String name)

Returns the Object represented by the specified name or null if unknown. Throws EvaluationException wrapping any exception thrown while resolving the name.

Package javax.faces.event

AbortProcessingException

An instance of this class is thrown by an event handler to terminate further processing of the event.

Synopsis

Class name:	javax.faces.event.AbortProcessingException
Extends:	javax.faces.FacesException
Implements:	java.io.Serializable

Constructors

public AbortProcessingException()

Creates an empty instance.

public AbortProcessingException(String message)

Creates an instance with the specified message.

public AbortProcessingException(String message, Throwable rootCause)

Creates an instance with the specified message and root cause.

public AbortProcessingException(Throwable rootCause)

Creates an instance with the specified root cause.

ActionEvent

An instance of this class signals that the user activated a component, e.g., a UICommand component.

Synopsis

Class name:	javax.faces.event.ActionEvent
Extends:	javax.faces.event.FacesEvent
Implements:	java.io.Serializable

Constructors

`public ActionEvent(javax.faces.component.UIComponent component)`
Creates an instance for the specified source component.

Methods

`public boolean isAppropriateListener(javax.faces.event.FacesListener listener)`
Returns `true` if the listener is an `ActionListener`.

`public void processListener(javax.faces.event.FacesListener listener)`
Calls the listener's `processAction()` method.

ActionListener

This interface is implemented by all classes interested in handling `ActionEvent` events.

Synopsis

Interface name:	`javax.faces.event.ActionListener`
Extends:	`javax.faces.event.FacesListener`
Implemented by:	All classes interested in handling `ActionEvent` events.

Methods

`public void processAction(javax.faces.event.ActionEvent event)`
Processes the event.

FacesEvent

This is the base class for all classes representing specific component events.

Synopsis

Class name:	`javax.faces.event.FacesEvent`
Extends:	`java.util.EventObject`
Implements:	`java.io.Serializable`

Constructors

`public FacesEvent(javax.faces.component.UIComponent component)`
Creates an instance for the specified source component.

Methods

`public javax.faces.component.UIComponent getComponent()`
Returns the source component for the event.

`public javax.faces.event.PhaseId getPhaseId()`
Returns the identifier for the request processing lifecycle phase when the event listeners shall be notified of the event. The default value is `PhaseId.ANY_PHASE`.

```
public abstract boolean
  isAppropriateListener(javax.faces.event.FacesListener listener)
```
Returns true if the listener is of an appropriate type for this event type.

```
public abstract void processListener(javax.faces.event.FacesListener listener)
```
Calls the listener's event processing method.

```
public void queue()
```
Calls the source component's `queueEvent()` method.

```
public void setPhaseId(javax.faces.event.PhaseId phaseId)
```
Sets the identifier for the request processing lifecycle phase when the event listeners shall be notified of the event. If set to `PhaseId.ANY_PHASE`, the listeners are notified in the same phase as where the event is queued.

FacesListener

This is the base interface for all interfaces representing specific component event listeners. It's an empty interface, used for type-safety only.

Synopsis

Interface name:	`javax.faces.event.FacesListener`
Extends:	`java.util.EventListener`
Implemented by:	Indirectly by all classes implementing a subinterface.

PhaseEvent

An instance of this class signals that a new request processing lifecycle phase begins or ends.

Synopsis

Class name:	`javax.faces.event.PhaseEvent`
Extends:	`java.util.EventListener`
Implements:	`java.io.Serializable`

Constructors

```
public PhaseEvent(javax.faces.context.FacesContext context,
  javax.faces.event.PhaseId phaseId, javax.faces.lifecycle.Lifecycle lifecycle)
```
Creates an instance for the specified phase, context and `Lifecycle` instance.

Methods

```
public javax.faces.context.FacesContext getFacesContext()
```
Returns the `FacesContext` instance.

```
public javax.faces.event.PhaseId getPhaseId()
```
Returns the `PhaseId` for the phase the event signals the beginning or the end of.

PhaseId

Instances of this class represent the request processing lifecycle phase. All instances are made available through public final static fields, with ordinal values in the order ANY_PHASE, RESTORE_VIEW, APPLY_REQUEST_VALUES, PROCESS_VALIDATIONS, UPDATE_MODEL_VALUES, INVOKE_APPLICATION, and RENDER_RESPONSE.

Synopsis

Class name:	javax.faces.event.PhaseEvent
Extends:	None
Implements:	java.lang.Comparable

Fields

public static final javax.faces.event.PhaseId ANY_PHASE
: The phase identifier for any phase.

public static final javax.faces.event.PhaseId APPLY_REQUEST_VALUES
: The phase identifier for the Apply Request Values phase.

public static final javax.faces.event.PhaseId INVOKE_APPLICATION
: The phase identifier for the Invoke Application phase.

public static final javax.faces.event.PhaseId PROCESS_VALIDATIONS
: The phase identifier for the Process Validations phase.

public static final javax.faces.event.PhaseId RENDER_RESPONSE
: The phase identifier for the Render Response phase.

public static final javax.faces.event.PhaseId UPDATE_MODEL_VALUES
: The phase identifier for the Update Model Values phase.

public static final javautil.List VALUES
: All instances in ascending ordinal order.

Methods

public int compareTo(Object other)
: Returns a negative integer, zero, or a positive integer if this object is less than, equal to, or greater than the specified object.

public int getOrdinal( )
: Returns the ordinal value for this instance.

public String toString( )
: Returns a String representation of this instance.

PhaseListener

This interface is implemented by all classes interested in handling PhaseEvent events.

Synopsis

Interface name:	`javax.faces.event.PhaseListener`
Extends:	`java.util.EventListener`
Implemented by:	All classes interested in handling `PhaseEvent` events.

Methods

`public void afterPhase(javax.faces.event.PhaseEvent event)`

Processes the event signaling the completion of a phase.

`public void beforePhase(javax.faces.event.PhaseEvent event)`

Processes the event signaling the beginning of a phase.

`public javax.faces.event.PhaseId getPhaseId( )`

Returns the identifier for the request processing lifecycle phase when the event listeners wants to be notified of the event. Returning `PhaseId.ANY_PHASE` means that the listener wants to be notified in all phases.

ValueChangeEvent

An instance of this class signals that the user changed the value of a component, e.g., a `UIInput` component.

Synopsis

Class name:	`javax.faces.event.ValueChangeEvent`
Extends:	`javax.faces.event.FacesEvent`
Implements:	`java.io.Serializable`

Constructors

`public ValueChangeEvent(javax.faces.component.UIComponent component, Object oldValue, Object newValue)`

Creates an instance for the specified source component with the old and new value.

Methods

`public Object getNewValue( )`

Returns the new value.

`public Object getOldValue( )`

Returns the old value.

`public boolean isAppropriateListener(javax.faces.event.FacesListener listener)`

Returns true if the listener is a `ValueChangeListener`.

`public void processListener(javax.faces.event.FacesListener listener)`

Calls the listener's `processValueChange( )` method.

ValueChangeListener

This interface is implemented by all classes interested in handling `ValueChangeEvent` events.

Synopsis

Interface name:	`javax.faces.event.ActionListener`
Extends:	`javax.faces.event.FacesListener`
Implemented by:	All classes interested in handling `ActionEvent` events.

Methods

`public void processValueChange(javax.faces.event.ValueChangeEvent event)`
Processes the event.

Package javax.faces.lifecycle

Lifecycle

An instance of a subclass of this abstract class manages the request processing lifecycle.

Synopsis

Class name:	`javax.faces.lifecycle.Lifecycle`
Extends:	None
Implements:	None

Constructors

`public Lifecycle()`
Creates an instance.

Methods

`public abstract void addPhaseListener(javax.faces.event.PhaseListener listener)`
Adds the `PhaseListener` to the list of listeners for the `PhaseEvent` this instance fires.

`public abstract void execute(javax.faces.context.FacesContext context)`
Executes all lifecycle phases up to but not including the Render Response phase, by invoking the phase processing methods on the root component as described in Appendix B.

`public abstract javax.faces.event.PhaseListener[] getPhaseListeners()`
Returns all `PhaseListener` instances registered with this instance or an empty array if none is registered.

`public abstract void removePhaseListener(javax.faces.event.PhaseListener l)`
Removes the `PhaseListener` from the list of listeners for the `PhaseEvent` this instance fires.

`public abstract void render(javax.faces.context.FacesContext context)`
Executes the Render Response lifecycle, unless the `responseComplete()` method has been called on the provided `FacesContext`.

LifecycleFactory

An instance of a subclass of this abstract class is a factory for a `Lifecycle` instance for a request.

Synopsis

Class name:	`javax.faces.lifecycle.LifecycleFactory`
Extends:	None
Implements:	None

Fields

`public static final String DEFAULT_LIFE_CYCLE`
The default lifecycle identifier: `DEFAULT`.

Constructors

`public LifecycleFactory()`
Creates an instance.

Methods

`public abstract void addLifecycle(String lifecycleId, javax.faces.lifecycle.Lifecycle lifecycle)`
Adds the provided `Lifecycle` instance mapped to the specified ID.

`public abstract javax.faces.lifecycle.Lifecycle getLifecycle(String lifecycleId)`
Returns a `Lifecycle` instance for the specified lifecycle ID.

`public abstract java.util.Iterator getLifecycleIds()`
Returns an `Iterator` over the IDs for all available `Lifecycle` instances.

Package javax.faces.render

Renderer

See Appendix C for a description of this class.

RenderKit

An instance of a subclass of this abstract class represents a collection of `Renderer` instances for a specific rendering language, e.g., a markup language like HTML or WML, and is a provider of a `ResponseStateManager` responsible for encoding view state in a response as well as for configured `ResponseStream` and `ResponseWriter` instances.

Synopsis

Class name:	`javax.faces.render.RenderKit`
Extends:	None
Implements:	None

Constructors

`public RenderKit( )`
: Creates an instance.

Methods

`public abstract void addRenderer(String family, String rendererType, javax.faces.render.Renderer renderer)`
: Adds the provided `Renderer` instance mapped to the specified family and renderer type combination.

`public abstract javax.faces.context.ResponseStream createResponseStream(java.io.OutputStream)`
: Uses the provided stream to create and return a new `ResponseStream` instance.

`public abstract javax.faces.context.ResponseWriter createResponseWriter(java.io.Writer, String contentTypeList, String characterEncoding)`
: Uses the provided `Writer` to create and return a new `ResponseWriter` instance for one of the listed content types (or the default if `null`) and the specified character encoding.

`public abstract javax.faces.render.Renderer getRenderer(String family, String rendererType)`
: Returns a `Renderer` instance for the specified family and renderer type combination, or `null` if none is registered for this combination.

`public abstract javax.faces.render.ResponseStateManager getResponseStateManager( )`
: Returns a `ResponseStateManager` suitable for encoding and decoding client-side view state information for the rendering format supported by this kit.

RenderKitFactory

An instance of a subclass of this abstract class is a factory for a `RenderKit` instance for a request.

Synopsis

Class name:	`javax.faces.render.RenderKitFactory`
Extends:	None
Implements:	None

Fields

`public static final String HTML_BASIC_RENDER_KIT`
: The default render kit identifier: `HTML_BASIC`.

Constructors

```
public RenderKitFactory()
```

Creates an instance.

Methods

```
public abstract void addRenderKit(String renderKitId,
  javax.faces.render.RenderKit renderKit)
```

Adds the provided RenderKit instance mapped to the specified ID.

```
public abstract javax.faces.render.RenderKit
  getRenderKit(javax.faces.context.FacesContext context, String renderKitId)
```

Returns a RenderKit instance for the specified ID, possibly customized based on the provided FacesContext (if any).

```
public abstract java.util.Iterator getRenderKitIds()
```

Returns an Iterator over the IDs for all available RenderKit instances.

ResponseStateManager

An instance of a subclass of this abstract class is responsible for encoding and decoding client-side view state information for the rendering format supported by a specific render kit.

Synopsis

Class name:	javax.faces.render.ResponseStateManager
Extends:	None
Implements:	None

Constructors

```
public ResponseStateManager()
```

Creates an instance.

Methods

```
public abstract Object
  getComponentStateToRestore(javax.faces.context.FacesContext context)
```

Returns an Object representing the component state extracted from the current request or null if not found.

```
public abstract Object
  getTreeStructureToRestore(javax.faces.context.FacesContext context, String viewId)
```

Returns an Object representing the component tree structure for the specified view, extracted from the current request, or null if not found.

```
public abstract void writeState(javax.faces.context.FacesContext context,
  javax.faces.application.StateManager.SerializedView state)
```

Writes the current position of the ResponseWriter for the FacesContext, in a format that ensures it's returned with the next request triggered from the view.

Package javax.faces.validator

DoubleRangeValidator

An instance of this class is used as a `Validator` for the range of a `Double` value.

Synopsis

Class name:	`javax.faces.validator.DoubleRangeValidator`
Extends:	None
Implements:	`javax.faces.convert.Validator,` `javax.faces.component.StateHolder`

Fields

`public static final String MAXIMUM_MESSAGE_ID`
: The message identifier for the message this validator creates if the maximum value limit is exceeded: `javax.faces.validator.DoubleRangeValidator.MAXIMUM`.

`public static final String MINIMUM_MESSAGE_ID`
: The message identifier for the message this validator creates if the minimum value limit is not reached: `javax.faces.validator.DoubleRangeValidator.MINIMUM`.

`public static final String TYPE_MESSAGE_ID`
: The message identifier for the message this validator creates if the value is not of the correct type: `javax.faces.validator.DoubleRangeValidator.TYPE`.

`public static final String VALIDATOR_ID`
: The identifier for this validator: `javax.faces.DoubleRange`.

Constructors

`public DoubleRangeValidator( )`
: Creates an instance.

`public DoubleRangeValidator(double maximum)`
: Creates an instance with the specified maximum.

`public DoubleRangeValidator(double maximum, double minimum)`
: Creates an instance with the specified maximum and minimum.

Methods

`public boolean equals(Object other)`
: Returns `true` if the other object represents the same converter as this instance.

`public double getMaximum( )`
: Returns the upper limit set or `Double.MAX_VALUE` if not defined.

`public double getMinimum( )`
: Returns the lower limit set or `Double.MIN_VALUE` if not defined.

`public boolean isTransient( )`
: Returns `true` if no state should be saved and restored for this instance.

`public void restoreState(javax.faces.context.FacesContext context, Object state)`
Restores the state for this instance from the provided value; an `Object` previously returned by the `saveState()` method.

`public Object saveState(javax.faces.context.FacesContext context)`
Returns the state for this instance as an `Object` to be passed to the `restoreState()` method when the instance is restored for the next request.

`public void setMaximum(double maximum)`
Sets the upper limit.

`public void setMinimum(double minimum)`
Sets the lower limit.

`public void setTransient(boolean isTransient)`
Sets the `transient` property value.

`public void validate(javax.faces.context.FacesContext context, javax.faces.component.UIComponent component, Object value)`
Validates the provided value to ensure it falls within the specified limits. Throws a `ValidatorException` with an instance of the appropriate `FacesMessage` if the validation fails.

LengthValidator

An instance of this class is used as a `Validator` for the length of a `String` value.

Synopsis

Class name:	`javax.faces.validator.LengthValidator`
Extends:	None
Implements:	`javax.faces.convert.Validator`, `javax.faces.component.StateHolder`

Fields

`public static final String MAXIMUM_MESSAGE_ID`
The message identifier for the message this validator creates if the maximum length limit is exceeded: `javax.faces.validator.LengthValidator.MAXIMUM`.

`public static final String MINIMUM_MESSAGE_ID`
The message identifier for the message this validator creates if the minimum length limit is not reached: `javax.faces.validator.LengthValidator.MINIMUM`.

`public static final String VALIDATOR_ID`
The identifier for this validator: `javax.faces.Length`.

Constructors

`public LengthValidator()`
Creates an instance.

`public LengthValidator(int maximum)`
Creates an instance with the specified maximum.

`public LengthValidator(int maximum, int minimum)`
Creates an instance with the specified maximum and minimum.

Methods

`public boolean equals(Object other)`
: Returns true if the other object represents the same converter as this instance.

`public int getMaximum( )`
: Returns the upper limit set or zero if not defined.

`public int getMinimum( )`
: Returns the lower limit set or zero if not defined.

`public boolean isTransient( )`
: Returns true if no state should be saved and restored for this instance.

`public void restoreState(javax.faces.context.FacesContext context, Object state)`
: Restores the state for this instance from the provided value; an `Object` previously returned by the `saveState( )` method.

`public Object saveState(javax.faces.context.FacesContext context)`
: Returns the state for this instance as an `Object` to be passed to the `restoreState( )` method when the instance is restored for the next request.

`public void setMaximum(int maximum)`
: Sets the upper limit.

`public void setMinimum(int minimum)`
: Sets the lower limit.

`public void setTransient(boolean isTransient)`
: Sets the `transient` property value.

`public void validate(javax.faces.context.FacesContext context, javax.faces.component.UIComponent component, Object value)`
: Validates the provided value, to ensure it falls within the specified limits. Throws a `ValidatorException` with an instance of the appropriate `FacesMessage` if the validation fails.

LongRangeValidator

An instance of this class is used as a `Validator` for the range of a `Long` value.

Synopsis

Class name:	`javax.faces.validator.LongRangeValidator`
Extends:	None
Implements:	`javax.faces.convert.Validator`, `javax.faces.component.StateHolder`

Fields

`public static final String MAXIMUM_MESSAGE_ID`
: The message identifier for the message this validator creates if the maximum value limit is exceeded: `javax.faces.validator.LongRangeValidator.MAXIMUM`.

`public static final String MINIMUM_MESSAGE_ID`
: The message identifier for the message this validator creates if the minimum value limit is not reached: `javax.faces.validator.LongRangeValidator.MINIMUM`.

public static final String TYPE_MESSAGE_ID
The message identifier for the message this validator creates if the value is not of the correct type: javax.faces.validator.LongRangeValidator.TYPE.

public static final String VALIDATOR_ID
The identifier for this validator: javax.faces.LongRange.

Constructors

public LongRangeValidator()
Creates an instance.

public LongRangeValidator(int maximum)
Creates an instance with the specified maximum.

public LongRangeValidator(int maximum, int minimum)
Creates an instance with the specified maximum and minimum.

Methods

public boolean equals(Object other)
Returns true if the other object represents the same converter as this instance.

public long getMaximum()
Returns the upper limit set or Long.MAX_VALUE if not defined.

public long getMinimum()
Returns the lower limit set or Long.MIN_VALUE if not defined.

public boolean isTransient()
Returns true if no state should be saved and restored for this instance.

public void restoreState(javax.faces.context.FacesContext context, Object state)
Restores the state for this instance from the provided value; an Object previously returned by the saveState() method.

public Object saveState(javax.faces.context.FacesContext context)
Returns the state for this instance as an Object to be passed to the restoreState() method when the instance is restored for the next request.

public void setMaximum(long maximum)
Sets the upper limit.

public void setMinimum(long minimum)
Sets the lower limit.

public void setTransient(boolean isTransient)
Sets the transient property value.

public void validate(javax.faces.context.FacesContext context, javax.faces.component.UIComponent component, Object value)
Validates the provided value, to ensure it falls within the specified limits. Throws a ValidatorException with an instance of the appropriate FacesMessage if the validation fails.

Validator

This interface is implemented by all validator classes.

Synopsis

Interface name:	`javax.faces.validator.Validator`
Extends:	None
Implemented by:	All standard and custom validators.

Fields

`public static final String NOT_IN_RANGE_MESSAGE_ID`

The message identifier for the message a validator creates if the value falls outside both the minimum and maximum value: `javax.faces.validator.NOT_IN_RANGE`.

Methods

`public void validate(javax.faces.context.FacesContext context, javax.faces.component.UIComponent component, Object value)`

Validates the provided value. Throws a `ValidatorException` with an instance of the appropriate `FacesMessage` if the validation fails.

ValidatorException

An instance of this class is thrown by a `Validator` implementation to signal a validation error.

Synopsis

Class name:	`javax.faces.validator.ValidatorException`
Extends:	`javax.faces.FacesException`
Implements:	`java.io.Serializable`

Constructors

`public ValidatorException(java.faces.application.FacesMessage message)`

Creates an instance with the specified message.

`public ValidatorException(java.faces.application.FacesMessage message, Throwable rootCause)`

Creates an instance with the specified message and root cause.

Methods

`public java.faces.application.FacesMessage getFacesMessage()`

Returns the `FacesMessage` instance, or `null` if none is set.

Package javax.faces.webapp

AttributeTag

This class is a JSP tag handler class for an action that sets a generic attribute of the component represented by the closest `UIComponentTag` parent tag handler.

Synopsis

Class name:	`javax.faces.webapp.AttributeTag`
Extends:	`javax.servlet.jsp.tagext.TagSupport`
Implements:	`javax.servlet.jsp.tagext.IterationTag`

Constructors

`public AttributeTag()`
Creates an instance.

Methods

`public int doStartTag()`
Sets a generic attribute with the name and value corresponding to this tag handler's attributes for the component represented by the closest `UIComponentTag` parent tag handler if this component doesn't already have an attribute with this name.

`public void release()`
Releases all references to acquired resources.

`public void setName(String name)`
Sets the attribute name.

`public void setValue(String name)`
Sets the attribute value.

ConverterTag

This class is a base class for JSP tag handler class actions that configures the component represented by the closest `UIComponentTag` parent tag handler with a `Converter`.

Synopsis

Class name:	`javax.faces.webapp.ConverterTag`
Extends:	`javax.servlet.jsp.tagext.TagSupport`
Implements:	`javax.servlet.jsp.tagext.IterationTag`

Constructors

`public ConverterTag()`
Creates an instance.

Methods

`protected javax.faces.convert.Converter createConverter()`
: Returns a `Converter`, configured based on tag handler attribute values. An implementation of this method can be provided by a subclass. This implementation creates an instance of the converter identified by the `converterId` attribute.

`public int doStartTag()`
: Calls `createConverter()` to create a `Converter` and configures the component represented by the closest `UIComponentTag` parent tag handler to use if the component was created while processing the JSP page.

`public void release()`
: Releases all references to acquired resources.

`public void setConverterId(String converterId)`
: Sets the `converterId` attribute.

FacesServlet

This class is a servlet that acts as the entry point to a JSF view. It creates all infrastructure instances and then asks them to process the request as a JSF request.

Synopsis

Class name:	`javax.faces.webapp.FacesServlet`
Extends:	None
Implements:	`javax.servlet.Servlet`

Fields

`public static final String CONFIG_FILES_ATTR`
: The name of the application context initialization parameter holding a list of JSF configuration files: `javax.faces.CONFIG_FILES`.

`public static final String LIFECYCLE_ID_ATTR`
: The name of the application context initialization parameter holding the class name of the `Lifecycle` implementation to use: `javax.faces.LIFECYCLE_ID`.

Constructors

`public FacesServlet()`
: Creates an instance.

Methods

`public void destroy()`
: Releases all acquired resources.

`public javax.servlet.ServletConfig getServletConfig()`
: Returns the `ServletConfig` instance.

`public String getServletInfo()`
: Returns information about this servlet.

```
public void init(javax.servlet.ServletConfig config)
```

Acquire all JSF infrastructure instances needed to process JSF requests.

```
public void service(javax.servlet.ServletRequest request,
  javax.servlet.ServletResponse response)
  throws java.io.IOException, javax.servlet.ServletException
```

Create a `Lifecycle` instance and ask it to process the request.

FacetTag

This class is a JSP tag handler class for an action that configures the component represented by the closest `UIComponentTag` parent tag handler with the facet component represented by its single child `UIComponentTag` tag handler.

Synopsis

Class name:	`javax.faces.webapp.FacetTag`
Extends:	`javax.servlet.jsp.tagext.TagSupport`
Implements:	`javax.servlet.jsp.tagext.IterationTag`

Constructors

```
public FacetTag()
```

Creates an instance.

Methods

```
public int doEndTag()
```

Returns `EVAL_PAGE`.

```
public int doStartTag()
```

Returns `EVAL_BODY_INCLUDE`.

```
public void release()
```

Releases all references to acquired resources.

```
public void setName(String name)
```

Sets the facet name.

UIComponentBodyTag

This class is a JSP tag handler base class that all JSF actions that represent a `UIComponent` instance that need access to the element body evaluation result extend.

Synopsis

Class name:	`javax.faces.webapp.UIComponentBodyTag`
Extends:	`javax.faces.webapp.UIComponentTag`
Implements:	`javax.servlet.jsp.tagext.BodyTag`

Fields

`protected javax.servlet.jsp.tagext.BodyContent bodyContent`
The variable holding the buffered `BodyContent`.

Constructors

`public UIComponentBodyTag( )`
Creates an instance.

Methods

`public int doAfterBody( )`
Returns the value of `getDoAfterBodyValue( )`.

`public int doInitBody( )`
This implementation does nothing. Can be overridden by subclasses to prepare for the body evaluation.

`public javax.servlet.jsp.tagext.BodyContent getBodyContent( )`
Returns the value of the `bodyContent` variable.

`public int getDoAfterBodyValue( )`
Returns the value to return from `doAfterBodyValue( )`, as established by a subclass. This implementation returns `SKIP_BODY`.

`public int getDoStartValue( )`
Returns the value to return from `doStartTag( )`, as established by a subclass. This implementation returns `EVAL_BODY_BUFFERED`.

`public javax.servlet.jsp.JspWriter getPreviousOut( )`
Returns the `JspWriter` for the parent tag handler.

`public void release( )`
Releases all references to acquired resources.

`public void setBodyContent(javax.servlet.jsp.tagext.BodyContent bodyContent)`
Sets the value of the `bodyContent` variable.

UIComponentTag

This class is a JSP tag handler base class that all JSF actions that represent a `UIComponent` instance that don't need access to the element body evaluation result extend.

Synopsis

Class name:	`javax.faces.webapp.UIComponentBodyTag`
Extends:	None
Implements:	`javax.servlet.jsp.tagext.Tag`

Fields

`protected javax.servlet.jsp.PageContext pageContext`
The variable holding the `PageContext` for the JSP page.

Constructors

public UIComponentTag()
: Creates an instance.

Methods

public int doEndTag()
: Renders the end of the component the tag handler represents. If the component's `getRendersChildren()` method returns `true`, calls `encodeBegin()` and `encodeChildren()`, and calls `encodeEnd()` independent on the `getRendersChildren()` value. This method also adjusts the children and facets for the component it represents, by removing children and facets created by conditional portions of the JSP page the last time it was processed but not processed this time.

public int doStartTag()
: Calls `setupResponseWriter()`, in case this is the first tag handler in the page. Calls the `findComponent()` method to locate the component this tag handler represents, creating it if it isn't already available in the view. If a new component was created, add it as a child of the component represented by the closest `UIComponentTag` parent tag handler, if any, by calling the parent's `addChild()` method. Calls `encodeBegin()`, unless its `getRendersChildren()` method returns `true`.

protected void encodeBegin()
: Delegates the call to the component this tag handler represents.

protected void encodeChildren()
: Delegates the call to the component this tag handler represents.

protected void encodeEnd()
: Delegates the call to the component this tag handler represents.

protected javax.faces.component.UIComponent
  findComponent(javax.faces.context.FacesContext context)
: Locates or creates the component the tag handler represents. An attempt to find the component is done by locating a parent `UIComponentTag` tag handler and asking it for its component. If this tag handler represents a facet, try to get a facet with the same name from the parent, otherwise try to get a child based on the component ID. If the component doesn't exits, creates an instance of the type returned by `getComponentType()`, calls `setProperties()` and adds the new component as a facet or child of the parent.

public javax.faces.component.UIComponent getComponentInstance()
: Returns the component the tag handler represents, if called between `doStartTag()` and `doEndTag()`.

public String getComponentType()
: Returns the component type the tag handler represents.

public boolean getCreated()
: Returns `true` if the component instance was created by this tag handler during the processing of this request.

`public int getDoEndValue()`
: Returns the value to return from `doEndTag()`, as established by a subclass. This implementation returns `EVAL_PAGE`.

`public int getDoStartValue()`
: Returns the value to return from `doStartTag()`, as established by a subclass. This implementation returns `EVAL_BODY_INCLUDE`.

`public javax.facet.context.FacesContext getFacetContext()`
: Returns the current `FacetContext` instance for the request.

`protected String getFacetName()`
: Returns the name of the facet this tag handler represents or `null` if it represents a regular child component.

`protected String getId()`
: Returns the `id` attribute value or `null` if not set.

`public javax.servlet.jsp.tagext.Tag getParent()`
: Returns the parent tag handler or `null` if none.

`public static javax.facet.webapp.UIComponentTag getParentUIComponentTag(javax.facet.context.FacesContext context)`
: Returns the closest parent `UIComponentTag` tag handler or `null` if none. This method uses a stack to keep track of the nesting level, even between included pages processed as part of the same request.

`public String getRendererType()`
: Returns the renderer type or `null`.

`protected boolean isSuppressed()`
: Returns `true` if the component is a facet, the component's `rendered` property is `false`, its parent's `rendersChildren` property is `true`, or the component's parent returns `true` from this method.

`public static boolean isValueReference(String value)`
: Returns `true` if the value is a JSF EL expression, i.e., is delimited by #{ and }.

`public void release()`
: Releases all references to acquired resources.

`public void setBinding(String binding)`
: Sets a component binding expression.

`public void SetId(String id)`
: Sets the id attribute value, to be used as the component ID for the component represented by the tag header.

`public void setPageContext(javax.servlet.jsp.PageContext pageContext)`
: Sets the `pageContext` variable.

`public void setParent(javax.servlet.jsp.tagext.Tag parent)`
: Sets the parent for this tag handler.

`protected void setProperties(javax.facet.component.UIComponent parent)`
: Sets the component properties and attributes corresponding to the tag handler's attributes. The default implementation sets the `componentId`, `binding`, `rendered`, and `rendererType` properties. Subclasses must call this implementation before processing the subclass-specific attributes.

public void setRendered(String rendered)
: Sets an explicit value or a JSF expression value for the rendered property.

protected void setupResponseWriter()
: Unless it's been done already, sets up the ResponseWriter for the current response.

ValidatorTag

This class is a base class for JSP tag handler class for actions that configures the component represented by the closest UIComponentTag parent tag handler with a Validator.

Synopsis

Class name:	javax.faces.webapp.ValidatorTag
Extends:	javax.servlet.jsp.tagext.TagSupport
Implements:	javax.servlet.jsp.tagext.IterationTag

Constructors

public ValidatorTag()
: Creates an instance.

Methods

protected javax.faces.validator.Validator createValidator()
: Returns a Validator, configured based on tag handler attribute values. An implementation of this method can be provided by a subclass. This implementation creates an instance of the converter identified by the validatorId attribute.

public int doStartTag()
: Calls createValidator() to create a Validator and configures the component represented by the closest UIComponentTag parent tag handler to use if the component was created while processing the JSP page.

public void release()
: Releases all references to acquired resources.

public void setValidatorId(String validatorId)
: Sets the validatorId attribute.

Identifiers for Standard JSF Messages

Most of the JSF default classes can be replaced with customized versions by declarations of implementation classes for with the identifier for the default implementation it replaces. This previous sections include all standard class identifiers for the standard validators and converters, and Appendix C includes identifiers for the standard components and renderers.

In addition to replacing default classes with custom classes, the text for all JSF messages can also be replaced by creating resource bundles containing the custom text for the standard message keys, see Chapter 7 for examples. This section contains subsections for all standard message keys along with the text (including message parameters, replaced by property values when the message is created) used by the JSF reference implementation.

javax.faces.component.UIInput.CONVERSION

A message with this summary text is created when an input value can't be converted to the data type of the bean property the component is bound to.

Sample text

"Conversion error occurred"

javax.faces.component.UIInput.REQUIRED

A message with this summary text is created when an input component has the required property set to `true` but no value is submitted.

Sample text

"Value is required"

javax.faces.component.UISelectOne.INVALID

A message with this summary text is created when the submitted value for a select-one component doesn't match one of the select item values.

Sample text

"Value is not a valid option"

javax.faces.component.UISelectMany.INVALID

A message with this summary text is created when the submitted value for a select-many component doesn't match one of the select item values.

Sample text

"Value is not a valid option"

javax.faces.validator.NOT_IN_RANGE

A message with this summary text is created when the value validated by one of the standard validators falls outside both the minimum and maximum value specified for the validator.

Sample text

"Specified attribute is not between the expected values of {0} and {1}"

javax.faces.validator.DoubleRangeValidator.MAXIMUM

A message with this summary text is created when the value validated by the standard `DoubleRangeValidator` exceeds the maximum value specified for the validator.

Sample text

"Value is greater than allowable maximum of {0}"

javax.faces.validator.DoubleRangeValidator.MINIMUM

A message with this summary text is created when the value validated by the standard `DoubleRangeValidator` is lower than the minimum value specified for the validator.

Sample text

"Value is less than allowable minimum of {0}"

javax.faces.validator.DoubleRangeValidator.TYPE

A message with this summary text is created when the value validated by the standard `DoubleRangeValidator` is of an invalid data type.

Sample text

"Value is not of the correct type"

javax.faces.validator.LengthRangeValidator.MAXIMUM

A message with this summary text is created when the value validated by the standard `LengthValidator` exceeds the maximum value specified for the validator.

Sample text

"Value is greater than allowable maximum of {0}"

javax.faces.validator.LengthRangeValidator.MINIMUM

A message with this summary text is created when the value validated by the standard `LengthValidator` is lower than the minimum value specified for the validator.

Sample text

"Value is less than allowable minimum of {0}"

javax.faces.validator.LengthRangeValidator.TYPE

A message with this summary text is created when the value validated by the standard `LengthValidator` is of an invalid data type.

Sample text

"Value is not of the correct type"

javax.faces.validator.LongRangeValidator.MAXIMUM

A message with this summary text is created when the value validated by the standard `LongRangeValidator` exceeds the maximum value specified for the validator.

Sample text

"Value is greater than allowable maximum of {0}"

javax.faces.validator.LongRangeValidator.MINIMUM

A message with this summary text is created when the value validated by the standard `LongRangeValidator` is lower than the minimum value specified for the validator.

Sample text

"Value is less than allowable minimum of {0}"

javax.faces.validator.LongRangeValidator.TYPE

A message with this summary text is created when the value validated by the standard `LongRangeValidator` is of an invalid data type.

Sample text

"Value is not of the correct type"

APPENDIX E

JSF Configuration File Reference

One or more configuration files are used to configure a JSF application. The main configuration file for an application is the *WEB-INF/faces-config.xml* file. Files in the same format can be bundled also within JAR files containing custom components, renderers, or any other custom JSF classes. See Chapter 13 and the description of the FactoryFinder class in Appendix D for details.

This appendix describes all elements that can be used in a JSF configuration file. The configuration file is an XML file, with the rules for which elements it can contain and how they must be arranged controlled by Document Type Definition (DTD) available online at *http://java.sun.com/dtd/web-facesconfig_1_0.dtd*. This DTD must be referenced in the document type declaration at the top of the configuration file, as shown in Example E-1.

Example E-1. JSF DTD element

```
<!DOCTYPE faces-config PUBLIC
  "-//Sun Microsystems, Inc.//DTD JavaServer Faces Config 1.0//EN"
  "http://java.sun.com/dtd/web-facesconfig_1_0.dtd">

<faces-config>
  ...
</faces-config>
```

All other elements in the configuration file must be enclosed within a <faces-config> element as shown in Example E-1.

Within the <faces-config> element body, top-level elements can be included in any order. Each top-level element is described in a separate section in this appendix. The top-level elements are all optional and can be included more than once, unless otherwise stated. Most top-level elements contain other elements.

I use syntax descriptions similar to those in the other appendixes to show the rules for the elements nested within top-level elements. The nested elements must be included in the order they are listed in the syntax description. Mutually exclusive elements are separated by vertical bars (|). Optional nested elements are embedded in square brackets ([ ]), followed by an asterisk (*) if more than one element of this type may be used. An element name followed by a plus sign (+) means the element is required, but it can be used more than once. For elements that accept predefined values, all values are listed separated by vertical bars; the default value (if any) is in bold font. Italics are used for element values that don't have a fixed set of accepted values. Element attribute values are described using the same syntax as element values.

<description>, <display-name>, and <icon>

These three elements provide information a development tool can use to describe the application. These three elements are not top-level elements themselves but can be nested within most top-level elements.

Syntax

```
<description [xml:lang="lang"]>description</description>

<display-name [xml:lang="lang"]>displayName</display-name>

<icon [xml:lang="lang"]>
  [<small-icon>iconPath</small-icon>]
  [<large-icon>iconPath</large-icon>]
</icon>
```

The `<icon>` element can contain a `<small-icon>` and a `<large-icon>` element, each with a context-relative path to an image file (GIF and JPEG formats are supported). The small icon must be 16x16 pixels, and the large 32x32. The `<display-name>` element can specify a name for the entity described by the parent element, and the `<description>` element a longer description.

You can use different versions of all these elements for multiple languages, each with a unique `xml:lang` attribute value ("en", for English, is the default value):

```
<icon>
  <small-icon>/images/small.gif</small-icon>
  <large-icon>/images/large.gif</large-icon>
</icon>
<display-name>The application name</display-name>
<description>
  A longer description of
  the application.
</description>
```

<application>

The `<application>` element declares replacements for various pluggable classes for the application. The top-level nested elements can be declared in any order.

Syntax

```
<application>
  [<action-listener>actionListener</action-listener>]
```

```
[<default-render-kit>defaultRenderKit</default-render-kit>]
[<message-bundle>messageBundle</message-bundle>]
[<navigation-handler>navigationHandler</navigation-handler>]
[<view-handler>viewHandler</view-handler>]
[<state-manager>stateManager</state-manager>]
[<property-resolver>propertyHandler</property-resolver>]
[<variable-resolver>variableResolver</variable-resolver>]
[<locale-config>
   [<default-locale>defaultLocale</default-locale>]
   [<supported-locale>supportedLocale</supported-locale>]*
 </locale-config>]
</application>
```

The <action-listener> element contains the fully qualified class name for a class implementing the javax.faces.event.ActionListener interface, used as the default ActionListener for the application:

```
<action-listener>
  com.mycompany.jsf.MyActionListener
</action-listener>
```

The <default-render-kit> element contains identifier for a default render kit to use instead of the JSF HTML basic render kit:

```
<default-render-kit>myFancyHTMLKit</default-render-kit>
```

The <message-bundle> element contains base name for the message resource bundle containing custom message texts for the JSF standard messages (see the java.util. ResourceBundle JavaDocs and Chapter 7 for details):

```
<message-bundle>myMessages</message-bundle>
```

The <navigation-handler> element contains the fully qualified class name for a customized javax.faces.application.NavigationHandler class:

```
<navigation-handler>
  com.mycompany.jsf.MyNavigationHandler
</navigation-handler>
```

The <view-handler> element contains the fully qualified class name for a customized javax. faces.application.ViewHandler class:

```
<view-handler>
  com.mycompany.jsf.MyViewHandler
</view-handler>
```

The <state-manager> element contains the fully qualified class name for a customized javax.faces.application.StateManager class

```
<view-handler>
  com.mycompany.jsf.MyViewHandler
</view-handler>
```

The <property-resolver> element contains the fully qualified class name for a customized javax.faces.el.PropertyResolver class:

```
<property-resolver>
  com.mycompany.jsf.MyPropertyResolver
</property-resolver>
```

The <variable-resolver> element contains the fully qualified class name for a customized javax.faces.el.VariableResolver class:

```
<variable-resolver>
  com.mycompany.jsf.MyVariableResolver
</variable-resolver>
```

The <locale-config> element contains one optional <default-locale> element declaring the default locale for the application and any number of <supported-locale> elements declaring additional supported locales. A locale is specified as a language code, optionally followed by a country code, optionally followed by a variant, with the pieces separated by a dash or an underscore:

```
<locale-config>
  <default-locale>en-US</default-locale>
   <supported-locale>fr</supported-locale>
   <supported-locale>sv</supported-locale>
</locale-config>
```

<factory>

The <factory> element declares replacements for the factory classes for the application. The top-level nested elements can be declared in any order.

Syntax

```
<factory>
  [<application-factory>applicationFactory</application-factory>]
  [<faces-context-factory>facesContextFactory</faces-context-factory>]
  [<lifecycle-factory>lifecycleFactory</lifecycle-factory>]
  [<render-kit-factory>renderKitFactory</render-kit-factory>]
</factory>
```

The <application-factory> element contains the fully qualified class name for a customized javax.faces.application.ApplicationFactory class:

```
<application-factory>
  com.mycompany.jsf.MyApplicationFactory
</application-factory>
```

The <faces-context-factory> element contains the fully qualified class name for a customized javax.faces.context.FacesContextFactory class:

```
<faces-context-factory>
  com.mycompany.jsf.MyFacesContextFactory
</faces-context-factory>
```

The <lifecycle-factory> element contains the fully qualified class name for a customized javax.faces.lifecycle.LifecycleFactory class:

```
<lifecycle-factory>
  com.mycompany.jsf.MyLifecycleFactory
</lifecycle-factory>
```

The <render-kit-factory> element contains the fully qualified class name for a customized javax.faces.render.RenderKitFactory class:

```
<render-kit-factory>
  com.mycompany.jsf.MyRenderKitFactory
</render-kit-factory>
```

<component>

The <component> element declares the implementation class for a component type.

Syntax

```
<component>
  [<description [xml:lang="lang"]>description</description>]*
  [<display-name [xml:lang="lang"]>displayName</display-name>]*
  [<icon [xml:lang="lang"]>
     [<small-icon>iconPath</small-icon>]
     [<large-icon>iconPath</large-icon>]
   </icon>]*
  <component-type>componentType</component-type>
  <component-class>className</component-class>
  [<attribute>
    [<description [xml:lang="lang"]>description</description>]*
    [<display-name [xml:lang="lang"]>displayName</display-name>]*
    [<icon [xml:lang="lang"]>
       [<small-icon>iconPath</small-icon>]
       [<large-icon>iconPath</large-icon>]
     </icon>]*
     <attribute-name>attrName</attribute-name>
     <attribute-class>className</attribute-class>
     [<default-value>defaultValue</default-value>]
     [<suggested-value>suggestedValue</suggested-value>]
     [<attribute-extension>extension</attribute-extension>]*
   </attribute>]*
  [<property>
    [<description [xml:lang="lang"]>description</description>]*
    [<display-name [xml:lang="lang"]>displayName</display-name>]*
    [<icon [xml:lang="lang"]>
       [<small-icon>iconPath</small-icon>]
       [<large-icon>iconPath</large-icon>]
     </icon>]*
     <property-name>propName</property-name>
     <property-class>className</property-class>
     [<default-value>defaultValue</default-value>]
     [<suggested-value>suggestedValue</suggested-value>]
     [<property-extension>extension</property-extension>]*
   </property>]*
   [<component-extension>extension</component-extension>]*
</component>
```

The <component-type> element declares a component type ID and the <component-class> element contains the fully qualified class name for the javax.faces.component.UIComponent subclass. These are the only mandatory elements:

```
<component>
  <component-type>com.mycompany.MyComponent</component-type>
  <component-class>
    com.mycompany.jsf.MyComponent
  </component-class>
</component>
```

The <attribute> and <property> elements provide information about the component's generic attributes and type-safe properties, respectively, that may be used by a development tool to help a developer use the component. They are optional but should be used at least for components used by a large group of developers. Subelements declare the name and the data type for the attribute or property, the <suggested-value> element declares a value a tool should suggest for the attribute or property, and the <default-value> the value used if none is set.

The extension elements for the attribute and property, as well as for the component, may be used for implementation-dependent elements.

<converter>

The <converter> element declares the implementation class for a converter.

Syntax

```
<converter>
  [<description [xml:lang="lang"]>description</description>]*
  [<display-name [xml:lang="lang"]>displayName</display-name>]*
  [<icon [xml:lang="lang"]>
     [<small-icon>iconPath</small-icon>]
     [<large-icon>iconPath</large-icon>]
   </icon>]*
  <converter-id>converterId</converter-id> |
    <converter-for-class>targetClassName</converter-for-class>
  <converter-class>className</converter-class>
  [<attribute>
    [<description [xml:lang="lang"]>description</description>]*
    [<display-name [xml:lang="lang"]>displayName</display-name>]*
    [<icon [xml:lang="lang"]>
       [<small-icon>iconPath</small-icon>]
       [<large-icon>iconPath</large-icon>]
     </icon>]*
     <attribute-name>attrName</attribute-name>
     <attribute-class>className</attribute-class>
     [<default-value>defaultValue</default-value>]
     [<suggested-value>suggestedValue</suggested-value>]
     [<attribute-extension>extension</attribute-extension>]*
   </attribute>]*
  [<property>
    [<description [xml:lang="lang"]>description</description>]*
    [<display-name [xml:lang="lang"]>displayName</display-name>]*
    [<icon [xml:lang="lang"]>
       [<small-icon>iconPath</small-icon>]
       [<large-icon>iconPath</large-icon>]
     </icon>]*
     <property-name>propName</property-name>
     <property-class>className</property-class>
     [<default-value>defaultValue</default-value>]
     [<suggested-value>suggestedValue</suggested-value>]
     [<property-extension>extension</property-extension>]*
   </property>]*
 </converter>
```

The <converter-class> element contains the fully qualified class name that implements the javax.faces.convert.Converter interface. If the converter should be accessible through an identifier, it's declared by the <converter-id> element. For a converter used for conversion of a particular data type, the <converter-for-class> element declares the fully qualified class name for the target data type These are the only mandatory elements:

```
<converter>
  <converter-id>com.mycompany.MyConverter</converter-id>
  <converter-class>
    com.mycompany.jsf.MyConverter
  </converter-class>
</converter>
<converter>
  <converter-for-class>java.util.Locale</converter-for-class>
  <converter-class>
    com.mycompany.jsf.MyLocaleConverter
  </converter-class>
</converter>
```

The <attribute> and <property> elements provide information about the component's generic attributes and type-safe converter properties, respectively, that may be used by a development tool to help a developer use the converter, the same way for the <component> element.

<lifecycle>

The <lifecycle> element declares lifecycle phase listeners.

Syntax

```
<lifecycle>
  <phase-listener>phaseListener</phase-listener>
</lifecycle>
```

The <phase-listener> element contains the fully qualified class name that implements the javax.faces.event.PhaseListener interface.:

```
<lifecycle>
  <phase-listener>com.mycompany.MyPhaseListener</phase-listener>
</lifecycle>
```

<managed-bean>

The <managed-bean> element declares a managed bean, which is created and populated by JSF when it's needed (e.g., when a value binding expression referencing it is evaluated) but it doesn't yet exist in the declared scope.

Syntax

```
<managed-bean>
  [<description [xml:lang="lang"]>description</description>]*
  [<display-name [xml:lang="lang"]>displayName</display-name>]*
  [<icon [xml:lang="lang"]>
```

```
      [<small-icon>iconPath</small-icon>]
      [<large-icon>iconPath</large-icon>]
    </icon>]*
  <managed-bean-name>managedBeanName</managed-bean-name>
  <managed-bean-class>className</managed-bean-class>
  <managed-bean-scope>
    none|request|session|application
  </managed-bean-scope>
  [<managed-property>
    [<description [xml:lang="lang"]>description</description>]*
    [<display-name [xml:lang="lang"]>displayName</display-name>]*
    [<icon [xml:lang="lang"]>
       [<small-icon>iconPath</small-icon>]
       [<large-icon>iconPath</large-icon>]
     </icon>]*
     <property-name>propName</property-name>
     [<property-class>className</property-class>]
     <map-entries>
       [<key-class>className</key-class>]
       [<value-class>className</value-class>]
       <map-entry>
         <key>key</key>
         <null-value/> | <value>value</value>
       </map-entry>*
     </map-entries> |
       <null-value/>] |
       <value>value</value> |
       <list-entries>
         [<value-class>className</value-class>]
         <list-entry>
           <null-value>/ | <value>value</value>
         </list-entry>*
       </list-entries>
   </managed-property>* |
     <map-entries>...</map-entries> |
     <list-entries>...</list-entries>
  ]
</managed-bean>
```

The managed bean name, the fully qualified class name, and the scope are declared by three mandatory elements: `<managed-bean-name>`, `<managed-bean-class>`, and `<managed-bean-scope>`.

Values for the bean's properties can be declared with `<managed-property>` elements, with a nested `<property-name>` element containing the name of the property, an optional `<property-class>` element declaring the property data type, and one element of type `<null-value>`, `<value>`, `<map-entries>`, or `<list-entries>` for the property value. The `<null-value>` element sets the property to null and the `<value>` element sets the property to the element content; either an explicit value or a JSF EL expression:

```
<managed-bean>
  <managed-bean-name>myBean</managed-bean-name>
  <managed-bean-class>com.mycompany.MyBean</managed-bean-class>
  <managed-bean-scope>session</managed-bean-scope>
```

```
  <managed-property>
    <property-name>myProperty</property-name>
    <value>myValue</value>
  </managed-property>
  <managed-property>
    <property-name>myDynamicProperty</property-name>
    <value>#{anotherBean.aProperty}</value>
  </managed-property>
</managed-bean>
```

A property of type java.util.Map is populated with the <map-entries> element, containing optional elements declaring the data types for the key and the value and one or more <map-entry> elements with nested <key>, <null-value>, and <value> elements. The key and value is converted to the declared key and value data types before the map entry is put in the Map.

Similarly, a property of type java.util.List of Object[] is populated with the <list-entries> element, containing optional elements declaring the data type for the value and one or more <list-entry> elements with nested <null-value> and <value> elements. The value is converted to the declared value data types before the list entry is added to the List or array.

A concrete implementation of the java.util.Map and java.util.List interfaces can also be declared as a managed bean. The <map-entries> or <list-entries> elements can be used to populate the entries of such a bean:

```
<managed-bean>
  <managed-bean-name>myMap</managed-bean-name>
  <managed-bean-class>java.util.HashMap</managed-bean-class>
  <managed-bean-scope>session</managed-bean-scope>
  <map-entries>
    <value-class>java.lang.Integer</value-class>
    <map-entry>
      <key>Apple</key>
      <value>1</value>
    </map-entry>
    <map-entry>
      <key>Banana</key>
      <value>2</value>
    </map-entry>
  </map-entries>
</managed-bean>
```

<navigation-rule>

The <navigation-rule> element declares a navigation rule for the default navigation handler.

Syntax

```
<navigation-rule>
  [<description [xml:lang="lang"]>description</description>]*
  [<display-name [xml:lang="lang"]>displayName</display-name>]*
  [<icon [xml:lang="lang"]>
     [<small-icon>iconPath</small-icon>]
```

```
      [<large-icon>iconPath</large-icon>]
    </icon>]*
   [<from-view-id>viewId</from-view-id>]
   [<navigation-case>
     [<description [xml:lang="lang"]>description</description>]*
     [<display-name [xml:lang="lang"]>displayName</display-name>]*
     [<icon [xml:lang="lang"]>
        [<small-icon>iconPath</small-icon>]
        [<large-icon>iconPath</large-icon>]
      </icon>]*
     [<from-action>actionBinding</from-action>]
     [<from-outcome>outcome</from-outcome>]
     <to-view-id>viewId</to-view-id>
     [<redirect/>]
    </navigation-case>]*
  </navigation-rule>
```

The optional <from-view-id> element limits the rule to the specified view ID or all views with IDs matching a pattern, for instance "/myViews/*", where the asterisk matches any characters. One or more <navigation-case> elements declares which view to select (the <to-view-id> element) depending on the action method (the <from-action> element) and/or the action method's outcome (the <from-outcome> element):

```
<navigation-rule>
  <from-view-id>/myView.jsp</from-view-id>
  <navigation-case>
    <from-action>#{myBean.myActionMethod}</from-action>
    <from-outcome>success</from-outcome>
     <to-view-id>/myOtherView.jsp</to-view-id>
  </navigation-case>
</navigation-rule>
<navigation-rule>
  <from-view-id>/*</from-view-id>
  <navigation-case>
    <from-outcome>error</from-outcome>
     <to-view-id>/myErrorView.jsp</to-view-id>
     <redirect/>
  </navigation-case>
</navigation-rule>
```

Omitting the <from-action> or the <from-outcome> element means that the view is selected regardless of which action produced the outcome or which outcome was produced, respectively. If the <redirect> element is included, the new view is requested through a redirect response.

<referenced-bean>

The <referenced-bean> element declares a bean that the application makes available in one of the scopes accessible to JSF. A development tool can use this information, e.g., include the bean name in a list of available JSF EL variables, and show all its accessible properties.

Syntax

```
<referenced-bean>
  [<description [xml:lang="lang"]>description</description>]*
  [<display-name [xml:lang="lang"]>displayName</display-name>]*
  [<icon [xml:lang="lang"]>
     [<small-icon>iconPath</small-icon>]
     [<large-icon>iconPath</large-icon>]
  </icon>]*
  <referenced-bean-name>beanName</referenced-bean-name>
  <referenced-bean-class>className</referenced-bean-class>
</referenced-bean>
```

The bean name (i.e., the name of the request, session, or application scope attribute where the application puts the reference) is declared by the <referenced-bean-name> element, and <referenced-bean-class> declares the fully qualified class name:

```
<referenced-bean>
  <referenced-bean-name>myDataSource</referenced-bean-name>
  <referenced-bean-class>javax.sql.DataSource</referenced-bean-class>
</referenced-bean>
```

<render-kit>

The <render-kit> element declares a custom render kit or additional custom renderers for the default kit.

Syntax

```
<render-kit>
  [<description [xml:lang="lang"]>description</description>]*
  [<display-name [xml:lang="lang"]>displayName</display-name>]*
  [<icon [xml:lang="lang"]>
     [<small-icon>iconPath</small-icon>]
     [<large-icon>iconPath</large-icon>]
  </icon>]*
  [<render-kit-id>renderKitId</render-kit-id>]
  [<render-kit-class>className</render-kit-class>]
  [<renderer>
    [<description [xml:lang="lang"]>description</description>]*
    [<display-name [xml:lang="lang"]>displayName</display-name>]*
    [<icon [xml:lang="lang"]>
       [<small-icon>iconPath</small-icon>]
       [<large-icon>iconPath</large-icon>]
    </icon>]*
    <component-family>componentFamily</component-family>
    <renderer-type>rendererType</renderer-type>
    <renderer-class>className</renderer-class>
    [<attribute>
      [<description [xml:lang="lang"]>description</description>]*
      [<display-name [xml:lang="lang"]>displayName</display-name>]*
      [<icon [xml:lang="lang"]>
         [<small-icon>iconPath</small-icon>]
         [<large-icon>iconPath</large-icon>]
```

```
        </icon>]*
        <attribute-name>attrName</attribute-name>
        <attribute-class>className</attribute-class>
        [<default-value>defaultValue</default-value>]
        [<suggested-value>suggestedValue</suggested-value>]
        [<attribute-extension>extension</attribute-extension>]*
      </attribute>]*
     [<renderer-extension>rendererExtension</renderer-extension>]*
    </renderer>]*
  </render-kit>
```

The <render-kit-id> declares an identifier for a custom kit, and the <render-kit-class> element declares a custom javax.faces.render.RenderKit class for the kit. If omitted, the renderer declarations apply to the default HTML basic render kit.

Each renderer is declared by a <renderer> element, with nested <component-family>, <renderer-type>, and <renderer-class> elements mapping an implementation class to the combination of the component family and renderer type (see Chapter 13 for details).

```
<render-kit>
  <renderer>
    <component-family>com.mycompany.MyComponent</component-family>
    <renderer-type>com.mycompany.MyRenderer</renderer-type>
    <renderer-class>
      com.mycompany.jsf.MyComponetRenderer
    </renderer-class>
  </renderer>
</render-kit>
```

The <attribute> element provide information about the component's generic attributes used by the renderer, which may be used by a development tool to help a developer use the renderer, the same way for the <component> element.

<validator>

The <validator> element declares the implementation class for a validator.

Syntax

```
<validator>
  [<description [xml:lang="lang"]>description</description>]*
  [<display-name [xml:lang="lang"]>displayName</display-name>]*
  [<icon [xml:lang="lang"]>
     [<small-icon>iconPath</small-icon>]
     [<large-icon>iconPath</large-icon>]
   </icon>]*
  <validator-id>validatorId</validator-id>
  <validator-class>className</validator-class>
  [<attribute>
    [<description [xml:lang="lang"]>description</description>]*
    [<display-name [xml:lang="lang"]>displayName</display-name>]*
    [<icon [xml:lang="lang"]>
       [<small-icon>iconPath</small-icon>]
       [<large-icon>iconPath</large-icon>]
```

```
      </icon>]*
      <attribute-name>attrName</attribute-name>
      <attribute-class>className</attribute-class>
      [<default-value>defaultValue</default-value>]
      [<suggested-value>suggestedValue</suggested-value>]
      [<attribute-extension>extension</attribute-extension>]*
    </attribute>]*
   [<property>
     [<description [xml:lang="lang"]>description</description>]*
     [<display-name [xml:lang="lang"]>displayName</display-name>]*
     [<icon [xml:lang="lang"]>
        [<small-icon>iconPath</small-icon>]
        [<large-icon>iconPath</large-icon>]
      </icon>]*
      <property-name>propName</property-name>
      <property-class>className</property-class>
      [<default-value>defaultValue</default-value>]
      [<suggested-value>suggestedValue</suggested-value>]
      [<property-extension>extension</property-extension>]*
    </property>]*
</validator>
```

The <validator-id> element assigns a unique identifier for the validator, and the <validator-class> element contains the fully qualified class name that implements the javax.faces.validator.Validator interface:

```
<validator>
  <validator-id>com.mycompany.MyValidator</converter-id>
  <validator-class>
    com.mycompany.jsf.MyValidator
  </validator-class>
</validator>
```

The <attribute> and <property> elements provide information about the component's generic attributes and type-safe converter properties, respectively, that may be used by a development tool to help a developer use the validator, the same way for the <component> element.

APPENDIX F

Web Application Structure and Deployment Descriptor Reference

A complete Java web application may consist of several different resources: JSP pages, servlets, applets, static HTML pages, JSF components, custom tag libraries, and other Java class files. Starting with Version 2.2, the servlet specification defines a portable way to package all these resources together with a deployment descriptor that contains configuration information such as how all the resources fit together, security requirements, etc. This appendix describes the standard file structure for a web application and how to use the deployment descriptor elements defined by the Servlet 2.4 and JSP 2.0 specifications to configure the application.

Web Application File Structure

The portable distribution and deployment format for a web application defined by the servlet specification is the Web Application Archive (WAR). All Servlet 2.2–compliant servers (or later) provide tools for installing a WAR file and associate the application with a servlet context.

A WAR file has a *.war* file extension and can be created with the Java *jar* command or a ZIP utility program, such as *WinZip*, as described at the end of this appendix. The internal structure of the WAR file is defined by the servlet specification:

```
/index.html
/company/index.html
/company/contact.html
/company/phonelist.jsp
/products/searchform.html
/products/list.jsp
/images/banner.gif
/WEB-INF/web.xml
/WEB-INF/lib/bean.jar
/WEB-INF/lib/actions.jar
/WEB-INF/classes/com/mycorp/servlets/PurchaseServlet.class
/WEB-INF/classes/com/mycorp/util/MyUtils.class
...
```

The top level in this structure is the document root for all application web page files. This is where you place all your HTML pages, JSP pages, and image files. A browser can access all these files, using a URI starting with the context path. For instance, if the application has been assigned the context path */sales*, the URI */sales/products/list.jsp* is used to access the JSP page named *list.jsp* in the *products* directory in this example.

Placing Java Class Files in the Right Directory

The *WEB-INF* directory contains files and subdirectories for other types of resources used by the application. Files under this directory aren't directly accessible to a browser. Two *WEB-INF* subdirectories have special meaning: *lib* and *classes*. The *lib* directory contains JAR files with Java class files, for instance JavaBeans classes, custom action handler classes, and utility classes. The *classes* directory contains class files that are not packaged in JAR files. The web application automatically has access to all class files in the *lib* and *classes* directories (in other words, you do *not* have to add them to the `CLASSPATH` environment variable).

If you store class files in the *classes* directory, they must be stored in subdirectories mirroring the package structure. For instance, if you have a class named `com.mycorp.util.MyUtils`, you must store the class file in *WEB-INF/classes/com/mycorp/util/MyUtils.class*. Another type of file that can be stored in the classes directory is the type of a resource properties file containing localized text, as described in Chapter 11.

The *WEB-INF* directory can also contain other directories. For instance, a directory named *tlds* is by convention used for tag library Tag Library Descriptor (TLD) files when they are not packaged in JAR files.

During development it's more convenient to work with the web application files in a regular filesystem structure instead creating a new WAR file every time something changes. Most containers therefore support the WAR structure in an open filesystem as well. The book example application is distributed as an open filesystem structure to make it easier for you to see all the files.

Web Application Deployment Descriptor

The *WEB-INF/web.xml* file is the Java web application deployment descriptor that contains all general configuration information for the application, in addition to the JSF-specific information in the *WEB-INF/faces-config.xml* file described in Appendix E. Some elements are especially important for a JSF application, namely the `<context-param>`, `<servlet>`, and `<servlet-mapping>` elements. See the subsections for these elements for what configurations you must and can set for a JSF-application in the *WEB-INF/web.xml* file.

The deployment descriptor is an XML file. Starting with Servlet 2.4 and JSP 2.0, the elements it can contain and how they must be arranged are controlled by a number of XML Schema documents. The main XML Schema document, which includes the others, is available online at *http://java.sun.com/xml/ns/j2ee/web-app_2_4.xsd*. This XML Schema document must be referenced in the root element of the deployment description, as shown in Example F-1.

Example F-1. Web Application Descriptor root element for Servlet 2.4/JSP 2.0

```
<web-app xmlns="http://java.sun.com/xml/ns/j2ee"
  xmlns:xsi="http://www.w3c.org/2001/XMLSchema-instance"
  xsi:schemaLocation="http://java.sun.com/xml/ns/j2ee
    http://java.sun.com/xml/ns/j2ee/web-app_2_4.xsd"
  version="2.4>
  ...
</web-app>
```

If you're not familiar with the intricate details of XML Schema and namespace declarations, just accept the fact that you must enclose all other elements in the deployment descriptor within a <web-app> element exactly as shown in Example F-1.

A JSF application can be deployed in a Servlet 2.3/JSP 1.2 container,* and the rules for the deployment descriptor for those specification versions are defined by a Document Type Descriptor (DTD), available online at *http://java.sun.com/dtd/web-app_2_3.dtd*. Most of the elements are the same between the two deployment descriptor versions, but the Servlet 2.3 DTD requires a fixed ordering of the top-level elements while the Servlet 2.4 XML Schema allows them to be declared in any order (see the DTD for details if you use a Servlet 2.3 container). Other than that, the only visible difference is at the top of the deployment descriptor. Example F-2 shows how it must look like for a Servlet 2.3 deployment descriptor.

Example F-2. Web Application Descriptor root element for Servlet 2.3/JSP 1.2

```
<!DOCTYPE web-app PUBLIC
  "-//Sun Microsystems, Inc.//DTD Web Application 2.3//EN"
  "http://java.sun.com/dtd/web-app_2_3.dtd">

<web-app>
  ...
</web-app>
```

Within the <web-app> element body, top-level elements can be included in any order if you're using Servlet 2.4/JSP 2.0 deployment descriptor. Each top-level element is described in a separate section in this appendix. The top-level elements all are optional and can be included more than once, unless otherwise stated. Most top-level elements contain other elements.

* Note that the examples described in this book use JSP 2.0 features and will not run in a Servlet 2.3/JSP 1.2 container unless the JSP pages are modified.

I use syntax descriptions similar to those in the other appendixes to show the rules for the elements nested within top-level elements. The nested elements must be included in the order they are listed in the syntax description. Mutually exclusive elements are separated by vertical bars (|). Optional nested elements are embedded in square brackets ([]), followed by an asterisk (*) if more than one element of this type may be used. An element name followed by a plus sign (+) means the element is required, but it can be used more than once. For elements that accept predefined values, all values are listed separated by vertical bars; the default value (if any) is in bold face. Italics are used for element values that don't have a fixed set of accepted values. Element attribute values are described using the same syntax as element values.

<description>, <display-name>, and <icon>

These three elements provide information a web container deployment tool can use to describe the application. As an exception to the rule that top-level elements can be included in any order, these three must be in the order shown here.

Syntax

```
<description [xml:lang="lang"]>description</description>

<display-name [xml:lang="lang"]>displayName</display-name>

<icon [xml:lang="lang"]>
  [<small-icon>iconPath</small-icon>]
  [<large-icon>iconPath</large-icon>]
</icon>
```

The <icon> element can contain a <small-icon> and a <large-icon> element, each with a context-relative path to an image file (GIF and JPEG formats are supported). The small icon must be 16x16 pixels, and the large 32x32. The <display-name> element can specify a name for the application, and the <description> element a longer description.

You can use different versions of all these top-level elements for multiple languages, each with a unique xml:lang attribute value ("en", for English, is the default value):

```
<icon>
  <small-icon>/images/small.gif</small-icon>
  <large-icon>/images/large.gif</large-icon>
</icon>
<display-name>The application name</display-name>
<description>
  A longer description of
  the application.
</description>
```

<distributable>

The <distributable> element is used to tell the web container that the application is designed to run in a distributed web container.

Syntax

```
<distributable/>
```

This element does not contain a body. A distributable application does not rely on servlet instance variables, static classes or variables, servlet context attributes, or any other mechanism for shared information that is restricted to one Java Virtual Machine (JVM). It also means that all objects placed in the session scope are serializable, so that the container can move the session data from one JVM to another. For more information about distributed applications, see the servlet specification or my book *JavaServer Pages* (O'Reilly).

<context-param>

Using the `<context-param>` element, you can define context parameters that are available to all components of the application (both servlets and JSP pages).

Syntax

```
<context-param>
  [<description [xml:lang="lang"]>description</description>]*
  <param-name>paramName</param-name>
  <param-value>paramValue</param-value>
<context-param>
```

The `<param-name>` subelement specifies the name and the `<param-value>` element the value. Optionally, the `<description>` element can be used for a description that can be displayed by a deployment tool:

```
<context-param>
  <param-name>jdbcURL</param-name>
  <param-value>jdbc:idb:/usr/local/db/mydb.prp</param-value>
</context-param>
```

The JSF specification defines the following context parameters:

`javax.faces.CONFIG_FILES`
: Optionally defines a comma-separated list of context-relative paths for JSF configuration files. See Chapter 13 for details.

`javax.faces.DEFAULT_SUFFIX`
: Optionally defines a suffix (file extension) for the JSP pages that contains JSF component action elements, to use a different one than the default (*.jsp*). If you define a nondefault suffix, you must also define that this suffix represents a JSP page, using the `<jsp-config>` element in a Servlet 2.4/JSP 2.0 container or an implementation-dependent mapping in a Servlet 2.3/JSP 1.2 container.

`javax.faces.LIFECYCLE_ID`
: Optionally defines a lifecycle identifier other than the default set by the `javax.faces.lifecycle.LifecycleFactory.DEFAULT_LIFECYCLE` constant.

`javax.faces.STATE_SAVING_METHOD`
: Optionally defines a state saving method other than the default (server). Valid values are `client` and `server`. See Chapter 6 for details.

<filter>

The <filter> element registers a filter component.

Syntax

```
<filter>
  [<description [xml:lang="lang"]>description</description>]*
  [<display-name [xml:lang="lang"]>displayName</display-name>]*
  [<icon [xml:lang="lang"]>
     [<small-icon>iconPath</small-icon>]
     [<large-icon>iconPath</large-icon>]
   </icon>]*
  <filter-name>filterName</filter-name>
  <filter-class>className</filter-class>
  [<init-param>
     [<description [xml:lang="lang"]>description</description>]*
     <param-name>paramName</param-name>
     <param-value>paramValue</param-value>
   </init-param>]*
</filter>
```

Nested <icon>, <display-name>, and <description> elements can optionally define icons and descriptions that can be used by a tool. The nested <filter-name> element defines a unique logical name for the filter, and the <filter-class> element the class name. A set of initialization parameters can optionally be defined by <init-param> elements.

```
<filter>
  <filter-name>accessControl</filter-name>
  <filter-class>com.mycomp.AccessControlFilter</filter-class>
  <init-param>
    <param-name>loginPage</param-name>
    <param-value>/login.jsp</param-value>
  </init-param>
</filter>
```

<filter-mapping>

A filter is mapped to either to a URI pattern or a servlet using the <filter-mapping> element.

Syntax

```
<filter-mapping>
  <filter-name>filterName</filter-name>
  <url-pattern>urlPattern</url-pattern> |
    <servlet-name>servletName</servlet-name>
  [<dispatcher>FORWARD|INCLUDE|REQUEST|ERROR</dispatcher>]*
</filter-mapping>
```

The <filter-name> subelement identifies the filter using a name defined by a <filter> element. A <url-pattern> or a <servlet-name> defines when the filter shall be invoked. If a URL mapping is used, the same values as for a <servlet-mapping> element can be used.

More than one filter may match a specific request. If so, the container chains them in the order the matching <filter-mapping> elements appear in the deployment descriptor.

Up to four <dispatcher> elements may be used to define for what circumstances the filter should be applied: FORWARD and INCLUDE mean it's applied for internal request made through the javax.servlet.RequestDispatcher forward( ) and include( ) methods, respectively; ERROR means it's applied when dispatching to an error page as part of the error mechanism; REQUEST means it's applied for regular, external client requests. If no <dispatcher> element is used, the default behavior is as if an element with the REQUEST value had been specified:

```
<filter-mapping>
  <filter-name>accessControl</filter-name>
  <url-pattern>/protected</url-pattern>
</filter-mapping>
```

<listener>

All the listener types defined by the servlet specification (as opposed to the JSF listener types) must be registered with a <listener> element.

Syntax

```
<listener>
  [<description [xml:lang="lang"]>description</description>]*
  [<display-name [xml:lang="lang"]>displayName</display-name>]*
  [<icon [xml:lang="lang"]>
     [<small-icon>iconPath</small-icon>]
     [<large-icon>iconPath</large-icon>]
   </icon>]*
  <listener-class>className</listener-class>
</listener>
```

The <description>, <display-name>, and <icon>, elements can optionally be used, the same as for many other top-level elements. The nested <listener-class> element contains the listener class name:

```
<listener>
  <listener-class>com.mycomp.AppInitListener</listener-class>
</listener>
```

<servlet>

The <servlet> element defines servlet class or JSP page details.

Syntax

```
<servlet>
  [<description [xml:lang="lang"]>description</description>]*
  [<display-name [xml:lang="lang"]>displayName</display-name>]*
  [<icon [xml:lang="lang"]>
     [<small-icon>iconPath</small-icon>]
     [<large-icon>iconPath</large-icon>]
   </icon>]*
```

```
    <servlet-name>servletName</servlet-name>
    <servlet-class>className</servlet-class> |
      <jsp-file>jspPath</jsp-file>
    [<init-param>
       [<description [xml:lang="lang"]>description</description>]*
       <param-name>paramName</param-name>
       <param-value>paramValue</param-value>
     </init-param>]*
    [<load-on-startup>startupValue</load-on-startup>]
    [<run-as>roleName</run-as>]
    [<security-role-ref>
      [<description [xml:lang="lang">description</description>]*
      <role-name>internalRoleName</role-name>
      [<role-link>roleName</role-link>]
     </security-role-ref>]*
  </servlet>
```

Most commonly, this element just associates a servlet or JSP page with a short name and specifies initialization parameters:

```
<servlet>
  <servlet-name>
    purchase
  </servlet-name>
  <servlet-class>
    com.mycorp.servlets.PurchaseServlet
  </servlet-class>
  <init-param>
    <param-name>maxAmount</param-name>
    <param-value>500.00</param-value>
  </init-param>
</servlet>

<servlet>
  <servlet-name>
    order-form
  </servlet-name>
  <jsp-file>
    /po/orderform.jsp
  </jsp-file>
  <init-param>
    <param-name>bgColor</param-name>
    <param-value>blue</param-value>
  </init-param>
</servlet>
```

The same servlet class (or JSP page) can be defined with multiple names, typically with different initialization parameters. The container creates an instance of the class for each name.

The `<load-on-startup>` subelement can tell the container to load the servlet when the application is started. The value is a positive integer, indicating when the servlet is to be loaded relative to other servlets. A servlet with a low value is loaded before a servlet with a higher value:

```
<servlet>
  <servlet-name>
    controller
```

```
    </servlet-name>
    <servlet-class>
      com.mycorp.servlets.ControllerServlet
    </servlet-class>
    <load-on-startup>1</load-on-startup>
  </servlet>
```

The <icon>, <display-name>, and <description> elements describe the servlet or JSP page, the same way as for other top-level elements.

<security-role-ref> elements, combined with <security-role> elements, can link a security role name used in a servlet as the argument to the HttpServletRequest.isUserInRole( ) method to a role name known by the web container:

```
<servlet>
  <servlet-name>
    controller
  </servlet-name>
  <servlet-class>
    com.mycorp.servlets.ControllerServlet
  </servlet-class>
  <security-role-ref>
    <role-name>administrator</role-name>
    <role-link>admin</role-link>
  </security-role-ref>
</servlet>
...
<security-role>
  <role-name>admin</role-name>
</security-role>
```

All role names defined by <security-role> elements must be mapped to users and/or groups known by the web container. How this is done is container-dependent. The <security-role-ref> element allows you to use a servlet that uses a role name in the isUserInRole( ) method that is not defined by a <security-role> element. A typical scenario where this can be useful is when you combine servlets from different sources into one application, and the servlets use different role names for the same logical role.

Finally, the <run-as> element can define the security role that the servlet should be presented as if it makes calls into an EJB container. The nested <role-name> value must be defined by a <security-role> element:

```
<servlet>
  <servlet-name>
    controller
  </servlet-name>
  <servlet-class>
    com.mycorp.servlets.ControllerServlet
  </servlet-class>
  <run-as>
    <role-name>admin</role-name>
  </run-as>
</servlet>
...
<security-role>
  <role-name>admin</role-name>
</security-role>
```

See the J2EE documentation for details about how to use this element.

JSF relies on a servlet that must be declared and mapped to a URL pattern. The servlet class name is javax.faces.webapp.FacesServlet, but you can use any symbolic name you want:

```
<servlet>
  <servlet-name>facesServlet</servlet-name>
  <servlet-class>
    javax.faces.webapp.FacesServlet
  </servlet-class>
</servlet>
```

<servlet-mapping>

The <servlet-mapping> element maps a servlet or JSP page to a URL pattern.

Syntax

```
<servlet-mapping>
  <servlet-name>servletName</servlet-name>
  <url-pattern>urlPattern</url-pattern>
</servlet-mapping>
```

Most containers support a special URI prefix (*/servlet*) that can invoke any servlet class that the container has access to, for instance the URI */servlet/com.mycompany.MyServlet* can invoke the servlet class com.mycomapany.MyServlet. This isn't mandated by the specification, however, so to make sure the application is portable, it's better to map a unique path to a servlet instead. Explicit mapping also simplifies references between servlets and JSP pages. The <servlet-mapping> element is used for this purpose. The <servlet-name> subelement contains a name defined by a <servlet> element, and the <url-pattern> contains the pattern that should be mapped to the servlet (or JSP page).

```
<servlet-mapping>
  <servlet-name>purchase</servlet-name>
  <url-pattern>/po/*</url-pattern>
</servlet-mapping>

<servlet-mapping>
  <servlet-name>sales-report</servlet-name>
  <url-pattern>/report</url-pattern>
</servlet-mapping>

<servlet-mapping>
  <servlet-name>XMLProcessor</servlet-name>
  <url-pattern>*.xml</url-pattern>
</servlet-mapping>
```

A pattern can take one of four forms:

- A *path prefix pattern* starts with a slash (/) and ends with /*, for instance /po/*.
- An *extension mapping pattern* starts with *., for instance *.xml.
- A *default servlet pattern* consists of just the / character.
- All other patterns are *exact match patterns*.

When the container receives a request, it strips off the context path and then tries to find a pattern that matches a servlet mapping. Exact match patterns are analyzed first, then the path prefix patterns starting with the longest one, and then the extension mapping patterns. If none of these patterns match, the default servlet pattern is used, if specified. As a last resort, the containers default request processor handles the request.

With the mappings defined here, a URI like */po/supplies* invokes the purchase servlet, */report* invokes the sales-report servlet (but note that */report/spring* doesn't, because an exact match pattern is used), and */eastcoast/forecast.xml* invokes the `XMLProcessor` servlet.

The JSF servlet must be mapped to a URL pattern. The **.faces* extension mapping pattern is recommended, but you can also use path prefix pattern, for instance */faces/**:

```
<servlet-mapping>
  <servlet-name>facesServlet</servlet-name>
  <url-pattern>*.faces</url-pattern>
</servlet-mapping>
```

<session-config>

The `<session-config>` element can customize session handling attributes. You must use only one element of this type in a deployment descriptor.

Syntax

```
<session-config>
  [<session-timeout>minutes</session-timeout>]
</session-config>
```

It contains just one subelement: the `<session-timeout>` element used to specify the default session timeout value in minutes. A value of 0 or less means that sessions never time out. Omitting the nested element means the container uses its own default:

```
<session-config>
  <session-timeout>30</session-timeout>
</session-config>
```

<mime-mapping>

The `<mime-mapping>` element can define the mappings an application requires.

Syntax

```
<mime-mapping>
  <extension>fileExtension</extension>
  <mime-type>mimeType</mime-type>
</mime-mapping>
```

A servlet may need to know which MIME type a file extension corresponds to, and such a mapping can be defined with this element:

```
<mime-mapping>
  <extension>wml</extension>
  <mime-type>text/vnd.wap.wml</mime-type>
</mime-mapping>
```

Most containers provide default mappings for the most commonly used extensions, such as *.html*, *.htm*, *.gif*, *.jpg*, and so on, but if you need to be absolutely sure that a mapping is defined for your application, put it in the *web.xml* file.

<welcome-file-list>

The <welcome-file-list> element can define an ordered list of files to look for in the directory and serve if present. If you use more than one element of this type, the container merges them.

Syntax

```
<welcome-file-list>
  <welcome-file>fileName</welcome-file>+
</welcome-file-list>
```

A welcome file is a file (or a URL mapped to a servlet) that the container serves when it receives a request URI that identifies a directory as opposed to a web page or a servlet:

```
<welcome-file-list>
  <welcome-file>index.html</welcome-file>
  <welcome-file>index.htm</welcome-file>
  <welcome-file>default.html</welcome-file>
  <welcome-file>default.htm</welcome-file>
</welcome-file-list>
```

When a directory entry request (a request for a URI ending with a slash) is received that does not match a servlet mapping, the container appends each welcome file name in the order specified in the deployment descriptor to the request URI and checks whether a resource in the WAR is mapped to the new URI. If it is, the request is sent to the resource. If no matching resource is found, the behavior is container dependent. The container may, for instance, return a directory listing an HTTP 404 status code (Not Found).

<error-page>

The <error-page> element can define pages that inform the user about various errors.

Syntax

```
<error-page>
  <error-code>errorCode</error-code> |
    <exception-type>className</exception-type>
  <location>pagePath</location>
</error-page>
```

A page can be specified for an HTTP error status code, such as 404 (Not Found), using the <error-code> subelement. As an alternative, the <exception-type> subelement can be used to specify a Java exception class name, to use a special page to handle exceptions thrown by servlets and JSP pages. The <location> subelement contains the context-relative path for the error page:

```
<error-page>
  <error-code>404</error-code>
```

```
    <location>/errors/404.html</location>
  </error-page>
  <error-page>
    <exception-type>javax.servlet.ServletException</exception-type>
    <location>/errors/exception.jsp</location>
  </error-page>
```

<jsp-config>

The <jsp-config> element embeds most elements dealing with JSP configuration. You must use only one element of this type in a deployment descriptor.

Syntax

```
<jsp-config>
  [<taglib>
    <taglib-uri>taglibURI</taglib-uri>
    <taglib-location>filePath</taglib-location>
   </taglib>]*
  [<jsp-property-group>
     [<description [xml:lang="lang"]>description</description>]*
     [<display-name [xml:lang="lang"]>displayName</display-name>]*
     [<icon [xml:lang="lang"]>
        [<small-icon>iconPath</small-icon>]
        [<large-icon>iconPath</large-icon>]
      </icon>]*
     <url-pattern>urlPattern</url-pattern>+
     [<el-ignored>true|false</el-ignored>]
     [<page-encoding>encoding</page-encoding>]
     [<scripting-invalid>true|false</scripting-invalid>]
     [<is-xml>true|false</is-xml>]
     [<include-prelude>filePath</include-prelude>]*
     [<include-coda>filePath</include-coda]*
   </jsp-property-group>]*
</jsp-config>
```

Nested <taglib> elements map the symbolic name for a tag library specified by the `taglib` directive in a JSP page to the location of the TLD file or JAR file that contains the TLD file. The <taglib-uri> element value must match the `uri` attribute value used in the JSP page and the <taglib-location> subelement contains the context-relative path to the library file:

```
<jsp-config>
  <taglib>
    <taglib-uri>orataglib</taglib-uri>
    <taglib-location>/WEB-INF/lib/orataglib_1_0.jar</taglib-location>
  </taglib>
</jsp-config>
```

With the introduction of the auto-discovery feature in JSP 1.2, this element is rarely needed. For more details, see Chapter 4.

Nested <jsp-property-group> elements define a number of attributes for a set of JSP pages. The set of pages is defined by one or more <url-pattern> elements, with the same pattern types as are valid for the <servlet-mapping> element. The other elements define the attributes shared by these pages.

```
<jsp-config>
  <jsp-property-group>
    <url-pattern>*.xml</url-pattern>
    <el-ignored>true</el-ignored>
    <page-encoding>Shift_JIS</page-encoding>
    <scripting-invalid>true</scripting-invalid>
    <is-xml>true</is-xml>
    <include-prelude>/copyright.txt</include-prelude>
  </jsp-property-grop>
</jsp-config>
```

An <el-ignored> value of true means that character sequences that look like EL expressions, i.e., starts with ${, are treated as template text instead of EL expressions. This can be useful when pre-JSP 2.0 pages must be used in a JSP 2.0 application. The default is true for an application deployed with a pre-JSP 2.0 deployment descriptor, and it's false for an application with a JSP 2.0 deployment descriptor.

The <page-encoding> element defines the file encoding for all matching JSP files.

The <scripting-invalid> element can be used to define an application-wide policy for use of the JSP scripting elements (i.e., Java code). With a value of true, a page that contains scripting elements is rejected at translation time.

A <is-xml> element with a value of true tells the container that matching pages are written as JSP Documents, i.e., as XML documents instead of regular JSP pages.

The <include-prelude> and <include-coda> elements provide for automatic inclusion of files during the translation phase. Files defined by <include-prelude> elements are included at the top of each matching page; files defined by <include-coda> are included at the end. The file location is specified as a context-relative path.

For more on all the <jsp-property-group> elements, see the JSP specification or my book *JavaServer Pages* (O'Reilly).

<resource-env-ref>

The <resource-env-ref> element declares an application resource accessible through JNDI.

Syntax

```
<resource-env-ref>
  [<description [xml:lang="lang"]>description</description>]*
  <resource-env-ref-name>envRefName</resource-env-ref-name>
  <resource-env-ref-type>envRefType</resource-env-ref-type>
</resource-env-ref>
```

In a complete J2EE-compiant container (i.e., one that supports other J2EE technologies besides servlets and JSP), the container can provide access to so-called administered objects through JNDI. Examples of this type of object are the ones used by the Java Messaging System (JMS) API. The <resource-env-ref> elements declares the JNDI path used to access the object in the application and its type, using nested <resource-env-ref-name> and <resource-end-ref-type> elements:

```
<resource-env-ref>
  <resource-env-ref-name>/jms/StockQueue</resource-env-ref-name>
  <resource-env-ref-type>/javax.jms.Queue</resource-env-ref-type>
</resource-env-ref>
```

Optionally, descriptions can be provided by the <description> element.

<resource-ref>

The <resource-ref> element defines JNDI accessible object factories for application objects.

Syntax

```
<resource-ref>
  [<description [xml:lang="lang"]>description</description>]*
  <res-ref-name>refName</res-ref-name>
  <res-ref-type>refType</res-ref-type>
  <res-auth>Application|Container</res-auth>
  [<res-sharing-scope>Shareable|Unshareable</res-sharing-scope>]
</resource-ref>
```

A J2EE-compliant container (and some web containers that support JNDI in addition to servlets and JSP) can also provide access to resource factories that produce the objects used in an application, such as a `DataSource` that produces `Connection` objects for database access. The <resource-ref> element defines these factories using the <res-ref-name> to specify the JNDI path used in the application, the <res-type> for the factory type, and <res-auth> to define whether the authentication is performed by the application (with the `Application` value) or the container (with the `Container` value). An optional <res-sharing-scope> element can be used to define if the objects produced by the factory may be shared or not (with `Shareable` and `Unshareable`, respectively, the prior being the default):

```
<resource-ref>
  <res-ref-name>/jms/Production</res-ref-name>
  <res-ref-type>/javax.sql.DataSource</res-ref-type>
  <res-auth>Container</res-auth>
</resource-ref>
```

As for most elements, <description> elements can provide descriptions in multiple languages to help the deployer.

<security-constraint>

The <security-constraint> element defines how and by whom resources can be accessed.

Syntax

```
<security-constraint>
  [<display-name [xml:lang="lang"]>displayName</display-name>]*
  <web-resource-collection>
    <web-resource-name>resName</web-resource-name>
    [<description [xml:lang="lang"]>description</description>]*
```

```
    <url-pattern>urlPattern</url-pattern>+
    [<http-method>GET|POST|PUT|DELETE|HEAD|OPTIONS|TRACE</http-method>]
  </web-resource-collection>+
  [<auth-constraint>
     [<description [xml:lang="lang"]>description</description>]*
     [<role-name>roleName</role-name>]*
   </auth-constraint>]
  [<user-data-constraint>
     <transport-guarantee>
       NONE|INTEGRAL|CONFIDENTIAL
     </ transport-guarantee>
   </user-data-constraint>]
</security-constraint>
```

The <security-constraint> element contains a <web-resource-collection> subelement that defines the resources to be protected and an <auth-constraint> subelement that defines who has access to the protected resources. It can also contain a <user-data-constraint> subelement that describes security requirements for the connection used to access the resource:

```
<security-constraint>
  <web-resource-collection>
    <web-resource-name>admin</web-resource-name>
    <url-pattern>/admin/*</url-pattern>
    <http-method>GET</http-method>
  </web-resource-collection>
  <auth-constraint>
    <role-name>admin</role-name>
  </auth-constraint>
  <user-data-constraint>
    <transport-guarantee>CONFIDENTIAL</ transport-guarantee>
  </user-data-constraint>
</security-constraint>
```

Within the <web-resource-collection> element, the resource is given a name with the <web resource-name> subelement and the URI patterns for the protected resources are specified with <url-pattern> elements. <http-method> subelements can also be used to restrict the types of accepted requests. This example protects all resources accessed with URIs that starts with */admin* and says that only the GET method can access these resources.

The <role-name> subelements within the <auth-constraint> element specify the roles that the current user must have to get access to the resource. The value must be a role name defined by a <security-role> element. In this example, the user must belong to the admin role in order to access resources under */admin*. How the role names are mapped to user and/or group names in the container's security system is container dependent.

A <transport-guarantee> element can contain one of three values:

NONE
: No special requirements. This is the default.

INTEGRAL
: Data must be sent between the client and server in such a way that it can't be changed in transit. Typically this means that an SSL connection is required.

CONFIDENTIAL
: Data must be sent in such a way that it can't be observed by others. This is also typically satisfied by an SSL connection.

<login-config>

The <login-config> element declares which authentication method to use for protected resources. You must use only one element of this type in a deployment descriptor.

Syntax

```
<login-config>
  [<auth-method>BASIC|DIGEST|FORM|CLIENT-CERT</auth-method>]
  [<realm-name>realmName</realm-name>]
  [<form-login-config>
     <form-login-page>loginPagePath</form-login-page>
     <form-error-page>errorPagePath</form-error-page>
   </form-login-config>]
</login-config>
```

For an application that uses the <security-constraint> element to protect resources, you must also define how to authenticate users with a <login-config> element. It can contain three subelements: <auth-method>, <realm-name>, and <form-login-config>:

```
<login-config>
  <auth-method>BASIC</auth-method>
  <realm-name>Protected pages</realm-name>
</login-config>
```

The <auth-method> element can have one of the values BASIC, DIGEST, FORM, and CLIENT-CERT, corresponding to the four container-provided authentication methods described in Chapter 5. The <realm-name> element can specify the name shown by the browser when it prompts for a password when the BASIC authentication is used.

If FORM authentication is used, the <form-login-config> element defines the login page and an error pages (used for invalid login attempts):

```
<login-config>
  <auth-method>FORM</auth-method>
  <form-login-config>
    <form-login-page>/login/login.html</form-login-page>
    <form-error-page>/login/error.html</form-error-page>
  </form-login-config>
</login-config>
```

For more about the FORM authentication method, see Chapter 5.

<security-role>

<security-role> elements are used to define the role names that the application uses.

Syntax

```
<security-role>
  [<description [xml:lang="lang"]>description</description>]*
  <role-name>roleName</role-name>
</security-role>
```

All names used in isUserInRole() calls, in <security-role-ref> elements and <auth-constraint> elements must be declared by a separate <security-role> element:

```
<security-role>
  <role-name>admin</role-name>
</security-role>
<security-role>
  <role-name>user</role-name>
</security-role>
```

Each role must be mapped to a user and/or group in the container's security domain in a container dependent way.

<locale-encoding-mapping-list>

The <locale-encoding-mapping-list> element defines mappings between locales and response encodings. If you use more than one element of this type, the container merges them.

Syntax

```
<locale-encoding-mapping-list>
  <locale-encoding-mapping>
    <locale>locale</locale>
    <encoding>encoding</encoding>
  </locale-encoding-mapping>+
</locale-encoding-mapping-list>
```

Unless a specific response encoding is been specified explicitly, setting the locale for a response also sets its encoding. The <locale-encoding-mapping-list> element allows you to define how locales map to response encodings, overriding the container's default mappings. The <locale> element contains the locale value as an ISO-639 language code, optionally combined with an ISO-3166 country code, separated by an underscore or a dash. The <encoding> element contains an encoding (charset) value recognized by Java.

```
<locale-encoding-mapping-list>
  <locale-encoding-mapping>
    <locale>en-US</locale>
    <encoding>UTF-8</encoding>
  </locale-encoding-mapping>
  <locale-encoding-mapping>
    <locale>ja</locale>
    <encoding>Shift_JIS</encoding>
  </locale-encoding-mapping>
</locale-encoding-mapping-list>
```

<env-entry>

The <env-entry> element is used to define simple objects, such as a String or Boolean, accessed by the application through JNDI.

Syntax

```
<env-entry>
  [<description [xml:lang="lang"]>description</description>]*
  <env-entry-name>entryName</env-entry-name>
  <env-entry-type>entryType</env-entry-type>
  [<env-entry-value>entryValue</env-entry-value>]
</env-entry>
```

The <env-entry-name> defines the JNDI name relative to the java:comp/env context and <env-entry-type> the type, which must be one of java.lang.Boolean, java.lang.Byte, java.lang.Character, java.lang.String, java.lang.Short, java.lang.Integer, java.lang.Long, java.lang.Float or java.lang.Double. The value can optionally be defined statically, using the <env-entry-value> element or be provided at deployment. An optional <description> element is also supported:

```
<env-entry>
  <env-entry-name>maxConnections</env-entry-name>
  <env-entry-type>java.lang.Integer</env-entry-type>
  <env-entry-value>100</env-entry-value>
</env-entry>
```

<ejb-ref>

The <ejb-ref> element is used to declare a remote EJB reference used by the application.

Syntax

```
<ejb-ref>
  [<description [xml:lang="lang"]>description</description>]*
  <ejb-ref-name>ejbRefName</ejb-ref-name>
  <ejb-ref-type>Entity|Session</ejb-ref-type>
  <home>homeInterfaceName</home>
  <remote>remoteInterfaceName</remote>
  [<ejb-link>linkedEJBName</ejb-link>]
</ejb-ref>
```

In a J2EE-compliant container, the <ejb-ref> element is used to declare EJB objects. The name (JNDI path), type (Entity or Session), home, and remote interface class names must be specified with the <ejb-ref-name>, <ejb-ref-type>, <home>, and <remote> elements:

```
<ejb-ref>
  <ejb-ref-name>ejb/Payroll</ejb-ref-name>
  <ejb-ref-type>Session</ejb-ref-type>
  <home>com.mycomp.PayrollHome</home>
  <remote>com.mycomp.Payroll</remote>
</ejb-ref>
```

An optional <ejb-link> element can be used to uniquely identify a specific bean if more than one EJB has the same name. In addition, an optional <description> element can be used to add a description of the EJB.

<ejb-local-ref>

The <ejb-ref> element is used to declare a local EJB reference used by the application.

Syntax

```
<ejb-local-ref>
  [<description [xml:lang="lang"]>description</description>]*
  <ejb-ref-name>ejbRefName</ejb-ref-name>
  <ejb-ref-type>Entity|Session</ejb-ref-type>
  <local-home>homeInterfaceName</local-home>
  <local>localInterfaceName</local>
  [<ejb-link>linkedEJBName</ejb-link>]
</ejb-local-ref>
```

The <ejb-local-ref> element serves the same purpose as the <ejb-ref> element but for local beans. It supports all the same nested elements, except that <home> is replaced by <local-home> and <remote> is replaced by <local>:

```
<ejb-local-ref>
  <ejb-ref-name>ejb/Payroll</ejb-ref-name>
  <ejb-ref-type>Session</ejb-ref-type>
  <local-home>com.mycomp.PayrollHome</local-home>
  <local>com.mycomp.Payroll</local>
</ejb-local-ref>
```

<service-ref>

The <service-ref> element declares a reference to a web service used by the application.

Syntax

```
<service-ref>
  [<description [xml:lang="lang"]>description</description>]*
  [<display-name [xml:lang="lang"]>displayName</display-name>]*
  [<icon [xml:lang="lang"]>
    [<small-icon>iconPath</small-icon>]
    [<large-icon>iconPath</large-icon>]
   </icon>]*
  <service-ref-name>serviceRefName</service-ref-name>
  <service-interface>jaxrpcInterfaceName</service-interface>
  [<wsdl-file>wsdlFilePath</wsdl-file>]
  [<jaxrpc-mapping-file>mappingFilePath</jaxrpc-mapping-file>]
  [<service-qname>wdslQName</service-qname>]
  [<port-component-ref>portComponentRef</port-component-ref>]*
  [<handler>portComponentHandler</handler>]*
</service-ref>
```

See the Servlet 2.4 and J2EE 1.4 web services specifications for details on how to use this element.

<message-destination-ref>

The <message-destination-ref> element declares a JMS message destination reference used by the application.

Syntax

```
<message-destination-ref>
  [<description [xml:lang="lang"]>description</description>]*
  <message-destination-ref-name>refName</message-destination-ref-name>
  <message-destination-type>typeName</message-destination-type>
  <message-destination-usage>
    Consumes|Produces|ConsumesProduces
  </message-destination-usage>
  [<message-destination-link>linkedDestName</message-destination-link>]
</message-destination-ref>
```

See the Servlet 2.4 and J2EE 1.4 messaging specifications for details on how to use this element.

<message-destination>

The <message-destination> element declares a logical name for a JMS message destination used by the application.

Syntax

```
<message-destination>
  [<description [xml:lang="lang"]>description</description>]*
  [<display-name [xml:lang="lang"]>displayName</display-name>]*
  [<icon [xml:lang="lang"]>
    [<small-icon>iconPath</small-icon>]
    [<large-icon>iconPath</large-icon>]
   </icon>]*
  <message-destination-name>destName</message-destination-name>
</message-destination>
```

See the Servlet 2.4 and J2EE 1.4 messaging specifications for details on how to use this element.

Example Application Deployment Descriptor

Example F-3 shows an example of a deployment descriptor (*web.xml*) file with the most common declarations needed for a JSF- application.

Example F-3. Example deployment descriptor file

```
<?xml version="1.0" encoding="ISO-8859-1"?>
<web-app xmlns="http://java.sun.com/xml/ns/j2ee"
  xmlns:xsi="http://www.w3c.org/2001/XMLSchema-instance"
  xsi:schemaLocation="http://java.sun.com/xml/ns/j2ee
    http://java.sun.com/xml/ns/j2ee/web-app_2_4.xsd"
  version="2.4>
```

Example F-3. Example deployment descriptor file (continued)

```
  <context-param>
    <param-name>javax.faces.STATE_SAVING_METHOD</param-name>
    <param-value>client</param-value>
  </context-param>

  <servlet>
    <servlet-name>facesServlet</servlet-name>
    <servlet-class>
      javax.faces.webapp.FacesServlet
    </servlet-class>
  </servlet>

  <servlet-mapping>
    <servlet-name>facesServlet</servlet-name>
    <url-pattern>*.faces</url-pattern>
  </servlet-mapping>
</web-app>
```

At the top of the file, you find a standard XML declaration and the `<web-app>` element, with the reference to the deployment descriptor schema. Next comes a `<context-param>` element that tells JSF to save state in the client. The `<servlet>` element maps the JSF servlet class to a name, and the `<servlet-mapping>` element maps the servlet to the recommended **.faces* extension pattern.

Creating a WAR File

A WAR file is an archive file, used to group all application files into a convenient package. A WAR file can be created with the *jar* command, included in the Java runtime environment, or a ZIP utility program such as *WinZip*. To create a WAR file, you first need to create the file structure as directories in the filesystem and place all files in the correct location as described earlier.

With the file structure in place, *cd* to the top level directory for the application in the filesystem. You can then use the *jar* command to create the WAR file:

```
C:\> cd myapp
C:\myapp> jar cvf myapp_1_0.war *
```

This command creates a WAR file named *myapp_1_0.war* containing all files in the *myapp* directory. You can use any filename that makes sense for your application but avoid spaces in the filename, because they are known to cause problems on many platforms. Including the version number for the application in the filename is a good idea, because it is helpful for the users to know which version of the application the file contains.

Index

A

We'd like to hear your suggestions for improving our indexes. Send email to *index@oreilly.com*.

B

C

F

G

H

I

H

I

J

M

Q

R

U

V

W

Z

About the Author

Hans Bergsten is the founder of Gefion Software, a company that focuses on Java services and products based on J2EE technologies. In addition to being an active participant in the JavaServer Faces (JSF) specification group, Hans has been a member of the specification groups for both the servlet and JSP specifications since their inception and contributes to other related JCP specifications, such as the JSP Standard Tag Library (JSTL). As one of the initial members of the Apache Jakarta Project Management Committee, he helped develop the Apache Tomcat reference implementation for the servlet and JSP specifications.

Colophon

Our look is the result of reader comments, our own experimentation, and feedback from distribution channels. Distinctive covers complement our distinctive approach to technical topics, breathing personality and life into potentially dry subjects.

The animal on the cover of *JavaServer Faces* is a Barbary ape (*Macaca sylvanus*). Despite its name, the Barbary ape is a monkey found in Algeria, Gibraltar, and Morocco, on the plains and in cedar and oak forests. Barbary apes are equally comfortable on the ground and in the trees. These tail-less macaques live in groups with multiple adults led by dominant females. Unlike most other monkeys, the males play an active role in caring for and playing with the young. Their fur is yellowish grey and brown with a pale underside; their diet consists of fruit, leaves, roots, and insects.

Barbary apes have played an interesting role in the political history of their environment: legend has it that Britain will never lose control of the Rock of Gibraltar while the Barbary apes remain in residence. For a time, the Barbary apes on Gibraltar were the responsiblity of the British Army; they even received medical care from the military hospital. Winston Churchill replenished the monkeys' population in 1942. The Barbary apes are Europe's only free-range monkeys, and their homes (Gibraltar, Morocco, and Algeria) have historically functioned as politically fraught transition areas between Europe and the Middle East. Apparently, the Barbary apes' pink faces have served to make them a resonant symbol of European imperialism.

Colleen Gorman was the production editor and copyeditor for *JavaServer Faces*. Sarah Sherman was the proofreader. Mary Anne Weeks Mayo, and Claire Cloutier provided quality control. Mary Agner and Jamie Peppard provided production support. Johnna VanHoose Dinse wrote the index.

Emma Colby designed the cover of this book, based on a series design by Edie Freedman. The cover image is a 19th-century engraving from the *Library of Natural History*, Volume V. Emma Colby produced the cover layout with QuarkXPress 4.1 using Adobe's ITC Garamond font.

David Futato designed the interior layout. This book was converted by Julie Hawks to FrameMaker 5.5.6 with a format conversion tool created by Erik Ray, Jason McIntosh, Neil Walls, and Mike Sierra that uses Perl and XML technologies. The text font is Linotype Birka; the heading font is Adobe Myriad Condensed; and the code font is LucasFont's TheSans Mono Condensed. The illustrations that appear in the book were produced by Robert Romano and Jessamyn Read using Macromedia FreeHand 9 and Adobe Photoshop 6. The tip and warning icons were drawn by Christopher Bing. This colophon was written by Colleen Gorman.

Keep in touch with O'Reilly

1. Download examples from our books

To find example files for a book, go to:

www.oreilly.com/catalog

select the book, and follow the "Examples" link.

2. Register your O'Reilly books

Register your book at *register.oreilly.com*

Why register your books?
Once you've registered your O'Reilly books you can:

- Win O'Reilly books, T-shirts or discount coupons in our monthly drawing.
- Get special offers available only to registered O'Reilly customers.
- Get catalogs announcing new books (US and UK only).
- Get email notification of new editions of the O'Reilly books you own.

3. Join our email lists

Sign up to get topic-specific email announcements of new books and conferences, special offers, and O'Reilly Network technology newsletters at:

elists.oreilly.com

It's easy to customize your free elists subscription so you'll get exactly the O'Reilly news you want.

4. Get the latest news, tips, and tools

www.oreilly.com

- "Top 100 Sites on the Web"—PC Magazine
- CIO Magazine's Web Business 50 Awards

Our web site contains a library of comprehensive product information (including book excerpts and tables of contents), downloadable software, background articles, interviews with technology leaders, links to relevant sites, book cover art, and more.

5. Work for O'Reilly

Check out our web site for current employment opportunities:

jobs.oreilly.com

6. Contact us

O'Reilly & Associates
1005 Gravenstein Hwy North
Sebastopol, CA 95472 USA

TEL: 707-827-7000 or 800-998-9938
(6am to 5pm PST)

FAX: 707-829-0104

order@oreilly.com
For answers to problems regarding your order or our products. To place a book order online, visit:

www.oreilly.com/order_new

catalog@oreilly.com
To request a copy of our latest catalog.

booktech@oreilly.com
For book content technical questions or corrections.

corporate@oreilly.com
For educational, library, government, and corporate sales.

proposals@oreilly.com
To submit new book proposals to our editors and product managers.

international@oreilly.com
For information about our international distributors or translation queries. For a list of our distributors outside of North America check out:

international.oreilly.com/distributors.html

adoption@oreilly.com
For information about academic use of O'Reilly books, visit:

academic.oreilly.com
